DREAMS
IN THE
MIRROR

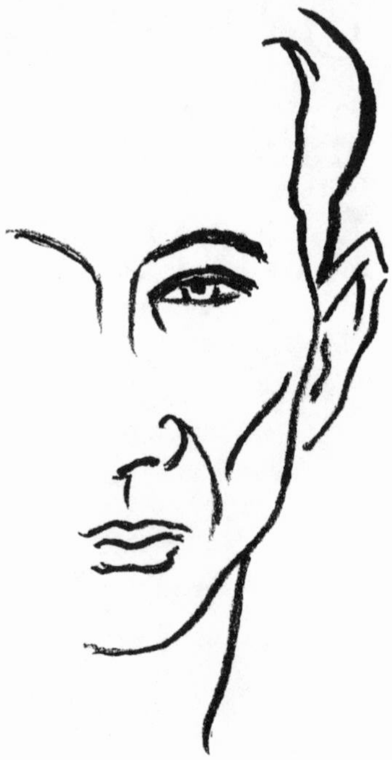

Richard S. Kennedy

DREAMS
IN THE
MIRROR

A Biography of
E. E. CUMMINGS

Liveright Publishing Corporation   New York

We acknowledge with thanks the kind permission of Nancy T.
Andrews and The Estate of Marion Cummings to reproduce the
poems and drawings of E. E. Cummings.

All drawings reproduced in this volume are by E. E. Cummings,
except where otherwise identified.

Designed by Earl Tidwell

Library of Congress Cataloging in Publication Data

Kennedy, Richard S
    Dreams in the mirror.
    Includes bibliographical references and index.
    1. Cummings, Edward Estlin, 1894–1962. 2. Poets,
American—20th century—Biography. I. Title.
PS3505.U334Z7   811'.5'2   [B]   79–18301
ISBN 0–87140–638–1
    2 3 4 5 6 7 8 9 0

FOR ELLA

Ἡδὺ θέρους διψῶντι χιὼν ποτόν, ἡδὺ δὲ ναύταις

ἐκ χειμῶνος ἰδεῖν εἰαρινὸν Στέφανον

Ἡδιστον δ᾽ ὁπόταν κρύψῃ μία τοὺς φιλέοντας

χλαῖνα καί αἰνῆται Κύπρις ὑπ᾽ ἀμφοτέρων.

Contents

Preface

This book has been long in the making. Its origins go back as far as 1963 and an honors seminar I taught at Wichita State University in Kansas, "E. E. Cummings and the Poetic Experiment of His Time." But my research began in earnest in 1969 at Houghton Library, Harvard University, which houses the voluminous Cummings papers, perhaps the largest collection in existence of the papers of an American writer, even larger than the Thomas Wolfe collection.

These materials provide a record which extends from Rebecca Haswell Cummings' description of the birth pangs attending her son's coming into the world, through millions of pages, up to the last words which E. E. Cummings wrote in a little blue notebook about the brightness of a late-summer delphinium.

The sheer bulk of material was so overwhelming that at first I planned to write the biography in two stages, the first volume of which, "E. E. Cummings: The Years of Innocence," was almost complete in 1976. But the exigencies of present-day publishing made it necessary for me to reduce the length of the biography and to pack the account of Cummings' life into a single volume. As a result, the present work is perhaps more readable even though it contains less information and less discussion of Cummings' poetry than I had intended.

That the book exists at all I have to thank Nancy T. Andrews, who holds the copyright to all her father's writings. She generously allowed me to quote from Cummings' works both published and unpublished, and I am extremely grateful to her not only for that permission but even more for allowing me to write the kind of biography I wished without censorship or obstruction. She herself is a poet and understands that freedom is necessary for creation. Even so, I should add that this book is in no way an "authorized" biography. Although Mrs. Andrews was kind enough to permit me several interviews and although she read through my typescript and corrected several errors of fact, she is not responsible for the opinions that I have set forth about her father. In fact, in three places in the work where she wished to offer an alternative interpretation of a situation, she has supplied a footnote signed "NTA," giving her own understanding of it, one of which presents a perspective of her stepfather, Frank MacDermot, rather different from that which would otherwise be seen in my pages.

I owe a heavy debt of gratitude also to George J. Firmage, Mrs. Andrews' representative, who not only granted permission to quote from Cummings' unpublished writings but has also contributed immeasurably to the accuracy of the Cummings poems which are printed here. He checked the text of each poem against its original manuscript or type-script version (and against Cummings' own published version in the few instances where that was the sole authority), and he prepared the copy for the printer. I am thus assured the same high standard of accuracy that attends the "Typescript Editions" of Cummings' poems published by Liveright or by the Marchim Press in England which he himself has edited.

I wish also to express my gratitude to Alfred Rice, the administrator of the estate of Marion Morehouse for allowing me to quote from the published writings of E. E. Cummings which were copyrighted in Marion Morehouse's name.

Jonathan Cape, Ltd. has granted permission to quote from Henry Reed's superb poem "Naming of Parts" from *A Map of Verona*.

Since this biography is based largely on manuscript sources, I owe much to the great research libraries which house Cummings material. My greatest debt is to the Houghton Library: to W. H. Bond, the librarian, for permission to quote from the Cummings collection; to Rodney Dennis, curator of manuscripts, and his cataloguer, Suzanne Currier, for giving me access to parts of the collection before it was indexed; to Marte Shaw, curator of the reading room, and her able staff for nine years of patient help. For permission to quote from Cummings material in the Humanities Research Center, University of Texas, I am grateful to William Holman, the librarian, and for her courteous assistance I remember with thanks Sally Leach, head of the reading room.

To the Clifton Waller Barrett Library and the Alderman Library of the University of Virginia I am indebted for permission to quote from Cummings' letters to S. A. Jacobs and John Dos Passos; to the Princeton University Library for Cummings' letters to John Peale Bishop; to the Massachusetts Historical Society for a letter and for the Hopkinson painting of Rebecca Cummings; to the Yale University Library and to Donald Gallup, curator of the American literature collections for access to and permission to quote from the *Dial* Collection; to the staff of the National Archives for their successful search for the documents relating to Cummings' imprisonment in France.

This project was given a great boost by an award from the National Endowment for the Arts which enabled me to travel to England to interview Nancy T. Andrews and Mr. and Mrs. Frank MacDermot and to visit La Ferté-Macé and other sites in France associated with Cummings during World War I. I am grateful to Nancy Hanks and her staff for their enlightened generosity.

But libraries and foreign travel could not provide all the essential information about Cummings and his career. I owe special thanks to a large number of his relatives and friends for their kindness and courtesy when I approached them for aid. Elizabeth Cummings Qualey, the poet's sister, very kindly gave me facts about her brother's early life and helped fill in a picture of Cambridge and New Hampshire in the 1900s, especially with her memoir, "When I was a Little Girl," a charming work, which I hope some day will be published. I am also grateful to her for reading and commenting on Chapters II, III, and IV of this book.

Dr. J. Sibley Watson and his late wife Hildegarde have provided invaluable help over a decade. In particular, they allowed me access to their large collection of Cummings' letters and have always been a source of accurate knowledge when I had questions. I owe them additional thanks for reading my chapters on Cummings at Harvard.

Two of Cummings' oldest and closest friends have been most generous with their help, Slater Brown and M. R. Werner. They have granted interviews, provided me with letters and documents, and answered many questions. Mr. Brown has kindly read and corrected facts in a dozen of the early chapters.

Other friends have been equally helpful with other portions of the book. Malcolm Cowley, Archibald MacLeish, and the late Allen Tate have all supplied helpful reminiscences of their friendship with Cummings. Jere Knight and Aline MacMahon have provided information about Marion Morehouse and about the period the Cummingses spent in

California. David Diamond and Lincoln Kirstein have told me about their friendship with Cummings and especially about the projected ballet production. Mr. Diamond has kindly read my chapter, "The Undanced *Tom*." Loren MacIver has given me many details about the long friendship which she and her husband, Lloyd Frankenberg, had with Cummings and Marion Morehouse.

Helen Stewart has not only given me a warm remembrance of Cummings but also allowed me to make use of the manuscripts of *i x i* and "Preface to Krazy," which Cummings had given her. Evelyn and Harry Segal, whom Cummings called "the dear seagulls," were extraordinarily gracious to me when I spent a weekend at their house, interviewing them and going through Mrs. Segal's journals and correspondence. I am especially grateful to Dr. Segal for obtaining for me Cummings' medical records at Strong Memorial Hospital. Mina Curtiss was particularly helpful in her reminiscences about Marion Morehouse.

I wish I had the space to acknowledge individually the one hundred and fifty-six members of the Harvard Class of 1915 who answered my inquiry about Cummings and his professors. But I can only name a few who contributed important information for my pages: Kenneth Conant and Robert Cawley (each of whom granted me an interview), Theodore Browne, Robert Holden, Roger Fenn, William Langer, Shirley Mason, Stearns Morse, Henry Murray, Harold Schroeder, Edwin B. Smith, Constant Southworth, Eric Stone, Warren Taylor, Roswell Whidden, and Benjamin Whitney. Two other Harvard friends of Cummings, though not of his class, supplied vivid details about Cummings' Harvard years: the late S. Foster Damon about Cummings' literary beginnings; and Philip Smith about Cummings' social life.

Any biographical project carried out over a long period brings one into contact with many fascinating people whom one comes to think of as real allies in completing the task. The following list of names comprises a group of what I think of as co-workers because of their help to me in answering questions by letter or in person or in allowing me to use materials in their possession: Louise Alger, Bernice Baumgarten, Eloise Bender, Jane Block of the University of New Hampshire Library. John Malcolm Brinnin, Douglas Bush, Mary Caffry, Esther Lanman Cushman, Robert A. Cushman, Julian Cornell, Cecil Derry, Elizabeth Dos Passos, Ruth DeQuoy (Town Historian of Temple, New Hampshire), Yvette Eastman, Mrs. Douglas Faulkner, Harriet M. Foley, J. C. Furnas, Amy Gozzaldi Hall, Franklin Hammond, C. Hugh Holman, Elizabeth Thaxter Hubbard, Howard M. Jones, Betty Kray, Rushworth Kidder, Walter Donald Kring, Professor Jean Lafond, James Laughlin, Mary Lynch of the Colebrook Public Library, Joseph MacCarthy, Elaine Orr

MacDermot, Frank MacDermot, Sister Patricia McKeon, Fern Malkine, Harold Mantell, Ruth Marshall of the Boston Public Library, Mary Meehan of the Harvard University Archives, J. W. Nystrom, president of Bennett College, Mrs. William O'Brien, David Perkins, Dudley Poore, Dagmar Reutlinger, Monelle Richmond, David Sinclair, Helen Schevill, Jack Sweeney, June Tilton of the Topsfield Historical Society, J. P. Vernier of the University of Rouen, Drs. Eleanor and Richard Wagner, and Edwin Williams, editor of the *Harvard Library Bulletin*.

Professors Mel Scott and Geraldine Knight Scott of the University of California, Berkeley, gave unstintingly of their time in a critical reading of my manuscript, and the book has been improved greatly by their suggestions. I was also privileged to have the distinguished American poet, Josephine Miles, read my manuscript. Her response to my views of Cummings' poetry was of great help.

I thank the John Simon Guggenheim Foundation for access to the letters and poems of Cummings which are in their files. I am also grateful to Harcourt Brace Jovanovich and to Rita Vaughan for their gracious gift of a Xerox copy of all the Cummings letters in their archives.

In our profession one can generally count on help from other scholars. But the late F. W. Dupee and George Stade of Columbia University made one of the most gracious gestures in the history of scholarly cooperation. They opened to me their files of the letters they had collected during the years of their preparation for *Selected Letters of E. E. Cummings*, which they edited in 1969. Their generosity thus saved me countless hours of correspondence. I owe deepest thanks also to Professor Jack Undank of Rutgers University for checking my handling of the French language and for answering questions about French slang in *The Enormous Room*.

I owe a special debt of gratitude to my own university for encouragement and support during the many years of my research and writing. Temple University provided me with a summer research grant in 1969 and a one-semester study leave in 1974 to assist me in carrying out my task. In addition, I have several times been allowed a reduced teaching load in order to provide time for research and writing. I wish to direct special thanks for this help to Dean George Johnson and to a series of department chairmen, Robert Buttel, Paul Jackson, and George Deaux.

For preparing the typescript I again have Temple University to thank, this time for the presence of Dorothy Mewha and her assistants in the Word-Processing Center, especially that ballerina of the typewriter keys, Nadia Kravachenko.

For his help and understanding over a long period of association, I propose a toast of thanks to Victor Schmalzer, my good-natured and perceptive editor at Liveright. For his concern and for the contributions of the staff at Liveright and at W. W. Norton I only wish I could express more adequately than these words can convey, my full appreciation.

My wife, Ella Dickinson Kennedy, has been a full partner in the making of this book. She accompanied me on interviews, guided my assessment of biographical problems, read and weighed every sentence of my composition. I trust her judgment as I trust no one else's, including my own. The book is dedicated to her as an expression of our partnership.

RICHARD S. KENNEDY

Temple University
May 1979

DREAMS
IN THE
MIRROR

I

An Introduction to Someone and anyone

> ... for I profess to write, not his panegyric, which must be all praise,
> but his Life.
>
> BOSWELL

"He was the most entertaining man I ever met," recalled Slater Brown, E. E. Cummings' companion in the ambulance corps in World War I and later his roommate in New York. "He was a dreadful show-off. Everything he did was a performance."[1] "He was the most brilliant monologuist I have ever known," wrote Malcolm Cowley of the Cummings he knew during the 1920's.[2] The descriptive phrases that others used about Cummings run in the same vein: "I have never been so royally entertained in my life," "the best talk I ever heard," "a brilliant analytical wit," "He played [the piano] like fireworks. He talked the same way"—all testifying about a fascinating human being and pointing up the way he used language.[3]

Archibald MacLeish, speaking of Cummings' visit to his house in a suburb of Paris in November 1924, remembered, "Cummings came out to lunch and produced one of his virtuoso performances."[4] It happened that Burton Rascoe, who was also a guest that day, set down a detailed impression of his talk: "E. E. Cummings was there and for eight solid hours he talked incessantly; but he was not boring; on the contrary, he was enormously entertaining. His head was a storehouse of remembered verses from Sappho in Greek, Laforgue in French, Horace in Latin, and Amy Lowell, Shakespeare, and Longfellow in English and he could weave the most incongruous quotations together spontaneously, with effects sometimes very funny and sometimes of a startling beauty. No one else had a chance to talk throughout the afternoon, during dinner, or after dinner; but no one minded this, because Cummings's flow of words was so entertaining. He even talked all the way into town on the train and was still talking when he asked to be dropped at a certain corner, on our way home in a taxicab."[5]

Cummings loved to play with words, usually witty combinations of the learned and the colloquial, scraps from ancient and foreign languages mixed with slang and bawdy phrase; it was a dazzling linguistic agility: puns, twisted slogans, topsy-turvy proverbs, incongruous literary allusions, sometimes in dialect, sometimes in mimicry of familiar public voices—he played so many roles it was difficult to perceive the real Cummings. But, more than just a captivating talker, Cummings had a special talent for converting this linguistic play into unique poetic structures and a style that was entirely new to poetry.

One key to his unique creations is the fact that he was a painter as well as a poet: ". . . in the beginning was the Eye (not the mind)," he declared.[6] He had drawn and painted ever since childhood and become a self-taught artist in both oils and watercolors by the time he left college. He carried a pocket sketchbook with him, especially on his travels, and his fingers were always busy with a pencil. Not only did this habit train his acute observation of life, but his visual orientation combined with his word play to produce unusual spatial arrangements of words in his poems and to allow the development of a personal style that was one of the most important contributions to the literary revolution of the twentieth century.

This happy conjunction of visual and linguistic expressiveness occurred at a time when it could best be nurtured. The influx of new art forms from Europe—cubism, fauvism, futurism in painting and sculpture and the unusual tonal combinations and rhythmic freedoms in music—encouraged him to join the revolt against realism; or to put it another way, it helped him to develop a sensibility that could express a new way of looking at reality. "The Symbol of all Art is the Prism," Cummings pronounced. "The goal is unrealism. The method is destructive. To break up the white light of objective realism, into the secret glories which it contains."[7] The result for Cummings was a new way of writing poetry.

He dedicated his existence to the arts: to creative manipulation of language and to lively visual arrangements of color and line. But since to make a living as a painter or a poet is scarcely possible for anyone in our time and in our nation, he had to live frugally and accept a great deal of help from his friends. "He thought a poet should be fed by the ravens," said his college friend, John Dos Passos, "and of course he was."[8] Toward the end of his life, however, he achieved a great deal more recognition than he expected and even reached the point at which he could support himself. But the recognition was so long in coming and the contrariness which seemed to be the necessary posture for his expression was so continuous that he developed an increasing sense of himself as alone and at odds with almost everyone around him.

The descriptions of Cummings as the vivacious monologist show him among intimates. Outside that circle he was very retiring, modest, protective of a tightly wrapped self. Indeed, even the mask of gaiety among close friends gave no hint of a secret self expressed only in his poetry or in his love letters. The sign of this private self was the lower-case "i," which he used to refer to the speaker in many of his poems. It stood for a vulnerable, sensitive antihero, wide-eyed with wonder before the world and readily assertive of his natural feelings, a figure corresponding to such characters as Pierrot, Petrouchka, and Charlie Chaplin's role of "the little tramp."

One mythic presentation which reveals that private self most clearly is a charming poem, redolent of wistful pathos, about a little being named "anyone" (both anonymity and uniqueness are there in the name), who lives in "a pretty how town." The poem makes frequent use of nursery rhyme language ("with up so floating many bells down"), which is appropriate to the world of innocence Cummings is creating. "anyone" is happy, indeed exuberant, in all his activities whether they succeed or not: "he sang his didn't he danced his did." But he is alienated from other people ("Women and men (both little and small)/ cared for anyone not at all") who are negative in their activities and standardized in their achievements: "they sowed their isn't they reaped their same." But anyone is loved by a woman named "noone," who joins him in his response to life no matter whether good or bad events befall: "she laughed his joy she cried his grief." Her name allows Cummings to express both the isolation that anyone feels and the love that the woman offers: "noone loved him more by more." This same doubleness applies to the response which follows the death of anyone: "one day anyone died i guess/ and noone stooped to kiss his face." It is a simple story, taking place in a mythic no-time, within the cycle of the seasons "autumn, winter, spring, summer," which is expressed as a refrain along with another refrain of grouped natural elements, "sun moon stars rain." The poem ends with the people of the world following their fruitless routines, as anyone and noone lie buried together absorbed into the natural world which continues its diurnal round:

busy folk buried them side by side
little by little and was by was

all by all and deep by deep
and more by more they dream their sleep
noone and anyone earth by april
wish by spirit and if by yes

Women and men(both dong and ding)
summer autumn winter spring
reaped their sowing and went their came
sun moon stars rain[9]

This was the central myth of Cummings' life, but "noone" knew it, unless it was one who loved him enough to be privy to his deepest feeling.

How far away from all this seems the general career of E. E. Cummings, the public figure who was one of the leaders of the literary revolt of the 1920's—the cubist painter, the dadaist dabbler, the daring linguistic experimenter, the ruthless satirist who heaped scorn on American culture.

And how infinitely far seems the E. E. Cummings of the final years, the curmudgeon of Patchin Place who yearned for an older time "before 'urbs' slaughtered 'rus' & movies-times-radio became the universally false & popular UNtaste of the moment";[10] the irrational grumbler who somehow blamed the Korean War on Franklin and Eleanor Roosevelt; the cantankerous naysayer who turned down President Kennedy's invitation to dine at the White House with a selected group of artists and writers (whom Cummings characterized as "70some crooks, punks, & preknowbellists.")[11]

This biography attempts to merge into one life story these various selves and some others too—the libidinous faun of New York and Paris, the Nature lover alert to the presence of her winged, footed, leaved, and petaled creatures, the spellbinding poetry reader widely acclaimed by a generation of college students, and the mystic attuned to a oneness beyond his coherent expression. But since human nature is so complex and the personality of a literary genius so enigmatic, a biographer cannot supply any easy explanation of this mixture of tendencies. Nor can any biographer ever account for genius. He can only chart the course genius took and describe why some of the changes and developments happened on the way. In a literary biography, this task includes showing why an author wrote the literary works he did and how his peculiarities of style and structure came to be. These general aims have guided the composition of this book.

The story of E. E. Cummings' life and the development of his art is a fascinating one not only because he was one of the leading American poets of the twentieth century but also because he was one of the unique personalities of his time. His biography is of special interest too as an American life story, for despite his hostility to American culture, he is as American as Concord Bridge and the Statue of Liberty. "The tradition, after all, in this nation is bucking the tradition," as Toby Olshin has so aptly phrased it. Our story begins in the Boston area, one of the two great cultural centers of the nation at the end of the nineteenth century, a place where breaking with tradition has always been as common as establishing it.

II

Origins

Know old Cambridge? Hope you do.
Born there? Don't say so! I was too.
The nicest place that ever was seen,
Colleges red, and common green,
Sidewalks brownish with trees between.

O. W. HOLMES

Rebecca Haswell Cummings' diary entry for October 14, 1894 begins, "Pains began at 12:30 A.M.—not severe—constant desire to make water— (3:45 A.M.) called Miss McMahon but there was nothing to be done . . . 7:30 Dr. arrived everything all right so he went back to breakfast and came back at 9:30—Examined again. Slight progress but nothing immediate so he went to bed being called at 1 as the pains were more severe—(I wept early in morning)—another examination—Everything all right but no hurry Dr. retired to dinner—Held on to Edward [her husband] and tugged—About 5 towels were arranged and I tugged as hard as possible —Later part of P.M. took lots of gruel—Miss McMahon saw child's hair at 4—Tug of war till 6 then very reluctantly took ether as Dr. Hildreth said it would be bad for the child to wait longer—Dr. Taylor gave the ether (20 minutes). Then Dr. Hildreth delivered the child with forceps —Boy born at 7—weighed 8 3/4 + pounds."[1]

Reading this passage, one realizes more fully what Edward Estlin Cummings meant when he later told an audience at Harvard that he was born "at home."[2] His father was present, the servants were running in and out, his mother felt secure in the familiar surroundings of 104 Irving

Street, Cambridge, Massachusetts. It was a good way to begin life. During his childhood he felt a special proprietary warmth about that house, too, because his father, Edward Cummings, told him that he had built the house "in order to have you in." It was a huge, three-storied, many-roomed structure with thirteen fireplaces, situated on the point where Irving and Scott Streets come together, not far from Harvard Yard.

The Cambridge of 1894 was an ideal place for a boy to grow up in —that is, if his parents were of old New England stock and his father was a Harvard professor or a professional man of standing. It was a self-conscious community. Although there was a good deal of light industry in East Cambridge, the townspeople were very much aware that Cambridge was the home of Henry Wadsworth Longfellow and of James Russell Lowell. Here too stood the Washington elm where the General took command of the Continental army, and, of course, Harvard University was known to be not only the oldest but also the best "college" in the country and President Eliot was regarded as a much more important figure than Mr. Cleveland or Mr. McKinley. Nearby Boston called itself "The Athens of America," but Cambridge knew that the cultural eminence of Boston rested in great measure upon the intellectual foundation of the Cambridge educational institutions. The Charles River, which wound past Harvard and Massachusetts Institute of Technology, was thought to resemble the Cam. The important clergymen of New England, whether liberal Unitarians or conservative Episcopalians received their training at the Harvard Divinity School or the Episcopal Theological School. The Irish (and Roman Catholicism) still did not count for much in Cambridge, and the Anti-Saloon League felt that they had something to do with that fact: Cambridge, by local option, had been dry since 1886.[3]

West Cambridge, the area around Harvard Yard and along Brattle Street and Garden Street, still retained some of the quiet charm of a New England village. President Eliot could be seen riding his bicycle to his office or Dean Briggs observed standing in Harvard Square, with his green book bag over his shoulder, chatting with a circle of students. Cattle browsed in the open fields near "Shady Hill," the Charles Eliot Norton estate, just a step away from 104 Irving Street. The inhabitants were prosperous and well established in a tradition of education and earnest citizenship. Books and essays were being written in a surprising number of the well-painted colonial-style houses, and cultural clubs or "evenings" (the Dante Club, the Query Club, the Junior Shop Club) flourished. Bliss Perry, who had come up from Princeton to teach at Harvard, has described the tone and quality of West Cambridge at the turn of the century very well:

In 1900 the gracious outward aspect of Old Cambridge was in harmony with its inner spirit. Brattle Street, and even the streets "just off" Brattle, looked as secure as an English cathedral close, and there was among its old American families the sense of continuity, of assured social position, which was a part of that English tradition which lingered in Boston and Cambridge until well into the twentieth century. Brattle Street was like an island in the stream of new and alien races swarming into Greater Boston; an island also in the stream of suburban Americans attracted to Cambridge by rapid transit, by the development of manufacturing interests, and by the growth of Harvard University. Possibly Old Cambridge could count fewer men of world-wide reputation than in 1850, and yet within half a mile of Craigie House [Longfellow's home] there were probably as many men of personal distinction as could be found anywhere in a similar radius, outside of the great European capitals.[4]

To be born in West Cambridge was like being born to multiple parents who were gracious, cultivated, and a little outdated, enjoying the comfort of middle age.

II

By the age of thirty-three, Edward Cummings had achieved a foothold in the social hierarchy of this city. He was a recently appointed assistant professor of sociology at Harvard, and as time went on, he reached a position of great respect in the whole area of Greater Boston: he left Harvard to become the Unitarian Minister of the South Congregational Church at the corner of Exeter and Newbury Streets in the fashionable Back Bay area of Boston. He was the dominant figure in the early life of his son.

The man whom young Estlin knew during this childhood and youth, that is from about 1898 to 1915, was a tall (six feet two), broad-shouldered, brown-haired man with striking features including a prominent nose and a full moustache. He spoke with a resonant, authoritative voice—occasionally somewhat pompous, Estlin began to think by the time he was in college. He was gay, informal, and kindly but forcefully masculine in manner. Some of his pictures show him in handsome profile with resplendent waves of hair and a black Windsor tie that makes him look like a *fin de siècle* poet. Other pictures show him in rugged camper's clothes, like a Leslie Stephen ready to climb a mountain. These pictures represent two sides of his nature, for he was a sensitive intellectual, able to be responsive to both beauties and sufferings; yet he was also athletic in constitution, with a personality affected by his physical muscularity, a striver, a leader, a fighter. Since his son did not inherit his father's physical make-up, he showed none of these aggressive tendencies. Because of this basic difference in temperament, there was bound to be more conflict than usual between father and son when the boy reached his teens.

During the years when his son was growing up, Edward Cummings presided over a large household. Besides Mrs. Cummings and the two children, Estlin and Elizabeth, there were, at one time or another, Edward's mother (Nana Cummings, the children called her); his unmarried sister, Jane Cummings; Mrs. Cummings' mother (Nana Clarke); her brother, George Lemist Clarke; two servant girls, frequently changing; and Sandy Hardy, the black handyman who came in by day. It was a happy, harmonious arrangement, and growing up in the midst of a model extended family, which included the servants who were also family, was a fortunate set of circumstances for the children.

Edward Cummings himself had grown up in humbler surroundings and in a less liberal-minded atmosphere. He had been born in a strict Congregationalist family on April 20, 1861, in Colebrook, New Hampshire, a little town near the Canadian border. He was the son of Edward Norris Cummings and Lucretia Frances Merrill and he was descended on both sides from early New England settlers, a hardy and vigorous series of farmers, tradesmen, and artisans. Not much is known about his mother's maternal ancestry, although on the Merrill side the line is traceable back to 1634 when Nathaniel Merrill, of French origins (the name had earlier been spelled "Merle"), settled in Newbury, Massachusetts, with his wife Susanna Jourdaine. The most enterprising of his descendants was Sherburn Rowell Merrill,[5] who eventually established himself in Colebrook as the owner of grist and starch mills and the proprietor of a general store. Lucretia Frances, the oldest of Sherburn's five daughters, was born in Woodstock, New Hampshire, April 7, 1838. When she married her father's partner in the Cummings and Merrill store, she brought a comfortable dowry to the marriage. She became, in time, Estlin's Nana Cummings, whom he would visit in her home by the sea at 135 Nahant Street in Lynn, Massachusetts. She was, for the Cummings children, the lovable Nana who came to live with them, who taught them to play the piano, and who played and sang for family gatherings, especially the old Scottish songs. She ended her days in 1923 in her son's home at 104 Irving Street.

Old Edward Norris Cummings, born April 3, 1837, in Canaan, Vermont, is remembered as a dour man who took his Calvinism seriously. The Cummings background was Scottish and the family claimed a Cummings ancestry that went back to the Red Comeyn, the clan leader who was killed by Robert the Bruce at the Church of the Friars Menorite at

Dumfries in 1306.[6] However that may be, the earliest information that can be traced in the ancestral line concerns Isaac Cummings of Ipswich, Massachusetts, in 1638, who eventually bought land and settled in Topsfield.[7] Four generations of the Cummings family farmed in Topsfield before the Revolution and before one name emerges with some distinction beyond the meager town records of ownership and vital statistics. Archelaus Cummings, born the youngest of eleven children, June 1, 1752, uprooted himself from Topsfield and migrated to Temple, New Hampshire, a new settlement in a remote and mountainous area twenty miles west of Nashua. Here he is first heard from at age twenty-three when in 1776 he signed the profession of intent to oppose the British by force of arms. In 1780 he is named as one of sixteen men who "marched on the alarm at Coos, at y[e] time Royalston was burnt."[8]

His grandson, Archelaus III, who was Estlin's great-grandfather, continued the spirit of migration and enterprise, and in his youth he wandered up to Canaan, Vermont, where the borders of Canada, Vermont, and New Hampshire come together. He was a shoemaker ("in the shoe and leather business," reads a euphemistic report),[9] one of a series of Cummings men who were clever with their hands. At twenty-two, he married Mary Fletcher, daughter of a prosperous sawmill operator in Colebrook. As seems proper for a man with plenty of lumber, Ebenezer Fletcher owned one of the largest houses in New Hampshire, and some time after the old man's death, Archelaus converted his father-in-law's house into a hotel, the Mohawk House, or as some local wags later called it, "The Hawk 'n Spit House." This explains an enigmatic note in the hand of Jane Cummings, who recorded that her brother John was born "at the old Cummings Tavern."[10]

The Calvinistic gloom of Edward Norris Cummings may have been the reaction of a son to the conviviality of a tavern-keeper father. (Nor was anything ever said about the Cummings Tavern at Irving Street, probably because grandson Edward was a minister and a strong temperance man.) In any case, the earliest view of Edward Norris Cummings places him in Colebrook in the late 1850s, where he was the part owner of a general store, "Cummings and Co." across the street from the Congregational Church of which he was a staunch member.[11] His son, Edward, who was to become Estlin's father, was born "over the store" in the spring of 1861 just as the first cannons of the Civil War began to roar.[12]

If traits can be passed on to descendants, it is important to note that Edward Norris had a streak of inventiveness. Family tradition refers to him as an "inventor" who worked out a form of mute pedal on the piano so that a youngster could practice his music lesson without driving the neighbors into fits. Nothing came of it. He also devised and produced

"Handifold," a mechanism for dispensing toilet paper in public places—and lost most of his wife's money. He was obviously a tinkerer and he had some odd notions about education. He taught his son Edward how to handle carpenter's tools and how to do mental arithmetic. But young Edward was not sent to school until he was eight and had to learn to read in a class of younger boys. Still, he had been trained sufficiently well in using his hands so that a few years later, after the family moved to Woburn, near Boston, he was able to earn wages working alongside a local master carpenter.[13]

The strains on the unsuccessful father were visited upon young Edward Cummings. The boy had to work at various jobs, mostly carpentering, but when he was graduated from Woburn High School in 1879, he went to Harvard where he became a student of philosophy, political science, and economics. He was graduated *magna cum laude* in 1883. In our day, he probably would have become a social worker or a bright young man in the Department of Health, Education, and Welfare. But in the 1880s, the ministry offered the best opportunity for social service. Edward Cummings went on to the Harvard Divinity School determined to be a preacher of the social gospel and a minister active in useful parish work.

But after two years in the Divinity School, he was disappointed with studies in theology and pulpit practicalities. He took his master's degree automatically, and he then enrolled with new enthusiasm in the Harvard Graduate School where he came to find, as he said later, that "sociology is more religious than most theology."[14] He performed well in his studies and was rewarded in 1888 with the Robert Treat Paine Fellowship, which allowed him to travel for three years in Europe, making a comparative study of the social and economic conditions of workers in Italy, Germany, France, and Great Britain. In London he worked at Toynbee Hall Settlement House in the slum district where the "Jack the Ripper" murders were being committed, and he joined the patrol that nightly helped the London police to guard the streets. After further study at the University of Paris and the University of Berlin, he was probably the best trained sociologist in the United States. When in 1891 Harvard established a post in this new area of study, Edward Cummings was chosen to fill it, the first instructor in sociology in the history of the College.[15] He felt settled in his new career now, and on June 25 he married Rebecca Clarke of Boston.

In the next few years, we find him publishing articles on such subjects as trade unions, cooperative stores, arbitration of strikes, penal codes, philanthropic institutions, and the social problems of the industrial revolution. As a lecturer and as a practical social worker, he soon became well known outside the academic community. He was on the board of the Boston Associated Charities. He was active in penal reform and in promoting the probation system, particularly for "penal aspects of drunkenness." It was probably his work at the Hale Settlement House that brought him into association with Edward Everett Hale, the energetic minister of the South Congregational Church and the author of that patriotic tale, "The Man without a Country."

The teachings and the character of Edward Cummings became so well known in Boston that when Edward Everett Hale was nearing retirement from his pulpit, the membership called Cummings as his associate minister to groom him as Hale's replacement. The Unitarian church was the only church that could have found a place for this Harvard professor who had never been ordained. Cummings was pleased with his new position, for it made it possible for him to be a strong moral force in society in a more direct way than was possible for a university professor. He knew from the outset that his church board approved of his spending half of his time dealing with social problems. In fact, he regarded this as the practical application of his religious beliefs and the fulfillment of the motto of the South Congregational Church, "That They May Have Life More Abundantly."

During the week, Edward Cummings saw more of his children than most fathers do, for he was in and out of the house all day. Although he did not make a practice of visiting the members of his congregation, he had a schedule of civic meetings and scattered activity in social work. When at home, he was working in his study, receiving callers, building fires, overseeing a lively family gathering at dinner, digging in the garden, and above all, busy at carpentry or masonry, constructing, repairing, improving, adding. He loved to have his children around him. He showed them how to use tools; he made things for them; he let them help, or hold, or just stand about and watch and ask questions or even tell stories while he worked. He seemed to be a combination of a scoutmaster and a friendly uncle rather than a minister.

But his impact on his son's development was forceful. He provided an example of power and success and excellence in his own life. He created and colored strongly an atmosphere in which Estlin's unique and valuable personality emerged. But more important, there are a few rather specific ways in which Edward Cummings' helped to shape E. E. Cummings the poet. Most prominent is the constant verbalization which was part of a minister's life. Then too, some of Edward Cummings' own habits of language were good for the ears and the mind of someone who was going to speak as a poet. He loved wordplay. His sermons had puns, had toyings with proverbs and mottos and slogans, linguistic ways to attract or surprise the minds of his parishioners. ("Judge Actions by their

Edward Cummings with Estlin and Elizabeth. HOUGHTON LIBRARY

People," "Worldliness is next to Godliness," "I want my church to be a layman's church," and so on). He dealt liberally in metaphor and in large controlling images. His sermon titles indicate it: "The Picture Puzzle of the Universe," "Mud Pies," "Spiritual Perennials." Much of this was a New England habit of mind, an emblematic view of the world we live in. But Edward Cummings went beyond it to create parables: "Invisible Barriers or the Bird in the Window," "The Parable of the Sugar Place" (a moral application of the process of maple-sugar-making), "The New Year Bank Account," "The Elevator or the Ups and Downs of Life," "The Railway Train Parable" (about the illusion of movement when you are standing still).[16] When his son in later years wrote *Santa Claus, A Morality,* he was following, and surpassing, his father's practice.

But the best thing that he did for his son was to create a happy childhood for him; in Estlin's words, ". . . no father on this earth ever loved or will love his son more profoundly."[17] This is good growing weather for anyone's formative years, be he poet or not.

Equally responsible for that happy childhood was Rebecca Cummings. She was a jolly, stout (up to 170 lbs. when Estlin was born), warm, motherly person, just five feet four inches tall—"a bouncy, bubbling person," as one of Estlin's friends remembered her.[18] She was loved by all the neighborhood children, some of whom were rather scared of

*Rebecca H. Cummings in 1892, oil
portrait by Charles Hopkinson.*
MASSACHUSETTS HISTORICAL SOCIETY

Edward Cummings' booming voice. She did not care for fashion and
believed in comfort in her clothes. She could not cook, she did not sew,
she had great difficulty with the household accounts. She enjoyed being
the companion of her husband and joining with him in all kinds of
activities, whether it be shingling the roof or playing tennis and fencing.
But she seems to have occupied herself chiefly in the care and entertain-
ment of the children. She sang to them, she read to them by the hour, she
taught them their letters, she took them on errands, she arranged games
and little surprises, she taught them how to keep diaries, she copied out
their school compositions on the typewriter.

She early learned to drive an automobile and delighted in going
about and in stopping to give rides to others. However, her social life
consisted mostly of interchange with relatives and neighbors and of meet-
ings of her Cambridge Mothers Club. In winter she enjoyed the snow and
in spring the flower garden. She responded to the abundance of summe
by picking blueberries, blackberries, and apples for preserving and for
jam and marmalade. Records of her pleasure in a colorful sunset, a kind
act, a child's achievement, her husband's writings, are scattered through
her diary. She felt her life experiences deeply and was easily moved to
tears. Estlin remembers seeing her at church watching Edward preach,
a tear creeping slowly down her cheek. Above all, her ability to relate

warmly to other human beings seems to have been widely recognized. "Mother knew how to enjoy people," wrote her daughter Elizabeth, "and always trusted them and saw the best in them. She had very firm ideas of her own and didn't mind if they had firm ideas that were quite different. She seemed to understand how people really felt about things and could always tell a big important thing from a little one, and she could see the fun in things even when the joke was on her."[19]

Before her marriage, she was Rebecca Haswell Clarke, born December 7, 1859, in Roxbury, Massachusetts. Unlike Edward she had distinguished forebears and her heritage of Unitarianism extended back to its New England beginnings. When one examines her maternal ancestry, one finds an interesting mixture of independent-minded adventurers and minor literary talents.[20] Susanna Haswell (married name: Rowson), the author of the first American novel, *Charlotte Temple*, was her great-great-great aunt. Susanna's cousin, Anthony Haswell, was a writer of political ballads during the American Revolution and the editor-printer of *Haswell's Massachusetts Spy or American Oracle of Liberty*. Susanna's half brother, Captain Robert Haswell went to sea young, was on board ships that first explored the coast of the Pacific Northwest, going up as far as Alaska, and was later on the *Columbia* when she became the "first vessel to carry the Stars and Stripes around the world" in 1790.

The Clarkes, on the other hand, were religious or political in their exploits. Rebecca's great-grandfather, Pitt Clarke, was a leader in the American Unitarian movement from his church at Norton, Massachusetts. In "A Pastor's Legacy," his own "confession of faith," he reports that he examined the Sermon on the Mount and found "nothing about three co-equal persons in the Godhead—nothing about the five points of Calvin."[21] In good Unitarian fashion he believed in the Holy Spirit as the spirit of God in the human heart. His son, John Jones Clarke, was more worldly; he went into law and, it was said, "argued more cases in the Supreme Judicial Court [of Massachusetts] than almost any of his contemporaries."[22] He became the mayor of Roxbury and later was elected to the State Legislature serving first in the House and then in the Senate.

It is clear that there was a good deal of linguistic ability, both spoken and written, in Mrs. Cummings' background and it is not surprising that she herself wrote verse and that her brother George was well-known at the Brookline Country Club for his witty *vers de société*. But all this refers to her maternal ancestors only. Almost nothing is known about the paternal side because of a family disgrace. Her name was not Rebecca Clarke but Rebecca Hanson. Her father, John A Hanson, forged his father-in-law's name to a check one day, and the outraged J. J. Clarke let him go to prison for it.[23] Other family troubles must have been present too, for Hanson's wife, Mary (Rebecca's mother), arranged to have her marriage of more than fifteen years annulled in 1873 by the Supreme Court of Massachusetts (no doubt, the case was argued by J. J. Clarke himself). She took her three children back to their grandfather's house in Roxbury and resumed the name Clarke. All this happened at a bad time for Rebecca: she was fourteen. This seems to explain something that she later told her children about her own troubled adolescence: "that when she was young she was painfully shy, didn't know how to enjoy people and didn't want to meet them and that she had to work very hard to overcome her shyness."[24] It also explains the secret sorrow that once in a great while she would reveal. Estlin remembers her reciting, with a wistful sense of inadequacy, Emily Dickinson's poem, "I'm nobody. Who are you?"

She was still unmarried at the age of twenty-nine when William James introduced her to one of his graduate students, Edward Cummings, in 1888. She was thirty-two by the time she was married. Although she was always somewhat unassuming, the fact that she developed into the wonderful woman who lives in everyone's memory as a perfect model of loving kindness is good testimony to the nurturing love that Edward Cummings gave her. They both are well deserving of the tribute that Estlin paid them years later in his Charles Eliot Norton lectures at Harvard: that it was "my joyous fate and my supreme fortune" to be born to them.

III

The Realm of the
Goat-footed Balloonman

In a well-planned play world in which the real world has been brought
down to manageable size, the child can manipulate and maneuver it
to suit his own whims. He can try his talents for structuring life.

FRANK and THERESA CAPLAN, *The Power of Play*

Since Mrs. Cummings' passion for diary-keeping extended to recording
separately the early events of Estlin's life, we have available the details
about such matters as his first smile, his first tear, his nursing habits and
the condition of his bowels. An account of interest is his first real trau-
matic experience—circumcision. He endured it very well, we learn.
"Cried lustily till Edward spoke to him telling him to bear it bravely.
Then the boy actually stopped crying."[1] He was christened by his father
at the age of two months. Although the name Edward was an old one in
the family, Estlin was new, in honor of J. Estlin Carpenter,[2] Edward's
companion in social work and religious studies in England, who was also
asked to be the boy's godfather.

The child loved music. His first word was "Hurrah," shouted
while joining in a chorus of "Marching Through Georgia." He de-
lighted in his music box. When he was two he could hum "Fair Har-
vard," "America," and other tunes. His second birthday also brought
letter blocks and a little blackboard. Four months later he knew all
the letters of the alphabet. Harvard associations were inculcated early.
He wore a crimson H embroidered on his white sweater and he loved
the statue of John Harvard, which in those days stood on the delta of
land at the confluence of Kirkland and Cambridge streets in front of

Memorial Hall. At the age of three he announced "when I get a 'ittle bigger, Mullah, I'm going to be a big college boy and go to college with Fader." He loved animals immensely and his artistic talents began to emerge early in his drawings of dogs, cats, elephants, giraffes, and other beasts. He took a calico cat to bed with him and later a dog named Jack, who often had to undergo repair. He had a remarkable rocking horse named Daisy Circus, who was also fitted with wheels for outdoor excursions.[3]

The spacious house that Edward Cummings had built for the child to begin his life in combined beauty, comfort, and convenience. The structure itself is in the best Colonial Revival tradition of Cambridge.[4] The height of its three stories is comfortably supported by the breadth of its façade, with two spacious window bays symmetrically placed on each side of a double-pillared porch and terrace. An entrance on each side of the house, one on Irving Street and one on Scott Street, made it possible for the broad face of the house to look out over the larger of two gardens. Thus, the porch, the two bay-windowed first-floor rooms and the two second-story master bedrooms all had a view of a sunny green area to the south. Here the well-trimmed lawn and flower beds were surrounded by fir, hemlock, and rhododendrons thickly planted for a privacy screen. The whole of this garden area was shaped like the prow of a ship where Irving and Scott streets joined together. The rose garden grew on the Scott Street side of the house outside Edward's study, catching the eastern sun. Begun with slips provided by Francis James Child (compiler of the Child's *Ballads*), it produced generous blooms of various shades, especially the dark "Jack" roses. Years later it supplied the controlling image for E. E. Cummings' poetic memorial to his mother:

> if there are any heavens my mother will(all by herself)have
> one.   It will not be a pansy heaven or
> a fragile heaven of lilies-of-the-valley but
> it will be a heaven of blackred roses
>
> my father will be(deep like a rose
> tall like a rose)
>
> standing near my
>
> swaying over her
> (silent)
> with eyes which are really petals and see

nothing with the face of a poet really which
is a flower and not a face with
hands
which whisper
This is my beloved my

                         (suddenly in sunlight
he will bow,

and the whole garden will bow)[5]

On the Irving Street side grew an apple tree and two cherry trees that delighted Estlin with their springtime bloom and with their limbs for climbing and swinging in imitation of circus acrobats.

Entering the house, one found a gracious entrance hall with a fireplace; three large rooms on the right all looking out upon the garden through the tall bay windows and large French doors; and an ample dining room straight ahead. All this space was cluttered with diverse evidence of family tastes and interests: antlers mounted on the wall (Edward's trophy, although his wife had now made him change his gun for a camera), a mounted seven-pound trout, stuffed birds including a loon standing upon the newel post of the stairway, portraits of Edward and of Rebecca (in an elegant Italian cloak) by Charles Hopkinson, a portrait of Nana Clarke by Chester Hale, a painting of a Norwegian fiord by Edward, a photo of Estlin on the Joy Farm horse, a tank of goldfish, a piano, a gramaphone, a marvelous sideboard with a mirror reflecting the napkin rings, the candlesticks, and the tea set; Edward's books lining his study, a plaster head of Jove, desks, a toy bench, window seats; and off to the left the pantry and the kitchen with its mammoth coal and wood stove with a hot water tank on the side from which water could be dipped for dishwashing. Near the laundry room, the back door led outside to the strange octagonal garage that Edward had built out of a series of discarded doors.

Upstairs, again the ample space and garden view, and the family pictures in four bedrooms, all of which had fireplaces. In the hall a dumb waiter which Edward, exercising the Cummings inventiveness, had constructed for hauling fireplace wood to the upper floors. Speaking tubes allowed communication between the downstairs and the upper floors. Besides the water closet, the upstairs area had a shower room and a bathroom, where the children often sailed their boats. On the third floor a skylight in the hall, five more rooms: servants rooms and rooms for fun and hobbies—Edward's darkroom, where he developed his photographs and a workroom, "the studio," with a carpenter's bench and tools.[6]

Sunday was the busiest day of the week for this family. They rose early and breakfasted on codfish balls. Then Edward Cummings cranked up the Ford and all drove off to the red-brick church. He posted the hymn numbers and donned his black gown while Mrs. Cummings greeted parishioners at the church door. The South Congregational Church had a semiprofessional choir directed by William Zeuch, a distinguished organist. For special religious holidays Zeuch would augment his group with guests from the Boston Symphony, so that sometimes strings, harp, and timpani rendered some of the best music of Boston's Sunday mornings. Edward Cummings, who wore his learning with ease, preached polished, down-to-earth sermons seasoned with wit, delivering them effortlessly in his sonorous voice. He led the congregational singing with vigor. The children endured the long service dutifully. Elizabeth brought her teddy bears to play with and Estlin sat drawing pictures. After the service, Edward Cummings went below to the ground floor where the South Congregational Citizenship Committee met, and he turned to the more immediate concerns of society. For their good behavior the two youngsters were allowed to go to the drug store for lemon phosphates and then to take the street car home alone. Later Mr. Cummings brought one of the congregation home for a typical American Sunday dinner featuring chicken and ice cream. Ginger ale was their champagne.

The area around Irving Street was mostly settled by Harvard professors and their families. Estlin's first playmate was Betty Thaxter, daughter of Roland Thaxter, professor of cryptogamic botany (and granddaughter of Celia Thaxter, the New Hampshire poetess). As he and his sister grew up, they played with Jack and Esther Lanman, children of Charles Lanman, the greatest Sanskrit Scholar in the country; with Francis and Alec James, William James's boys; with Catherine and Helen Taussig, children of Frank W. Taussig, head of the department of Economics. One need not think that the youngsters scribbled in Sanskrit or botanized and philosophized, but their play was marked by a little more awareness of tradition and more imagination than usual.[7]

Holidays were still communal affairs in those days. The neighborhood children were all invited in to see Professor Josiah Royce's Christmas tree and share some goodies on Christmas morning. The children organized parades on Memorial Day. May Day was an occasion for dressing up, especially for little girls, and leaving May baskets at neighbors' doors. At May parties they marched two by two in ceremony, chose and crowned a May queen. Estlin was usually involved in the group activities and he was quite an entrepreneur in producing shows.

One program began with a toy tableau of Elizabeth's dolls, Scene II was a skit featuring Estlin's dog Rex as a "fierce bull dog," Scene III was "The Hold Up."

The inspiration for many of these programs was the circus, which became for E. E. Cummings in later years the symbol of dedicated and uncorrupted artistry. His father or his Uncle George took him to Forepaugh and Sells Brothers Circus (where he once rode on an elephant), to Ringling Brothers, and on one glorious occasion to Barnum and Bailey where he saw the sideshows for the first time—the freaks and the swordswallowers. Best of all was Bostock's Animal Show with Captain Bonavita "and his matchless group of 27 forest-bred African lions grouped for the first time in one arena." Still extant is Mrs. Cummings' season ticket to "Estlin's Great Animal arena (Positively not transferable if presented by other person)." This perhaps admitted her on February 10, 1901, when the six-year-old advertised himself as "Edward Estlin Cummings and his matchless group of 32 elephants little and big." A later development announced on its "Programm" a whole series of acts, the first being "ESTLIN CUMMINGS AND HIS MATCHLESS GROUP OF TWO ELEPHANDS AND TWO LIONS PRESENTING THE MOST WONDERFUL EXHIBITION OF ITS KIND EVER SEEN IN THE HISTORY OF THE WORLD."[8]

West Cambridge was not fully built up around the turn of the century. The streets were not paved, and a herd of cattle being driven down Kirkland Street to the Brighton Abatoir would raise great clouds of dust. There was a great deal of open space for the children to play in near the Cummings house, for the area had been part of the Charles Eliot Norton Estate.[9] As a consequence, the beautifully planted acreage of deciduous and coniferous trees around the Shady Hill mansion known as "Norton's Woods" (about thirty-five acres) was available as a local wilderness for exploration and games. A stream ran through it feeding "Norton Pond," which in winter made a perfect skating rink at a spot now occupied by the Harvard Divinity School. Besides this, the older boys iced a toboggan slide, and others built snow forts for snow ball battles. Another winter sport was "punging," that is, hanging on to the back of sleighs that drove by, the genial drivers of which (icemen, milkmen, and other delivery folk) often slowed down so that the children could catch hold. Greater excitement was generated from time to time by the nearby firehouse, from which the plunging horses pulled clanging firewagons led by a barking Dalmatian.

Most of the good weather fun was in spontaneously organized games of cops and robbers, prisoner's base, blindman's buff, follow the leader, hare and hounds (with chalk arrows drawn on the sidewalk or bits of paper dropped in the woods), fox and geese, "still pond" (their name for

E. E. Cummings, oil portrait by Charles Hopkinson about 1902. HOUGHTON LIBRARY

the game of statues), and later on, scrub (a form of baseball usually known as three o' cat). "It was a real neighborhood," declared one old inhabitant, "the kind you don't find anymore."

Much of the after-school play centered in the Cummings yard, partly because of its space and partly because after play the children could retire to Estlin's tree house. Edward had built an enviable construction, six feet by six feet by six feet, not counting the extra height of the roof. It had a porch and railing, and it held some children's furniture, including a little stove on which Estlin was allowed to cook. "after school went up in Estlin's tree house," wrote Esther Lanman in her diary, "we made toased and cooked some apples and had a few peanuts then we poped corn." Her diary for 1908 (she was ten years old) mentions "Estlin's house" twenty-two times. Just beyond the place where Irving and Scott Streets formed a point, a third, Farrar Street, joined them from the east and at the center stood "tree square," as the children called it, a small island of greenery with a tree that served as "goal" for hide-and-seek and other games. Spring thaws filled a low spot in the street there with a huge puddle, a "mud-luscious" site. In years to come, the memory of this annual occurrence plus the advent of the balloon-seller, blowing his whistle, and the remembered joy of childhood play would coalesce to inspire E. E. Cummings' best known poem, "in Just-/spring" and to convey his sense of a time when the world was "puddle-wonderful,"

> and bettyandisbel come dancing
>
> from hop-scotch and jump-rope and
>
> it's
> spring
> and
>   the
>
>   goat-footed
>
> balloonMan   whistles
> far
> and
> wee

This idyllic world had, however, the limitations of homogeneity. The children had fear and distaste for the poorer youngsters of the working class, the Cambridge "muckers," who were growing up in a tougher world of fighting, rock-throwing, and jeering. Estlin, who was small and slight of build, was afraid of them when he met them in Harvard Square. In the same category were the "Somerville Micks," who sometimes invaded the neighborhood or Nortons Woods. Somerville, formerly a part of Charlestown but now a separate city, was a crowded area of tradespeople and factory workers, mostly Irish, who by settling outside Boston were demonstrating upward social mobility. Its border, Beacon Street, ran along one side of the Norton Estate. The professional offspring in Cambridge hated and despised these intruders, who sometimes engaged them in snow-ball fights or name-calling sessions. "We were a snobbish generation," recalled one of Estlin's playmates.

Not all the fun of growing up took place in Cambridge. Since the Cummings family lived in the annual rhythm of academic life, they were free to spend their summers away from Irving Street. In Estlin's early life the family went to the seashore at Lynn, where Edward kept his sailboat, the *Actress*, and where his mother and his sister Jane could help Rebecca look after the child. But Rebecca did not care for the sea, and sailing made her sick, so in 1899 the family bought a farm in the Sandwich Range of the White Mountains near Silver Lake, New Hampshire, from a farmer named Ephraim Joy. Joy Farm, as they called it, with its hand-cut floorboards and plastered walls was about one hundred years old at the time of purchase.[10] By the time Edward Cummings had finished making additions and improvements, the sixty-foot-wide farmhouse had new second-story dormers and a fifty-foot porch with a striking view of Mount Chocorua and its sister peaks. Both the "reception room" and the dining room had fireplaces. There were two double bedrooms, one with a fireplace, and six smaller bedrooms plus two in the barn. The farm had its own well and the kitchen had provision for hot water, but there was no electricity. Two hundred feet from the house, Edward had built himself a study in the woods and Estlin had a small house, this time on the ground, for his times of retreat. Edward also built a dam in a nearby stream in order to create a pond for bathing and swimming and for teaching his children to paddle a canoe.

Every June the family members boarded the train with the servants, the dog, pet rabbits, children's toys, books, trunks, suitcases, and lunch boxes for the all-day ride up to Madison, New Hampshire. The farm-house was as fully populated as the Cambridge house with most of the relatives plus, usually, Rebecca's best friend from childhood days, Emma Billings Hathaway ("Aunt Emma"). Sandy Hardy joined Mark Nicker-son, the tenant who worked the farm, in a bedroom in the barn. During the summer, many visitors came up from Boston, and many friends from Cambridge who had summer "camps" in the area around Silver Lake and Conway dropped in. Nearby neighbors were Samuel Crothers, minister of the Cambridge Unitarian Church, and his family, who had a farm called "Crothers Croft."

For Estlin, Joy Farm was a boy's paradise. The farm had quite a domestic menagerie, a horse named Thomas à Kempis, two or three cows (Estlin learned to milk), a varying number of pigs, hens, a goat named Nan who could pull a small cart, and a charming, independent-minded donkey named Jack, whom Estlin learned to ride. "When my soul—myself's own self—wasn't wandering pasture and woodland," he recalled years later, "it's home was the barn. Savagely hand-hewn timbers . . . not a spike in the whole structure."[11] Swallows nested in the roof and mice in the feed box. It had a sweet-smelling hayloft where the children built hay forts and had hay fights.

All around the clearing of the hayfields stood huge boulders for climbing and sliding and for stalking behind while playing Indian. One

The Barn at Joy Farm, early 1900's: Sandy Hardy, Rebecca Cummings, Estlin on horse Thomas à Kempis, Elizabeth with her cat on Jack Donkey, family friend with dog Rex.
HOUGHTON LIBRARY

year Estlin set up a wigwam for his Indian games and for outdoor sleeping. Estlin became quite an expert on caterpillars and on butterflies. Edward taught the children how to find their way through the woods by both compass and woodcraft. At the farm, a log book recording the daily events was faithfully kept, mostly by Rebecca, and each volume of it reflects, in Sterling North's phrase, "a memoir of a better era."

Occasionally the family went up to Joy Farm for a winter holiday of skiing, snowshoeing, and roaring fires. In 1904, for instance, they went up for a New Year's weekend and Estlin invited the Crothers girls for a New Year's feast. Rebecca prepared a menu in French:

> *Bouillon en Tasse*
> *Boef roti et fritte à la Madison*
> *Pommes de Terre roti en cindres*
> *Pommes en puree*
> *Olives d' Espagne*
> *Patés de Beaucoup de Choses*
> *Des Oranges Glaciés en Panniers*
> *Champagne à la Madison*
> *Educators à la Boston*[12]

In 1910 Edward built a summer home, mostly with his own hands, on the shore of Silver Lake itself, and the following year Joy Farm was leased. But Estlin never ceased to love it and in 1929 his mother deeded him the farm. He returned there every summer for the rest of his life.

II

Estlin's schooling began at home. He was taught to read and write by his mother. He had been read to daily since he was two, and it was not long before he was printing his own name on the pictures he drew. He could write a short letter by the age of six. Mrs. Cummings showed him how to keep a diary, at first, writing the brief diary entries for him, while Estlin drew pictures illustrating the activity.[13] The first entry is May 19, 1900: "In bed with cold. Played with my music box. Cold rain. Read Robinson Crusoe. Looked at picture cards. Had a good night. Eat a good breakfast, two dropped eggs, two pieces of toast one orange." A little later, May 22, he records going to his first circus, "Saw jaguars, hyena, bear, elephants, baby lions, and a father lion, baby monkeys climbing a tree." So on it goes. On his sixth birthday he records, "Had a good birthday. Rode to church. These are my presents." There follow pictures of books, paint box, ice cream freezer, fishing pole, goldfish, gloves, and carpenter's tools: saw, hammer, square, and screw driver.

By the following March, he begins to write out his own entries, "I am going to be Happy Light and Free said Sun God Jesus Ligh and Free." His own entries consist mostly of the date, the weather conditions and "A good day." A long account of a performance of Bostock's Animal Show is again written out for him by his mother. As the years went by, his reading and writing exercises became more regularized, for Mrs. Cummings purchased the standard textbooks for him to use.

It is not certain when Estlin's formal schooling began. Under the Cambridge system, pupils went three years to Primary School (there were only a few kindergartens); then followed Grammar School in a pattern of six years—grades 4, 5, 6, 7, 8, 9—or four years—the "skipping" grades A, B, C, D—depending on the child's progress.[14] It seems that Edward Cummings agreed with his father about not having children go to school too early. Elizabeth Cummings states that she did not start school until she was nine years old.[15] Estlin was apparently not sent to Primary School at all.

It was probably as late as September 1902 when he first went to Miss Webster's School, a private establishment on Appian Way, on a site now occupied by a Radcliffe College building.[16] Classes began with the Lord's Prayer and a reading from the Bible (as required by Massa-chusetts law) and Estlin was distressed one day when he had a nose-bleed during the prayer. From descriptions given by those who at-tended Miss Webster's School it sounds as if classes were conducted in a very informal way and that the emphasis was on the three R's with a lot of creative play in arts and crafts (Estlin's 1903 report card even gives him a grade in "Baskets"). Estlin seems not to have remembered very much about it, except that one day he wept at the blackboard because he did not know how to do an arithmetic "example". It appears that he had not learned enough elementary arithmetic at home, possibly because Mrs. Cummings herself did not care for it. His own dislike for mathematical abstractions seems to have begun here and stayed with him all his life. This may have contributed to his later hatred of science, technology, and quantitative measurement.

In September 1904 this small, very blond, very smiley, very shy youngster changed to the Agassiz Public School at the corner of Oxford and Sacramento Streets (the present structure replaced the old one in 1914). Because of his high level of reading comprehension, he was placed in the 7th grade, although he was still not ten years old. A report from the principal, Maria Baldwin, still survives, dated October 28, 1904. "In all his work, except arithmetic, he is quite the equal in attainment of the seventh grade pupils." She pointed out that he needed more confidence in doing arithmetic problems by himself, that he is rather used to "the individual teaching to which he has been accustomed" and this "makes these little appeals for help seem quite the natural thing. . . . He is a most loveable little boy and we are glad that he is part of our little community."[17] One of Estlin's school papers covered with exercises in fractions has on the back a drawing of an Indian with a bow and arrow: he would have much preferred to be off with Leatherstocking. Another paper with long problems in addition and multiplication has a note by his teacher, Edith C. Arey, "You are improving,"[18] and by the end of the year he was promoted to the skipping grade C.

For each grade, the Cambridge School Committee established a list of poems which the pupils were required to memorize. Estlin's school notebooks record that in his time at Agassiz School, he mastered such pieces as Emerson's "The Concord Hymn" and "Forbearance," Hunt's "Abou Ben Adhem and the Angel," Longfellow's "The Legend Beautiful" and "January," Whittier's "The Corn Song," Scott's lines beginning, "Breathes there a man with soul so dead," Browning's "Home Thoughts from Abroad," and Emerson's lines from "Voluntaries" about "When Duty whispers low, *Thou must.*"[19] The lists were heavy on the New England poets and on versified expression of patriotism, duty, and brotherhood. The custom was an admirable one for establishing a sense of communal values and for upholding the importance of verse. For Estlin Cummings it not only reinforced the encouragement to write verse that he was getting at home but it also had a curiously ironical outcome: he absorbed the New England and Victorian commonplaces so thoroughly that they supplied him with unmoving targets for later satirical sharp-shooting and they provided well-known phrases for him to burlesque in his satirical epigrams.[20]

Maria Baldwin herself was Estlin's next teacher. She was a short, stout mulatto woman with a motherly manner. Her soft mellifluous voice read aloud such works as the Cambridge School Committee recommended: Scott's *Lady of the Lake,* Macaulay's *Lays of Ancient Rome,* Charlotte Yonge's *Book of Golden Deeds,* Scott's *Ivanhoe,* Towle's *Life of Pizarro,* and other works.

The Agassiz School was so small that it could not offer the 9th or the D grade; so Estlin and his classmates transferred to the old Peabody School at the corner of Linnaen and Avon Streets—four stories of solid brick which has since been replaced.[21] Here Estlin struggled in mathematics with Frederick Cutter, the principal, but the teacher he chiefly remembered was a prim, white-haired spinster, Miss Charlotte A. Ewell, who taught American history and English. Under her tutelage, he read such works as *Julius Caesar, As You Like It,* and Andrew Lang's *Tales of Troy and Greece,* and outlined in extensive detail the story of the *Iliad* and of the *Odyssey,* book by book. A few of his compositions from this period survive, all on historical topics—one on "Lincoln," others on "London," on "Daniel Webster," and on "Free Trade and Protective Tariff."[22]

There was, of course, the usual list of selections to memorize. Estlin records such pieces as Holmes' "The Chambered Nautilus" and "Old Ironsides," Longfellow's "The Ship of State" and the great sonnet "Nature," Emerson's "The Rhodora," Brutus' speech, "There is a tide in the affairs of men," Lincoln's "Gettysburg Address," an extract from Webster's "Washington," Gray's "Elegy," Bryant's lines from "Thanatopsis" beginning "So live, that when thy summons comes." Altogether it was a first-rate body of material. Miss Ewell drilled her youngsters to recite in unison with appropriate gestures in order to train them for their performance on graduation day.[23] (Miss Ewell's pupils can still recite them today—and sometimes do at Cambridge dinner parties.) This year provided an even greater occasion, the centennial of Longfellow's birth; so on February 27, 1907, there was a special celebration in all the Cambridge schools which included at Peabody a group recitation of "The Psalm of Life" and a declamation of "Excelsior." E. E. Cummings parodied these poems in his verse and in his letters all during his writing career ("COURAGE he said and pointed to his GOGGLELESS GLIMS").[24]

Estlin was ill frequently and absent a great many times during the year. Thus, there was some difficulty about his passing geometry, but finally he did graduate with his class. At an elaborate ceremony, the girls in their white dresses and the boys in their knickerbockered suits recited in unison "Build Me Straight" from Longfellow's "Building of the Ship," and E. Estlin Cummings recited Henry Holcomb Bennett's "Hats Off! The Flag Is Passing by." The program included choral singing, musical solos, a recitation of "A Task for Each Generation" (from a speech by Theodore Roosevelt), and an address by the Reverend Edward Cummings. At the end the mayor passed out the diplomas and everyone sang the Peabody Hymn, three stanzas about the founding of the colonies and the ideals of freedom and brotherhood.[25] It was a memorable occasion for the Cummings family.

III

But Estlin was still being educated at home. As a child he was surrounded by a plenitude of books and reading matter. Besides the *Boston Transcript* and the *Boston Herald* and the adult periodicals like the *Atlantic Monthly* and *Harper's Weekly*, his own magazines, *St. Nicholas* and *The Youth's Companion*, came regularly to the house. He was presented with books on every pretext and was read to every evening until well into the grammar school years.[26] The Cummings family had a happy custom too of group reading, especially in the long evenings at Joy Farm, where all would listen while Rebecca or Aunt Jane read aloud Scott's *Quentin Durward*, *The Monastery*, *The Abbot*, *Anne of Gerstein*, *Kenilworth*, and *The Talisman* (for which Estlin provided painstakingly careful illustrations), Jane Porter's *The Scottish Chiefs* (the Cummings heritage provoked much interest in Scottish material), Dickens' *Christmas Carol*, *David Copperfield*, and *The Old Curiosity Shop*. Not much poetry was served up this way, except for Longfellow's *Hiawatha* and the ballads from Percy's *Reliques* (Estlin identified himself, because of his name, Est-lin, with "The Heir of Lynn").

In later years, Estlin remembered that he read or was read such varying works as *The Arabian Nights*, Bullfinch's *The Age of Fable*, *The Iliad*, *The Odyssey*, *Robin Hood*, *King Arthur and His Knights* (both the lavishly illustrated Howard Pyle version and the Andrew Lang version, which was sent by godfather Estlin Carpenter from England), *Froissart's Chronicles* (Sidney Lanier's abridgment), *The Three Musketeers*, *Westward Ho*, *Lorna Doone*, *The Deerslayer*, *Tom Sawyer*, and *Tom Brown's School Days*. Jules Verne was another favorite: *Twenty Thousand Leagues under the Sea*, *Around the World in Eighty Days*, and *The Mysterious Island* (for which he provided additional illustrations). There were plenty of western stories: some about Daniel Boone, Davy Crockett, Kit Carson; Clarence E. Mulford's *Bar 20 Days;* and, most important, a book about Buffalo Bill which his father had picked up at an auction. He knew *Treasure Island* so well that in 1925 he was able to type out, from memory, a two-page synopsis accurate in every detail and character's name.[27]

Animal stories, especially those by "Enearst Tomphon Seton," as Estlin spelled the name, were high on the Christmas list, and Kipling's *The Jungle Book* took on special significance. Ever since he was a tiny boy Estlin had a singular liking for elephants, which he came to associate with his father (who carried him about, who had big ears). Drawing pictures of elephants became a repeated pastime. At length, the situation became reversed in the role-playing with his father, so that Estlin became in imagination Kipling's elephant Kala Nag, and his father became little Tomai, the elephant boy who took care of him. "Take me with you, O Kala Nag," his father would say at bedtime.[28] In later years the elephant became his totem: he collected dozens of elephant figures, and for special people he signed his name accompanied by an elephant drawing.

Very early in his childhood Estlin merged the literary and the visual in his creative outpouring. He was constantly drawing—with pencil, crayon, chalk, paint, or even scratching in the dirt with a stick. He drew trains, ships (even Roman galleys and Viking ships) racing cars, Indians, merry-go-round horses, wild animals of all sorts, soldiers and sailors of various historical periods (including the Boer War and the Russo-Japanese Battle of Port Arthur).[29]

But very soon his pictures took their inspiration from his reading, and among hundreds that survive, some have dates. In March 1902, he drew Hiawatha and his canoe; in February 1903, Sitting Bull and Buffalo Bill; on the day after Christmas 1903, Achilles in armor; in February 1904 scenes from *Ivanhoe*.[30] As this practice continued, it became connected with writing out versions of the stories themselves. But to see the beginnings of this literary development we must go back in time.

The first combination of writing and drawing after the early diary entries is an alphabet book which Estlin composed, under his mother's supervision: "D is for the Duck," "O is for the Ostrich," and so on, with appropriate pictures.[31] His first real story, rather a brief one, is carefully printed out underneath a sketch of an entrapped deer. "A stag was running about in the field when suddenly he was caught in a trap. He called for his to farmers and his cowboys." Other little stories survive, one called "Joy Farm" about catching a woodchuck, another called "Bunny Cottontail," and another, "Abdullah and Redruff," about two boys on a hippopotamus hunt. The retelling of stories he was reading begins during the King Arthur period in the fall of 1903 when he had just turned nine years old. He labored to produce reams of pages which go through the story of the Sword in the Stone, of Gareth, Gawain, Tristam, Galahad, and other knights. The illustrations are quite elaborately done in the manner of Howard Pyle and each one has its caption—for example, on October 24, 1903, for Sir Gareth, "Faugh Sir You Smell of ye Kitchen." Pages survive, too, of the same sort of treatment of Robin Hood.[32]

The next step was taken with stories that were not synopses but were still derived from the reading. "For Henry and England," with illustrations, is set vaguely in the time of Henry II, and it begins with two friends, Austin and Danby, who while journeying to London meet Robin Hood. Another, "For God and Queen" is about Henery Dureward, whose father has been knighted by Queen Elizabeth. One dated November 28, 1905, and entitled "A Son of the Sea" concerns Largile, a French fisherman who lives alone because he "was thought a traiter by his countrymen, yet not for crimes, not for anything more than an act committed on a friend's behalf." It runs forty-one pages. Another story, done more in the style of the *Youth's Companion,* seems to have been inspired by *The Mysterious Island*—about a boy who goes up in a "baloon" ("He, Jack Main was a 'scientific' boy,—much laughed at by his fellow associates who were true 'country boys' "). He was still doing his historical narratives toward the end of grammar school days. Forty pages, dated January 19, 1906, "In Cromwell's Time," tell the story of Edward Longwood, who comes from a Royalist family but who serves as a colonel (at age eighteen) in Cromwell's army. One Table of Contents, illustrated by figures and scenes from the book, shows plans for a wide-ranging series of boys stories:

1. Under the Stars and Stripes at Manila, or Young Americans in the Spanish War.
2. For British or Boers, or Young Fighters in South Africa.
3. Fighting the Boxers, or Yankees against Chinamen.
4. Fighting for Japan, or Boy Fighters against Russia.
5. On Board the "Mary Ann"; or Boys at Sea.
6. Fighting the new way, or young submarines.
7. Two to one, or the modern pirate.
8. What they did for themselves, or wrecked and alone.
9. Gold and the West; or, young "49'ers."
10. In the north with Nansen, or to latitude 87°.

Estlin's continued literary activity, accompanied always by numerous drawings, gives evidence that Rebecca Cummings had under her guidance a special artistic personality, one who hated to see a piece of paper remain blank. His immediate impulse was to fill it, whether with words or with lines and shapes did not matter.

What we have been seeing in this glimpse of E. E. Cummings' first dozen years are the principal forces that operated upon his developing personality. He was both verbal and visual in expressive inclination and ability, and these tendencies were encouraged by his father and especially by his mother. His parents fostered the exercise of mind and imagination, thus helping him to become responsive to symbols and patterns. They were providing ample means for play, that simplest of manifestations of the joy in being alive which creative people feel. They were inviting him to explore and discover both himself and the world about him and to express freely what he found.

At the same time, the whole ethos of Cambridge was coloring his values—imbuing him with a sense of its traditions: with the sense of duty to the group, the community, the state, and with the endorsement of order and heirarchy. The way of life of the Cummings family, however, ran somewhat counter to the Cambridge demands for submission to the group. Estlin's mother was a quiet but strong-minded person who showed him a way of being an individual without having to be over-assertive about it. His aggressive father, the self-made man, was more socially oriented, but he still displayed a strong individualistic drive for his son to emulate. A conflict need not have developed between these two sets of values, but given the kind of ego Estlin had and given the nurturing that was provided for that ego, he was very likely to clash with a twentieth-century urban society that was ever-increasing in its pressures for conformity. Meanwhile, there was a family atmosphere of love and approval in the home and a class atmosphere of solidarity in the community, both of which strengthened his psyche for whatever positions it would take. There was also the middle-class American literary and artistic heritage that he absorbed through his reading and his schooling—not indeed very rich or remarkable but sufficiently pervasive to nurture the future poet and at the same time provide a coherent cultural complex that he would later try to modify.

IV

Longfellow's
Latest Disciple

Look, then, into thine heart, and write!
Yes, into Life's deep stream!
All forms of sorrow and delight,
All solemn Voices of the Night,
That can soothe thee, or affright,—
Be these henceforth thy theme.

H. W. LONGFELLOW

Rebecca Cummings wanted her son to be a poet. In 1894 when Estlin was still an unnamed embryo in her womb, the Cummings family lived at 96 Brattle Street, across the street from Craigie House, the home of Henry Wadsworth Longfellow and already a national shrine. Indeed, the fame of Longfellow was even international: he was the only American writer who had ever been accorded a memorial in the Poets' Corner of Westminster Abbey. A little further west, just off Brattle Street, was Elmwood House, the home of James Russell Lowell, who had just recently died. In an atmosphere like this, rhyme and meter seemed to hang in the air. Like other citizens of West Cambridge, Mrs. Cummings thought of Cambridge as a focal area of New England culture, halfway between Boston, with its literary urbanity represented by Oliver Wendell Holmes, Thomas Bailey Aldrich, and the celebrated authors whose Brahminism fluttered from the pages of the *Atlantic Monthly,* and Concord with its transcendental eminence represented by Emerson, Channing, and Thoreau, whose wisdom had been absorbed in the serenity of nature.

Mrs. Cummings had been surrounded by verse all her life. She treasured a group of poems written by an early relative or friend of the family, one of which described her great-grandmother, Rebecca Jones, as having:

> Resistless virtue, sentiments refined;
> Ennobled feelings and a generous mind.[1]

She kept a commonplace book into which she copied her favorite poems, such as Wordsworth's Immortality Ode, several of Shakespeare's sonnets, Browning's "Evelyn Hope," many poems of the New England poets, several from Adelaide Proctor, several from Tennyson, an extract from Bailey's *Festus*—altogether a collection that reflected a varying taste but one with a decided leaning toward themes of religion or social uplift.[2] She read nursery rhymes and jingles to Estlin very early, and by her singing and playing platters on the music box, she developed his sense of rhythm. Her efforts paid off sooner than one might expect, for on April 18, 1898, Estlin, at the age of three uttered his first rhyme:

> Oh my little birdie oh
> With his little toe, toe, toe![3]

She encouraged these little productions and when the diary-keeping began in 1900, there were regular entries in which she wrote out the little verses he composed. The first is dated December 14, 1900, when he was six. "It is a sunny day Read about milk in Holland. Drow a camel on Dec. 11, 1900. Every thing is still except the bushes which rustle in the wind.

> In the shining sunlight
> Bushes rustle there
> In the shining sunlight
> Daisy is so fair."

A little later, December 20, we find:

> On the chair is sitting
> Daddy with a book
> Took it from the book case
> Beaming in his look.[4]

As time went on, Estlin composed verses for valentines, for Mothers' Day, Christmas, birthdays, national holidays, and for other occasions, such as the death of his uncle's dog, Jack, who had been killed by an automobile:

> Only a dog, to me a friend
> As dear as many friends can be,
> Faithful hoeric [*sic*] to the last,
> True to his master and to me. . . .[5]

Stacks of prejuvenilia still exist, for Mrs. Cummings saved every scrap. The verse writing continued all through the grammar school years and developed more variety in the themes and in the poetic forms that Estlin imitated. Several poems celebrate spring or the outdoor life in the fashion of poems he read in *St. Nicholas* magazine ("Merry Spring has come at last,/All the dreary winter's past"); one gives us a character speaking in the New England dialect of Lowell's *Biglow Papers* to complain about the noise and pollution of the automobile; several are religious; some grow out of his school work, such as one on Lincoln; one is a comic poem about his father's sermons and another celebrates the visit of Theodore Roosevelt to Harvard:

> Teddy's come to Harvard like
> An ordinary man;
> I'd like to see a feller
> Insult him if he can. . . .

There are even some memorial verses, for Nana Clarke had died, as had a cousin Sarah. The best of these develops a central metaphor very solemnly, in the manner of Longfellow's "Nature":

> As rooms are separated by a curtain,
> So are our lives; yes, like those rooms; the first
> Is this our present life; the second is
> Our life to come,—our better life in Heaven;
> The separating curtain,—it is death.

In 1906 he copied into a small composition book the best of the work he had written in the past two years. It was his first volume of verse.[6] Estlin's singsong lines are not remarkable. What is remarkable is his unceasing attempt to write in verse and to live up to what he conceived to be the Cambridge tradition. We have already seen how the Cambridge schools revered their local authors. Besides all the memorizing, Estlin developed an awe about the role of the poet, and Longfellow became one of his childhood heroes. As early as the years at Agassiz School, he had written an essay about him which began, "Who is there in the State of Massachusetts, who has not heard of, and admired, the good, kind, Longfellow? I trust there is no one. Shame to him who does not love the great poet."[7] His discipleship had begun.

If Estlin's verses up to this time are in no way illustrative of the promise to come, one prose composition, also included in the 1905–1906 collection, does show a delicate handling of language that had not appeared before. This piece, entitled "The River of Mist," is reminiscent of Wordsworth's sonnet, "Composed upon Westminster Bridge." It is dated November 25, 1906—halfway through his year at Peabody School when he was twelve years old. It combines a sensitive response to a natural scene and a rather insipid religious reverie in the Longfellow manner:

> Stretching away to westward the great river lies quiet beneath me. So still it lies that it seems as if it had not yet awakened from the delicious sleep brought on by the silence of night. A little distance from the shore a boat is moored on its glossy surface,—perfect to every detail the reflection glimmers below it. All is still and sombre and wonderful, as dawn gives way to daylight and night to morning.
>
> As I stand leaning over a rail of the old wooden bridge that spans it, I give full play to my imagination, and gaze ahead into the morning fog that rests above its polished surface. And as I gaze, gaze into the deep white mist, my thoughts turn from earth to heaven, from mankind to my God. Far away, beyond the limits of that stream that fades into the atmosphere, I can see a great celestial river and a great celestial land. Ah! How my fancy pictures it,—how vivid and how real it seems! How plainly I can see into the inestimable future! And how I doubly worship the Great Power that has created all this. How wonderful and how marvellous it all is! How sweet is this unconscious dreaming of the soul. . . .[8]

This linking of religious feeling and emotional response to the natural world, a common form of Unitarian religiosity, was to become more fully developed during his high school and college years.

II

In September 1907, Estlin entered the Cambridge Latin School, the college preparatory branch of the Cambridge High School. It stands, an impressive, three-story, yellow-brick structure, with the names Homer, Virgil, and Euclid carved upon its facade, about fifty feet from the English High School and is now connected to it by a linking building.[9] During the time Estlin attended, the Latin School had about 480 pupils and 25 teachers ("masters" and "mistresses"). It was equal in quality to the Boston Latin School, and its graduates did as well or better in college than those from the more prestigious preparatory schools like Phillips Exeter, Groton, or Brown and Nichols. It offered both a four-year and a five-year program of study, but almost all students took the five-year course, which was required for admission to Harvard College. Harvard changed its requirement in 1911 and allowed four-year students who could pass its entrance examinations to be admitted: Estlin and his friend Robert Cawley were the first two students from Cambridge Latin School who went on to Harvard under this new plan.

When he entered Latin School, Estlin was still only twelve years old and rather small for his age. "God forgive us for our short Cummings" was the teasing prayer of one of his classmates.[10] He followed a rigorous course of study that had a very heavy emphasis on ancient and foreign languages. Besides routine study of English, algebra, and geometry, he took four years of Latin, four of French, and two of Greek.[11] Yet what gave the program its distinctive classical emphasis was that classes in Latin and Greek met every day, whereas the others met only on alternate days, and beyond that, the three-year course in history was composed of one year of ancient history,[12] one of Greek history, and one of Roman history.

The nineteenth-century flavor of this curriculum is even more evident when we note that Estlin took no science course during these four years.[13] However that may be, it was a fortunate situation for Estlin Cummings, the future poet, for here he built the foundation of that linguistic ability which marked his whole literary career. The language study made him intensely aware of the range and possibility of the English language; it made him conscious of literal meanings, of etymological roots, and of cognates and related words in ancient and foreign languages. It stretched his vocabulary and embedded a sense of syntax in his very bones. More than this, he became aware, through his beginning study of three languages—which was extended to five at Harvard—of the way systems of linguistic communication work; in other words, he came to understand linguistic theory in a practical way.

Estlin's language study was pursued, according to the planned program, in a very sensible way. In the first year he began only one language, Latin. (But, alas, using Collar and Daniell, a deadly book with paradigm after paradigm to memorize.)[14] In the second year, while he got into Caesar (four books of *The Gallic War*) and a little Ovid and Nepos, he began his second language, French. In the third year, he marched with Caesar and sailed with Aeneas; he took both French II and III, reading such standard classroom pieces as Mérimée's *Colomba*, Hugo's *La Chute*, and selections from La Fontaine's *Fables;* and he began the study of

Greek, using White's *First Greek Book,* an intelligently arranged textbook
(given the terrible difficulty youngsters have in learning Greek) which
based its daily reading exercises on a continuing narrative, a simplified
version of Xenophon's *Anabasis.* [15]

In his Greek classroom, Cummings met a man who affected the
course of his studies for years. Cecil T. Derry, newly come from taking
his A.M. degree in classics at Harvard, became one of the most beloved
teachers in the history of the Latin School. A jolly little Christmas elf of
a man, scarcely taller than Estlin himself, he made him love the study of
Greek. He encouraged classroom fun with the language, and responded
enthusiastically to Estlin, who was by this time beginning to exhibit wit,
and to the cartoons which the boy drew in the margins of his homework
papers. He also encouraged him to write out some of his translations in
verse and thus began a practice which Estlin followed over the next few
years. Since he was a bachelor, his pupils became his children—or, more
accurately, his younger brothers, for he was very much like a boy himself.
Because of these features of his personality, he was able to infect his
pupils with his own love of Greek culture.[16] By the end of the next year,
when he had taken the class through an undiluted *Anabasis* and portions
of the *Hellenica,* he had inspired Estlin to major in Greek at Harvard.

This final year saw Estlin going through four more books of the
Aeneid and beginning that meaningless exercise, prose composition in
Latin. French seemed more lively with Corneille's *Le Cid,* Racine's
Athalie, and Molière's *L'Avare,* and the writing exercises in Bouvet's
composition textbook seemed more meaningful. With his facility in lan-
guage, he really mastered French in his three years in Latin school. He
never studied it further in college; yet he passed an oral examination in
French during his freshman year at Harvard, he could read a French
novel in the original for Bliss Perry's fiction course, he could read Ver-
laine, Rimbaud, and Mallarmé with his college friends who were discov-
ering modern poetry, and he wrote several poems in French during those
years.

Estlin's English courses at Latin School were shaped largely by the
Harvard Reading List, and that list was not the equal in imaginative vigor
to the reading he was doing at home. He studied, for example, *Silas
Marner, The Vicar of Wakefield,* a heavy dose of Irving—*The Sketch Book,
Tales of a Traveler,* and *The Life of Goldsmith*—*The Idylls of the King* (selec-
tions in second year, the whole in third year—as if it had been written
in Greek), several books that he had read at home years before: *Quentin
Durward, David Copperfield,* and *Henry Esmond,*—and (oh dreariness, when
a boy has raced through Andrew Lang) Pope's *Iliad.* No wonder he chose
not to concentrate in English when he started at Harvard.

The students in the Cambridge High Schools published a monthly periodical, the *Cambridge Review,* which contained essays, stories, verse, local jokes, school gossip, and some official announcements. Estlin, quiet, shy, and small, took a while to adjust to the new institution, but the *Cambridge Review* captured his interest early (he already had rejection slips from the *Outlook, Youth's Companion,* and *Atlantic Monthly*). He began writing for it in his second year, and by his last year he was the literary editor.[17] No one could call his stories and poems very significant. Two essay-stories which are supposed to be funny are rather labored. Two melodramatic stories are scarcely worth comment, but there are three more stories each of which reflects, in a way, Estlin's concern about his small size, his lack of athletic ability, and his worry about what this could mean in being attractive to girls.

"The Story of a Man and a Pack of Cards" follows the fortunes of a cheater, first in college and then in the Far West. The note of interest does not lie in the story itself but rather in a character's name: Kingston Clarke, a ranch owner who is a friend of the narrator. When Estlin was a child he had an imaginary friend named Kingston Clarke, an adventurer who had invented a flying machine that circled the globe. Kingston always called Estlin "Ned," which the boy conceived to be a manly, regular-fellow name rather than the something peculiar which his parents had fastened on him. "So long, King." "So long, Ned," the reply would come.[18] Now, a decade later, King was still associated with the strenuous life of adventure.

The next story, entitled "The Little Quarter," was about the exploits of a very small but lightning-fast football player who was quarterback and captain of the team. The boy is forced to quit football and go to work to support his widowed mother, but he returns for the big game, which his team wins just as the little quarterback is injured. He has saved the day but he will be paralyzed for life. Rebecca Cummings wept over the story. The fantasy seems to reflect Estlin's yearning for heroic recognition combined with self-pity for the bad luck of not having the physique to gain it in athletics. A third story, "Blind," which won second prize in the annual fiction contest for 1910–1911, tells of a poet who has become blind and turns to music for his artistic expression. In the end, he wins the favor of the beautiful girl whom he cannot see and in so doing beats out his rival, who is an athlete. In this final year at school, the fantasizer has more confidence in the power of art.

Estlin's poems published in the *Review* do not substantiate that confidence. Most are merely jolly poems about the seasons, such as a ballade on "The Coming of May" and a verse tribute to "Skating." Estlin's first published poem, however, is noteworthy for the generosity of spirit it shows. The headmaster, William F. Bradbury, had been his mathematics teacher, and Estlin hated master and subject alike. For Mr. Bradbury's retirement in February 1910, Estlin wrote a sonnet to the "leader and teacher" who was departing. In the sestet, he forgives everything:

> Now when we find ourselves about to lose
> Your leadership, whose strength will ever dwell
> In us and by us to the very end,
> We know no better title we can use
> In wishing you a final fond farewell,
> Than that which fits you best,—our faithful friend.

When the sonnet was published, the printer had omitted the word "you" from the last line. Estlin was furious.[19] The event planted in his heart an everlasting distrust of typesetters. Given the peculiarities of his mature verse, it was a good suspicion for him to have. In later years when he was publishing in periodicals, he demanded and got galley-proof, eight, ten, a dozen times if necessary, before he was satisfied that all was correct.

III

But Estlin was writing better verse than what he published in the *Cambridge Review*. One poem written during his second school year in 1909 has a pleasing boldness in its irregular line length and has more play with sound than has been usual in his verse exercises:

> A chilly murky night;
> The street lamps flicker low,
> A hail-like whispering rain
> Beats 'gainst the streaked, bleak pane
> The sickly, ghostly glow
> Of the blurred, blinking, wavering, flickering light
> Shines on the muddy streets in sombre gleams
> Like a weird lamp post on a road of dreams.[20]

But it tapers off into a Longfellovian lesson for the reader.

Later that year he attempted some quiet descriptive pentameter lines with run-on flow and irregular rhyming, called "The Great White Sleep," probably inspired by Emerson's poem, "The Snowstorm," which he had once memorized:

> The dying embers of the fire glow,
> The darkness veils the silent world outside,
> The clouded air is full of falling snow,
> And it is Christmas night. The white flakes glide
> Through the black atmosphere without a sound,
> In dumb procession. As upon a couch
> Is laid an enfolding drapery, the sky
> In silence lays upon the naked ground
> Her pure white mantel from on high.
> The laden bushes, cold and cheerless, crouch
> To the hard earth, as Heaven's white robe comes down.
> The mournful trees in leafless silence bow
> Before the numbing pressure of the cold.
> All earth is drear, and chill, and dormant now,
> Crowned by the winter with a cold, white crown,
> And nature, like the year, is growing old. . . .[21]

Again the application, however: "So e'en with us" etc. God will bring the Great White Sleep to us someday. Estlin followed the Cambridge models.

He attempted some narrative verse too: one piece on the battle of Waterloo, another about Alexander the Great, and another a legend of the curse of the Indian chief Chocorua upon Cornelius Cromwell, a Puritan intruder upon his lands. These are in the best Longfellow historical manner, especially "The Legend of Mt. Chocorua," which, with its terse exposition and its voice echoing the historical period, suggests *The Tales of a Wayside Inn:*

> Cromwell, you recollect, had died and all hope of Protectorate
> > Had slipped away from the nerveless hands of his weak-headed
> > > > son,
> The second Charles had mounted the English throne, and his
> > > > round-head-hate
> > Had driven some 'cross seas,
> > While others on their knees
> > Groveled round the royal feet,
> > At the blood-stained mercy-seat
> Sponging for a loser's pardon from the foeman who had won.
> But we had sworn to bow the knee but to Cromwell and to God,
> So we fled from servitude, and we left old England's sod,
> > And the human crop a-ripening on the trees.[22]

Sometime in the summer of 1909, the fruits of the last year or two were again gathered in a volume of thirty-seven poems. The table of contents groups them as "Songs of the Seasons," "Songs of the Great Outdoors," "Songs of the Immortal Soul," "Songs of the Past" and so on.[23] Longfellow would have been pleased with the achievement of this fourteen-year-old.

At some point, probably in the fall of 1909, uncle George Clarke gave Estlin a copy of Thomas Hood, Jr.'s widely reprinted book, *The Rhymster* or *The Rules of Rime*.[24] With this guide in hand, the boy experimented a good deal with form, especially during the summer of 1910. As early as December 4, 1909, he had written a rondeau, a rather difficult thirteen-line form that allows only two rhymes to be used (and in a prescribed order) and demands that a four-syllable refrain based on the first four syllables of the poem be worked in after lines eight and thirteen. As the months went by he wrote sonnets, villanelles, triolets, ballades, and intricate stanza forms. He seems to have taken real joy in the patterning. At the same time he seemed increasingly to enjoy playing with sound. Here, for example, is a poem dated July 27, 1910, entitled "Summer Song":

I

Warm air throbbing with locust songs,
Warm clouds screening the heavens' blue rifts,
Warm sun shadowing over-head cloud drifts,
Warm sky straining, earth-tethered, at her cloud-thongs.

II

Far away
A thrush's silver trills,
Far away
The murmur of a river's rills,
Drumming of the thunder fist,
Coming of the rain mist,—
Peeping,
Creeping,
Leaping,
Sweeping,
O'er the weeping,
Hot hills.[25]

He still has the didactic impulse, but there is surprisingly little of it. Estlin's adolescent idealism seems to have been largely siphoned off into religious poems—poems in praise of God's glory and goodness, expressions of the value of the good life (including admonitions to himself), prayers for help in the struggle against temptation, and vows of self-dedication to art as well as to good deeds.

As one might expect, they have a distinct Unitarian coloration; that is, they address themselves to a powerful but loving God and they have none of the traditional Christian references to Jesus. "Holiest, most mighty, O most sacred one," begins one poem, "Whose smallest aim is all infinitude/Whose mind can tilt the globe—whose thought can weld/Earth into stars with superhuman fires. . . ."[26] Some take the form of hymns that Estlin heard in church: "Teach us O God thy hallowed ways."[27] When he is writing in this vein, the verses have an artificial quality, that of material manufactured for parental approval. He takes a sensible turn when he asks in another poem, "God, make me the poet of simplicity/Force and clearness."[28] Whenever he takes this direction, he can produce an effective religious poem. It takes only a few colloquial phrases to envigorate religious verse:

> God,Thine the hand that doth extend
>   The booby prize of failure,and
> The victor's chaplet in the end.
>   God,thine the hand.
>
> God,mine the power to die or live,
>   To find the earth-fruit sweet or sour,
> To take and keep,or take and give.
>   God,mine the power.
>
> God,keep me trying to win the prize;
>   Pamper me not,though I be crying.
> Though snickering worlds wink owlish eyes,
>   God,keep me trying.[29]

The summer of 1910 brought an increase in poetic activity. From a few surviving fragments of his diary at Joy Farm, it appears that Estlin's daily practice was to go off by himself into the woods or up the mountain to the "big boulder" and write "an idyll."[30] A number of poems that carry dates come from this period. "All the world goes to the circus" in June celebrates one of his favorite pastimes. June also saw an "Ode to Sculpture" ("O sculpture, canvas of virility"). Several nature poems are dated July and August: "Summer Song," "A lustrous blur of moon," "Nature's face/Is bright/With the dewy tears/Of sleep." The summer was also a period for religious poems: "How wondrous is kindness," "In Daemone Deus," and probably many others which are not dated.[31]

The conjunction of nature poems and religious themes in Estlin's writing takes its rise from the Unitarian tradition which in both England and America had its development alongside the Romantic movement in literature. Visitors to Unitarian churches have always been struck by the fact that the hymns are more likely to be about the birds and bees or the spacious firmament on high than about anything they have heard in other Protestant churches. Many are the works of the New England poets set to music, and, of course, Samuel Longfellow, Henry's brother, was the chief hymn writer for the American Unitarian Association.

Estlin's poetic activity continued through the next year and in early 1911 he compiled another collection of the verses he had written—175 in number.[32] Variety of stanza form, variety of mood, and great variation in quality mark this group of poems. Estlin was venturesome in playing with line-length and rhyme—for instance in an unusual stanza form like this:

> Gray
> Is the world this morn.
> Worn
> Almost quite away;
> Mourn,
> Earth, and be forlorn,
> Bray
> Trumpet of the victor, as to fray.[33]

He had also learned to merge the effects of slant rhymes, word repetition (in a kind of half sestina), alliterative pattern, and concrete imagery into an understated poem of aspiration—in which form helps to create tone —as in his poem "After Glow", written in the summer:

> Blue water, and behind.
> Benevolent orange sky,
> And gentle sheep that troop
> From their huge fields of cloud,
> Hurrying, headed all
> Homeward across the heaven,
> Unto the western folds,
> Where stands upon a hill,
> Calling with gentle voice,
> One cheery shepherd-star.

Stand still, O shepherd! I,
With many other feet
And many, many flocks
From all the purple earth,
And all the yellow heaven,
Am coming, hurrying home,
Lifting mine eyes to thee,
And listening for thy call
Across the fragrant fields,
Adown the quiet world.

Grey water, yellow sky;
Alas! my star is gone,–
Departed, over the hill.
And all the flocks that heard
Their shepherd's call, and I,
Pause, midway in the rich
And honeyed middle heaven,
Sniffing the luscious sweet;–
No star, no shepherd.   Shall
We lag in the middle way?

No.   On, ye flocks!   And I,
Who heard his call, and saw
His tender, starry face,–
Down the soft, padded mead,
O'er fair, alluring fields,
Along ambrosial lands,
Away into the sun,
Will follow, follow him,
And farther, farther on,
And up, up, over the hill![34]

But at the same time, his great sheaf of verses contain a preponderance of doggerel—that is, lines of verse which have so many irregularities that one loses all sense of rhythm. In addition, the collection contains many utterances of lamely expressed thoughts about the goodness of the Creator, the beauties of the countryside, and the ingratitude of mankind for the gifts of life.

Why this heaping up and indexing of so much literary trash? No doubt the attempt to produce a poem a day during the summers and other vacation periods can account for the accumulation, and perhaps the hope that the half-caught mood could later be revisited and improved, may account for the hoarding of the material. But since throughout E.E. Cummings' career he published much poor stuff and neglected to print many superior pieces, it appears his literary judgments about his own work were always uncertain.

IV

What kind of boy was this who was earnestly trying to become a poet? It is usually difficult for a biographer to capture much of the developing personality of anyone at an age as early as this, but E. E. Cummings left so many records of his life that we get a number of glimpses of what he was like during the Latin School period. Since he was younger and smaller than his classmates, he was rather quiet and retiring at school. He was dutiful about his lessons, yet not outstanding—his grades all four years were in the eighties, sometimes in the seventies, never in the nineties. Except for one attempt at crew, he participated in no organized sports (it was just as well—Cambridge Latin lost almost all of its football, baseball, and hockey games every year). At home he was livelier, especially up at the farm and at Silver Lake where the family now summered in a roomy cottage surrounded by woods right on the lake shore. He was becoming a good mimic, able to recount an experience and catch the phrases and inflections of all speakers so accurately that the family members collapsed with laughter.

He loved and admired his father and tried to follow the precepts of goodness that he heard from the pulpit. He ushered at the church, passed the collection plate, attended the citizenship class after services. He was devoted to his mother and consulted her about his friends, his lessons, his thoughts. He adopted her patterns of social play—in referring to people by their initials and in using allusions to family jokes and family reading. He was kind to his little sister, although he resented her place as Edward Cummings' favorite. Since he was an underling in the school hierarchy, he enjoyed being the kind, older boy in his own neighborhood and the leader in their local games.

But he began to enjoy being by himself, too, especially in the summer. He liked to roam the woods with his dog Rex and to read or write in his retreat at Joy Farm or in his new tree house at Silver Lake. He began to be known as a youthful poet. His mother records in the Joy Farm log for July 19, 1910: "Read Mrs. Standish some of Estlin's poems which she thought very remarkable."[35]

He began to wonder about sex and about girls. He was awed by the repressive attitude toward sex that his father took and, as a consequence, learned more from Sandy Hardy, who instructed him about rabbit-breeding in the barn at Joy Farm, than from his father. He meditated on the adultery of Lancelot and Guinevere in *The Idylls of the King* and puzzled about the dismissal of a servant girl from 104 Irving Street. He began to experience some of the guilty tensions of the minister's son who has sexual fantasies, and occasionally this tension was expressed in his verses, as in "A Father to his Son":

> It's up to you my son, to kill this thing.
> You're tempted by the devil which is lust. . . .[36]

Lest these generalizations outline too strongly the portrait of a conscientious grind at school, an oversheltered child at home, we may look at two incidents which provide more depth for the picture. They reflect two rather different sides of his character. The first one is an act of youthful heroism, described by Elizabeth Cummings in her manuscript "When I was a Little Girl."[37] One day in the summer before Estlin's last year at Latin School, he and his sister went out on Silver Lake to try out a patented folding canoe that was supposed to have two air-filled cushions fastened in it to keep it afloat if it overturned. The cushions were not in the canoe, so Estlin took along a life preserver that was guaranteed to keep a full-grown man afloat. As they crossed the lake, Estlin's dog Rex snapped at a hornet that was buzzing around them and he overturned the canoe. Both canoe and life preserver sank, leaving the children holding on to two boxes that they had used for seats in the canoe. Rex swam off for shore, but becoming confused and frightened, he returned to the children. Apparently tired and desperate, he climbed on to Elizabeth for support and the child went underwater. Estlin shouted at the dog to no avail. Rex climbed onto Elizabeth again as soon as she came up to the surface. Estlin swam over, pulled Rex off his sister, and struggled with him as the dog tried to clamber up onto him. Finally, he had to drown his dog in order to save his sister and himself.

As luck would have it, Edward Cummings and other family members had gone out for a motor boat ride. Seeing two bobbing heads in the distance, they headed over to warn the swimmers that they were out too far for safety. In this chance fashion, the children were rescued, and, ever afterwards, Edward Cummings kept the two boxes in the lake cottage as a remembrance of the accident. "I keep them to remind me whenever things seem to me to be too bad," he said.

The next day Estlin found Rex's bloated body where it washed ashore and carried it home in his arms. The family buried him with

ceremony and Edward Cummings erected a cement marker. Estlin went
off by himself and gave his grief to a poem which began:

> Rex, you and I have loved each other
>   As dog and man
>   Only can,
> And you have given your silent best,
> With silent cheerfulness to me,
> And now that our great mother
> Holds your poor body to her breast
> I come to give you my best, you see,
> Dear dog, to that pure Rex whom we,
> We two, know lies not here at rest.[38]

A poem about the death of an animal is generally considered unaccept-
ably sentimental. But when the author is a youngster, it becomes an
altogether different poem in its effect. Estlin never had another dog after
Rex.

The second incident is not at all dramatic. It is only an entry in
the Joy Farm log which Estlin recorded. It is an account of a trip that
he and his father made to the farm during March of 1911 to build a
new maid's room into the farmhouse. It not only reflects the affec-
tionate cameraderie of father and son but it also shows that Estlin
was becoming able to convey in prose his high spirits and his enjoy-
ment of play in language:

March 28:
    Dad and I arrived after a pleasant session in the choo-choo. . . . After
talking over different plans for the new maid's room we had a crack-a-jack
supper of beans bacon canned pairs (for me). . . . After supper a gale set in,
and while I wrote up the Joy Farm book, raged and ramped like a whash-ho
zephyr.

March 29:
    [after skiing and building]. We lunched on soup—it was fine!—and
buttered shredded wheat things, toasted. They were awfully good but
whiskery. I didn't recover from one whisker for some time. . . .

March 30:
    We closed the month and our stay simultaneously by completing the
side of the new room—at least Dad did. After dinner on beanhamegg, Dad's
"sensationally" satisfying invention, we cleaned up all shipshape and de-
parted on snowshoes for the short-cut-foot. . . . It remains only to be said:

1) that we supped on cheeze-&-doughnuts, orange, 2 bananas, 2 crackers [on the train]. . . .

2) Yours Truly never enjoyed a winter trip to Joy Farm more.

To which I affix my 'and seal.

E. Estlin Cummings
President of the
Boostem Serial Co.
Butter Creek, Mich.
USA
"There's a Reason"³⁹

At age fifteen he was coining his own words like "whash-ho zephyr" and squashing others together to form new ones like "beanhamegg." He was conscious of characteristic phrases that could supply some of the trappings of a literary role and he knew how to establish an ironical distance from that posturing. Also, in his parodying of advertising slogans he was already girding up for satirical assaults.

Although the graduation exercises on June 14, 1911, took place in Sanders Theater of Harvard's Memorial Hall, they held none of the glories of the Peabody Graduation day for Estlin and his parents. He was just one of two hundred and two graduates of Cambridge High and Latin School (as the recently amalgamated school was now called).⁴⁰ Although he felt that he was making some real progress with his poetry and although he had been admitted to Harvard, he was still pretty much of a child—sixteen years old, perhaps the smallest boy in his graduating class and one who was still held very close to the bosom of his family. His poem "On Being Sixteen" had ended with the words "Thou art man,"⁴¹ but it would be some time yet before he could believe it.

V

The Harvard Experience: Studies

On let us go, to survey
Yon glittering city of Pallas,
Home of the warrior, home of sobriety,
Home of religion and mystical piety,
Darling of Hellas;
City of fanes with welcoming portals,
Giver of gifts to the Blessed Immortals:
Temples and images, holy confessionals,
Worship and honor in tuneful processionals.

ARISTOPHANES, *The Clouds*

When Estlin Cummings entered college in September 1911, Harvard had just completed a period of unprecedented development and expansion under President Charles W. Eliot which had changed it from a college with an attached "Scientific School" and Law School and a barely attached Medical Faculty into a real university with a graduate school, nine professional schools, several museums, and an observatory. The College, which was still the heart of this educational complex, had doubled its faculty to almost two hundred and its student body to about twenty-two hundred. President Eliot's educational experiment, the elective system, had just been abandoned, because a faculty committee had discovered that students were mostly enrolling in elementary courses or in large numbers of courses within a single department. The chairman of that committee, Professor A. Lawrence Lowell had become the new president of the university, and students were now required to plan a program of "concentration and distribution" of their studies so that a liberal spread of related courses supported the educational strength of a major field.[1]

The student population still came largely from New England. Although Harvard had not yet begun its policy of recruiting a national student body, the expansion of admissions had begun to produce a more democratic mix in the entering classes and to leaven the conservative Brahmin lump that Harvard had been at the time Eliot took over as president. Not all the faculty were happy about this. Cummings' first Greek instructor told him that he was glad to have moved to Princeton because at Harvard he "had men like yourself sitting next to some little rough-neck Irish Catholic or Polish Jew, and the problems of teaching a course in poetry to such a heterogeneous agglomeration was not by any means a simple one."[2] Nor was everyone overjoyed about the expansion. Yet no one could quarrel with the fact that Eliot had assembled a distinguished faculty. Nowadays, any decade between 1890 and 1930 is usually referred to as Harvard's Golden Age. Although a number of the Olympian figures like William James, George Santayana, Francis J. Child, and Charles Eliot Norton had retired or were about to retire by the time Cummings entered on the scene, many of the great professors were still in the full vigor of their careers.

Cummings remained at Harvard for five years.[3] He took an A.B. degree, "magna cum laude in Literature especially in Greek and English" in 1915. (But he did not realize his ambition to be elected to Phi Beta Kappa as had his father and his Uncle John.) He stayed on one more year to earn an A.M. degree in English in 1916,—really more like a fifth undergraduate year since there were no special examinations and no master's thesis. In his freshman year Cummings decided to concentrate in classics and he took courses in modern languages and literature to augment that concentration. Study in some other fields was required for distribution. He complied but took no pleasure in study of the sciences or economics.

He studied only one year of philosophy, the full range of the History of Ancient and Modern Philosophy under young Ralph Barton Perry. His notes indicate diligent study but he did not do well. He earned only a D⁻ on his first examination in early Greek philosophy—Pythagorus, Democritus, and others. When he went on to Plato (whom he found more poetic), Aristotle, and the Stoics, he pulled the grade up to a B for the fall term; but in the spring term he fell back to a gentleman's C. This performance is not surprising. Cummings had a creative personality, and disciplined intellectual analysis was not to his liking. As time went on, he came to express open scorn for philosophers and reminded others that Mallarmé had told Degas, "One doesn't write poetry with ideas: one writes poetry with words."

Language study involved words. Cummings began his classics program in freshman Greek with Homer's *Odyssey,* Books VI, VII, VIII, IX and X, many passages of which he rendered into English hexameters. He went on to Euripides' *Hippolytus* and *Medea* and Aristophanes' *The Acharnians* and *The Frogs.* Theodore A. Miller, a graduate student in classics from Rochester, New York, was his first instructor in Greek, and he became the first of a series of mentors who would act as father-surrogates for Cummings during the next dozen years.

"Dory" Miller soon noticed young Cummings' zest for language and his unique performances in translation. He found himself preparing his classes with young Cummings in mind as his ideal student. Unlike many classics teachers, he had a real taste for poetry and he was delighted with the verse translations that Cummings attempted for him—for example, "Medea Mater," a rendering of the betrayed Medea's anguished words just as she is about to kill her children, which was set up in terza rima. It begins in this way:

> My sons, my little sons! ye go to dwell
>   In a city of many homes, a city vast,
> But mother at the gates must say farewell.
>
> Into another country am I cast
>   Afar off, never to be reached by ye,
> Hot-foot with joy from portals unsurpassed.[4]

The poem is not coherent, nor is it completely accurate in its translation (or poetic paraphrase) of Medea's speech, but it shows in individual passages that Cummings was able to rise to his material and was able in his phrasing to express heroic grief and passion.

Although Miller was seven years older than Cummings, the two became intimate friends by the end of the year. As a warm-hearted teacher and someone perhaps even inspired by the Socratic ideal of bringing to birth beauty of the mind, he discussed Cummings' studies, his reading, his poetic experiments, and he soon began to advise him about his creative work in general. He spoke scornfully of Longfellow and led the young man to the medieval French masterpiece, *Auccassin et Nicolette,* to Tennyson and Swinburne, and to Shelley and Keats. It seems unbelievable that Cummings could have aspired to be a poet and never have heard of Keats, yet it was Miller who made the introduction and wrought a change in his life, altering the values of 104 Irving Street by putting before him Keats's creed, "I am certain of nothing but of the holiness of the heart's affections and the truth of Imagination. What the Imagination

Theodore "Dory" Miller aboard the Watson yacht.

COURTESY J. S. WATSON, JR.

seizes as Beauty must be Truth."[5] and by upholding the sacredness of pure aesthetic pleasure. When Keats replaced Longfellow as his archetypal poet, Cummings came also to accept the romantic view of the poet as the tortured genius whom society rejects or alienates, a view which he held for one reason or another for the rest of his life. Keats "was as truly crucified as Christ was," Miller told him in one of his rather gushing letters, and suggested plans for the two of them to visit Keats's grave the following summer.[6]

But Miller was also eager to give every encouragement to Cummings' classical studies. He introduced him to Catullus and Horace, and he presented him with gifts at Christmas and on birthdays, volumes of Sappho, of Anacreon, and of selections from *The Greek Anthology*.[7] Although Cummings did not mark up these handsome volumes the way he did his textbooks, he certainly must have treasured the gifts, for they came with warm inscriptions[8] from the first person outside his family who fully engaged his affections. One may guess that he browsed through these volumes frequently during his college years and after, especially that fascinating collection of Hellenistic epigrams, *The Greek Anthology*.

The books represent clear evidence that he was familiar with Greek lyric poetry. In the poems of Sappho, whose *Hymn to Aphrodite* he quoted in a Harvard lecture in 1952,[9] Cummings had an inspiration for the kind of direct and intense expression of love which he gave voice to throughout his career. In Anacreon and *The Greek Anthology* he had a host of models for epigrammatic verse, a poetic mode which he turned to frequently during mid-career. The epigram is a short poem which makes a point incisively, usually by wit or linguistic play. Anacreon (sixth century B. C.) is known mostly for his amatory epigrams and drinking pledges, which are composed with great skill. *The Greek Anthology* or *Anthologia Graecae,* contains a great variety of the form: love poems, dedications or prayers to the gods, epitaphs which comment on the value of the dead individual's life, gnomic wisdom, private satirical attacks, and comic views of human behavior. These poems with their brevity and thrust represent, along with the work of Catullus and Martial, a very old tradition that Cummings later joined.

Miller also showed him some sides of Boston that Cummings had not been acquainted with before. He took him to Greek restaurants like the Athenia and the Parthenon (he could speak some modern Greek) and introduced him to such Middle Eastern exotica as yaoorti (yogurt), shish kebab, and eggplant cooked in sesame oil. Cummings also recalled that one of the first erotic experiences of his life occurred when he and Miller went to see Otis Skinner's extravaganza *Kismet* and watched the naked harem girls dive into a pool on stage. Miller came up to Silver Lake in the summer and participated in all the hiking, swimming, and minor construction around the new cottage. He went sketching with Cummings up Mount Chocorua. He looked over the accumulated collection of verse and gave him thoughtful criticism. This important friendship lasted through Cummings' junior year at which point Miller left Harvard for a teaching position at Princeton.[10]

Second-year Greek covered Thucydides' *History of the Peloponnesian War,* Books VI and VII, Aristophanes' *The Birds,* Aeschylus' *Prometheus Bound,* and Sophocles' *Oedipus Tyrannus.* Cummings' professor, C. P. Parker was an expert in Greek and Roman philosophy, but his interest in classroom instruction was so intense that he devoted most of his time to early undergraduate courses. He too encouraged Cummings in his verse translation. On one occasion, he mailed to Cummings' mother the rendering of the Choral Ode from Act I of *Oedipus Tyrannus* that the young man had written for him.

Cummings took no further course in Greek until his senior year when he enrolled in Greek 6 and read some Greek oratory and a good deal of drama, Aeschylus' *Choephoroe (The Libation Bearers),* Euripides' *Bacchae,* Sophocles' *Elektra* (plus an independent reading of Euripides' *Elektra*). Chandler Post, his professor, held appointments in three departments, Classics, Romance Languages, and Fine Arts. He was a peppery man who sometimes terrified the undergraduates when he fired questions at them. Greek 6 was no mere series of sessions in translation. Post lectured on Greek history and Athenian politics, on Greek drama and the literary characteristics of the three great tragedians. Cummings was so impressed with him that he enrolled the following year in Post's course, The Art and Culture of Spain, even though he was supposed to be a graduate student in English. The course was an educational treat, the best possible way to absorb the character of a people, through their art and literature. Here he learned more about painting than he did from any other source in his whole career. Reams of notes remain from the lectures on art history, architecture, and analysis of individual works of painters and sculptors.[11] John Dos Passos had also recommended the course to Cummings and their friendship became cemented in a mutual response to Post and to Spanish culture. Their experience with Post led to their spending the month of April 1921 in Spain, touring Salamanca, Seville, Toledo, and Madrid.

Cummings' interest in classical studies was largely confined to Greek, for he felt that the Roman literature lacked intensity. He only took one Latin course, Latin B in his sophomore year, in which he slogged through Livy, Books I and II of the *History of Rome,* before he gained relief through Terence's *Phormio* and *Andria.*[12] The worthwhile part of the year was the time spent with Horace, and once again Cummings was able to work with verse translation. Horace's odes have always been favorites with translators because of his clarity of language and the challenge of capturing his elusive moods as he develops the great commonplace themes of life and death. For these reasons, perhaps, and because he himself liked best to write lyric poetry, Cummings delighted in working with Horace, and in so doing, he produced three of the best poems he had yet written. For example, his version of Ode IV from Book I begins:

> The fetters of winter are shattered, shattered
> And the limbs of the earth are free,—
> Spring, and the breeze that lovest the lea!
> And the old keels—gaping and tempest-battered—
> Men roll them down to the sea.[13]

What he has produced is a creatively free translation. In the first line he has developed his own metaphor to express the rather straightforward "Solvitur acris heims" (Sharp winter is breaking up) and goes on to expand it further in line two, which has no Latin equivalent at all in the Horatian poem. Further, Cummings' lines about "the old keels—gaping

and tempest-battered" are a poetic elaboration of the abbreviated state-
ment "trahuntque siccas machinae carinas" (the engines drag dry keels)
and he has pictured human action responding to the change of season, not
the machines doing the hauling.

He takes one more liberty to make the Horatian poems his own: he
eliminates the complicated pasticcio of mythological allusion, yet at the
same time he holds to the spirit of the ode he is working with. Ode VI
from Book IV, an invocation to Apollo begins (as the Loeb translation
gives it): "O God, whom Niobe's offspring came to know as the punisher
of boastful words, whom the robber Tityos felt and Phtian Achilles when
well-nigh victorious over lofty Troy, mightier than others, yet no match
for thee, though he was the son of sea-born Thetis and shook the Dar-
danian towers, fighting with his awful spear"—and so on for two more
paragraphs. Yet Cummings' delicate rendering of this poem cuts through
all that tangle to give us the simple invocation:

> O,blessed of the gods,
> Shield of the race of Rome,
> Are Faith and Fame at odds?
> Thy smile is Spring.—O,too long thou dost roam,
> > From home.

> As a fond mother stands,
> Seeking with prayerful eyes
> O'er sea and sinuous sands
> Her long-departed son,for whom black skies
> > Arise,

> So doth this land of ours
> Yearn for her mighty son;
> All lapped in fruit and flow'rs,. . . .[14]

As we have seen, Cummings very early enjoyed writing poems about
the seasons—especially the coming of spring. His three best Latin trans-
lations involve spring, and two of them are tempered with that sad
Horatian awareness that the natural cycle brings death too, to human
beings. Here is his handling of the work that A. E. Housman, declared
to be the most beautiful poem in ancient literature, Ode VII, Book IV:

> Farewell,runaway snows!   For the meadow is green,and the tree
> > stands
> > Clad in her beautiful hair.

New life leavens the land!   The river,once where the lea stands,
   Hideth and huggeth his lair.
Beauty with shining limbs 'mid the Graces comes forth,and in glee
                                                            stands,
   Ringed with the rhythmical fair.

Hope not,mortal,to live forever,the year whispers lowly.
Hope not,time murmurs,and flies.
Soft is the frozen sod to the Zepher's sandal,as wholly
   Summer drives Spring from the skies,—
Dying when earth receives the fruits of Autumn,till slowly
   Forth Winter creeps,and she dies.

Yet what escapes from heaven,the fleet moons capture,retrieving;
   When through Death's dream we survey
Heroes and kings of old,in lands of infinite grieving,
   What are we?   Shadow and clay.
Say will rulers above us the fate tomorrow is weaving
   Add to the sum of today?

Hear me:whatever thou giv'st to thine own dear soul,shall not
                                                          pleasure
   Hungering fingers of kin.
Once in the gloom,when the judge of Shades in pitiless measure
   Dooms thee to journey within,
Birth,nor eloquent speech,nor gift of piety's treasure
   Opens the portal of sin.

Never,goddess of chasteness,from night infernal thou freest
   One who for chastity fell.
Ever,hero of Athens,him who loved thee thou seest
   Writhe in the chainings of Hell.[15]

"The portal of sin" and "writhe in the chainings of Hell" represent
terminology far too Christian for the Roman underworld, but the rest of
the poem does justice to the original. Once more, Cummings engages in
poetic development while following the general Latin guidelines: the
gentle apostrophe, "Farewell, runaway snows," for the more declarative
"Diffugere nives" (The snows having fled); the more concrete image, "the
meadow is green," for "redeunt iam gramina campis" (already the grasses
return to the fields); and the more lively personification, "the tree stands
clad in her beautiful hair," for "[redeunt] arboribusque comae" (and the

leaf-hair returns to the trees). On it goes, with Cummings displaying a really poetic mind thinking even more metaphorically than his master. "Nos ubi decidimus quo" (When we have departed to the place where) becomes "When through Death's dream we survey," and "manus avidas . . . heredis" (the avaricious hands of the heir) becomes the ringing consonance of the "hungering fingers of kin." In keeping with his practice about allusions, Diana, Hippolytus, Theseus, and Pirithous disappear from the poem, and more general statements replace what they stand for.

Translation is excellent training for a young poet. His motif is supplied to him, suggested phrasing guides him, and like a painter with a model standing before him, he can concentrate on what is essential, his technique. The meanings and the sounds of the words in their patterns must then be sought out to bring the model into being, not merely to represent but to be given new dimension and proportion in an aesthetic life of its own. Cummings' efforts in translating passages in the Greek drama were useful to him, especially when he worked with choral odes, but his achievement with the Latin lyric poetry shows him to have profited most from playing with metaphorical language within the immense metrical and stanzaic variety of the Horatian form of ode.

No other courses in Latin appealed to him and he turned instead to the modern language which is its most direct descendant, Italian, a decision which led to a major educational experience in his senior year: a full year of Dante under Charles H. Grandgent.

Grandgent, a philologist, a literary historian, and an interpretive critic, was the foremost Dante specialist in the English-speaking world. He had prepared an annotated edition of the *Commedia* which has become standard in this century.[16] Besides numerous short studies in Dante, he was just completing his critical and historical book, *Dante*, at the time Cummings enrolled in Italian 10, the Dante course.[17] The first semester of work included study in the culture of the Middle Ages, the history and politics of Florence, the nature of allegory, and the reading of *Il Convivio, De Monarchia, La Vita Nuova* and the early cantos of *La Divina Commedia;* the second semester was devoted to a close reading of the entire *Commedia.*

Grandgent was not a stimulating lecturer and there were those who found that his "rhythmic, musical, soothing"[18] voice put them to sleep. But not Cummings. He was intensely interested in the material of the course and he sat, an alert figure, in the front row. He took extensive lecture notes and he set down careful reading notes on a series of Dante studies by Norton, Grandgent, E. G. Gardiner, and R. W. Church. He drew elaborate diagrams of Dante's Hell, Purgatory, and Paradise with the allegorical details minutely placed in the scheme. He also became

fascinated with the character of Dante and with the psychological phe-
nomenon of his injecting his personal life—his likes and dislikes, his
enemies and his ideal loved one—into his vast cosmic poem. A sonnet that
he wrote at the time embodies this response and his general admiration:

> Great Dante stands in Florence,looking down
> In marble on the centuries. Ye spell,
> Beneath his feet who walked in Heaven and Hell,
> "L'Italia." Here no longer lord and clown
> Cringe,as of yore,to the immortal frown
> Of him who loved his Italy too well:
> Silent he stands,and like a sentinel
> Stares from beneath those brows of dread renown.
>
> Terrible,beautiful face,from whose pale lip
> Anathema hurtled upon the world,
> Stern mask,we read thee as an open scroll:
> What if this mouth Hate's bitter smile has curled?
> These eyes have known Love's starry fellowship;
> Behind which trembles the tremendous soul.[19]

The course provided Cummings' first critical exposure to allegory
and his first serious understanding of the medieval mind. For a young
man brought up in a religious household and with adolescent emotional
leanings toward religiosity, Unitarianism must have seemed meager.
Now the richness and complexity of the religion of the medieval church
which was brought vigorously to life in Dante's masterpiece offered deep
emotional appeal. He was also thrilled by the Platonic idealism of the
Vita Nuova (and its dramatization in the *Commedia*), for it matched the
youthful idea of the sacredness of womanhood that he still held in the fall
of 1914. Dante's world-view in general intrigued him. Ever afterward he
drew upon this fully detailed Christian mythic view for his verse, and in
the 1930s he used Dante's allegorical scheme for his narrative, *Eimi*, the
most elaborate work he ever wrote.

The other modern language Cummings studied was German, begin-
ning with grammar and elementary reading in his freshman year
(breathes there a student of German who has not read Storm's *Immensee?*)
and going on to spend a year with the great literary historian and founder
of Harvard's Germanic Museum, Kuno Francke, for the course, History
of German Literature in Outline. Cummings was not attracted to Ger-
man culture, feeling it lacked the freedom and looseness of the French
or Italian ways of life. The fact that Professor Francke was a Prussian

chauvinist and an admirer of Kaiser Wilhelm did not help the situation much. In his final year Cummings enrolled in a similar cultural introduction, The History of Russian Literature, given by the Russian exile, Leo Wiener. Here he read a number of Russian novels and therefrom he absorbed an awareness of the Russian soul which served him well in his bewildering tour of Soviet Russia in 1931.

II

Although Cummings' concentration was nominally in classics, he never took the full six year-long courses which were required, probably because he had exhausted his interest in Latin. He found Greek literature more to his taste but three years of Homer and the dramatists seemed the cream of Greek studies, and other courses stressed the Greek philosophers, Greek philology, or Greek literary history. He was interested in literature, not in classical civilization. He therefore finished out his concentration with courses in English and Comparative Literature.

The course with the grandest title was taught by William Henry Schofield, the man who created the department of Comparative Literature: The Literary History of England and its Relations to that of the Continent. The attention paid to the chivalric romances must have attracted Cummings (he referred to it as the "Romance literature course"),[20] for he went on to take the second half-course—which carried itself only as far as the Elizabethan period. This view of early European literature as a whole must have been good for him, and this kind of learning was congruent with his tendency toward cultural spread in the study of five languages plus the courses in Spanish and Russian culture. He continued to read indiscriminately in all of the major European literatures after he left college.

The great figure he encountered in the English department was George Lyman Kittredge when he enrolled in the famous English 2, "Shakspere (six plays)." Although most literature courses at Harvard had become an unconsummated marriage of lectures and assigned readings, the Kittredge method was different. It was chiefly a combination of historical criticism and *explication de text*. After initial lectures on Shakespeare's life, on the Elizabethan theater, and on the distinctive features of the period, he spent a month or more on each of six selected plays. Some students took the course twice in order to cover twelve plays. Cummings read *Julius Caesar, Henry IV, Parts I and II, Macbeth, King Lear,* and *All's Well that Ends Well* (and in good old Cambridge fashion had passages to commit to memory in each).[21]

During class periods Kittredge, who looked like a New England version of George Bernard Shaw, offered a series of running footnotes on the plays. Each significant word or line was scrutinized for its linguistic origins, its meaning at the time, its allusive reference to mythology or history or Elizabethan custom, its reflection of Renaissance ideas, its relevance to the particular passage or to the play as a whole. But most student recollections depict him in the classroom as playing a well-rehearsed role of omniscient scholar: an imperious eagle-eyed old man hurling penetrating questions or answering queries with authoritative scorn as he lifted his well-trimmed white beard in the air.

Anecdotes about him abound, and words like god, prophet, or patriarch occur in most of them. In one, Kittredge, invited to an afternoon tea, is met at the door by a maid who shrinks back in alarm at his startling appearance exclaiming, "My God." "Not God, madam, Kittredge," he replies as he strides across the threshold. When he wished to cross the street in Harvard Square, he stopped the thronging traffic by stepping forth with his gold-headed cane raised like Moses holding back the Red Sea waters. Cummings himself in a memoir of a classroom incident refers to him as "Zeus."[22] Yet Kittredge could be humble in the presence of greatness: "If you gentlemen will not remove your hats in the lecture hall for me," he would say, gesturing toward a bust on his left, "then please do so for Homer." Cummings relished the flamboyant individualism of the performance and he adopted some of the Kittredgean amused arrogance for his own roles in public assemblies.

Under another Shakespeare scholar, William A. Neilson, Cummings studied Chaucer. Neilson, a genial Scot, trained both at Edinburgh and at Harvard, was a specialist in medieval literature and Elizabethan drama. He was shortly to desert Harvard to become president of Smith College. His assistant in the course, young F. N. Robinson, was later to succeed him at Harvard and to become the foremost Chaucerian of his time. Under these two teachers, Cummings' delight in Chaucer was fostered, as well as his further pleasure in chivalric romance and allegory. Neilson had the right sense of humor for teaching Chaucer, and he communicated to the students his lively pleasure in reading the work even though he used the Kittredgean method of minute examination of the text.

Cummings returned to Neilson in his graduate year for a half-year course in The Nature and History of Allegory. The lectures began with distinctions among literary terms—allegory, myth, parable, personification, metaphor, symbol. The readings began with the Bible and medieval allegories, such as the *Roman de la Rose, Piers Ploughman,* Gower's *Confessio Amantis,* and *Everyman;* then moved up through Spenser and Bunyan to

satirical allegories such as the *Dunciad* and *Gulliver's Travels;* and at length
to romantic works such as *Endymion, Prometheus Unbound,* and (for Cum-
mings the third time) *The Idylls of the King.*[23] Cummings was already
familiar with the emblematic habit of mind, from the New England
tradition that surrounded him and from his father's sermons. But his
study now showed him the means of providing further dimension to
stories, plays, renderings of ordinary incident—and all of this in a variety
of presentation, from didactic preachments to subtle illuminations. His
first important work, *The Enormous Room,* was to employ *Pilgrim's Progress*
as an allegorical narrative device.

The English professor in whose classes Cummings sat most fre-
quently was Bliss Perry, perhaps the most popular lecturer in the Col-
lege. He was a vigorous, masculine figure, very much interested in
sports: an ardent trout fisherman and a former baseball player at Wil-
liams College, who now taught the students to "bat the curves" of
Emerson's poetry.[24] Although he had done graduate work at the Uni-
versities of Berlin and Strassburg, he was not so much a scholar as a
man of letters.

In his sophomore year, Cummings enrolled in Perry's fall-term
course in Lyric Poetry. Perry lectured on verse forms, gave facts of
biography and literary history, and occasionally would read poems aloud.
William Langer remembers that Perry's approach to lyric poetry was "a
very manly one" and that "whenever he read a poem he got up from his
chair, threw back his shoulders, and read in a measured, very effective
manner."[25]

The textbook for the course was Raymond Alden's *English Verse,
Specimens Illustrating its Principles and History,* a splendid, sensible treat-
ment of the subject. Besides identifying all the metrical forms, Alden
gives the theory behind accent in lines of verse. Besides defining asso-
nance, alliteration, and onomatopoeia, he discourses on tone quality,
especially tone-color (German *Klangfarbe*), by means of which sounds of
words can increase their expressiveness. From Alden's book, Cummings
learned a great deal more about stanzas and meter than he had from *The
Rhymster.* He read samples of English lyric poetry from Chaucer up to the
1890s and was introduced to many poets he had not known before, includ-
ing such sweet singers as Waller, Herrick, Lovelace, and Carew. He liked
Perry well enough to study further under him, and with additional
encouragement from Dory Miller, he signed up for the half-year course
in Tennyson. It was very thorough, covering all of Tennyson's verse
including the plays, but Cummings (one more time, *The Idylls of the King*)
grew very tired of Tennyson and scribbled Hudibrastic couplets for his
classmates:

Dear God, be kind to Tennyson,
He did no harm to anyone.
For queen, for country, and for Thee
He wrote for all eternity.
He led an exemplary life
Having children by his wife.
Dear Lord: let Keats and Shelley wait.
Make Tennyson thy laureate.[26]

He did not return to Perry until his graduate year, but then took two courses in a vain reaching out for more contact with modern literature and with the principles of literary criticism. The first, Types of Fiction, made use of Perry's own textbook, *A Study of Fiction.*[27] In the first half-year the students read short stories, mostly American, and then went on to novels, continuing through the year in rather scattered fashion to read such works as Defoe's *Captain Singleton,* Scott's *The Bride of Lammermoor, The Deerslayer, Old Goriot,* Hugo's *Les Travailleurs de la Mer, Uncle Tom's Cabin, Middlemarch, The Scarlet Letter, Madame Bovary, The Return of the Native, Anna Karenina.*[28] Cummings wrote a term paper for Perry in which he dealt with a scattered series of works: Defoe's *Captain Singleton,* Le Sage's *Gil Blas,* Richardson's *Pamela,* Fielding's *Joseph Andrews,* Goethe's *Werther,* and Saint-Pierre's *Paul et Virginie.* Whether it was the fault of the student or the teacher, and one may suspect it was both, the paper had no center. Unable to draw all this reading together to support any thesis, Cummings made it a long impressionistic meditation that moved from one book to another as he dreamed of them in his study. Perry wrote, "Very clever but don't do it again."[29]

The second course, entitled The English Critical Essay, which ran during the spring term, began with Montaigne and Bacon and moved up through literary history to Arnold and perhaps Pater. Cummings seems not to have learned anything from this course either. By the time he came to write his long paper in April 1916, he was unable to produce a critical essay himself and he wrote a long clever satire entitled "MS found in a Bottle,"[30] in which he parodied the styles and attitudes of a great variety of authors. He created a situation in which William Dean Howells presiding over a literary gathering introduces George Eliot, who is going to discourse on "My Favorite Insect and Why." Present are Balzac, Flaubert, Melville, Dreiser, Amy Lowell, Poe, Hawthorne, Henry James, Tolstoy, and others, all of whom make comments in characteristic fashion. Parody is a form of literary criticism, but Perry could not see it. He refused to put a grade on the paper because it was not the kind of term report he expected.

One may observe here something deficient in the Harvard program, as well as something lacking in the early twentieth-century literary scene in general. In his English studies under Kittredge, Neilson, and Grandgent, and to some extent in his classical studies, Cummings learned the method of historical criticism very well; that is, he learned the way to read a literary work by acquainting himself with the period in which it was produced and the circumstances that produced it. It is an essential beginning for the understanding of earlier literature. Also from Grandgent and Neilson he learned the rudiments of literary interpretation. But there was no one on the faculty who could deal in a critically intelligent way with the literature of the previous century, which included the richest efflorescence since the Renaissance. One need not blame Harvard. In no other college or university could such a critic be found. And President Eliot's instincts were right in reaching out for the editor of the *Atlantic Monthly* (Bliss Perry) in order to put someone on the faculty who supposedly could speak authoritatively about modern literature.

Cummings' failure to learn anything from Perry about aesthetic criticism or about making literary judgments reminds us that there was really no sound method of aesthetic analysis before I. A. Richards or the Vanderbilt critics in the 1920s. There was literary theorizing about the nature of art, there were interpretations of literary texts, there was some literary categorizing. But in aesthetic criticism—the study of literary works as beautiful objects achieving their significance through a delicate interplay of elements, especially style and structure—the modern world had not really gone beyond Aristotle's *Poetics*, which had been rigidly misapplied since the Renaissance, or beyond Horace's *Ars Poetica*, which, echoed by Sidney, Dr. Johnson, and others even down to the present, regarded literature as a kind of teaching. Coleridge's theorizing about the nature of poetry was brilliant but it had never had any application and remained to be rediscovered in the 1930s. Arnold was a man of good taste with a question-begging method of making literary judgments. What can we expect at any college or university in the early decades of the twentieth century when the task of making literary discriminations arose, except personal impressions? Cummings went on after college to write book reviews for the *Dial* and critical attacks and parodies in *Vanity Fair* and to make pompous pronouncements in his later life to friends and to audiences of college students, but he never was able to apply any other criterion than his own personal response as to whether or not a work was, as he called it, "alive."

III

Yet in an adjacent area, the teaching of composition, Harvard made a discernible contribution to Cummings' future career. Harvard had a long tradition of emphasis on writing, especially creative writing. Even during the days of President Eliot's elective system, the one required course was English A, Rhetoric and English Composition, Oral and Written, under the direction of A. S. Hill, whom Grandgent called the "high priest of correctness and conformity to good usage."[31] In fact before 1910, the Harvard English Department had much more renown for its teaching of composition than for its teaching of literature, and in their composition courses, students were encouraged to write verse and fiction as well as good expository prose. In addition to the student newspaper, the *Harvard Crimson,* and the satirical magazine, the *Harvard Lampoon,* the undergraduates supported two rival literary periodicals, the *Harvard Advocate* and the *Harvard Monthly,* both of which published verse, fiction, essays, reviews, and literary polemics. As a result of all this literary opportunity, an astounding number of Harvard men became writers of some renown. Those from the 1900–1918 period alone make a long list: Conrad Aiken, Frederick Lewis Allen, Robert Benchley, S. N. Behrman, Earl Derr Biggers, Heywood Broun, Rollo Walter Brown, Van Wyck Brooks, Witter Bynner, Stuart Chase, Malcolm Cowley, S. Foster Damon, Bernard De Voto, John Dos Passos, T. S. Eliot, Arthur Davison Ficke, John Gould Fletcher, Herman Hagedorn, Robert Hillyer, Henry Herbert Knibbs,[32] Walter Lippmann, John Marquand, Samuel Eliot Morison, Robert Nathan, Charles Nordoff, Eugene O' Neill (as a special student), John Reed, Alan Seegar, Edward Sheldon, Stuart Sherman, Harold Stearns, Wallace Stevens (who did not graduate), Arthur Train, John Hall Wheelock, John Brooks Wheelwright, Willard Huntington Wright (S. S. Van Dine). And, of course, E. E. Cummings, who enrolled in English A in 1911, studied the principles of argumentation, read Burke, Lincoln, and Bryce, analyzed speeches, compiled vocabulary lists, wrote weekly themes, gave both prepared and extemporary speeches, and was excused from the prescription after one term. "Learn to write by writing," his section leader told the class.[33] No need to tell Estlin Cummings, who had been scribbling since he was five. "Cultivate the forming of figures of speech. They may serve the highest and humblest uses." This was news, and young Cummings diligently recorded images and tropes whenever he had leisure.

Part way through Cummings' college career, something happened to his verse that moved it beyond Keatsian richness to a decadent overripeness, and the same thing befell his prose style whenever he was trying to evoke an imaginative situation or indeed, even when he was only trying to say something impressive about art or literature. It seems reasonable to connect it with a happening he described many years later.[34] One day, Josiah Royce stopped Cummings on Irving Street and said, "Estlin, I understand that you write poetry. Are you perhaps acquainted with the sonnets of Dante Gabriel Rossetti?" When the young man said no, Royce took him into his house, sat him down in the study and began to read him the Willowood sequence from *The House of Life*. Cummings was enthralled by the music and by the calculated exaltation in Rossetti's treatment of love themes. Over the months, he read Rossetti and became familiar with his career. Gradually he developed a wish to become a poet-painter like Rossetti. As a budding poet, it was the worst thing that could have happened to him. Longfellow did no harm to a school-boy poet, but Rossetti was a disastrous influence for a maturing young man —and especially the style of the sonnets in *The House of Life*.

Rossetti's style attempts to imitate a medieval allegorical mode, thus it is full of archaic words and constructions and it makes frequent use of references (not quite personifications) to capitalized abstractions such as Love, Death, Life, Oblivion, Hope, Soul, God, and the like, with the idea that these references will bring emotional vibrations or lend profundity to what is being expressed. In this Rossetti style, religious language and mythological allusion are plentiful. In addition, it indulges in a highly self-conscious piling up of figures of speech, sometimes quite strained in their relevance to the poetic situation, and it frequently employs language of far greater intensity than is appropriate. Soon Cummings was writing that way. His "Water-Lilies" sonnet, with Rossetti-like vagueness and artificiality, begins:

> Behold—a mere like a madonna's head
> Black-locked, enchapleted with lilies white;
> By Him the Prince of Artists in Earth's sight,
> Eons ere her most ancient master wed
> With Immortality.[35]

And a little later when he was writing love poetry, he was going into musical swoons like this:

> I miss you in the dawn, of gradual flowering lights
> And prayer-pale stars that pass to drowsing-incensed hymns,
> When early earth through all her greenly-sleeping limbs
> Puts on the exquisite gold day.   The Christlike sun

> Moves to his resurrection in rejoicing heights,
> And priestly hills partake of morning one by one.[36]

It would not be worth commenting on if this had been only one more imitative phase that Cummings passed through, but it was not. This style, reinforced by the interest that many of the young Harvard literati took in the English decadents of the 1890s, continued to appear in some of his poems for the next decade. Whenever he wrote a sonnet, the chances were great that the spirit of Rossetti would hover over him ready to descend and cloud his expression.

Theodore Miller, the first person Cummings ever encountered who could give him helpful criticism on his poems, cautioned him about loose usage of words, and he recommended after Cummings' sophomore year that he take a course in expository writing "in order to clear up your tendency to obscurity in poetry."[37] Cummings did not take his advice until his senior year when he enrolled in Dean LeBaron Russell Briggs's English 5, Advanced Composition. Briggs was no doubt the best loved professor in the Harvard yard. He was a very kind, gentle, gracious human being, very slight of build, very boyish in appearance even into his middle years, exhibiting a modest charm enlivened by a delightful sense of humor. He had attended Cambridge Latin School and went on to study Greek at Harvard. Cummings must have felt a strong identification with Briggs because of his own frail appearance and his Cambridge background.

Briggs's course in Advanced Composition drew a mixed group, for it was open to both undergraduate and graduate students. Some students enrolled to improve their means of expressing their ideas, but others appeared with embryonic short stories in their folders or an outline of a grandiose project, perhaps even a half-finished novel. A few had been working in verse and, like Cummings, had compiled little stacks of unpublished poems. Briggs, very sensibly, did not believe one could teach writing. A teacher could only encourage the writer, give him plenty of practice, and see that he received comment on what he produced, both from professor and from fellow-student. His thought was "he had kept a diary himself and had profited by daily writing. Why should not students write a little every day?"[38] Students wrote short essays on all aspects of their thought and observation, at every class meeting, Tuesday, Thursday, and Saturday, for at least twenty-five or thirty minutes. Briggs gave careful attention to each paper. "He had an old-fashioned schoolmaster's concern for neatness of language," said John Dos Passos, "a Yankee zest for the ship-shape phrase, an old-fashioned gentleman's concern for purity of morals . . . and a sharp nose for sham and pretense."[39]

Many of Cummings' short essays survive, carefully marked up by Briggs and graded in his peculiar manner with an o, a y, a z, or some such hieroglyphic, the meaning of which he never would divulge to his students. These essays are not very promising. For instance, Cummings produced this little allegory on October 20, 1914:

The Unwelcome Diety [Sp]

There is but one God on the pillar of Art. He is dressed in unspeakable magnificence. A crown is upon his temples, and that crown touches the farthest of the faint stars. The smoke of his worship is a curling column of soul, [Briggs: *I am pretty sceptical about this*] making sweet the temple of the world.

He is the God of all things beautiful. A red dove flutters about his head, and a white dove murmurs at his feet; and shy thoughts build their music into his temple.

He is the God of all things terrible. A blue snake writhes upon his right hand, and a black snake smiles between his knees, and dark dreams nest silently in his temple. . . .[40]

On it goes for a couple more tedious pages. Briggs offered this comment: "It is hard to produce satisfactory work of this nature in so short a time. You have done—all things considered—remarkably well,—but you don't command perfect confidence as to your own sturdy knowledge of your meaning (e.g. line 5)."

Sometimes at the class meeting, Briggs read a student theme aloud, made comments, called for further criticism, and after that the class members wrote their little essays about the paper they had heard read or about the discussion they had listened to. In addition, long papers, six or more pages, were to be written outside of class eight times during a term. A few of Cummings' longer pieces are still in existence and they show that Briggs began to clean up Cummings' prose style with frequent marginal comment and a general over-all admonition for each essay. One of these, dated October 13 [1914], "The Young Faun" is an overwritten scenario inspired by the ballet "The Afternoon of a Faun," which drew Briggs's polite rebuke "Now and then I suspect you . . . of putting in some details for sound's sake—of indulging yourself in that for which English 5 is one of the best remedies."[41]

Briggs himself had a charming prose style, casual, witty, in the best tradition of good conversation, and as a teacher of composition he held up standards of clarity, precision, and economy for his students. Thus the preciousness of Cummings' over-ornate style drew many judicious reprimands: "You show literary and poetic feeling; but to me, at least, you are foggy. You write as if you put down combinations of such words as you associate with poetry and hoped they would mean enough to pass muster. Sometimes they have poetry that burns through the fog; sometimes they seem ill-advised, not quite normal, as if caught from writers who lack a man's strength. Probably this comment strikes you as unintelligent Philistinism: yet I also love poetry; and I don't like to see a man with poetic talent—choosing false gods."[42]

One of the long themes, perhaps from the later part of the college year, shows an improvement in style and some appreciation for economy in expression: "The Poetry of Silence," on Chinese and Japanese poetry.[43] At the end of the year, the members of the class voted on the best story of the year, and Cummings' story for children, "The King" was awarded second prize. It was a story about a little boy who takes a toy elephant to bed with him at night.[44] Briggs had discouraged Cummings' pursuit of the decadent style in prose. Cummings' major paper of the year, a twenty-seven page discourse on "The New Art" (which was to have a surprising future) gained Briggs's praise, "An interesting and able essay, showing a sense of style, good power of analysis, love of the subject, and a courage and persuasiveness of treatment." The paper received a grade of y x w z y.[45]

Study at Harvard University did not make an intellectual of E. E. Cummings, nor would he have welcomed such a label. But it did make him one of the best-educated young men in the country. The training in classical and modern languages gave him the ability to use English with great skill, not for analytical discourse but for creative expression in unique ways. His exposure to a variety of cultures, Greek, Roman, Italian, German, Spanish, and Russian, and especially to British culture from its beginnings to the twentieth century, enriched his whole existence for the rest of his life.

His program of study shows only one serious omission: his failure to take any work in the history department, a mistake that weakened his understanding of the past and deprived him of a proper perspective on his own time. This lack was partially remedied by the time spent with literary and cultural history—but even that kind of historical study has its deceptions, for art and literature reflect their time obliquely and spottily. In any case, this comment about history is really only a quibble, for the courses in history would have been given through lectures in large halls where a huge assembly of students seated alphabetically was methodically taking notes, an educational procedure that makes very little impression. In later years, Cummings never mentioned anything he supposedly learned from lectures. He spoke only of his study of languages and his study under Kittredge, Neilson, and Grandgent—both kinds of instruction which focused carefully on specific texts and examined passages in their relationship to each other or to the whole. The classical and foreign language classes were small; the classes in Shakespeare, Chaucer, and Dante were large, but the educational procedure was similar. Still, for all of its value and with all of its limitations, the formal course work was only part of his education. For E. E. Cummings, the poet, his practice in writing, his work in verse for Dean Briggs during his graduate year, and his association with a few lively and intelligent fellow students—all of this in conjunction with being weaned away from 104 Irving Street—contributed most to his development as a writer and to his growth as one of the distinctive personalities of his time. A full account of this other side of his education requires another chapter.

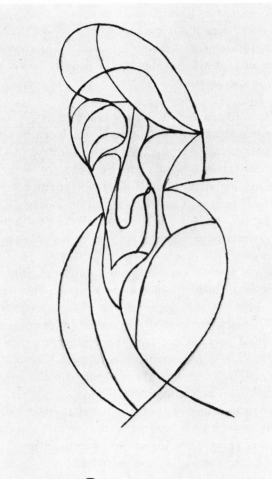

Dante

VI

The Harvard Experience:
Verse, Friends, Rebellion

> .... we must make the distinction between primary creativeness
> and a secondary creativeness. The primary creativeness or inspira-
> tional phase of creativeness must be separated from the working out
> and the development of the inspiration. This is because the latter
> phase stresses not only creativeness, but also relies very much on just
> plain hard work, on the discipline of the artist who may spend half a
> lifetime learning his tools, his skills, and his materials, until he
> becomes finally ready for a full expression of what he sees.
>
> ABRAHAM H. MASLOW

During the five-year period at Harvard, a profound change took place in
Estlin Cummings' personality. If we look at a long introspective state-
ment which he set down in a notebook midway through his freshman
year, we will see that it shows him clearly as a dutiful youngster (he was
still only seventeen) devoted to his parents, inclined toward Unitarian
piety, proud of his friendship with the decorous Dory Miller, and hopeful
about his future social conduct and achievement. He was living at home
in Cambridge, not in a Harvard dormitory. Even the prose style of the
passage suggests a nineteenth-century New England ethos:

> I am a young man living in an advanced and cultivated era, surrounded
> by things lovely and of good report. I have a strong mind, a healthy body,
> resulting from years of careful and devoted watching by father and mother,
> and a high reputation, everywhere I go, as a gentleman. My friends are pure,
> high-minded girls and clean, manly fellows. My father is a man who has

worked out his own success by toil and pluck, who has maintained as a lasting gift to his son a noble soul and well-developed body. He is a man who never allowed the faintest suggestions of temptation to grip him, and expects the high and pure of his son. My mother is a woman who has kept herself strong and pure for me alone, who has built upon me, her first child, a wonderful frame of utter love and endless aspiration, whole [*sic*] lives only as I live, hopes as I hope, and falls only when I fall. I worship a God unutterably merciful and vitally human, and who embodies all the good that I have not won and all the vast strength I have not attained. He is within as well as without, and his voice is all too small for my soul as I write. I thank him when I do right, pray for help when I err, and ask forgiveness when I sin. I avow my self to be His son as well as my parents' son; He is my first and primal Parent. . . .

One friend have I of whom I speak out lovingly from my heart at all times. He is a man at college with me, older, wiser, and of perfect chivalry toward woman and man. I love him as I love no other friend; I worship him for good, and imitate him for worthiness. His life, also, has grown into mine. The honor of his friendship he has placed with perfect confidence in my trembling hands; if I do wrong, I commit an unfaithfulness to him who I admire most of my friends. If I do right, his the glory equally with the deed's.

It is important that I should realize this fact: I am of the aristocracy of this earth. All the advantages that any boy should have are in my hands. I am a king over my opportunities. No one can take away from me the possibilities of growth founded on the firm rock of inherent advantage and power.[1]

By the time he was five years older, Cummings was in full rebellion against his father, he hated Cambridge, he scorned the prevailing American attitudes and tastes, and he associated with a lively, spree-drinking, girl-chasing group of young men who were apprentices in the new artistic movements of the twentieth century. He also had begun to develop a distinctive poetic style and was well on his way to becoming an iconoclastic modern poet. The story of that change is a fascinating one which combines the ordinary pattern of a young man's rejection of his father's dominance and the unique course of one young American who became a follower of the new artistic tendencies of his era.

Estlin Cummings had come to Harvard with good literary habits. He wrote poems as often as he had time free from his studies. Some were dreadful. Others had only a few worthwhile lines. With continuing practice and experiment he could not help but grow as a poet. From time to time during the year he was able to produce successful poems which exhibited the firm control that he had demonstrated in "After Glow" at the end of his preparatory school years.

The big change during his freshman year came with the discovery of Keats, and when the leisure of summer arrived, Cummings began to study the poems closely. A surviving diary-entry for July 9, 1912, contains page upon page of commentary on images or lines from *Lamia*. His notes the next day, July 10, offer a series of "Impressions Which Various Vowels Give The Ear"—such as:

   1. o long—largeness
      Ex. "robe" is ampler than "garment."

   2. ow (as in "how")—heaviness
      Ex. "round weight" outweighs "circular weight."

   3. Two short vowels in succession,
      i.e., in two succeeding words, give the idea of strained, compressed.
      Ex. "hid scent" and "held breath" (Lamia).[2]

During the summer, he compiled lists of images either to hoard away for the future or merely to stretch his capacities for metaphor. "Slowly the mountain climbs into the sky," "A little warbler writes his twitching flight/Across yon parchment sky," "Huge logs sleep, bearded with their own decay." So on he goes, filling the pages of his workbook.

He attempts to draw upon imaginative depths by trials of free association in response to a summer scene:

A little pensive smoke—the robins, like dead leaves, go flying southward—the shelldrake harrows the lake—see where with outstretched lips the trunks embrace—around his brows the halo of divine unhappiness—the panting stars (like a dog)—How good to see the sun; Even through the rain—Married to memory—And all the trees painted a vivid green by rich rain—Would every man were Plato to his God—Old saints Robed in the untransparent garb of prayer—Sun, moon, earth—God, God, God!!—Nature with hoary eye stares at us from the dark as we intrude (Phosphorescent wood)—Her eyes knelt there in prayer before him—ashes of roses; ashes of angels. Sunset: shades of vivid color change and rise and fall—as if the day writhed alive upon his pyre.[3]

The words pour out for three more pages.

This increased awareness of imagery accompanied a new phase of Cummings' poetic expression that can best be called Keatsian because he displayed a linguistic exuberance reminiscent of Keats's descriptive style, although he was also prone to lapse into Rossetti-like lushness. During the summer he wrote a series of descriptive poems, most of which he published during the next year in the *Harvard Advocate*. Most of them were sonnets but two were exercises in one of Keats's favorite forms, Spenserian stanzas.

The presence of Dory Miller helped. He visited Silver Lake in July and looked over Cummings' work; later the two carried on a correspondence about some of the poems, including some that Cummings never published. One entitled "The Paper Palace" was an unusual piece about a colony of wasps, beginning "A clan of imps—morose and ugly things"[4] and going on to set up in contrast a description of the delicate nest they build. Some of the poems fell into the Pre-Raphaelite style. Miller was tactful in his criticism but warned Cummings that he found too many of the poems "forced—over-elaborated." His favorite, however, was a sonnet entitled "Fame Speaks," a tribute to the poet whom he and Cummings admired most:

> Stand forth, John Keats!   On earth thou knew'st me not;
> Steadfast through all the storms of passion, thou,
> True to thy muse, and virgin to thy vow;
> Resigned, if name with ashes were forgot,
> So thou one arrow in the gold had'st shot!
> I never placed my laurel on thy brow,
> But on thy name I come to lay it now,
> When thy bones wither in the earthly plot.
> Fame is my name.   I dwell among the clouds,
> Being immortal, and the wreath I bring
> Itself is Immortality.   The sweets
> Of earth I know not, nor the pains, but wing
> In mine own ether, with the crowned crowds
> Born of the centuries.   Stand forth, John Keats![5]

The only phrase Miller questioned was "virgin to thy vow," which made him uncomfortable.

The peak achievement resulting from the combination of Miller's friendship and the influence of Keats came about when Cummings worked out a free translation of the sequence in *Aucassin et Nicolette* in which Nicolette descends from her prison tower. The obvious model for the style is "The Eve of St. Agnes." The richness of the poem consists not only in the languorous diction appropriate to the romantic moonlight scene or in the echoing alliterative consonants among the waves of assonance but also in the complexity of images that grow one out of the other in surprising intricacy. For instance, the nighttime scene in which Nicolette appears at the tower window to drop down the rope of twisted cloth for her escape is introduced in terms of the opening of a lily, which is further likened to a maiden awaking at dawn as the sun touches her (it). Yet, the light is really moonlight seen as fire burning to a snowlike whiteness when it falls upon the figure of Nicolette, whose harmony of movement is likened to delicate musical vibration when she lets the rope fall and slides down it—as silently as one of the dew drops which the opening lily had revealed:

> And as an opening lily, milky-fair,
> When from her couch of poppy petals peers
> The sleepy morning, gently draws apart
> Its curtains to reveal the golden heart,
> With beads of dew made jewels by the sun,
>
> So one fair, shining tower, which like a glass,
> Turned light to flame, and blazed with silver fire,
> Unclosing, gave the moon a nymph-like face,
> A form whose snowy symmetry of grace
> Haunted the limbs as music haunts the lyre,
> A creature of white hands, who, letting fall
> A thread of lustre from the opened wall
> Glided, a drop of radiance, to the grass.[6]

Brilliant in its way, but alongside this, the clarity and precision of his Horatian translations during the same year seem lost. Was it the medievalism of *Aucassin et Nicolette* or the medievalism of Keats that sponsored this luxuriance? Keats, more likely. After this, there seemed no where to go except down the Pre-Raphaelite path. Cummings needed some new models. But the time he had spent drilling himself in imagery was not wasted.

II

When Cummings began to publish his work in the two literary magazines at Harvard, the editorial staff of each rival group hoped to enlist this new talent in the service of its own periodical. The rules were such that no one could be elected to an editorial board until he had published three items in its issues. So eager were the men of the *Harvard Advocate* to have Cummings join them that they accepted and published three of his poems (including "Of Nicolette") in one month. In spite of this opportunity he really wanted to join the *Harvard Monthly,* which had the superior reputation for the quality of its verse. Founded in 1885 by George Santayana and others, the *Monthly* had published the early verse of such figures as William Vaughn Moody, Bliss Carmen, John Hall Wheelock, and Edwin Arlington Robinson. Its aspirations were quietly asserted on its masthead: "The aim of the Monthly is to publish the best literary work produced by students of the University." In the spring of his sophomore year, Cummings was pleased to get a letter from the secretary, Scofield Thayer, telling him that he had been elected to the board of editors of the *Monthly*.[7]

Because Cummings lived at home, he had taken very little part in the varied social life of the Harvard Yard during his first two years. He was not a joiner: he stayed away from the special interest groups and certainly he was too unsophisticated to be part of the poshocracy of the waiting clubs and final clubs. He is remembered as someone who occasionally appeared at a smoker which his class held at the Harvard Union—a straw-haired youth, quiet but friendly, with an engaging smile, rather preferring to remain on the fringe of the festivities. But when he began his association with the *Monthly*, he gradually made new friends and he began to be drawn into a very different atmosphere from that surrounding Dory Miller.

S. Foster Damon, a handsome, blond-haired enthusiast of the arts from Newton, who was two years older than Cummings, became his guide to all that was modern in the arts. Damon seemed interested in everything. He was a musician, president of the Harvard Music Society, and editor of the *Harvard Music Review*, which was a first-rate periodical, a real testimony to the good taste, maturity, and curiosity of the Harvard aesthetes. He taught Cummings to play the piano (Estlin could already play ragtime by ear) and to write music. He introduced him to Debussy, to Stravinsky, and to the delightful satiric piano sketches of Eric Satie. He took him to the El Greco exhibit at the Fogg Museum, for he considered El Greco "modern."[8] He made him acquainted with the French Impressionists, with Cézanne, and with *Les Fauves*, all of whom had a decided impact on Cummings' later poetry. He took him to the Armory Show in 1913 when it traveled to Boston, and Cummings was ecstatic over the sculptures of Brancusi. He took him to New York after a Harvard-Yale boatrace and Cummings was overwhelmed by the "modern Babylon," a different kind of visit from the one he had made years before with his father. Damon was an editor of the *Monthly*, he wrote poetry, he wrote an article on the history of free verse and received a letter from Amy Lowell about it. He took an interest in Wilde, Shaw, Maeterlinck, Whistler, Pirandello. He subscribed to *Poetry* magazine and read Sandburg, Masters, and Lindsay. He owned a rare copy of Gertrude Stein's *Tender Buttons*, which delighted and bewildered

Cummings. He owned a copy of Pound's anthology *Des Imagistes* (H.D., Aldington, Flint, Joyce, Hueffer) and by this means brought the Imagist Movement into Cummings' ken. He organized the Harvard Poetry Society in 1915. Besides providing all this cultural excitement, he opened the way to some old-fashioned college activities too: he took Cummings out drinking for the first time in his life. Estlin consumed several seidels of dark beer in Jake Wirth's sawdust-strewn restaurant on Stuart Street and ended the evening, much to Damon's mirthful scorn, hanging over a bridge and puking into the Charles River. In his senior year, Cummings wrote a hexameter sonnet for Damon, a rather precious piece, celebrating their mutual intoxication with the music of Debussy:

S. F. D.
In Memory of Claude o'Dreams

Behold, I have taken at thy hands immortal wine
The fume whereof is ecstasy of perfect pain,
Which is more sweet than flowers unknown uttered of rain,
More potent than the fumbling might of the brute brine.
Lo, my pale soul is blown upon far peaks with thine,
Steeped in star-terrible silence, at whose feet the plain
Murmurs of thought and time's illimitable refrain,
Upon whose brows eternity setteth high sign.

This thing hath been, by grace: one music in our souls,
One fane beyond the world, whence riseth sacrifice
Unto that god whom gifts invisible appease.
So be it when sunset's golden diapaison rolls
Over our life—then shalt thou, smiling, touch the keys,
And draw me softly with thee into Paradise.[9]

Another new friend was amiable, modest, generous John Dos Passos, dark as a gypsy, with thick-lensed glasses and a slight stutter. Like Cummings, he was drawn to language study—Latin, Greek, French, German, Spanish—and he specialized in English and Comparative Literature. Like Cummings, he tried his hand at drawing and painting and he earnestly worked out verses, both traditional and modern in their manner, which he published in the *Monthly*. His social consciousness had not yet awakened. Immersed in Henry James and the French Symboliste poets, he was in his aesthetic period and still had no thought to tell his professors "to go take a flying Rimbaud at the moon."[10] In these college years, Dos Passos and Cummings formed a lasting friendship which overrode all their later and considerable differences in social views.

More assertive and opinionated was Scofield Thayer, a student of philosophy and literature three years ahead of Cummings, who was secretary to the editorial board of the *Monthly*. A native of Worcester, Massachusetts, he had attended Milton Academy, where he had been remotely acquainted with T. S. Eliot. He had traveled extensively in Europe with a tutor before coming to Harvard. Although he left Harvard in 1913 to spend two years at Magdalen College, Oxford, he returned for graduate work in 1915–1916 and was again an active member of the *Monthly* staff. Whereas Damon and Dos Passos had met Cummings in the Harvard classroom (seated alphabetically, the last of the C's and the beginning of the D's), Thayer sought Cummings out because he admired his poetry. Although he did not see Cummings during the 1913–1914 college year, he invited him to his Mother's "cottage" at Edgartown, Martha's Vineyard, in the summer of 1914 (the first of many such invitations) in order to renew their acquaintance, and he corresponded with him during the following year. Thayer was an extremely handsome man, very pale, with carefully groomed black hair and dark eyes that sparkled with irony. He dressed elegantly, he spoke with precision and wit, a little suppressed smile flickering around his full curving lips, and he moved and gestured as if powered by a heavy charge of nervous energy. He was equally interested in literature, painting, and aesthetic criticism. He was as fully acquainted as Damon with the new trends in the arts, especially in Wilde, Beardsley (he later built an extensive collection of his prints), Symons, Lautrec, Picasso, Brancusi, the Post-Impressionists and Cubists in general, Joyce, and Eliot. Although he wrote verse himself, he was more of an arbiter of taste than a genuinely creative person. As Cummings put it, "He lived for the honor of art."[11] He had inherited a fortune at an early age and hoped to use his money in the world of publishing in order to make an impact upon the aesthetic values of the American public. Meanwhile, he was a cultural force in Cummings' development. He presented him with a copy of Willard Huntington Wright's *Modern Painting* in spring 1915, a study of painting from the Impressionists to the Cubists, which Cummings marked and annotated like a textbook.[12] It was Thayer who was to bring the major works of Joyce and Eliot to Cummings' attention. Cummings, in flattering joke called Thayer "Williard Huntington Wright, Jr.," and in his graduate year at Harvard he addressed a sonnet to him (with reference to a piece of Wilde's poetic prose which Thayer had shown him). The tone of the poem reveals Cummings' adulation of Thayer, who was soon to replace Damon as his mentor:

W. H. W., Jr.

In Memory of "A House of Pomegranates"

Speak to me, friend! Or is the world so wide
That souls may easily forget their speech,
And the strong love that binds us each to each
Who have stood together watching God's white tide
Pouring, and those bright shapes of dream which ride
Through darkness; we who have walked the silent beach
Strown with strange wonders out of ocean's reach,
Which the next flood in her great heart shall hide?

Do not forget me, though the sands should fall,
And many things be swept away in deep,
And a new vision uttered to the shore,—
If afterdays bespeak me not at all,
Nor other's praise awake my song from sleep,
Nor Poetry remember, anymore.[13]

Another friend from Rochester, New York, who had come to
know Cummings through Dory Miller, was tall, quiet, shy J. Sibley
Watson, a man as loyal, dependable, and unassuming as Thackeray's
Captain Dobbin. He was to become Cummings' closest friend
throughout his lifetime. He wrote short stories, criticism, and verse
translations from the French, all of which were published in the
Monthly. But his self-effacing personality made him difficult to know.
He was "anonymous," Cummings said, "monosyllabic," even "myste-
rious"; yet for all the other-worldly detachment he exhibited, he had a
deeper understanding of the world and of human beings than Cum-
mings' other friends. And he did participate in the literary life of the
Harvard Yard and in occasional nightime gambols. Late in his Har-
vard career, Cummings scribbled out a sonnet to Watson, in a light
and not entirely sober moment:

Softly from its still lair in Plympton Street
It stole on silent pads, and, raping space,
Shot onward in a fierce infernal race,
And shivered townward on revolving feet[.]
Skidded, fortuitously indiscreet;
And now a lady doth its bosom grace
And now the 'phone, tingling its wild disgrace
Telleth that hearts be broke and time is fleet.

O Watson, born beneath a generous star[,]
Oft have I seen thee draped upon a bar[;]
Thou might'st have slain us with a bloody couteau
And
O Watson, moriturus te saluto,
Infinite in thy fair beatitude;
But you could not do anything so rude[.][14]

Although he was the same age as Cummings, Watson was two classes
behind him. Yet, it was he who introduced Cummings to modern French
poetry—to Verlaine, and Rimbaud—and who extended his acquaintance
with Mallarmé; these were three poets whose attitudes and whose experi-
ments with form were to make their impact on Cummings' work a few
years later. Like Thayer, Watson inherited great wealth, and in the 1920s
he and Thayer became owners of the *Dial*, a magazine which in time
served as a new focal point for the *Harvard Monthly* group and won them
an international readership.

Long-faced Stewart Mitchell, "The Great Auk," as he was called,
came to know his classmate, Cummings, when he was editor-in-chief of
the *Harvard Monthly* in 1915–1916. He was a charming, witty young man
from Cincinnati, of somewhat more scholarly inclination and orderliness
and efficiency than most of the *Monthly* editorial board. In 1920 he joined
Watson and Thayer as managing editor of the *Dial*.

Arthur Wilson, a classmate of Cummings from Junction, a tiny town
in Texas, was another editor of the *Monthly*. At the time Cummings was
elected to the board, Wilson sent him a note telling him he was mightily
disappointed that the *Advocate* had been given the privilege of publishing
"Of Nicolette."[15] He and Cummings became close during the following
year when they both were enrolled in Briggs's English Composition
course. Wilson painted and wrote fiction. He is chiefly remembered at
Harvard for a minor scandal. When his short story, "The Girl Who
Advertised," was published in the *Monthly*, December 1914, it stirred the
wrath of the parietal authorities at Harvard, for it employed a few realis-
tic references they disapproved of.[16] Wilson, as well as Damon, helped
Cummings to explore Boston night life and to move beyond a little beer
in a restaurant to something stronger at the Woodcock Hotel or Healy's
Palace.[17]

The literary influence of the new friendships and the familiarity
with modern art and literature do not seem to crop up much in Cum-
mings' writing during his senior year. For Briggs's course in English
Composition, he submitted a number of poems but he held himself

within established forms, sonnets, haiku, ballads, couplets or stanzaic patterns. One exception and the one real triumph was the haunting ballad, "All in green went my love riding/On a great horse of gold/Into the silver dawn." In its irregularity of line, it showed a real freedom from discipline that Cummings had not allowed himself up to this time. Six well-scratched-up pages in his working notebook attest to the care which he devoted to this piece.[18] When it was published in the *Monthly* the following year, it met with praise from professors and fellow-students alike.[19] The first display of sympathy with the modern sensibility that appears in his writing came in the term paper he submitted to Briggs in the spring entitled "The New Art." As we might expect, it is a critically naïve piece of work. It is descriptive and impressionistic, indicating familiarity with the artistic works rather than ability to discourse maturely about them. But what is surprising is the range of the discussion into the areas of painting, sculpture, dance, music, and poetry; and what is remarkable is the fact that an undergraduate in 1915 should have such a comfortably discursive acquaintance with so much of the avante garde activity in the arts.

In the essay, he undertook to point out "the continuous development from Realism to Monet and from Monet to Duchamp-Villon" and the Cubists, and to show the interconnections among the new tendencies in the visual arts, music, and literature.[20] He begins with a consideration of Monet and the "broken color" technique, moves on to Cézanne and the Post-Impressionist emphasis on form, to the primitives Van Gogh and Gauguin, to Matisse's handling of line as a logical continuation of Impressionism, and on to "that peculiar phase of modern art called indiscriminately 'cubism' and 'futurism,' " at which point he offers a detailed discussion of Brancusi's "Mlle. Pogany" and "The Kiss" and of Duchamp-Villon's "Nude Descending a Staircase."[21] For connections between art and theater and among art, music, and dance, he describes the Gordon Craig production of "Caesar and Cleopatra" and Anna Pavlova and her company in the performance of "Les Preludes" with "futuristic" sets and costumes by Bakst. When he comes to music, he writes about Sibelius' Fourth Symphony, Stravinsky's "Le Sacre de Printemps," the works of Debussy and Satie, and finally Schönberg's "Five Orchestral Pieces."

The consideration of visual images and sounds leads naturally to a look at the new poetry. Several of Amy Lowell's poems from *Sword Blades and Poppy Seeds* are set down and admired for their "overleaping the barriers of convention": their grotesquery, their "brutality," their synaesthesia, or their "childish spontaneity and fearlessness." Finally Gertrude Stein and some quotations from *Tender Buttons* are trotted out as the ultimate triumph over realism, the "subordination of the meaning of words to the esthetic significance (i.e. beauty) inherent in the words themselves." A recurrent motif throughout the essay is the hostility which Boston audiences had displayed toward the new art.

Cummings was pleased with his achievement and with Briggs's inexplicable but approving grade, and he decided to carry the battle for the new art into the camp of the Philistines. He revised his essay, cut it drastically, and submitted it to the class marshals in competition for a "commencement part," an oral presentation at the commencement ceremonies, along with the Latin oration and the valedictorian's address. It is testimony to the enterprising spirit of the class of 1915 that this unusual commencement part was chosen, for it reached far over the heads and beyond the tastes of the usual audience of parents and alumni who packed Sanders Theater every year at this time. Thus on June 24, 1915, Estlin Cummings stood once more on the platform at graduation time.[22] He had come a long way since "Hats Off! The Flag is Passing By." He fully enjoyed the unconventionality of his subject, "The New Art." He had planned to refer to Marcel Duchamp-Villon's "Nude" as a "phallic fantasy," but his father forbade it. Still, he took his presentation seriously, delivering it earnestly in his rather high voice. The spirit of mischief was there, nonetheless. President Lowell had continuously been embarrassed by his sister's poetry. Now he "turned to brick"[23] when Cummings read the lines:

> Why do the lilies goggle their tongues at me
> When I pluck them;
> And writhe and twist,
> And strangle themselves against my fingers,
> So that I can hardly weave the garland
> For your hair?
> Why do they shriek your name
> And spit at me
> When I would cluster them?

The audience hitherto somewhat bored by all the aesthetic palaver took amused interest at the President's discomfort. Cummings looked rather startled by the sounds of surpressed laughter. "But," as he later recalled, "what really brought down the house was Gertrude Stein's *Tender Buttons.*" He had recognized already that Stein stood at the outer limits of literary expression, and his speech even posed the question, "How much of this is really Art?" But in a note written later, Cummings confessed that such Steinian topics as:

2) Salad Dressing and an Artichoke
　　Please pale hot, please cover rose, please acre in the red
　　　　stranger, please butter all the beef-steak with regular feel faces.

had been provided merely as " 'comic relief' for a long and learned 3 act treatise." It worked. Uncontrolled laughter swept over the hall. What must have been regarded as a tedious presentation was greeted at the end with "flattering applause."[24] Cummings was learning early how to handle audiences.

III

It had taken Estlin Cummings a long time to become a member of his Harvard class, and in a way he never did. He was two years younger than most of his classmates, and since he lived at home and much under the surveillance of his parents, he seemed less mature than the other college men and rather outside the social scene. As a result, scarcely anyone in the class of 1915 remembers him at college. During his first two years he was quiet and retiring in all social situations. When he did make friends, his acquaintance was limited to the group which published the *Monthly* or the members of the Poetry Society. He was here displaying a characteristic that marked his whole life—the avoidance of the crowd and the selection of a very few friends to whom he was intensely loyal. In company with his new friends, he gradually began to discover Boston, which was now more easily accessible since the new subway had been built out as far as Harvard Square, and he would sometimes stay overnight in Foster Damon's room after a concert, a dance, or a late-night ramble. In his senior year, his father allowed him to move into Thayer Hall and take advantage of the special privilege of the senior class to live in Harvard Yard. He began to experience more independence. He had his own checking account: a few remaining stubs indicate that during the two years he lived in Thayer Hall he went to theaters, movie houses, symphonies, recitals, the opera, he saw Pavlova and Nijinsky, he dined at the Parthenon, Posillipo's, Gee Fong, Venice, Sorrento, the Copley Plaza and other restaurants Greek, Armenian, and Italian. He now began to experience some of the alcoholic and sexual adventure common to a college boy's life.

He had grown taller, moving toward his full height of five feet, eight-and-a-half inches. His hair was still blond, he was light-skinned, and frequently plagued with acne. He had begun to develop a slightly Oriental look. His cheek bones were high and his eyes set wide above them seemed to narrow or slant. He carried his chin high as if to give himself more height and this habit sometimes made him seem aloof. But his alert hazel eyes and engaging smile quickly banished this impression, and his eager enthusiasm about all aspects of his new life gave his face a glow.

His unofficial career at Harvard, he later declared, was "getting acquainted with the fair sex."[25] The acquaintance had actually begun long ago and even led to Charles Eliot Norton's coachman chasing him and two little neighbor girls out of the bushes when they were about six years old. However that may be, his college pursuit of local beauty began with his going by invitation to the Brattle Hall dances, where the boys were aware of four categories of girls: pre-debs, debs, post-debs, and LOPH's (Left on Papa's Hands). Cummings, rhythmically talented, became a very good dancer and sufficiently adept at the Tango and the Maxixe that he and Dorothy Chester, a girl he knew through his father's church, entered a contest at the Boston Theater. He also enjoyed the unorthodox dances like the Turkey Trot and the Bunny Hug that were somewhat frowned on at Brattle Hall.

Damon's roommate, Philip Smith, a genial young man from Jamaica Plain, used to go to barn dances and road houses in the summer with Cummings. Whenever they approached a pair of girls for dancing, Cummings always got the pretty one and Smith ended up with the lemon. Smith remembers Cummings' love for fast motor cars and a series of tricks he would play when joyriding with his friends. When Smith would take the wheel, Cummings liked to climb out on the running board, scramble onto the hood for part of the ride, and then pass over to the driver's running board to cheer him on from there in his steering.

One of Estlin's first loves was Amy de Gozzaldi, a dark-haired, dark-eyed beauty, the daughter of a Cambridge teacher of foreign languages. Amy, two years older than he, was an actress in the productions of the Cambridge Social Dramatic Club, which also performed at Brattle Hall.[26] Cummings met her when he played the part of Micah Dow in J.M. Barrie's play *The Little Minister* in May 1910, and came to know her better when he played Ernest Bennet (the second footman) in Jerome K. Jerome's *The New Lady Bantock* in May 1913. One part of the action called on Cummings to kiss Amy, who played the leading role of Lady Bantock, but she intimidated him by her sophistication. At rehearsals the director continually encouraged him to be more bold. At length, on the night of performance he outdid himself in a kiss that he remembered for months. During the course of production, Cummings felt somewhat outpaced for Amy's regard by the elegant young man who played Lord Bantock, T. S. Eliot. But in the end he achieved a subtle triumph. A custom prevailed in the Cambridge Social Dramatic Club that the men would present gifts to the leading lady on the night of performance. Eliot brought a gorgeous bouquet of roses, but Cummings brought the ultimate gift, a poem—which later appeared in the *Harvard Monthly:*

> Do you remember when the fluttering dusk,
> Beating the west with faint wild wings, through space
> Sank with Night's arrow in her heart? The face
> Of Heaven clouded with Day's red doom
> Was veiled in silent darkness, and the musk
> Of summer's glorious rose breathed in the gloom.
>
> Then from the world's harsh voice and glittering eyes,
> The awful rant and roar of men and things,
> Forth fared we into Silence. The strong wings
> Of Nature shut us from the common crowd;
> On high, the stars like sleeping butterflies
> Hung from the great gray drowsy flowers of cloud.[27]

Cummings was always more ready than Eliot to address a lyric to a lady.

He continued to see Amy, stopping by to see her (too shy to come to tea), taking her for a ride in the family Ford, or taking her dancing at the Copley Plaza, where he introduced her to gin fizzes. He paid her the honor of taking her to the circus. He was allowed such liberties as an embrace while they rode the Scenic Railway at Revere Beach. But he shortly became more attracted to a beautiful golden-haired girl from Brookline, who was attending Miss Haskell's School. Her letters to Cummings in 1915 show her to be a warm, vivacious young charmer, almost a character out of an early Scott Fitzgerald story. She was enthusiastic about parties, dances, clambakes, card games, tennis, boating, swimming, much pleased with her new roadster (a Scripps-Booth with bright red wire wheels) devoted to her little dog Scottie, and struggling to be a proper New England girl and to keep her passionate nature under wraps. In her letters she would lapse into French whenever she touched on a delicate subject (". . . c'était justement parce-que je vous aime *si* beaucoup que j'ai hésitée hier soir, comprends-tu?")[28] She called Cummings "Billiken."

He took her to dances, to Revere Beach, to baseball games, for moonlight drives around Fresh Pond. He visited her at the seashore during the summer. He wrote poems to her, including a long one, in which his ardor overcame his powers of poetic expression. (It began "Never to utter / The wonder of you; (O God!) the wonder of you—")[29] Another, also in *vers libre* but in the decadent style he was affecting during his senior year, displayed the intensity of his youthful passion but it was disciplined by a pattern of near-haiku stanzas:

There is a moon
Sole in the blue night,
Amorous of waters tremulous;

Blinded with silence
The undulous heaven yearns
Where in tense starlessness

Anoint with ardors,
The yellow lover stands in the dumb dark,
Svelt and urgent.

(Again, love,
I slowly gather of thy langorous mouth
The thrilling flower.)[30]

He gave her a copy of Wilde's "Salome" for Christmas.

They had many long intense discussions about their private thoughts, about love, about sex, about their families, and they shared some cuddling intimacies. But she sensed that Cummings was not ready to commit himself to her future. In fact, she worried about all the young men who paid her attention: "I mean this perfectly alright, so don't get offended, but Estlin, I have never yet been quite sure whether the men I know have *souls*. . . . Some people seem to consider a girl or a woman as being merely a 'toy' and some women and girls consider a man just the same thing. I, for one, entirely believe that such a thing as the 'platonic friendship'. . . . cannot exist. *But* (and a large 'but') don't any men love a girl for anything besides physical attraction?"[31] They drifted away from each other during 1916.

Cummings and his friends respected the chastity of the Cambridge and Brookline girls they knew. When they wanted more excitement they picked up girls in Central Square in East Cambridge or on Tremont Street in Boston. But, even so, there were limits. When Cummings reached a furtive hand inside the dress of one of these casual partners, she sternly told him, "Closed for the winter." His mother was very understanding about the freedoms of the automobile age. On Sunday mornings she patiently swept the hairpins out of the Ford so that the Reverend Edward Cummings would not have to remonstrate.[32]

Some notes survive to give us a glimpse of one of these late-night, (not very romantic) outings. One evening in December 1916, Cummings and Foster Damon had dinner in Boston and afterwards bumped into three friendly shop girls on the street. Cummings had encountered one of them before at Revere Beach (he had nestled with her in the back seat of his father's Ford and had been apprehensive about their demeanor when a policeman strolled by across the street). They took the girls to the Hayward Restaurant and drank gin rickeys, then whiskey sours. Damon was embarrassed by a smutty story one of the girls told and went off to get more drinks. When he returned he discoursed for their amusement in a sort of Russian double-talk pretending to be a foreigner. At midnight they sought another place but found it closed. A "chauffeur" approached offering to drive to the Cedarcrest Inn, where dancing and entertainment were available. On the way in the automobile, some mild petting ensued, made awkward by the situation that there were three girls and by the fact that one of the girls became sick from the mixture of drinks and upchucked out the car window. Upon arrival the sick girl retired to the rest room while the others drank and danced. At one point, Damon went to the piano and rolled out a polonaise and Cummings followed the act with "Poor Butterfly." The ride home was attended by some indiscriminate petting and quarreling until one by one the girls were dropped off in South Boston. Cummings recorded the evening in great detail, especially the conversation and phrasing of the girls as they gossiped, talked about their work, or offered back-seat protestations ("oo, just a minute, a *button's killing me,* dear; honest i'll let you put it right back").[33]

Another escapade from this period has been recounted in so many versions that it has become a piece of folklore about Cummings. The central feature of these stories is the threat of a family scandal on an occasion when the Reverend Edward Cummings' Ford was found parked outside a brothel. Cummings' own notes, written years later, give the following information about the episode. One night Cummings was taken by Arthur Wilson down to the area around Scollay Square to visit one Marie Hayes, whose bad reputation was apparently known to the police. Wilson became very drunk, and Cummings departed in search of some oranges to help his friend sober up. While he was gone, the police came upon the Cummings automobile with its clergyman's license plates parked outside Miss Hayes's apartment. They blew its horn to summon the owner, and getting no response, "had it towed away," so the notes read, "to a garage (from which I subsequently got it: cynical remarks, grins, at me, by cops the next morning)." He had gone down to the police station with Jack Churchward, a young friend whom he knew through the South Congregational Church. "Jack and I went into the station, gave the Captain some of (his father's) cigars . . . at trial, slipped the clerk of the court $5 and he showed me in ('you wait outside'—to Jack)."

The clerk said something to the Judge "about my being young 'we all of us make mistakes' . . . [Judge:] WHAT WERE YOU DOING AT THAT HOUR OF THE MORNING IN THAT APARTMENT (address?)—; answer: "Why to tell you the truth I was stopping with a sick friend' . . ."[34] He was able to say it with great sincerity because it was true.

All this sort of activity appears to fall into the classic pattern of the young man getting some wild oats ready to broadcast. But for Cummings it has additional significance. It was for him the discovery of a sphere of life so different from the high-minded atmosphere of the South Congregational Church and of 104 Irving Street that it seemed as exotic as chivalric romance. It was an extension of life into new areas of experience so different from the middle-class culture of Cambridge that it had the shock to provoke creativity. As time went on he would draw upon it for his writing. He continued to seek out the forbidden pleasures of drink and its release from the inhibitions of New England puritanism and to reach out for sexual titillations which his parents would have regarded as dangerous or vulgar. He continued to explore the seedier side of Boston, to frequent the saloons of Washington Street, to visit Scollay Square with its drunks, its prostitutes, its down-and-outers, its Salvation Army preachers, and to attend the Old Howard, the burlesque theater with its crude parodies of popular songs and its broad comedy sketches (girl with stuffed donkey and cat: "You can pat my ass but you can't stroke my pussy").

But not all of his amusements involved drink or sex. He discovered new delights in the popular arts in general. He observed with studied fascination a variety of popular performers: clowns, acrobats, side show spielers, performing animals (a poem addressed "To a Little Seal," which he had seen at Keith's vaudeville theater, begins "Thou of the body beautiful/Born of God's pure joy/Unto the happy sea/For frolic and shining play"),[35] tap dancers, ragtime piano virtuosos, chorus girls, singers of sentimental songs—and sought them out in the various places they performed: circuses, carnivals, amusement parks, vaudeville houses, moving picture palaces, charity bazaars. Even in the streets. For example, one of his notes catches a moment as he responded with a rush of pleasure to an organ grinder and his daughter:

> The most beautiful face I ever saw I saw at 7 o'clock on this evening of Friday December 1st, on Washington near Eliot, on right hand side as you go to the Parthenon. An oldish Italian with a moustache was turning the crank of the hurdy gurdy; he would speak to her, and she'd lean back smiling against it. She was so beautiful that I did not dare look at her or even give her money.
> God will there be hurdy gurdies in heaven?[36]

IV

It is against this background of Cummings' new freedom from family restraints, of his adventures in the livelier Boston precincts, and of his studying people who were different from the Cambridge elite—together with his growing acquaintance with revolutionary painting, music, and literature—that we can see what took place in Cummings writing during his final months at Harvard while he was enrolled in Briggs's course, English Versification, a course designated as "primarily for graduate students." Year after year the course drew the most interesting young literary men at Harvard. In the spring term of 1916, thirty students enrolled (ten, including Cummings, were graduate students). Among the group were Joseph Auslander, Briggs's favorite, who kept quietly to himself but later published six volumes of verse; S. N. Behrman, who dropped out to become a dramatist rather than a poet; Foster Damon who became the biographer of William Blake and Amy Lowell; Robert Hillyer, the conservative of the class and foe of *vers libre*, who was to win the Pulitzer Prize in 1933 for his *Collected Verse;* Stewart Mitchell, editor-in-chief of the *Harvard Monthly;* and Dudley Poore, who became a free-lance writer and an associate of Dos Passos and Cummings in New York during the twenties.[37]

Briggs's procedure was the same simple formula he followed in English Composition, a lot of writing by the student and a lot of comment in the classroom. The textbook for the course, as Dudley Poore remembers, was A. W. Ward's *English Poets* in four volumes, containing "abundant examples of everything from Chaucer to Tennyson." Briggs's assignments required students to produce examples of all the different verse forms, "exact to the point of imitating faults and mannerisms such as the 'dids' Marvell relied on to fill out a verse. The best of these Briggs would read aloud and comment on. Some of them might not have displeased Max Beerbohm."[38]

A good many of Cummings exercises and notes from this course survive, testimony to his continuing seriousness about versifying and to his skill in shaping language to each new form. One composition book holds many pages of his notes on such matters as stanza forms, the difference between the Pindaric and Cowleyan ode, and the scansion of classical forms such as Sapphics, Alcaics, and the various choral odes. He has written an imitation of the early alliterative verse, "When in the northland new is the spring-tide;" he has produced hexameters, blank verse, Alcaics, rime royal, Sapphics, heroic quatrains: he seems to have been tireless.[39]

But his favorite way to fulfill these assignments was to turn out parodies. He gets his hexameters underway for one exercise in this fashion:

> O Ella Wheeler Wilcox, thin patient and very
> *Very* prolific child of the scarcely famouser Sappho
> Why, when I read thy verse, is my heart encircled with loathing.

His heroic couplets "After Dryden" carry out a long satire about Theodore Roosevelt and the Kaiser. Another uses the couplets in the manner of Pope. Still another, "I saw the author of Christabel," is done in the bouncy irregular meters of Coleridge's experiment. In his trial of Whitmanesque verse, he scarcely had to parody—his imitation almost sounds authentic as he declaims the assertions:

> I sing the world imperfect! I worship men and women,
> God being shown me in them, from day to day immortal.[40]

Briggs was rather conservative about form and felt uneasy one day when Cummings produced a startling fourteen-line poem in couplets which were highly irregular in meter and line-length:

> When God lets my body be,
> From each brave eye shall sprout a tree;
> Fruit which dangles therefrom
> The purple world will dance upon.
> From my lips that did sing
> A flower shall bring forth the spring,
> Which maidens whom passion wastes
> Will lay between their little breasts.
> My strong fingers beneath the snow
> Into strenuous birds shall go;
> My love walking in the grass
> Their wings will touch, e'er they pass.
> And all the while shall my heart be
> With the bulge and nuzzle of the sea.[41]

It was what Scofield Thayer called one of his "mortuary pieces." Briggs's comment reflected his troubled response, "Almost too much variety,—or rather, too many licences of doubtful worth. E.g., your six-syllable verses. Variety in distribution of accent is, of course, good if not too unsteadying." Nor did he care for some of the phrasing: "The bulge and nuzzle of the sea," he found "bold rather than happy." On "wastes" and "breasts" as a rhyme he grudgingly conceded, "This will do for a rhyme if need be." Although Briggs did not recognize it, Cummings had produced his first really singable lyric. The strangeness of some of the tropes had thrown Briggs off and he vented his discomfort in comments about mechanics. During the past few years, Cummings had grounded himself so solidly in traditional verse that he could build upon it, yet do so uniquely. The poem was a variation on the sonnet form with three four-line units and a final couplet. Its diction and rhythmic irregularity drew upon the English Renaissance tradition of song that ran all the way from Wyatt to Carew as well as upon the idiom of folk song. Briggs did not approve of the flower being laid "between the little breasts," but the image is common in folk ballads, such as "Lady Alice." All in all, the poem can produce in a reader or hearer that feeling of recognition combined with surprise which is the mark of successful originality in art.

Cummings was loosening up as a result of all this exercise. In the midst of the routine, he suddenly tossed off another poem which was entirely different from his previous work. It made skillful use of slang and it worked a raucous description of a tavern brawl into swift, running tetrameter couplets:

> In Healey's Palace I was sitting—
> Joe at the ivories, Irene spitting
> Rag into the stinking dizzy
> Misbegotten hall, while Lizzie,
> Like a she-demon in a rift
> Of Hell-smoke, toured the booths, half-piffed.
>
> I saw two rah-rahs—caps, soft shirts,
> Match-legs, the kind of face that hurts,
> The walk that makes death sweet—Ted Gore
> And Alec Ross; they had that whore
> Mary between them.   Don't know which,
> One looked; and May said: "The old bitch
> Lulu, as I'm a virgin, boys!"
> And I yelled back over the noise:
> "Did that three-legged baby croak
> That you got off the salesman-bloke?"
>
> The beer-glass missed.   It broke instead
> On old man Davenport's bald head.

I picked a platter up, one-handed.
Right on her new straw lid it landed.
Cheest, what a crash!
                     Before you knew,
Ted slipped the management a new
Crisp five, and everyone sat down
But May, that said I'd spoiled her gown,
And me, that blubbered on her shoulder,
And kissed her shiny nose, and told her
I didn't mean to smash her...Crowst,
But I was beautifully soused!
I think Al called me "good old sport,"
And three smokes lugged out Davenport.[42]

For the first time, Cummings was trying out the new freedom of diction and subject matter and disciplining it within a standard verse form. Briggs did not know what to make of it. His comment: "So far as four-accent verse goes, this is all right (March 8 was a day for heroic couplets). Please don't forget that a clean subject is never harmful."

Since Briggs was conservative about meter, line, and diction, he was not overjoyed about the direction that modern poetry was taking. For him, Matthew Arnold's freedom of line offered about as much deviation from poetic norms as he liked. Some of the work now coming out in *Poetry* magazine and in *Others* (Alfred Kreymborg's new monthly which welcomed work by unpublished authors, the "others" who did not appear in *Poetry*) was not to his taste, especially Sandburg and Lindsay in their use of slang. He also felt uncomfortable about the notoriety and influence of President Lowell's sister Amy. Some of the students like Robert Hillyer and Joseph Auslander agreed with him, and a running argument took place in the classroom with Damon and Cummings leading the opposition. At the end of the spring term 1916, Cummings carried his side of the contention over into a major paper, forty-seven pages long, "The Poetry of a New Era."[43] It is not a critically sophisticated work but it shows the trend of his taste and the kind of reading that he had been doing.

The essay is really an elaboration of the section in his discourse on "The New Art" that was devoted to poetry. It points to the dawn of a new spirit of art that had been gradually lighting up the sky for almost a quarter of a century, but that the English-speaking public had only become aware of "after the 1912 Cubist Exhibition." Cummings refers to W.H. Wright's article on modern art in the January issue of *Forum* which describes the further developments in the work of Matisse, Picabia, and the English Vorticist school. In poetry, Cummings names Mallarmé and Whitman as precursors of the new spirit of revolt against dead tradition; he admires Masters, Brooke, and Masefield for being upholders of "the spoken word" in poetry; he calls Pound and Lowell the Picasso and Picabia of the new poetry; and he singles out the Imagist school for special praise. Among the poems that he copies out are Aldington's "The Poplar Bromios," Eliot's "Rhapsody on a Windy Night" (he particularly admires the use of detail and the introduction of ordinary objects such as the "toothbrush" into the poetic scene), F. S. Flint's "Fragment," H. D.'s "The Garden" and "The Pool" (he thought she was a man), Amy Lowell's "The Traveling Bear" and "Stravinsky's Three Orchestral Pieces, Grotesques for a String Quartet," Pound's "The River Merchant's Wife: A Letter," "Liu Che," and "Fan Piece for her Imperial Lord," (he praised the spirit of "oriental condensation" in these and other poems from *Cathay*). His final pages are reserved for "the two greatest poems," Pound's "Doria" and "The Return."

Cummings wanted to be part of the modern movement. What the essay shows is the variety of poetic expression he had before him as models. As time goes on we see him trying on one influence after another but he was really looking for a style all his own. Chiefly he sought a diction and phrasing which would be unusual when compared to the common notion of what was appropriate for poetry. Among the parodies that he wrote during the term is a piece referring to Kreymborg's magazine. It reveals that he was aware of and able to imitate the various styles of contemporary poets but that he sought for his own poetic expression something entirely different. In this instance he uses for his own style a mixture of long, Latinate, somewhat learned terms and a colloquial phrase in describing a commonplace situation:

"OTHERS"

William D.   "Scorn not the sonnet, critic"?   Any one
Howells   Can do it, Amy Lowell says.   By by,
                 Poesy!   I wipe my broken-hearted eye;
                 The days of minstrelsy are surely done.
                 The "Spoon River Anthology" has won
                 The sympathy of all our smaller fry;
                 No one could call the muse of *vers libre* "shy"!
                 Nowadays rhymesters have to shoot and run.

Amy Lowell   Well well,
                        I don't know after all but what
                        'Tis better so.
                        Perhaps
                        The ancient forms are really getting stagnant,
                        And need
                        Rep-
                        lenishing from the newer well.
                        Tut
                        Tut!
                        You know it never rains but what
                        It storms—
                        And after all,
                        These new bards have
                        The pep!

Vachel Lindsay   Time was, I cursed the newer charioteers
                        Who drive the wain of Art at break-neck pace;
                        Time was, I thought th' entire human race
                        Had been absorbing much too many beers;

John Masefield   Time was, I felt assured that this round earth
                        Was really going straight, straight, straight to H-ll;
                        Time was I thought of leaving home and hearth
                        For gaudy climes of gelded culture ... Well,

Robert Frost   I was quite wrong, and I will tell you why,
                        And you will be surprised,—I'll wager that.
                        You see it was like this.   Yesterday I,
                        Opening the kitchen door, saw our old fat

E. Estlin   Phlegmatically feministic cook
Cummings   Weeping great buckets over Rupert Brooke![44]

Note that after the free-verse sample he has pressed the Lindsay-Masefield-Frost-Cummings lines into sonnet form.

Although Dean Briggs did not encourage free verse, the students were writing it anyway, and over the next few months of 1916 Cummings began to develop a whole series of new and unusual poems that he showed to his friends in the Poetry Society but did not publish in the

Monthly. In a list of poems which he labeled "Index 1916,"[45] compiled apparently in the summer, Cummings gathered his best work of recent vintage, arranged according to verse or stanza form—sonnet, ballade, villanelle, Alexandrine, blank verse, and so on. The largest group, fifty-nine poems, is headed "D.S.N." (Designatio Sine Nomine?) and it includes all his unrhymed poems in such forms as haiku, *vers libre,* and long Whitmanesque lines. Many texts of those poems which are listed still survive. Some of them are early versions of poems which were later published in *Tulips and Chimneys.* For instance, his best known poem, a nostalgic harkening back to childhood games presided over by a disguised nature god, appears in this form:

> In just-Spring
> When the world is mud-luscious
> The queer old baloon-man
> Whistles far and wee,
> And Bill and Eddy come pranking
>
> From marbles and from piracies,
> And it's Springtime.
>
> When the world is puddle-wonderful
> The little lame baloon-man whistles
> Far and wee,
> And Betty and Is'bel come dancing
>
> From hop-scotch and still-pond and jump-rope,
> For it's Springtime,
> And the world is ooze-suave,
>
> And the goat-footed baloon-man
> Whistles
> Far
> And
> Wee.[46]

Some others are grouped together as "Impressions,"—and on these poems the influence of the new art is everywhere evident. "Stinging gold," for instance, shows that Cummings has combined the principles of impressionism (the emphasis on the rendering of light and color; the free-verse technique as a literary form of "broken brushwork") and the principles of imagism (compression, precision, the rhythms of common speech, the presentation by means of images):

> Stinging gold
> Swarms upon the spires,
> Silver chants the litanies,
> The great bells are ringing with rose—
>
> The lewd fat bells.
>
> And a tall wind
> Is dragging the sea for a dream,
> For soon shall the formidable eyes
> Of the world be
> Entered
> With sleep.[47]

In his images, Cummings has been providing the "freshness and novelty" that T. E. Hulme called for in modern verse.

At one point while he grouped and regrouped his poems, he had established one category of "Odes." Only one page remains, containing, "Spring, slattern of seasons" and "Humanity/I love you." The first of these, in less tightly curbed free verse, represents one of Cummings' distinctive approaches to a subject. He takes a traditional theme (the praise of spring), makes use of the traditional device of personification, and employs the archaism of the second person singular in his address —and then selects detail and chooses language that runs counter to the tradition. Yet the details are appropriate: spring is a muddy, sloppy time and the effects that the season brings upon the natural world should not always be prettified. This is the way the poem begins:

> Spring, slattern of seasons,
> Thou hast muddy legs
> And a soggy petticoat;
> Drowsy is thy hair,
> Thy eyes are sticky with dream,
> And thou hast a sloppy body
> From being brought to bed of crocusses;
> When thou singest with thy whisky voice
> The grass rises on the head of the earth
> And all the trees are put on edge.

and it ends in this way:

> Spring,
> Of the dissolute slobber of thy breasts
> And the indecent jostle of thy thighs
> I am so very fond,
> That my soul inside me
> Hollers;
> For thou comest,
> And thy hands are the snow
> And thy fingers are the rain,
> And I hear the screech of dissonant flowers,
> And first of all I hear your stepping,—
> Freakish feet,
> Feet incorrigible,
> Ragging the world.[48]

Certain surprises in the images go beyond the novelty of the Imagist school into the wrenching world of Cubism: The cross-over of senses and associations in "the screech of disonant flowers" and the reversal of expectations in the slobber of breasts and the jostle of thighs.[49] More than anything else that was startling for the time, however, was the joyous spirit of basic sexuality. Four years of trial had to pass before Cummings could get the poem published in a magazine.

One poem in the D.S.N. list pushes into real innovation in technique. Perhaps the very fact that Cummings was working with cubist imagery released some additional creativity. At any rate, it is the first time he tried using verbs as nouns. He introduced the device into a poem about sunset in the city in which the harshness of the cityscape is depicted through twisted and distorted word usage, through architectural images that are made to suffer, and through the imagery of noise, breaking, scraping, colliding, shouts and crashes:

> Writhe and gape of tortured perspective,
> Rasp and graze of splintered horizon,
> Crackle and sag of planes,
> Clamors of collision,
> Collapse;
> As peacefully
> Lifted

> Into the frightening beauty of sunset
> The perfect young city,
> Putting off dimension
> With a blush,
> Enters the becoming garden of
>
> Her agony.[50]

With a few changes in word and in typographical arrangement, this new contribution to modern poetry became "Impression II" in *Tulips and Chimneys* seven years later.

V

The giant steps into new realms of expression that Cummings was taking indicate that he was looking at the world from new perspectives and that he had begun opening new aspects of himself and considering who and what he was. All this had to begin with a change in his view of his home life and his new attitude toward his father. In earlier years the relations between father and son were excellent, but the close relations and the supervision had to give way if Estlin was to mature emotionally. There were two difficulties, however, and very normal ones indeed.

First, Edward Cummings continued to treat Estlin as a child. He still called him "Chub," a nickname derived from "cherub," the wallpaper pattern in the room he had occupied in childhood. Besides the name, his manner of talking to Estlin, telling him what to do, cautioning him about his behavior, responding to his ideas—all these communicative signals reflected an address to a youngster. As Edward had grown older, he had become more dogmatic about his beliefs in the way to live life, and since he was a minister, he had adopted a more didactic tone, although his views were certainly not conservative. He became then, in his son's eyes, more preachy. The aphorisms Estlin had heard as a child ("If you don't like doing something, act as though you did and pretty soon you will," "Smile before breakfast and shine inside") now sounded dreadful. (He had long ago removed the motto he had chosen from a list of his father's and placed in decorated letters over his study table: "Anything worth doing at all is worth doing well.") Since Edward Cummings loved his son deeply, he wanted to share his experiences and guide them. He constantly thrust himself into Estlin's affairs and unwisely so. When Estlin invited visitors to Silver Lake, Edward wanted to join their company—go on a hike, go in a boat, sit with them in the evening. As a consequence, Estlin built himself a tree house down the lake to which he could retreat. Ever since late adolescence, he had been becoming more and more withdrawn and secretive in order to protect himself from the dominance of his father.

The second difficulty was Estlin's own view of himself, especially in comparison to his father. His sister had inherited Edward's broad shoulders and height. Estlin, measured against the wall regularly and in vain, did not grow much until the middle of his college career, and "slight, delicate, nervous"[51] he felt dwarfed by his father's height and bulk and awed by his strength. He was also overwhelmed by the fact that his father had so many accomplishments. In one frequently quoted summary of his father's many activities, Estlin, many years later, made him sound like a real American hero, a combination of Benjamin Franklin and Daniel Boone:

> He was a New Hampshire man, 6 foot 2, a crack shot & a famous fly fisherman & a firstrate sailor (his sloop was named The Actress) & a woodsman who could find his way through forests primeval without a compass & a canoeist who'd stillpaddle you up to a deer without ruffling the surface of a pond & an ornithologist & taxidermist & (when he gave up hunting) an expert photographer . . . & an actor who portrayed Julius Caesar in Sanders Theatre & a painter (both in oils & watercolours) & a better carpenter than any professional & . . . a plumber who just for the fun of it installed all his own waterworks & (while at Harvard) a teacher with small use for professors — . . . & my father was a servant of the people who fought Boston's biggest & crookedest politician fiercely all day & a few evenings later sat down with him cheerfully at the Rotary Club & my father's voice was so magnificent that he was called on to impersonate God speaking from Beacon Hill (he was heard all over the common). . . .[52]

Given this father-son situation, it is a wonder that Estlin ever made much of a success as a human being at all. But the rebellion gradually began to take place. At first in trivial ways. Estlin was troubled with acne, especially on his back and chest. Embarrassed by his appearance, he refused to go to the Sargent Gymnasium for physical exercise, and in spite of his father's remonstrances he would not explain why. Soon after when he was in college he refused to wear long underwear in the winter, and no amount of argument could sway him. He no longer went regularly to church or to the citizenship class for young people. He began to bathe less frequently, a turn of events that especially irritated his father, who held "We can't all of us be honored by titles and degrees but we can all be Knights of the Daily Bath."[53] He began to be careless in his dress and appearance. (His mother occasionally stole his shoes and shined them.) He did not change his underwear frequently enough nor did he care about rips and tears in it. His parents, troubled about appearances, asked him "what if he were taken up in an accident."[54] His beard was light because he was very blond and he did not begin to shave until later than most men, nor did he have to shave every day during these early years. Yet, when he lived at Thayer Hall, he slacked off in shaving and occasionally had a scraggly, unshaven appearance.

Although he indulged in these gestures against his early training, he could turn himself out well for his own social purposes. He began, too, to hold himself straight with his shoulders back to give himself his fullest height. He began now his habit of holding his chin high in an almost arrogant pose. The postures were those of a young man of new self-confidence. Certain details of his social life, although unknown to his father, ran directly counter to his father's principles. His drinking was the chief activity in opposition to his father's temperance work and also to oft-stated paternal sayings ("I'd never give a penny to a son of mine who drank").[55] In his wandering into Scollay Square with its pimps and prostitutes or in his visits to the old Howard burlesque theater, he invaded territory his father, who was a supporter of the Watch and Ward Society, would very much have wanted him to avoid.

But there was a real change in Estlin's attitude toward his father's attributes. Once he had admired his father's sonorous voice. Now he thought he talked too loud. Once he looked to his father as wise, solemn, all-knowing. Now he thought him rather pompous and overly dependent on the *Boston Transcript* for his opinions. The repressive approach to sex that was common in the household, as well as in Cambridge in general, contributed to further estrangement. Estlin's father talked to him only once about sex and only years after he had learned all the secrets of this adult province from Sandy Hardy and from his friends. He had begun occasionally to masturbate and he felt very guilty about it—somehow before both God and his father. He even reflected his struggle in a poem "Never any more, My God."[56] Later he heard some folklore to the effect that masturbating caused acne, but in his worry he could not go to his father. Instead he inquired of Dr. Hutchinson, the college physician, asking if acne was caused by wet dreams.

At this time, Estlin began to dredge up out of his memory subjects for grievances against his father, and they invariably involved his mother. He remembered his father's jibe at his mother's fatness—an ironical remark about "that swan-like neck"—and the tears in her hurt eyes. He remembered overhearing his father scolding his mother for her mishandling of the household accounts, referring to his "hard-earned money" and pointing out that she had not brought a cent to their marriage. "All this overheard by me," Cummings noted, "who am (supposed to be) doing my lessons in library. I REVOLT ag my F: would like TO KILL HIM." When he read Tennyson's "Guinevere" in *The Idylls of the King* he considered that Arthur's self-righteous reproaches to the queen sounded, "exactly like my F's to my M."

One other incident that he vaguely recalled borders closely on what Freud called the primal scene. One night in the bedroom near his own he heard his mother cry out "Edward," and years later he conjectured about what he had thought it meant and what his response was. "What happened a) to make her cry out in room betw. rooms b) afterwards?—her room (=doors locked) did I get out of bed & listen at the door-jamb —or even open the door silently—& hear . . . & did I thereupon, white, trembling with terror, decide I'd never take any more of my F's hypocrisy [?]"[57]

The clearest break came in a scene after the episode about the impounded automobile. On that night, Marie Hayes, having been told by the police the name of the owner of the automobile that was being towed away, telephoned Edward Cummings at 3 A.M. "Eddie?" she inquired in a somewhat drunken voice and then reported what had happened. When Estlin arrived home, he was met by Edward Cummings standing on the stairs in his pajamas and bathrobe, denouncing him for his keeping such low company. Edward waked Rebecca to participate, telling Estlin how much he should be ashamed for having disgraced his mother—his mother "who went down to the gates of death to meet you" [that is, in giving birth to him]. Estlin countered with the argument that Jesus was no snob toward sinners—prostitutes and other unfortunates. He would not submit to being the subject of a sermon. Later in the argument, Edward threatened to throw him out of the house. When Estlin replied, "Go ahead," Edward burst into tears, and in his disillusionment about his son, cried, "I thought I'd given birth to a god!"[58]

Although there can be no doubt of Edward's heart-felt grief, his rhetoric and theatrics diminished the respect he had held in his son's eyes.

This period of Oedipal crisis was hard on both father and son. Later in life Estlin was fully aware of the range of attitudes that he had harbored about his father: "My father was a true father—he loved me. And because he loved me, I loved him: first, as a child, with the love which is worship; then, as a youth, with the love that gives battle; last, as a man, with the love which understands."[59] That understanding was far in the future. Estlin had thrust him aside as an authority figure. Yet as the Harvard years revealed, he was still dependent on some intellectual authority. He merely turned to other father-figures like Dory Miller or

Foster Damon for guidance and support. His full maturity would be slow in coming. He would pass through a succession of surrogate fathers in the years to come.

His turning to aestheticism and the new art was congruent with his breaking away from the dominance of his father's views. The result was a release of creativity. What happened in his own writing ran parallel to the rebellion against his father, and only as territories of his life became freed did a unique personal style in his verse begin to emerge. As this development continued to take place, it was accompanied by his ever-vigorous challenge to established opinion and traditional forms of expression in the American literary scene. That, for a while, was another form of the battle with his father. The Oedipal wrestling bout was renewed off and on over the next decade, with Edward Cummings taking most of the falls. But Estlin's struggle with the American public lasted the rest of his life.

VII

The Poet Finds
a Patron

The applause of a single human being is of great consequence.
SAMUEL JOHNSON

When his year as editor-in-chief of the *Harvard Monthly* drew to a close, Stewart Mitchell wanted to organize another kind of publication. Some high-quality verse had appeared in the magazine and had been discussed in Dean Briggs's classroom, and he felt that it deserved a permanent place between hard covers. He and six of his fellow poets decided to publish a book of verse as a cooperative venture. Each would contribute a handful of poems and the authors would appear in alphabetical order, Cummings, Damon, Dos Passos, Hillyer, Mitchell, Poore, and Cuthbert Wright, another former editor of the *Monthly*. Hillyer insisted that his friend, William Norris, who was the head of another literary society, the Signet Club, be invited to publish with them. Thus it came about that by early fall 1916 Mitchell had compiled a collection entitled *Eight Harvard Poets*, which he brought to Lawrence Gomme, owner of the Little Book Shop Around the Corner at 2 East 29th Street in New York. Since a number of volumes of verse had been launched from this shop, it was a respectable publishing source, but each of the Harvard poets had to agree to buy thirty copies to insure sales and eventually John Dos Passos' father had to put up the money to guarantee full publishing costs.[1]

The eight poems which Cummings chose to publish fall into two groups. Four were sonnets of a rather ordinary sort; the other four were in free verse and were arranged unusually on the page, reflecting the fact that Cummings had been playing around with form during the summer.

It all started with Ezra Pound. When Damon had shown Cummings

Stewart Mitchell, pencil drawing by E. E. Cummings.

Pound's poem "The Return," it had made a profound impression on him. He was moved by the linguistic expressiveness of the piece, which used modern diction and oblique treatment for a classical subject, the decline in the power of the gods. But the arrangement on the page, he said, "the inaudible poem—the visual poem, the poem for not ears but eye—moved me more."[2] The poem does not look very unusual to us today:

> See, they return; ah, see the tentative
> Movements, and the slow feet,
> The trouble in the pace and the uncertain
> Wavering!
>
> See, they return, one, and by one,
> With fear, as half-awakened;
> As if the snow should hesitate
> And murmur in the wind
>   and half turn back;
> These were the "Wing'd-with-Awe,"
>   Inviolable.
>
> Gods of the winged shoe!
> With them the silver hounds
>   sniffing the trace of air!
> Haie! Haie!

> These were the swift to harry;
> These the keen-scented;
> These were the souls of blood.
>
> Slow on the leash,
>   pallid the leash-men![3]

Still, the lines which begin uncapitalized in the middle of the page give a sense of tentative separation from the line above without the isolation of standing by themselves. And the use of space above the last line-unit offers a guiding pause and thus some dramatic emphasis before the final descriptive phrases. In Pound's 1915 volume *Cathay*, which Cummings had singled out for praise in "The Poetry of a New Era," the poet had used similar spacing for his verse lines.

For Cummings this freedom of spacing represented a release from formal bonds, and he saw, as he sat at the family typewriter trying out visual arrangements, that there were immense possibilities for expressiveness in the combinations and the separations of the words on the page. Beyond this, he had for some time recognized the needlessness of capitalizing the first letter of each new line of verse: he had seen that the Greeks capitalized only the first letter of the first word in a poem and sometimes not even that. At the same time, he had noticed in reading the comic strips, especially his favorite Krazy Kat, that capitals were used for emphasis.[4] As for punctuation, the purpose of which is to guide and clarify meaning for a reader, he realized that its absence could create significant ambiguities and complexities. His "Crepuscule" as published in *Eight Harvard Poets* makes use of all of these new considerations in its opening lines:

> I will wade out
>   till my thighs are steeped in burn-
> ing flowers.
> I will take the sun in my mouth
> and leap into the ripe air
>   Alive
>   with closed eyes
> to dash against darkness
>   in the sleeping curves of my
> body
> Shall enter fingers of smooth mastery
> with chasteness of sea-girls
>   Will I complete the mystery
> of my flesh

The arrangement of the lines on the page seems sometimes merely arbi-
trary—the break in "burn-ing," for instance, is badly placed. Perhaps the
printer was responsible, for there was some fuss and some correspon-
dence about the typographical difficulties of one of Cummings' poems.
But the effect of capitalizing "Alive" (it was to become Cummings' favor-
ite word) is easily evident. Since "Shall" and "Will" carry their own
emphasis without capitalization, it is possible that this is a private Har-
vard joke, for the correct usage of "shall" and "will" was an obsession
with Dean Briggs. The absence of a period after "mastery" allows the
phrase "with the chasteness of sea-girls" to be a part of both the statement
before and the statement after it.

The last of the poems, "Epitaph," (Cummings later dropped the title)
was a little masterpiece, the most important poem he had written up to
that time. It is a poem about innocence betrayed or the vulnerability of
beautiful things, but it is expressed by means of a classical subject, the
abduction of Persephone by Hades and treated in the new technique he
had developed:

> Tumbling-hair
>   picker of buttercups
>   violets
> dandelions
> And the big bullying daisies
>   through the field wonderful
> with eyes a little sorry
> Another comes
>   also picking flowers

It is an image in action, presented with elliptical brevity. Persephone is
pictured right at the outset as a wind-tossed flower among the other
more common blossoms. The alliterated "big bullying" seems not to
apply to daisies, and we do not understand it until we reach the end of
the poem and carry it over to the advancing Hades. Because there is no
punctuation, the phrase "through the field wonderful" applies to the
field flowers in one way and in another way to the god Hades. In fact,
the missing punctuation, together with the capitalizing of "And," al-
lows the eyes of the daisies as well as of Hades to be "a little sorry."
Only at the last word—which takes us back to the first image—can the
poem be understood. Only then can the archetypal story be recognized,
reinforced, one hopes, by the reader's remembrance of Milton's Satan
coming upon Eve:

oft stooping to support
Each flower of slender stalk, whose head though gay
Carnation, Purple, Azure, or speckt with Gold,
Hung drooping unsustain'd, . . .
mindless the while,
Herself, though fairest unsupported Flow'r,
From her best prop so far, and storm so nigh.
Nearer he drew. . . .[5]

Lawrence Gomme may have fretted about the typography of some of the poems, but Cummings had been considering even more radical arrangements—for instance, a format in which the eye might travel back and forth across the page in a kind of English-Hebrew combination:

I will wade out
srewolf gninrub ni depeets era shgiht ym llit
ym ni nus eht ekat lliw I
mouth
and leap into the ripe air
Alive
seye desolc with
to dash against darkness
in the sleeping curves of my
yretsam htooms fo sregnif retne llahs ydob
with chasteness of sea-girls. . . .[6]

The inventive spirit of old Edward Norris Cummings, the tinkerer, seems to have awakened in him.

One more stylistic innovation was ventured in the poem "Crepuscule." For the first time Cummings tried the first-person singular pronoun "i."[7] As chance would have it, this little startler was never published, for the copy editor apparently took it as a typing error and corrected it. But since this pronoun later became Cummings' special mark, we should look at the origins of this usage. For a number of years, the Cummings family had frequent dealings with a man of all work named Sam Ward. He looked after the cottage at Silver Lake during the winter, cared for the boats, repaired ice damage, took down weed growth, cut firewood, and his wife Mae opened the house and cleaned it before the family arrived for the summer. Sam and his wife were barely literate, and his letters reporting the chores that he had carried out, especially his spelling and capitalization, gave the Cummings family much amusement. None of the early letters survive, but a later example can serve to illustrate his way of writing:

> i am sending Bill up to nov 17 i have the house finished all but painting the new Boards that came in sight to keep them from cracking i have the ice Houstop on and can finish that in a couple of days now i had to git Some more joice and some flashing to finish the Work around the chimleys the Woodshed the End next to the ice House is all gon and the side next to the garden is all rotten at the bottom and fell out in the feald i have piled the Wood over and i shall have Boards to board them up again.[8]

Sam was an honest, self-reliant, hard-working, genial, ungrammatical fellow with a fund of folk wisdom (Cummings was later to write a tribute to him, an elegy for Sam, "rain or hail"[9]), and now, just at the time that Cummings was scrutinizing language and was taking an interest in the behavior of people who were outside his social sphere and was rebelling against the middle-class style of living, Sam's primitive means of expression appealed to him. The small "i" seemed appropriate to Sam's humble position and to his individuality, and Cummings began, more and more, to use it himself for the new role he was fashioning for his life. He began, more and more, to subvert all the conventions of punctuation, capitalization, and syntax, like a linguistic Thoreau trying to discover what the essential operations of language were. But the small "i"s had further significance. Cummings was small himself, especially alongside his father, yet by acknowledging his littleness with the lower-case "i", he became different, became in fact unique, and therefore made himself outstanding. It was a symbolic procedure that was to develop into a pattern of behavior and eventually to manifest itself in multiple ways, social, political, and artistic.

II

Some of Cummings' friends were getting married. Sibley Watson married the ethereal, artistically talented Hildegarde Lasell of Whitinsville, Massachusetts, on Cummings' twenty-second birthday, October 14, 1916. His letter to Watson, written "le matin apres la nuit avant" reveals that he celebrated the double occasion with a splendid champagne drunk, that he was singled out at the wedding dinner by Harper Sibley:

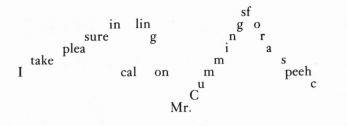

and that his drive back to Cambridge was rather slow "because partly 2 of my hands had or were fallen off and partly because something tinny had tumbled from the Ford at Wellesley." He arrived unscathed for a dawn breakfast at the Waldorf restaurant, "being a virgin of circumstance from the waist up."[10]

The wedding that made a greater impact upon his personal life had taken place earlier on June 21, 1916, in Troy, New York. Scofield Thayer had met Elaine Orr, a demure, soft-spoken student from Miss Bennett's School, when he was traveling in England, and they became engaged in the winter of 1915–1916. In the spring he invited Elaine to Cambridge to meet some of his Harvard friends. Cummings saw her for the first time in March and came to know her better when he joined her and Scofield for lunch and an afternoon at the theater (Galsworthy's *Justice*) on May 20. He was deeply stirred by her quiet loveliness as soon as he met her, a feeling that was to grow until, in time, she became for him an object of worship. As chance would have it, Thayer asked him to write an epithalamion for the wedding day. Cummings set to work immediately to provide something in the best Greek tradition, yet with his own stylistic touches. It was his first commission, a work unique in Cummings' whole productive career, and was published first in *Tulips and Chimneys*. It now stands as the opening poem in his volume, *Complete Poems*, twenty-one strophes of eight lines each in intricately rhymed pentameter.

Except for one other, "Epithalamion" is the longest poem he ever wrote. In its exuberance it exhibits the kind of romantic Hellenism that would have rejoiced the hearts of Keats and his circle. Choked with mythological allusion, it begins in an elevated Pindaric manner, with an address to natural personifications—earth, rain, sky, wind— and ends traditionally with a plea to Aphrodite for the poet himself, "I beseech thee bless/thy suppliant singer and his wandering word."

After Cummings finished the poem, he delivered it to Thayer at luncheon at the Hotel Touraine on the Saturday before the wedding. Thayer ordered a bottle of the legendary Chateau d'Yquem sauternes for the occasion, although he himself drank scarcely more than a sip

*Scofield Thayer, pencil
sketch by E. E. Cummings
about 1916.*
HOUGHTON LIBRARY

of anything alcoholic. After lunch, Estlin, rather giddy from consuming the whole bottle of wine, handed his composition to Thayer, who taking it with a welcoming flourish proceeded to read the poem aloud:

> Thou aged unreluctant earth who dost
> with quivering continual thighs invite
> the thrilling rain thy slender paramour
> to toy with thy extraordinary lust. . . .

Thayer's voice resounded through the room, from which all other diners had departed. Estlin shrank with embarrassment as the waiters looked questioningly at them while going about their table arrangements, but Thayer pressed on, through lush, erotic imagery to the throbbing passage describing Danae's response to Zeus, who comes to her bed disguised as a shower of gold:

> Danae
> saw the night severed and the glowing throng
> descend, felt on her flesh the amorous strain

of gradual hands and yielding to that fee
her eager body's unimmortal flower
knew in the darkness a more burning rain.

The culminating point of dismay for Estlin came when Thayer reached the line, "Lover, lead forth thy love unto that bed." "Ah," he said, "now we come to the interesting part," and continued to declaim in an even more sonorous voice. Cummings thought his attitude about his bride-to-be was rather coarse, and this behavior somewhat altered his opinion of Thayer.

But the epithalamion caused further reverberations in Cummings' life. With the regal magnificence that was a characteristic of his patronage, Thayer sent him a check for $1000, an extraordinary sum (the equivalent of $10,000 in the money of today). It provided Cummings with enough money to be economically independent of his father and to launch himself in a life of his own choosing. Edward Cummings was outraged that Estlin would accept money from a friend: he felt that the poem should have served as a wedding gift. This did not trouble Estlin. Phil Smith vividly recalled hearing a long and earnest discussion between Estlin and his Harvard friends about the morality of having a patron. By now, Estlin had made up his mind: if the great poets and painters of earlier times accepted patronage, he was ready to follow their example.

Estlin had wanted to leave Cambridge and Boston for some time. He felt that the environment of the Unitarian Church, of Cambridge mothers' clubs, of Irving Street neighborliness, of Harvard paternalism, of the culture represented by the *Boston Transcript* and the New England household poets was smothering him. He had lived all his life within a book's throw of Harvard Yard and the spirit of Apollo—or of Hestia—had ruled. He needed some Dionysian release. The one trip to New York with Damon had convinced him that he wanted to live there in the midst of its heterogeneous cultural stimulation.

He thought of taking a job somewhere in the world of journalism or publishing. He had hoped to find something on the staff of a magazine through Bliss Perry's help, but he did not get much encouragement. He wrote to the *New York Post*, which had published one of his poems, but there was no opening. He ran down to New York in June taking with him a general letter of introduction from Amy Lowell, but his interviews led nowhere. "I begin to feel like the 'questing beast' of Malory," he wrote to his parents.[11] He returned to New England for the summer, and during the fall he stayed at home and worked on his poems or his cubist experiments in painting, although he was chafing to leave Cambridge. His friend, Phil Smith, remembers the situation at 104 Irving Street as

generally uncomfortable for Estlin during this time of his changing atti-
tudes: "In the Cummings household when I knew them there was old
Mrs. Cummings, his Aunt Jane Cummings, both of whom were critical
of Estlin, and for about a year there was a boarder [Mr. Philip Davis, a
neighbor whose house had burned down], who did not approve of Est-
lin's writings. It was a very 'churchy' atmosphere lightened only by
Estlin's mother, a bubbly, seemingly happy person."[12]

Estlin announced that he wanted to take a flat in Greenwich Village
and devote himself to painting, a plan which irritated his father, who
worried openly about whether Estlin could ever support himself as an
artist. In the back of Estlin's mind, however, was a retreat for serious
literary purpose. When he had seen the Forbes-Robertson production of
Hamlet at Sanders Theater in April, he had been thrilled to his very
bones. "I was also never so impressed," he set down in his tables, "that
conversational language is the very greatest of all mediums." At that time
he began to lay his plans. "I saw that to write Hamlet one must fathom
life completely in his heart, & thus pitilessly spurn the world for months
—a winter, say, in a N.Y. garret, seeing no one."[13] He had enough money:
the Thayer check plus $500 which his godfather Estlin Carpenter had
deposited in his account years ago. Yet, the Cummingses were a close-knit
family, and Estlin was not so independent as to leave his parents' home
without the excuse of a job that took him to the alluring city. So the
autumn of 1916 dragged on.

VIII

The Emergent Styles

There is something antic about creating, although the enterprise be serious.

JEROME BRUNER

These months at home were not wasted time. As matters turned out, it became one of the most creative periods of Cummings' life, for during the months from June 1916 to January 1917, he consolidated the basic styles that were to be characteristic of his future work. He had no courses to read for, no papers to write, no routines to follow. While he waited for answers to letters about jobs, he was free to play with his typewriter and to investigate further all the interrelationships among the new arts to which he had so recently been exposed. As some of his notes show, he tried occasionally to theorize about what he was doing.

He became enthralled by Cézanne and aware of the revolution in painting which he had brought about. Through the writings of Pound he became acquainted with the sculpture of Henri Gaudier-Brzeska, and he set down notes from his theorizing about lines and planes. In his writing he began to push further the visually directive ways of handling verse, and he attempted to impose form onto material which had not usually been treated in poetry. "Poets," he asserted, "(with the exception of some few geniuses like Shakespeare) have felt it necessary, in order to give stability to their efforts, to avoid the language (which means the life) of everyday, and cultivate a hothouse style suitable to the elevation of well-preserved thoughts which they dared express."[1] In order to avoid that hothouse style and to capture instead the life of everyday, he considered any language, any subject, to be available for use. The earliest of his radical experiments that can be dated is jotted on an envelope with the postmark June 29, 1916.[2] It presents a dialogue of a man trying to pick up a giggling girl on the street. When he gave it typewritten form, it began this way:

> lo kiddo
> hehe
> wer gon
> hehe
> busy tnight gertie
> saywho dythink ytalkin to
>> sink that stuff[3]

On it goes with its attempt to record street talk and to render it phonetically. Sometime later he typed it out again in a visually different form. This time it had the title "Death and the Young Girl."[4] Hades no longer stalked the meadow; he had come to the city. In this latest version, the dialogue was much the same, but even though Cummings had allegorized it, he lost interest in it and left the poem in an unfinished state.

A distinct tendency in the new painting was to reduce the emphasis on subject or motif and to concentrate on form. Cummings was not willing to go as far as Gertrude Stein, but he was trying to diminish the importance of motif by choosing banal, unremarkable situations or verbal exchanges for these exercises and to focus attention on visual patterns or patterns of sound. He felt that he was moving far enough away from the conventions of poetry that he would sometimes speak of a "fait" instead of a poem and refer to an artist as a "faiteur." One dialogue about two friends greeting each other on the street he worked over three times, rephrasing and rearranging, trying to use his typewriter for visual composition. His first draft, written in pencil, has the comment scribbled on the side, "Lines should differ in spacing."[5] He tried it out on the typewriter and then noted at the bottom of that version, "how about getting movement by dividing words, i.e. composing by syllables."[6] The third version shows that he has learned how to use spatial arrangement: to suggest hesitation, surprise, emphasis, and other aspects of tone.

logeorge
      lo

            wellifitisn't eddy   how's the boy

grandhave you heard

                shoot

                              you knowjim

goodscout   well

   married

   the hellyousay
             whoto

     'member ritagail

do i remember rita   what'sthejoke

                         well

                              goddam

     don'ttakeit too hard old boy

sayare you kidding me   because if you are   by hell
   easyall george   watchyourstep old fellow

   christ

       that   that

mut[7]

Notes and marks prepare for a fourth version, but Cummings was apparently dissatisfied and abandoned it at this stage.

At the same time that he was trying out visual arrangements, he was eager to integrate them with sound patterns. In one of these trials he lined up a series of fourteen vowel sounds and arranged the words of a dialogue in columns underneath them, each syllable placed according to its sound. The dialogue of the poem (or "fait") is a littled muddled, but since it reflects a drunken recollection, that may be all right. What is surprising is the new interest that the triviality of this talk takes on when it is given this patterned form:

```
            two        brass      buttons off
            your       scar let              coatlo
                       ret    taone          old   dint
                       ed                           and
        a   new                   one
            you                           don't              re
                       mem
                 ber
            you   were       drunk
                       when
    i                  askedret  ta    for                      the
                                       rose  in
                 her                                             hair
            you   can't                        havethatshe
    smiled                                     lar    riehe
                                               give          methe
            bloom
        aint                                   itpretty
                       but                     kid
            you        gut
        a
    knife              yes             op'   nit   thanks
    my                                                   teeth
        aint                          strong  it's        the
            booze      gets  'm                      and   she
                                                     hands methe
            two        brass      buttons
                       nev
                 er                             drink
dear
```

The Cummings family home, 104 Irving St., Cambridge.

Although no really significant product had resulted, Cummings wondered whether or not he was on the brink of a discovery. His comment at the bottom of the page shows that he wanted to see what made his sound pattern different from that found in musical expression. "Note: in Music there are (12) units which differ in pitch, corresponding to the (19) vowel sounds; BUT the representation of the occurrence of any and all these units by a common symbol, whose form (or picture) changes only to portray prolongation, confers a suitability to horizontal progression, which does not exist in the case of a fait where the sounds (units) are presented by visible equivalents (generally speaking) calling for vertical progression."[8] He next tried the same dialogue in a horizontal progression as if it were written on a musical staff. But there was no new opening up of relationships. "Inferior because no reversal of direction," he noted. It also lacked "logic of arrangement of vowels in an order, to juxtapose parts of different words."[9]

Another and more successful "fait" which uses this visual arrangement is a presentation that is easier for a reader to apprehend, because the piece is not so long and because, being more limited in the range of vowel sounds, it is not so wide either:

            the sky

            was   can dy

    lu   mi

            nous   ed

                            i
            ble

                spry   pinks

                shy   lem

            ons

                                    greens

        cool

    choco   lates

            un   der

a   lo

        co

        mo   tive   s pout

                        ing

            vi

    o   lets[10]

The form is more appropriate here because we have a descriptive poem. What happens to us then is that we have one kind of visual experience while another is being described to us. The result is something of a visual chord, though perhaps dissonant. The piece has its limited success. But,

all things considered, the over-all feeling is that it is a gimmicky perform-
ance and cannot offer any more aesthetic pleasure than a group of skillful
ice skaters attempting to dance. These word-ventures we have been look-
ing at were mostly failures. Nevertheless, playing with sound and sylla-
ble this way taught Cummings to be on the watch for the new complexi-
ties and the multiple meanings that can emerge through spatial arrange-
ments.

But he was going in still other directions to explore sound patterns.
Probably he remembered Scriabin's chromatic scale, for he tried making
analogous tables for vowel sounds. He drew up charts and designs based
upon the color wheel and on variations in sound frequency. He compiled
lists of consonant combinations, "primal," "intermediate," and "final,"
such as br, bl, dr, dzh, and so on. He then combined them with vowels to
form words like breast, bless, blabbed, rabble, labor, drink, riddle, lad-
der.[11] Pondering on such compilations, he drew out arrangements of
sound for verses that look as if they had been composed by a computer.
Sometimes the motifs are ugly, with ugly sounds to match: plenty of
glottal and labial stops and choked with grunting back vowels. Here is one:

> of bunged mug
> blousy gob
> glued lipped
> muddle lidded
>
> ole liz
> goggle glimmed
> bag bodied
> pimple bummed
>
> slow slob-
> bers down
> babble belly
> blubber boobied

He has carefully noted the consonant combinations and the sequence of
vowel sounds (ŏ-ŭ-ŭ-ow-ĭ-ŏ-ŭ, etc.) and marked down the repetition pat-
tern of vowels as if he were recording a rhyme scheme:

> a b b
> c d a
> e d
> b b d d[12]

and so on.

As time went on, he began to take some of his D.S.N. poems and revise them, working out a visually directive arrangement on the page and sometimes cutting them drastically, trying to follow Pound's injunctions against superfluous words. "In just-/Spring," "Stinging/gold swarms," and "Writhe and/gape of tortured/perspective" were all given this treatment. Cummings' growth as a poet really becomes evident in this work of revision. Not only could he improve upon some old lines, but sometimes he even created a new poem out of an old one. This recasting of one's old work is a very difficult feat. It requires a revisit to a felt moment of the past and an attempt to retrieve something out of the false or feeble expression of what was felt.

An instance worth examining is what Cummings did with a poem written in November 1914, his senior year at Harvard. He had apparently been reading Whitman or Sandburg (*Chicago Poems* was a treasured volume of these early years) and was attempting a "city" poem in long free-verse lines. I have marked in brackets the lines and phrases that he kept now that he was revising the poem in 1916; the rest he threw out:

[The hours rise up, putting off stars, and it is dawn.
Into the street of the sky Light walks, scattering poems.]

[On earth a candle is extinguished; the city wakes,
With a song upon her mouth, having death in her eyes.]

[And it is dawn: the world goes forth to murder dreams;]
And one shall buy with gold, and one shall pay with tears;
A white flower wither; a pale child weep.

[I see in the street where strong men are digging bread.
And I see] the shining shops, and [brutal faces of people.]
[Contented, hideous, happy, hopeless, cruel] people,
Cursing and laughing, dying and living, side by side.

Then I look up and behold palaces of business,
Floor on floor and house on house seeking heaven.
There is not a single room but is full of flying thoughts,
There is not a single tower but speaks the tongue of the world.

And I turn to look upon the shouting wharves and the docks.
Every ship is a soul, stepping the living sea.

Then I pass the mart and muster of commerce, seeing the place
Where dwells my brother, the Fairy, and my dear sister, the
                                Broad,
Whom I greet well, and make to them profound obeisance,
Because their feast is dust, and their apparel pain,
Being immensely rich in priceless misery.

For the king of life is this bent spouse of hopelessness,
And the queen of the world is this pale bride unto despair.
Him I salute, and her I salute, saluting God.

Now is a candle lighted on earth; [the city sleeps,
With death upon her mouth, having a song in her eyes.]

The day is done: [the hours descend, putting on stars.
Into the street of the sky Night walks, scattering poems.][13]

What is left is only a skeleton. The narrative of the speaker's walk
through the city is gone, leaving only an observer's brief impression.
The sentimentalizing about the homosexual and the prostitute is gone.
Gone too is the social posturing. When he creates the new piece by
removing all the excrescences, he adds one new element in the middle,
the frail man who stands before the mirror. Printed later in *Tulips and
Chimneys* as "Impression IV," the refreshed poem appears on the page
in this form:

        the hours rise up putting off stars and it is
        dawn
        into the street of the sky light walks scattering poems

        on earth a candle is
        extinguished   the city
        wakes
        with a song upon her
        mouth having death in her eyes

        and it is dawn
        the world
        goes forth to murder dreams. . . .

        i see in the street where strong
        men are digging bread

and i see the brutal faces of
people contented hideous hopeless cruel happy

and it is day,

in the mirror
i see a frail
man
dreaming
dreams
dreams in the mirror

and it
is dusk   on earth

a candle is lighted
and it is dark.
the people are in their houses
the frail man is in his bed
the city

sleeps with death upon her mouth having a song in her eyes
the hours descend,
putting on stars. . . .

in the street of the sky night walks scattering poems

The rearrangement has one immediate effect: it slows up the poem and
thus contributes to the dream-like quality of the vision. It also breaks up
the experience of the city day into appropriate units. Certain words are
isolated, "dawn," "wakes," "the world," "man," "dreaming," to focus our
attention on the principal features of the action. The addition of the frail
man is most important, for it emphasizes the main theme which was
extricated from the distracting tangle of detail in the early version. The
poem is about the value of dream—dream in the sense of the vision of
some ultimate reality which is beclouded by the world. The "poems" that
are scattered are the materials for the dream. They are always available;
daytime destroys them but night nourishes them. The frail man is the
image of a poet, the perceiving dreamer, a projection of Cummings him-
self.

We have followed Cummings' explorations and trials long enough to
be able to say that he has developed three principal styles. They some-

times merge together and thus are not always distinct from one another. But they are frequently different enough in technique or attitude that they can be defined or characterized. They form the basis of most of his future work. The first is a lyric and mythic style. It is mythic in the materials it makes use of and in its idealized approach to them. It is concerned with the cycles of the natural world or the essential rhythms of human life. It deals with such subjects as sunrise, sunset, snowfall, springtime, the life of plants, the flow of rivers, the changes of the moon, the eternal presence of the stars. It also deals with birth, childhood pleasures, idyllic love, sexual fulfillment, the serenity of age, death, and a possible afterlife. In so doing, it makes use of archetypes: imagistic concepts such as the garden, the poet, the mistress, the wanderer, the clown. The style is lyric in that it expresses an emotion directly or it employs its mythic procedures in songs or in singable stories. In technique, it is visually directive with spacing and alterations of conventional grammar and punctuation in such a way as to contribute to significance. Sometimes it is economical, as in "in Just-/spring," even elliptical, as in "Tumbling-hair"; sometimes it flows more freely as in "the hours rise up putting off stars and it is," but most always it has fresh, novel images, simple diction, casual conversational phrasing and syntax, and it is presented on the page with visual guidance for a reading which flows smoothly along to create its delicate impression or modest assertion. Much of Cummings' most enduring work employs this lyric-mythic style, which I will call his Apollonian style.

The second style that can be isolated I will call his Satyric style, using this spelling because it suggests that the style is used at times for an expression of libidinous energy as well as for criticism of folly or vice. Its range is extreme. At the low or naturalistic end of the scale, the attitude toward life or society is merely rejection, and the result may be descriptive ugliness (the exercise "of bunged mug" is an example). At the high end of the scale, a later development for the most part, wit and high spirits indulge in gentle mockery (as in the pastiche of parodies, "Others") or make fun of human follies. Or when the gentleness is set aside, a sincere and ruthless invective denounces evil or viciousness. It is the obverse of the Apollonian style as I have described it, especially in the attitude toward sex, which is treated as a dirty but necessary physical function. If the Satyric style is in any way mythic, it employs only the demonic approach, for it reflects a dark view of human behavior and a hostile attitude toward society. Its materials are pompous, stupid, hypocritical, squalid, corrupt, or mendacious people and the places they are found, whether it be a tastelessly decorated office or a furnished room. It focuses on professors, polititians, fake artists, advertisers, salesmen,

clubwomen, drunks, prostitutes, policemen, generals, and national lead-
ers. The technique Cummings usually follows is to take a well established
verse form—such as the ballade or the sonnet—and to treat the subject
(which will be inappropriate in the customary use of the form) within the
confines of its formal discipline. This creates an immediate ironical con-
trast between subject matter and form. Other times he will employ a
loose, almost doggerel-like meter and rhyme. "In Healey's Palace" is an
example. Cummings does not work very often with the Satyric style in
this early period. He had not yet seen enough of the world or its vice and
folly to write much in this vein. He would bring this style to its perfec-
tion during the period when he was on duty in the U.S. Army.

A third style which had been emerging has been called "modernist,"
even by Cummings himself.[15] The term is unsatisfactory because it has
been so loosely used in literary history and criticism and because the
so-called "modern" movement in the arts came to an end in the middle
of the twentieth century. In the final quarter of the century, it seems
preferable to use a term that has no chronological associations. I am going
to call this third style Hephaestian, which seems appropriate since He-
phaestus was a craftsman, and in working at the forge he was engaged
in bending, breaking, twisting, mending, reshaping—manipulations
which describe well what the "modern" artist was doing to his materials.

Cummings was continuing to read all the criticism he could find on
the new movement in the visual arts, and he had begun to try his hand
at the new painting styles himself. Although he had done water colors
all his life, he began to work with oils during the time he was living in
Thayer Hall and was now continuing at home in "the studio" on the
third floor of the house. He had never had any art lessons beyond the kind
of instruction encountered in arts-and-crafts exercises in school. But at
Harvard he had friends who painted and whose example and whose
criticism helped him. Dos Passos, also living in Thayer Hall, was an
excellent colorist. Arthur Wilson painted. A new acquaintance, Edward
Pierce Nagel, stepson of Gaston Lachaise, the sculptor, was majoring in
art at Harvard and kept up on all the new tendencies in painting and
sculpture. But whether or not Cummings had ever taken up the practice
of painting seriously, he was deeply responsive to the new directions in
art and eagerly discussed them with his friends Foster Damon and Sco-
field Thayer. In the recent months he was trying to incorporate this new
spirit into his verse technique, and he gradually developed his Hephaes-
tian style. It took the form of elliptical statements, fragmented expres-
sion, surprise in the images and shock in the juxtapositions, wrenches and
distortions of diction, and violations of expectations in linguistic usage.

One instance of a successful poem in this style shows excellent use of visual arrangement. The action of the poem, a man reading a letter, is outlined in the silhouette of the poem on the page: all the descriptions of the man are on the left side of the page, the excerpts from the letter are on the right, and the description of the handwriting is placed in between, as if linking the man and his letter:

mr. smith
is reading
his letter
by the fire-
light

   tea-time

      smiles friend smith

no type bold o's
      d's gloat
      d's gloat
      droll l's twine
      r's rove

    haha

       sweet-hearts
       part fellow
       like darl- write
       i dream my try ned ma
       thinks
       right thing will be still
       till death
       thine

blows ring

strokes nose   P
toasts toes   S
       kiss

But the more intricate patterns of repetition and of comparison and contrast are presented by means of sound—mostly vowel sound. "Vowels are contagious," Cummings observed.[17] For example, short and long "i"

sounds play back and forth from "like" all the way down to "thine," with
many combinations of repeated sound in between, such as "thinks" and
"thing" and the rhyming words, "will," "still," and "till."

The sounds of the words establish subtle connections to reinforce
their meanings: sweethearts who call each other darling are parting;
dreams and death are the two contrasting extremes of the love affair—
hoping and ending. Also in this sequence, the words "part" and "till
death" create an irony if the phrase "till death do us part" creeps into the
reader's mind. Again, although the letter is rationalizing the break-up of
the love affair, the sounds connect and intensify the irony that love ought
to prevail: what is "right" is to be "thine," and the "thing" "will" "still"
continue "till death."

The orderliness at the end of the poem is appropriate to mr. smith's
unruffled response to the letter. His composure, toasting his toes by the
fire, takes us back to the cozy tea-time picture in the opening lines. All
this, following the emotionalizing in the letter, communicates mr.
smith's cynicism, which the reader now understands. The "ha ha" with
which he looked at the handwriting appears hard-hearted alongside the
distress and concern of "ma thinks," "try ned," and of all the love phrases
in the letter. The postscript at the end of the letter is tagged on to the
end of the poem. Although the "i" and "s" sounds formally round out the
structure by a return to sounds in the opening line, "mister" and "smith,"
the postcript also underscores all the final irony of contrast between the
emotional pitch of the letter and mr. smith's unmoved comfortableness
by the fire.

This is the kind of creation that Cummings wanted most to give his
energy to—the kind of product that he had in mind when he said, "The
day of the spoken lyric is past. The poem which has at last taken its place
does not sing itself; it builds itself, three dimensionally, gradually, subtly,
in the consciousness of the experiencer."[18] In its view of human life and
society the Hephaestian style might see either the idealized or the de-
monic vision of existence that we identified in the other two styles, but
what often emerges is an ambiguous attitude toward life and its
phenomena. The scene he depicts may be full of stress, as in "Writhe
and/gape of tortured/perspective," or the people he describes may be
entangled in life's demands as in "mr. smith," but the linguistic treatment
will be so unusual that the reader is kept at a distance from the subject
and will be pleased by the aesthetic manipulations.

Although Hephaestus was a craftsman, he did not always move
gracefully, for he had been lamed. There is a characteristic sense of strain
about this third style, not only at this period when Cummings was first
starting to work with it, but throughout his career. At times, in later

poems, even his linguistic distortions become habitual and fail to offer surprise—that is, too many times he seems to supply automatically a mixture of the organic and the mechanical in order to suggest cubist angularity or disjunction: flowers are "punctual" or "correct," the moon or the trees are "accurate" or "exact." Nevertheless, when the style is under control, it can produce much more complex and therefore more aesthetically valuable work than either of the other two styles. As we shall see.

II

One day late in 1916, Cummings met Professor Neilsen by chance and was asked if he wanted a job with Collier's. He was ecstatic at the offer, picturing himself working for Mark Sullivan's weekly magazine, but he soon found he was mistaken. It was the publishing branch of P.F.Collier in New York, which sold books by mail, and he was to do desk work dealing with correspondence. Still, this was his chance; so he accepted the position and reported for work in New York City on January 1, 1917, somewhat uncertain about "the dismal project of warming a wooden chair for 3 and 4 hour intervals."[19] The Collier's office was at 416–430 West 13th Street in Greenwich Village. At least, he would be living and working in the area of the city where one breathed the air of art and literature. He worked for Mr. F.J. Reynolds answering inquiries and arranging book orders. Business was not brisk and in his slack time he read some of the books (among others, *Crime and Punishment* and the *Elder Edda*), or he wrote letters.

Or poems. For one poem, some notes on P.F.Collier stationery survive to give us as close a look as we can get at the creative process in action. On January 11, Cummings was reading the *New York Sun,* and his eye fell upon a report of the death of William F. "Buffalo Bill" Cody. In the midst of some notations he was making about books, he began scribbling phrases. On one sheet are the words "Buffalo Bill is Dead," an echo of the headline, and above it is the unusual synonym "defunct."[20] On another sheet are notes which show Cummings working out much of the phrasing for a poetic portrait of Buffalo Bill. The trials and changes reveal that at first Cummings was in a nostalgic mood remembering a childhood hero "who used to ride a white horse and shoot pidgeons/with his long hair like reindeer moss on the old stone of his face." Gradually, the portrait takes on action: Cody "breaks one two three four five pidgeons before one fell" and his hair is now "streaming" from his face. He takes on more heroic qualities, too. He rides "a smooth silver stallion," and death is asked "how d'you like him, death/he had you always in his eye." The hint of a tone of impudence creeps in at the bottom of the page when Cody is, first, "the brave old boy" and then "the blue eyed boy." On the page, Cummings plays with the "one two three four five" in different spatial arrangements trying to suggest the experience of witnessing the marksmanship.[21] That is all the manuscript can tell us, but the directions are fairly clear. It moves next, presumably, to the final version with its words pressed together to convey breathless speed and with its jaunty conclusion. It was, to be sure, a *fait* which defies categorizing:

> Buffalo Bill 's
> defunct
>> who used to
>> ride a watersmooth-silver
>>> stallion
> and break onetwothreefourfive pigeonsjustlikethat
>>>> Jesus
>
> he was a handsome man
>>> and what i want to know is
> how do you like your blueeyed boy
> Mister Death

If the days in the office were tiresome, everything else about the adventure was, in his word, "superb." He had moved in with Arthur "Tex" Wilson, who had been in New York for a year trying to write stories and to do some painting. As they looked for permanent quarters to share, they really did have a garret one night—with no water (they shaved out of a tin pail which they filled in the basement). They soon found a pleasant Village studio with a ten-foot ceiling at 21 East 15th Street, one "enormous room" as Cummings termed it, twenty by twenty, with a kitchenette in the corner. It had a peephole in the door and they told their friends they had rented a former gambling den. It also had such luxuries as a fireplace and a piano.

Without delay, he was exploring the city. His first letter to his mother reported, "I have already met several aggressively intellectual people of the literary world, visited a "Mills House" (where the city sleeps its vagabonds for a nominal amt.—a huge institution), and dined several times divinely upon foods of diverging nationalities."[22] The Woolworth building, tallest in the world since 1913, was a special marvel: whenever he saw it, he "smelled white violets."[23] On the first Sunday he tramped the full length of Fifth Avenue.

Another result of his move to New York was that he began painting in earnest. He set up an easel and acquired a palette, tubes of color, linseed oil and some canvases, and he spent many evenings from eight to midnight trying to become an American Cubist. When he wrote home he especially asked for Wright's book on *Modern Painting* and Eddy's book on *Cubism and Post-Impressionism.* One painting he was working on he described to his parents as "3 figures heaving on a lever. Find the three figures and get a nickel cigar."[24]

He did not last long in the office routine. On February 25 he quit, explaining quite frankly to Mr. Reynolds, "I am pursuing that course which, after long and serious consideration, I am thoroughly and definitely convinced is best for my own welfare, not to mention that of the department in which I have had the honor to be employed. My ability, if I have any, certainly does not lie in the direction indicated by a career in the publishing business, even though the environment be as pleasant a one as Collier's affords."[25] Reynolds was generous. He accepted the resignation with a letter of regret and a check for two weeks' pay. To all appearances, Cummings had never been serious about the job but had only used it as an excuse to ease himself out of 104 Irving Street without hurting his parents too much. He heaved a sigh of relief. "I can't express to you," he wrote home, "how excellent a thing it is to be my own master (instead of the alarm clock's servant)."[26] Edward Cummings had nurtured in Estlin a New England spirit of independence but he had never dreamed that the independence would extend to the rejection of regular paying work. He worried deeply about his son's future.

Meanwhile, the New York life was good for young Cummings. The lively confidence that he had begun to develop in the last two years at Harvard now became a self-reliant effervescence. He sang at his easel, he invited friends to tea or to late-evening parties. He talked a creative stream—puns, literary allusions, fantasies, mimicry, dialect. He drank himself into euphoria and entertained everyone, drawing elephants, joking, or pounding on the piano while he sang, "Who'll pay the rent for Mrs. Riiiiiip Van Winkle when Mr. R. Van is away!"[27]

He settled in comfortably, writing home for all of his manuscripts that he had accumulated in the drawer of a trunk and for some of his favorite books (among them Sandburg's *Chicago Poems,* issues of *Others,* Blake's poems, *The Story of the Volsungs, The Mabinogion,* Plato's dialogues, Alan Seegar's poems ("perhaps I can give him to the landlady"), and the *Oxford Book of English Verse*). He rented a typewriter and worked with his new verse techniques. For Cummings, it was a period of creative flow. If he was not sitting at his typewriter, he was standing before his easel. "Did I tell you of a quick-portrait of A.W.?" he reports home. "2 new pictures have since seen the light; and I am beginning to feel happier, inasmuch as I now invariably desire to throw away the-thing-before-last as soon as the last is done."[28] Or if he was out of the studio, he was alert for the new sensations, and his hands were always busy recording them. He jotted notes of poems on envelopes or on paper napkins—once even on a chip of wood. Or he sketched with pencil in a pocket notebook. He was growing artistically. He was happier than he had ever been in his life.

But the weather turned round, and all was swept away when the U.S. entered the European war on April 6, 1917.

IX

The Pacifist Warrior,
1917

In 1917 there happened to be a larger than usual number of apprentice writers, including some of exceptional talent, who were still in American colleges or had lately been graduated. They were in most respects like other young Americans of the middle classes, but they also had characteristics, good and bad, that set them somewhat apart. They had more imagination than most of their contemporaries. They had more vanity—why else should they try so hard to be published?—more initiative and curiosity, more sympathy with foreign cultures—especially French culture at the time, owing to their literary admirations —and more eagerness for experience. They wanted to see everything so they could write about everything.

MALCOLM COWLEY

The Reverend Edward Cummings was the head of the World Peace Foundation. He had been drawn toward peace work through Edward Everett Hale, the minister whom he succeeded at the South Congregational (Unitarian) Church, and he had become a trustee of the Foundation in 1910 and executive secretary in 1916. In his sermons he had long preached peace. His socio-theological position, which he called "The Religion of the Star," had as its symbol not the cross but the star of Bethlehem that marked an occasion of joy and celebrated a new spirit of peace and good will to all living creatures. His optimism was shattered when the European war broke out and dragged on mercilessly. But he did not have the temperament for disillusionment. His response was to throw himself more vigorously into peace work and he developed a new vision of an international religious organization that would have the religious breadth of the Unitarian Church and the secular scope of the League of Nations. In his notes for sermons one finds references to "The Family of Nations," "The Religion of Worldliness," "The Kingdom of Heaven on Earth," "World Patriotism," "The Church of World Peace." The most fascinating elaboration is found in an outline in 1915 beginning "Wanted! A Supernational Religion," in which he described the "Religion of Jesus Pacified or Peacemaker." The creed is "Blessed are the Peacemakers"; its symbol is the Star of Bethlehem; its motto is the angel's song, "Peace on Earth, Good Will to Men." Its calendar would begin in 1915, "The Year of the Peacemaker"; later years would be designated A.P.[1]

During his college years Estlin Cummings seemed oblivious to the cataclysm that was disrupting European civilization, nor did he take any interest in politics or international affairs like the men in the Socialist Club at Harvard. He did turn aside occasionally from his preoccupation with aesthetic problems to express his sympathy with war-ravaged peoples or to show his basic antiwar feelings. In the fall of 1914, he produced a sentimental poem, "From a Newspaper August 1914," for Dean Briggs's course, English 5. His father later had copies of it typed with a new title, "The Casualty List," and inserted into the pages of *Eight Harvard Poets*.[2] Estlin's sympathy for the devastated Belgian nation and his horror at the brutality of the Germans toward the "franc-tireurs" comes out in another piece that he planned for Briggs's class, a play set in a tiny village near Louvain. The hero is a schoolteacher. The German invaders come, all the villagers retreat to the school house, a shot is fired at the approaching Germans, all the villagers are threatened with death unless they reveal who fired the shot.[3] Although the play apparently did not get written, its drafts engendered the feeling which took shape in a blank verse poem, "Belgium," written for Briggs's class.[4] In a revised and cut version, "Belgium" became the first poem that Cummings published outside student periodicals. It appeared in the *New York Post*, May 20, 1916:

> Oh thou that liftest up thy hands in prayer,
> Robed in the sudden ruin of glad homes,
> And trampled fields which from green dreaming woke
> To bring forth ruin and the fruit of death,
> Thou pitiful, we turn our hearts to thee.
>
> Oh thou that mournest thy heroic dead
> Fallen in youth and promise gloriously,

> In the deep meadows of their motherland
> Turning the silver blossoms into gold,
> The valor of thy children comfort thee.
>
> Oh thou that bowest thy ecstatic face,
> Thy perfect sorrows are the world's to keep!
> Wherefore unto thy knees come we with prayer,
> Mother heroic, mother glorious
> Beholding in thy eyes immortal tears.

His best antiwar poem from the Harvard years was never published or distributed. It is a Hardyesque piece, probably written for Briggs in the spring of 1916:

> All is over,—a shrug from the world's broad shoulders,
>   What more?
> There is earth to bury a corpse. Is a nation's sword-
>   edge dull[?]
> The world will whet it again, and a skull is only
>   a skull;
> And what cares the priest for a little stain on the
>   altar floor?
> 'Twill wash; it is only War.[5]

Support for the Allied cause was strong in the Harvard Yard. Former President Eliot in public statements was openly urging that the United States intervene on the side of the Allies. An ugly turmoil developed when Professor Hugo Münsterberg spoke out for Germany, and angry alumni and wealthy donors demanded his dismissal.[6] The controversy was soon swirling in the pages of the *Harvard Monthly*. Norman Hapgood in an article entitled "Germany's Disease" attacked German-Americans, and especially Hugo Münsterberg and Kuno Francke, for their defense of Germany's aims. Kuno Francke, invited to reply, wrote an article entitled "Germany's Hope," praising Kaiser Wilhelm and German "national consciousness." But the pacifists were shortly dominating the argument. J. Sibley Watson in an article, "Fair Play," denounced the attacks on Münsterberg and pointed to the "Pan-Slavism" of Russia as contributing to the outbreak of war. R. W. Chubb wrote "The Position of the Internationalists in Europe," a pacifist treatise, and "Meeting the Jingoists," a criticism of ex-president Eliot and others.[7] President Lowell, Dean Briggs, and other voices of reason succeeded in restoring calm and reminded everyone of the principles of academic freedom. Cummings' response to all this passionate conflict of ideas was merely a set of satiric verses, "God Mit Everybody."[8]

As reverberations from Europe rolled across the Atlantic and the campaign for "preparedness" developed, President Lowell urged Harvard men to attend the Plattsburg military training camp for officers in the summer, a policy which led to the establishment of the course in Military Science at Harvard in the spring of 1916 for those who had completed the summer training. Cummings' parody of the Harvard hymn, "Fair Plattsburg, thy sons to thy discipline throng,"[9] reflects the fact that 864 Harvard men enrolled for the fall term.

When he went to New York in 1917, he continued his mild interest in the peace movement. He attended a huge antiwar rally at Madison Square Garden in March and observed with some scorn the mounting war fever all around him. The ambiguous attitude of Cummings and his pacifist friends comes out in a letter that Damon wrote to Cummings revealing his response to the historical forces which were gathering momentum: "What will *you* do if we go to war? I am *so* sick, So SICK of that eternal question. Enlist, I suppose."[10] They had good reason to feel apprehensive, as the unrestricted submarine warfare took its toll of United States' ships and Wilson broke off diplomatic relations with Germany. Yet, when Wilson's war message to Congress called for the United States' entry into the war, declaiming "that the world must be made safe for democracy," and when war was declared on April 6, they all very gradually got into uniforms of one sort or another. Arthur Wilson joined the army as a flyer. Damon, captain of the Harvard fencing team, became a bayonet instructor at the Plattsburg training camp. Dos Passos and Hillyer joined the Norton-Harjes ambulance group and Dudley Poore the American Ambulance Field Service. Conscription soon swept up others. Later in the spring, all the thirty-odd men in the Poetry Society except three or four "were in khaki."[11]

During his restless autumn in Cambridge, Cummings had considered joining the French ambulance corps but ended up going to New York instead. Now that war was declared, his ever-alert father wrote to him pointing out all the alternatives to conscription, recommending that his son volunteer and get a choice of service. But Estlin had already made an investigation of his own. He had talked at length with Dillwyn Parrish, a friend of Edward Nagel's who had just completed a tour of duty with the Norton-Harjes Ambulance Service, a Red Cross unit serving with the French army, which had been organized by the Cummings' former neighbor at Shady Hill, Richard Norton. Cummings made up his mind quickly. On April 7, the day after the declaration of war, he volunteered for Norton-Harjes, a decision made on characteristic grounds: desire to govern his own destiny and fascination with new experience. As he wrote his father: "I'm glad to be out of here by the 1st of May, when everybody is to be tabulated on pink, violet, yellow, (and I dare say orange) cards, for the benefit of conscription. It will mean everything to me as an experience to do something I want to, in a wholly new environment, versus being forced to do something I don't want to & unchanging scene. I only hope I shall see some real service at the front."[12]

The choice of the ambulance service by young intellectuals and especially by young literary men is quite understandable. They usually were pacifist by inclination and this was noncombatant duty. They were classed as officers, yet did not have to bear the burdens of command or the responsibilities of giving orders to others. The ambulance service carried all the prestige of dangerous military duty with a minimum of risk. It required no long, dull training period; anyone could drive a car (except Dos Passos who had to get driver training before he was eligible). They signed on for only six months, and if they did not like it, they could get out, rather than having to endure two to six years of service. Most important, they would share in the experience of their time, yet do so on their own terms with the least amount of regimentation and the maximum amount of freedom. They could then speak or write with accuracy and authority about that common experience.

On April 17, Cummings formally signed up with the Ambulance Service. He scurried about for a day or two getting a kit together and having his father arrange his letter of credit for him. Cummings asked Wilson to ship his belongings home, to distribute his paintings among his friends, and to store the poems with his own gear. On April 28, Rebecca Cummings came down from Cambridge, and she, Wilson, Nagel, and Parrish saw Estlin and the others off on board the *Touraine*, a handsome French passenger liner. The peacemaker, Edward Cummings, pleased and feeling some pride and reflected glory, sent a telegram:

> As I said in advance
> I envy your chance
> of breaking a lance
> for freedom in France
> by driving and mending
> an ambulance
>
> Best love and luck a soldier ever had,
> From Betsy, Mother, Jane, Nana, and Dad.[13]

Cummings relished every moment of the departure. As the ship moved out of the harbor, he scribbled the notes for a poem, "Looking back one saw the real that was New York, a leonine uproar of rose in the unpunctual stupidity of heavenless heaven."[14] Gazing about from his first-class cabin, he worked out another poem[15] on a piece of ship's stationery:

> the   saintly
>   sweetness   of
>
>
>   sea
>   blowings from the   unimaginable
>
>
>   gulls
>   lift   ing   in
>   curviness

II

It turned out to be a rough passage and Cummings was seasick for the first few days. He struck up acquaintance among the recruits with a trio from Columbia University: William Slater Brown, who was to become his bosom friend; Edgar Guy Lemon, a friendly red-head; and a law student named O'Brien ("a Mick from Cambridge," Cummings identified him). When Slater Brown first saw Cummings, he was wearing a long fur coat and a crushed "Harvard" hat (from J. August, Harvard Square) and he needed a shave. He was getting a light for his cigarette from Red Lemon. He looked more like a 1920's caricature of Joe College than an ambulance driver. When they all went to the bar for a drink, Cummings recognized Brown as a former neighbor, whose family had rented the Thaxter house next door for a year. Brown was two years younger than Cummings, the son of a country doctor in Webster, Massachusetts, a town which had been founded by his great-great-grandfather, Samuel Slater, who established cotton mills there. Brown felt just as smothered by Webster as Cummings did by Cambridge, and he had left home to study journalism, and, later, English and French literature at Columbia University. During the voyage he and Cummings developed a close friendship because of their likeness in taste and temperament. Brown was a stocky, dark-haired, high-spirited young man with a droll wit and a forthright tongue. He too was a pacifist. He and Lemon had just returned from Washington where they

William Slater Brown, 1917.
COURTESY SLATER BROWN

had participated in an organized effort to stop the Congress from declaring war.

After a ten-day passage and a little thrill going through the U-boat zone, the ship docked at Bordeaux and the group entrained for Paris. Brown and Cummings were in a separate car from the others and did not notice when their unit all got off at the wrong station. They rode on to the Gare d'Orléans and got off with the American Ambulance Field Service men, and on their own they sought out the Norton-Harjes headquarters at 7 rue François Premier. After a long hike with their gear, they found the office closed, and taking the advice of a "scrub lady," they put up at the Hôtel du Palais, an ideal site on the right bank of the Seine, along the Cours-la-Reine behind the Grand Palais. Although they reported in at the Norton-Harjes office the next morning and got instructions about ordering their uniforms, they were allowed to stay put in their hotel. The outcome of these mishaps is that Cummings and Brown became separated from their group and that the Norton-Harjes headquarters lost track of them. As a consequence, they enjoyed a splendid five-week holiday in Paris.[16]

The war seemed far removed. Except for uniformed men on leave and the lameness or disfigurement of the café waiters, Paris showed little sign of it. The daily bustle of trade and leisure prevailed, theaters were open, restaurants were crowded. Paris exhibited a holiday gaiety. It was Cummings' favorite season, spring. The horse-chestnut trees were in bloom and the darkness of the night seemed to intensify their fragrance. Looking across the Seine from their hotel, Brown and Cummings could see Mansart's magnificent dome of the Hôtel des Invalides floating in the May sky. Leading to its esplanade was another sight that made Cummings smell white violets, the Pont Alexandre III with its carefully wrought, art-nouveau lamps. The hotel was only a short stroll from the Louvre and from the Rond-Point of the Champs-Elysées, where he and Brown took their *petit déjeuner* every morning while reading *Le Figaro* and *Le Matin.*

They browsed among the stalls of the *bouquinistes* along the river, bought prints by Cézanne and Matisse, and when Brown told Cummings about Amy Lowell's *Six French Poets,* which he had been reading in New York, they searched for books of poetry by Rémy de Gourmont, Henri de Régnier, and Paul Fort. They went to Les Ballets Russes and saw Stravinsky's *Petrouchka* more than once. On May 18, they saw the premiere of Erik Satie's *Parade* with Cubist sets by Picasso. When the audience booed Satie's ballet, Cummings got angry and shouted abuse at the crowd. At the Olympia Music Hall they admired the dancers and acrobats. But mostly they tramped about all over the city.

They leaned on the parapets along the sparkling Seine and watched the barges float by. They rode up the river in a *bateau-mouche.* They strolled through the Jardin de Luxembourg and watched the children riding on the merry-go-round and buying balloons from an old woman. They gazed their fill at the Impressionist paintings in the Luxembourg Museum. They wandered up to Montparnasse, then over to St. Germain-de-Prés—and had drinks at Les Deux Magots. They listened to the organ at Notre Dame and studied the sculpture on the façade (Cummings sketched the Virgin). They lounged in a café at the place de l'Opéra and listened to the pleasant clop-clop of the carriage traffic. They sat in their favorite restaurant, Etablissement J. Chartier, on the rue du Louvre and watched the soldiers go by with their girls. They sought out "the best and wildest of restaurants—wild, I would say, as regards food," Cummings assured his mother, "for other wildness there is none during the duration of this state of affairs known as la guerre."[17] One wild place became another favorite when they discovered the delights of eating couscous at Sultana Cherque's Oasis Restaurant on the rue du faubourg-Montmartre. And they climbed to the top of Montmartre and gazed over the sunlit city. To Cummings, Paris was a "divine section of eternity."[18]

Cummings' sketchbooks show the great variety of things that caught his eye, mostly the ordinary sights of everyday Parisian life: soldiers, sailors, newsboys, children in the Champs-Elysées jumping rope, swinging, watching a puppet show *(Guignol),* women carrying long loaves of bread, a man with a top hat, another with a fez, a man on crutches, another sweeping at the Taverne Royale, another with a basket ("Les saucissons sont bons"), a blind man crossing the street at the Madeleine, a woman picking up coal on the boulevard des Italiens, countless horses, wagons, carriages. Cummings considered buying a "painting outfit." He tried to become even more Parisian by growing a small, somewhat faint moustache.

One of the features of Paris that struck the young men immediately was the freedom of sexual pursuits. They lost no time getting over to the Folies-Bergère to admire the beautiful bodies on stage. At first, Cummings was taken aback by the importuning of the prostitutes in the promenade area and felt a combined attraction and repulsion. In a letter to Parrish, he described the women of Paris, whom he judged as very ugly, but went on to say that "the whores are very beautiful with their diseased greenness, slobbering on the tight Americans and Englishmen between the acts of the Folies-Bergère—with the smell of their many deaths about them."[19] As time went on, he came to recognize that since prostitution was not illegal in France, the street women had a place in the Gallic society which gave them a limited respectability similar to that accorded to chorus girls, night club dancers, and burlesque queens in the United States. The hotel was not far from the area where many of the women had their rooms, and as he and Brown roamed the streets and promenaded on the Grands Boulevards, they came to know several of them who stopped in the bistros and cafés where they went for food and wine. He changed his report about Parisian women, declaring to his Mother that Paris had "the finest girls God ever allowed to pasture in the air of this fresh earth."[20] In time, they had attached themselves to two beautiful Parisian whores, whose beat ran between the place de la République and the place de l'Opéra. Cummings' girl was Marie Louise Lallemand and Brown's was her partner, Mimi.

Compared to his Harvard friends, Cummings had a late sexual development. Even though he had gained freedom of action at Harvard and in New York and despite an eager sexual interest which brought him into titillating proximities, he was still a virgin at the age of twenty-two. A Cambridge upbringing and life in a clergyman's household had created a heavy layer of inhibition. At 104 Irving Street as in many other middle-class Cambridge homes, the subject of sex was treated with solemnity. It was an activity associated only with marriage and reproduction. Any sex outside of wedlock was viewed with sternness or with sorrow. Estlin knew to whom his mother was referring when she spoke of "those women," and he caught the attitude clearly when his father spoke with a snort of disgust about the "loose relations" of some of the summer visitors at the Mohawk House in Colebrook.[21]

A mixture of hygienic caution and moral admonition had surrounded his training in the care of his body. Estlin had been told as a child never to touch his genitals unnecessarily and to take plenty of cold

*Marie Louise Lallemand asleep; her friend
Mimi at a picnic, chewing a stem of grass,
pencil sketches by E. E. Cummings.*

showers in the summer. A family story, probably passed on to him by his
mother later with some amusement, indicates how closely she checked on
her son as a child. One night when she heard him stirring restlessly in
bed, she inquired maternally, "What are you doing, Estlin?" "Turning
the handle," came the sleepy reply. In addition to all this, the Harvard
experience had included dire warnings about venereal disease. In the
freshman class in physiology, lectures carried the full terrifying details
to students. When Cummings heard the treatment for syphilis described,
he added a slogan to his notes, "Salvarsan. God bless that man!"[22]

His relationship with Marie Louise was, then, a strange affair. He
and Brown wined and dined and squired the girls around. They took
them to a revue at the Concert Mayol. They even took them out to the
country for a picnic at Nogent-sur-Marne. They paid attention to them
as if they were American dates, which is to say they treated them like
ladies. Yet, at the same time, they paid them their fees when they spent
time with them in their rooms. The women responded happily to this
treatment: they thought of these young men as their special American
friends, "Edouard" (Estlin was too difficult) and "Bel." On one occasion,
they invited Brown and Cummings to their apartment at 8 rue Dupetit-
Thouars for dinner, an unusual practice for Parisians in the first place,
but most unusual for these undomestic women of the streets.

As time went on, Marie Louise developed a real crush on Cummings
and he, in turn, felt deeply about her. Thus it came about that, with Marie

Louise, Cummings had a sexual initiation of a quality he would never have found in Boston. But the warnings of Physiology 1 were too strong. He knew how she supported herself and he was afraid of venereal disease. As a result, he never gave himself fully to his beautiful Parisian companion, even though on at least one occasion he shared her bed for the entire night. She was the only frankly passionate woman he had ever known, and it was for him his first real love affair. Yet he could not completely shake off a sense of guilt. Beneath an appointment that she wrote into his notebook, "Samedi midi place de la republique statue," he jotted some verses:

> Chérie, I suggest we've sinned
> Against the world and not the wind
> Nor give the sun and moon a damn
> If you are and if I am.[23]

Although their uniforms finally were finished, he and Brown did not wear them. They were rejecting, in an understandable way, all the evidences of the war that they could. They tried to take advantage of their Paris layover with the fullest enjoyment—and to isolate it in time, as if it were intensified by an awareness of death outside the city's perimeters. In his notebook, Cummings penciled some notes for a poem, "My lady Death whose smile is unto me."[24] But their stay in Paris could not last forever. Someone in the Norton-Harjes headquarters found their address again. M. Harjes, the French banker who was Richard Norton's partner, summoned them himself and rebuked them for not reporting in regularly, and they were sent to their units at the front. Cummings had been scheduled to go to a "de luxe Harvard section" (Brown's words), but when he found that Brown was to be sent to a different unit, he requested to stay with his friend. They gathered their gear and said good-bye to their girls, promising to write. Underneath Marie Louise's address, Cummings wrote a somewhat light-hearted sonnet, with a little touch of sentiment in the last portion:

> goodbye, Betty, don't remember me,
> pencil your eyes dear, and have a good time
> with the tall tight boys at Tabari'
> s, keep your teeth snowy, stick to beer and lime,
> wear dark, and where your meeting breasts are round
> have roses, darling, its all I ask of you,—
> but when the light fails and this sweet profound
> Paris moves with lovers, two and two,

bound for themselves,—when passionately dusk
brings softly down the perfume of the world,
(and just as smaller stars begin to husk
Heaven), you, you, exactly paled and curled,
with mystic lips take twilight where I know:
proving to Death that Love is so and so.[25]

III

They arrived at *Section Sanitaire XXI* on June 13 in Germaine, a small
village between St. Quentin and Ham from which the Germans had
withdrawn in the spring. The unit of about fifty men was equipped with
twenty vehicles, large Ford and smaller Fiat ambulances, the drivers of
which were assigned in pairs. *S.S. XXI* was attached to the French army
and was ordered to one military unit or another as necessary. The daily
procedure was to send certain ambulances for duty near the front, while
others were held in reserve in the village. After a period of duty the whole
section would withdraw to another village or town for *repos*. Since the
sector to which *S.S. XXI* was assigned was very quiet during the three
months that Cummings and Brown stayed there, most of the time was
spent *en repos*.

The usual boredom and seemingly useless work of an inactive mili-
tary unit filled the days. The unit moved from one muddy village or town
to another, Nesle for a week, Noyon for a week, Jussy for four days,
Chevincourt for two weeks, Assevilliers for two weeks (it was now late
August). Cummings tried to outwit the censor in hinting to his parents
where he was—"a place hardly *germain* to my malcontent," "a place so
quiet that Dickens' 'little Nell' might be read as daily work," "what might
be called a *Juicy* place," "The Road of the Sweet Ladies" [Chemin des
Dames]. He wrote to "ma Marie Louise, ma grande chérie" describing the
details of their arrival and the woods and the fields of poppies around
Germaine, and he assured her of "l'Amour dans le coeur d'un amant."[26]

It is difficult to assess Cummings' behavior during this tour of duty
with *S.S. XXI*—whether one should call it childish petulance or justified
outrage—but either way he was very unhappy. There was no action,
much time was spent cleaning the mud from the vehicles, the food was
poor. He did not get along with anyone except Brown. In a letter written
June 18 from Nesle, a village near the English sector, he reported the
following routine: "Cleaning-up of cars follows 'breakfast' (= salt-peter,
colored black to resemble coffee, whose mission Dad will gladly explain,
and 'bread' = amorphous hunks of crust with dried up ossification of a
pale yellow nature in the middle). At 10:30 those who are 'going on post'

eat; others at 12. 12–2 repose. Then cleaning-up again (or refuse shoveling, etc.) till supper,—the inspection of cars comes every other day,—and after supper, drill—then bed. I refuse to describe the food. Suffice it to say that its consistency, when it enters (as well as color, form, smell, etc.) is identical with same when it exits."[27]

His letters over the next weeks make up a full budget of complaint. He and Brown did not get on well with the men in their unit, Midwest-erners, who were put off by their New England accents and regarded them as "effete Easterners and probably fairies," Brown recalled.[28] Nor did they get along much better with their *chef de section*, John T. Phillips, a New Yorker, who continually found fault with their unmilitary ways. They were not used to discipline; they had not been given any indoctrina-tion training; they were volunteers for positions that carried the status of officers but they were treated as enlisted men in the unit; they were both still in the stage of rebelling against parental authority. Trouble was bound to ensue.

They showed their distaste for their comrades by holding aloof and spending time with the eight Frenchmen who were assigned to their unit as cooks, auto mechanics, and menials. Unlike the other men in the unit, they spoke French readily, having had expert instructresses in Paris, and in the next months they used this ability well to fraternize with the *poilus*, the ordinary French soldiers, of the nearby units. From them, they heard all the gossip of the French army, they heard all the bitterness that boiled up in the ranks, and in particular, they heard details about the best-kept secret on the Western front, the mutiny in the French army after General Nivelle's disastrous campaign on the Aisne. Their talk about what they heard and their pacifist views in general did not go down well with the Americans in *Section Sanitaire XXI*.

They showed their scorn for their *chef de section* (a new one now, Harry Anderson, a garage mechanic from the Bronx) by managing to be unshaven, unwashed, and generally unkempt and by giving him a good deal of insolence. As a result, Cummings and Brown were taken off the driver assignments and spent most of their time washing muddy vehicles. When the time came for a few brief leaves in Paris, Anderson did not even include their names in the lottery. Cummings' chagrined response to this discrimination was to blow a mouthful of cigarette smoke in Anderson's face. In the army such a situation would not have arisen. An intelligent, inexperienced college graduate, drafted and made to serve under an oafish sergeant, would have been given sufficient training to tolerate the rigid hierarchies of the military service. But the Norton-Harjes Ambulance Service had no standards or traditions to regulate the troubled relationships among men who had different backgrounds and values. Cummings was outraged by the daily treatment accorded to him and Brown. He vowed not to renew his service contract when the six months were up.

But they were getting the first-hand experience of the war which they were curious about when they joined. They saw the beautiful rolling countryside, its greenery destroyed, churned into mud or feebly surviving trees. They saw the shell-marked and bullet-pocked walls and buildings in the serene little villages where they were stationed—Chevincourt with its ancient church and its winding, hilly, walled streets; Roupy, which was a ruin of rubble; Assevilliers, a crossroads near the Somme in the British sector, watched over by a tall brick and stone church. Chance has preserved a report that Brown sent home of a walk that he and Cummings took when they came upon "a tiny little chapel hidden among some willow trees." Within they found a partly destroyed Madonna and child and a variety of verses and prayers scribbled on the walls. " 'Respectez la Vierge Mutilée car elle ne peut se defendre.' On another side of the wall was written a fierce denunciation of war, the Government, the Chamber of Deputies and it ended with 'Vive la Paix.—Vive le petit peuple.' It was a riot of ideas and creeds."[29] They observed the dogged patience of the French rural folk, especially the women, who continued to carry on their lives as best they could—to care for their livestock, bear their children, pray to God, and conduct their funerals.

They were able to spend time talking with the fighting men of France (although invited to dine with officers, they always preferred the *poilus)* and drinking wine with them when they could. This was another violation of the wishes of Anderson, who discouraged association with the French and wanted "to show those dirty Frogs what Americans were like" by keeping spic and span and pretending superiority. Cummings and Brown preferred relaxation and mud-stained, grease-stained uniforms—and wine when they could get it. They were welcomed and questioned by the French, especially as they displayed a friendliness that had not usually been found among the English in that sector. One time in Chevincourt, they had a hilarious drinking session with the neighboring French soldiers, who wanted to learn songs in English. Brown and Cummings did not know the words to most of those which were requested, but Cummings improvised anyway. Brown remembers himself and Cummings standing on a table, with Cummings leading the singing:

> And to her maidenhead
> He softly softly said:
> It's a long way to Tipperary
> It's a long way to go.

It is amusing to find Cummings, the striver for individual rights and freedoms, the foe of authority, the friendly, unpretentious ambassador to the ordinary Frenchmen, denouncing his compatriots as "Typical Americans."

Their letters were censored. Both the section commander and the French authorities had the responsibility, but after a time Cummings felt that perhaps one or another of the *chefs de section* had stopped his letters because of his forthright criticism of them; so in August he began to write home in French, for Anderson could not read the language. He indulged himself in even more specific abuse of his superiors. Of Anderson, he wrote "Le présent chef de la section, avant, sous-chef, est un homme assez stupide, sans éducation. . . ." Richard Norton's visit to the camp did not hearten him: "C'est un homme maigre, plutôt grand, qui cause sans mouvoir la bouche, a un oeil obscurci par le monocle; dans un mot, un âne agréable et sans raison d'être. . . . Merde pour lui."[30]

But censorship proved to be a source of real trouble. Brown and Cummings, having heard of the Lafayette Escadrille, had hoped perhaps to get out of their ambulance unit by joining the French army as aviators. On the advice of a friendly French lieutenant, they naïvely wrote a joint letter to the undersecretary of French aviation volunteering their services but expressing their reluctance to kill Germans.[31] This strange proposal alerted the censors, who then watched their outgoing mail carefully. Cummings also wrote to Richard Norton on August 30 requesting that he and Brown be allowed to join "an ambulance section which we understand is being formed in America for service in Russia."[32]

Brown's letters caused more suspicion. He was writing to friends in the United States, and, in a manner that looks like a deliberate teasing of the censors, he reported a good deal of the gossip of the French troops. He reported that "the French soldiers are all despondent and none of them believe that Germany will be defeated."[33] This and other opinions about the spirit of the troops and the progress of the war made him appear dangerous to the jumpy French intelligence authorities. They ordered the arrest of Brown and his accomplice. The oddity of Cummings' arrest merely because he was Brown's friend made Cummings think that Anderson, too, played some part in that decision. His suspicions about Anderson were right. The French security officials had come to Anderson with questions about Brown and Cummings, and Anderson had told them "he believed Brown was a bad man." He also reported some hearsay from another ambulance driver named Rotopan "that Brown was a German spy." Anderson then signed a three-page report about the matter for the French.[34]

IV

On Sunday, September 23, 1917, *Section Sanitaire XXI* was encamped at Ollezy, a hamlet near the Somme southeast of Ham, a peaceful spot dominated by an enclosed farmyard beside a shell-ruined church. Cummings, wet and muddy, was cleaning an ambulance when suddenly the meticulously attired Ministre de Sûreté of Noyon arrived with two helmeted gendarmes and took him and Brown in separate cars to the Noyon gendarmerie for questioning. Although Cummings was interrogated for a long time and in extensive detail about his background, there seemed really no evidence that he was a spy or a traitor. But the trio of examiners asked him one final question, "Do you hate the Germans?" and Cummings refused to say yes. He would only reply "No, I like the French very much."[35] Nor would he say that he believed in the atrocities attributed to the Germans. There was a lifetime of character-molding behind this crucial stance, plus a touch of plain New England stubbornness. Throughout the questioning, Cummings would not dissociate himself from his friend, although it was clear that Brown's provocation of the censors was the cause of the difficulties. He also displayed a sufficient confidence not to be intimidated by the arrest, by the strange surroundings, or by his realization that his American superior had cast him into alien hands. Finally, he would not knuckle under and agree to an opinion that he did not hold, even to get himself free of dangerous accusations.

He was told he would have to be detained and was locked up in a cell for the night. All at once, at a late hour he felt a flood of warmth as he heard a familiar tune whistled from somewhere in the jail, a theme from Stravinsky's *Petrouchka*. He replied by whistling another theme. After a second night in jail, he was taken by rail in company with two *gendarmes* to Creil, a railroad junction north of Paris, for another night in jail, where he amused himself by loudly singing all the French songs he had picked up from the troops. The next day he was taken to Paris and from there to Southern Normandy, where his rail journey ended at Briouze, a town about 150 kilometers west of Paris.

He was being sent to a Dépôt de Triage in the nearby town of La Ferté-Macé, a kind of waiting station for aliens who were suspected of espionage or whose presence was generally undesirable during time of war. They all were waiting to be examined by a commission which came every three months to look over their cases. Those who were found innocent or harmless were set free or deported to their own countries; doubtful cases were sent to a concentration camp for the duration of the war; those deemed to be spies were turned over to the military for trial. At La Ferté-Macé there were both men and women among the prisoners.

The men were mostly petty criminals who, having fallen afoul of the law again, were interned as undesirables. Some were felons in the same situation. A few were innocents who had lost their papers or had encountered some mishap that brought them into the hands of the police. The women fell into two groups: wives or female relatives of the interned men, and prostitutes who had wandered into the war zone or other areas where they were forbidden. It was a kind of international house for unfortunates, dissidents, and social misfits.[36]

When his train arrived in Briouze, Cummings was not sure where he was. When the *gendarmes* told him he was bound for La Ferté-Macé, he understood them to say Marseilles. Now after a twelve-kilometre hike at night from Briouze to La Ferté-Macé, he realized that he was at the end of his bewildering journey, somewhere way out in the country several hours by train west of Paris.

La Ferté-Macé was a pleasant little Normandy agricultural center among the hills, near the popular watering place, Bagnoles-de-l'Orne. Its twin-towered church, portions of which went back to the twelfth century, overlooked a market square that was busy each morning with the sale of fruit, vegetables, butter, cheese, and eggs—a very different scene from the battered villages of Picardy and Champagne. Its inhabitants at the time were conservative, religious householders, tradesmen, and farmers, all of whom hated and feared the presence of the internment center in their town. The Dépôt de Triage itself was a grim, grey, stone three-building complex, formerly a seminary (closed in 1906), comprising two three-story structures and a large chapel, surrounded by a seven-foot stone wall.

Cummings was taken to this Dépôt late at night, subjected to another but briefer interrogation and then placed for the night on a mattress of straw. When he awoke, he found himself in a huge chapel-like room eighty by forty feet, with slender arched windows, which on three sides of the room were boarded over, and with a vaulted ceiling twenty feet high supported by a series of wooden pillars, alongside most of which were pails overflowing with urine. With him were about forty men of a variety of nations and tongues, French colonial, Belgian, Dutch, English, Spanish, Polish, Russian, Norwegian, Turkish, and Arabic. Also present was his friend, William Slater Brown.

Cummings remained three months in this internment center, an experience which later provided him with the material for his first published book, *The Enormous Room.* For the early part of this period he and Brown regarded it as the same kind of exciting adventure as their sojourn in Paris had been. The daily routine was dull enough: up at 6:30, down from their third floor confinement room to a mess center for meals (bread

Dépôt de Triage at La Ferté-Macé: The Enormous Room is on the top floor of the building on the right. The chapel is on the left. COURTESY SLATER BROWN

and coffee, bread and soup of potatoes and vegetables, three times a week braised meat), periods of exercise in a courtyard at the rear of the compound, sleep at 9 P.M. or earlier when darkness fell. But coming to know the people was as fascinating as the time spent with the French *poilus.* Since the prisoners had the solidarity of men who suffer a common fate, Cummings and Brown were readily accepted into the group. Thus they felt a paradoxical relief in having escaped from the enmity and harassment of their compatriots into the hearty friendliness of a society of international outcasts. The whole experience gave Cummings an opportunity to know intimately men of classes and nations he never would have encountered anywhere in his life. He had his notebooks with him, and he made entries against the day when he would draw on this material for his writing. His letters to his parents contain none of the grousing that colored his description of life in *S.S. XXI.* In fact, he declared, "I am having *the time of my life!*"[37]

The Dépôt de Triage at La Ferté-Macé was for Cummings a microcosm with its own peculiar customs, values, and attitudes. Hostility toward all authority was necessary to give meaning to daily life—toward the guards *(plantons),* toward M. Gaillan, *le Directeur,* and all his administrative aides, toward the examining commissioners, toward the French government, toward the governments of all the nations who were at war and thus responsible for the situation of present imprisonment. The days were much the same in the little world, broken in their monotony only by the arrival of newcomers and the departure of friends, by the arrival of packages, by changes in the weather which interfered with the court-yard exercise, or by whatever little incident could make the days differ —a fight, an illness, an airplane flying over, the biweekly shower. Or by punishments that were meted out for infractions of the rules: the solitary confinement of a person in a small room, *cabinon* (Cummings spells it *cabinot*), without a mattress and with a bread and water diet.

The presence of the women on the first floor caused some diversion for the men. There were constant attempts to see them, talk to them, pass notes to them. Their promenade in their courtyard provided a third-floor spectator pleasure, although only a tiny corner of their exercise area could be seen. Forced attendance at mass on Sunday was a break in the schedule, but the prisoners did not enjoy the occasion. The priests were another arm of authority and their preachments were regarded as false, foolish, or hypocritical. In *The Enormous Room* Cummings gives a glimpse of the congregational attitudes:

> —And then One *Dimanche* a new high old man with a sharp violet face and green hair—"Vous êtes libres,mes enfants,de faire l'immortalité—Son-gez,songez donc—L'Eternité est une existence sans durée—Toujours le Paradis,toujours l'Enfer"(to the silently roaring whores)"Le ciel est fait pour vous"—and the Belgian ten-foot farmer spat three times and wiped them with his foot,his nose dripping;and the nigger shot a white oyster into a far-off scarlet handkerchief. . . .[38]

Cummings' war experiences were not typical. In the same way that *Section Sanitaire XXI* was not a real army unit, the Dépôt at La Ferté-Macé was not a real prison, although the guards were instructed to shoot anyone who tried to escape. The confinement was not intended as punishment without opportunities and privileges, and a few trusted in-ternees were actually allowed to live in the town. Prisoners who could afford to pay were able to secure private rooms in one of the two Dépôt buildings. Cummings had plenty of money in his letter of credit but he and Brown chose to share the lot of the other men. A canteen was available for those who had extra money to buy food and supplies. Cummings and Brown bought some tobacco, chocolate, and candles, and later, occasionally, eggs and butter, but they did not use their money very much—it would be a *gaucherie* in the prison society.

This amorphous state of affairs plus the oddity of the fact that these American volunteers were now under arrest gave a sense of absurdity to their life, especially when they had contacts with the outside world.

Cummings' old Greek teacher from Cambridge Latin School, Cecil Derry, wrote him a letter to wish him well in the ambulance service telling him how proud the school was about his volunteering. Derry reported that "over one hundred of our boys" were in service already.[39] Both of them had a birthday celebration in the fall, Brown's twenty-first and Cummings' twenty-third. They and their new friends regaled each other with cups of chocolate. He and Brown indulged in a great deal of discussion of art, literature, and aesthetic theory, especially abstract art and modern French poetry, and Cummings made a color chart in his sketchbook by sticking leaves and pieces of colored paper or tinfoil into slots in its pages (it still exists in the guarded vaults of the Harvard Library).[40]

Cummings continued to write poems. In his large notebook, one finds a number of poems which became a part of his *Tulips & Chimneys* manuscript, including "God gloats upon her stunning flesh," "Doll boy's asleep," "When unto nights of autumn do complain/earth's ghastlier trees," and "When citied day with the sonorous homes/of light swiftly sink in the sorrowful hour."[41] He and Brown sent to Brentano's bookstore in Paris for a set of Shakespeare (Everyman edition), which was received with great joy.[42] But the store was unable to supply them with a volume of Blake's poems (Brown was especially fond of Blake and one of his censored letters had included a request to a friend in New York to send him an edition of his work). Thayer wrote to say that he was going to take Cummings' poems out of Wilson's custody and was going to try to get some of them published.[43] Cummings first published poetry in book form, in *Eight Harvard Poets*, appeared while he was imprisoned.[44]

V

On the morning of October 17, Mr. and Mrs. Cummings were stunned at the receipt of a cable from Richard Norton:

EDWARD E. CUMMINGS HAS BEEN PUT IN A CONCENTRATION CAMP AS A RESULT OF LETTERS HE HAD WRITTEN STOP AM TAKING UP THE MATTER THROUGH THE EMBASSY TO SEE WHAT CAN BE DONE.[45]

Edward Cummings' reaction was an immediate letter to Estlin full of sympathy, advice, and an offer to make any necessary restitution himself. Considering the fact that he knew absolutely nothing of what the charges were, it is a remarkable expression of his love and understanding:

You and I have a longstanding debit and credit account running through many years; and there is still a big balance in your favor. Once by your courage and address you saved from drowning two lives that were dearer to me than my own—as they still are. I told you then that if you ever made a fool of yourself—and who of [us] does not soon or late?—You could remind me of that debt, and draw on that account, and I would honor the draft. And I will.

You poetic and artistic chaps are so afraid of being conventional and commonplace that you often hide your real emotions under a camouflage of words that is sometimes about as difficult to make anything out of as a cubist portrait of a "Nude descending the stairs."

He went on to say that if the authorities wanted to discipline someone he would be glad to be their subject and that although he was too old to drive an ambulance he would be glad to replace his son in the service by being a chaplain and he would give them all the patriotic language that they desired. And finally:

I know the real stuff you are made of. No child of your mother could ever lack courage or patriotism. You have plenty of both. All you need is a chance to prove it.

Ask for another chance. The fate of civilization is at stake in this terrible war.[46]

After cabling Norton to take action and proposing that he himself come to France if need be, he sat down to compose a letter to Norton, this one full of insight as to what could have happened. He told Norton that he did not know the circumstances but that Estlin's letters always showed love for France and affection for French soldiers. "Sometimes he grumbles unreasonably and says things he does not mean and does not expect to have taken seriously—just for the sake of giving the unpopular side a hearing; but he knows perfectly well that I do not take him seriously—though I fear the censor might."[47]

The same day, another cable went to Estlin, care of Norton, urging him to follow Norton's advice and to "TAKE THE GREATEST CARE FOR MY SAKE."[48] It was signed by Rebecca. Presumably Estlin received it, for he sent a long reassuring letter home on October 24 in which he declared that imprisonment at La Ferté-Macé meant "days spent with an inimitable friend in soul stretching probings of aesthetics, 10 hour nights (9 P.M.–6:45 A.M.) and fine folk to converse in five or six languages beside you —perfection attained at last." Moreover, he wanted no intrusion by others on his behalf. He insisted that "I see the thing thru, alone, without any monocled Richards, American ambassadors, or anything else. Nothing under H. can change my resolve, and everybody but me, i.e., Gods, men, women, & children had best keep butted out!!!!"[49]

Time passed without anything but meaningless reassurances and explanations from Norton, until he cabled on November 6, "IMPOSSIBLE FOR ME TO DO MORE FOR YOU STOP ADVISE USING ALL INFLUENCE TO STIR AUTHORITIES TO more vigorous action."[50] Edward Cummings turned to another friend, George Weston Anderson, the former attorney general for Massachusetts and now the head of the Interstate Commerce Commission in Washington. He sent him all the correspondence that he had had with Norton, told him Norton had given up and had recommended other sources of influence be used. Anderson went into action immediately. Secretary of State Robert Lansing was brought into the case and he cabled the U. S. Embassy in Paris for an immediate investigation. Correspondence went back and forth. Norton became involved again and sent further reports. Little by little Edward Cummings got the story of the reasons behind the arrest and received assurances of the innocence of his son. But still no word came about his release.

On November 21 came a report from Norton that Estlin would be released shortly. But this good news was clouded by a cruel confusion originating from a misread Navy report. The Paris Embassy cabled that Estlin had been lost at sea when the *Antilles* was torpedoed by submarines. The message was absurd because the newspapers had reported the sinking of the *Antilles* as long ago as October 17, a time when the Embassy officials were still trying to get information on Estlin's imprisonment. But Edward dared not disbelieve the worst. He kept the official report secret from Rebecca because she had just received word of the death of her brother George. He took only one step to prepare her for the horrible possibility of Estlin's death: he called her attention to the newspaper stories of mid-October that "H. H. Cummings, casual civilian" was on the passenger list of the *Antilles*. Meanwhile he cabled Norton in Paris to check the source of information that the embassy sent, and he got his friend Anderson busy in Washington checking the Navy report.

Ignorant of the official cable containing the false news, Rebecca wrote Estlin on November 23 that "Poor Father" was staggered by the newspaper accounts about H. H. Cummings and "nothing will persuade him that it is not you—I never saw a man change as he has done in these two days of intense anxiety."[51]

Nor was his anxiety completely relieved the next day when an official correction came from the State department that it was an H. H. Cummings and not E. E. Cummings who had gone down on the *Antilles*. Edward's long letter to Estlin, November 29, tells of the mental anguish he endured: "Dearest Chub, This is Thanksgiving day. It is one of the most thankful of all such days in my life. . . . because your double letter of October 14 and 24 brought me what I wanted more than anything else in the world,—final and convincing proof that you were safe and sound somewhere in France at some date later than October 17." After telling him the details of the false alarm, he revealed how he had passed the three days with his lonely secret. "So down I went into the depths of Hell, and suffered as [I] did not suppose I was capable of suffering,—until my tortured soul had nothing worse to dread. These were days that seemed like years of agony, when I would have given all I had or hope for in exchange for the right to believe that you were safe."[52]

The entire episode further shook Edward Cummings' faith in the government officials. Nor was it restored just because the State Department sent a correction of the false report. Estlin was still in a French prison camp. On December 8, Edward Cummings sat down and wrote a letter to President Wilson. Lincoln used to deal with individual cases during the Civil War—why not the idealistic Woodrow? Edward Cummings arranged for the letter to be hand-delivered from Anderson's office to the White House on December 10. Although Edward never received a reply, it appears that White House pressure was brought to bear on the case. The State Department fired off another cable to France on December 15 asking for a full report from the Embassy.

Time had dragged on at La Ferté-Macé. Cummings and Brown had been examined by the visiting commissioners as long ago as October 17. Cummings was confronted with excerpts from Brown's letters, which indicated, that the writer "was not a hater of Germans or a lover of war,"[53] and he went through questions similar to the earlier scene in which he denied hatred for the Germans. The commission decided that Cummings should be set free but would not be allowed to leave the country. He could choose his place of residence in France but would live classified as a refugee under government surveillance for the duration of the war. It took two months for that decision to be made and communicated to La Ferté-Macé in a dispatch on December 8 from the Ministre de Sûreté in Paris.[54]

Meanwhile Estlin continued to keep up the spirits of the home folks by the cheeriness of his letters. In one that the French authorities confiscated (and still remains in the archives of the Department of Orne), he told his father:

> Our life here is A 1. Never have I so appreciated leisure. I continually write notes on painting, poetry, and sculpture, as well as music; and the Muse Herself has not been unkind. My days, spent in delightful discussions with my good friend, whose tastes so happily coincide with my own, remind

me of the mental peregrinations of your favorite Socrates, insofar as they
have already illumined many dark crannies in the greatest of all sciences—
Art.

Their only lack, he declared, was "good smoking tobacco."[55]

The choice of a place of residence for the duration of the war Cum-
mings apparently discussed with some of his fellow prisoners, especially
Charles Bragard, an English artist who had long lived in France and had
known Cézanne. He chose Oloron-Ste.-Marie, in the Pyrenees near the
Spanish border. His choice was recorded on December 17 and he began
his long wait for the Minister of the Interior to approve. Brown was not
so fortunate. The commission decided that he would be sent to the con-
centration camp at the College of Precigné, Sarthe, for the duration of
the war.

No matter how happy-go-lucky the early weeks of imprisonment at
La Ferté-Macé had been for them, time and privation depleted that spirit.
The food was really inadequate. Sometimes they supplemented it with
an egg cooked over a candle. Sanitary conditions were so bad that it was
a good thing Cummings and Brown were not overfastidious people. The
"medicine major" in his report during autumn 1917 declared it an un-
healthy situation for an average of forty to fifty men to be living in dirt,
"some being sick, diseased, stiff with cold and complaining of rheuma-
tism or worse."[56] In mid-December Brown developed scurvy and Cum-
mings found a rash on his face and an infection on his hand. But it was
not until Brown left on December 14 that Cummings lost his sense of
adventure and fascination. He became more and more depressed until the
time of his release.

In the meantime, the efforts of the American Embassy paid off. On
the afternoon of December 18, a telegram arrived signed jointly by the
Ministry of the Interior and the Foreign Office ordering that Cummings
be freed and sent to Paris to report in at the American Embassy.[57] He left
by train on December 19 after warm good-byes from his old friends at the
Dépôt de Triage but feeling somewhat in a daze about the new turn of
events and about the loss of his friend Brown. His excitement mounted
as he approached Paris over the wintry fields, although he felt weak after
his three months on prison fare. Good food and a bath at the Hôtel
Saints-Pères were deep luxuries. He was distressed at the number of fleas
he brought with him from the enormous room. In the morning he walked
into the Embassy wearing his fur coat and his crushed Harvard hat.
Everyone was very cordial. He put in a good word for Brown with
Ambassador William Sharp, who later took steps for Brown's release.

Hasty arrangements were made for sailing to the United States on

December 22 aboard the *Espagne*. But Cummings had plans for those two
nights in Paris. He would spend them with Marie Louise Lallemand, and
after what he had been through, he was not going to worry about vene-
real disease. He had received one letter from her at *S.S. XXI*, in which she
said she was ill and had to go to a hospital. Now he went to her apartment
but his knock found no answer. For two days he searched the wintry
Grands Boulevards from the place de la République over to the boule-
vards Montmartre and des Italiens down to the place de l'Opéra and in
the cafés and bistros in the area, but he could not find her. He left a note
for her at her address, telling her he would return to Paris as soon as he
could. He asked her to write and gave Scofield Thayer's address in New
York for his mail.[58]

He spent his last evening drinking champagne at the Sultana
Cherque's restaurant in the warmth of the only association he had in
Paris and at closing time he was taken home by a woman named Berthe,
a waitress at the restaurant. This was his last night in France and he was
determined not to return to the United States without a fully consum-
mated sexual experience. Although he was weak from his imprisonment,
he took her "faute de mieux." It was an experience important enough that
he tried to record it in a poem. But his usual forms would not do. The
appropriate form he took from Mallarmé's *Poëmes en Prose*, thinking per-
haps of "Le Phénomène Futur," and the next day he jotted his notes on
a tiny little pad that he picked up at the Embassy. When he typed it out
the following month, it had taken this expression, with its toughness of
detail and its oddness of image not completely hiding his intensity of
feeling:

The moon-hit snow is falling like strange candy into the big eyes
of the little people with smiling bodies and wooden feet
hard thick feet full of toes
left-handed kiss

I think berthe is the snow, and comes down into all corners of
the city with a smelling sound.   The moon shines all green in
the snow.

then saw I 1 star cold in the nearness of sunset.   the face of this
star was a woman's and had worked hard.   the cheeks were high and
hard, it powdered them in a little mirror before everybody saying
always nothing at all.   The lips were small and warped, it
reddened them.   Then one cried to it & it cried Je viens and
went on looking at itself in the little mirror saying always

nothing—Then I ask the crowding orange—how is that star
called?   she answers Berthe,
changing into a violet very stealthily
O with whom I lay
Whose flesh is stallions
Then I knew my youth trampled with thy hooves of nakedness

23 years lying with thee in the bed in the little street
off the Faubourg Montmartre

tongue's cold wad knocks[59]

   He sailed the next day, vowing, as he had written to Marie Louise,
to return to the city which had captured his heart. But he never found
Marie Louise again. Did she ever get his note in which he said, "Si tu
penses que j'ai oublié les jours et nuits que nous avon passé ensemble, tu
te trompes, Marie Louise. . . . Jusqu'à mon retour, acceptes ces baisers!
Edouard"?[60] He memorialized her in a poem he wrote during the next
year, in which he assembled a collage of street talk and the voices of her
sisters, the ladies whom he and Brown had courted:

              little ladies more
              than dead exactly dance
              in my head,precisely
              dance where danced la guerre.

              Mimi à
              la voix fragile
              qui chatouille Des
              Italiens

              the putain with the ivory throat
              Marie Louise Lallemand
              n'est-ce pas que je suis belle
              chéri? les anglais m'aiment
              tous,les américains
              aussi. . . . "bon dos,bon cul de Paris?"(Marie
              Vierge
              Priez
              Pour
              Nous). . . .[61]

X

A Wartime Interlude

> But damn it, I don't see enough miscellaneous folk and especially
> yourself or burlesque shows, or reviews, the opera Aida, the traffic cop
> at 42nd and Fifth Avenue . . . or the pickles that ripen in April under
> the L on the East side or anything.
>
> DOS PASSOS to Cummings

Hildegarde Watson was pained to see that Cummings had lost his smile.
He had arrived aboard the *Espagne* on January 1, 1918 and had been met
by his mother and Sibley Watson, who brought him back to the Watson
place at 127 East 19th Street (the smallest house in New York) for a
welcome-home luncheon. Cummings had lost weight, he had a rash on
his face, and he showed Watson an ulcerous lesion on his leg. He seemed
sober and serious, partly because he was suffering from a vitamin defi-
ciency but partly too because of the story he had to tell. Hildegarde
missed the high-spirited conversational flow that Cummings used to pro-
vide. But Rebecca Cummings, in her somewhat dowdy Cambridge finery,
unshakable as Plymouth Rock, was the dominant genial spirit of the
luncheon table, overjoyed at her son's return.

Edward Cummings, who arrived by train later, was thankful to the
Unitarian God that his son had come home safely. But his feeling of joy
and relief was tempered by his anger at the Red Cross for its irresponsi-
bility, at the Embassy for its bumbling, and at the French government
for its abuse of an American citizen who had volunteered to help France
in her darkest hour. Even after the reunited family returned to Cam-
bridge, Edward was brimming with fulminations and vaguely consider-

ing an international law suit. For evidence he had a heap of documents that he had accumulated during his efforts to free his son. When he heard the details of what Estlin had gone through, he urged him to write it down so that he would have a full eyewitness account. In a letter to Arthur Dehon Hill, another friend in Washington who had been trying to help out, Edward declared his intention to make his complaint public and hoped "it would get serious attention." "If I am wrong, and American citizens must expect to suffer such indignities and injuries at the hands of other governments without any effort at remonstrance and redress by their own government, I believe the public ought to know the humiliating truth. It will make interesting reading. It remains for my son to determine what action he will take."[1]

He and Estlin had many argumentative discussions about it. But the man of action could not convince Estlin that he should participate in any lawsuit. To satisfy his father's desire, Estlin finally entered into a contract with him. He would write out his story of the imprisonment if his father promised not to use it in any legal action. His father agreed to pay him for his time. Although it is not clear what sum of money was settled on, there are some indications that it was a $1000 Liberty Bond.[2] This arrangement also helped temporarily to soothe Edward's worry about his son's ability to support himself. It would give Estlin more time to come around to accepting a job and settling down.

With the good food and loving care at home, Estlin began to return to his old self. In the third floor studio, he was soon painting, and he began to look over his notebooks and sketchbooks, to transcribe by typewriter some of the poems he had written in Paris and La Ferté-Macé, and to draw upon his experiences in France for new productions. He worked on some prose-poems that ranged from high to low in subject matter, one on the age of chivalry, one about Berthe, and another, in French, a monologue in which a slightly drunken whore mourns the death of two sisters in the trade but pictures them at an eternal party with the boy-angels in the heavenly café ("Et toujours on dansera, on songera, et on s'enivera de nektar le plus coûteux, au son des harpes dorées de mon propre orchestre qui joue dans le café du ciel toute la nuit, et le dimanche compris.")[3] He composed other poems in French, both in rhymed stanzas and in his visually directive free verse.

If Cummings' memory sentimentalized Parisian *cocottes,* his view of their American counterparts was quite otherwise. A poem he began to work on soon after he arrived shows him ready to exercise his Satyric style. The poem, see-sawing between attraction and revulsion, is not very successful. Probably, as pencilled revisions indicate, it was still unfinished, but certain devices are quite effective, such as the working of an ugly scene and fragments of dialogue into the intricate rhyme scheme of a Petrarchan sonnet:

> She smiled.   She was too full of Bud and siph
> to be pretty,even at a distance.   These made her
> only beautiful....Now,as she laid her
> five fingers on the unwhite stiff
> cloth,I breathed.   With her sat a stiff
> I'd seen before somewhere or other.   Her pimp
> was watching from the bar—her eyes went limp
> and big,so blaming big it was as if ...
> and hungry....   "So,he says to me Girlie
> he says,you're all in from them rye-highs.
> Cut it.   I give him a glawnce,and I says,Jawn
> I says..."   My spine scuttled,fed by pale curly
> memories;I started half to rise,
> and the curtain of the booth was drawn.[4]

The concluding lines provide a surprising tingle, brought about by Cummings' use of suggestion, including the ellipsis, "as if . . .". This has helped to pull our attention away from the unattractive scene and place it on the paradoxical response of the speaker: he catches his breath; when her eyes go limp, he is unable to complete his thought; and finally when he hears her voice, he remembers her. We are provoked into wondering what his stirred remembrance was, but that is all: the curtain closes on the scene and on the poem.

Soon, much to his parents' disappointment, Cummings was ready to return to New York and to rent another studio. Since he was still eligible for the draft, his father was full of advice and suggestion about his future. Edward urged him to join other Harvard men by volunteering for officer's training at the Plattsburg military camp. Estlin would have nothing to do with it, and the whole matter ended in a shouting match on the stairway shortly before he departed to resume the life he had left in New York the previous year. It must have been about this time that Cummings wrote at the end of his La Ferté-Macé notebook a long satirical diatribe, in which a father remonstrates with his son about his whole pattern of behavior. Since it mocks a great many of Edward Cummings' phrases and arguments, it reveals the deterioration which had taken place in the relationship between father and son:

> My son, for you are still my son, tho' had I known a son of mine
> would turn out so I would have spilled my seed upon the ground rather

than beget him. I tell you that your previous conduct is the direct result of the steadily increasing selfishness to which you were becoming more and more prone. As long as you remained at home, you were sensitive to pure ideals. When you went to college we began not to understand you. You fuddled your mind with tobacco, altho' I gave you the benefit of my experience on the subject. You refused to promise not to indulge in alcohol, thereby breaking your mother's heart. You evaded all my entreaties to go to the gymnasium to make your body strong. You took less and less personal care of yourself, tho' I assured you of what everybody knows, namely that a man is judged by his appearance. Finally you picked your friends unwisely, tho' a man's compagnons are a criterion of his tastes.

I threatened, I begged, I went down on my knees to you. I said to you: It is quite evident that you have no respect for me, your father; then go to your teachers, professors, to men like Perry, to men whose opinions you do respect; ask their advice. You virtually spat in my face. I cried to you: treat me like a dog, me your father, he's an old codger, a fool, not up to the times, old fashioned in his ideas, but for God's sake remember your mother who went down to the gates of Death to get you, who suffered every sacrifice that you might be strong and well. I said to you: Look at her, your Divine Mother, she is crying. You are breaking her heart. You answered in your cavalier way that it was not your fault that you were born.

Now you come to me in this dreadful hour, when your country calls you to sacrifice your time, your petty pleasure, your occupation, your life if need be, to the Cause of Justice and Right, and you dare to tell me that you refuse to answer that call, that your business is more important than everybody's business, that you will not give yourself to Save the World, will not avail yourself of the Greatest Opportunity that the World has ever given a young man to prove himself worthy of the sacrifices that have been made for him by his parents. For *you do not belong to yourself.* Your mother wanted to have more children, but I said to her, we will have only 2 children, but they shall be eagles. Before you were born even [,] we began making sacrifices for you. We denied ourselves the ordinary comforts of existence that you might be well nourished and pure-minded. You owe your strong body to your mother; when I chose her for my wife, I was thinking of the Child To Be & I took a fine strong healthy woman, none of your cocktail-drinking, cigarette-smoking, flat-chested society dancers who could no more cook a piece of toast than they could deny themselves a ball. Finally your frankness, you never took us into your confidence, your mother and I told you often that our lives were bound up in yours, that by keeping this unmanly silence you were depriving us of life itself.

When you were at college I begged you to make the most of your chances to cultivate an acquaintance with the great minds of the world, chances to study under well known people come from all parts of the world: you showed a brutal indifference, a criminal laziness. Still I did not hurry you. I asked you to try as many fields as possible. I told you that you could take your *time*, that I would back you in any field you chose to settle down in. My son, no one has been more proud of you when you were your true self than we have been. No one has taken such great pleasure in your poetic and artistic achievements as has your mother. I have been often proud of you, always too fond of you, nearly always confident that your better nature would finally assert itself. I have prayed that I might wake & find the ever-widening gap between us all a hideous dream, that after all, the end of my whole life had not been denied me; the companionship of my son working at the same things, side by side, comrades. There is nothing that I have desired as I have this: I have prayed for it every night & that you might see the light at last as I have seen it—shaking off the scales of unmanliness & laziness & worthlessness from your eyes & standing forth ready to give everything for the Truth. . . .

The Son:

>   You broke away from your father in marrying my mother.
>   My country is inside me.[5]

It is a pathetic document in the war between the generations.

Cummings arrived in New York at the end of February and by early March he had sublet from Dillwyn Parrish "the best studio in New York" in a little wooden house at 11 Christopher Street in Greenwich Village. It had three rooms, a bedroom, a kitchen with a three-burner stove and an oven, and a large workroom with five tall windows; it was completely furnished with couches, chairs, pots and pans. Slater Brown had returned from Europe, released by the French authorities through the combined efforts of his uncle Paul Bartlett, of Senator Henry Cabot Lodge, and of Estlin, who had explained the case at the Embassy. Brown was now at home in Webster, Massachusetts, recovering from scurvy and malnutrition which had even caused some of his teeth to fall out. The two friends made plans for sharing quarters in New York.

When Brown came to the city in April, he was immediately drawn into the circle of Cummings' Harvard friends: Sibley Watson, who was now attending Medical School at New York University; Scofield Thayer, who was now an associate editor and financial backer of the *Dial*, a Chicago-based fortnightly periodical with literary, social, and political concerns which was about to move its offices to New York; Arthur Wilson, who was temporarily back from military training in the South; Edward Nagel, who had not been drafted and was trying to develop as a painter; and anyone else from the *Monthly* group who happened to pass through town. A new addition to the circle was Nagel's stepfather, Gaston Lachaise, who was on his way to becoming one of America's important sculptors. He had been born and trained in Paris but his romantic

pursuit of a heroically proportioned American woman had brought him
to the United States. It had also brought him to the expedient of working
in the studio of Paul Manship and the commercialized production of civic
sculpture and bas-relief so that he had very little time for his own creative
work. Despite the great difference in their ages, Cummings and Lachaise
became good friends, for they each had a romantic enthusiasm for artistic
creation.

During the time Cummings and Brown shared studios in New
York, they were able to live very cheaply. The rents they paid were
from $15.00 to $30.00 per month, and the cost of a restaurant dinner
was twenty-five to thirty-five cents, sometimes with table wine. Above
all, their wants were modest and they could always dine happily on
tea and pilot biscuits if they fell short of money. As the months went
by, they engaged in the same kind of exploration of the city that they
had carried out in Paris. They dined frequently at Khoury's Restau-
rant at 95 Washington Street on the Battery for they loved Middle
Eastern food: shish kebab, stuffed vine leaves, and the Syrian ways of
cooking eggplant that brought tears of sensual joy to Cummings' eyes.
They spent many evenings at the Roumanian Hall, an upstairs estab-
lishment that featured Middle Eastern music, including the Kanoon (a
large zither, plucked not strummed), a hefty belly dancer, and the fas-
cinating sight of a line of Greek men delicately pacing through the
handkerchief dance. They became well known to the proprietor, Has-
san, and to other habitués, to whom they gave their own special
names, such as The Fairy Man or The Baboon (a young man who
came around selling nuts from a tray held by straps around his shoul-
ders). They went to Bertolotto's, Fortunio's and other Italian restau-
rants for ravioli, risotto, zabaglione—and ample supplies of tart red
vino da pranzo (often made by the proprietor himself). Cummings
liked to try out his command of Italian at least once a week in one
place or another, and they were always well received—sometimes
even into a local card game.

They went frequently to Minsky's National Winter Garden, up-
stairs at Second Avenue and Houston Street, to see the current bur-
lesque show. They loved the strippers, particularly one named Cleo,
who at "an advanced stage of dance" would exclaim, "Burn my
clothes,—I'm in heaven." But their real favorite was the leading co-
median, Jack Shargel, whom Cummings ranked above Chaplin. One
of the simple-minded routines that Shargel frequently repeated sent
Cummings into childlike delight. Here is his own description of it,
phrased in the overly transcendent language which he later employed
when praising aspects of the popular arts:

... a beauteous lady (weighing several hundred pounds) hands the super-Semitic, black-derbied, misfit-clothed, keen-eyed but ever-imposed-upon individual called Jack Shargel a red rose—Shargel receives her gift with a gesture worthy of any prince; cautiously escorts the flower to his far from negligible nose; rapturously, deliriously even, inhales its deep, luxurious, seductive, haunting fragrance; then (with a delicacy which Chaplin might envy) tosses the red rose exquisitely, lightly, from him. The flower flutteringly describes a parabola—weightlessly floats downward—and just as it touches the stage there is a terrific, soul-shaking, earthquake-like *crash:* as if all the glass and masonry on earth, all the most brittle and most ponderous things of this world, were broken to smithereens.[6]

The part Cummings liked best was the way Shargel smelled the rose.

Another of their favorites was Mr. Moscowitz, who performed on the cymbaloon, a kind of East European xylophone, at his restaurant. He was a sober-faced Roumanian who took himself very seriously whether he was playing one of Lizst's Hungarian Rhapsodies or "Hello Central, Give Me No-Man's Land. My Daddy's There."

A letter from Dillwyn Parrish has preserved a memory of an especially Pickwickian scrape that Cummings got into during this spring because he liked to climb up to contemplate the stars from the roof of 11 Christopher Street: "Do you remember taking a midnight stroll with Dos over the rooftops and losing your way? You returned by the wrong trap door; got into a houseful of screaming ladies; were chased by the police; ended innocently drinking milk at No. 11 while old Mrs. Ryan held officers at bay on the narrow stairway?"[7]

With Brown or Watson, Cummings wandered all over the East Side, his eyes sparkling at the ethnic exotica of the teeming streets—the peculiar clothes, hats, scarves, window pots, pets, children's games, pushcarts, food shops. His ears were titillated by Hebrew, Yiddish, and a chorus of the immigrant dialects of English; he wrote his mother that he was trying to learn both Russian and Yiddish.

At tea-time most afternoons, he and Brown could be found at 3 Washington Square beside Elaine Thayer's fireplace. All of her husband's friends loved her and she made her apartment a kind of social center for them after work at the end of the day. This kind of gathering with friends for tea in the afternoon or for drinking in the evening was the social life Cummings enjoyed most.

He was spending most of his time painting at an easel which was, he told his mother, "as big as a house." He was now developing his cubist technique more fully, much inspired by some of the things he had seen in Paris, especially Picasso's sets for the ballet, *Parade.* He described his work and his general technique to his mother in this way: "[The pictures] are organizations of colour and line, presentative, semi-abstract, and abstract. Figures often are taken in design, more often machineryish elements."[8] The word "presentative" here is his own apt term, indicating that he was well aware that "nonrepresentative" was an imprecise description because in his work he did use representations of objects. What he did was to give them new life in new relationships by unusual placement or surprising juxtaposition, in the same way that he used recognizable words in his poems but placed them in arrangements that made them part of a new and unusual whole.

Scofield Thayer had contracted for a cubist work and Cummings produced a painting which he entitled "Traffic" and which he described to his father as "a fairly large organization of spinning, jerking, and generally petulant chromatic planes, the effect of whose mating upon the gentle spectator might be said to produce a sensation analogous to that obtained by peeking into a dynamo-room of a large electric station."[9] Another of what his father called "fourth-dimension crazy-quilt" pieces was an interpretation of the Brooklyn Bridge. Lachaise very much approved of it ("These forms are beoot'fool," he told his pleased young friend). Cummings felt that "he honoured me by seeing a fitness of form to color in it." A third painting was one his father had contracted for, a little less angular and busy than his cubist efforts. "Poetic," Lachaise called it.[10]

He was not neglecting his poetry, but he did not spend as much time on it as he did on his painting; poetry was easy for him. Brown could not understand why Cummings should busy himself with painting, an area of endeavor in which he had much less skill than in writing. Cummings argued that since it was harder for him to paint, it was artistically more important to achieve something in the more difficult medium. Nevertheless, he had not lost his interest in poetry, and the time he spent painting even gave him a new perspective on his literary work. He was revising the poems he had already written, he told his mother in April, and by this he probably meant that, among other changes, he was rearranging them spatially on the page. But there were fresh poems too. One batch was made up of very short statements or scenes, composed without rhyme or meter but with careful attention to vowel and consonant patterns. He fastened them together with a ring binder and wrote on the cover "Most significant poems Everything is in arrangement Sounds not words Purity for the first time," adding as an afterthought for whomever he might allow to see them," P.S. Spacing sometimes corrected by numbers; or by ‿, meaning that the syllables must be written as one."[11]

There is no certainty what poems were included in this batch but several seem identifiable because they were typewritten on Cummings' new typewriter, they have holes punched through the margins of the page, and they were found among other materials from this period. They vary in their effectiveness. Some are mere bagatelles, like "ta/ ppin/ g/ toe."[12] But one incisive little city vignette that he discarded he should have kept and included in *Tulips and Chimneys*. A few notes survive that show how it came to be written: they give us another glimpse of Cummings in the act of creating—or at least show us the origin and selection of materials that he shaped into a poem.

One night in his wanderings he had been approached three times by street-walkers or their agents—or he had overheard their solicitations. When he returned home, he made notations of the dialogue and a brief description of each one of the women:

1) Hotel?
  Is that all you want to do?
  Yes.
  I'm wet. Let's do something, go somewhere.
  That's the only place I can take you.
  Well, let me take you, somewhere; a show.
  I guess not. Thank you.

2) Want to spend seven dollars kid?
 Seven dollars.
 Two for the room and five for the girl.
 Give me time to think it over.
 Sure.
    —Did you hook the bo?
    No.
 Comin'?
 Well. I guess not.
 I'm sorry.
    —Didn't have the seven!

3) What do you say honey, want to go?

1) dark, perfect olive complexion, slight, 14–15. Voice sweet (Irish?)

2) peroxide, doll, heavy, gold smile unhuman manner

3) plain, flat, washedout, frail
 womanly accent[16]

Out of these casual observations he fashioned one of his visually directive pieces:

                    wanta
                    spendsix

                    dollars Kid
                              2 for the room
          and
                              four   for the girl
                    thewoman wasnot

                    quite Fourteen   till she smiled
                                                                    then
          Centuries   She
                                            soft ly
                    repeated
                    well   whadyas ay
                              dear
                              wan
                              taspend

                    six

          Dollars[17]

Visually, the poem moves down, expands outward as it does so, and then
contracts as the return is made to the opening words. The capitalization
draws out certain special connections. Capital "Kid" is the customer, but
the capital "Fourteen" emphasizes that the whore is almost a child. Capi-
tal "Centuries" sharpens the contrast with capital "Fourteen," and capi-
tal "Dollars" reminds us what the whole pathetic human encounter is all
about.

    Cummings was writing sonnets too, a good many of them tough,
cynical exercises in his developing Satyric style. One of the best, later
published in *Tulips and Chimneys,* has an opening line that reads like a
police description:

          "kitty". sixteen,5′1″,white,prostitute.

          ducking always the touch of must and shall,
          whose slippery body is Death's littlest pal,

          skilled in quick softness. Unspontaneous. cute.

the signal perfume of whose unrepute
focusses in the sweet slow animal
bottomless eyes importantly banal,

Kitty. a whore. Sixteen
                     you corking brute
amused from time to time by clever drolls
fearsomely who do keep their sunday flower.
The babybreasted broad "kitty" twice eight

—beer nothing,the lady'll have a whiskey-sour—

whose least amazing smile is the most great
common divisor of unequal souls.

Although some of the unusual sonnets he was writing at this time
are marked by ugliness and squalor, others are really in the anti-Petrar-
chian tradition of Shakespeare's "dark lady" sonnets, providing intellec-
tual pleasure through their complex ironies. One of these, later published
in *&*, is full of tough-minded assertions that run counter to the conven-
tion of the poet's extravagent praise of his mistress:

my girl's tall with hard long eyes
as she stands,with her long hard hands keeping
silence on her dress,good for sleeping
is her long hard body filled with surprise
like a white shocking wire,when she smiles
a hard long smile it sometimes makes
gaily go clean through me tickling aches,
and the weak noise of her eyes easily files
my impatience to an edge—my girl's tall
and taut,with thin legs just like a vine
that's spent all of its life on a garden-wall,
and is going to die.   When we grimly go to bed
with these legs she begins to heave and twine
about me,and to kiss my face and head.

Thayer gave him the greatest encouragement in what he was doing.
Not only did he commission paintings but also on his trips to Chicago
he brought Cummings' poems to Martyn Johnson, the editor of the *Dial*,
and to other members of the editorial board and urged publication. When

they did not like the earlier poems which Thayer had on hand, he asked Cummings to send more recent ones. The current sonnets met similar disfavor. "Your sordid verses are now profaning the office-building gentility of the Dial," Thayer wrote in May 1919, and he reported on the results of showing them to Johnson. "He liked the several mortuary pieces, but as I had expected, was discreetly silent as to my favorites 'Kitty' and 'The Grape-Vine lady' ['my girl's tall']." The next day Thayer sought response to one of Cummings' new spatial arrangements at a board meeting, hoping for support from Merrill Rogers, a former editor of the *Monthly,* who was now also working for the *Dial:* "The appeal to my visual imagination I sprang on the board when I blew in this A.M. Merrill Rogers glassed it for some considerable time. Afterward he tried rodently to slip off. Cornered he 'lowed it was pretty queer poetry."[18]

When the *Dial* moved its headquarters to New York in June, Thayer arranged a meeting between Johnson and Cummings. Some hopes were raised that Cummings would at last get some work published, but not great hopes. As Cummings wrote to his father, "He will take some stuff, he says, tho' what stuff troubles him, or rather his Georgian anatomy. Another man dead—if not from the neck upward, at least downward."[19]

But other forces had already begun to intrude into Cummings' life. On May 6 the Cambridge Draft Board sent him notice that he was placed in Class 1, "Subject to call for service."[20] The imminence of his being drafted into the army increased when General Crowder with the approval of President Wilson issued his famous "work or fight" order, "requiring all men of draft age who were habitual idlers or engaged in non-essential industries, to appear before their Local Boards before July 1, 1918 and explain why they were not working in essential industries or find occupation therein."[21] His father soon had advice and recommendations for a job for Estlin in the Boston area and he also reminded his son that he had once considered volunteering for "aviation." Estlin's response was quick and negative, "I would rather die than leave New York at this moment. . . . I should worry about General Crowder. Also the work-or-worry bill, which will not go into effect until July 1 anno domine, etcetera. Meanwhile my presence here on this spot and moment is requisite to my absolute and individual success in existence."[22] Later he teasingly proposed going to Silver Lake and claiming to be a New Hampshire farmer and an essential food-raiser. As for his staying in New York, Lachaise assured him he would not be classed as an idler as long as he stayed away from "poo-lhawlz."

Yet he did worry. He reported to his mother that Foster Damon was two pounds underweight and therefore rated 1C or special service." "Am thinking of dining on lemon peels for a fortnight in imitation but on second thought consider shredded wheat more efficacious."[23] He was concerned too about the increasing excesses of patriotism which he observed all around him in New York. "Little children mouth the bloody-thirstily-inspiring words of 'over there, over there' 'so what are you going to do to win the war' etc. ad infin. Moovies show reels where ex-soldiers about-to-commit-traitery are so moved by the patriotic appeal of babies in nightgowns that they weep bitter tears—and go out and kill Mexicans! A grim looking bunch of dames sits collectively in a booth on 14th shrieking faintly at everyone 'buy a stamp," while o'er their sacred heads ring the printed words 'Help to make the Kaiser's coffin,' or some such reference to the 'Baby Killer.' How fierce we are."[24] And the call did come: he was drafted in July. He was sworn in at Cambridge City Hall and scheduled to leave for the Camp Devens training area on July 24. A poem that he had written during the spring seemed to take on additional ironic meaning now that he had lost his liberty:[25]

               a Woman
                    of bronze

          unhappy
                              stands

          at the mouth
          an oldish woman
                                   in a night-gown
                         Boosting a

          torch
          Always

                    a tired woman
                    she has had children
                                   and They have forgotten

               Standing

                         looking out
          to sea

XI

Private Cummings,
1918

Today we have naming of parts. Yesterday
We had daily cleaning. And tomorrow morning,
We shall have what to do after firing. But today,
Today we have naming of parts. Japonica
Glistens like coral in all of the neighboring gardens,
　　　And today we have naming of parts.

This is the lower sling swivel. And this
Is the upper sling swivel, whose use you will see of,
When you are given your slings. And this is the piling swivel,
Which in your case you have not got. The branches
Hold in the garden, their silent, eloquent gestures,
　　　Which in our case we have not got.

HENRY REED

Camp Devens was situated about forty miles west of Cambridge in the midst of small farms with bounteous fields and flourishing orchards. In the previous century, Bronson Alcott had established his utopian community, "Fruitlands," nearby, and his daughter Louisa May had scampered over its hills with joy. The army camp lay between the villages of Shirley and Harvard, which, with their simple elegance and their tall white-spired churches, are two of the most picturesque spots in all New England. But Cummings saw none of this beauty. Here he was imprisoned, as he later noted (mistaking one letter on his typewriter) "for the most eerrible 6 months of my life . . . wonderless: vs wonderful F[erté] M[acé]."[1]

During the initial examining and screening, he classified himself as an "artist," a "specialist in Cubism," and when asked his preference for kind of duty, he put "Interpreter."[2] Nevertheless, he was assigned to the 3rd Company, 1st Battalion, Depot Brigade and given infantry training. Because of his education and his scores on the psychological testing, he was selected, shortly, to attend a training school for officers and NCO's. He objected vociferously. He wanted no rank or responsibility. The role of "i," the non-hero, the frail man who stares into the mirror, would not allow it. "No officer's job for this weevil-dodger,"[3] he wrote to his mother. Yet with all his reluctance to serve in the army, he did not have the difficulties that attended his tour of duty in *Section Sanitaire XXI*. He was appointed acting corporal (a job that he got away from as soon as possible) and he soon fell into the discipline of a soldier's daily life.

One may be surprised at the dislike he held for the heterogeneous collection of men in his barracks, whose language he described in this way: ". . . some speak an exquisite brogue, others Italian, Spanish, others Lithuanian, Swedish, Polak, Russian. Unfortunately most speak Central Square English (a la Cambridgeport)."[4] It seems as if he so resented his loss of freedom that he could not possibly see any exotic fascination in this American mixture as he once had in his fellow-prisoners at La Ferté-Macé or in the ethnic mix of lower Manhattan. "Out of 250 more or less male bipeds with whom I cohabited night and day," he later recalled, "our unhero could only find a pair of human beings[;] one named Coty, sold Ward's Bread from a truck[,] the other, named Oscar Perry—from whom I learned all I don't know about education—could neither read nor write & signed with a cross."[5] Since he was entered on the company roll as Edward Cummings, his barrack-mates called him "Eddie."

What he really loathed, however, was the constant indoctrination of hatred for the Germans. At bayonet practice: "Don't forget you men want to have guts at *both* ends of your guns." "Yes, we don't want any *helmets* as souvenirs, we want *guts*, we prefer 'em, we can use 'em for fertilizer."[6] ". . . don't stick it in the chest, it's hard to pull out. Stick it in the bellies, and Don't Stick It In Deep, stick it in *A Little Way. There's nothing better than to see a Bosch die.*" At general instruction: ". . . the word Kamarade doesn't mean anything to an american any more. . . . Of course when they have ammunition, they fight, and when they run out of it, they throw up their hands."[7]

There was, of course, plenty of ordinary army routine to complain about: the tasteless, overcooked food, the constant drill, the hikes with a full pack, the marching in the rain or sleeping in the field in the rain when the tents leaked. Yet all the military hardening built his body up to the finest physical fitness of his life. In September when the epidemic of "Spanish influenza" swept the camp, he did not succumb. There were so many cases that the health authorities quarantined the camp and seriously considered closing it down altogether. In Cummings' company, a large number of men were stricken and six of them died.

Given this collection of troubles and resentments and given the general situation of Cummings' pacifist leanings, it is surprising that he was able to get through his six months of army training without getting into serious difficulty. But his experiences in France had wrought a psychological change, a toughening that brought a new maturity. In fact La Ferté-Macé and Camp Devens seem to have provided both the time and the psychic challenge for Estlin to formulate a philosophy of life. Perhaps the word, philosophy, is too grandiose a term for the collection of views by which he began to govern his life at age twenty-four, but it is a convenient word for the personal value system which had begun to take shape and which he began to articulate in 1918 in a way that he had never done before. For clear understanding it will be helpful to identify, by listing, those values most important to him:

1. Experience. Cummings was reaching out for the fullest range of experience within his personal sphere. The five years at Harvard had introduced him to such a huge panorama of human life from Homeric Greece down to the complexities of modern life that he could hardly wait to flee the classroom and the Cambridge restrictions in order to sample the world in all its intensity and in all its extremes, good and bad. That was why he loved New York and sought to know its immense variety. That was why the exposure to Paris seemed like an ascension to heaven. Moreover, the perplexities caused by the war and the changes in the social scene made him feel that he could never accept any older person's assessment of a situation. He must have the personal experience himself. He was distinctly conscious that nothing could be as direct an experience as the immediacy of sensation. He recognized that the reasoning processes that brought about judgment might or might not be warped by cultural forces but that, right or wrong, judgment was ultimately dependent upon the senses. "I should think myself cheated," he wrote to his mother, "if I allowed my humanly-sentimental-mind to interfere, one *iota,* with the sealed letters of sensation brought to my soul by these eyes, these ears, this nose & tongue."[8]

2. Creativity. Cummings had already planned to spend his life creating beautiful forms as a painter and as a poet. But in the creative life, he valued the process more than the product. The doing, the action was the valuable experience. More than this, he valued skilled creativity in all activities of life: Mr. Moscowitz improvising on the cymbaloon, Cleo

performing a *danse du ventre* at Minsky's, the cook at Khoury's Restaurant creating moussaka, as well as Nijinsky dancing in *L'Après-midi d'un faune* with the Ballets Russes, Erik Satie composing *Trois morceaux en forme de poire,* or Joyce taking Mr. Bloom into the realm of Hades through an Irish cemetery. He felt the same way too about people who had a creative style of living, like Slater Brown, who was continually doing the new, surprising, spontaneous thing.

3. Uniqueness. Cummings was aware that the experiences of life will bring out an essential self, an individual personality that is like no other being in the world, and he hated any stifling of that uniqueness by those who encouraged imitation. This was why he held himself away from other Americans—the bulk of his Harvard classmates, the men in *Section Sanitaire XXI,* the soldiers in his company at Camp Devens. He found them too much alike and too ready to follow patterns of behavior which were urged on them by authority or by the consensus of the multitude. He liked the misfits and eccentrics of La Ferté-Macé. He liked people who had no pretentions, who had a simple confidence in themselves, and who were not afraid to say what they thought or felt. He preferred people like Oscar Perry, a butcher by trade and a deer hunter by avocation, who was as uncultivated as a backwoodsman but who displayed a basic mother-wit unsullied by education. This romantic preference for uncultured simplicity is closely associated with the next value.

4. Primitiveness. Cummings liked unsophisticated people and from the days of his early wanderings in Boston until the end of his life he spent a great deal of time observing and listening to ordinary folk: waiters, handymen, country people, delivery men, shopkeepers, street merchants, derelicts—and children. He was here following the American romantic tradition. When he had waited for the draft rather than enroll for officer's training, he had consciously chosen, he said "to 'take a chance' with the guys-born-in-mangers rather than with ginks born in silk shirts."[9] He had an instinctive sense that privilege corrupts. He associated goodness with the little man, the one who is helpless in the hands of authority. He admired the nonhero and identified himself with that classification.

5. Freedom. We have seen plenty of evidence already that Cummings valued freedom of thought, expression, and action. The direction of his whole creative life demanded it. He had opposed all efforts—whether by his father, by Harvard, by the United States government or other authority—to restrict his course of life. His opposition to authority was alerted and strengthened by the experiences in France, but it was to increase in his life to the point at which he felt himself to be much more a citizen of the world than a United States citizen and he came at length

to oppose all social structures, regarding them as potential threats to his freedom.

6. Independence. Although Cummings wanted to be free from specific authority, he also wanted to be independent of society in general. He consciously held himself off from groups. About the only people he would now align himself with were other inner-directed individuals like himself. He hated demands for social conformity of any sort—whether it be in speech or dress or behavior or mode of thought. The whole tenor of his artistic career sounded a hostility to what was established, or to what was accepted without question. Since life in the United States was to become increasingly urban and since most of his future years were to be spent in the largest city in the nation, he would find mounting pressures for conformity in the urban ethos, and he would become increasingly unhappy with the life that he observed around him.

7. Recognition of reality. The values of freedom and independence were, paradoxically, subject to limitation by Cummings' own realization that chance and the determining forces of nature affect all human beings and that an artist wishing to experience life intensely and to observe it in all its complexity must submit himself to the physical and social restrictions suffered by the ordinary man. Here was the real maturity he brought back from France. This new outlook was the reason why we find in his letters from Camp Devens none of the spoiled-child pouting, although he offers plenty of understandable objection to his situation and to what he finds repellent in the training of men to be cruel.

Many aspects of this recently formulated code of personal behavior are embodied in a couple of letters from the late summer of 1918. On September 11 he wrote to his mother expressing a defense of the aristocratic uniqueness of the artist. He states that if John Doe, crushed among the hoi polloi, hates the army life, Doe would pull strings to try to get out and into a higher position. "I say—to hell with John Doe. Do you think that I have suffered for nothing the obligatory conscription and all the evils which accompany a complete separation from all I hold to be life? Not on your tintype; as Uncle George ecstatically would remark. I say: the artist is merely the earth's most acute and wiley observer of everything under the sun. Mankind intrudes itself. (Draft). Does the artist duck? Nix. Does he let Major Abbot, KCB, EZ, etc. come between him and the new angle on destiny? Like fun he does. Nor President W, nor Napoleon Buonaparte. The artist keeps his eyes, ears, & above all his NOSE wide open, he watches, while others merely execute orders he *does* THINGS. By things I do NOT mean wearing gold bars or pulling wires or swallowing rot-in-general or nonsense-in-particular. I mean the sustain-

E. E. Cummings on leave from Camp Devens, 1918. HOUGHTON LIBRARY

ing of his invisible acquaintance with that life which, taken from his eyes, makes itself a house in his very-brain-itself. On the pergolas of that house his soul will lounge gorgeously while his arms & legs do squads right. . . . not for all the lead pipe in Solomon's mines would I dare negate the invisible, and derail my destiny by swerving from the polished and trite tracks on which my 'neighbors' have so generously placed my unoffending cow-catcher."[10]

Another letter which reflects a similar position is more shrill, even slightly incoherent. His father had been trying to argue him out of some of his complaints by reminding him that he had been drafted because he refused to take a job in a war industry or to volunteer for Plattsburg. Estlin replied with a mock sermon, preached on the text: "an' brer rabbit he lay low." Here are a few of his "ferocities":

The question naturally arises: why, then, "Detester of Discipline," didst thou not pick-and-choose, instead of letting them put something distinctly over on thee, whence even now thou dost uplift thy pale shrill accents like unto a drowning rat held under the boisterous faucet of freedom?

My answer: because I am he who would drink beer and eat shit if he saw somebody else doing it, especially if that somebody were compelled to do it.[11] And I would think myself partially cheated of the expensive adventure of the universe did I not take a chance with Tim, Vittorio, Alexos. And their kin and kith.

. . . So noone would be allowed to take my place? And come here in my stead? And enjoy the privilege of "dying" (or more correctly, living) for democracy—very well; by the Iaveh, noone shall come out of the valley and the mountain with the same music in his eyes as me.

. . . by god. Mine is the perspiration of my own existence, and that's all I give a proper and bloody damn for. As for the "results," "fruits," and other painful and necessary etceteras, be they unto whomsoever may want 'em. They are no concern of mine—but the SWEAT is! And I would not change it for anyone else's sweat under heaven.[12]

This position of romantic individualism has some contradictions in it, such as his simultaneous admiration for and scorn of ordinary human beings, but it represents the general outlook that he would maintain, with occasional modification, for years to come.

II

Cummings proclaimed that he suffered inexpressible boredom at Camp Devens. Yet away from the stimulation of Manhattan friends and far from the distractions of city life, he went through another important creative period in his life. During the evenings or on Sundays, he spent time at the Camp Devens library or at the YMCA recreation hall, reading, writing letters, writing poems, and writing essays. Some release of energy may have come from his recent restatement of independence from his father, and some stimulus may have come from the time he was spending with the work of James Joyce. He was reading *Dubliners*, which Thayer had sent him, and he responded eagerly each month to the installments of *Ulysses* which had been appearing in *Little Review* since March.

He was theorizing a great deal about the new developments in literature and art, work which culminated in two essays, one on Joyce and the other "in acrobatic language," as Thayer called it, on modern art. Neither of these essays has survived, although the one on Joyce was apparently submitted to the *Dial* just before a change of editorship in December 1918, and the one on art bequeathed some of its notions to an essay on Gaston Lachaise in 1920. All that remains of these two essays is a flotsam of notes and drafts written on Camp Devens stationery and on other sheets from the same period. These fragments reveal what he understood about the artistic movements in which he hoped to participate and also how his aesthetic theorizing at this formative stage in his career linked up with his recently formed philosophy of life.

The most distinctive feature of these notes is his idea that the new movement in art mingles the arts of music, dance, poetry, painting, and sculpture with one another or adapts the techniques of one of the arts with another. A trial beginning for one essay reads this way: "Looking back upon the last few years one cannot but feel it pleasant and even natural that the many, solemnly convulsed by an important reality called war, should regard with suspicion the actual and significant dancings of the few whose obsession is the hearty fragilities. It is more than agreeable to find this authentic cellular renaissance particularly flowering upon the putrescence of American ideals. And to distinguish in the vivid plastic tumult certain vital musical gestures is (to speak frankly) thrilling. I may as well avoid misunderstanding by giving these vital musical gestures their proper names. They are:

Brancusi (especially the polished brass Mlle. at the
    last Independent)
Ezra Pound (σωρια) [doria]

Gleizes (skyscraper motifs)
The best of Matisse (before he imitated Matisse)

T. S. Eliot (Preludes and Rhapsody on a Windy Night)
Schoenberg (Five Orchestral Pieces)
The Woolworth Building
The Russian Ballet (Parade, Till, L'Après Midi, and
    Petroushka)

To this list of genuine phenomena the months have latterly added James Joyce (Ulysses)." He goes on to say the list could be extended to include Nijinsky, Robert Edmund Jones, Bakst, Picasso, Satie, Debussy, Strauss, and Stravinsky. The three groupings in the first list he labels "melodic gesture, harmonic gesture, and orchestral gesture," by which he apparently means to distinguish three different degrees of complexity.[13]

Another aspect of the mingling has to do with the sensations of the viewer or the reader, not only taste, touch, sight, smell, and hearing but also what he calls "organic sensation"—kinesthetic sensations: of weight, resistance and position, of all forms of pressure or pain, of the sense of balance in the inner ear, and so on.[14] He is interested in the way that the arts call upon, mix, or even confuse the various sensations. He is concerned with exquisite perceptions and the feelings which arise from them. He refers to this whole psychic faculty of feeling as "the Tactile."[15]

In an attempt to illustrate some of these ideas about the value of experiencing a work of art as opposed to "thinking" about it, he discourses on his own early "knowledge" of Cézanne's work. One day, he tells us, he passed by a gallery off Fifth Avenue where he saw "La Montagne Sainte Victoire," which had been the frontispiece in Wright's *Modern Painting.* Suddenly he "felt." The picture made him dizzy, made him feel a whirling nausea. The picture "touched" him.[16]

Besides his attraction to Cézanne and to Cubism ("an overdose of architecture on the human form,") he was especially taken by Futurism because of his appreciation of movement in art. Balla and Duchamp "paint the fact of motion." He is ready to declare that "the highest form of Composition is the Squirm, it is made of Creeping, Stretching, Gliding, Shrinking, Gripping. As emphasis tends toward angularities, the composition Wags, Hops, Bounds, Fiddles, Sprints, Fumbles, Trembles and Struts."[17]

His brief summary of the history of twentieth-century art presses together a great many of these ideas and crowns it all with his most praise-bestowing adjective "alive," a word which combines for him concepts of identity and being ("is"), of movement, warmth, vigor, power, and joy. ". . . after the death of The Man of Aix [Cézanne] european painting blew up in two places—Subject exploded so violently as to be carried piecemeal into psychology, while the explosion of Technique was straight up in the air and its denouement the precept of the perpendicular. . . . Then out of "the wreck of Formula" developed "the present state of art" which is described as a group of "isms" loudly contending with one another.[18]

As one might expect there is a clear carry-over from critical and theoretical jottings of this sort to the verse that he was writing. During this six-month period, Cummings produced a large number of the poems that appeared in his first three published volumes. They represent further development of his Hephaestian style into experimental complexity, especially in ways that provide mixtures—subtle mergings or violent conflicts—or in ways that create movement. His fascination with Cubism continues to crop up. Most notable is his poem "Picasso," which is a tribute to the artist in language that attempts to express a response to his achievement and to suggest the manner in which he achieved it: the sculptural dimensioning of his geometrical technique, the clash of his intersecting planes, and the intellectuality of his analytical approach:

Picasso
you give us Things
which
bulge:grunting lungs pumped full of sharp thick mind

you make us shrill
presents always
shut in the sumptuous screech of
simplicity

(out of the
black unbunged
Something gushes vaguely a squeak of planes
or

between squeals of
Nothing grabbed with circular shrieking tightness
solid screams whisper.)
Lumberman of The Distinct

your brain's
axe only chops hugest inherent
Trees of Ego,from
whose living and biggest

bodies lopped
of every
prettiness

you hew form truly[19]

The Cubist stimulus is also present in an item ironically entitled "Crepuscule," as if it were a quiet Impressionist painting. A prose-poem this time, it is a linguistic rendering of the delirious sensation of being swallowed in the rush-hour throng while surrounded by Wall Street sky scrapers. It begins in this way:

at the ferocious phenomenon of 5 o'clock i find myself gently decomposing in the mouth of New York.   Between its supple financial teeth deliriously sprouting from complacent gums,a morsel prettily wanders buoyed on the murderous saliva of industry.   the morsel is i.

Vast cheeks enclose me.

a gigantic uvula with imperceptible gesticulations threatens the tubular downward blackness occasionally from which detaching itself bumps clumsily into the throat A meticulous vulgarity:

a sodden fastidious normal explosion;a square murmur,a winsome flatulence—. . . .[20]

Although "Picasso" deals with concepts and "Crepuscule" is a descriptive poem, both are characteristic of Cummings' work during 1918 in their jarring juxtapositions. He called the effects of this interplay and conflict between words and their appropriate realms of meaning "the Rhythm of Sense." Each is as full of surprise as a Stravinsky score. And like Stravinsky, Cummings had difficulties being accepted by the public. The *Dial* editors would not touch the prose-poem. "Your crepuscular morsel which you forwarded through me," wrote Thayer from the New York office, "is altogether three or four hours too late in the obscurities of the evening to be perceptible to any of our bunch."[21]

Another prose-poem from this period and one which goes beyond description into incident is "i was sitting in McSorley's," about an evil apparition in a saloon, but its emphasis is still upon conveying experience. It is a remarkable piece in which Cummings managed to merge images of sight, sound, and smell while employing echoing patterns of vowel and consonant in a complex orchestration. For example, the following verse paragraph brings into conjunction the metallic lights of the bar equipment and glassware, the smell of beer and cigars, the sizzle of beer foam, the phrases and gestures of talkers at the bar, a strain of music, the mouth-noises of spitting, belching, and hiccoughing:

the Bar.tinking luscious jigs dint of ripe silver with warmlyish wet-flat splurging smells waltz the glush of squirting taps plus slush of foam knocked off and a faint piddle-of-drops she says I ploc spittle what the lands thaz me kid in no sir hopping sawdust you kiddo he's palping wreaths of badly Yep cigars who jim him why gluey grins topple together eyes pout gestures stickily point made glints squinting who's a wink bum-nothing and money fuzzily mouths

take big wobbly foot-steps every goggle cent of it get out ears drib-
bles soft right old feller belch the chap hic sum-more eh chuckles
skulch. . . .[22]

Cummings' method of preparation for a piece like this was to com-
pile extensive lists of words which have rhyme and consonance, like dint,
grin, point, glint, squint, and wink, or words which begin or end in a
common joining of similar consonant sounds, like piddle, spittle, topple,
wobble, dribble, and gobble.[23] He then consciously composed his poem
as a sound-painting. Another composition, this time a collage of urban
sounds interrupted continually by the word "Peace," was probably in-
spired by the hullaballo of the false armistice announcement. He called
it simply "Noise."[24]

Although these poems reflect Cummings' memory of New York City
and its melange of sound, he can also be aware of quieter sounds. "SNO/
a white idea" gives us the sound that snowflakes make as we:

> (hear little knives of flower
> stropping sof a.   Thick silence)
>
> blacktreesthink
>
> tiny,angels sharpen:themselves
>
> (on
>   air)[25]

For the first time here in "SNO" we have some experimental peculiari-
ties of punctuation. He explained later in a letter to Thayer "Note punc-
tuation exemplifying a theory of my soul that every 'word' *purely* consid-
ered implies its own punctuation."[26]

Another series of poems take their rise from the fact that Cummings
was in a state of sexual turmoil. After his sexual initiation in France and
after his situation of sexual freedom in New York, he found himself
cooped up in an isolated army camp where passes off the base were
available only once a month. Most of these poems in the Satyric style are
sonnets, as if Cummings unconsciously sought to curb their libidinous
vigor by imposing a strictness of form upon them. Much of their aesthetic
interest lies in the ironical clash between the traditions of the sonnet and
the coarseness of their subject matter. The pages of his Camp Devens
notebooks are filled with work sheets for such poems as "the bed is not
very big," "in making Marjorie god hurried," "if i should sleep with a

lady called death," and "life boosts herself rapidly at me."[27] Frequently too the pages are festooned with sketches of copulating couples. He would develop one of these sonnets by jotting down a few metaphorical phrases and then working them into a partially rhymed series of lines using some unifying motif. The following draft employs a number of military images:

> my deathly body's deadly Lady
> smooth-foolish,exquisitely tooled
> (becoming exactly pash Gladys grips
> with chuckles of supreme sex
> me;inviting my gorgeous bullet to vex
> the groove hugely intuitive.
> And the sharp ripples of her brain bite
> fondly into mine,as the slow give
> of hot flesh takes me in waves of craziest light....
> hello central,give me no man's land.[28]

This piece never went any farther but some of its phrasing and its linguistic ideas turn up in later sonnets.

One difficulty which troubles the success of many of the poems is Cummings' own uncertain attitude toward sex. Cummings' guilt about sex emerges in images of disgust that he visits upon sexual partners in these sonnets. Her kiss has "dirty colors," her body is a "trite worm," her "ugly nipples" are "squirming in pretty wrath," her hair resembles horse droppings ("a sufficient pillow shoveling/ her small manure-shaped head"). Sexual coupling is "the square crime of life," and sometimes will involve a "friendless dingy female frenzy." Despite cleverness of phrasing, material of this sort cannot sit well beside delicate images such as "upon the room's/ silence I will sew/ a nagging button of candlelight."[29] Thayer, who had more critical sense than Cummings, should have helped him with these aesthetic problems. But he only encouraged Cummings by enthusiastic responses. Thayer too like many of the middle-class young men of this time who had broken away from the puritanical attitudes of earlier decades had his own tensions and insecurities about sex, which he often expressed by a posture of cynicism.

One way of dealing with problems posed by this kind of subject matter is by joke or parody which will lighten or deflect any grossness. Work sheets for one of Cummings' best known sonnets in the Satyric style show that he had begun it as a sexual memory from France, and associated it with military imagery:

'y avait une fois . . . the slipshod mucous kiss
of her riant belly's fooling bore.[30]

When he reworked it he struck on an even more audacious phrasing:

O It's Nice To Get Up In,the slipshod mucous kiss
of her riant belly's fooling bore
—When The Sun Begins To(with a phrasing crease
of hot subliminal lips,as if a score
of youngest angels suddenly should stretch neat necks
just to see how always squirms
the skilful mystery of Hell)me suddenly

grips in chuckles of supreme sex.

In The Good Old Summer Time.

He was drawing upon lines and phrases from a comic song made popular
on the music hall stage by the rich Scottish burr of Harry Lauder:

Oh, it's nice to get up in the morning
When the sun is beginning to shine
And it's three or four or five o'clock
In the good old summer time.
But when the sky is murky
And it's cloudy overhead,
Oh, it's nice to get up in the morning
But it's nicer to stay in bed.

This device allowed him to play throughout the poem with a pattern of
allusion that refracted the sexual directness.

Many of his attempts to versify with sexual materials at this time are
less direct. The Parisian memory of Marie Louise Lallemand and her
friends which danced in his head became the poem "little ladies more"
with its images of beautiful or delicate attributes, "the ivory throat," "la
voix fragile," and the body like "une boîte a joujoux," and with its mix-
ture of street talk and prayers. Another, and this time a sonnet, "perhaps
it is to feel strike" uses the controlling metaphor of the fisherman and his
seeking through paths and woods to find the experience of a quiet natural
sport. The sonnet "my naked lady framed" makes the comparison be-
tween an artistic representation and a real-life presence and builds to-
ward its affirmation of life and love-making.[31] It is probably safe to say

that, given Cummings' temperament and his own special ways of creating, the important and deeply felt sexual experiences of his life provided the basis of his more delicate and more successful erotic poems. He did hold in memory at this time one very serious love relationship that will be described in the next chapter.

III

Cummings' attitude of grim fatalism about being in the army ceased abruptly as soon as the armistice was declared. If the war was over, he wanted to get out immediately, but the United States decision-makers, fearing to flood the labor market, allowed only a gradual release of the soldier population. Cummings had been willing during the national emergency to accept the lot of the guys-born-in-mangers, but he had "not the slightest intention," he protested, "of making the manger my hometown for Eternity; simply because that was not in the contract between The Powers and me."[32] But the weeks dragged on. There were still drills and marches, one of which was a long hike over glare ice. One day in December the officers forced two companies to have a snowball battle and Oscar Perry was smacked between the eyes with a hard one. The commander tried to cope with the unrest among the men by ceaseless training maneuvers. He gave a speech telling them that "we never know when we'll be needed."

Cummings had a special grievance because of a peculiar set of circumstances that befell his company. He had been assigned, after initial training, to the 73rd Infantry Division, Depot Brigade. One day early in the fall, a call had come for volunteers who would be sent to fighting units in Europe within two months. Cummings responded. He was attracted, probably, by the opportunity to see France again and he was eager to be done with the boredom of Camp Devens. He was assigned to the 12th Infantry Division. Now in December, all the soldiers in the Depot Brigade were being discharged, whereas those on duty with the 12th Division were considered "regulars" and were not being returned to civilian life. What is more, the 12th Division did not go overseas but was scheduled to continue training at Camp Devens for another four months. On top of all this, Cummings and others who were agitating for release and for exercise of their rights were put on K.P. with threats of its being permanent.

New York was much in his thoughts. Brown, whose poor dental condition kept him out of the army, wrote regularly, giving news of their friends and detailed reports on his own doings. One letter described a fight at the Roumanian restaurant:

There was a great row in the Roumanian Hall upstairs, so that everyone bellowed and roared except the fée with the powdered face, and nice hands, and myself. The new dancer who is smaller than my woman, and who does not look like the Goddess of Pigs when she plays the tambourine, was insulted by a very drunk man who was talking to Hassan. It was a tremendous argument about virginity, at least I suppose it was, and the dancer became so wrathy that she flung a chair and would have thrown another if the baboon hadn't held her. Then the witch came in and said to the dancer, "Let me speak to you." But the drunken man began bellowing again and the dancer tried to throw another chair. Finally all the musicians suddenly decided to leave. So they packed up their instruments and left. Ten minutes later the baboon returned lugging the canoun which he took out of its case. When he had finished all the musicians filed back, as if returning from a bar, and everything started once more.[33]

And on another occasion:

Eight drunken men at the Rue Rest. upstairs danced. And they put the ones who couldn't stand up in the middle where the rest could hold them up. But there was a sailor with very black hair, who could speak only a little English. He was tight. . . . and tossed a chair so that it cleaned two tables of glasses and bottles.
The baboon treated me to an anisette, asking how you were.[34]

Cummings longed to be back in the old haunts of carefree New York, roaming its streets whether in the shadow of the Singer Building (second in height to the Woolworth) or in the populous tangle near Washington Square. Yearnings of this sort, along with Brown's letters, led to his composing a sonnet of remembrance:

by god i want above fourteenth

fifth's deep purring biceps,the mystic screech
of Broadway,the trivial stink of rich

frail firm asinine life
            (i pant

for what's below. the singer. Wall. i want
the perpendicular lips the insane teeth
the vertical grin

            give me the Square in spring,
the little barbarous Greenwich perfumed fake

And most,the futile fooling labyrinth
where noisy colours stroll. . . . and the Baboon

sniggering insipidities while i sit,sipping
singular anisettes as   One opaque
big girl jiggles thickly hips to the kanoon

but Hassan chuckles seeing the Greeks breathe)[35]

On December 31, he wrote to Charles Anderson, a family friend in a government office in Washington and asked for advice. The information that Anderson sent him spurred him to apply for discharge on the grounds that his occupation was suffering because of his continued duty in the military service. The climax of his struggle to get out came when his captain, in the presence of the other officers, called him in to tell him that he was turning down the application and Cummings argued his case angrily. "After much mental fisticuffs, in which "sir" and "private" disappeared, he asked, 'Cummings, do you consider that you've got as good a right to apply as the other men who put in?' 'As far as dependency goes I am not qualified to say'—quoth I. 'But for the occupational part I consider that I have as good a right as anybody in this company.' I added that I was probably the most ill-fitted man to be here, and the most un-at-home. 'The army wasn't made to suit temperaments,' he remarked. I was shaking in every muscle at this time."[36]

What counted most for Cummings in the confrontation was a contract which he had made with Thayer to produce four pictures for a sum of $600. Payment was to be made upon delivery of all four but he had only completed three of them by the time the draft call came. His strong-willed arguing bolstered by his "superior information" from Anderson, won him his case. He was given his final physical examination on January 14 and discharged on January 17, 1919. He was still just Private Cummings and rather proud of the fact that he had never advanced to first class.

XII

Elaine

Then answer'd Lancelot, 'Fair she was, my King,
Pure, as you ever wish your knights to be.
To doubt her fairness were to want an eye,
To doubt her pureness were to want a heart—
Yea, to be loved, if what is worthy love
Could bind him, but free love will not be bound.'

ALFRED TENNYSON

Cummings' life as a poet and a private in the United States Army had an underside that we have been neglecting and it is time to examine it. As long ago as spring 1918, he had fallen in love with Elaine Thayer. Their developing love affair became, then, part of a strange triangular relationship. Estlin and Elaine never engaged in any deceit about it with Scofield Thayer, and all three were, so Cummings maintained, "now and always . . . the best of friends."[1] This reaching out for happiness in what seemed a very civilized and accommodating way led eventually to the marriage of Estlin and Elaine, to extraordinary complications about their child Nancy, to some terrible grief and stress, and to some searing psychic damage for Cummings and, it seems probable, for others as well.[2]

A look into the past will be helpful if we are to bring any understanding to this distressing human entanglement. Elaine Eliot Orr was the second daughter of Caroline Gale and Alexander Orr, a wealthy owner of paper mills in Troy, New York. She was born April 9, 1896 and grew up with her sisters, Constance and Alexis, in a household of mercantile grandeur, like one of Henry James's American heroines. Her life was

visited early by grief: she lost her father when she was eight years old and
her mother a few years later. An uncle, Edward Gale, became the guard-
ian of the three orphaned children. Elaine was educated in Troy and at
the Westover School in Middlebury, Connecticut. In 1911 she transferred
to Miss Bennett's School, Millbrook, N.Y., a finishing school for the
daughters of notable families, established in a turreted English Tudor
manor amidst the hills of Duchess County. Many of the girls at Miss
Bennett's owned their own horses, which were cared for in a "Riding
Center" that contained fifty-two box stalls and a number of show rings,
where Elaine won several ribbons in "equitation." Tea was served for-
mally every afternoon. Here Elaine received instruction in social graces
and course work that amounted to a junior college education. Among
other subjects she studied French and music and she took an intense
interest in dramatics. In 1916 the school literary magazine, the *Hexagon*
printed her one-act play "The Things That Are and the Things That
Were," a strange piece set in a European Shrine of Our Lady to which
the troubled come and pray. It involved a chivalrous soldier, captured for
desertion, who falsely confesses to a murder he did not commit in order
to save the life of a young girl who had accidentally shot an aggressor.[3]

In 1915 Elaine met Scofield Thayer while on a European summer
holiday. She was by that time a demure, graceful, soft-voiced young lady,
chic in dress and perfect in coiffure, with delicate brown hair, pale
cheeks, and wide luminous eyes. Thayer fell in love with her immedi-
ately. When they were married the following June, Elaine was scarcely
twenty years old.

As we have seen, Estlin Cummings was introduced to this beautiful
creature in spring 1916 shortly before her marriage. He paid her his first
homage by sending her a drawing of an elephant. He was so charmed by
her flowerlike fragility that he rejoiced in Thayer's union with a girl who
"would make any man faint with happiness." Cummings' feeling gave
energy to the "Epithalamion" that he wrote for their wedding, and it
even seemed to grow into a state of his being in love with both of them.
He sent the following sonnet to them during their honeymoon trip to
California:

S.T.

O friend, who hast attained thyself in her,
Thy wife, the almost woman whose tresses are
The stranger part of sunlight, in the far
Nearness of whose frail eyes instantly stir
Unchristian perfumes more remote than myrrh,

Whose smiling is the swiftly singular
Adventure of one inadvertent star,
(With angels previously a loiterer,)

Friend, who dost thy unfearing soul pervert
From perfection of its constancy
To that unspeakable fellowship of Art—
Receive the complete pardon of my heart,
Who dost thy friend a little while desert
For the sensation of eternity.[4]

The Thayers were enchanted. "The poem is really corking," Scofield replied from Santa Barbara, "and Elaine and I thank you from the bottom of our heart. It is not to have lived in vain, thus to have occasioned beauty. 'Whose smiling is the swiftly singular adventure of one inadvertent star (With angels previously a loiterer)' is completely worthy of that smile which is now always with me."[5] They exchanged letters and snapshots during this period and Scofield even sent Cummings a life-sized photograph of himself.

The Thayers did not return to New York until October 1917, but during that fifteen months something withering had happened to their relationship. Scofield appeared to have lost interest in Elaine, and under his hard satirical manner she had shrunk into an accommodating player of the wife and hostess role. Their living arrangements showed it plainly. On their return Scofield reoccupied his former apartment in the Benedict, a luxurious apartment building at 80 Washington Square East reserved for bachelors only, and he hired a valet. Elaine "just to be neighborly" (Scofield's blithe phrasing) moved into a pleasant tree-shaded first-floor apartment at 3 Washington Square North, which Scofield had decorated with rich draperies and brocaded furniture. He bought her a piano and hoped to help her to fulfill her desire of going on the stage. As for their marriage, he declared that love should be free and that a mere social institution should not interfere with sexual adventure. He also wanted more time alone so that he could do some writing.

For Greenwich Village the arrangement was not unusual. Both before and after the war the middle-class young people who gravitated there began to live the emancipated Bohemian life with all the sexual freedom and equality and whatever living arrangements such a life allowed or demanded.[6] Yet in Thayer's case it does seem surprising, for he had not married a career woman or an assertive feminist; he had won a wife whom some people viewed as a Gibson Girl and others as a fairy princess. As time went on, Elaine found herself married not just

Elaine and Scofield Thayer, summer 1916. HOUGHTON LIBRARY

to Thayer but to Thayer's friends. Beginning in 1918 her apartment be-
came a social center for their gathering, especially at tea time. "She was
the Blessed Damozel," John Dos Passos remembered, "the fair, the lov-
able, the lily maid of Astolat. To romantic youth, she seemed like a
poet's dream. Those of us who weren't in love with Cummings were in
love with Elaine."[7]

Dos Passos' remark allows us to pause for a moment to consider the
sexual coloration of the *Harvard Monthly* group and the friends they had
gathered around them in New York and in the offices of the *Dial*. Only
one of them, Stewart Mitchell, was an overt homosexual. Nevertheless,
an innocent homoeroticism marked their devotion to each other: their
intense loyalty when a friend was in need, their eager promotion of a
friend's artistic career, and their genuine enjoyment of each other's
company. Their heterosexual drives were strong but they seemed still
to be outgrowing a sexual immaturity brought about, to a great extent,
by the repressions of the American home and church and by the ethos
of the boy's school and men's college, where the friendship of young
fellows together is the basis of life and any attention to women is a
secondary matter, even a diversion. Elaine provided a sisterly presence
for these young men but she was beginning to feel lonely in her mar-
riage.

When Thayer became associated with the Chicago *Dial* in 1918, he
was out of town a great deal and Cummings began to spend more and
more time with Elaine. One of her letters containing a reminiscence
reflects some of the ways in which Cummings tried to keep her cheered
up. "I remember how you used to come to 3 [Washington Square] insist-
ing that I go dancing or on parties with you & B. & you would stay until
you had persuaded me to join you. Always I was the one who did not
want to walk in the evenings or go to a restaurant but prefered to stay
at 3 alone. If you couldn't get me out you had everybody at 3 & raised cain
till all hours."[8] In May, Thayer seems even to have sent Cummings a
check to cover some of the cost of entertaining Elaine. One paragraph of
a letter reads: "For the time, energy, and other things you have expended
upon Elaine, I think it only right you should have some reimbursement.
However, I will add that while she's a nice kid I do sometimes find her
a bit expensive."[9] Ironically this letter was written about the time that
Elaine's relationship with Cummings had begun to be more intimate.
Since Elaine was lonely and in need of cherishing, it is scarcely surprising
that one night when chance found them in her bedroom at 3 Washington
Square, she gave him such a look of invitation that he could not believe
what was happening. "She couldn't mean me! that I would Desire her—
Because she is Another's and Belongs to Another Person," spoke the

voice of social inhibition. He did not touch her. He turned and walked out.

Besides the attitudes toward adultery and loyalty that Cummings had been brought up with, there were other intimidations. In spite of his attraction to Elaine, he still felt somewhat in awe of the refinements that her wealth and social training had created. Her taste in dress, her perfume, her grooming, her ease in the presence of luxury, her handling of servants in public places, her ability to make any man she spoke with think he was the most important person in the room—all this social presence was far removed from the middle-class plain living and high thinking of his Cambridge upbringing and even farther removed from the easy frank sexuality of the lower-class women, both French and American, with whom he had had relations before. Thus in this affair he was not an aggressor and the full relationship with Elaine developed very slowly. He was gallant, flattering, solicitous, tender, caring—abject in his idealization of her beauty and her doll-like vulnerability. After Thayer's coldness and sharp-tongued witticisms this kind of chivalry was what Elaine needed. There followed a long period of hesitant, gentle caresses and mutual sexual restraint until Elaine herself had to initiate their union.

But, of course, an important reason for Cummings' unassertiveness had been his respect for Thayer's position. The conflict between his love for a beautiful woman and his loyalty to a friend and patron had been an ordeal for him, but now he solved his problem in a literary way. His imagination imposed the pattern of medieval courtly love upon it. He thought of himself as a Lancelot loving a Guinivere (the fact that she was an Elaine blended with no difficulty), who was married to his liege lord, King Arthur. After he was drafted and stationed in an army camp, his emotional fire intensified and he became even more completely the languishing courtly lover. He sloughed off some of his sexual energy, as we have seen, writing poems about prostitutes and lustful couplings. But that energy was also being sublimated into tender love sonnets inspired by Elaine. During this period he wrote such pieces for her as "when you went away it was morning," "i have found what you are like," "perhaps it is to feel strike," "my love is building a building," and others which became part of his *Tulips & Chimneys* manuscript.[10] It was for Elaine that he composed the finest erotic poem he ever wrote:

> i like my body when it is with your
> body.   It is so quite new a thing.
> Muscles better and nerves more.
> i like your body.   i like what it does,

> i like its hows.   i like to feel the spine
> of your body and its bones,and the trembling
> -firm-smooth ness and which i will
> again and again and again
> kiss,   i like kissing this and that of you,
> i like,slowly stroking the,shocking fuzz
> of your electric fur,and what-is-it comes
> over parting flesh.... And eyes big love-crumbs
>
> and possibly i like the thrill
>
> of under me you so quite new

These were the products of restless, sometimes ferocious longing, such as the following fragment of a sonnet suggests:

> tonight i am going to have a big bounding
> panther shaped dream only of you
> leap,creasing the moist high ferns of
> my brain:and the bright confounding
> eyes of this dream,and the sly
> brutish paw-poems of him making love-
> shaped noises in the sharp jungles of my
> blood....)   Me musically shall pursue
> into dawn[11]

Scofield Thayer appeared to treat the whole situation with sophisticated cooperation, since he said that people should be as free in their sexual pursuits as in any other area of expression and action. He himself was interested in seeking out other women. But, above all, he took the position that Cummings was his friend, who was only following the course that proximity and circumstances had fostered. Beyond this, he even arranged for Cummings to see Elaine when he obtained a weekend leave from Camp Devens, as a surviving note to Cummings makes clear: "Your apocryphal letter received. That we may understand each other more adequately, can you make your appointment with E. E. [i.e. his wife, Elaine Eliot Thayer] for New York instead of Boston? Should you do so I shall study well my exits and entrances. I have written E. E. of the possibility. Wire her if you can and when you can. If you can get to Boston but not N. Y., entrust all to her ear. She can (on occasion) be faithful."[12]

The cynical joke about faithfulness indicates that beneath the façade of sophistication lay an awareness of something that Thayer felt uneasy about. Cummings, in spite of his self-justification in the role of chivalrous rescuer, felt some guilt and confusion about the affair too. It may have revealed itself when he wrote poems dwelling upon sexual ugliness and squalor. But one excellent poem emerged from his sense of guilt, once again taking form from a literary source associated with courtly love, the story of Paolo and Francesca. Their story, one much like that of Lancelot and Guinivere, is most familiar to readers in Dante's version of it in the *Inferno*. Dante shows them as adulterous lovers who will spend eternity together but who must do so in the second circle of Hell. Cummings' sonnet veers away from the pathos that Dante gave to this episode. Its spirit is twentieth-century jauntiness: the cosmic and religious references are only a stage setting for his oblique statement of a willingness to give all for love:

> chérie
>   the very,picturesque,last Day
> (when all the clocks have lost their jobs and god
> sits up quickly to judge the Big Sinners)
> he will have something large and fluffy to say
> to me.   All the pale grumbling wings
>
> of his greater angels will cease:as that Curse
>
> bounds neat-ly from the angry wad
>
> of his forehead(then fiends with the pitchforkthings
> will catch and toss me lovingly to
> and fro.   Last,should you look,you
> 'll find me prone upon a greatest flame,
>
> which seethes in a beautiful way
> upward;with someone by the name
> of Paolo passing the time of day.[13]

Although he sent a copy to Elaine, he never published the poem. Did he think, in spite of its light tone, that it was too clearly a reflection of an old-fashioned attitude toward adultery?

It seems evident from Brown's letters to Cummings that Elaine was once again lonely after Cummings had departed for Camp Devens, because he writes frequently of having dinner with her or spending an evening with her:

I saw Elaine & S. Monday night. Scofield said it was a great day for liberalism. (T.[heodore] R.[oosevelt] having passed on)[14]. . . .

At eleven I rose to leave, for I thought Scofield was weary. But he rose too, and as we started out Elaine called me back & wanted to know how you were.

It seems (I don't remember whether I vowed silence or not) that she is rather hurt because you wrote "premeditated?" in a letter referring to colors.[15] I said you probably didn't mean it, and she said you probably didn't either. But life is Probable as U know.

We discussed Bessie [Brown's and Cummings' dog] & her whorey brood, Elaine expressing a desire to have one of the puppies. But I told her that if the offspring were anything like their mother her carpet would be kapoot in a few hours. She wishes to have a dog to lead about on a string, but unless she can have someone house break the beast I do not see how she can manage it. I should like to see S's valet taking the dog out to piss.

Elaine played some French songs for me. Au clair de la lune. Veilles Chansons pour les Petit Enfants.

Finally being unusually sober I left at an early hour & wandered home to my room lighting two candles & reading De Rerum Natura until my atoms began to disintegrate.[16]

None of Cummings' letters to Elaine from this period survive, but a draft of a letter is scribbled into a notebook. It tells us something about their relationship and, more importantly, reveals something about a self that Cummings did not openly show to others—a self which appears in certain poems but gets lost in the thicket of other selves which peep out of the multitude of his creations. This particular self is a little boy who is wistful, powerless, full of yearning, who indulges in rituals to make wishes come true. He is related to Charlie Chaplin's little tramp gazing shyly, soulfully out of the corners of his eyes at his secret beloved. And to the victimized puppet Petrouchka. And to Ignatz mouse in the Krazy Kat comic strip. And to Jack Shargel smelling the rose. In the role that Cummings adopts in this letter to someone he loved, he reveals the self represented by the lower-case i:

Elaine—
 i come in to the woods to write you, for this Sunday didn't rain, and first i draw a picture (that might be you and me—somehow) Then i don't know; but sud-den-ly. . . . and afterwards i came all-up with my Mouth full of moss.
 i had tried queer & little tricks to make your letter Kum (one was stepping-high every day in a certain place between the piano-corner & the board where the superiors sit and gurgle their three times swill)
 and it never Kam; but till one day—and that one day they moved away

the piano! that day i'd had kept all in my overcoat pocket a letter to Watson. So i sed, if the letter i want Kumz, i won't post this one to him) Then it Kam, and i laughed and did.

it colours here, where i lie, & things of reds & chromes & 5 eyes rattle & swish over me into my ears, my eyes. they call it—l'automne.

i told Watson i'd seen you when i did, just because i liked his-hair-over-his-eyes, and he was unhappy for me, and because i like him. he said he was to be at 6 [Washington Square]. i climbed on the radiator & sat there & he drove till a Mrs. Colonel was afraid of her reputation, so i got in back again, & i liked that packard. (It was deep and noiseless. And Watson drove because i drove a little & punctured a tire immediately.) and someway i swallowed Things i never thought i'd tasted before. (they were so Good) in a little pink room, too. but he would take only one. and another woman gave me hers, so i felt creepyish & pleasant like walking to W. Sq. North after zubaphone (keeping somebody perpendicular beside me [end of page][17]

In his dealing with society, its institutions and organizations, Cummings had matured, but in his emotional life he still felt like a little boy, an identity role which I will call the *petit garçon*.

In some respects, Elaine too seemed something of a little girl. Only one of Elaine's letters between 1916 and 1923 remains. It was written to Cummings while he was at Camp Devens. A representative passage from it has some of the *petite fille* quality:

W.[atson] & H.[ildegarde] left now having had tea. It rains very much. And W. said he liked the Sq. better than before and H. said its just like London, don't you think? And Berget was out so I got tea & was still scared of the upper part of my stove so couldn't make toast. . . .

Some things have made me very sorry—& gee I try not to speak to you of anything I hope. Maybe tomorrow I shall get a letter from you saying you won't be in N.Y. on fur low [.] I heard W & Sco talking over the telephone & it was about you & as I was on W's end I heard almost nothing except that it was about you & I thought maybe they had heard you weren't going to get fur low or something. But I couldn't ask W & may not see Sco till hours and hours.[18]

Estlin and Elaine, as their language in letters to each other defines them, were babes in the woods. The wood had been entered and darkness would soon begin to fall.

After Cummings was discharged from the army in January, 1919, he and Elaine were able to resume their association for a temporary period of happiness, but it turned into consternation when in May or June Elaine discovered she was pregnant. For the first time some of the moral perplexities of the Thayer-Cummings arrangement had to be faced. All three of them knew that it was Cummings' child. What should be done? It was too late for a divorce, and besides, Cummings was not emotionally ready for marriage or financially able to take on the cares of family life. Even if he could have supported a wife and child, Elaine herself may not have been sure of what she wanted. Thayer urged a convenient solution to the problem, an abortion, and Cummings agreed.[19] Elaine balked at an operation, so they consulted a friend who was just then finishing his medical studies, for advice about other measures. The friend very reluctantly recommended some medication that might bring about a miscarriage. But it did not work. Elaine's pregnancy continued unimpeded.

By midsummer, the Thayers were at Edgartown with Scofield's mother at the family cottage. Thayer was prepared to have the child as his own; Cummings stayed on in New York daubing paint on his canvases. In mid-July Cummings was invited to Edgartown and everything seemed much the same—summer beach sports, riding about in Elaine's new automobile, an "Owen Magnetic." Elaine, scarcely showing her pregnancy, looked breath-takingly beautiful. When Cummings went up to Silver Lake in August, he spent one afternoon on the lakeshore writing the longest poem he ever composed in his life, his tribute to Elaine, "Puella Mea," in which he declared that she surpassed the loveliness of all the great beauties of legend and literature.[20] Yet throughout the poem there hovered a dark awareness—it took the form of a Keatsian theme that beauty must die:

> Eater of all things lovely—Time!
> upon whose watering lips the world
> poises a moment(futile,proud,
> a costly morsel of sweet tears)
> gesticulates,and disappears—
> of all dainties which do crowd
> gaily upon oblivion
> sweeter than any there is one . . .

But Elaine seemed not to be his puella. The pregnancy drew the Thayers closer together and created a distance between Estlin and Elaine. He stayed at Silver Lake and, later, in the fall did not devote much time to her but spent most of his evenings drinking with Brown. As December approached, poor Elaine fell back on the attentions of her sister, Constance, for her two men seemed not to care about her. Cummings stayed away, and Thayer had another baby, the *Dial* magazine, to absorb his life, for he and Watson had recently purchased it and taken editorial control.

The child was born December 20, 1919. There is almost no information available which records any details or any feelings about the new baby girl. There is only one note among Cummings' papers about Elaine's confinement, "She is estranged from me Thayer takes care of her —hospital." His letters right up to December 19 are full of other concerns —about his manuscript-book of poems, about some line drawings for the *Dial*, about the galleys for the January 1920 issue which Mitchell misplaced. Among the Cummings papers there is one note from Thayer dated December 21, 1919. It probably accompanied a check for some of Cummings' contributions to the *Dial*, but it may have been one of Thayer's tough-minded jokes. It says only "For value received S.T."[21]

Years later Brown recalled a few details of the occasion: "I was with Cummings in New York when Nancy was born. As we were going out to dinner, or perhaps returning, Cummings made a phone call and returned to say that Elaine had given birth to a girl and that 'Thayer was very pleased.' I had more than a strong suspicion that Cummings knew he himself was the father but from his remark I gathered that I was to refer to the girl as Thayer's."[22]

Nothing was ready for the baby at 3 Washington Square. There was no layette: she had to wear doll's clothes and shoes. Her crib was a bureau drawer. We get only one glimpse of her in the earliest weeks and of Cummings' own confession of surprised pleasure in her appearance. In a letter to his sister Elizabeth, February 3, 1920, he reported, "Elaine Thayer's daughter looks just like a doll—she has ever so much very long hair which Mrs. Thayer has Dutch-cut and the result is extremely becoming. I never knew how much nicer a baby could be with hair."[23]

Elaine's child was eventually named Nancy. She was not christened. Cummings in a letter to his mother May 22, 1920, mentions that the "little Elaine" just escaped baptism on the occasion of that ceremony for Michael, the new baby boy of Sibley and Hildegarde Watson. In early 1920 there continued to be some distance between him and Elaine. Elaine was very occupied with her new motherhood, her sister was in and out frequently, she had a nursemaid living in the apartment as well as her own French maid. Perhaps Cummings was awed and perplexed about the situation: he was the father of a child he could not acknowledge. At any rate, he seemed to feel no ties; and he and Brown began to consider plans to take jobs aboard a ship bound for faraway places.

In the summer Thayer made a gesture of reunion, writing to Cummings at Silver Lake that his wife was going to visit near Boston and suggested that Cummings come down to see them. In October, Cummings, still at Silver Lake and hard at work on his narrative of La Ferté-Macé, wrote to Mitchell, "Have you seen Elaine lately? I hear from her that everyone is having a cold, & she escaped pneumonia—as she says

Elaine in front of her apartment at 3 Washington Square, winter 1920, just after Nancy was born. COURTESY NANCY T. ANDREWS

'softly.' I should like to see her kid. Give her & *her* my love when you see her, please.[24] Some renewal of the association had taken place though he apparently took little interest in the baby. In the winter, Cummings was once again spending evenings with Elaine and their love affair rekindled. During this time and for the next few years while their association lasted, Cummings remained faithful to Elaine, despite many sexual opportunities offered to him by other women. He was, in Brown's words, "a one-woman man."[25]

XIII

Some Firsts

A young man of twenty-five is the Lord of Life. . . . at the very least
he wants to be the greatest fighter in the world, which would take
courage and not cunning; and at the very most he wants to be the
greatest poet, the greatest writer, the greatest composer, or the great-
est leader in the world—and he wants to paint instead of own the
greatest painting in the world.

THOMAS WOLFE

After his discharge from the army in January 1919, Cummings spent the
next two-and-a-half years in New York and despite the complications of
his private life, this was the period during which his career as both poet
and painter was publicly launched and during which he wrote his first
book-length work in prose. Since he had been limited to drawing and
sketching during the months at Camp Devens, he turned his full ener-
gies to painting as soon as he returned to New York. Even back in
December he had let his parents know that painting supplies would be
welcome as Christmas gifts: canvas, stretchers, oil paints—he supplied a
long list.

Mid-February found Cummings and Brown settled in a large studio
on the fourth floor at 9 West 14th Street. It was a climb of 74 stairs to a
huge one-room studio with no running water. They descended to the
floor below for toilet and washing needs and hauled buckets of water up
the stairs for cooking and dishwashing. There was no heat but they had
a gas cooking stove and a small fireplace in which they burned cannel
coal. Cummings had very few possessions besides his clothes and painting

equipment. But Brown, who was once again enrolled at Columbia, had a great many books on the premises and friends soon supplied a scattering of furniture.

Cummings worked at his painting earnestly, including a sign for the Italian restaurant of his friend "Joe," who discussed Dante with him every time he and Brown came in for dinner. He had completed three drawings, nudes, for Thayer's newly decorated "black room" in his bachelor apartment. Thayer, ever the patron, also hung Cummings' paintings and tried to interest Walter Pach and Leo Stein in making a purchase.[1] For one work, Cummings tried to describe the experience of coming into being that he hoped it would communicate:

This is not the painting of forces. It is Force the painter Himself. Or—not painting but Forcing, if the verb be felt as intransitive. It is the Selfing of things. You have doubtless had the common experience of sitting in a dusk-nibbled room, say Elaine's, the probable room-full-of-furniture is not disintegrating; there is integrating delicately a cubic pulp. The nouns are gone, the adjectives have fainted, an adverbial stress seizes (i am still talking about the room). There is what we mistakenly call a moment, a point Now, a Verb = Is. Distinctness. or: this cubic pulp SELFS.[2]

But he was tackling new compositional problems now, following the futurist aim to get motion into his cubist work. He had asked his father to ship some of his old paintings down from Cambridge and he was "reorganizing" one called "Coney Island Side Show." The stimulus perhaps was his meeting Joseph Stella, the American Futurist, whose best known works featured the whirling activity of amusement parks or the graceful arcs of the Brooklyn Bridge.[3]

He was planning to enter two works in the spring show of the New York Society of Independent Artists, a happily democratic organization open to anyone who paid the six dollars annual dues. The Society had been established in 1917 by William Glackens, Charles Prendergast, and Walter Pach. Among its directors were a number of painters whom we think of now as early American moderns, George Bellows, Marcel Duchamp (he had moved to New York), John Marin, Man Ray, and Joseph Stella. Every year the Society sponsored an exhibition to which members were allowed to send two paintings. They guaranteed the exhibitors "that whatever they send will be hung and all will have equal opportunity." Their motto was "No jury, no prizes."[4] The art critics of the day still displayed a good deal of hostility toward "extravagant modernism," and the Independent Show each spring was one of the chief battlegrounds. Cummings was ready to join the contest in 1919 with two abstract works. One entitled "Sound" "looks like a lot of circles going on a bat," he told his mother, the other called "Noise," "is more swimming-ish."[5]

The show was held in the roof gallery of the old Waldorf-Astoria Hotel from March 28 to April 14 just about a month before Elaine discovered she was pregnant. Over a thousand works were on display placed in alphabetical order according to the artist's name, and opening night brought a crush of over two thousand visitors. Cummings relished every aspect of his first exhibition: the hubbub of the viewers, the exchange of congratulation among friends, the appearance of the reviews (his name was not mentioned), the continuing return to the gallery with Elaine, Nagel, and Brown to digest the variety of the work on display and to note which pictures were sold. His excitement reached its peak when Lachaise reported to him that Albert Gleizes, one of the high priests of the Cubist movement, "was TAKEN OUT OF HIS FEET" by the two Cummings paintings. After the exhibition closed, he was nominated (although he was not elected) to be one of the twenty directors of the next year's showing.[6] Later in the spring he entered another exhibition at the Penguin Gallery. He bubbled with suppressed glee when Horace Brodsky, the man who supervised the arrangements, asked "Which side is up?" as Cummings brought in "Sound Number 2."[7]

Edward Cummings was elated by the news that Estlin sent along. "My paternal pride is gratified by the appreciation which your work is receiving. I am glad things are going well. Your opinion of the human race ought to improve proportionately." He went on to offer Estlin money anytime he was in need and placed a standing offer for a painting "at the regular exhibition price." He urged him to come home any time "at my expense" and to come up and take over one of the cottages at Silver Lake during the summer (besides Abenaki, Edward owned two other places on the lake).[8]

This letter was characteristic of him both in his generosity of spirit and in his continuing desire to share more fully in his son's life. The previous year when Estlin had sent his mock sermon to him and counseled him to "worship the . . . billiken of Silence,"[9] he later added his hope that "D.D." had not been too "fachéd" [angered] by his forthright utterances. Edward Cummings had been very hurt but he displayed his usual tolerant good nature in a long reply to his son, assuring him that he was not angered by the

> "Fourth of July Declaration of Independence"—as you so properly style the sonorous paragraph conveying the impression that you intend to exercise

your inalienable right to do as you d.p. with what you regard as your *own* —and no questions answered! No matter how civil or innocent or customary such questions may be in the everyday business relations of normal human beings. A word to the wise! *Verbum sap!* and I am *Saphead* enough to read the D. P. declaration without getting too much *fâché.* I am glad to have you recognize the provocation, however. . . . Besides, I feel that under the laws of heredity I have a certain responsibility for your Romanesque traits, as well as for your Spartan virtues! I do have that feeling of gratitude towards you, which has been aptly described as a *lively sense of favors yet to come.* For I confidently expect to be gratefully remembered by the world as the *Father of my Son! Don't forget that*—even if your inalienable right to make a fool of yourself now and then is not recognized so fully and cheerfully as you think it should be. . . .

Incidentally, referring for a last time to what you call your declaration of independence, it may interest you to know that you are, so far as I know, the only member of our family who believes in the inalienable right to do as he likes with his "own"—and no questions answered! The partnership which I crave so earnestly & affectionately is based on the opposite assumption—that everything is *ours,* nothing *mine.* You remember perhaps my favorite story of the old (Russian) woman in *Hell,* who would have got out & brought all the other damned out with her—if she *had said ours* and not mine! Well, I will tell it to you another time! The point is that there is a Hell of a difference between the *mine* and *our* theories of life![10]

Over the months, letters from Edward Cummings continued to make offers of one kind or another, to buy pictures, to frame pictures, to buy clothes for Estlin—even to send twenty-five dollars to Harvard in his name when the alumni association sought contributions. Estlin invariably refused the offers, for he was wisely aware of his father's propensities for interference and he had long known that "every gift is a swop."[11] Most of the time his refusals were cheery, as in the simple plea to "let me go my own way in my flannel shirt and my ideas."[12] At other times, they were sandwiched in among sharp criticisms of his father's remarks about politics and foreign affairs.

This whole area provided another ground of contention between father and son. Edward Cummings upheld the idealism of Wilson and supported the U. S. policy of opposition to the Bolshevik supremacy in Russia, and his letters would usually contain a sentence or two on the current international situation. Estlin and his friends were Socialist in their sympathies; even the wealthy Scofield Thayer had once voted a Socialist ticket. They deplored the red-baiting of the postwar years, especially the activities of Attorney General A. Mitchell Palmer, who arbitrarily ordered the arrests of radical agitators. Estlin's letters to both parents during 1919 strongly supported the Soviets and he urged them to read articles in the *Nation* or books like John Reed's *Ten Days That Shook the World.* His letters occasionally contained clippings of news stories or editorials which would support his position. During the Civil War in Russia Estlin greeted the defeats of Admiral Kolchak's White Russians with scornful satisfaction. History seemed to vindicate his disillusion-ment with the capitalist countries. When the Versailles Peace Conference ignored the most important of Wilson's Fourteen Points, Cummings gave a snort of cynical expectation. He was also an eyewitness to one part of the May Day riots of 1919 in New York when the U. S. soldiers and sailors disrupted the May Day meetings of Socialists and trade union groups and destroyed the new offices of the Socialist daily newspaper, the *Call,* at 112 Fourth Avenue. "My faith in humanity, as you call it," he reported, "was somewhat battered by the kaki (khaki?) clad hoodlums of our well known Uncle and their lightsome badinage on May Day. I witnessed one scene my self—the attack on The People's House which is just a block up [7 E. 15th St.]. The helpless and worsethanhelpless, if not conniving, gen-darmes did, however, nobly redeem themselves that night—a spectacle of interest which Nagle and I attended at Madison Square Garden—i.e. prevented uniforms from entering to attack the Mooney Protest meeting. The mounted police rode again and again at the inspired naval and army patriots. . . . I suppose that you know that one woman is blind and many people injured from the attack on The Call office, May 1."[13] As for a contribution to Harvard, he told his father, he would prefer to contribute to the Soviets.[14] Exchanges of this sort continued over the next couple of years.

Estlin spent the summer of 1919 at Silver Lake painting, with his family, taking time out in mid-July to visit Thayer and the expectant Elaine on Martha's Vineyard. After he returned to New York in the fall, he began to give some attention to his poetry. Since no magazines had accepted any of his poems for publication, he decided now to try book publishers. After all, Lawrence Gomme had come through handsomely for the eight Harvard poets. Estlin began to assemble a book-length manuscript of the work he most wanted to see in print. If no publisher would take it, at least he would have his work in readable form and he could pass the manuscript around among friends as the Elizabethan poets used to do. The title he chose was *Tulips & Chimneys,* an example of the disparate pairs of words that he and Brown enjoyed putting together: "lilacs and monkeywrenches," "creeds and syringes," "hangmen and tea kettles," and so on.[15] He was determined to keep the ampersand in his title and not allow it to be written out as a word.

II

Thayer and Watson had been able to purchase the stock of the *Dial* because Martyn Johnson had faced increasing financial difficulties as owner and publisher of the magazine. They saw an opportunity to take over a periodical that had the general respect of the public and to drop its social emphasis and turn it into an international magazine of the arts. Thayer became the editor-in-chief and Watson became the publisher.[16] As Elaine prepared to give birth in December, Thayer and Watson began drawing in former members of the *Harvard Monthly* staff to prepare the *Dial*'s first issue for January 1920. Stewart Mitchell, who had come to New York in the fall, was named managing editor. Cummings set to work to produce four line-drawings. He also turned over his *Tulips & Chimneys* manuscripts to Thayer "and bade him allez-y" to choose whatever poems he wished to publish. Thayer proved almost as wary as Martyn Johnson, at first; nor did he select his "favorites," "Kitty" and "The Grape Vine Lady," for the January number. At length, he picked out some less startling but still characteristic Cummings pieces.

When the new *Dial* went on sale during the Christmas season (just at the time Nancy was born), it contained Cummings' first publications in his new style, seven poems, including "little tree," a Christmas poem for children; "Buffalo Bill's"; "when god lets my body be"; "O Distinct," a cubist love song in which, among other things, "the square virtues of oblong sins" dance; and "when life is quite through with" a poem about endings, with the delicately ironic handling of a Wordsworthian Lucy motif:

> when all's done and said,and
> under the grass
> lies her head
> by oaks and roses
> deliberated.)

Sibley Watson's mother went into a righteous-Christian fit over the expletive "Jesus" in "Buffalo Bill's," perhaps the common reaction of the average American reader of the time. But the editors were making clear just what kind of readers they were addressing. In the April issue they stated flatly: "The Dial . . . cannot be everything to everybody. It is non-political and has no message for the millions." Cummings' four line-drawings were an example of the unconventionality of the *Dial*'s approach. Art in America did not usually include a representation of Jack Shargel, hand on derby, with coattails flying, nor did it stoop to include

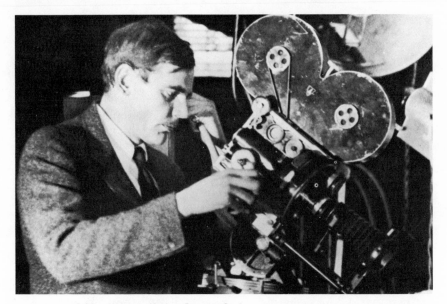

Sibley Watson filming Lot in Sodom. COURTESY J. S. WATSON, JR.

women dancers with firmly planted legs doing the shimmy.

The following month Cummings made a new kind of contribution to the *Dial,* an essay in art criticism entitled "Gaston Lachaise." The piece does not say anything critically significant about Lachaise but it has a special importance because this was the first time Cummings put into print any aspects of his theory of romantic individualism. Even the language reflects the values that Cummings had begun to articulate at Camp Devens. As he develops his appraisal of Lachaise and his work, the "good" words that appear are "original," "intense," and "naïve"; the bad words are "secondhand," "superficial," and "self-conscious." Beyond this, Cummings employs a metaphorical scheme using grammatical terms in order to communicate his notion of good art. A good artist will produce "verbs"—that is, those representations that are "alive," that have vigor and power; a poor artist will produce works which are "nouns" (indeed, "soggy nouns")—that is, those representations that are "dead," that turn us into unfeeling spectators. Further, he sees Lachaise's work as having "integrated simplicity" and he places him in the good company of "the child who has not yet inherited the centuries and the savage whose identity with his environment has not yet become a prey to civilization." In order to respond fully to the work of such artists one must achieve "the negation of thinking" and reach "the child's vision."[17]

Cummings had worked very hard to produce his essay, using enough paper "to fill a ragman's contract."[18] Lachaise was delighted. When consulted about whether some of the slurs on his sculptor-employer, Paul Manship, might get him into trouble, Lachaise said, "Print it. It's troo."[19]

Since Cummings was moving to romantic extremes in his literary outlook, it is no wonder that he had difficulty with his next essay, a review of T. S. Eliot's *Poems, 1920,* in the June issue. Although he worried it through nine drafts and Thayer (or was it Mitchell?) made him revise it still further,[20] it is an inadequate treatment. Although Cummings perceived Eliot's mastery of sound and praised his achievement of "oral rhythms," he could not offer any analysis of Eliot's technique and had to resort to quoting passages. Certainly not much is accomplished by his saying that Eliot is "alive" and that Pound is a "peppy gentleman" nor by his quoting lines from "Rhapsody on a Windy Night" and then refusing to say anything about them because "this is one of the few huge fragilities before which comment is disgusting."[21] Cummings did not write any more reviews for the *Dial.* Nor was this turn of events due to any dissatisfaction on the part of the editors. It is clear that this was Cummings' own decision because he turned down an opportunity to review his favorite modern poet, Ezra Pound's *Hugh Selwyn Mauberly* later in the year.[22] This was wise. Cummings had no capacity for critical analysis, and once he had set down his few aesthetic ideas, he had nothing left to say.

Although he was out of his orbit with the Eliot piece, he had the previous month enjoyed a triumph when work in his best vein appeared in the May number. Thayer had chosen from his manuscript five poems in honor of spring: "in Just-," "spring omnipotent goddess," "but the other," "O sweet spontaneous," and a more recent composition than the other four, "into the strenuous briefness." This last poem is not, strictly speaking, about spring but rather a forthright affirmation of life, expressing a joyous response to ordinary existence yet also seeing what inevitably lies beyond spring. The speaker charges, glides, swims into life's rewards and just as ebulliently anticipates their ending:

> into the strenuous briefness
> Life:
> handorgans and April
> darkness,friends
>
> i charge laughing.

Already the contrasts are being set up: "briefness," "darkness." The natural cycle of the day is another metaphorical paradigm ending with sunset (death):

Into the hair-thin tints
of yellow dawn,
into the women-coloured twilight

i smilingly
glide. I
into the big vermillion departure
swim,sayingly;

The facing up to the "vermillion departure" brings about the simplest summary of what life is, expressed in a tone of restrained jauntiness:

(Do you think?)the
i do,world
is probably made
of roses & hello:

(of solongs and,ashes)

Edward Cummings was among the first to write his congratulations and to confess his pleasure in recognizing the "little lame balloonman" of "in Just-" as "a Cambridge bit of Spring furniture." He went into detail about the "strenuous briefness" poem: "Hellos and Roses with their parenthetical shadow of so longs & ashes is a masterly touch," but he objected to the word "slobber" in "Spring omnipotent goddess" and hoped it was a misprint.[23]

In reply, Estlin declared that "into the strenuous briefness" was his favorite among the lot and felt confident "that its technique approaches uniqueness." "After all," he added, "sans blague and Howells, it is a supreme pleasure to have done something FIRST—and 'roses & hello' also the comma after 'and' ('and,ashes') are Firsts." The refusals and blocks against publication were behind him now. His distinctive style and manner of presentation were being seen all over the country, and what is more, the problems he encountered with Lawrence Gomme and his typesetter were no longer a worry. "I am extraordinarily . . . lucky in having what amounts to my own printing-press in Thayer and Watson —by which I refer to the attention which such minutiae as commas and small i's, in which minutiae my Firstness thrives, get at the hands of these utterly unique gentlemen."[24]

Another "first" during the spring was a notice of his painting by an art critic. He had entered two large canvases in the Independent Exhibition for 1920, which was held from March 11 to April 1. The opening was even more crowded and jostling than before; 3000 visitors pushed their way through. The reviewer for the *New York Times* complained that it was almost impossible to see the exhibition. Once again Cummings was offering visual renderings of aural experience. One painting 40 x 40 was entitled "Sound Number 5"; the second, which in execution was, he said, "somewhere near what I want" was a 42 x 36 work called "Noise Number 5." This year his work apparently had more effect, for he was able to report to his mother that he had caught the attention of S. Jay Kaufman of the *New York Globe and Advertiser*, who recommended that an exhibition be held for abstract art only and added: "In any such exhibition paintings by E. E. Cummings should be included."[25] In the area of the arts the Spring of 1920 had not gone too badly.

III

Cummings' work on his account of imprisonment in France had strung out over a couple of years now. His first efforts in 1918 had been interrupted when the U.S. Army took him to Camp Devens. After that, he received an occasional prod in a letter from home and he would reassure his father that the "French Notes" were in hand, although "by no means in final shape."[26] At Thanksgiving time in 1919 he had told his mother, "As for the Story Of The Great War Seen From The Windows Of Nowhere, please don't expect a speedy conclusion."[27]

In May 1920, the building at 9 West 14th Street was about to be pulled down, and Cummings and Brown began to consider their summer plans. Travel seemed like a good idea. They were disgusted with the political scene in the United States. They were especially outraged by the passage and ratification of the Eighteenth Amendment to the U. S. Constitution, which forbade the sale of alcoholic drink in the country. The Volstead Act to enforce it had been passed over Wilson's veto and had gone into effect on January 16, 1920. The young men first considered an excursion to the Orient, but later their rather vague plans became more specific in the hope to take jobs on a ship bound for South America and then through the Panama Canal to the West Coast.

Edward Cummings tried to discourage the departure. He urged them to come to Silver Lake where Estlin could finish the "French Notes." He even offered board, lodging, and salary if Estlin would come up to New Hampshire and help him compile a book of sermons. When these entreaties failed, he tried to persuade them to travel to South America as passengers rather than seamen and offered to buy their passage and add $500 for expenses. The answers were all no, until Estlin and Brown found themselves unable to get jobs on outbound ships. They had moved into temporary quarters at 109 Waverly Place ($5.00 a week for the two of them, "Thus is the H[igh] C[ost] of L[iving] knocked in the beezer by the goddess Art.")[28] Summer in the city was hot. They finally gave in and went to New Hampshire in mid-July.

Cummings brought his La Ferté-Macé manuscript and his typewriter with him and decided that now was the time to finish what he had promised to do. Brown would join him later and be on hand to help him remember details. The writing had gone slowly in the past because he was really taking pains with it. In consenting "to 'do the thing up,' " he explained to his mother, "I did not forgo my prerogative as artist, to wit —the making of every paragraph a thing which seemed good to me, in the same way that a 'crazy quilt' is made so that every inch of it seems good to me. And so that if you put your hand over one inch, the other inches lose in force. And so that in every inch there is a binding rhythm which integrates the whole thing and makes it a single moving Thing InItself."[29]

His routine at Silver Lake was to work during the day alone at a campsite on "Hurricane Point," away from the cottage, then to canoe back to the cottage for a swim and for dinner and socializing, including frequently an argument with his father at the table. Then, taking some fruit and bread for breakfast, he would return to his tent for the night. He had to work alone, he explained, because he was trying to duplicate his own verbal flow: "I surely find it impossible to determine anything, in 'prose' at least, which I cannot mouth to myself—hence need for solitariness."[30] Even when Brown came up to Silver Lake, he worked alone—nor did he show his pages to Brown as he went along. In this way, as the weeks went by, he managed to complete about three pages a day.

He had brought along several French sketchbooks to help him recapture the details. Unfortunately they contained almost no written notes at all. Most were filled with sketches from Paris and the small French towns where the ambulance unit had been stationed. A couple had a few visual reminders of La Ferté-Macé, sketches of guards and inmates or views from the exercise yard.[31] One held the color chart which he and Brown had made by arranging bits of colored paper, tinfoil, and leaves, stuck through slots in the paper. All this was not much help. One large notebook had been his workbook for his poetry and his ideas on art. Besides about thirty poems, it contained notes on sensations, colors, light, and music; images and phrases placed under such headings as Autumn, Snow, Sunset, Twilight; lists of distant sounds ("dimanche—porcelain chimes—sanitary noise"); impressions of the S. S. *Touraine*, Bordeaux, Paris (Montparnasse, Notre Dame, The Louvre), Noyon, and Compiegne; memories of the details and furnishings of 104 Irving Street; musical compositions ("Dance of the Bread Crumbs" "Prison Symphony"); lists of French rhyme words; lists of English words with common combinations of consonants; and a list, entitled "Argot," of French slang terms. Again, except for the argot, not much help. Only one page had notes about the prison quarters and a few of its inhabitants. He had apparently tried to record a few of his first impressions, "Awoke among men fighting and farting in 5 languages," and then gone on to a few cryptic entries.[32] With so few aids and with no day-to-day diary or notes of events, he was working largely from memory, and when he reached the point where his nonhero arrived at the internment center, he turned to a series of character sketches, for which Brown gave invaluable help.

When the Cummings family left for Cambridge in September, Estlin and Brown stayed on at the lake and Edward Cummings took a large chunk of the manuscript to Boston with plans to have his secretary typewrite a fair copy. This was the first time Estlin had allowed anyone to see his work. Edward was startled and pleased by the originality of the style, and any misgivings he may secretly have held about Estlin's future in the literary world were now thrust aside. On October 2 he wrote that he had just finished reading through the chapters he had in hand. "It is superlative stuff—I am sure now that you are a *great writer*, and as proud of it now, as I shall be when the world finds out."[33]

Estlin worked on into the fall, and in a final burst of energy he completed the narrative in the last part of October, just before the snow came. After his return to New York, he continued to exchange batches of manuscript with his father and he brought the concluding portion with him for typing when he went home for Christmas. He had also selected a series of pencil drawings to illustrate the book. Brown had read it and approved. John Dos Passos, who had just returned from his long stay in Europe, was genuinely enthusiastic about it. Already his friends were suggesting publishers.

Estlin tried to place it with Harper's but got only a nibble of interest about serial publication in their magazine. In Boston, Edward tried Houghton Mifflin and the Atlantic Monthly Press without success. He arranged through a family friend to have the manuscript read at Scribner's but they eventually turned it down. Finally, one of Cummings' friends in Greenwich Village, Mary Heaton Vorse, called it to the attention of Horace Liveright of Boni and Liveright. By this time Estlin was losing interest, and as the weeks went on, he left the matter of publication in his father's hands.

Although 1920 was an eventful year for Cummings, he had been discouraged lately by the number of refusals that his painting and writing had encountered. When he looked at his situation as a painter, he had to admit, "I have exhibited twice at the Independents and once at the Penguin and noone whom I do not know personally has bought one of my pictures."[34] Stewart Mitchell had peddled *Tulips & Chimneys* to six publishers but met six rejections. In October, Estlin contemplated his twenty-sixth birthday and faced up to dispiriting realities. He was dependent upon his father for money and his friends for publication. He wrote to Mitchell gloomily: "In the 26th year of my age, without a book published, without a molecule of worship or confidence outside of those whom I $\frac{\text{can}}{\text{cannot}}$ that is to say $\frac{\text{have}}{\text{haven't}}$ drunk under the table—id est, my friends . . . I, then, totally unworshipped and completely untrusted with those tinily profound exceptions, do on my 26th birthday (aujourd-'hui) accept dollars two hundred and sixty from an enthusiastic father; also a furcoat; also a charge-account at 'The Continental Clothing House' also (sequitur) a pair or two of shoes and maybe a hat, also (it is on the way) a pair of corduroy trousers—!"[35]

To be ready for the Independent Show of 1921, he slaved over a 40 x 40 canvas called "Noise Number 10," only to have it singled out for attack by an art critic: "The linoleum school . . . though assertive [has not] been numerous. Its large patterns of lovely hues still make cheerful havoc of an occasional wall. Jay Van Everen's design will catch the eye on entering. It pretends a Mayan suggestion. E. E. Cummings displays a theme of eccentric ovates. He calls it a 'noise' and numbers it."[36] As late as 1921 the American critics and gallery directors could still react strongly against the new movement in the arts. Later in the spring, a Cummings painting was refused admission to a show at the Wanamaker Gallery by the director, Miss Ruby Goodnow, who stated that she "drew the line at abstract art." At length, Lachaise browbeat her into hanging the work, but its name was not listed in the catalogue.[37]

The negative responses to his La Ferté-Macé book early in 1921 did nothing to raise Cummings' spirits and he began to think of travel again. He became more eager to leave the United States as he discussed possibilities with John Dos Passos and Griffin Barry, a young journalist who had journeyed to Russia with John Reed. Dos Passos had finished *Three Soldiers* and a book of travel sketches, *Rosinante to the Road Again,* and he was waiting to hear from publishers about both of them. He decided that as soon as he was free he and Cummings should go on a hiking tour of Portugal and Spain and then take the train up to Paris. Cummings had $1000 for completing his part of the bargain in writing about his prison experiences; so he was ready to go, especially to return to France. Although Edward Cummings was full of worries and advice and reminders about typhoid innoculation and small pox vaccination, he made arrangements for a letter of credit for Estlin's European travels.

Cummings had longed to return to the city he had fallen in love with in 1917 and now there were new attractions as well. Paris, rather than New York, was becoming the center for American artists, a situation partly caused by the fact that a favorable exchange rate for the dollar made it possible for writers and painters to live cheaply in Europe. He was determined to settle in Europe for an extended period: "Will be gone a year or a century," he told his parents. But he had additional reasons for a trip to Europe just now, for Elaine was making some important changes in her life.

The Thayer marriage, even if only a façade, did give Cummings' child a name. Notes from Scofield to Cummings had been saying such things as "Elaine I do not profess to understand" and "So far as I know Elaine is alive."[38] Indeed, he appeared to be backing away from her to make way for Cummings. In January 1921, he seemed even to make a public declaration of the situation when he published Cummings' poem, "Puella Mea," in the *Dial*. Shortly after, he and Elaine reached an agreement for a French divorce. Both would travel to Paris and establish separate residences there in July. Elaine would charge desertion and he would not contest it. He had scheduled the rest of the summer for travel in Germany and Austria to meet new artists and literary figures and secure their work for publication in the *Dial*.

When Estlin chose the spring of 1921 for his departure, he had in mind to be on hand when the Thayers arrived in Paris for their amiable divorce proceedings. He hoped to be the principal man in Elaine's life once again. Elaine and Brown saw him off when he left New York in March to catch his ship in New Bedford, and he arranged to meet Elaine in Paris as soon as she and Nancy arrived.

He and Dos Passos sailed for Lisbon on the Portuguese freighter *Mormugão* on March 15. He took very little luggage but he did include a copy of the *Tulips & Chimneys* manuscript and a portable typewriter. He left the war book with his father, who was eager to continue the search for a publisher. It would be many months before Boni and Liveright accepted it and entered into correspondence with Edward about details. Edward enjoyed all the arrangements hugely and wanted to take part in the publication. He supplied an "Introduction" written from a father's point of view, which included his letter to President Wilson. Liveright suggested that the book be titled "Hospitality," which Edward thought too cynical. He himself favored "Lost and Found," but he sent Estlin a long list of possible titles. With a sure sense of its symbolic suggestion, Estlin cabled back, "TITLE OF BOOK THE ENORMOUS ROOM."[39]

XIV

The Great War Seen from the Windows of Nowhere

> . . . and then, said they, we will, if the day be clear, shew you the Delectable Mountains, which, they said, would yet further add to his comfort, because they were nearer the desired haven . . .
>
> JOHN BUNYAN, *Pilgrim's Progress*

With *The Enormous Room* Cummings had produced a unique work. Here was a story of oppression, injustice, and imprisonment presented in a high-spirited manner as if it were a lark. Nothing in the book is handled in any way that could be expected—the experience is peculiar, the linguistic style is experimental, the mingling of French words and sentences with the English is a practice that no modern literary work had attempted, the characters are a crew of incredible grotesques, and, finally, Cummings even forbids the reader from interpreting his release and return home as a "happy ending."

All this is most appropriate for a work whose central theme is romantic individualism. Cummings had tried, less successfully, to set forth his outlook on life when he wrote his essay on Lachaise in the *Dial.* In his autobiographical narrative, however, he skillfully upholds the child's vision of the world when he considers human behavior and he even carries it to the heights of political anarchism, seeming to echo Thoreau's basic position, "That government is best which governs not at all." In the book, Cummings mounts a symbolic attack upon all governmental structures whatsoever; indeed, he offers the proposition that authority of any kind stifles the development and the expression of individual being.

In *The Enormous Room,* Cummings is quite explicit about what that essential being of each person is. Different words have been used for centuries to describe an essential self—Socrates called it a daimon, Plato called it a psyche, Duns Scotus called it thisness, Shelley called it genius, Bernard Shaw called it life force, Freud called it id. Cummings called it an "IS." One can best understand what he means by looking at a series of notes that he jotted down sometime in 1921:

> IS = the cold 3rd singular of the intense live verb, to feel.
> Not to completely feel = thinking, the warm principle.
> incomplete thinking = Belief,the box in which god and all other nouns are kept.[1]

Once we recognize the pejorative coloration that he throws over the word "belief," we can understand more clearly his description of the IS as he applies it in *The Enormous Room* to the character named Zulu, who exhibits "an effortless spontaneity":

> There are certain things in which one is unable to believe for the simple reason that he never ceases to feel them.   Things of this sort—things which are always inside of us and in fact are us and which consequently will not be pushed off or away where we can begin thinking about them—are no longer things;they,and the us which they are,equals A Verb;an IS.[2]

The book, without ever saying so, presents the narrator as an IS in action. In discussing the book I am going to refer to the narrator as C. in order to distinguish my comments about him as a character from those about Cummings as the creator of this work.

The structure of *The Enormous Room* is fairly simple, dividing into three main parts. Part I covers the arrest of C. and his journey to the detention center at La Ferté-Macé. It jumps right into the incident of the arrest without any preliminaries and later we gradually learn the details of the conflict that arose between Mr. A., the *chef de section* of the ambulance unit, and the narrator and his friend B. The bouncing jollity of Cummings' language scarcely hints of C.'s predicament as he is driven off to Noyon by car, escorted by a helmeted soldier. But when the driver's hat blows off and C. helpfully starts to get out to retrieve it, he is in for a sudden shock. The soldier draws his pistol to stop him. The narration continues to be ebullient, however, through the next episodes: his eating *déjeuner* under detention, his being searched, and his interrogation at a security hearing in the *Gendarmerie.* During the questioning he passes his first test: he refuses to be in any way deferential toward his examiners and when he is asked the crucial question that will determine his case, "Do you hate the Germans?" his own Socratic daimon rises up and forbids him to say, yes.

When the door of his jail cell in Noyon slams upon him, he has no misgivings. "I put the bed-roll down. I stood up. I was myself." The whole sequence of his first day in jail reverberates with joy, although the grimmest details are available for an indulgence in self-pity. When he inspects a toilet can in the corner of the cell, he is filled with a sense of human companionship upon finding a recently deposited turd. It reminds him of Robinson Crusoe's discovery of a footprint in the sand. Such is the emphasis on life in this book that an animism frequently transposes things into beings: the toilet can get a name, Ça Pue (It Stinks), and becomes an animate presence in the cell.

He soon has the pleasure of more company, "a little silhouette" who comes along the windowsill and nibbles at a piece of his chocolate. "He then looked at me, I then smiled at him, and we parted, each happier than before." Night falls; a sliver of a moon appears—another animation, feminine this time, not Madame la Lune, as in the song, but Mademoiselle. He is happy. Imagination provides him company, "My friends: the silhouette and la lune, not counting Ça Pue, whom I regarded almost as a part of me."

As the series of ordeals continues, a literary development takes place which adds extra dimension to the work. Cummings begins a series of allusions to Bunyan's *Pilgrim's Progress,* the best-known allegory in English literature, and this continues throughout the book. Bunyan's story of Christian, who leaves home, wife, and children, setting out on a journey to the Celestial City, is filled with allegorical episodes. Christian falls in the Slough of Despond, he is imprisoned in the castle of the Giant Despair, he has to do battle with the monster Apollyon in the Valley of Humiliation, but at length he reaches the Delectable Mountains, and attains the Celestial City.

But Cummings does not use Bunyan's work as a structural device the way Joyce did with the *Odyssey.* He does not duplicate all the episodes and significances of *Pilgrim's Progress.* He merely employs an accumulation of allusions in order to elevate and intensify the misadventures that befall the narrator. Because of the reference to *Pilgrim's Progress,* the heavy load of gear which C. has to carry on his three-day journey to La Ferté-Macé is seen to be like the burden that Christian must carry and thus becomes heavier and mythically more credible (150 pounds is the weight given) as C. staggers with it from station to station. The muddy area of the ambulance unit in which he and B. are stuck without getting any *permission* [leave] is made muddier and more dispiriting by the allusion to the

Slough of Despond. The cruel Directeur at La Ferté-Macé seems the more threatening because he is referred to as Apollyon. And so on. But these are selective allusions and we should not read the whole narrative in terms of Christian's journey or to look among the characters for representations of Mr. Worldly Wiseman, Mr. Facing-Both-Ways, and all the rest of Bunyan's personifications.

This raising of the narrative above the level of realism has made possible other variations in the fictional mode. As C. makes his way to La Ferté-Macé in the custody of the two stupid, prodding *gendarmes*, he is given help and comfort by a series of strangers, and Cummings lets the characters take on a mythic nimbus by using the language of religious supernaturalism. On the train another prisoner, a "divine man," humble in speech and demeanor, helps him with his burden and shares with him his wine and sausage. A kindly woman in Noyon who serves him food and offers comforting words is revealed to be the *marraine* [godmother] of all the prisoners: "I love them and look after them. Well, listen:I will be your marraine too." When the train reaches Paris, it is a holy place: The people on the streets are "divine," a motherly woman sells C. coffee, a "sacredly delicious" brew. All these figures draw strength from association with Christian folklore, which is full of tales of sudden appearances of saintly helpers or even of Jesus himself. In a scene no doubt inspired by the episode in which Christian is relieved of his burdens when he stands before a cross, Cummings arranges a final beatification for the narrator himself, carrying the religious identification a good deal farther now than he has with the minor characters. In a passage full of cubistic obliquities, he identifies the suffering C. with the Christ figure and the two *gendarmes* with the two thieves who were crucified on either side of Him. The scene takes place at night near the end of the journey to La Ferté-Macé when the prisoner and his guards come upon a large roadside shrine:

I banged forward with bigger and bigger feet. . . . Uphill now. Every muscle thoroughly aching,head spinning,I half-straightened my no longer obedient body;and jumped:face to face with a little wooden man hanging all by itself in a grove of low trees.

—The wooden body clumsy with pain burst into fragile legs with absurdly large feet and funny writhing toes;its little stiff arms made abrupt cruel equal angles with the road. About its stunted loins clung a ponderous and jocular fragment of drapery. On one terribly brittle shoulder the droll lump of its neckless head ridiculously lived. There was in this complete silent doll a gruesome truth of instinct,a success of uncanny poignancy,an unearthly ferocity of rectangular emotion. . . .

Who was this wooden man? . . . I had seen him before in the dream of some mediaeval saint,with a thief sagging at either side,surrounded with crisp angels.   Tonight he was alone;save for myself,and the moon's minute flower pushing between slabs of fractured cloud.

I was wrong,the moon and I and he were not alone—a glance up the road gave me two silhouettes at pause.   The gendarmes were waiting.

Part II of the book begins in the Dépôt de Triage when C. wakes to find himself in the new world of *The Enormous Room* and is reunited with B. It is a world in which everything is upside down. Although they are imprisoned, it is "the finest place on earth." It is a fine place for B. and C. because they have escaped from the oppressive ambulance unit, but it is a fine place for the group as a whole because they are in a limbo away from the world at war. In the world outside, it is suggested, the Schoolmaster was perhaps considered a corrupter of youth for telling "the children that there are such monstrous things as peace and goodwill." Civilization is seen as a bad kind of development for nations, compared to a place like Algeria, "uncivilized, ignorant, unwarlike." The harsh rule of the Dépôt de Triage and the oppression and injustice that it perpetrates are very gradually seen as symbolic of all governmental structures.

In spite of the earnest social criticism, the thematic emphasis in *The Enormous Room* is rather upon affirmation and particularly upon the values of individualism and the virtues of primitivism. Most of the prisoners are not real criminals but mere unfortunates: soldiers who overstayed their leave, sailors who missed their ships, a man who stole four cans of sardines, aliens who could not understand the stringencies of French wartime rules, whores who violated some wartime regulations. The characters who become friends of B. and C. are simple, gentle, harmless people—even Christ-like. They are especially pathetic because of their vulnerability—they are weak, or small, or crippled, or illiterate, or mentally deficient—and they are in one respect or another childlike. Monsieur Auguste the little Russian is only five feet tall and he likes to sing a song about the quacking of a duck. The Wanderer is a tall bearded gypsy but he will sob his heart out over the sale of his favorite horse or be struck dumb with misery over the separation from his wife and children. He is the first of the specially venerated companions whom C. has designated as Delectable Mountains, and these men have an even more primitive quality than the others.

One of the Delectable Mountains, the Zulu, cannot communicate with C. by means of language, for he is a Pole who knows neither French nor English. Yet since he is categorized as an IS, his essential being can communicate itself easily by a roll of an eye or a twitch of the mouth. He moves about wraith-like, appears mysteriously with gifts of food, and stands imperturbable in the midst of alarms and confusion.

Since the Four Delectable Mountains are presented in order of increasing veneration, the most Christlike and the most childish are reserved to the last. Surplice is, B. and C. think, Polish, but nebbish is a word more applicable. He is the one who is always ignored, forgotten, silent in the background—except when selected out for group derision and teasing (his tormentors call him "Syph'lis") and, then, he is wide-eyed with wonder that anyone would notice him. He has an intuitive talent for music, and a childish toy, the harmonica, is his special instrument. As the characterization develops he becomes an archetype of the Holy Fool. He is "intensely religious" and so oblivious to the things of this world that he does not know there is a war going on. What Cummings emphasizes is his ignorance of the terrible things that civilization has developed—like submarines. He is childlike in his naïveté and oblivious to dirt, as if he were a three-year-old still picking up anything he finds on the floor or still fascinated with paddling in feces. Surplice sweeps up the spilled sand from the spitting box; he salvages the saliva-soaked cigarette butts for his pipe; he voluntarily carries down to the sewer daily the pails of solid excrement. He is filthy: "he has, in fact, an unobstreperous affinity for excrement; he lives in it; he is shaggy and spotted and blotched with it; he sleeps in it; he puts it in his pipe and says it is delicious." In exhalting Surplice to saintliness, Cummings seems to add to the number of the beatitudes, "Blessed are the befouled for they shall be the shining ones." On the occasion of Surplice's departure, Cummings indulges in one of his poetic flights. He has the narrator sing a private hymn for him and arrange a vision of his apotheosis:

> For he has the territory of harmonicas,the acres of flutes,the meadows of clarinets,the domain of violins.   And God says:Why did they put you in prison?   What did you do to the people?   "I made them dance and they put me in prison." . . . And He says:O you who put the jerk into joys,come up hither.   There's a man up here called Christ who likes the violin.

If the holy child Surplice is pathetic, Jean Le Nègre is the comic child, full of natural high spirits. He likes to pretend—he tells outrageous stories of his life and exploits. He reads aloud nonexistent news out of a newspaper. He carries on a hilarious conversation with a friend through the imaginary telephone of a stove pipe. But he can also throw tantrums or have periods of the sulks. Like a highly sensitive but overly strong boy on the school playground, he reacts to peer pressure, and when he feels group criticism for his breaking the nose of the Fighting Sheeney, he does not defend himself when set upon by that vengeful man and his sidekick.

In developing the character, Cummings intensifies the feeling about Jean by beginning with high jinks and then dropping down to the troubles that beset him. The sequence is brought to its crisis in the account of an unjust punishment of solitary confinement. It is here that Cummings brings in poignantly the basis of the child's emotional disequilibrium. He wails, "Everybody puts me in the cabinot because I am black" and smashes his head against a pillar. C. cements his friendship with Jean by defending him against the punishment and, when he is powerless to prevent it, by personal gifts including the coat off his back. It is one of those moments, frequent in American literature, of interracial masculine bonding.

Cummings makes one variation here in the portrait-pattern of the distinguished four. Jean is afforded a triumphant conclusion. Cummings describes his fighting off four guards and throwing them about, whereas with kindly treatment they might have handled him with ease. The little Belgian with the paralyzed arm controls him easily in the midst of that melee by means of a few soft words of friendship. The character sketch ends with the most personal of Cummings' apostrophes addressed to Jean:

> —Boy,Kid,Nigger with the strutting muscles—take me up into your mind once or twice before I die(you know why:just because the eyes of you and me will be full of dirt some day).   Quickly take me up into the bright child of your mind,before we both go suddenly all loose and silly(you know how it will feel).   Take me up(carefully;as if I were a toy)and play carefully with me,once or twice,before I and you go suddenly all limp and foolish. Once or twice before you go into great Jack roses and ivory—(once or twice Boy before we together go wonderfully down into the Big Dirt laughing, bumped with the last darkness).

Part III picks up the narrative again and moves the story to its conclusion. Change comes with the verdicts of the examining commission. B. is sent to a permanent prison and C. is to be freed but placed under surveillance in a French town. With this turn of events, C.'s mental attitude changes too. With the departure of B., the Dépôt is no longer "the finest place on earth." C. goes about in a numbed state, captured, we might say, by the Giant Despair. From those clutches he is rescued by a *deus ex telegramma:* he is ordered released to the American embassy and sent on his journey home. The final allusive detail comes when C's return by ship to New York is described as if it were a cubist view of the spires of the Celestial City: "The tall, impossibly tall, incomparably tall, city shouldering upward into hard sunlight leaned a little through the octaves of its parallel edges. . . ."

II

A narrative of the sort we have just examined would have had its vogue in the 1920s and then faded into the obscurity of a wartime document were it not for the fact that it was written by a poet. The selectivity and pace of the narrative are commendable, but it is the language that makes it memorable. Cummings brings his narrative alive by recording sensations whenever he can. He makes us see and smell and sometimes hear, taste, and touch. We experience vividly the daily life in the Dépôt de Triage—its oozing walls, its overflowing pails of urine, its encrusted dirt, its greasy soup, the piercing cold, the noise and confusion.

The linguistic exuberance of the style is in harmony too with the philosophy of individualism and it immediately comes into conflict with the prevailing wartime rhetoric. On the very first page, Woodrow Wilson's pronouncements are made fun of in the summary of the trouble with Mr. A. "To borrow a characteristic cadence from Our Great President:the lively satisfaction which we might be suspected of having derived from the accomplishment of a task so important in the saving of civilization from the clutches of Prussian tyranny was in some degree inhibited, unhappily, by a complete absence of cordial relations between the man whom fate had placed over us and our selves. Or, to use the vulgar American idiom, B and I and Mr. A. didn't get on well." As the narration goes on, the slanginess gives vigor, and the occasional lift into formal circumlocution provides irony. More than this, lively and unusual figures of speech abound. C. waits in a moment of excitement: "my blood stood on tiptoe"; a *gendarme* gets ready for duty: he "buckled on his personality." Surplice speaks with a "shrugging voice"; an ineffective and isolated prison guard stands "like a tragic last piece of uneaten candy in his box at the end of the cour"; the gypsy's little son has "lolling buttons of eyes sewn on gold flesh."

There is no standard narrative style. Cummings tries out everything. We have, for instance, impressionism, a style invented by the French novelists and developed by Joseph Conrad, in which the impressions are recorded as falling on the consciousness of the narrator. This is a view of the jail at Gré:

> A wall with many bars fixed across one minute opening.   At the opening a dozen,fifteen,grins.   Upon the bars hands,scraggy and bluishly white. Through the bars stretchings of lean arms,incessant stretchings.   The grins leap at the window,hands belonging to them catch hold,arms belonging to them stretch in my direction—an instant;then new grins leap from behind and knock off the first grins which go down with a fragile crashing like glass smashed:hands wither and break,arms streak out of sight,sucked inward.

That style carried further can become interior monologue, a very good means for conveying unusual states of mind. Here is the narrator, dazed by his sudden release, leaving La Ferté-Macé by train:

> A wee tiny absurd whistle coming from nowhere,from outside of me.   Two men opposite.   Jolt.   A few houses a fence a wall a bit of neige float foolishly by and through a window.   These gentlemen in my compartment do not seem to know that La Misère exists.   They are talking politics.   Thinking that I don't understand.   By Jesus,that's a good one.   "Pardon me,gentlemen,but does one change at the next station for Paris?"   Surprised.   I thought so.

He tries out his synaesthetic style, in which he merges, linguistically, the words which apply to one of the senses with those which apply to another (the sort of thing he had done in the prose-poem "i was sitting in mcsorley's"). For example, the description of C.'s first observation of the prison chapel when the *Surveillant* leads him through it in the darkness:

> The shrinking light which my guide held had become suddenly minute; it was beating,senseless and futile, with shrill fists upon a thick enormous moisture of gloom.   To the left and right through lean oblongs of stained glass burst dirty burglars of moonlight.   The clammy stupid distance uttered dimly an uncanny conflict—the mutterless tumbling of brutish shadows.   A crowding ooze battled with my lungs.   My nostrils fought against the monstrous atmospheric slime which hugged a sweet unpleasant odour. Staring ahead,I gradually disinterred the pale carrion of the darkness—an altar. . . .

There are passages, too, as we have seen, that are somewhat like set pieces, done in variations of his cubist style—the description of the roadside crucifix and the culminating portions of each of his views of a Delectable Mountain.

It is this linguistic display, along with the allusions to *Pilgrim's Progress* and the hints of a mythic dimension, that takes *The Enormous Room* out of the humble category of the war memoir and that keeps it out of the work-a-day category of the realistic novel. It is then merely a prose work of literary art. There had never been anything quite like it before and there has never been anything like it since.

XV

Europe, 1921–1924

Juxtaposition, in fine; and what is juxtaposition?
Look you, we travel along in the railway-carriage, or steamer,
And, *pour passer le temps*, till the tedious journey be ended,
Lay aside paper or book; to talk to the girl that is next one;
And, *pour passer le temps*, with the terminus all but in prospect,
Talk of eternal ties and marriages made in heaven.

A. H. CLOUGH, *Amours de Voyage*

When Cummings embarked for Lisbon in March, 1921, he was to remain
in Europe for the next two and a half years. It was a period of wandering,
of trying to decide what kind of a life he wanted with Elaine, and of
marking time with his poetry and his painting. Although he said on one
occasion, "I was a painter in New York and a poet in Paris," this was only
one of his mannered assertions. He worked in both the visual and literary
arts no matter where he lived. Paris was now to be his headquarters, but
in the thirty-two-month period he wrote and sketched in every country
in Western Europe except Holland.

The voyage to Lisbon on board the *Mormugão* was a three-week
crossing, with plenty of good wine and Portuguese cookery. Dos Passos
worked on translations from *The Greek Anthology* and Camoëns' *The Lus-
iads*: Cummings wrote poems, drew pictures, and theorized about lan-
guage and color in his notebooks. At night they read aloud from Brooks
Adams' *The Degradation of the Democratic Dogma*, a treatise on American
history which they both hated.[1] Their approach to Iberia began with a
dawn view of the Azores and an offshore scent of lemon blossoms. Their

John Dos Passos in the 1920s.

visit ashore at Fayal provided them with a scene of black-hooded women and black-caped men and a Good Friday procession. After a stop in Madeira, they debarked in Lisbon and then traveled up the coast to Coimbra and Oporto. Cummings' notebooks are filled with sketches: churches, an oxcart, a Quixotic windmill, a hand-drawn funeral hearse, ships in harbor, uniformed soldiers, dancing gypsies, a "pissoir", cafés with meditative drinkers in wide black hats.[2]

From Oporto they headed inland to Salamanca, but their proposed hiking trip through Estramadura was disrupted when Cummings developed a toothache which got worse as they traveled south by train to Seville. There a Spanish dentist lanced his ulcerated gum and saved the trip for Cummings. He began now to enjoy Spain hugely, the Alcazar in Seville, the great toreador Belmonte in a bullfight, the annual springtime fair with all of its Andulusian color. He described it to his mother:

I wish you could have seen the feria; the streets crammed with carriages in which the most exquisite girls rode, each with her mantilla, superb scarlet and vermillion—such shawls you never imagined—such huge combs, such amazing dresses. At night the various clubs gave dances in the open, in little pavillions side by side along certain streets. Men and girls stood up with castanets, swaying, twisting, stamping; spectators seated in a ring clapped in time; there was music and often singing. Millions of lanterns—streets full

of toys—groups of bright balloons—victorias, laughter, andora hats, har-
monicas, and a splendid merry-go-round on which Dos suggested we ride
as a parting achievement—so we sat our pigs (wonderful pigs, with a triple
sea-sick motion) in the light of lanterns and the laughter of thousands of
people.[3]

They headed back north past fairy-tale castles on hilltops, arriving finally
in Toledo with its ancient twisting streets, which they found to be the
most fascinating city in Spain. They marveled at the elaborate facade of
the Cathedral (which Cummings sketched), at the Gothic splendors of
San Juan de los Reyes, and, above all, at Santo Tomé, which held El
Greco's magnificent "Burial of Count Orgaz," a painting that Cummings
later declared contained "more aesthetic intensity" than the entire Uffizi
Gallery in Florence.[4]

Judging from his sketchbook, which contains some drawings of
women with lifted skirts displaying themselves, one might conclude that
both the travelers explored the sexual traffic of Spain too, but later testi-
mony indicates that Dos Passos was still in a very early stage of sexual
development. In his notebook from the 1920's, Edmund Wilson recorded,
years later, a story that Cummings had told him about the Spanish trip:

> When we got to a town, Cummings said, I'd want to go out to the square
> or somewhere to see if I could find something (he meant a girl). Dos would
> never go with me—he'd say, "I'll just stay here in the hotel, I think." One
> day I said to him: "Dos, don't you ever think about women?" No. "Don't
> you ever dream about sex?" No. What I went through with that man! He'd
> wake me up in the night groaning and throwing himself around in his sleep.
> I'd say, "What's the matter, Dos." He'd say, "Why, I thought there were
> some beautiful wild swans flying overhead." One day I said, "You know
> sometimes sex appears in dreams in very much disguised forms. You may
> be dreaming about sex without knowing it. Tell me one of your dreams—
> what did you dream about last night, for example?" He said, "Why, I
> dreamed I had a bunch of aspawagus and I was twying to give it to you."
> This . . . evidently stopped Cummings in his tracks.[5]

By May 1 they were in Madrid, which they did not care for—even
the Prado, which had too much eighteenth-century work and too many
massive Rubens's displays for Cummings' taste. They turned northeast,
stopping at Segovia's breath-taking Alcazar, going on through Burgos up
to the Basque country. Spain, protected by the barrier of the Pyrenees,
had not become involved in World War I and was, therefore, an area of
Europe that seemed unspoiled—unchanged from its picturesque unso-
phisticated past, especially in the rural Basque provinces. Cummings

loved the Basque people, both here and across the border in the French
Basque country. His sketches show them with their oxen and goats,
wearing their large characteristic berets. He was fascinated by their
peculiar language, which is thought to be something like the original
Indo-European. "They speak a tongue or patois approximating Es-
quimaux and don't seem to care whether it hails snows or merely piddles.
Nothing can persuade me that these folks are inhibited."[6]

They crossed the border and went on to the French Basque seaside
town of St. Jean de Luz, where they met Dos Passos' friend, John Howard
Lawson, who was later to be one of America's first expressionist play-
wrights. After a train journey inland which afforded some spectacular
vistas of the Pyrenees from the little *Chemin de Fer du Midi,* they stopped
at Oloron. Cummings wanted to see the town he had selected for intern-
ment just before his release from La Ferté-Macé. They shipped their
baggage on to Paris in Lawson's care and took a train which twisted its
way up to Accous, a village at the head of the well-traveled mountain
pass, Col d'Iseye. From here they started out on foot to cross the Pyre-
nees, although warned that the pass was dangerous at this time of year,
"la neige est mauvaise: elle est douce." Because of the snow they missed
the pass and ended up facing a precarious drop. But on they went, "Dos
went first, waist-deep; I lowered the baggage . . . then I followed 'in his
steps'. . . . A little way and I had to sit down and empty [my] shoes,
because my feet burned with cold. From then on said feet were all right,
and we went rushing and tumbling downward in a *tree-men-doos* way, as
Lachaise remarks. . . . we started down again, down a perpendicular
meadow, in this position [sketch of them sliding seated] which we held
to for nearly 3/4 of an hour—my pants-seat disappearing rather rapidly."
In this position they followed the historic route that travelers and armies
had tramped for centuries. They ended up in Biel, a village with picture
book houses and brightly costumed peasants. After this they reverted to
travel by train and arrived in Paris by mid-May.[7]

II

It was springtime once again when Cummings returned to his favorite
city. He set down a series of impressions of its Maytime scents, planning
perhaps to convert it all into a sonnet (rhyme words are scribbled in the
margin):

Along the river trees are letting go scarcely and silently wisps, parcels of
incense, which drop floatingly through a vista of talking moving people;

timidly which caress hats & shoulders, wrists and dresses; which unspeak-
ingly alight upon the laughter of men & children, girls & soldiers. . . . People
smile, moving gaily through the twilight to the Gingerbread Fair [foire aux
pains d'espices]. I go along too. i slowly go up the vista among the hats &
soldiers, among the smiles & neckties, the kisses & old men, wrists and
laughter. . . .[8]

He was soon settled at the Hôtel Marignan, 13 rue du Sommerard, where
he had a huge room, sparsely furnished, (with unpredictable plumbing
down the hall) for 150 francs ($12) per month. He began roaming the city,
reacquainting himself with its variety. He leaned upon the Pont des Arts
watching barges, rowers, *bateaux-mouches*. He gazed contemplatively at
Notre Dame cathedral, noting a beggar on its steps. As his sketchbooks
show, he wandered about observing the flower sellers, children playing
in the Luxembourg Gardens, a funeral procession (black horses drawing
the hearse), lean men, fat men, crippled war veterans, men in capes,
women with large carefully styled hats, double-deck omnibuses, donkey
carts, a street fair with a man who ate glass, a snake woman, and other
performers.[9] A penciled self-portrait shows that he had regrown his
moustache now.

At first, he was with Dos Passos and sometimes with Dos's friends:
Lawson and his sister Adelaide, Cuthbert Wright and Dudley Poore
(both of whom he had known from the *Harvard Monthly*). He also ran into
Dory Miller, but their tastes seemed very different now: Miller did not
care for modern art and literature and spoke patronizingly of the *Dial*.
When Dos Passos left for the Middle East on the Orient Express, Cum-
mings spent his time alone until the Thayers arrived. Scofield was travel-
ing with Slater Brown, whom he had hired as a private secretary, a job
which entailed everything from taking dictation to picking up girls on
the street (a suggestion that Brown never carried out).

Thayer entertained the impecunious Cummings for dinners and
musical shows (they both ranked the Folies-Bergère very highly), and
promised to introduce him to Ezra Pound. Cummings diffidently held
back until one night by chance they met Pound on the street, red hair and
beard flamboyantly ruffled. Cummings and Pound took to each other
immediately, especially because of Pound's "inborn sense of chivalry"
and his great courtesy in questioning Cummings about his work and his
ideas on poetry and art. At the end of the evening they left Thayer at his
hotel on the rue de Rivoli and Pound, "feline, pantherlike," walked
Cummings across the bridge to the left bank, questioning and lecturing.
Cummings, suddenly embarrassed about his Spartan hotel room, bid him
good-night on the boulevard Saint-Germain and made his way to the

Marignan alone, stunned with hero-worship. It was the beginning of a life-long friendship.[10]

The Thayers' divorce went through on July 25, and Scofield settled on Nancy a sum judged not so generous as to be a danger to marriage later. However, as a result of the 1929 depression, two-thirds of it was lost by the time she came of age. Elaine would accept no money for herself from Thayer. He left for Germany and Austria on July 31 to seek material from German artists and writers and to consult Freud in Vienna about his psyche. Thayer's reading in Freud had made him aware that he had certain neurotic tendencies and he felt flattered that Freud found his case interesting enough to accept him as a patient. He did not return to the United States until 1924, a situation which caused Watson and the managing editor of the *Dial* considerable difficulty and eventually ended Thayer's position as "editor maximus" of the magazine.

Cummings had been seeing Elaine even before Scofield's arrival, for she, Nancy, and the nurse had appeared in Paris at the end of June. For the first time Estlin began acting a little like a father. Nancy was one-and-a-half years old, scarcely more than a baby, but she was walking now. She began to seem more of a person to him: he called her Mopsy. When he strolled with her in the Bois de Boulogne he was filled with delight as she told him "the most amazing stories."[11]

Estlin adored Elaine anew and now that she was free he began to spend part of every day with her. Because his purse was slim and she was well-to-do, he felt very awkward about the disparity in their styles of living. But his cherished philosophy of individual uniqueness served him well and he found her willing to share his simple pleasures and humble haunts, although he lived near the Sorbonne on the left bank, the student quarter, while she lived at the Hôtel d'Iéna near the Etoile, a very fashionable section of the city. He called in the afternoon, went out to the Bois de Boulogne with her and Nancy, took her to tea and occasionally stayed on later in the evening before going back to the Hôtel Marignan and his companionship with Brown, who had recently joined him there.

In August he and Brown accompanied Elaine and Nancy on a trip to England to visit Elaine's sister, Alexis Orr. They left Elaine with Alexis at Dover and had a few days for the usual tourist's exploration of London. Cummings seems to have enjoyed most the British Museum and the National Gallery, to which he returned three times. Elaine came to London on at least one excursion, and she later met her two hovering travel-companions for the channel crossing, a tour through Belgium, and the return to Paris.

Edward Cummings was in Europe during this summer of 1921 in

connection with the War Relief work of the World Peace Foundation. Estlin had turned down his father's generous invitations to travel with him at the end of the summer, so Edward came to Paris during September. The big news he brought was that Boni and Liveright had accepted Estlin's book about La Ferté-Macé. Estlin seemed less interested in this turn of events than his father did. He was happy to leave the final negotiations in Edward's hands, and he set off on a bicycle trip to Italy with Brown as soon as his father left.

The two friends departed September 28 and pedaled to Auxerres, Autun, Lyon, and over the Alps to Turin, Genoa (October 11), Pisa, and down to Rome and finally Naples by November. His sketchbooks are filled with visual reminders of poplar-lined roads, church façades and spires—including the Romanesque marvel at Vezelay—and landscapes of the countryside in Beaune and Pommard.[12] The *vin du pays* was superb. They became good cyclists and made excellent progress; in fact, one day they covered 112 kilometers. They did not linger long in any city: even in Rome they stayed only a day and a half "& left after visiting the Capella Sistina, Tomb of Hadrian, Catty combes, etc. etc." In Naples they boarded a train for the return trip and arrived in Paris by the middle of the month, in time for Cummings to receive a copy of the contract from Boni and Liveright. He sent back instructions about the title page, "Name of Author, E. E. Cummings (not E. Estlin, not Edward E., not Edward Estlin)" and was explicit about the handling of any objectionable obscenities *"No words changed.* In cutting use dash ——— e.g. '——— it,' said etc. (not 'chuck it,' said etc.)"[13]

A report to his mother, shortly before Elaine returned to the United States, makes his association with her sound happy but uncommitted. "B. and I have fine parties with Elaine and Mopsy (who runs extraordinarily fast, and is now learning English, having long since created a new language and being cognizant of French in addition.) We take her to the Merry go round, the little one in the Champs-Elysées—or give her tea in state at Fouquet's, or simply all 4 promenade together in a lofty manner and to the amazement of each other and the gendarmes."[14]

After she left, he was living by himself in the Hôtel Havane, near the place St. André des Arts, one of the most picturesque corners in all Paris. Here he had the "best chambre" he had yet found in Paris, although he later discovered that the hotel was "literally a demi-bordel, half its rooms being rented many times over, every night."[15] He lived very cheaply. In a detailed account to his father, who supplied the money he was living on, he figured that he spent 1024 francs ($85) a month, not counting dental bills. He was drawing and painting daily, enjoying Parisian cuisine (especially at his favorite restaurant La Reine Blanche across from the Cluny Museum on the boulevard Saint-Germain), and generally feeling exuberant. "I eat snails almost daily, oysters biweekly, mussels weekly, mermaids once a month."[16]

III

Now that he had one book accepted, he considered it more likely that he could find a publisher for *Tulips & Chimneys*. Since Stewart Mitchell had no luck in his efforts to place it the previous year, Cummings now decided to revise his table of contents, and in particular he considered it prudent to withhold several of the sonnets whose sexual explicitness had possibly scared off publishers who feared a censorship battle. By the time he finished, he had compiled a remarkable volume of 152 poems. This book never saw publication, in Cummings' lifetime, in the full assembly and arrangement that he desired. Its contents were eventually scattered through three books of poems published between 1923 and 1925. But it is important here to describe this 1922 version of *Tulips & Chimneys* in order to make clear what a remarkable collection of modern poetry Cummings was trying to put before the public. The volume, including all the poems, is available at last under its true title (that is, with the treasured ampersand) in the Liveright edition, 1976, edited by George J. Firmage.

Since it is a first book of poems, it contains a good deal of apprentice work from the college years. The Keatsian exercise, "Of Nicolette," is here. There is a group of poems under the heading "Orientale" which come from the Harvard days—pieces such as "my love," which imitates "The Song of Songs," and "i spoke to thee/with a smile," which had once appeared in the *Harvard Monthly* under the title "Out of the Bengali." In the group called "Amores," some poems, notably "into the smiting" and "the glory is fallen out of," had in the Harvard days been written in long free-verse lines; now Cummings has given them varied pacing and additional interest by making the lines shorter. Not all apprentice work need be inferior. The group of poems entitled "Songs" has pieces from Briggs's classroom, such as the ballad "All in green went my love riding," and "when god lets my body be." The group entitled (after Debussy), "Chansons Innocentes" includes the paean to springtime in Cambridge "in Just-" as well as the imagistic triumph "Tumbling-hair."

After some doubts, he included the two long occasional poems. "Epithalamion", written for the Thayer wedding, leads off the manuscript. It is possible that Cummings later felt this intense formal declamation in the Hellenistic mode may have been a dragon at the gate which chased

"View from My Room," Hôtel Havane, rue St. André des Arts, pencil drawing by
E. E. Cummings, 1922. HOUGHTON LIBRARY

off prospective readers, for he omitted it from his *Collected Poems* in 1938.
"Puella Mea," the tribute to Elaine, is more sophisticated.

The mature work in *Tulips & Chimneys* is found mostly in the groups
entitled "Impressions," "Portraits," "Post Impressions" and in the three
sections of sonnets. The "Impressions" are descriptive poems mostly
employing the Apollonian style, which, appropriately for the impressio-
nistic manner, deal with effects of light. "The hours rise up putting off
stars and it is" and "stinging" are both placed here, as well as "the sky
a silver," the description of a spring shower which dissolves into a mist:
the opening image presents the April morning as if it were a Debussy
"Impression" for the piano:

> the sky a silver
> dissonance by the correct
> fingers of April
> resolved
>
>   into a
> clutter of trite jewels
>
>
> now like a moth with stumbling
>
> wings flutters and flops along the
> grass collides with trees and
> houses and finally,
> butts into the river

The "Post Impressions," written in the Hephaestian style, have
more unusual experiments with spacing, diction, punctuation and gram-
mar. The prose-poem "i was sitting in mcsorley's" is here. Another
prose-poem about a street scene with a hurdy-gurdy and a monkey builds
to a startling fantasy when the speaker projects himself imaginatively
into becoming the monkey. It is a wholly successful poem adapted to the
petit garçon role:

(if you toss him a coin he will pick it cleverly from,the air and stuff
it seriously in,his minute pocket)Sometimes he does not catch a piece
of money and then his master will yell at him over the music and jerk
the little string and the monkey will sit,up,and look at,you with his
solemn blinky eyeswhichneversmile and after he has caught a,penny
or three,pennies he will be thrown a peanut(which he will open
skilfully with his,mouth carefully holding,it,in his little toylike hand)

and then he will stiff-ly throw the shell away with a small bored
gesture that makes the children laugh.

But i don't, ... tiniest dead tunes crawl upon my face my hair is
lousy with mutilated singing microscopic things in my ears scramble
faintly tickling putrescent atomies,

and

i feel the jerk of the little

string!the tiny smiling shabby man is yelling over the music i under-
stand him i shove my round red hat back on my head i sit up and blink
at you with my solemn eyeswhichneversmile . . .

The identification was not difficult. Dos Passos said, "Cummings had a
way of looking like a chimp at times."[17]

The "Portraits" have stylistic variety ranging from the ironic nostal-
gia of "Buffalo Bill's" to an exuberant Satyric tribute to Marj which
begins:

> between the breasts
> of bestial
> Marj lie large
> men who praise
>
> Marj's cleancornered strokable
> body   these men's
> fingers toss trunks
> shuffle sacks spin kegs they
>
> curl
> loving
> around
> beers
>
>   the world has
> these men's hands but their
> bodies big and boozing
> belong to
>
> Marj. . . .

The sonnets are divided into three groups. The "Sonnets—Realities"
are all tough-minded pieces. Most of them come from the Camp Devens
period when Cummings had felt an intense pressure of sexual frustration.

These are the most interesting of the sonnets because of what Cummings does in playing around with the form. One, however, is a "goodbye to Cambridge" sonnet reflecting on the lack of response to life and to beauty that he attributed to the people of his native town. Even in its first line this poem about the Cambridge ladies contains a wickedly compact metaphor which suggests that their ideas and attitudes are, like the fittings of so many furnished rooms, the worn, shabby, and ill-matched hand-me-downs of others:

> the Cambridge ladies who live in furnished souls
> are unbeautiful and have comfortable minds
> (also,with the church's protestant blessings
> daughters,unscented shapeless spirited)
> they believe in Christ and Longfellow,both dead,
> are invariably interested in so many things—
> at the present writing one still finds
> delighted fingers knitting for the is it Poles?
> perhaps.   While permanent faces coyly bandy
> scandal of Mrs. N and Professor D
> ....the Cambridge ladies do not care,above
> Cambridge if sometimes in its box of
> sky lavender and cornerless,the
> moon rattles like a fragment of angry candy

The moon, the only object of beauty in Cambridge, is neglected, as if it were the last undesirable chocolate in the box.

Much less interesting are the "Sonnets—Unrealities," the most idealized and traditional among the sonnet groups, although two written on board the S.S. *Touraine* as it traveled to France through submarine-infested waters in 1917, have considerable power. One, "come nothing to my comparable soul," is a consideration of death; the other "a connotation of infinity," is a cosmic meditation.

The "Sonnets—Actualities," almost all love poems, have a freshness which reflects their origins: most of them were written for Elaine. They begin with a casual conversational assertion worked into the line: "when my love comes to see me its/ just a little like music," or "it is funny you will be dead some day" or "let's live suddenly without thinking." As they go on, they become more complex as they introduce startling images or unusual syntax. When they are easy to comprehend, they are pleasant and when they are difficult, they are worth spending time on in order to absorb the intricacy of the statement. For instance, "yours is the music for no instrument" turns on an allusion to Dante's *Inferno*. Francesca has told Dante that her love for Paolo began when they were reading the story of Launcelot and Guinivere together and suddenly "la bocca mi bacio tutto tremonte" ([he], trembling all over, kissed my mouth). Once this allusion is understood, the rest of the meaning of Cummings' poem reveals itself: the poet and his lady risk all eternity for love ("in this at least we have got the bulge on death") just as Paolo and Francesca had done.

When we stand back from *Tulips & Chimneys,* we see that it divides stylistically into those poems which look back and those which look forward. There are lyric renderings (tulips) in standard or free verse, and there are responses to the modern world (chmineys) in sordid urban scenes or in linguistically explosive handlings of conventional poetic subjects. The collection is in this way a transitional landmark in the progress of twentieth-century expression in verse. It deserved publication.

Zooming through Paris on his way back from Persia in February 1922, John Dos Passos stopped to see Cummings. With his usual willingness to help a friend, he offered to take the manuscript back to New York and seek a publisher.[18] He was an established author now with three books in print and he wielded some influence. Cummings himself had his first book just about to be launched. Surely this was a good time to try. As for accepting any changes in his book that a publisher might ask for, Cummings was willing to be flexible about some matters, but on a few important points, as he wrote later that year to John Peale Bishop, he would hold firm: ". . . provided the arrangement isn't changed, I'm meek as to omissions—Not misprints or improvements, however happily conceived by however brilliant minds. . . ." The title was another item that he insisted upon. The ampersand which had been a "first" in a poem in the *Dial* he intended to be a "first" in book titles: "on this," he declared, "I am portland cement and carrara."[19]

IV

Since Elaine was the most important woman in the world to Cummings, his occasional indifference to her and Nancy in the last two years is inexplicable unless we recognize that even after the birth of Nancy he had not matured emotionally in any noticeable way, although he was now twenty-seven years old. He never thought of Nancy as his own child but only as Elaine's. As for Elaine herself he regarded her as his girl—someone he loved, yet someone he could easily leave behind when he wanted to go off on a jaunt with Dos Passos or Brown. How-

ever that may have been, Elaine's absence in the winter of 1921–1922 seems to have made an impact upon him. Their letters from this period have not survived, so we cannot know what he expressed to her or why she returned to Europe in the spring of 1922. All we know is that she carried Estlin's Christmas presents to his parents back to New York for him and that in January Mrs. Cummings made a trip to New York especially to meet her and got a first look at Mopsy.[20] One wonders whether or not the golden-haired child reminded her of Estlin twenty-five years earlier in Cambridge. She and Elizabeth knew that Nancy was Estlin's daughter.

Cummings' own scattered notes about his life in Paris that winter make clear that he tried to live a monogamous existence, which he thought of as being faithful to Elaine. He was almost successful. If he had not been celebrating dionysically with Brown on New Year's Eve, he would not have abandoned his resolves and taken up with an attractive street-walker in the place Pigalle. But he was remorseful the next day— and so terrified of venereal disease that he gave up tobacco and drink for eighteen days in a ritual of protective superstition.

Winter was lonely without Elaine and it was probably at this time that he wrote the following sonnet about their rendezvous near the merry-go-round horses *(chevaux de bois):*

> along the brittle treacherous bright streets
> of memory comes my heart,singing like
> an idiot,whispering like a drunken man

who(at a certain corner,suddenly)meets
the tall policeman of my mind.
                                        awake
being not asleep,elsewhere our dreams began
which now are folded:but the year completes
his life as a forgotten prisoner

—"Ici?"—"Ah non,mon cheri;il fait trop froid"—
they are gone:along these gardens moves a wind bringing
rain and leaves,filling the air with fear
and sweetness.... pauses.   (Halfwhispering.... halfsinging,

stirs the always smiling chevaux de bois)

when you were in Paris we met here[21]

As spring came on and Brown left for New York, he was alone once
more. He longed to see Elaine and when word came that she would
return in May, he numbered the days till she and Nancy arrived. This
time Elaine had reservations at the Hôtel Wagram on the rue de Rivoli,
right across the river from Cummings' modest left-bank quarters. On the
morning of their reunion, his first glimpse of her walking toward him in
the Tuileries Gardens was an experience that he remembered as "my
life's most magical moment." The summer companionship which fol-
lowed seemed to him "perfect bliss." But he still preferred the role of
lover to that of husband. Thinking of himself as dedicated to "my work,"
he shied away from any permanent ties. Elaine came to his room at the
Hôtel Havane, which, if it was a "demi-bordel," seems not the most
suitable place for long-range happiness. Nevertheless, day after day they
strolled down the rue St. André des Arts with their arms around each
other, as was the young Parisian fashion, and did not look back or ahead.
    One of his unpublished poems from this period conveys his experi-
ence of being another self through her love:

                    look
                    my fingers,which
                    touched you
                    and your warmth and crisp
                    littleness
                    —see?do not ressemble my
                    fingers.   My wrists hands
                    which held carefully the soft silence

```
of you(and your body
smile eyes feet hands)
are different
from what they were.   My arms
in which all of you lay folded
quietly,like a
leaf or some flower
newly made by Spring
Herself,are not my
arms.   I do not recognise
as myself this which i find before
me in a mirror.   i do
not believe
i have ever been these things;
someone whom you love
and who is slenderer
taller than
myself has entered and become such
lips as i use to talk with,
a new person is alive and
gestures with my
or it is perhaps you who
with my voice
are
playing.[22]
```

Nancy was two-and-a-half years old, an age at which children be-
come more interesting to indifferent fathers, and her vocabulary was
increasing daily. Cummings was charmed by this loquacious pixie, and
he drew pictures for her, bought balloons, took her to the Luxembourg
Gardens, and in general enjoyed some of the special insight into human
development that a parent can have. But it was still not a real father's role:
he resembled more the genial uncle who comes and goes. Even so, he
became more a part of Elaine's little family (Nancy, Eva Prior, the per-
sonal maid, and Winifred Rudy, Nancy's English nurse) than before. In
the afternoons, he would sit drinking beer in the Tuileries Gardens with
them while Nancy skipped about, and in the evenings, he and Elaine
would dine outdoors at the place du Tertre on top of Montmartre. In
June he accompanied Elaine's household to Pornic, a seaside resort on the
north coast of France, but he had to return to Paris shortly to travel with
his parents.

Once again Edward Cummings had an international conference to attend in Venice and this time Rebecca Cummings was making the European trip with him. Estlin arranged rooms at the Hôtel Havane, although he warned his mother that this was a "tough district." He took special pleasure in showing her his favorite spots and even persuaded both parents to attend the music hall, Concert Mayol, with him. For the next few weeks he toured Italy with them, going to the Italian Riviera, Venice, and Rome before they took ship for Boston in August.

V

When Elaine had come to Paris in May, she had brought with her four copies of *The Enormous Room,* which had just appeared in New York. As Estlin began to read through it, he discovered that an editor at Boni and Liveright had cut out several sections, had translated many of the French phrases and passages into English, and had left a scattering of misprints. When Edward Cummings had been unable to persuade his son to return to the United States to supervise the publication (Estlin had rejected the whole idea of making a "temperance cruise"), he himself read the proof. He saw the changes that had been made but approved their publication in order not to delay getting the book before the public. Now Estlin scribbled a sizzling letter to the publisher in which he declared that the book should be "immediately suppressed, thrown in a shitoir"[23] unless the errors were all corrected.

These problems did not trouble reviewers, however, for the book was well received. The *Boston Sunday Globe* treated it in a special feature on the front page of its Editorial and News Section, May 21, with the headline, "Harvard Man, Son of Prominent Preacher Reveals His Terrible War Experience, Involving High Officials." With pictures of Estlin and Edward and additional news stories about the background of the book, it occupied a full page. Louis Kantor, a friend of Brown, reviewed it for the *New York Herald Tribune* and was able to comment on the book with the full knowledge of Cummings' verse and art work that had appeared in the *Dial.* After a brief summary of how Cummings came to be prisoner in the "enormous room," he devoted the bulk of his long review to a discussion of the prose style and, in so doing, placed Cummings in the center of the new movement in the arts. This is a sample:

> Now Cummings, the artist, the poet . . . has recorded veraciously the life, buttered in his humor, of that room for three months. It is not a continuous record, nor does it read as smoothly, say, as the vapid biographies of Floyd Dell. It is jerky, rather like a Chaplin movie.

Cummings sees human beings, their surroundings, mental and physical, as pictures, makes language describing, representing those pictures. His writing, at first reading, may seem sketchy, but so in a different fashion is the writing of James Joyce in "Ulysses". . . .

It is true that often Cummings is obscure, that is to say, his sentences wriggle off in a dozen different directions; a phrase is suspended, help-lessly, between two rows of . . .; a paragraph is too obviously expressionis-tic; some phrases are pressed too hard—the word "neat," for example, has its nice edge worn off with overuse; the smell of the stench in La Ferté-Macé is smeared over Mr. Cummings' words a little too frequently and with too apparent a pleasure, perhaps I ought to say too *realistically* and make him furious; a thought is often unkindly deserted before completion, and often nuggets of beauty are tarnished by haste, carelessness, or buried in an arid page.

But I have come to praise Cummings not to bury him. I know of these shortcomings, but they are those of an artist—an artist who is experimenting with *form.* Show me another young prose writer who has the brains or daring to *play* with the language—and I don't mean by that the tortured, if clever, mimicry of, say, Ben Hecht. I can find the veins of pure gold in Cummings' composition with an unhasty eye; show me another young American prose artist in whose composition gold can be mined without a patient pickaxe.[24]

As time went on, reviewers responded to both the matter and the manner of the book with great praise: "It is the sort of book that should be read if this world is to be ordered a bit more intelligently,"[25] "One is conscious of a sensitive, pitying, and ironic mind,"[26] "[The book shows] an aware-ness of the knockabout vitality, vigor, raciness, authenticity, humor, po-etry and vividness of the American language."[27] "It is writing created in the ear and lips and jotted down,"[28] and so on. Cummings ought to have been grateful to Liveright for taking a chance on his unusual manuscript, but instead he spent his fury making ethnic slurs on "Boni's Yiddisher chum" for "mutilating" his book or for failure to send royalty payments on time.

Meanwhile, his poetry had become better known. The *Dial* con-tinued to publish poems from *Tulips & Chimneys* and Mitchell persuaded Frank Crowninshield of *Vanity Fair* to print eleven poems from the manuscript in December 1922. Poems also appeared in Harold Loeb's *Broom,* Gorham Munson's *Secession,* and in the Communist literary organ, the *Liberator,* while Claude McKay was editor. By April of the following year, he received word that Dos Passos had persuaded Thomas Seltzer, the father-in-law of Albert Boni of Boni and Liveright, to publish a selection of his poems under the title *Tulips and Chimneys.*

He was now sure that his dream of following the career of an artist would not come to an end, that he could continue to share fully the life of the writers, painters, and magazine editors he was talking and drinking with in Paris—John Peale Bishop, the poet and critic; Gilbert Seldes, who had replaced Mitchell as managing editor of the *Dial;* Alfred Kreymborg, who now edited *Broom* with Harold Loeb; Lewis Galantiere, the translator and critic who contributed the "Paris Newsletter" to the book section of the *New York Tribune;* Malcolm Cowley, poet, critic, and associate editor of *Broom* and *Secession;* Louis Aragon, a leader of the new Paris Surrealist movement, and, of course, Ezra Pound.

His father did not cease urging him to return to the United States and settle down into some kind of regular paying job in publishing or journalism, nor stop accusing him of his lack of consideration for those at home. He offered to pay his passage; he pleaded with him to come at least to share a few weeks of the family summer at Silver Lake. But he also reminded Estlin that he was his financial backer and remonstrated with him about the money he lent to Brown. Estlin's replies were just as shrill as ever.

> Let me also state that while fully realizing the ignominy attaching to one who, unlike yourself, cannot enjoy the satisfaction of asking his son to not forget that he has been working for half a century, and earning his own living most of the time, and the living of a lot of other people to boot (end of quotes)—a satisfaction impossible for the twain more or less simple reasons (a) I am not, have never been, and do not anticipate being self-supporting (b) I have, to my own knowledge, no son just at present—the present writer has always been, is, and in all human and supernatural probability will remain, so everlastingly sure of and stuck on himself that the decline and fall of Roman Empire, President Harding's message to the Indians, and the invention of the cotton gin . . . cannot, by comparison to his personal pride, matter one iota subscript.[29]

He would not even accept his father's congratulations on the critical success of *The Enormous Room* as evidence that he ought to write more autobiographical narrative: "Allow me to reiterate that what I have already published in the *Dial* (drawings, poems, essais) and shall in future (Watson has taken more, here in Paris; besides a great bunch which he bought for himself) is worth 30 (triente) Enormous Rooms to me."[30]

At this time, he was counseling his sister Elizabeth, who had graduated from Radcliffe and wanted to leave home for an independent life of her own. "Big Chief Abenaki" was on the warpath about it. Estlin's advice to her is a slangily phrased epitome of the philosophy of life that he had worked out for himself, which reflects some additional developments, such as his reading of Freud and his adopting the Dada principle that the destruction of traditional values is a necessary preliminary to creation. One long letter was composed as a lay sermon with five heads:

1) Never take anyone's word for anything.
2) The only sincerity is perspecuity (one's perspecuity "is self-sufficient growth, a piece-of-thing-in-itself, irresponsible to anyone outside the ego").
3) To destroy is the first step in any creation.
4) Never be afraid.
5) Sex is everything ("when I see you I shall expect you to be conversant with two books: The Interpretation of Dreams and WIT and the Unconscious. Both are by FREUD."[31]

In later years Elizabeth expressed her deep gratitude to Estlin for having helped her to escape the possessiveness that Edward Cummings exercised over her. She acknowledged that Estlin was the only person in the world who understood the problems that her hovering parents created for her, and whose advice she could have accepted.[32]

Elaine stayed in Europe during the winter of 1922–23, and in January Cummings joined her entourage for another trip to the French and Italian Riviera and later Venice and Rome, where he became aware, for the first time, of the bullying presence of the Fascisti. Because of the political change he was glad to leave Italy and he journeyed alone to Austria to see Scofield Thayer in March. This was his second visit to Thayer in Vienna and he found some odd behavioral developments were taking place in his old friend. Although Thayer had remained in Vienna to be near Freud, he continued to direct the operations of the *Dial,* leaving the details to the managing editor. But he was more arbitrary than ever in his likes and dislikes and quarreled with Watson over printing excerpts from Pound's *Cantos,* which he thought were inferior and pretentious contrivances.[33] It is likely that at this time Thayer put pressure on Cummings to marry Elaine, for Thayer consulted Freud for his opinion on the matter.[34]

Giving up his habit of independent life was only one of the problems Cummings would face in such a marriage. Elaine lived in a luxurious style and she had tastes and social interests that were far removed from what Cummings thought worthwhile. She had other American and British friends whom Cummings despised and whom he referred to as the "Rue de Rivoli crowd," and she enjoyed dancing and partying and traveling to resorts with them. In the summer of 1923, her holiday plans took her and Nancy to Biarritz on the French Basque coast. Cummings turned up but, hostile to her posh surroundings, he settled instead in the nearby village of Guéthary. He took a servant's room on the fourth floor of the Hôtel Juzau, for which the charge, including full pension, was $2.50 per day ("My Bolshevik proclivities are tickled," he told his father).[35] This low-cost proximity to Elaine is typical of their association during these months in Europe. Cummings never lived with Elaine but always had a place of his own, usually without bath. He seemed to be tagging along in her life rather than being a full part of it. But he had very little money to exist on and he refused to live on Elaine, even though he was quite willing to accept money from his father.

His attachment to Nancy had grown deeper. In 1923, when she was three-and-a-half years old, he was spending more time than ever with her. She was finally old enough to go to the circus and Cummings took her to see the Fratinelli clowns and acrobats at the Cirque Médrano. He was even able to have her meet an elephant named Nancy. In the Tuileries Gardens he invented a game to play with her called Elephant Ball. At other times, carrying her on his shoulders, he was reliving all the old elephant play he had known with his father. Once, someone took a photograph that was to make its impact in Athens years later. "Mopsy is amazinger whenever I see her," he wrote home, "now very beautiful with the most energy ever dreamed of by anyone."[36] His letters give an occasional glimpse of them at play; for instance, one picture of Nancy dancing while he and Dos Passos play on the harmonica.[37]

Elaine and Nancy returned to New York in late September, 1923. Cummings, alone, away from them, and somewhat immobile because of a sprained ankle, sat at his typewriter and, during the next two months, took a long voyage of self-exploration. He had been reading Freud and perhaps pondering his discussions with Thayer and others about the psychoanalytic process, for he typed out pages of notes drawing upon early memories of his father, his mother, other relatives, family servants (especially nursemaids who took care of him) remembrances of details of the family house, of Joy Farm, of Abenaki, family sayings, playmates, school friends, games, illnesses, accidents, deaths, early sexual interests, phobias, theatrical performances and shows, memories of schools and teachers, of books that he read, of his first responses to music, of his drawing and coloring, lists of identifications and associations with words and names. He even asked his mother about names and dates. Later in the United States he consulted the Joy Farm logs to stimulate additional remembrances. It seems likely that this kind of self-scrutiny was preliminary to some momentous decision in his life. Perhaps the exercise removed some emotional blocks and encouraged an assessment of values that moved him toward his marriage with Elaine and his adoption of Nancy.*

Other events made their contribution too. Early in October Estlin received word that Nana Cummings had died. He was surprised to discover that she had left him a legacy of $1000 in her will. Shortly after that came news of the publication of Thomas Seltzer's edition of *Tulips and Chimneys*. He was now officially, though precariously, established as a poet. And Edward Cummings added $1000 to his letter of credit as a congratulatory gift to celebrate the publication. Estlin was suddenly richer by $2000. At about the same time, Elaine wrote Cummings asking him to return to the United States. That was all that was needed, apparently: "I am following the suggestion of a friend," he told his father, "with whose daughter I am anxious to exchange greetings." His intentions were, he went on to say, to live in New York for a while. "One's tastes have not, I fear, materially changed; am still convinced that am primarily a painter, that New York is one-fine city, that snow is more beautiful in winter than is rain, that Alfred Dunhill's Smoking Mixture Makes Pipes Prettynearly Palatable, that prohibition is a profoundly promiscuous petty-fogging or preambulatory curse."[38] He had also heard from friends that the prohibition laws were winked at in Greenwich Village.

We do not know what happened during that winter in New York to bring about a decision. Elaine still lived at 3 Washington Square North; Estlin rented a studio at 50 1/2 Barrow Street on the west side of the Village. He renewed his life with Elaine and Mopsy and apparently began to change his notion that Mopsy belonged only to Elaine: he planned Christmas celebrations with them. Thayer had returned from Europe too and there are some indications that once again he had some

---

*It is extremely odd that I remember absolutely nothing about the later of these years from one to five, which my father describes in such companionable and idyllic terms; and perhaps even more extraordinary that my one dim recollection of "Cummings" (probably during 1926) should have seemed in no way connected to me. The only personality from the past completely familiar, vividly friendly and most lovable was Dos Passos; I would have known Dos anywhere, though I believe I never saw him after 1925 till once, about 1950; he was just the same.

Something my father told me later on, suggests why he might have needed very carefully to cover up a blow which really fell much earier than it was seen to fall, and which he was perhaps totally unable to face. In his words to me: "One day when we were all together" (I think he meant with his friends present) "you suddenly asked Elaine 'where is my father?' She looked around the room while I held my breath, then said sweetly 'your father is a little bird!' Then she laughed, so gaily! and at that moment I was transfixed— I died utterly and forever, knowing it was irrevocable . . ." Perhaps she did not see what he saw; perhaps she never did.—NTA

influence on Elaine and urged her to marry Cummings. In any case, the proposal that the marriage should take place finally came from Elaine herself, and Cummings, always following her lead, was happy to be pushed to make up his mind. It was an unusual arrangement hedged with a protective clause: Estlin and Elaine each wrote on a sheet of paper that if either of them should ever desire to end the marriage the other would not oppose a divorce. With this mutual pledge exchanged, Cummings sent the news to his mother on March 15, 1924. It probably was the first word that Edward Cummings heard that Mopsy was Estlin's child:

> In writing you, I am fulfilling a desire which you've often expressed: that I should tell you before I married. Accordingly, I tell you that Elaine & I are going to be married immediately. The least complicated way is for me to apply for a license in New York & be married on the same day. Naturally, I should prefer that father marry us at 104 Irving Street—without gifts, fuss, or festivities, & with only yourself, Elizabeth & Aunt Jennie present. But I don't know whether father will like to officiate when he understands that our idea in marrying is principally this: once married, I can adopt Mopsy, becoming legally the father of my own child—a proceedure [sic] which, for various incredibly intricate reasons, was not feasible before. Incidentally, you may be sure that, so far as Thayer is concerned, there was never the slightest deceit involved, & that we three (Elaine, Thayer, & myself) are now & always have been the best of friends.
>
> What I do know is, first: that you and Elizabeth, having seen Elaine and Mopsy, have a different view of the situation from father; second, that you both will realise that I am unspeakably proud of Elaine and Mopsy.
>
> In case father prefers, under the circumstances, not to marry us, please wire me immediately, or let father or Elizabeth wire me immediately, simply "no." If he would like to marry us (in Cambridge) wire "yes," and "one day" if the application for a license & the marriage itself can take place on the same day, as it can in New York.

Rebecca Cummings noted on the envelope of this letter, "Edward Married Elaine and Estlin in the study at 104 Irving St. Wednesday *March 19, 1924* at about 12:30 P.M. Elizabeth, Jennie & I as witnesses."[39]

XVI

Disaster

The girl whose boy-friend starts writing her love poems should be on her guard. Perhaps he really does love her, but one thing is certain: while he was writing his poems he was not thinking of her but of his own feeling about her and that is suspicious.

W. H. AUDEN

Marriage did not seem to change the way Estlin and Elaine lived their lives, except that Estlin was now privileged to stay the night at 3 Washington Square for the first time in their six-year relationship. Even from the outset he did not act in a very husbandly manner. On their wedding day at the Hotel Copley Plaza in Boston he did not know how to arrange the room service, so he let Elaine handle the mechanics of hotel living. On the train, he did not know how to deal with the porter. Back in New York, he maintained his studio at 50 1/2 Barrow Street, and even after he moved in with Elaine some time later, he continued to follow his independent habits of living. He slept till noon, breakfasted, and then went out to the *Dial* office, or to *Vanity Fair* to see Crowninshield, or to his studio to paint or write, or sometimes just to spend the day with his friends, returning at teatime to be with Elaine and play with Nancy. Usually other friends would join them. Nancy was a great favorite and all the young men treated her like a little princess. It was an open secret among them that Nancy Thayer was Cummings' child, although Elaine saw to it that no one ever said so. In the words of one new friend, she was "the spitting image" of her father.

As the warm days came on, Estlin spent more time with Nancy, sometimes taking her to the Central Park Zoo or to F. A. O. Schwartz's toy store. Nancy was four and a half this spring and Estlin had begun making up stories for her, a routine which she found delightful. One especially charming one was about a little girl called I.[1]

In the evening he and Elaine would go out to dinner, usually to his favorite speakeasy-restaurant, Marte's, at 75 Washington Place. Sometimes they went to the theater but most of the time they socialized at one of their friend's apartments. Dos Passos gives a good picture of some of these alcoholic evenings during which "Cummings was the hub":

> After a couple of brandies on top of the wine Cummings would deliver himself of geysers of talk. I've never heard anything that remotely approached it. It was comical ironical learned brilliantlycolored intricatelycadenced damnably poetic and sometimes just naughty. It was as if he were spouting pages of prose and verse from an unwritten volume. . . .
>
> His mind was essentially extemporaneous. His fits of poetic fury were like the maenadic seizures described in Greek lyrics. . . . Those New York nights none of us wanted to waste time at the theater when there was a chance that Cummings might go off like a stack of Roman candles after dinner.[2]

Elaine often wanted to go to bed long before Cummings. Sometimes she would prevail on Dos Passos to see her home while Cummings continued to drink, give mock declamations, sing, pound the piano. It was a euphoric period for Estlin. He possessed the two human beings he loved most, yet he was free to pursue his work. Although he assumed no family responsibilities, he had them "to love, to praise, to be proud of." Adoption procedures went ahead: on April 24 Nancy Thayer legally became the daughter of Edward Estlin Cummings, although she did not use the Cummings name, nor was she told of the adoption.

In the midst of this happiness, a family tragedy occurred. Elaine's sister, Constance, traveling by train from Virginia caught a bad cold, which turned to double pneumonia while she was in her New York hotel. Although she seemed to be recovering, her fever suddenly became worse and she died. Elaine was distraught, and in the painful confusion of all the dealings with the undertaker and the hotel manager and in making the arrangements for a funeral in Troy, Cummings was of no practical help at all. She began to wonder what kind of a husband she had taken on for her future.

In the aftermath of Constance's death, there were numerous problems in settling her estate, some of which involved her sister Alexis,

Nancy, pencil sketch by E. E. Cummings. HOUGHTON LIBRARY

who lived in England but was now traveling on the continent. "Just whereabouts in Europe she may be we're not sure," Cummings informed his mother. "Probably—since there are any number of important papers to be signed without delay—Elaine will leave for Paris in May, with Mopsy, and Eva and Mopsy's nurse Winifred, and spend the summer-months abroad, returning next autumn to New York. But, even with the best of success, the settling of the estate will probably drag on for some time. . . . Elaine is, naturally, tremendously tired; but I hope that in a few days she will have recovered from the strain of last week's happenings."[3]

When Elaine left for Europe in May just two months after the wedding, Cummings remained behind, painting vigorously and enjoying an increasing reputation as a poet and iconoclast. Lincoln MacVeagh of the Dial Press looked over the remaining poems in the 1922 *Tulips & Chimneys* manuscript and selected forty-one for a published volume ("by the simple process of rejecting the rest," Cummings observed.)

For *Tulips and Chimneys,* Thomas Seltzer had gingerly avoided the most experimental of the poems and passed over those whose subject matter might startle readers who were still shocked by a writer like Theodore Dreiser. Now, MacVeagh in his selection tiptoed past such dangers as "between the breasts" and "twenty-seven bums give a prostitute the once/-over." "When my beard is white with dotage, etc.," Cummings complained in a letter to his mother, "the entire Tulips & Chimneys may possibly have made an appearance per 71 different selective passages conducted by 407 publishers."[4] To avoid this continuing selection process, he consulted with his new friend S. A. Jacobs, who was a printer, about issuing the remaining poems in a "private publication," and by these means, he was told, he would avoid any censorship problems brought on by the clamors of John S. Sumner, executive secretary of the New York Society for the Suppression of Vice.

Since in this case he did not have to worry about timorous publishers, he decided to restore the poems that he had withdrawn for the 1922 revision. In this way, some of the most startling of his "Sonnets—Realities" were finally to see print, such poems, for example, as "her careful distinct sex whose sharp lips comb" and "in making Marjorie god hurried." He also added a few other poems he had written in the last couple of years, including "Paris: this April sunset," a tribute to the beauties of a crepuscular cityscape, and "here is little Effie's head/ whose brains are made of gingerbread," a rollicking view of judgment day with "god" seen as a puzzled and somewhat stupid monarch of eternity. For the title of the book, he chose the ampersand which Seltzer had denied him in *Tulips and Chimneys.* His privately printed volume would be *&*. The volume chosen by MacVeagh, entitled *XLI Poems,* and *&* were to be published in the following year, 1925.

The book of poems which Seltzer had issued the previous October had met a different critical reception from that given to *The Enormous Room.* To be sure, there were some friends who understood what he was doing. Slater Brown, reviewing *Tulips and Chimneys* in *Broom,* discussed the relations between Cummings' poetry and modern painting,[5] and Sibley Watson (writing under his pseudonym W. C. Blum) in the *Dial* offered an analysis of Cummings' linguistic innovations.[6] But most reviewers were hostile to the "eccentric system of punctuation" (Louis Untermeyer's phrase) and allowed praise only for the more traditional poems like "Puella Mea" or "Epithalamion." Nevertheless, Cummings must have been pleased to see that some critics who had been troubled by his work when they encountered it earlier in magazines were now being won over—like Robert L. Wolf, reviewer for the *New York World,* who said, ". . . it is a very disconcerting thing to be compelled to admit, reluctantly, that [*Tulips and Chimneys*] is very good, that it is extraordinarily good, that it contains, in its own individual and unprecedented style, as beautiful poems as have been written by any present-day poet in the English language. When I first read Mr. Cummings' poetry, some years ago in magazines, it inspired me with rage and scorn; from which it appears that disgust is a half-way station on the road to admiration. . . ."[7]

The *Dial, Vanity Fair,* and *Secession* had continued to accept his poems for publication and he now also found a welcome at the *Little Review,* Chicago's most prestigious little magazine, and at Ford Maddox Ford's *transatlantic review.* Having friends in the editorial office sometimes helped. Pound was working for the *transatlantic review* and Cummings had shown him some work in Paris, "Pound liked the poems, and is taking 4 out of 5 (the 5th being too rough for the Hinglish Sensor)." Slater Brown was still on the staff at *Broom,* which under Matthew Josephson's editorship had taken on a Dada coloration. Cummings contributed to the Dada spirit with "Five Americans," sonnet-portraits of five prostitutes, and, later, the most zany piece of prose he had ever passed off as a poem, "Will i ever forget that precarious moment?" (Sample: "A crocodile eats a native, who in revenge beats it insensible with a banana, establishing meanwhile a religious cult based on consubstantial intangibility.")

He had found time, too, to get a painting hung in the spring Independent Artists show—another explosion, "Noise Number 12."

II

Sometime in June, Cummings received a bewildering letter from Elaine. She had fallen in love with an Irishman (Cummings sometimes referred to him as an Englishman), a fellow passenger on the ship going to France, and she wanted a divorce. Cummings, dazed, could not believe what he read. But he took an optimistic view that this was some momentary infatuation and that a reconciliation would take place after her return. He had by this time moved out of his Barrow Street studio and set up his easel in the "nursery," a back room at 3 Washington Square. He was there at work on a painting of Mopsy, when suddenly without notice Elaine appeared.

Cummings was stunned to discover that she had a rock-hard determination to leave him. "Just as soon as she set foot on board that boat," he reported to his mother, "she knew she was through with me."[8] Although she seemed never to waver in her decision to untie the marriage knot, Estlin could not accept his rejection, despite their agreement to part if married life was not a success; and an anguished struggle between her and Estlin dragged on for six months before it ended finally in a divorce in Paris. Cummings' ordeal can be reconstructed from the vast body of writing he accumulated about the break-up. In his attempts to exorcise his grief he tried to write an autobiographical novel about it, modeling his narrative on the section of Proust's *Swann's Way* entitled "Swann in Love." His "non-hero," Edward Seul [French: for alone], undergoes deep distress during a love affair with the beautiful Heloise. Later Cummings tried to write a play about it, in some drafts of which he used the real names of the participants. In addition to these semifictional outpourings, his letters and notes are full of his analyses and meditations on this, the most devastating psychological blow of his life. For the first time in his life, a challenge arose, so personally overwhelming that he could not rise to meet it with his customary high spirits. By the time the year was out, he had undergone an alteration in personality: never again was he so exuberantly happy-go-lucky; never again did he possess the unshakable self-confidence of youth.

Elaine had met Frank MacDermot on board ship; he was a senior partner in the American branch of Huth and Company, a British firm of merchant bankers, and had been living in the United States for the last three or four years.* Elaine continued to see him in Paris, and traveled back to New York with him on the *Majestic*, cancelling her plans to remain in Europe during the summer.

---

*At this time Frank was slim, dark-haired with light blue eyes, and very good-looking; the eleventh child of a self-made man, a Roman Catholic who became Attorney-general for

There is no record of the reasons for her precipitate action, only statements that she did not love Cummings any more and that her mind was unshakably set on divorce. Nevertheless, one can speculate about some of the causes that brought about the change of heart. The recent months had no doubt revealed fully his blindly self-centered existence. He professed to love her, yet he neglected her, as if she were a beautiful statue to whom he could return at his whim to offer homage. He declared that he loved Nancy, but he treated her less like his child than like a toy to be taken out for amusement. Further, there was the extreme contrast in their ways of living. He was continuing to follow his Bohemian habits, never taking any interest in his living accommodations, never dressing in any way except haphazardly (she had insisted that he buy a suit of dinner clothes but he had never once put the outfit on). He refused to live on her money yet would not get a job that could provide an income which would allow him to join her in her style of living—that is, a daily existence which included servants, fine clothes, dining out in elegant surroundings, social entertainment and interchange with her wealthy friends. In fact, he disapproved of her friends, as he did of anyone outside his own circle of writers and artists.

There were also some deeper concerns. Whether she recognized it fully or not, Elaine had two children on her hands, for Estlin was to a great extent being mothered. He had always been diffident and passive in his relations with her, letting her make the decisions, but when he married her he became even more dependent. After the marriage, she brought him to live in what he thought of as *her* apartment. She managed all the details of the household, gave orders to the maids, looked after Nancy, arranged for coal to heat the apartment and food and drink for meals, made travel plans. She had all the economic power; he was not even able to provide for Nancy. In the only long letter of Elaine's that survives, we can read, both in her references to the past and in her manner of trying to buck Estlin up, that she had grown from a *petite fille* into a mature person and that he was still the *petit garçon*. The letter was written just before the final divorce proceedings and in response to Estlin's having sent her a volume of Freud and some typewritten notes interpreting her and himself as neurotic personalities:

Ireland in a Gladstone government, who had also been a defender of Parnell. Frank had left Oxford a classicist and historian with a magnificent eighteenth-century legal mind; he very soon came to loathe banking. He always cared deeply for his unhappy country, characteristically proclaiming the only efficient form of government to be 'a benevolent autocracy'! He was later to write the definitive biography of Wolfe Tone.—NTA

Doesn't it appear odd to you that you are so anxious to have an inferiority complex! It does to me. Why ever so long ago when I had never heard of the words I was struck by your objections to being placed as a controlling personality. Do you remember how people used to refer to the Cummings group, & when you were told that B & N & sometimes Mitchell were following your example in the way they lived, dressed, drank, etc, you were most upset. There was a discussion about how they always walked a little behind you & I remember after that you took care to stay back of them. It was then S. T. began speaking of it as the Brown group which it obviously wasn't.

Personally I think you have a personality the exact opposite of inferior. When you are drunk or particularly happy (& therefore not trying to act a part) you always do the most extraordinary things. The years at Christopher Street (early part of time) & later at 14TH St. you were happy. You walked on the edge of the roof though you knew I was sick with fright. You kept everyone drinking long after they wanted to stop, etc. etc. . . .

You are pretending to yourself that I rule you in order to prove to yourself how effectually you have hidden your ego. In prison & again in the army you forced yourself to be placed at the lowest level & ignored all chances to be anywhere else for the simple reason that you liked to pretend you were like everyone else & so succeeded in making yourself miserable.

Again, now, you try to be like a child & refuse to accept things as a man would. And the sentence you wrote in for me seems to apply in your own case. You disregard the pleasure principle "that is—you make life as hard & disagreeable for yourself as you possibly can, in order to enjoy your unhappiness and the nursing of other people." The greatest pleasure you could feel at this moment is to be entirely free of me & feel yourself once again happy & not depending on somebody else for each contented moment. You don't look up your friends you don't go to theaters you don't seek distraction anywhere because you want to make yourself miserable thinking over & over again situations which will make you seem to be a failure & therefore in the lowest place. You ignore your work which is the one outstanding proof of your success in life.

Life seems to me to be full of the desire to repeat things & to do something new. One or the other is always in the acendancy [sic]. You who live as an advanced poet & reactionary [she means rebel] at other moments fall back into an inability to adjust yourself to a change in your private life.

As to myself, I grant you that I may be neurotic. But the difference is, between us, that I am not trying to make myself miserable, rather am I attempting to be constructive & to make life more happy. Within the last few years I have continued to gain strength of character. I am no longer a passive person to the point of misery. I know where I stand. And I know what I want. And most difficult of all, I know when I have made a mistake & the unfortunate thing now is that you whom I like should have to suffer too.[9]

When one considers what a short time their married life lasted, one might guess that in additon to other dissatisfactions, Elaine finally realized her "mistake" during the time when Estlin was proving so ineffectual after the death of Constance. Here was a time when she really needed help and Cummings was unable to take charge of anything. In her life in general, Elaine was a woman who wanted to be taken care of, but Cummings was not ready to do it.

However all this may be, Cummings himself could not accept what his friends pointed out to him, namely, that the incompatibility of their modes of life had caused the trouble between them. He could not abandon the idea that he had been sexually inadequate in some way. He filled pages with interpretations of their life together searching for the origins of his inferiority. He chastised himself for his ignorance of female sexuality, for his supposed inability to give Elaine satisfaction. Or he developed far-fetched psychoanalytic interpretations that involved Thayer, or Elaine's dead father, or even Mary McKenna, the nursemaid at 104 Irving Street when he was four years old.

During the days that followed, he was so psychologically crushed that he was thrust back into childhood again and turned to his father for help. While Elaine was in Williamstown for a week, Edward Cummings came down to New York with the intention of putting some spine into his son. Full of self-confidence himself, he urged Estlin to fight the situation, even to attack MacDermot physically. He growled about how he would beat up any man who came fooling around *his* wife, and, it seems, offered to take care of MacDermot if Estlin wanted him to. He also urged the advice of a good lawyer and suggested a suit against MacDermot for alienation of affections. In analyzing his problem, Estlin considered the irony that it was the Christian training by his father that lay behind his meekness: "My terrific handicap, my great trouble: I was brought up under this motto: Oh, how sublime a thing it is to suffer and be strong, instead of brought up To WIN!"[10]

He did not want to fight in the manner that Edward counseled, for it was not in his nature to do so. What he really wanted was to win back her love by promising that he would alter his ways. The night Elaine returned from Williamstown she found him dressed in his dinner suit and she did not even recognize him.

Hoping time might alter her resolve, he asked her to wait a year before making the decision. But she continued to see MacDermot in New York and to put the pressure on Cummings for her freedom. He desperately sought advice and comfort from parents and friends. He went to Cambridge to see his mother, he went to Gloucester to see Mitchell, he went up to Robin Hood, Maine, to see Nagel and Lachaise at their summer place. Sibley Watson came to Boston to meet him and drove him to his summer camp in the Adirondacks. Here, talking out his misery in the company of the gentle Hildegarde and the laconic Sibley, he found more psychic relief than he had known for weeks. That night he slept out under the pine trees and woke the next morning to the murmur of a nearby brook. Years later he wrote his remembrance to Hildegarde: "I've never forgotten & shall, I hope, never forget my dying night alone in your forest, with healing of fragrance under & around me; & my waking into a mystery of rebirth."[11] He returned with the Watsons to New York feeling refreshed and ready to face his problems.

It was the end of July by now and Cummings finally agreed to give Elaine a divorce. One of his principal worries was the fact that in the family of a minister, even a Unitarian minister, a divorce was looked upon as a social disgrace. Sensitive to his father's feelings, Estlin broke the news in a judiciously phrased letter, and pointing out that for ease and speed the best alternatives were a Nevada or a Paris divorce, he asked which course he should follow. "Don't forget that—whatever suffering you may justly lay claim to—you cannot possibly approximate mine. For this reason, if for no other, I have the right to act as seems to me necessary. I repeat that I am consulting you here as a token of my appreciation for your efforts for me, and for no other reason. Only I can & do realize what I have lost, & what I am losing."[12] His father wired back "PARIS PREFERRED."

Estlin then telegraphed Elaine and followed up with a letter in which he told her that he could not allow his father's feelings to stand in the way. She replied, trying to soothe him and at the same time to help him hold to the decision he had made: "I am glad in your letter to see that you did realize that to take refuge in another person wasn't getting you anywhere. And after all that's the point [,] you're going to be happy & you never will be till you live, yourself. . . . I do understand that you feel very much alone. But it's nice too, to be so, its not always scary."[13]

One last try, almost a ridiculous one, at changing Elaine's mind was a request to Scofield Thayer that he talk to her. In response Thayer invited Cummings to Edgartown in order to hear the story but in the end he took the expected position that people should do what they want and refused to interfere. On the basis of his Freudian outlook, Thayer diagnosed that Cummings did not have sufficient sexual interest in Elaine or he would fight for her. This kind of talk only coincided with the private self-criticism that Cummings had been indulging in all month. His papers are filled with notes like the following, which he scribbled on an envelope:

either
>   1) give her the divorce &   live
>   kill myself
>   2) not agree to divorce & know that she will stay with McD. . . .
> she is a very fine person
> she is finer than i
> but is it lack of aggresiveness, cowardice, that I did not attack the man?[14]

Cummings had obtained from Watson a 38-caliber pistol and cartridges, possibly with a view to defending himself, if necessary. According to jottings found among his papers, he also considered suicide several times and sat writing out the pros and cons of killing himself. On at least one occasion he wrote a suicide note. The highly literary posing revealed by its language casts doubt on what his intentions really were, but the theatricality in some of his threatening gestures sprang from a desperate attempt to express and accept his own pain. On one occasion, he came to 3 Washington Square and in Elaine's presence drew out the pistol and pointed it at his temple. After a moment he lowered it crying, "I musn't because you are finer and because of Mopsy." He then proceeded to unload the cartridges onto the carpet. At times, he considered shooting Elaine first and then himself, but the thought of the child always stood in the way of a violent catastrophe.

Other times his behavior was very mild and he seemed eager to act the part of a gentleman. Several entries in his notes give details of a meeting with MacDermot carried out in a formal, overcivilized manner, during which Cummings agreed to help Elaine obtain the divorce. They even shook hands in a gentlemanly way as they parted.

In mid-August when Elaine brought Nancy back from Williamstown, he packed all his things and moved completely out of the apartment and into the Hotel Lafayette, but he continued to see her day after day and to worry out the details of their sundered life. In the course of their talks he became calm and resigned about the turn of events. A letter to his parents reveals his complete capitulation:

Dear Mother and Father—
 Sorry not to have written you before: have been more than occupied in finding out the truth concerning Elaine and myself.
 Only now, incredible as it may seem, do I realize that I never attempted to understand the person for whom I thought I cared most in life, & who understands me better than anyone alive. Once to understand this person is, for me, at last to understand myself: I owe her everything fine in my life —I have hurt her more than anyone but myself, perhaps, can ever know— there remains only 1 course: one way: to show her how deeply I comprehend

my own selfishness & how perfectly I recognize her own fineness—to help her, so far as I can help her, in the divorce.

I appreciate, you may believe, the telegram & your attitude of agreement with me.

Have met "the man" twice since I saw you—have explained that I feel unworthy of Elaine & am therefore absolutely trying to aid her to free herself, with the understanding that, once divorced, her life is entirely her own affair—& I have shaken hands.

I hope that my point of view is clear to yourselves. It can be summed up in one sentence.

Anyone so magnificent as she should be allowed to entirely live. (Compared with her life, my own does not so much as matter to the wearer). . . . I never before realized how lucky Mopsy is & will be in having Elaine for a mother![15]

On August 25, their last evening before she sailed for Paris on the *Aquitania,* they dined together at Marte's and then said a quiet good-bye back at the Washington Square apartment. Elaine was full of sober, sometimes bitter, reflections on her life. Cummings preserved a good many of them in his notes. "One thing I know. I owe [Thayer] everything, he gave me the lesson of my life, the shaking up of my life." "I'm tired of everyone's unhappiness. And I've decided. I'm going to be happy." "You can't do anything if you've got a pain in your stomach, but you can if you've got a pain in your heart." "I don't like people who want to be understood." "I'm not sorry for anything. I wouldn't change one thing. I've been happy & I've been unhappy. I don't regret a single thing." "Nobody gets what they want." "Nobody lives for anybody else. Everybody lives their own life." [In response to Estlin's reference to Aristophanes' myth (in Plato's *Symposium*) of the split sexes as halves searching for the other half:] "People don't meet their soul-mates in this world. I don't believe in *one* person, I don't believe there's just one person." She was still apprehensive of Cummings' cooperation in getting the divorce and told him firmly that if he did not give it to her, she would take Nancy and go away and he would never see either of them again. When the ship sailed, Estlin sent a dozen roses.

Cummings needed a place to live but seemed helpless to act for himself. At length, Watson provided him with a third-floor room at 4 Patchin Place, a quiet, tree-shaded court near the old Jefferson Market at Sixth Avenue and 10th Street. It was small and without cooking facilities except for a wood-and-coal stove for heating water, but it had good light for his painting and the court itself with its iron gates was quaint and charming. The novelist John Cowper Powys occupied the next room on the third floor and Watson had rented the other room in order to insure peace and quiet for Powys. Cummings would maintain living quarters in one or more rooms at 4 Patchin Place for the rest of his life.

Despite the quiet tone of those last days before Elaine's departure, Cummings continued to feel unhinged about his agreement to the divorce. He had given his word before marriage that he would free her if she wanted to leave him and he had given it again when he promised to go to Paris for the divorce arrangements. But now that she had gone, he began to consider bitterly what had happened and to blame himself immoderately for cowardice and for a general lack of self-assertiveness his whole life through, a pattern of behavior which he thought had led to his present degradation: "The crisis of my life arrived: I acted exactly as might have been foreseen—forced suddenly to think for myself, to face a terrifying situation, to act on my own initiative, I immediately took refuge in the comforting idea: "E is fine, perfect, can do no wrong, is beautiful, right" with the corresponding COMPLETE INFERIORITY COMPLEX TO MYSELF. . . . THE MORE MY NOSE WAS RUBBED IN THE MERDE the more obedient, babyish, weeping, suicidal I became. In proportion, as I softened and disintegrated E became hard and pitiless."

He was in this mood when he received her cable:

ARRIVED SAFELY BE IN PARIS NOVEMBER FIRST.
ORR.

He drafted a reply (which he did not send): "Thank you very much for 'Arrived Safely.' The rest[,] including the signature, succeeds perfectly in giving me the impression that you consider myself as so much dirt."[16] By way of preparing himself to be more aggressive in Paris, he signed up for a course of boxing lessons at Kid Rogers' Gym at 117 West 14th Street.

When he arrived in Paris November 1, the Hôtel Havane was again a convenient place to stay, for Elaine and Nancy were living in an apartment at 45 quai Bourbon on the Ile St. Louis. One month's residence was all that was required for a French divorce and he and Elaine had agreed that he would establish himself and she would claim desertion. She had already sent him a check for his passage and expenses.

The very first afternoon he spied Nancy and her nurse, Winifred, in front of Notre Dame. He kept a detailed account of the day, possibly to send in a letter to his parents about their grandchild, who was now nearly five:

Saw them looking & ran to them taking off my hat. Nancy & I took a taxi up to Barbès, the beginning of the fête forain de Montmartre. . . .
Rode with her on child-merrygoround pigs. Then went on and she told

Nancy, age 5.

me to play a red & green [sketch of whirling game[so I did, betting on red, & won: "I lot." N. selected a red [sketch of a party snapper] She wanted to know what "win" is.

Then we came to a "human octopus"—outside, on a stand, a monkey holding a guinea pig. Nancy said: "Look at his ears!" of the monkey; & "is it alive?" of the guinea pig.

They played "throw-ball" into a spinning basket and Nancy won a stick of nougat candy. Then she rode the bicycle "child-vigor" tester. Then back to the pig merry-go-round for another ride.

They then took a taxi to the flower market and bought a bouquet of red roses for Elaine and went to 45 quai Bourbon, where they put the flowers in a vase.

Elaine came in & went stiff when she saw me . . . and told N. she wanted to speak to Estlin & told N to go into the inner room & N went in.

I said: Have you seen your friends? (Judge, Coudert, first reconciliat meeting of the divorce).

She told me about it & I wrote down in my address book data about myself which she had given; lest our stories conflict.

I began to feel faint & queer all over.

I told her "nice dress"—she "no" . . . I told her about Nancy at the fête & that I had had a beautiful day: as I looked into her eyes I knew she was moved . . . I said "I'll say goodnight" & went into the inner room, where

Nancy was standing before a kind of glowing stove, naked; Winifred wiping her dry after a bath. I kissed N. on her hair & she said "We'll go up there again"—"one day" & I said, "I'd like to" & "We'll settle that." She waved to me—"goodnight" twice.[17]

He thanked Elaine for letting him play with Nancy, and happened also to remark that he felt sick when Elaine said that he didn't love Nancy when she was a little baby and that now he wanted to get credit for something Elaine had done alone. But he soon controlled his feelings and asserted that what Elaine thought of him did not matter but that something else did matter, now—his child. Very gradually his concern about Nancy, who had been kept out of town all summer when he was in New York, became the center of a new attempt to get Elaine to change her mind. Now in Paris, he saw Nancy whenever Elaine would allow it, although he spent most of the days looking up friends like John Peale Bishop and Lewis Galantiere. In mid-November he sent Elaine a new proposal:

Twice, at 3 Washington Square, you told me that *you loved Nancy more* than anyone else—*more than you love McD.*

HERE IS YOUR CHANCE TO PROVE THAT.

Nancy's future (as well as your own future) depends—as you recently pointed out—on her being safe from scandal.

I agree with you entirely, and regret anything which I may have—unintentionally—done or said which might jeopardise her happiness or yours.

It is perfectly obvious that, since Nancy loves us both, there is only one way to assure her happiness, and that way is: for you and me to love each other and live together.

If this should be impossible, there is still something which can be done to help Nancy—you can remain my wife in name. In this way, Nancy, at least, is protected from scandal-mongers.

It is understood that—whether you care to live with me or merely to remain my wife in name—I insist on contributing to Nancy's support, beginning with $100 a month and working up as I am able to give more.

THE VERY WORST THING *which you could do, so far as both Nancy's and your own reputation are concerned, is: to divorce me at this time.*

As you yourself pointed out—the social world (into which you are planning so merrily to plunge) differs from the artistic world, and one difference is: the social world keeps up a façade of respectability. I believe that your observation is perfectly correct.

I go on record as pointing out to you that IN DIVORCING ME AT THIS PARTICULAR MOMENT you will *endanger Nancy's future,* will put yourself in a very difficult position socially, and will, eventually, unless I am much mistaken, harm the career of the person whom you profess to love.

Elaine scoffed at this new tack. A few days later she returned the letter to him: her view of his new tack was, "all this parent stuff is tommyrot."

Cummings' mental equilibrium was still unsteady. He had brought his gun with him and he carried it around in his coat pocket. One day at quai Bourbon as he climbed the stairs and approached Elaine's door, he thought he heard MacDermot's voice. In a fury of jealousy he got an impulse to fire at him through the door. He told the story a number of times in later years as a parable of how the distraught mind can be deceived, and it varied in its details. Here is one version: "I was once standing in front of a door waiting for it to open so I could kill the man who opened it. I knew he was inside, I knew it for my ears heard a voice which my mind told me was his. I can almost remember pushing the button of the bell with my left hand because the other was in my right outside overcoat pocket. Being cautious or cowardly . . . I was going to shoot him through my pocket with a thirty-eight Remington automatic pistol. I'd pried back the safety catch. Now my forefinger lived like a tendril around the trigger. Silence. Then steps. Every[thing] my life had before been was about to die in that illimitable silence—when the door opened & in the doorway stood a kindly middleaged lady who was a dear friend of both my girl and me, at that moment perhaps my staunchest friend. The only friend my girl and I had in common happened to be calling on my otherwise quite alone girl."[18]

At length the day came when the divorce proceedings took place. He was charged with deserting his wife and with having told a process server who requested his return, "Tell Mrs. Cummings to leave me alone. I have retrieved my freedom, I intend enjoying [it] to the full, I have organized my life without her, my decision is irrevocable."[19] He was present in the court with his lawyer, M. Jean Lenoir, but he seems not to have been called on for any testimony. The decree was issued December 4 in favor of Elaine.

Cummings did not see her again before he sailed home on the *Leviathan*. She sent him a note saying that she hoped he would ask her to dinner before returning to the United States. But they were divorced now. Cummings' thoughts were on Nancy. On the envelope of another letter from Elaine, he jotted some notes for a poem:

good bye dear & next time when I feel a little better we'll ride on the donkeys & next time on the pigs maybe or you will a bicycle & i will ride a swan &

next time when my heart is all mended again with snow & repainted with
bright new paint we'll ride you & I
& next time
I'll ride with you in heaven with all the angels & with the stars & a new moon
all gold between me & you & we'll ride together good bye dear you & i both
of us having yellow hair quietly will always just touching each other's hands
ride.[20]

On the voyage across the Atlantic he kept taking his pistol apart and
putting it back together again.

XVII

The Struggle for Nancy

Promise great things; promise and do not pay.
                    Guido da Montefeltro in DANTE's *Inferno*

Hurt and dejected, Cummings returned to the United States to spend the
Christmas of 1924 in Cambridge. His parents were dismayed to learn that
he had allowed the divorce to go through without securing any parental
rights with respect to Nancy.[1] Elaine had promised him free access to the
child, but in conspiring about the story of his desertion, she had cau-
tioned him not to say anything about the child in order to avoid complica-
tions. Now, almost too late it seemed, the Cummings family began to try
for a custody agreement, and they took a peculiar approach: Estlin threat-
ened to appeal the divorce decree on the grounds that no mention had
been made of Elaine's previous divorce nor of the child. From December
21 to February, telegrams flew back and forth across the Atlantic between
Edward Cummings and J. B. Robinson of Coudert Brothers, Edward's
Paris attorney. In time Robinson's pressure on Elaine produced some
results. On January 26, she cabled Estlin, who was now in New York:

> HAVE RECEIVED YOUR REQUEST THROUGH COUDERT FOR WRITTEN CONTRACT RE-
> GARDING NANCY STOP AM WILLING SIGN CONTRACT GIVING YOU UNLIMITED RIGHT
> OF VISIT AS AGREED BUT NOT LEGAL CUSTODY FOR ANY PART OF YEAR STOP APPEAL
> TO YOU NOT GO BACK ON WORD.[2]

Elaine's feeling that any plea from her would make Cummings do as
she wished was right. Not waiting for legal advice he cabled some

conciliatory reply (which has not survived) and as a consequence began to weaken his case. Robinson sent an angry cable two days later:

> CONSIDER YOUR CABLE TO WIFE PREJUDICIAL TO SUCCESSFUL APPEAL STOP WIFE WILLING YOU HAVE UNLIMITED RIGHT VISIT CHILD BUT CONSIDER CHILD SHOULD LIVE WITH HER IN VIEW OF YOUTH AND FACT YOUR CIRCUMSTANCES DO NOT PERMIT FURNISHING REAL HOME STOP CONSIDER SUCCESS APPEAL DOUBTFUL STOP AM RELUCTANT TO TAKE CASE STOP CABLE US RETAINER ONE THOUSAND DOLLARS.[3]

Estlin became subdued and Edward cabled the retainer. A few days later good news came from Paris:

> WIFE SIGNED FOLLOWING AGREEMENT YOU HAVE CUSTODY 3 MONTHS CHOSEN BY HER STOP YOU HAVE RIGHT VISIT BALANCE OF YEAR YOU SUPPORT CHILD WHEN WITH YOU IF DISAGREEMENT ABOUT SCHOOLS ARBITRATORS TO DECIDE.[4]

The signed contract came in mid-February. The arrangement brought joy to grandparents and father alike. Their plan was that Nancy could spend three months each year at Silver Lake, for Estlin's bachelor existence in furnished rooms in New York was clearly no atmosphere for a child. An abundance of love in the bosom of the Cummings family plus the healthful New Hampshire summer weather seemed an ideal situation.

II

Cummings had moved back into the room at 4 Patchin Place. At first, he was very lonely and given to a sinking heart when he saw an object in his room that reminded him of Elaine: his Japanese slippers, his black muffler (both gifts from her), his tea kettle,—or when he woke to see the three photographs of Nancy on his mantel. He still kept the gun beside his bed.

Gradually as weeks passed he fell back into his old routine. He woke every day about noon, rose, shook down the ashes in his stove, stoked it, and heated some water for tea. After a morning clean-up and a smoke from his pipe, he went out and walked down to the Battery for a meal at Khoury's—an odd breakfast: baba gahnouj (mashed eggplant with garlic and sesame oil) for fifteen cents and a plate of leban (Syrian yogurt) for five cents:

Float

ing
ly)
    i
        (in Khoury's warm

ish
)look

ing at thousands of
winter afternoons, through a
sometimes
a window In khoury
's

womB

for Ladies and Gents
like Restaurant
(always in Whom faces)
o ra mi

(sleep tick
s clock and
occasionally upon the)

perdreamhapsing
(floor cats drift)[5]

He returned to his room to write or paint all afternoon, then would go
out to seek a friend. Sometimes he went to Nagel's and took a warm bath,
sometimes to see Dos Passos or Mitchell or Brown (who was planning to
get married and trying to buy a farm near Pawling, New York). After
tea, gossip, and talk about the current issue of the *Dial* or *Vanity Fair* or
Broom or about what the Theater Guild was up to, they would go out to
a late dinner—perhaps to Passerini's, one of their favorites, where wine
was served in teacups, "like cups of blood"—and on to a speakeasy and
synthetic gin till late hours.

There were some new associates too, people who were to go in and
out of Cummings' life over the years. One was Hart Crane, the young
poet from Cleveland, Ohio, who lived near Dos Passos over on Columbia
Heights just across the Brooklyn Bridge. Crane fulfilled Cummings idea
of what a poet should be like: in later years he recalled him with fondness
and admiration, "There's just one word for Crane: hearty. I never knew
such a hearty so & so; & Dillon [*sic*] Thomas is the only person who has

ever reminded me of Hart. [Hart's] mind was no bigger than a pin—
which didn't make any difference (& may even have been an advantage)
for he was a born poet; whereas the mind's function is to take apart, to
distinguish between, to separate, break up, analyze, poets work & play as
whole human beings."[6] Cummings would call on him sometimes in
Brooklyn, where Crane in his apartment played the victrola constantly,
mostly jazz but occasionally Scriabin and Ravel. Both poets liked toys.
Crane showed Cummings a glass globe, containing a tiny house, which
would produce a miniature snowstorm inside when it was turned upside
down. Cummings resolved to get one for Nancy. At night, Crane rivaled
Cummings in boisterous revel at the Greenwich Village parties.

Another personage, more of a hanger-on to the Harvard group, was
Joseph Ferdinand Gould, a graduate of the class of 1911, who had gone to
New York and degenerated into a full-time bum. Joe was a forerunner
of the "street people" of today, the educated drifters who live on the
crumbs of an affluent society. He was a dirty, ragged, evil-smelling,
dwarfish man with a scraggly beard who lived on hand-outs from friends
or strangers. He came around regularly, asking for "anything that's bum-
able," and the Village literary folk would give him change or a pack of
cigarettes or an article of clothing—sometimes they would provide a meal
at a diner or a drink at a speakeasy. Joe told everyone that he was writing
"The Oral History of Our Time," made up of conversations he had
heard. "What people say is history," he maintained. He claimed his first
draft was already eleven times longer than the Bible and much more
interesting. He always carried a cardboard letter-file filled with papers
and composition books which contained fragments of it. Since he was a
genuine bum he had no place to call his own; in good weather he slept
in doorways or on benches and in cold weather in flophouses or on the
floor of someone's studio.[7] Cummings was fascinated by Gould because
Joe, completely without material possessions, lived the authentic roman-
tic life and because he exhibited boldly his own personal uniqueness, like
one of the Delectable Mountains of La Ferté-Macé.

Less colorful was Allen Tate from Winchester, Kentucky, an elegant
and courteous man, five years younger than Cummings, who was just
beginning his career as a poet and critic. Cummings was drawn to him
for his lively wit and courtly manner.

A most important new friend, M. R. Werner, was a New Yorker who
had been at the Columbia School of Journalism with Slater Brown. Be-
spectacled Morrie Werner was a witty but warm-hearted fellow who had
knocked around the world a good bit in his young life. He had served in
a hospital unit in France during the War and had been a newspaper man
in China and Japan. Now he wrote biography, for which he trained as

an obituary editor for the *New York Tribune*. In 1925 he published a success-
ful book on P. T. Barnum, and was now at work on the life of Brigham
Young. After Brown married Sue Jenkins and moved to the country,
Werner and Cummings became very close, even though their habits of
life were widely different. Werner was a disciplined researcher and
writer, at work every morning by 9 A.M. He could not keep the late hours
with Cummings.

Companionship and work were bringing about Cummings' recovery
from the psychic bruising of the previous year. He was posing "from the
collar up" for Lachaise, who was preparing to cast a bronze head of
Cummings. He was proofreading both of his new volumes of poetry, *XLI
Poems* and *&*, during January. He had decided to dedicate *&* to Elaine,
probably because of the many sonnets he had written for her. He warned
his mother about the explosive material in the book, though: "Note: this
concatenation of poems, if found in a Cambridge bookstore, or on a table
in the Cummings, Sr., home, would cause liberal arrests lawsuits may-
hems and probable massacres. Ver. Sapie. etc.)"[8] He was finishing a 39 x
60 "abstract" painting for the Independent Show on March 6, "Noise
Number 13," a work that made a powerful impression on the directors of
the exhibition, for they printed a photograph of it in the 1925 exhibition
catalogue. This was the third Independent Show in which Cummings
had exhibited. His spirits seemed to be recovering sufficiently for mis-
chief, too. He arranged for a rug made by Mae Ward, Sam's wife, to be
sent down from New Hampshire and he entered it in the exhibition
under her name as a work of art. (In 1926, he would enter a doormat from
104 Irving Street.)

Cummings had also begun writing comic sketches for *Vanity Fair*:
mock interviews with millionaires and heiresses; parodies of movie sce-
narios, of drama reviews, of letters to the editor; spoofs of all sorts. One
item, "Why Calvin Coolidge Laughed" was an explosion of free-associa-
tion nonsense, which later became Chapter I of his Dada-esque book,
[*No Title*]. Most of these pieces appeared under the "psoodnim," C. E.
Niltse, a reversal of his own name and initials. Frank Crowninshield, the
editor, took great pleasure in this work and commissioned regular ap-
pearances. "I also need a lot of what we call 'turns.' That is, down the
back material. I could pay $40 for these, and could use a good many. They
run to about 1100 words. They should be rather light; perhaps a little
dialogue, or short plays, or satires, or nonsensical verse—a letter from a
debutante, diary of a motion picture actress; what to eat in New York
Restaurants; Head Waiters I Have Known; the Horrors of Dining Out;
Wild Society Women I have met; If Benjamin Franklin went to Holly-
wood. I could use a lot of these and you could sign two or three different

M. R. Werner, pencil drawing by E. E. Cummings, HOUGHTON LIBRARY

Anne Barton, pencil sketch by E. E. Cummings. HOUGHTON LIBRARY

"Noise Number 13," oil painting by E. E. Cummings, 1925. HOUGHTON LIBRARY

names to them."⁹ Crowninshield sent letters of praise month after month and assured him, "I can't get enough of you, because you have exactly the touch we need."¹⁰

Although these items amused the casual reader of the 1920's, they were ephemeral pieces which no longer strike much of a spark. Cummings hated writing them but he needed the money. After all, he was counting on being a father to Nancy for three months of the year and perhaps even paying the wages of Winifred during that time.

Earlier in the year, John Dos Passos had introduced Cummings to Mrs. Muriel Draper, wife of Paul Draper the pianist, and mother of Paul Draper, Jr., who was to become a popular American dancer in the 1930's. Since Mrs. Draper collected artists and writers for her personal patronage, she was exactly the sort of woman to take over Cummings and to assist him with his problems. She arranged a meeting with Judge Richard Campbell, who advised Cummings throughout the custody struggle and who examined the contract that Elaine had signed. It was, in his opinion, "absolutely binding." For a short period Mrs. Draper provided both love and care that helped to restore Cummings to a proper sense of himself. Years later, looking back upon the months of emotional imbalance, he concluded that his "suicidal anguish" was actually part of his own enjoyment of the emotional involvement with Elaine: "while always feeling within me, that all this was false & forced —that I was deliberately sucking the last semidrops of poison out of an otherwise empty experience; suffering as deeply as possible for fear that if I ever stopped suffering I'd be nobody—lose myself. Such was this period of self-inflicted pain."

Estlin had come a long way towards recovering his balance by the time Elaine returned to the United States in early April. She and Mac-Dermot had married in a civil ceremony and they were preparing to live outside New York City in Tuxedo Park. In a letter of April 7, she thanked Cummings perfunctorily for dedicating *&* to her, and she invited him to come and visit Nancy. But as soon as he asked for a specific day, Elaine denied his request, declaring that Nancy was in a nervous state and troubled with nightmares. It appears that MacDermot had begun to object to Cummings' visitation rights. Perhaps he had become troubled because Nancy Thayer so clearly resembled Estlin Cummings, and feared that the social set into which he and Elaine were moving might ask embarrassing questions about this scandal-prone woman. He wrote several notes or letters to Cummings asking him to meet him at the Hotel Brevoort or the Racquet and Tennis Club, and he stopped by Patchin Place at least once. The upshot of these conferences was a complete change in the position that MacDermot had taken the previous year when

Elaine was pleading with Cummings not to contest the divorce. At that time, he assured Estlin "so far as the child is concerned that will be entirely between Elaine and yourself—I shan't interfere," and "so far as I am concerned, you can see as much of the child as you like." He saw no reason why three month's custody should not be arranged. Now, in a letter of May 4 he introduced restrictions: "I am still willing that you should see as much of Nancy as is consistent with Elaine's good name." He would allow the visits, "always provided that you are moderate in your proposals & that you do not endanger Elaine's reputation."[11]

Difficulties were arising about the custody question too. When MacDermot called at Patchin Place he told Cummings, "I'll give you a tip. You can take it for what it's worth: by insisting on your rights this year you'll jeopordize whatever hopes you have of seeing the child as much as possible. Even if Elaine, by some freak of fate, consented to being separated from the child this summer, I should fight it tooth and nail."[12] Further, he threatened to take Elaine and Nancy to live in Ireland if Cummings tried to enforce the custody contract.

From what evidence remains in notes and letters, it looks as if Cummings had not been able to see Nancy even once since her return. Since he had been refused access to Nancy at Tuxedo, he asked to have her brought to New York. He received only a curt telegram, "IMPOSSIBLE TILL ABOUT THE MIDDLE OF SEPTEMBER." Left to himself, he seemed defeated, but once again Edward Cummings, the outraged grandfather deprived of any sight of his grandchild, entered into the conflict. He was so angry about what had happened that he did not care whether he was addressing Estlin as his thirty-year-old son or as a bumbling kid:

Dear Chub,

I am returning herewith your letter to W[atson], which has interested me greatly.

I am not in the least surprised that E & Co. have repudiated the Paris contract, and refused to grant you the access to and partial custody of your daughter which was the price of the un-contested court proceedings. They are running true to form. And so are you. First they find you don't mean business in regard to the three month custody. Encouraged by that, they next refuse access. Finally, they ask you to call it all off and give up your daughter forever, turn her over to the tender mercies of an unspeakable cad, who has every reason to look upon her as a perpetual embarrassment,—and has no scruples of any kind except safety-first.

I am not in the least surprised that nothing came of your serio-comic interview with "Co," and that nothing came of W's friendly intervention. All such procedure is simply calculated to confirm E & Co in their well-grounded conviction that you are not to be taken seriously; that promises, agreements, and legal contracts made with you can always be squirmed out of by "diplomacy."

My advice has been from the first that you face the facts, realize what you are up against, and enforce your legal rights by strictly legal impersonal procedure. That means:

1. That you stop having serio-comic conferences and correspondence with E & Co, and conduct all negotiations via, or with the oversight of, a reliable attorney;

2. That you make clear in approved legal phraseology that you intend to enforce and execute to the limit your parental rights of custody, visitation, etc., guaranteed by the Paris contract;

3. That you intend that the child shall know her own name, father, grandparents and other relatives; and that she shall be so known by other people;

4. That you think this open recognition of name, and kinship is a fundamental right of the child, and something so vitally important that "making good" or "taking root" in Tuxedo—or any other place this side of H———is contemptible in comparison;

5. That you have instructed your attorney,—in view of the threat to live abroad if you insist on your rights—to apply to the courts for an order or decree restraining E & Co from evading the terms of the Paris contract by taking the child out of the country without formal consent of the court or legal agreements providing for the custody and access stipulated;

6. That you are prepared to take all necessary legal steps to insure your rights of visitation, custody, guardianship under the Paris agreement;

7. That E & Co have got to realize that there are now and always will be socially inconvenient aspects of the situation which they have insisted on creating; but you have no intention of sacrificing the child to their futile social ambitions and stupid efforts to conceal the unconcealable.

This means business. Anything else is melodrama or worse. . . .

As for seeing the Co, I am at your service, provided that I have the services of a first class lawyer to draw up some such ultimatum as I have indicated, and to assist me in presenting it.

I shall be only too glad to be responsible for all legal fees involved in the above recommendations.[13]

Reinspirited Cummings took his father's advice and sought help from Judge Campbell on August 6. He was able only to see a certain William McCool, who was the Judge's associate, and thus "I had the pleasure of telling my tale of sin and woe afresh," he wrote his father on August 27. "I found all this singularly exhausting but am 'recovering my natural buoyancy of spirits' under the influence of the delicious

Autumn weather. Never did like the 'old Army game' (force, etc.)"[14]

McCool told him that "the contract isn't worth the paper it's written on." He pointed out that it was a contract drawn by Elaine's lawyer and nowhere provided for a situation in which she might refuse to grant the three-month's custody but only provided arbitration in the case of a disagreement as to what time of year the custody might take place. Further (Cummings summarized) courts always favor the mother. "Granted the tender years of the child, and the fact that the mother is neither poor nor immoral, I would have not one chance in a hundred of winning my case before an Irish Catholic judge in the state of New York. But, added that the mother is wealthy, can give the child advantages of travel, educations, and *a home*, and moreover can provide a father for the child (alias the present husband), I would have not one chance in a million of winning. (I am an artist, not wealthy, live by myself, etc.)" McCool advised, however, that Cummings go to MacDermot and tell him he has "consulted counsel" and "intend an immediate showdown," and thus "see just how hardboiled he is."[15]

Cummings had meanwhile received a letter from Hildegarde Watson reporting that Nancy, who was now five-and-a-half, had been left with Mrs. Florence Thayer at Edgartown. Hildegarde had seen her and was worried about the child's response to the new marriage. Estlin hastened to Edgartown but met with a stiff rebuff from Mrs. Thayer. He was denied the chance to see his child because Mrs. Thayer so deeply resented his part in her son's divorce.[16] Stewart Mitchell, who accompanied him to Edgartown, worried him further by his speculations that Elaine was planning to take the child out of the country.

Estlin really felt beaten, and in his desperation he even contemplated snatching the child. Once again he sought his father's help, for he conceded that "I am not one thousanths as clever as Elaine." A letter to his mother reveals a psychological weariness. "It seems to me that father's brains (which I have ever admired, unlike my own) plus the life which he has given to society in the economic sense of that word ought to rise up, here, and somehow (my own apologies for brains are static) magnificently Save The Day before it's too late—mind you, he may know a Boston lawyer who's a genius; and he is a famous man whereas I am a small eye poet. I feel that something *can* be done. That something should be done I know . . .; am alas also aware that should Nancy be taken out of this country, you and father would be thoroughly cheated—hence the matter is actually your concern, now, as well as mine."[17]

Just exactly what kind of pressure Edward or he exerted on MacDermot or what unforseen events took place we do not know. But some arrangement for visiting seems to have taken place by Christmas. Some of Cummings' notes for episodes in the story of Edward Seul focus on visits to Nancy and her response to the box of paints which he had sent as a Christmas present. One episode labelled "2nd time" describes Seul (Cummings) watching Nancy as she skips in a circle and then hops about on one leg. He inquires if she has used the paints. He asks her to paint him a sunflower and promises then to write a letter, "Dear Miss Nancy, I have the honor to report that I thank you very much." He kisses her hand good-bye. The next time, Seul sees her in Central Park playing jump-rope and "it stirs the inner fringes of his heart." He speaks to the nurse, then talks with Nancy and finds she is going to the country the next day. He bows good-bye with a courtly manner, and suddenly she kisses his hand before she turns to leave. These scenes reflect dates early in 1926; Nancy was now six years old. All this time it appears that Elaine never wavered in her determination to keep from her the knowledge that Cummings was her father in any sense of the word.

Some of Cummings' zeal in his striving for custody or visitation rights was now distracted by other interests in his life. He had found a new girl friend, Anne Barton, and during this year, 1926, they traveled in Europe from April through July. When he returned to America, Cummings went to Silver Lake for the month of August. But in the fall, the MacDermots were again posing difficulties about visiting. A letter from Elaine, October 26, informed Cummings that they were moving from Tuxedo into the city. "Therefore it will be much easier to arrange a meeting once we get to New York. I don't like dropping Nancy about for a day in town." She added that Nancy was now riding horseback. Cummings may not have felt happy about Nancy joining the horsey set so young. He sent her a book of stories the next day.

What happened to prevent Cummings' visits in the autumn of 1926 is a matter for guesswork. Three possibilities suggest themselves. First, Elaine fell ill. She suffered, at some point, two paralyses of the hip and the hints are that the difficulty was psychosomatic.[18] A report form Dos Passos that "Elaine seemed less oppressed by the oppressable than before &, in general, more healthy," suggests that her third marriage had become a somewhat thorny bed of roses.[19] Second, Cummings and MacDermot disliked each other so thoroughly that Estlin's distaste for painful encounters discouraged him from applying for visits. Third, and most of the evidence points this way, the MacDermots were determined to prevent contact between father and daughter. As time went on, Christmas and birthday gifts from Estlin or the grandparents or Aunt Elizabeth were acknowledged only by Elaine, never by Nancy. Elaine specifically requested that any gifts be sent in wrappings addressed to her and not to Nancy. Estlin's valentines to Nancy were probably destroyed. What

Elaine in the late 1920s.
COURTESY NANCY T. ANDREWS

was being carried out appeared to be a planned campaign to keep all knowledge of Estlin's existence from Nancy and to wipe all memory of him from her mind. The culmination was reached when MacDermot arranged for the return of his family to Europe in the spring of 1927.

Just before they left, Elaine asked Cummings if he would legally cancel his adoption of Nancy. When she did not hear from him, she wrote to his mother, asking her to use her influence upon him. Rebecca replied but sent her letter first to Estlin for his approval:

Feb. 23, 1927

My dear Elaine:

I have thought very carefully over your request that I influence Estlin to cancel his adoption of Nancy and I am strongly of the opinion that it would not be wise for him to do so for N's sake as well as his own—

You say "the adoption is in any case ineffective" "because you have undertaken all duties and expenses"—The reason it is "ineffective" is not far to seek—As you know I have been, and still am, ready and eager to have N at any time and to pay her expenses while she is with me—You have always refused to let her come, even for a visit, and E has been repeatedly denied, even his right to see her.

You will pardon me if I cannot see that to be E's daughter will be "injurious" to N and I personally think "skeletons" are better not "shut up in closets." In any case, let me assure you that he and I stand ready to accept our responsibilities for Nancy and to do our best for her.

Sincerely yours,
Rebecca H. Cummings[20]

Perhaps as bait for Estlin, Elaine allowed a visit in early March. Or perhaps it was Elaine's attempt at an opportunity for personal persuasion, a method that had always been successful in the past. In any case, it did not work out as she hoped, although Cummings did get some time with his daughter, who was now seven years old. A description of the afternoon has been preserved in Cummings' letter to Rebecca reporting the details:

I've seen Nancy!

She looked pale, and Elaine said she was underweight and small for her age—you may imagine my reaction—but Nancy and I had a wonderful time walking up and down the room, joking, imitating each other, and making fun of things in general. Then we drew pictures for each other—eight of hers are now on my mantelpiece here.

Elaine was present throughout. She seemed rather nettled at first (probably by your excellent letter;[21] inasmuch as she made no allusion to it) then sad, and later more natural, when Mitchell came in. MacDermot arrived last and also got over a somewhat stilted attitude, even to the extent of showing me a Lachaise statuette and imbibing a scotch highball with RSM and myself. (Yesterday I wrote him as follows: "Dear MacDermot—my sincere thanks for your hospitality yesterday—Cummings"). Mitchell had been invited on his own and didn't expect to see me at all; but immediately sensed his part and took care of the MacDermots conversationally, so that Nancy and I could play together. After a while, Nancy went to have supper, but she came back and drew with me again; then she told MacDermot that she was going to run down stairs to the door with me and Mitchell if he'd wait upstairs; and he encouraged her, to my pleasure.[22]

It is perhaps on this occasion that Cummings got a rare chance to hear Nancy sing. The record is a brief reminiscence that he set down in a letter to her the year before he died. He recalled "a decorous visit I once

made to a Mr. and Mrs. MacDermot: during which you were somewhat
(it seemed to me) ostentatiously invited by the former to sing. Your pluck
was wonderful! You hated being made to show off, but your singing
teacher's reputation was at stake & you didn't hate me; so you sang.
. . . The song was enchanting—"tiens! me voilà c'est polichinelle, [a
mere puppet], mesdames"—& you sang it not only correctly but beauti-
fully."[23] She did not know that she sang for her father.

The MacDermots were making a permanent move to Ireland. Estlin
had seen Nancy, at most, only three or four times in the two years since
the divorce. The Cummings grandparents had not seen her at all since
the marriage, nor did they ever see her again in their lives. Nancy Thayer
grew up surrounded by comforts and "advantages," but she was denied
the warmth of their love and the exaltations of a yearly sojourn in a
child's summer paradise in New Hampshire. She grew up not knowing
that her mother had once been married to the American poet, E. E.
Cummings, or that he and not Scofield Thayer was her real father.

XVIII

Anne and *Him*

Let the mad poets say whate'er they please
Of the sweets of Faeries, Peris, Goddesses,
There is not such a treat among them all,
Haunters of cavern, lake, and waterfall,
As a real woman. . . .

KEATS

The story of Estlin and Nancy has obscured our awareness of other spheres of Cummings' life. Although 1925 was full of personal stress, it had been a year of literary success. The two volumes of verse, *XLI Poems* and *&*, had a better reception than *Tulips and Chimneys,* even though widespread recognition of his achievement would be a long time coming. At the end of the year, while in the midst of his struggles over visiting rights, Cummings was chosen to receive the *Dial* award "for distinguished service to American letters." The award carried a money prize of $2000, enough in those days for a writer to live on for a year. He was in select company. The three literary figures who had been honored by the award earlier were T. S. Eliot, Sherwood Anderson, and Marianne Moore.

Boni and Liveright were encouraged by his successes too. When the first printing of *The Enormous Room,* 2200 copies, had sold poorly, they had offered the remainder to the author at thirty cents a copy. Edward Cummings bought one hundred, planning to send a copy to each member of the United States Senate, until Estlin with earnest pleas dissuaded him. Now, Horace Liveright felt that sales would pick up and he restored the price of $2.00 for the copies still on hand. More than this, he contracted with Cummings, early in 1926, for a volume of poems. He asked him to provide an introduction as a help for readers to understand the peculiarities of his style. Cummings gave the news and an explanation of the title of the book to his mother: "am now confronted by the task of making my Voice Weedable for the Gwate Amewican Publick—that is, am supposed to edit my new collection of poems, write a preface, explaining same, and submit to publishers, No sinsh. Particularly as this (coming) volume is entitled: IS FIVE (short for: Twice Two Is Five, hasten to add.) But even so, how will M. et Mmme. Everyone compwehend?—such is the curse of awithmetic."[1]

By the time he had finished writing it, he had not fulfilled Liveright's desire. He had produced another statement about the value of process over product, "If a poet is anybody, he is somebody to whom things made matter very little—somebody who is obsessed by Making."

The book itself does not show any distinct development beyond the mature work in the *Tulips & Chimneys* manuscript. We can perhaps detect, among the epigrams, visual experiments, and samples of verbal play, a slight increase in the amount of satire. A group of antiwar poems helps to create this impression. One, in a tetrameter trot, reflects on the sacrifices of the ordinary soldier and the rewards of privileged officers who held desk jobs:

> . . . braving the worst,of peril heedless
> each braver than the other,each
> (a typewriter within his reach)
> upon his fearless derrière
> sturdily seated—Colonel Needless
> To Name and General You know who
> a string of pretty medals drew
>
> (while messrs jack james john and jim
> in token of their country's love
> received my dears the order of
> The Artificial Arm and Limb). . . .

Another antiwar poem, and one which is most characteristic of Cummings, has his nonhero at the center, Cambridge ladies in the background, a father-figure huffing and puffing his opinion, and a reminder of the information that Estlin had passed on to his sister Elizabeth about the importance of sex. All this presented by means of a burlesque of wartime activities on the home front:

my sweet old etcetera
aunt lucy during the recent

war could and what
is more did tell you just
what everybody was fighting

for,
my sister

isabel created hundreds
(and
hundreds)of socks not to
mention shirts fleaproof earwarmers

etcetera wristers etcetera,my
mother hoped that

i would die etcetera
bravely of course my father used

to become hoarse talking about how it was
a privilege and if only he
could meanwhile my

self etcetera lay quietly
in the deep mud et

cetra
(dreaming,
et
  cetera, of
Your smile
eyes knees and of your Etcetera)

Of the satiric pieces not associated with the war, "POEM,OR
BEAUTY HURTS MR.VINAL" is the most celebrated. It caused a minor con-
troversy when it first appeared in the little magazine, *S4N,* in Novem-
ber 1923, drawing an angry letter of protest and later another letter by
Matthew Josephson in defense. The technique of the poem shows
how Cummings could use the fragmentation of quotations in the
manner of the collage. Pound and Eliot had been doing it with classi-

cal references. Cummings takes advertising slogans jumbled with lines
from patriotic songs:

> take it from me kiddo
> believe me
> my country,'tis of
>
> you,land of the Cluett
> Shirt Boston Garter and Spearmint
> Girl With The Wrigley Eyes(of you
> land of the Arrow Ide
> and Earl &
> Wilson
> Collars)of you i
> sing:land of Abraham Lincoln and Lydia E. Pinkham,
> land above all of Just Add Hot Water And Serve—
> from every B.V.D.
>
> let freedom ring . . .

But the poem directs its satiric attack at popular American poets.
The Mr. Vinal of the title was Harold Vinal, editor of *Voices,* a poetry
quarterly which was a stronghold of the old guard and which took a
position against harshness of expression and other displays of "the mod-
ern distemper." Cummings lashes out at any poets who, because they
follow tradition, are dull:

> i would
>
> suggest that certain ideas gestures
> rhymes,like Gillette Razor Blades
> having been used and reused
> to the mystical moment of dullness emphatically are
> Not To Be Resharpened. . . .

The poem is filled with scatological jokes. For instance, Cummings
refers to the American songsters as "indigenous throstles," knowing full
well that the scientific name for the throstle or thrush is "turdus musi-
cus." In the end, he pictures them as constipated children straining to
produce their poetic efforts. (He takes the final advertising slogan from
Colgate toothpaste):

littleliverpill-
hearted-Nujolneeding-There's-A-Reason
americans(who tensetendoned and with
upward vacant eyes,painfully
perpetually crouched, quivering, upon the
sternly allotted sandpile
—how silently
emit a tiny violetflavoured nuisance:Odor?

ono.
comes out like a ribbon lies flat on the brush

Although this was the era when *Main Street* and *Babbitt* were causing a stir, Sinclair Lewis was never so cleverly fierce as this.

As with all his books of poems, the sales for *Is 5* were slim. His principal source of income was, and would be for the next year, *Vanity Fair*. For Frank Crowninshield and Douglas Freeman, his "well-intentioned nit wit employers,"[2] he continued to perform comic "turns."

There was a new development in another area of Cummings' life: during 1925 he was able for once to do something for his father and to appear as someone other than a mere heedless youth. Sometime during the year, Edward's church merged with the First Church in Boston at 64 Marlborough Street. The First Church had great prestige because it had been the place of worship for the founders and leaders of Massachusetts Bay Colony—such men as Hutchinson, Winthrop, Bradstreet, Endecott, and Cotton—but it had a dwindling membership. It also had a splendid building, whereas the drab, brick South Congregational Church had really only one asset, a Skinner organ. When the pewholders of the South Congregational Church voted to merge with the First Church and move the Skinner organ down to Marlborough Street, Edward Cummings, now 64 years old, was really out of a job, although he was awarded the post of Minister Emeritus. In return for some of the support Edward had given him during his year of griefs, Estlin now had a chance to bolster his father. The occasion, one day in Cambridge, is recorded in a reminiscence:

He came quietly down the front door steps (& I was standing in the little piece-of-yard near the garage-made-of-doors) moving as if he were full of darkness. Suddenly I decided to try an experiment; & I said:

"You can only see that you've lost the church, but that isn't so." He looked at me. "In losing the church" I said "you've entered the world. You're a wordly person; why deny it?" We stood face to face. "Only a small part of you could possibly fit in that church" I said almost angrily "—all the rest

of you had to remain outside. You're like a child who shut his finger in the
door. Now the finger's out of the door & that finger hurts you but it won't
hurt you long. And what if it hurts horribly—you're free! Now you can
move, love, be & do things; because you are yourself again: now (for the first
time in years) you're really you. And I know this really you—he's all sorts
of people, who can do any number of things & do them beautifully. Believe
me, instead of feeling sorry the church let you go, I thank heaven it did. I
think getting out of the church was the very best thing that could have
happened to you. I congratulate you" I said to him. "I feel every thing's
fine!"

His great shoulders straightened, he began to grow high; his head
climbed nobly into the sunlight: & his wonderful voice said slowly, "if you
feel that way about me, I'll feel that way." Then he smiled. He drew me
tenderly to him.[3]

Estlin was trying to put matters into proper perspective. Edward, at
age sixty-four, was still Executive Secretary of the World Peace Founda-
tion, and he could also look forward to years of opportunity for involving
himself in civic betterment.

II

One night in mid-1925, Morrie Werner had introduced Cummings to a
strikingly attractive young woman named Anne Barton, who worked off
and on as a fashion model. Anne had been recently divorced from Ralph
Barton, the New York caricaturist and cartoonist, best known perhaps
for his illustrations in Anita Loos's book, *Gentlemen Prefer Blondes,* one of
Liveright's most popular publications. She had been born Anne Min-
nerly, the daughter of Leroy Minnerly, a policeman, in 1899 in New York,
and later moved with the family to Ossining, a town fifty miles up the
Hudson River. Since her parents were poor, she had gone to work early.
Without any special education or training, she had nothing to help her
make her way in the world except her looks, and when she was old
enough to live on her own, she returned to New York to exploit her one
asset as an artist's model. In 1917 at the age of seventeen she married Ralph
Barton, who was then a struggling young artist, and had a daughter by
him in 1921. Although Barton was a notorious womanizer, the match
lasted until 1923, when he openly took up with Carlotta Monterey, the
actress who played the lead in O'Neill's *The Hairy Ape.* Anne decided that
she had had enough and sued for divorce. She was awarded the custody
of the child and alimony. At the time Cummings came on the scene in
1925, she had just broken off an affair with the son of an Italian admiral

Anne Barton, 1927.

and she was looking for another man. She and Cummings, both very much in need of affection, were attracted to each other from the moment they met. The earliest item in their correspondence that survives is a telegram from Anne to Estlin dated July 10, 1925:

THANK YOU KIND SIR MIDNIGHT.

Cummings was soon a frequent caller at her apartment, 55 Charles Street, not far from Patchin Place and their love affair developed quickly.[4]

Anne was very different from Elaine, not only in economic and social background but in personality and temperament. She was witty and vivacious, mischievous, much given to laughter. She loved parties, good jokes, the attentions of men. She had the kind of female allure that made every male in a room aware of her as soon as she entered. She drank heavily and smoked incessantly, leaving behind her heaps of crushed, lipstick-stained cigarette ends. She dressed smartly rather than elegantly and in snapshots or in paintings seems to represent accurately the Greenwich Village flapper of the 1920's. Unlike Elaine, she loved to pose for Cummings. It is possible that her willingness was partly responsible for the change in style in Cummings' painting which began in the mid-twenties. After 1925 he entered no more Noises or Sounds in the Independent Artists shows; he sent nudes, portraits, landscapes.[5]

Anne's piquancy stimulated Cummings, bringing out his own liveliness, and her jollity quickened his wit and pulled him away from his recent indulgence in loneliness and self-pity. She was also, as he later remembered, his "first real introduction to sex" and a welcome replacement for his idealized worship of Elaine. Nor was she in any way the mothering caretaker. Thus Cummings' life with Anne began to develop him away form the *petit garçon* he had been in his first marriage. None of his letters to Anne survive, but one draft of an early note to her, on Hotel Brevoort stationery, shows that he played a rather different role in their intimate communications. He was now the romantic poet who lives with a heightened awareness of the natural world and its changes of season and who calls to his beloved to join him:

> Anne, I wish you would come. A tall slippery lady in a white dress whose name is Madame Ilneige has postponed spring. The flowers in this room, the heavy yellow flowers, and the narcissus whose exquisite smell is of pudeur; they do nothing. They remember you[,] doing nothing. The flowers do nothing cleverly on my table, and a little measly snow tumbles in the dark air, and that high voice of my heart suddenly stops like an Arabian song. You will come. I do not know what day it is, and the white stupid face of the clock stops at three minutes past seven. (I shall not wind it because you are coming.)
>
> Did anyone believe in spring? The boy-limbed girl has put on her pajamas to go to bed, to go into the little dusty couch and lie with her lover. . . . and they will do nothing and feel one another turn in the dark, and in the light they will do nothing but look at one another, and they'll talk fooling and smile to each other.
>
> Just now it is snowing a little; the flowers of my room, which wait for you, they know you will come, (oh yes!) the white charming flowers and the big dumb flowers know—
> Fleur lourde,
> that is my heart[6]

But Anne was also the cause of much anger and bitterness because she was not ready to be faithful to one man. In fact, at the time her love affair with Cummings began, she was already involved with an older man named Douglas, a "merchant prince" as Cummings called him, who gave her financial support and promised to settle some money on her daughter, Diana. Cummings apparently closed his eyes to the fact that Anne regularly exchanged her sexual favors for Douglas's patronage and tried to pretend to himself that Douglas was only a fatherly advisor.

Although he had very little money, Cummings was able to give Anne one thing that the merchant prince did not have time to provide, a personally guided trip to Europe, and he made arrangements as soon as he received the money from the *Dial* award. In late March 1926, he took her and Diana to France aboard the *DeGrasse,* the "writers and artists" ship. He was able to introduce the woman he loved to Paris in April (alas, it was cold and rainy) and to Italy in June, including Venice, his favorite Italian city. When they returned to the United States in July, Cummings went up to Silver Lake to work on a play. Meanwhile Anne became very domestic. She cleaned and redecorated the Patchin Place studio and bought a new bed. Although she had lunch with Douglas as soon as she returned and although she allowed him to buy her three dresses, purses, and other articles, she reported it all to Cummings in a letter of July 14, saying, "I wish I were with you. I miss you terribly—I love you very much now—I have no doubt about it—and the realization that I do makes me happy."[7]

The months with Anne began to change Cummings's patterns of living. Since she was a party girl, he now spent increasingly more time in drinking and conviviality, especially with literary and theatrical figures in Greenwich Village studios or the better-known speakeasies. Marte's at 75 Washington Place became a real hangout for him. "You could always find him there," Werner said. Edmund Wilson included Cummings and Anne on his list "for an ideal party." Hart Crane recorded an account of a wild evening with them, "a riotous competition" in which he "won the cocktail contest" and afterwards spent a night in jail for having insulted a policeman. The next day, he continued, "I was good and mad. Made an impassioned speech to a crowded court room, and was released at 10 o'clock without even a fine. Beer with Cummings in the afternoon which was almost better than the evening before, as C's hyperbole is even more amusing than one's conduct, especially when he undertakes a description of what you don't remember. Anyhow, I never had so much fun jounced into 24 hours before, and if I had my way would take both C'gs and Anne along with me to heaven when I go."[8]

Anne's companionship was especially valuable to Cummings during the period of his troubles with the MacDermots over Nancy. She helped him to become resigned to the difficulties of dealing with them and to settle his mind to the point that he could undertake new literary work. He had not been creating anything to speak of in 1925, except essays and comic sketches for *Vanity Fair.* Both the novel and the play about Edward Seul and Heloise were obviously therapeutic exercises and after a time were put aside, but the attractions of doing some work in dramatic form remained. The twenties were exciting years in the American theater. The Theatre Guild and the Neighborhood Playhouse had both been bringing the new European drama to the American audience, and the Little Theatre Movement—especially the Provincetown Playhouse on Mac-Dougal Street in Greenwich Village—was encouraging new American playwrights.

Since Cummings had been spending time with both John Howard Lawson and John Dos Passos, he no doubt heard them discussing their expressionistic experiments in drama. Lawson's *Processional* was produced by the Guild in 1925 and Dos Passos' play, *The Moon is a Gong,* was produced at Harvard the same year and with its new title, *The Garbage Man,* was given a New York production in March 1926. Both of these plays, as well as Elmer Rice's *The Adding Machine,* 1923, gave a special American flavor to expressionism. Although the principle of "expressing inner experience by means of external action" was the acknowledged aim, their plays made use of humor, and their satire had a comic lightness. Both Lawson and Dos Passos introduced one more element—an attempt to make use of the forms of the American popular theater. Lawson described *Processional,* which was a play about a strike, as a "jazz symphony of American life" and declared that his technique was "essentially vaude-villesque in character." Dos Passos' play, which was about a young man and a young woman who are seeking to free themselves from the deter-mining forces of society, also has the episodic form of the vaudeville revue.

The play that Cummings wrote in 1926 is in this American expression-istic tradition, although at first he was as somber as Strindberg because he was trying to present Freudian ideas in symbolic action. In his first approach, his main character, Edward, represents consciousness or the ego. He is in love with Anna, who represents Beauty as well as a sexual goal. Also attracted to Anna is Jan, who represents the subconscious (in an even earlier draft he was the Janitor, who lived in the basement). Edward, who is a playwright, is frustrated both in his attempts to win Anna and in his artistic endeavors. Jan, who is never seen by his rival Edward, has more success with Anna, and Edward is planning to shoot him (or, in other pages, to shoot himself). Anna, in some drafts of the play, is drawn to Jan and unfaithful to Edward; in other versions, she is Ed-ward's lover but has a hysterical fear of pregnancy. In some drafts Jan is a hunchback (because the unconscious is not associated with thinking but with "hunches.") The final product, which is unnecessarily complex, is never completely clear in the ideas that it presents, but one aim is quite evident. In a series of scenes which draw upon the circus side show, the vaudeville revue, and the burlesque show, Cummings was attempting to present the realm of the unconscious—the unconscious thoughts of both Edward and Anna.[9]

As Cummings worked in 1926, the play took its final form, which was published under the title *Him* in 1927. By now, the main character, named Him, is a new manifestation of the nonhero, the lower-case i; he is Everyman and Anybody but he is an artist, a playwright. In the action, he is struggling to bring his play into being and has developed a case of writer's block. In a parallel action, his girl friend, whose name is Me is seen under anaesthetic on the operating table, giving birth to a child.

In the hospital scene, which keeps recurring throughout the play, sit three figures, rocking and knitting, and carrying on a weird gossipy conversation made up of slogans, twisted proverbs, and non sequiturs. They represent the three Fates, who in Greek mythology, are the dieties of childbearing. The jumble of their talk with its illogical mixture of the folk wisdom of the ages and contemporary references to American manu-factured products can be thought of as the psychic flotsam of Me's uncon-scious.

The next scene, set in a "Room" in the apartment of Him and Me, begins a series of discussions between the two, bearing on the problem that Him is having writing his play and on his difficulty in apprehending reality. Me, on the other hand, is concerned about their relationship and about his preoccupations which cause him to neglect her (Cummings put a great deal of Elaine into Me). Throughout this scene and later, he keeps looking in a mirror and making reference to another self who is the Man in the Mirror, (Again, some aspects of Jan have been transfered to the Man in the Mirror—Him even draws a pistol in front of him at one point.)

The dialogue between Him and Me leads eventually to Him's show-ing parts of his play to her, although the play has not been written by Him but by the Man in the Mirror. We thus move to Act II, a series of nine (corresponding to the nine months of pregancy) vaudeville skits many of them quite amusing, especially in performance rather than in reading. Yet each carries some kind of symbolic suggestion that has to do with identity or sexual personality or psychic problems of one sort or another. For instance, in Scene VI an Englishman enters staggering under a trunk marked "Fragile." He tells an inquiring detective that the trunk is his unconscious. When the detective wants to know what's in it, the Englishman tells him he doesn't know. After a good deal of verbal play about that idea, the detective opens the trunk, looks in it, and keels over from the shock of what he sees. In another scene (recognized at the time as a parody of O'Neill's *The Great God Brown*), two businessmen named Bill and Will, wear masks representing each other. In the course of a lot of dialogue like "Who are you?" "You mean 'Who am I?'", the masks and identities become exchanged and confused. Another scene involves a Negro ensemble singing "Frankie and Johnie"—in a version supplied by Edmund Wilson. A censorious figure like John S. Sumner arises from the audience to stop them just as they are about to utter a vernacular term for penis. After a hassle, he is frightened out of the theater when Frankie, a forthright black woman, shows him an amputated penis wrapped in a napkin ("The best part of the man / who done me wrong").[10]

There is no coherent scheme of ideas that the sequence of skits offers —and this is a distinct weakness in the play. The skits, then, constitute a kind of topical or intellectual revue. What Him says of his play is accurate, "It's about anything you like, about nothing and something and everything, about blood and thunder and love and death—in fact, about as much as you can stand."

As the play proceeds, every time the "Room" set is shown, the audience sees it from another side so that, in time, all four walls have been moved around in sequence. This emphasis on the walls leads to questions about breaking out beyond the walls into reality. In Act III, we are given the final psychic fantasy, a circus side show, presided over by a hunchback barker. It represents, one may guess, Me's psychic processes just at the end of childbirth. The barker introduces each of the eight freaks, the tattooed man, the missing link, the fat lady, and so on, and finally (note the number nine again) the Oriental dancer, Princess Anankay (Greek: for Necessity), who is guaranteed to [I translate the dialect] "boost your splendiferous bowlegged blueeyed exterior out of the peagreen interior of pinkpurple superconscious fourteen million astral miles into the prehensile precincts of predetermined prehistoric preternatural nothing." But when he pulls the curtain, there stands Me holding a newborn babe in her arms. The crowd recoils. Him utters a cry of terror. The Three Fates shout, "It's all done with mirrors."

We return to the Room for a final scene, and Me's thinking turns out to be about the fact that the Room has only three walls. She points to the fourth (the audience) and invites Him to consider escape out of the Room by means of letting the true world in through that wall.

Even in the few portions of the play we have been considering, we can see that *Him* has a good deal to do with bringing to birth.[11] But what it has to say about giving birth to artistic creation is puzzling. Further, the questions, why Him is terrified by the sight of Me as a mother, why nothing is ever said about the baby in that scene or later (was it a stillbirth and not childbirth?),[12] and why such a mechanical resolution of the playwriting problem is offered in the final scene, give us pause about the wholeness of Cummings' play. Cummings put a great deal of himself into *Him,* but even though he was quite aware, as some of his notes show, that the climactic revelation of Me with the baby is like an Oedipal moment of recognition,[13] still he was not aware of something else: that his own early response to Elaine and her baby had been re-enacted by Him. At this point of Cummings' career, it appears that neither his personal nor his creative life were sufficiently under control for him to be able to unify the fascinating assembly of parts which make up this highly personal play. It remains a conglomeration of brilliant insights, will-o'-the-wisp digressions, moving poetic speeches, tiresome verbal nonsense, provoca-tive ideas, and what Crowninshield had called "turns."

In the fall of 1926, Cummings had just given the final version of *Him* to a typist when a family tragedy occurred. On November 2, when Ed-ward was driving Rebecca Cummings up to Silver Lake, they ran into an early snowstorm in the Ossippee Mountains. Blinded by the snow, he failed to see a train coming at a grade crossing. In Estlin's words, this is what happened: ". . . a locomotive cut the car in half, killing my father instantly. When two brakemen jumped from the halted train, they saw a woman standing—dazed but erect—beside a mangled machine; with blood 'spouting' (as the older said to me) out of her head. One of her hands (the younger added) kept feeling of her dress, as if trying to discover why it was wet. These men took my sixty-six year old mother by the arms and tried to lead her toward a nearby farmhouse; but she threw them off, strode straight to my father's body, and directed a group of scared specta-tors to cover him. When this had been done (and only then) she let them lead her away."[14] She was taken to a nearby hospital at Wolfboro, New Hampshire, where, by candlelight because the snow had brought down the electric lines, her injuries were treated and her head stitched.

Down in New York, Cummings and Anne were enjoying a small party at Werner's apartment. Elizabeth came in and asked to speak to her brother in another room. When they emerged, Estlin's face was drawn. "It seems my father has been killed," he said to the others in a solemn voice. He and Elizabeth took the train north and the next day were at Rebecca's bedside. Her skull had been fractured, she was scarcely alive. The surgeon, Dr. Clough, did not expect her to live but thought that in five days they would know if recovery were possible. With the presence of her children to inspire her will to live, she gradually improved. But she kept complaining, as time went on, that she felt something strange in her head. Estlin called in a consultant who recommended she be moved to a Boston hospital. Two weeks after the accident, she was moved to Peter Brent Brigham Hospital by ambulance, where after X-rays it was decided to reopen the wound. The next day, she triumphantly showed her children the dirt and splinters that had been sewn into the wound the first time. "You see?" she said. "I was right."

Another occurrence lent sadness to the end of 1926. Scofield Thayer, who had been behaving more and more strangely, had succumbed, despite the ministrations of Freud, to a breakdown and was now under private care. He was never capable of managing his own affairs again. To what extent the Estlin-Elaine affair contributed to his condition one cannot be sure.

III

Cummings placed *Him* in the hands of a literary agency, Brandt and Brandt. But as usual his friends tried to help his career along. Marianne Moore, who was now the managing editor of the *Dial*, had always thought highly of Cummings' work, even of his essay on Lachaise. She now asked the agency if the *Dial* office might look over the play, and upon reading it, she wrote to Watson with an opinion, "Some of it seems to me as imaginative and expert as anything of his I have read; and some of it to the contrary."[15] She recommended that they print one scene, the first dialogue between Him and Me. Watson read through the script and decided to publish additional scenes, including the circus side show and the conclusion, although he was worried about giving readers material that would go over their heads. Miss Moore replied in her own forthright way: "I am willing, in the case of Mr. Cummings, to thrust on subscribers what I think they won't like—because the work has my complete aesthetic approbation. (The trunk scene has not, but I should like to do by Mr. Cummings as handsomely as possible)."[16] These excerpts from *Him* appeared in the August 1926 issue of the *Dial,* and Miss Moore also chose to reproduce the photo of "Noise Number 13" which had appeared in the Independent Artists exhibition catalogue the previous year. Soon afterward, Boni and Liveright, who were now becoming Cummings' chief publisher, went out on a limb and issued the entire script in book form, even though it still had no producer in 1927.

Meanwhile the agency and friends like Mrs. Draper were trying to find a producer who would stage it or a backer who would invest in it. Lawrence Langner, one of the directors of the Theatre Guild, was interested but was worried about some of its obscenities. At the same time, the Provincetown Playhouse, which prided itself on being "a home for young creative talent," was looking for a new playwright to replace Eugene O'Neill, who had graduated to Broadway. Henry Alsberg, one of the directors, thought he had found one when he read Cummings *Him,* but he had a hard time convincing the other members of the production staff: "Few of them could discover what the play was about."[17] They were also discouraged by the fact that it would be expensive to stage. It had a cast as large as a musical revue, and it called for a great many changes of set. The cramped little theater at 133 MacDougal Street had no wings and no overhead fly space, thus it would be a complex undertaking to stage a play with twenty-one scenes. Even the "Room" scene which recurred five times had to be turned around each time it appeared. Nevertheless, the executive board decided to take a chance on the Cummings' script, and James Light, who was selected to direct the play, sat down with Cummings and Eugene Fitsch, the set designer, and worked out ways that the action could be handled and the 105 parts could be played by 30 actors. Henry Alsberg said later that Cummings was "the only playwright he ever dealt with who was reasonable, decent, and intelligent, etc."[18]

For Cummings the production provided a series of experiences just as thrilling as the early exhibitions of the Independent Artists. He hung about for rehearsals and talked like an interpretive drama coach to William Johnstone, the young actor who played Him. He fell vicariously in love with Erin O'Brien-Moore, the young beauty who played Me. He dined or drank with the members of the cast across the street at Sam Schwartz's Black Knight Club and spent many hours talking with Jimmy Light, who became one of his best friends, and his wife Patti, whom Cummings found powerfully attractive. Since the play was far too long, he had to cut it, and Helen Deutsch, remembering the shaping of the play during rehearsal, felt that it became more intelligible.

The play opened on April 18, 1928, to a bewildered but responsive audience. Cummings had tried to prepare them by a "Warning" printed on the program, which advised, "Relax and give the play a chance to strut its stuff—relax, stop wondering what it's all 'about'—like many strange and familiar things, Life included, this Play isn't 'about,' it simply is. ... Don't try to enjoy it, let it try to enjoy you. DON'T TRY TO UNDERSTAND IT, LET IT TRY TO UNDERSTAND YOU."[19] He was hoping to get across the notion that the play was not a product but an opportunity for an experience—and each person might experience it differently.

The regular Broadway reviewers, with the exception of John Anderson of the *New York Journal,* threw vegetables and dead cats: a sample, "Fatiguing, pretentious and empty" (Alexander Woolcott); "For utter guff, this Cummings exhibition has never been surpassed within the memory of the oldest play-reviewer operating in Manhattan" (George Jean Nathan); ". . . Mr. Cummings' attempt . . . to chew up *Processional* and Frank Sullivan and Ring Lardner and Mike Gold and Jean Cocteau into one great looney quid and squirt the juice at us" (Robert Littell).[20]

But the audiences liked the play, for the production had real zest. The response was largely to the burlesque sketches and vaudeville skits, but some of the Dada nonsense and verbal pyrotechnics were just as fascinating to listen to as a Cummings monologue, and symbolic significances floated forth to haunt the mind. The Village audiences—intellectuals, Bohemians, academics—liked the play, and some people returned more than once. It ran to full houses (200 people) for 27 performances, though it made no money for the Playhouse because production costs were so high. It provided a fine climax for the 1927–1928 season.

During its run, the board issued a pamphlet entitled *him and the critics*, which set the harsh opinions of the Broadway reviewers against the views of several New York intellectuals (including some of Cummings' friends)—Conrad Aiken, William Rose Benét, S. Foster Damon, Waldo Frank, Paul Rosenfeld (the music critic for the *Dial*), John Sloan (the distinguished naturalistic painter), Edmund Wilson, and Stark Young. Gilbert Seldes wrote an introduction, asserting, "There is very little obscurity about the essence of *Him*."[21] He felt that the play was misunderstood because it presented serious themes through the technique of the burlesque show and the circus. The board hoped that a literary controversy about the play would entice subscribers for their next series. They announced another Cummings play for the 1928 season. Although Cummings was not able to bring that play into being, it was announced again for the 1929 season. Richard Lockridge, writing in the *New York Sun*, May 13, 1929, was one of those who were intrigued. "The anticipation of another play by the author of 'Him' is enough to sustain one through any summer's theatrical starvation. Not that it is certain to be successful, or even articulate. But almost certainly it will precipitate another such joyous literary dog-fight as resulted from 'Him' 's publication and subsequent presentation last season. Ladies and gentlemen usually most quiet and considerate snarled at one another. . . . The debate brightened things up immensely, at a time when things rather needed brightening. Now, if Mr. Cummings will only write a 'Her'."[22]

IV

"I'm through with Anne," Cummings had written to his mother on September 4, 1927. "Needless to add I stood as much as I could—then retreated. I think this will (if anything) help her." This is only one of a good many letters and notes that display the difficulties that Cummings had been having with Anne. When their relationship began, Anne had tried to break off her arrangement with Douglas, but she found herself unwilling to do without the money that he supplied, and Cummings thus found himself like Thayer, years before, having to put up with another man in his woman's life. Time might have eliminated this source of trouble but Anne had other serious emotional problems. She went through periods of excessive drinking. She suffered depressions during which she threatened to throw herself out the window or wished that a bus would run over her. She had come from a very troubled home situation and had even been a victim of the incestuous attentions of her father. No doubt this lay behind her emotional upset in general and her promiscuous behavior in particular. But Cummings loved her and grieved that he could not control her wandering. He sloughed off some of his bitterness in notes for a poem that he scribbled on the back of an envelope: "She was a woman upon whom many men might go, as if she were a ship; she took them somewhere. . . . And she was a woman into whom many men might go as many breaths inflate a balloon (which we admire for a moment) which is held for a moment & released: whereupon it jumps and exhausts itself, falling sillily, flops. And it must be reinflated."

In September 1927, "Anne's present capers" were being carried on around Peter Finley Dunne, the son of the famous American humorist of the Theodore Roosevelt era. "Mr. Dooley's descendant," Cummings called him. It was one thing for Cummings to have to ignore her traffic with Douglas but quite another to have her frisking with other men too. A week later they had made up their quarrel, for Cummings was deeply bound to her and she swore that she loved him very much. But Cummings never knew how long these reconciliations were going to last.

Rebecca Cummings, who was now in the process of moving to New York to live at 83 Washington Place, was very kind to Anne and very tolerant of her son's new love affair. She did what she could to keep them together. She invited them up to Silver Lake to stay in one of the cottages or at the farm. In this way little Diana was able to have a real summer vacation and a more stable family situation with a real father-figure in the household. What Nancy had lost, Diana gained, and she loved the summers at the farm and the swimming and boating in Silver Lake in the same way that Estlin had. Diana was six when she first came to the farm in 1927. Cummings had three pet rabbits waiting for her when she arrived. She and Estlin (her "dear Comi") began to be more close now. Yet Estlin, although ready to be her playmate, was still not ready to give his heart to her as fully as he had to Nancy. His whole relationship with Anne was too precarious. We can get some idea of the uncertainty of their future from the following summary in a letter to his mother on September 17:

Anne is, to use her own words "just rapidly desintegrating." . . . Wants money, but wants it handed to her in the shape of "support" by a *husband.* The only thing which could possibly keep us together now is her love of Joy Farm. For, according to Anne, everything which she does (down to the slightest move) is *in relation to Diana;* and Joy Farm she wants as a place in which to have Diana of a summer. So long as I am moneyless I don't count. Particularly since she (rightly) wishes to get rid of a father-substitute whom she's known for years, who has money, buys her giddy things, pays her rent, promises that he'll give Diana $50,000—all on condition that she plays up to him to the extent of dining and taking advice and being bossed etc. I advised her to *earn* her way out of this mess—and what a mess!—but no; she lacks the ambition to do that; or rather, she thinks she's too good to work for her living again and good enough to get a rich husband. The trouble is, therefore, that *she wants to take money from a man she loves.* Cure: get rid of a moneyless beloved, I should say! (For my year's work with Vanity Fair seems to have taught me that I'm no supporter of a wife, let alone myself). And it's no small sum that'll do the trick: big money wanted. Oh how big. I am sincerely disappointed by her discouragement.[23]

Their future seemed impossible. Anne was determined to have money, especially for Diana's sake, and Estlin was set in a pattern of life that would never allow him an adequate income.

By the time a week had passed, something had been done to pull Anne out of her low spirits. She was on a ship headed for France. Just how Estlin arranged to send her is not clear. There are hints that he sold off a timber lot at Joy Farm to buy Anne's passage.

She returned on the *Homeric* the morning of October 22, almost hysterically gay. Cummings was unable to meet the ship because only one pass onto the pier was allowed per passenger and her "merchant prince" had secured that. All day he dispatched notes to her asking her to break away and come to Patchin Place. She showed up about 4:30 P.M., reporting that she never felt so well, that ever since she left she had drunk nothing but champagne. She enjoyed herself tremendously, never laughed so much, her laugh rang out all over the *Homeric.* She had the constant attentions of men, beginning with the voyage over on the *Ile de France.* Cummings inquired if she slept with people, only to hear that she had confined her favors to one man, "o-o-o *so* handsome." She was not sorry. She was glad she did it. She needed to do it. Cummings thanked her for telling him, thinking wryly that he provided the occasion for cuckolding himself. But when he discovered that she and her lover looked so much alike that everyone thought they were brother and sister and when she referred gaily to its incestuous overtones, he became repelled and worried.

Because of his real estate purchases at Silver Lake and some modest investments, Edward Cummings had accumulated a rather good-sized estate and it was all left to Rebecca with the understanding that Estlin and Elizabeth would, of course, share in any family wealth. After his father's death Estlin, who had been awarded a $1000.00 legacy, had told his mother he wanted nothing more, no gifts, no share, the money was all to be kept by her. Now, faced with the emotional disturbance of the woman he loved and a sense that he, too, needed some better way of governing his life, he told Anne that he would underwrite the expense of her psychoanalysis. "I did this knowingly," he told his mother, "and in me right mind because you spoke of getting me the vast some of too thousand dollars out of the estate. For that some, we could both be analyzed (independently). Won thousand should suit [Dr. A. A.] Brill (supposed to be America's foremost, translated Freud's Traumdentung, etc.) and Brill should suit Anne. I'd prefer Watson's man Kempf myself. Of course, Anne thinks that a thousand will impoverish me, but damned if I do! In case Brill worked pro me—a slight chance, but a big one—I might be spared my own analysis. The proposition is a sporting one, neither more nor less. I love Anne and I should like her to be happy in herself—I've done my best; all I can do now is to let a better mind than mine—an impartial mind—do its best. She deserves her freedom, if that's to be her fate, or I deserve her love, if that's to be my fate. This must seem a dreadful thunderclap to you—with my previous O-no-I-don't-want-any-cash cries still prevailing in the unequal wind; in which case I'm sorry. All is, I need to give her this present."[24]

Cummings had been deep in Freud during the previous year. He had been reading, or rereading, *A General Introduction to Psychoanalysis,* the summary that Freud made of his theory in a set of lectures at the University of Vienna and his first book published in the United States (by Liveright). He had read, and recommended to both parents, Freud's new book, *Totem and Taboo.* He had been, as we have seen, earnestly trying to adapt the action of his play to the Freudian scheme of ideas. It is not surprising that he considered analysis at this crucial point of his life with Anne. A number of people he knew had turned to analysts with satisfactory results. Edward Nagel, Mrs. Lachaise, Sibley Watson, all had successful consultations. Thayer's case was the only failure he knew.

Rebecca Cummings came through generously with the money, but Dr. Brill turned out to be too hard-headed, even cynical, for both Estlin and Anne. Brill told her:

> Douglas supports her on the income of a large sum which he will leave to Diana "provided A. does not marry." (Anne)

Therefore she must marry someone with as much money as Douglas has or more.

Women need luxury.

I have no right to interfere with her promiscuity, since I have not enough money to compete with Douglas—albeit my objections are normal.

All women who have had sexual relations with their father are promiscuous always.

For a large sum he could analyze her & *perhaps* remove her father complex—but this would be useless unless she had money, so let her come back to him after she's married money!

She is neurotic, but has no neurosis. "A victim of circumstances—" "unhappy childhood."

"In short," Cummings reported to his mother, "he sized her up as a golddigger. This did not please A. as you may guess. Nor did it please your humble servant."[25]

He himself went to an analyst the next day "to lay bare my problem," though he was uncertain about what it was and why he was doing it. "I merely go because I feel right in going ahead." It is doubtful that Anne continued her course of analysis with Brill, but there is some evidence that Cummings continued to visit an analyst for at least a few sessions. A postscript to his mother records, "Have seen the psychiatrist. He's very nice—I think there's still a chance!"

Whatever the details may be, Anne continued to cause difficulties. One report in a letter to his mother December 30 gives a distressing picture of what Cummings had to bear (Anne had been visiting her mother in Ossining, New York, for Christmas):

> Thank you for the letter and review! I certainly needed cheering.
>
> Mary (Rody's girl) just dropped in with Anne. Anne was an entirely different person—scarcely able to sit still because she's been drunk for so long—venomous when she wasn't malicious—telling of one mean deed after another with relish—in short, more destructive, more unhappy, than I've ever seen her in my life (and I've seen her quite both). The mania is certainly at its height (or rather depth).
>
> I managed to keep clear—at least I think I did. . . .
>
> I actually feel that the only thing for me is to pray, and I do. Hope you will join me![26]

Cummings tried another approach to his problem of settling Anne down. In a very calculating way he turned to another woman in order to make Anne jealous (at least, this is what he reported to his mother.) Cummings met Emily Vanderbilt through Muriel Draper at a New

Year's Eve party when he was "investigating uptown" for the first time
in his New York life, and he continued to see her during January and
February, 1928. This happened just at the time Emily was divorcing
William H. Vanderbilt. Tall, blond, aggressive Mrs. Vanderbilt was an
extraordinarily beautiful woman. She seemed to be especially attracted
to literary men. She was later involved with Scott Fitzgerald and with
Thomas Wolfe, who used her as a model for his character, Amy Carleton
in *You Can't Go Home Again.* Reports depict her as a neurotic, unpredict-
able, sensation-seeking person. Just now her picture was appearing all
across the nation in an advertisement in which she, as Mrs. Vanderbilt,
endorsed Old Gold Cigarettes. But her letters to Cummings show her
simply as a vivacious personality who also liked to write poems.

Uptown life and Park Avenue towers (Babylonian, he told her) were
not really Cummings' style, but the brief love affair perhaps restored
some confidence after the treatment he had been receiving from Anne.
"So far the lady has played me straight," he confided to his mother, "(it
being understood that the word V[anderbilt] attracts me and the name
E. E. Cummings her, we get on very well.)"[27] He was later to comment
that she had the most beautiful breasts of any woman he had ever seen,
and he was a good judge of these matters.

Whether Anne became jealous or whether she became fascinated
with all the activities of the play production during the spring of 1928 is
uncertain. Whatever the reasons, she and Cummings came back together
again, and on May 28 when he had gone up to Silver Lake without her,
she wept because she missed him so much. Five weeks later, a happy
family group, Estlin, Anne, Rebecca, and Diana, all sailed on the *Suffren*
to Europe, where they spent the summer, mostly in Paris. Rebecca's
presence perhaps should have been more of a cause for Anne's jealousy
than if Emily Vanderbilt had come along, for Estlin and his mother had
drawn even closer since the death of Edward and since she had moved
to New York City. But Rebecca was such an amiable being that her
presence was more likely a deterrent to any troubles or quarreling be-
tween the young couple. She was also able to play a benign grandmoth-
erly role for Diana, whom she had come to love and who could now
occupy the space in her heart left sorely vacant after the loss of Nancy.

Cummings' activities are harder to follow when he is not writing
letters to members of his family. Nor did he have many publications at
this time. He was probably trying to write another play for the Province-
town Players and not succeeding. But something finally drove him late
in the year to undertake a full psychoanalysis with Dr. Fritz Wittels, a
Viennese disciple of Freud who had just come to the United States and
was lecturing at the New School for Social Research. A letter of Decem-

ber 28, 1928, mentions in passing, "The analysis made a leap and a bound today Wittels (as usual) being a genius."[28] Bills for $425 and $550 dated February 4 and March 1, 1929, indicate that he had thirty-five conferences with Wittels in January and February and four sometime earlier.[29]

Notes scattered throughout Cummings' papers attest to the fact that Dr. Wittels bolstered Cummings enormously in dealing with his problems. He is referred to as another father, as someone who saved his life, as someone who set him free. It is apparent that Wittels' method both reinforced Cummings' own philosophy of individualism and helped him to stand firm and live out this philosophy. He was, it seems, an extremely wise and gentle human being. Cummings left only one brief characterization of him. He is described as "a plump baldish lively and loyal man, who had sacrificed his own career (as a writer) to become a disciple of Freud; he symbolizes for me the merciful (the miraculous) non-necessity for any convention, any rule or rote or repetition —the privilege of one particular individual to (entirely on his own) explore some totally new dimension; he is the poet of Freedom & Opening; his tenderness is fearless." He and Cummings remained friends for the rest of their lives.

We can only guess from a few notes jotted down at the time what Cummings discovered about himself and what he learned about coping with his problems. But a few things are certain. He was made to face the fact that he lacked moral courage in dealing with others as long as he continued to play the role of a child, and feared the responsibilities of a man's life, which demand caring for others. Cummings was considering whether or not he could assume the responsibilities of marrying Anne and being a real husband for her. We can infer some of this from some fragmentary jottings that come from this period:

> rebelling *as a child* ("I won't marry because you want me to")
> If I could *stop fighting* with my father (dead) about marriage I *could fight* with the substitutes for my father (alive) e.g. MacDermot, Dunne
> I have never grown up
>   assumed the responsibilities of a man
> I prefer to have a mistress because it won't hurt me so much when I lose her (as, a wife)
> I won't fight for her.
>   to help her.[30]

Wittels treatment, it seems, brought Cummings to the point where he no longer feared giving himself fully to a beloved one, for within three weeks, he wrote to his mother, who was visiting Aunt Jane in Cambridge:

> I feel like marrying Anne! Please keep it a *secret*—but please also let me have my divorce papers (aren't they in the Cambridge safe deposit vaults?) as she says we must show our proof of asunder (respective) in order to legally unite (collective). . . . When are you coming in? (Anne insists that your presence is indispensable!)
>
> We plan to sail on the Holland American S.S. Niew Amsterdam about April 13th—also *sub rosa*. [31]

There were so many difficulties in finding all the right papers, even having to cable the French divorce court, that the wedding could not take place for a few more weeks, during which time the news even reached Walter Winchell's gossip column, "e.e. cummings, the playwright (who spells it that way) is plotting to elope to Yurrup with Anne Borden, one of Ralph Barton's exes."[32] Finally on May 1 the marriage was celebrated at All Souls (Unitarian) Church, Fourth Avenue at 20th Street, by the Reverend Minot Simons. John Dos Passos was best man; Rebecca and Elizabeth were witnesses. There had been a lot of drinking in the tense weeks before the wedding. Edmund Wilson, who was invited to the wedding breakfast at the Hotel Brevoort has left a description which, even allowing for the harsh manner of his notebooks does not bode well for the marriage:

> *The Cummings Wedding.* Dos with his withered bachelor's button— drinking at Hoboken—they had been stewed for days—married in what they called "the church of the Holy Zebra"—Dos had put them through it —Cummings had taken several baths, one after the other: he had felt his arms and legs getting numb as if they weren't there—Ann went to sleep and slept for days and couldn't wake up—awful moments just before the cere- mony (Cummings' mother and sister were there) when, after everything had been nonchalant and amiable, they all suddenly began snapping at one another.
>
> The sad German band—we had them come to the table and play the wedding march.—Cummings looked unusually washed and well and carried things off with an excellent easy distinguished manner.[33]

After two days at the Brevoort, they sailed for Europe and Paris in the spring. They planned to place Diana in a convent school to cultivate her French while they traveled on an extensive honeymoon trip. The "easy distinguished manner" which Wilson observed was a world away from the timid uncertainty which Cummings had displayed with Elaine at the Hotel Copley Plaza five years earlier.

XIX

Anne and Russia

The dictatorship of the proletariat is a continuation of the class strug-
gle under new conditions. The dictatorship of the proletariat is a
stubborn fight—bloody and bloodless, violent and peaceful, military
and economic, pedagogical and administrative—against the forces and
traditions of the old society.

PROGRAM OF THE COMMUNIST INTERNATIONAL, 1928

The honeymoon trip had an inauspicious beginning. Whether by chance
or by arrangement, the Cummings' ménage met Ralph Barton and his
fourth wife, Germaine Taileferre,[1] upon arrival in Paris, May 11. Over the
years Ralph had maintained intermittent and troubled relations with
Anne. He reluctantly provided support for Diana and occasionally made
it possible for Anne to take her on vacation trips, particularly to Kansas
City where the child could see her Barton relatives. He was, however, an
admirer of Cummings, and since he was a cartoonist, he had a fellow-
craftsman's appreciation for Cummings' line drawings which had ap-
peared in the *Dial* and *Vanity Fair*. Cummings responded well to Barton.
One of his notes reads: "I like RB much better than I expected (because
I see in him S[cofield] T[hayer]—Anne exaggerated; he's not a villain; she
made him one, it was all *her* fault."[2] The two couples and the child were
frequently together during the next few days. Barton was happy to spend
time with Diana; and Anne, Cummings observed with a twinge of jeal-
ousy, seemed pleased to sit at the head of Barton's table again on a day
when Germaine was ill.

Cummings made a set of notes in one of his sketchbooks which records the first part of this European trip. In it, his early days of marriage are seen as having the motif "On to New (honeymoon) vs. Back to Old (child, money)." Germaine talked the Cummingses into traveling by car on a joint motor trip to the South of France; thus Estlin soon found Anne, Diana, and himself in a chauffeur-driven Citroën winding down through the French "massif," stopping at La Puy (with its needle-spired church of Saint-Michel-Aiguille perched high on the pinnacle of a gigantic rock), moving on to Toulon, where Barton owned a villa, and then after a few days returning to Paris through Lyons. The whole trip was marked by too much drinking and punctuated by troubles and quarrels. Barton was tottering on the brink of divorce from Germaine, who split off from him part of the time and would have nothing to do with him. Barton was also so unstable in psyche that Cummings recommended that he seek help from Dr. Wittels.

The newlyweds had their quarrels too, as the notes reveal: "fight (I beginning to assert my independence: you come on home, that's what you said to *me* last night, when I wanted to drink more). SCENE. TEARING UP WEDDING CERT[IFICATE] etc.³ Cry: It's all a hideous mistake! I'm going back to Douglas. GOING BACK AMERICA DOUGLAS."⁴ Other conflicts arose over Diana, who at age eight after an irregular life was getting hard to handle. Cummings would not back up Anne's impetuous outbursts when the child misbehaved. Life calmed down finally after they left the Bartons. They placed Diana in a French convent for a month while they took a honeymoon journey to Austria. By July 20 they were all three back in the United States and absorbing New Hampshire serenity at Silver Lake.

During the next two years, Estlin and Anne spent an unusual amount of time in Europe, perhaps to save money. They would stay in New Hampshire until late fall, then travel to France during the winter, returning in spring to Joy Farm. Mrs. Cummings had given the Joy Farm property to them, and the deed was recorded in their names as joint owners. This was the first time in her apartment-dwelling life that Anne felt she had a real home and she responded fully to possession. In June 1930, she altered, redecorated, and refurnished the entire downstairs area of the house, and Estlin bargained with a local mechanic for an electric generator, run by a gasoline engine, so that they could have electricity at night. She bought a hen and a dozen chicks. She acquired two dogs, Chew-Chew and Tippy. Estlin built a playhouse for Diana. For himself, he built a study out in the woods "perched on an elephantine boulder and three trees." Anne called him to meals with a horn. "N. B. What a shock not to be a bachelor," he wrote his mother.⁵

Since Anne loved entertaining, they had a succession of guests during the summers of 1930 and 1931, among them John Dos Passos, who brought his new wife Katy; Gilbert and Amanda Seldes (Seldes set down his impressions of the White Mountains for his column in the *New York Journal*); Monroe and Mary Hall and their baby Mike. "Rody" Hall, who worked for the State Department, had come to know Cummings through his sister, Amanda Hall Seldes. He was awed by writers and worshipped Cummings, who in turn was awed by Hall because he was such a huge specimen of a man, "the last of the wielders of the two-handed sword."[6] Other visitors were Morrie Werner, who was pleased to have brought Estlin and Anne together, Hart Crane (probably the last time Cummings saw him alive), who brought Lorna Dietz, and, of course, Rebecca Cummings. Not all of the city folks appreciated the country as much as Anne. When Hart Crane and Lorna Dietz visited, they turned their backs on Mount Chocorua and spent all their time playing the victrola.[7]

II

In 1930, Werner, who had recently finished his biography of William Jennings Bryan, was free to travel, and he and Cummings planned an extended trip to Russia together. The educated people of the generation that served in World War I had all taken an eager interest in the development of the Soviet Union. Since they were highly critical of the industrial nations in which they lived and of their leaders who had brought civilization to such mass butchery in the war, they increasingly admired the Bolshevik government which had pulled out of the war and then gallantly fought to maintain itself against the interfering forces of England, France, and the United States. We have already seen Cummings taking this position in the letters to his father in the early 1920's. But very few people had visited Russia and seen what was happening there, for the situation of being beleaguered by the Great Powers had created an isolationist paranoia on the part of the Soviet leaders. Access to or observation of Russia under the Reds was tightly restricted, and almost all the information that was given to the world came carefully filtered from headquarters in Moscow or from specially selected visitors like Lincoln Steffens, whose statement, "I have seen the future and it works," was the most widely publicized comment on Russia in the 1920's.

During its first decade the Communist regime established itself firmly, and by 1929 the government announced its first Five-Year Plan to strengthen the economy. The new experiment in social planning fascinated European and American intellectuals, especially those like Cummings' New York friends, who, during the 1920's had professed socialist ideals. ("We were all socialists then," said Werner). The young people who followed the arts were particularly curious about the government-sponsored theater and film production in Russia and about the educational efforts to bring workers to museums, theaters, and lecture halls (the so-called proletcult program). Flippantly irreligious themselves, they were not troubled by the suppression of religious freedom and rather applauded the idea of substituting cultural programs for religious ceremonies. Now, in the 1930's, the Soviet-reported successes of the Five-Year Plan seemed triumphant in contrast to the economic depression that had just begun to spread over Europe and the United States. The picture of enlightened government appealed even more strongly to Americans than to young Europeans, for the United States had a heritage of idealism, and the recent years in their own country had shown them only a parade of closed-minded mediocrities like Harding, Coolidge, and Hoover at the head of their own nation.

Cummings did not have the money to make the Russian trip with Werner in 1930, but he maintained his interest even after Werner had returned with a first-hand account of the dismal and barbaric conditions that he had seen in the Soviet Union. This report contradicted the propaganda disseminated by Russia and the Communist Party of the United States and piqued Cummings' curiosity. Dos Passos had been enthusiastic when he returned from Russia in 1928. In the fall of 1930, as Estlin and Anne were getting ready to spend the winter in Europe, John and Katy Dos Passos came to Joy Farm for Cummings' thirty-sixth birthday on October 14. Dos had just finished writing *Nineteen Nineteen,* the novel in which he celebrated the Russian Revolution and excoriated the Western nations for their territorial politics at the Peace Conference. If Estlin never got an earful about Dos's Russian trip before, he certainly did now.

Estlin, Anne, and Diana left for Europe in November. During December they traveled from Paris to Lausanne to Munich to Vienna to Budapest to Prague to Berlin, where they spent Christmas in the suburb of Charlottenburg and Anne created a small Christmas tree out of parsley. The peak experience of all this travel was a trip to Rouen in January. When Estlin saw "the crazy houses and lacey gothics of Jeanne d'Arc's martyr-village," he said, "[it] made me wonder again at France; which certainly has more in it than the rest of creation multiplied by itself."[8]

Back in Paris, the Cummings family settled down in a rather small apartment at 32 bis rue du Cotentin. Here Estlin worked at his painting and made the final adjustments for a new volume of poems. Its title was W, a grafitto meaning "Viva" which is often seen scratched on walls in Latin countries ("Vive Briand," "Viva Mussolini," etc.) Boni and Liveright had already contracted to publish it and Cummings mailed the manuscript back to S. A. Jacobs, the printer who had come to be his special typesetter.

The particular circumstances that surrounded his decision to visit Russia before returning to the United States are not clear but people whom he had met in Paris no doubt influenced him. He had been spending some time with the Surrealist poet Louis Aragon, who had joined the French Communist party and who had recently visited Moscow. He had been seeing Mikhail Larionov, the painter who was the principal designer for Les Ballets Russes, and his wife, the painter Natalya Goncharova. He had met Ilya Ehrenburg, the Russian novelist, and he had been talking with some "pro-communist Americans" in Paris. Suddenly, in March, he cabled his mother inquiring if he still had $1000 in his bank account. It appears that there never was any plan for Anne to accompany him on the trip. Cummings knew that she was not capable of enduring a Spartan existence, and all the reports about Russia described grim living conditions.

He applied for a special "without-party" visa so that he could go where he wished instead of being herded about with a group of tourists, seeing only what the officials wanted him to see. Cummings had hoped to get to Moscow before May Day, but he had difficulties getting a visa. Only after Dos Passos, who was then traveling in Mexico, sent a wire to the Russian Embassy on Cummings' behalf did the visa come through. While he waited, Cummings studied Russian at the Berlitz School or at the apartment of his teacher, a native of Odessa who had fled after the revolution. He had to work very diligently at it, for even with his facility for languages, he found it harder to learn than Greek. With the help of his teacher he compiled a little grammar and phrase book to take along on the trip.

Shortly before he left Paris, Cummings had a surprise encounter with Elaine and Frank MacDermot at the Café Select in Montparnasse. Anne was not present, for she was in Switzerland placing Diana at a convent school for the spring. It was a tense but unruffled meeting. They, and the John Peale Bishops, who were with Cummings, had a drink together and exchanged news. Elaine had "recently produced a boy," who was named Brian. She inquired after his mother, his sister, Thayer, Mitchell and other friends, but did not once mention Nancy.[9] One wonders why Estlin did not ask.

For Anne, the timing of Estlin's trip to Russia was unfortunate. Just before or just after his departure in early May she discovered she was pregnant. The evidence about the situation is sparse and obscure. Generally speaking, Anne did not want another child at this time and Estlin was very reluctant to take on any more responsibility than he had. It is possible that after some family mulling, they decided to have Estlin go ahead to Russia since all the plans had been made and to have Anne try to find an abortionist in Paris. The pregnancy is not mentioned in her early letters to Cummings, dated in mid-May, but the abortion is discussed in her letter of May 31 as if she had already told him her plans about it before.[10] On the other hand, Cummings' mail did not always reach him in Russia and he may have heard the first news of her condition in that May 31 letter, for a very obscure reference is made in *Eimi,* the book about his Russian tour, to a telegram that he sent June 3, which said, DONT OPERATE UNLESS REASON.[11] Whatever the details may have been, it was a bad time for Anne to be alone and this occurrence, no doubt, put further strain on the marriage.

III

When Cummings left Paris for Moscow on a long train journey via Berlin, Warsaw, and Negoreloe, Poland, he was traveling toward what some members of his generation thought of as "The Future of Mankind."[12] His dissatisfactions with American culture made it just possible that he might judge Russia as having a better society in the making. Yet his philosophy of individualism ran so completely counter to collectivism that he must have known he would loathe what he found. At any rate, he had to see for himself. He secretly kept a diary from May 10 to June 14, and we are thus able to know the daily happenings and his responses. This diary formed the basis of his book *Eimi,* which was published in 1933.

Cummings' troubles started as soon as he arrived in Moscow. Ehrenburg, the novelist, had made special arrangements by telegram for Cummings to be met at the railroad station by the Russian dramatist, Vladimir Lidin. But Lidin did not appear, and having no one to give him guidance, Cummings fell into the hands of Intourist, the official travel agency for foreigners, which placed him at the Hotel Metropole, a deluxe hotel for foreign visitors which was far beyond his means. He was well aware of the irony: after traveling second-class all the way from Paris, he ended up surrounded by luxury in the Workers' Republic.

All his life, people had been coming to Cummings' rescue and in Russia there was no exception. The first of his guides was Henry Wadsworth Longfellow Dana, a professor studying the Russian theater who happened to be staying at the Metropole. Cummings had known Dana in Cambridge and chanced upon him the very first day. For the next week, Dana showed Cummings around, took him to the theater, intro-

duced him to Moscovites both American and Russian, made telephone
calls for him, and in his fussy, effeminate way (some of the Americans
called him "Mrs." Dana behind his back), he mothered Cummings at
every turn.[13] If Cummings was going to draw conclusions about what he
saw, Dana was as much a hindrance as a help, for he was, in Cummings'
phrase, a "New England idealist" and a "justifier" of the Soviet regime.

Moreover, he could do nothing to help Cummings find cheaper
housing. The Russian housing bureau assigned him a one-room dwelling
space but he found he would have to share it with an old woman. Another
American couple, Mr. and Mrs. David Sinclair (Upton Sinclair's son),
offered Cummings the unit they were vacating in a newly built housing
structure, but warned him of their dissatisfactions—no running water,
bedbugs, and close proximity to an evil-smelling communal toilet. Even
the unfastidious Cummings found, upon inspection, that he could not
endure it.

In spite of his difficulties he was cheerful, as a letter to Anne copied
into his diary reveals:

Dear Anne:
     There is an Arabian Nights church here which you should see some day
[St. Basil's]. The rest you'd hate—except (?) pas des belles femmes. Fortu-
nately for myself, for was not met at train, blundered into Dana at the Hotel
Metropole (his specialty is theater) & have been under the professorial wing
ever since. Was (am) quite right in guessing nobody's given (written) any
idea of hereabouts—either they've been seen through non-hereabouts eyes
(e.g. M R W[erner]) or haven't been seen at all (e.g. New Masses). Li'l me's
already acquainted with a) high life—my room costs 5 dollars a day, 1 dollar
being for breakfast with eggs & jam b) ikons (racket) c) "slums" d) theatres
e) powers that be f) literature—&—life etc. Have not yet presented a single
letter, incidentally: shall begin tomorrow.
     There isn't any toilet paper, lunch occurs about 3 (afternoon), dinner
= a pastry snatched in lobby (if lucky), museums move around with amazing
rapidity, street cars are only (except violent busses) plausible form of taxi,
everybody male (except étrangers) wears a cap & doesn't shave (unless a
high-high-high official possibly), food either vile or (I haven't tried the other
extreme yet) with nothing whatever, nobody has any sense of "efficiency"
or "time" or "comfort," there's a radio in every room of this hotel but I've
heard not one elsewhere, the eglises have crosses or double eagles, & I
imagine to have missed Moscow in 1931 would have been for me a curse
unparalleled. So probably, on the whole, "en tout cas" MRW[erner] was
right in his letter-remark to us re Rah Shah.
     Last night Prof. D. took me along (w. his elderly translatrix) to a show
called Necktie. A great many gents have the First Finger of their right hand

bandaged. [Cummings is here possibly hinting that a GPU agent with a bandaged finger is following him.] Lenin's mausoleum is imposingly Pyramidical. There's a dome which looks like a French tickler. Have not seen one faggot & hear they're hard to find.

On the other hand, "the feminine" simply does not exist—(at least, not yet!) Females smoke, wear too short skirts, are huge or dumpy or both—with the exception, maybe, of actresses who (for propaganda purposes) make up as gay gals. Such are a mere fraction of my early impressions, madame.

You photograph amazes ye lofty chamber; the bronze elephant frightens ye silent radio.

Write me "Intourist."

Love![14]

Although Cummings customarily found delight in unusual or exotic places, the delight was partly supplied by colorfulness and vitality. Now, in Moscow, farther than he had ever traveled, the drabness and dreary-spirited earnestness began gradually to depress him. The dirt and dilapidation, the substandard living conditions that he saw everywhere, and the overpowering stink of human bodies in trolley cars, cafés, and public buildings created an atmosphere of grey life. The theater which should have provided liveliness was weighted down with propaganda pieces. Even the technically brilliant productions of Vsevolod Meyerhold that he saw, *Roar China* and *The Last Decisive,* smelled of proletcult.[15]

Early in the first week, he visited Mrs. Lili Brik, the sister of Elsa Triolet, Louis Aragon's wife, and delivered some bourgeois luxuries—perfume, necklaces, cosmetics—and a stack of Parisian magazines. Here he enjoyed his first good dinner, "a magnificent meal!! Cognac, red & white wine (old, from Caucasus)"; he met his first "hero of work," a much be-medaled young man in uniform; and he met his first GPU official, "I thought there was something about him—besides, he didn't have as many medals as S[oldier] no. I. Also, hostess, from couch, had repeated (in R.) my remark about Proletcult as if to vindicate my presence".[16] It was well into the second week before he could move out of the Metropole. Some kind Americans, Mr. and Mrs. Charles Malamuth, took him into their apartment, rooms in a former mansion, where he was able to sleep on a couch in Malamuth's study.

By this time another distinctive characteristic of Soviet Russia had begun to trouble him. The dirt and stink of Moscow did not really matter greatly. He had, after all, put up with a lot in his life, including La Ferté-Macé and the run-down hotels of the Left Bank in Paris—nor were Greenwich Village and even Patchin Place models of American sanitation. But he began to feel oppressed by the sense of fear and the awareness of being watched that permeated the Moscow air. He observed an absence of laughter and enjoyment and a sense of guilt about pleasure. When he received no mail in two weeks, he suspected that the Russian censors were holding up both his outgoing and incoming letters. He began to conceive of Russia as another Enormous Room, this time covering one-sixth of the earth.[17]

The Malamuths were able to relieve some of this developing dread. Charles Malamuth, a professor of Slavic languages from the University of California who had taken a job as a newspaper correspondent, was a genial, six-foot man of good will married to Joan London (the daughter of Jack London), whom Cummings described in his diary as "the best-looking (California) girl that I have seen in R.")[18] Although Malamuth had once been sympathetic to the socialist experiment, his experience in Moscow had convinced him that the revolution had turned out wrong and that the dictatorial authorities were crushing the spirit of the Russian people and warping the minds of the young. Here at the Malamuth household, everyone was frank and open, and Cummings relaxed his tensions and felt especially soothed by the gracious presence of "J," as she asked him to call her.[19]

During his three-week stay in Moscow, Cummings met with many courtesies from writers and journalists, both American and Russian. Nicolay Efros, a theatrical critic and president of the Writers Club, invited him to lunch and introduced him to Sergei Tretyakov, the author of *Roar China,* and to Vsevolod Meyerhold, the celebrated theatrical producer and director of Moscow's Theater of the Revolution. Vladimir Lidin invited him to dinner (he claimed to have been unable to identify Cummings at the railroad station). Meyerhold asked him to tea and later arranged to have him see a rehearsal of his next production. Victor Eubank, the bureau chief of the Associated Press, entertained him and the Malamuths at a dinner that included a postprandial musical presentation of gypsy songs and dances. His opportunity to meet Maxim Gorky went awry, although he did attend a theatrical festival honoring the old man. Nor was an occasion suitable for meeting Walter Duranty.

These rather formal occasions were not unlike meetings with artists and writers in any European capital. What gave Cummings the real flavor of Soviet Russia was the experience of daily life: trying to find housing, exchanging currency at the bank, riding the often "too comrady" street cars, asking directions ("I don't know" was the commonest reply), watching officially guided groups being lectured or herded about in museums, buying matches, walking through the park (there were no lovers), seeking his mail (only one letter in three weeks), and struggling to obtain a permit to travel, an exit visa, and a railroad ticket. He did not visit any Soviet factories—he had seen enough of them in America—but he did join one

Intourist-sponsored tour of a prison (immaculate, efficient, grim). He sampled a full range of cultural entertainment, from several nights at theater, opera, and musical concert down to a Soviet circus, which was a disappointment, "2 clowns, sad, costumeless, almost makeupless". Also, the fourth act was a "terrific dose of propaganda = soviet sailor & (tart) émigrée, pompous quatrains, Mala. translates:—she makes every objection to 5 yr. plan, he counters."[20]

Cummings did not hear from Anne for weeks, and when he did, the news was not good. She had received word May 21 that Ralph Barton had shot and killed himself. Barton had left a note which mentioned personal problems, including fears for his mental health, and money worries. He had by now gone through four divorces. Since he left no will, it was necessary for Anne, as the mother of his child, to return to the United States to claim any insurance for Diana and to oversee the sale of his furnishings and personal effects. At the same time, she had not been able to discover an abortionist in Paris and was preparing to leave Europe to have the operation done in New York. Douglas, who had been in Toulon, happened to turn up in Paris just at this time, and it is likely that he accompanied Anne back to New York and was on hand to help out during her time of need. In her letter, however, Anne made no bitter reflections of blame upon Estlin for his absence nor did she even ask him to alter travel plans. She only sent her love and her wishes for reunion. "As for Joy Farm!!" she added, "I hope it and you will never leave me again."[21]

Cummings' itinerary included travel to Kiev to see a little of "Old Russia" and then to Odessa because his Russian teacher had asked him to carry, if possible, a few gifts to her mother. This southward journey by train provided experiences which reinforced Cummings' feelings about Russia, his affection for its people and his loathing for it as a police state. Twice on the train, he encountered the GPU in action. He was rather circumspect about recording such matters in his diary, even using the code letters ØBK to refer to the GPU. The first entry is a very brief description of the treatment of his compartment mates: "Between two places—comes here incident of ØBK—(search every compartment—I in aisle not approached; he afraid for his 'little document,' then (p[ass] p[ort] being Am[erican]) apologies—but of woman under him asked Why she's carrying man's clothes—'You're not a man.')"[22] When he expanded this material in *Eimi*, he recorded his own fears: "This comrade may have supposed that he knew something about fear. He may possibly have for weeks inhabited Moscow (that citidel of guilt). And yet every memory of those most merciless vibrations bows to when tovarich Gay Pay entered. . . ." He described the fall of terrified silence over the whole of the chattering second-class passenger car as, ruthlessly, with no showing of credentials, no asking permission, the two GPU officials searched the baggage or spoke their orders, "open this," "give me your papers," and finally terrorized the poor woman, traveling with her children, who was bringing some clothes to her husband.[23]

The second incident occurred two days later on the train to Odessa. Cummings was awakened in the middle of the night by his traveling companions who were "telling me to do something w. my suitcase." When he sat up he found himself "looking into and [against?] a young immaculate officer w. revolver on hip." He started to get up, but was then told, in German, to remain quiet. Puzzled and perplexed he meekly replied, in Russian, "Thank you," only to be told "No thank you. Stay quiet." ("I: spaseeba. He: Nyet spaseeba; bleiben Sie rühig. What does this mean? Friendly or not?")[24] By the time he expanded the incident in *Eimi*, he had decided it was not.[25]

That was one extreme. The other was his first real opportunity to fraternize freely with ordinary Russians. With the confusions of Russian railroading, Cummings found himself traveling third-class from Kiev to Odessa, crammed, suitcase and typewriter to boot, into a compartment with seven friendly Russians, one of whom spoke German. At length, with the help of Cummings' cigarettes and a great deal of natural Russian curiosity, they were all communicating eagerly and Cummings was the center of attention. They helped him to buy food. One drew a Ukrainian landscape in his notebook. Finally, one even gave up his sleeping-space down the car so that the Americanitz could stretch out for the night. Cummings dozed off hearing them talk together, "he said he was a writer and a painter, but he's a worker. Good. And that's his schreit machine. Ah, hah."[26]

During a six-day stopover in Odessa, he was befriended by an un-named American travel agent, referred to in his diary as "G" (for gnome), a New Haven man who had lived in Russia for twenty-two years. Cummings found Odessa more relaxed than the other cities, and he rejoiced to see the young people going through the evening ritual of promenade on the boulevard overlooking the harbor and dancing to sprightly music. The highlight of his sojourn, in a grotesque, even Dantesque way, was a visit to the nude mudbaths of the Black Sea. "Masquerade-effect—here and there (nose & lip) or all over, smeared w. dried black slime folk. Some droll, others hideous. P. S. on entering beach, 1st thing we almost stumble over is 50 yrs. old vast woman, stark n., lying on back w. piece of cloth betw. flabby legs; bosoms slopped. Next her, asleep on stomach, almost-as-huge-woman—Beside her, sitting up on one elbow, fat black-smeared man (imp. to tell trunks or mud!)[27]

He would have left Odessa sooner but he was awaiting a ship scheduled to sail for Istanbul on June 8. The steamship *Franz Mering* was Cummings' final Russian experience and it was typical: the departure was delayed a day and a half after he went on board, the food was inedible, and the crew was expansively amiable. One of the officers "gentle, kind (horse-face)" made friends with Cummings as he gazed out over the horizon, "magnificent twilight, forms of destiny, few evening stars, the following hills of wake & cry of mown waters, space, a throbbing heart of light."[28] The mixture of feelings he experienced in getting out of Russia was the common one that citizens of democratic nations have confessed when leaving totalitarian states: of constriction removed from the chest and a chance to breathe deeply, of elation at the return to a different world, and of relief at the escape from some nameless dread.

Turkey had its confusions for Cummings—and its beauties: both St. Sophia and the Blue Mosque were impressive enough for a visit on both days of his stop-over, and in St. Sophia this nonreligious American even offered a prayer to life and creativity. He then booked a *wagon-lit* on the Orient Express back to Paris, to wake three days later in France noting that even in paradise it rains. Estlin picked up Diana from her Swiss school, and by early July the little family was back together at Joy Farm for a good summer. Anne felt that the Swiss convent had helped Diana accept parental discipline more readily. She was happy, too, to have her stresses behind her and her husband back on home ground. If his absence during her abortion and at the time of Barton's suicide was held against him, she does not seem to have shown it. Estlin and Anne regained that lively and loving companionship which characterized their marriage at its best. Estlin's letters to his mother tell that they entertained a stream of visiting friends and that Anne was a joyful, triumphant hostess.

XX

The Ordeals of
Olaf and Estlin

As bad actors cannot sing alone, but only in a large company, so some
men cannot walk alone. Man, if you are worth anything, you must
walk alone, and talk to yourself and not hide in the chorus. Learn to
bear mockery, look about you, examine yourself, that you may get to
know who you are.

EPICTETUS

Even though Cummings had been traveling off and on between 1926 and
1930, he still had his hand in a variety of literary and artistic undertakings.
His book without a title had first appeared in *The New American Caravan*
for 1929, an annual edited by Alfred Kreymborg and Paul Rosenfeld,
dedicated to promoting the work of younger American writers. [*No Title*]
was then published in book form by Covici-Friede in 1930.[1] This little
improvisation, made up of nine chapters, each preceded by a rather
amusing line drawing, is Cummings' least satisfactory work. Conceived
as a kind of bagatelle, it assembled nine nonsense stories, all of them
delivered in a straight-faced narrative manner which never leads any-
where and which deals every few sentences with a new set of characters.
Its principal stylistic feature is the blithe intermixture of clichés, prov-
erbs, slogans, puns, and nonsequiturs. Here is a sample:

Once upon a time,boys and girls, there were two congenital ministers to
Belgium, one of whom was insane whereas the other was six-fingered.
They met on the top of a churchsteeple and exchanged with ease electri-
cally lighted visiting cards and the one who was not steering picked a rose

and handed it to the waitress with the remark:"Urinoir gratuit." The other declared dividends. He was immediately escorted,under pressure, by seven detectives disguised as consumptive highwaymen,to a nearby railroad trestle,where in the presence of the mayor his head was lovingly and carefully removed and emptied of molasses candy. Such was the shock produced by this amazing discovery upon the next of kin of the defunct that all four,attired in crêpe de Chine nightgowns, gradually rose to a height of ninety degrees Farenheit clapping their hands frequently. At that,a bareback rider named Jenny Wells proceeded in full view of all present to cross Niagara Falls on a clothesline stretching perpendicularly from the Woolworth Building to the Eiffel Tower. . . .[2]

A little of this goes a long way—but, alas, the book was 63 pages long.

A very important publication followed in January 1931, Cummings' collection of representative art work entitled CIOPW, initial letters which stand for charcoal, ink, oil, pencil, and water color. It is a handsome volume for its time, even though all the paintings had to be reproduced in black and white. It has a distinct autobiographical flavor, the subjects representing the personal world of E. E. Cummings. There are drawings of acrobats, burlesque dancers, Jack Shargel, Chaplin, elephants, Coney Island, a merry-go-round; portraits of Anne, Diana, Werner, Joe Gould; cartoons of Seldes, Thayer, and Watson; and landscapes of the Tuileries, the River Seine, Joy Farm, and Mount Chocorua. He was especially pleased with the way Jacobs had managed to reproduce the watercolors.

As for his poems, not many appeared in periodicals. The *Dial* had ceased publication in 1929, three years after Thayer had to withdraw from it, and Estlin had quarreled with the editors at *Vanity Fair* in 1927. When they asked him to make changes and rewrite "The Frenzied Franc," a piece in which he was directly critical of the French manipulation of the franc at the expense of the United States, he became annoyed. Crowninshield complained that the *Vanity Fair* office had many associations with the French people that would be disturbed. Cummings seems to have intentionally challenged these sensibilities again and caused stir in the *Vanity Fair* office when he wrote "Why I like America," an essay in which he (uncharacteristically) took the position that "America is more alive than France." He went on to ask:

"Where in the entire smallness of France or in the unmitigated amplitude of anywhere else, can you find a painter 'like' John Marin, a sculptor 'like' Gaston Lachaise and a phenomenon 'like' Niagara Falls?" But by "more alive" the present writer meant something which does not contain itself in such adjectives as "efficient" and "progressive." He meant that France has happened more than she is happening, whereas America is happening more than she has happened. . . .

America makes prodigious mistakes, America has colossal faults, but one thing cannot be denied: America is always on the move. She may be going to Hell, of course, but at least she isn't standing still. The same cannot be said of la République française. . . . More and more, indeed, the world realizes that France does not move because she is sick."[3]

Cummings was not really welcome at *Vanity Fair* unless he could be light and amusing. He did no more work for them after August 1927. In December 1930, however, Cummings made friends with Edward Titus, a wealthy patron of the arts (the husband of the beautician, Helena Rubinstein), who was the editor of *This Quarter*, "a magazine of left-bank activities." He lent Cummings a studio in which to work when he was in Paris and he asked him to contribute material for his magazine. Over the next couple of years he published several of Cummings' poems in four issues of *This Quarter*, including some which reflect Cummings' depressed periods when he was at odds with Anne, poems such as "you / in win / ter who sit / dying thinking . . . ," "in a middle of a room / stands a suicide / sniffing a Paper rose . . . ," and the wistful sonnet which begins:

> nothing is more exactly terrible than
> to be alone in the house,with somebody and
> with something)

>   You are gone.   there is laughter

> and despair impersonates a street

> i lean from the window,behold ghosts,

>   a man
> hugging a woman in a park. . . .

All these poems appeared later in *ViVa*, which was published in October 1931. This was Cummings' best book since the first *Tulips and Chimneys* compilation, and one which shows that his life with Anne, despite the quarrels and jealousies, had released, or at least permitted, creativity again. Its pages show much more experiment with spacing and typographical play than any previous volume and, in general, an attitude toward freedom of form that Cummings expressed shortly before he sent the manuscript of *ViVa* to Jacobs for setting: "There are two types of human beings children & prisoners. Prisoners are inhabited by formulae. Children inhabit forms. A formula is something to get out of oneself, to rid oneself of—an arbitrary emphasis deliberately neglecting the invisible and significant entirety. A form is something to wander in, to loose oneself in—a new largeness, dimensionally differing from the socalled real world."[4]

The over-all scheme Cummings worked out for *ViVa* is based on the number seven. The book contains seventy poems; every seventh poem is a sonnet, except that the last seven poems are all sonnets. That makes a total of fourteen sonnets, corresponding to the fourteen-line stanza of the sonnet. Beyond this, Cummings follows a development which is common to all his early books of poems since *Is 5*, a tendency, as he described it later to Francis Steegmuller "to begin dirty (world: sordid, satires) & end clean (earth: lyrical, love poems)".[5] *ViVa* has not been appreciated as fully as it should be because it also begins with complicated linguistic experiments and ends with sonnets. Many reviewers and readers probably became discouraged and never reached the second half of the book—in fact, the opening poem warns the casual reader off the premises.

The volume begins with a complex presentation of modern mass-humanity, proliferating itself, and then it moves on to a mixture of satires and linguistic puzzles which deal with such subjects as a drunk in a bar, the inhabitants of a cheap hotel, a panhandler, a double suicide, a bespectacled female from Cambridge, and other scenes and characters from urban life. There is plenty of variety, including even a mock elegy on the death of President Harding:

> the only man woman or child who wrote a
> simple declarative sentence with seven grammatical
> errors "is dead"

The variety goes beyond subject matter to language. The range is from private poems, or in Cummings' phrase, poems "from the cognescenti," to those which are more clearly related to schools of modern painting, like Poem III in which Cummings describes one of his own Futuristic canvases, such as "Noise Number 13":

> Concentric geometries of transparency slightly
> joggled sink through algebras of proud
>
> inwardlyness to collide spirally with iron arithmetics

Even the sonnets in this early part of the book involve linguistic manipulation, especially Poem XXI which interweaves words in order to suggest a prohibition-time drinking scene:

> helves surling out of eakspeasies per(reel)hapsingly
> proregress heaandshe-ingly people
> trickle curselaughgroping shrieks bubble
> squirmwrithed staggerful unstrolls collaps ingly
> flash a of-faceness stuck thumblike into pie. . . .

Among the satires, one about the treatment of a conscientious objector is the most hard-hitting antimilitary piece Cummings ever wrote. One day at Camp Devens, Cummings had come into the barrack and found "a big blond perfect stranger" lying on a bunk reading *Religio Medici* by Sir Thomas Browne. His name is lost to history but in recalling his brief acquaintance Cummings gave him the name of Olaf. He was awaiting an interview with the commanding officer of the camp, for although he was willing to do the dirtiest chore in camp he was unwilling to touch a gun. Cummings became acquainted with him and found him delightful—full of humor and good will. After Olaf returned from his confrontation with the commanding officer, he was laughing. Cummings asked him what happened and got the full story. The commanding officer, being unable to shake Olaf's attitude toward violence, asked him, "What would you do if some German came through the window and raped your sister?" Olaf, laughing, reported his reply to Cummings, "I told the truth. Sir, I have no sister." Olaf was taken away the next day and Cummings saw no more of him, although the rumor came back that he had been sent to the Army prison at Fort Leavenworth.[6]

During the months at Camp Devens, Cummings heard enough from army regulars to realize that Olaf would be brutalized at Fort Leavenworth for his pacifistic stance. He remembered what a certain "lieutenant-inspector" told him about military prisons: "You men ought to take a look at what they do to a man at the military prisons, Jay, New York; Leavenworth, Kansas; Fort Angel(?) California. I've been to all of them. When a man comes to Fort Jay, the first thing they do is give him a g. d. fine beating. They black his eyes for him. They do that on principle down there."[7]

Something in the late 1920's, perhaps the flood of literary protest about the Sacco-Vanzetti case, brought Olaf back from the past. Cummings' own memory of the man plus some imaginative work with the reports of the prison treatment merged with his still-remembered anger

at the Camp Devens officers and noncoms. As a result, he produced the
mythic story of the martyrdom of St. Olaf at the hands of super patriots:

> i sing of Olaf glad and big
> whose warmest heart recoiled at war:
> a conscientious object-or
>
> his wellbelovéd colonel(trig
> westpointer most succinctly bred)
> took erring Olaf soon in hand;
> but—though an host of overjoyed
> noncoms(first knocking on the head
> him)do through icy waters roll
> that helplessness which others stroke
> with brushes recently employed
> anent this muddy toiletbowl,
> while kindred intellects evoke
> allegiance per blunt instruments—
> Olaf(being to all intents
> a corpse and wanting any rag
> upon what God unto him gave)
> responds,without getting annoyed
> "I will not kiss your fucking flag"
>
> straightway the silver bird looked grave
> (departing hurriedly to shave)
>
> but—though all kinds of officers
> (a yearning nation's blueeyed pride)
> their passive prey did kick and curse
> until for wear their clarion
> voices and boots were much the worse,
> and egged the firstclassprivates on
> his rectum wickedly to tease
> by means of skilfully applied
> bayonets roasted hot with heat—
> Olaf(upon what were once knees)
> does almost ceaselessly repeat
> "there is some shit I will not eat"
>
> our president,being of which
> assertions duly notified

threw the yellowsonofabitch
into a dungeon,where he died

Christ(of His mercy infinite)
i pray to see;and Olaf,too

preponderatingly because
unless statistics lie he was
more brave than me:more blond than you.

Olaf has a special place in Cummings' pantheon of little people crushed by authority.

Halfway along in *ViVa*, at Poem XXXVIII, the natural world abruptly banishes the urban setting with an excellent, visually rendered poem about an electrical storm:

n(o)w

       the
how
     dis(appeared cleverly)world
iS Slapped:with;liGhtninG
!

 at
which(shal)lpounceupcrackw(ill)jumps

of
    THuNdeRB
        loSSo!M. . . .

The poems which follow deal with stars, birds, flowers, twilight, and other of Cummings' favorite phenomena. The mood of the book has changed too and the people are of quite another sort. The poem to his mother ("if there are any heavens . . .") is number XLIII. Love poems begin at Poem LIV and continue to the end of the book. Among them is the exquisite "somewhere I have never traveled, gladly beyond / any experience," which employs the motif of the speaker opening and closing like a flower. If there is any doubt about the intensity of feeling to which Anne carried him, this poem dispels it. The volume reaches its climax with the theme of love triumphant over death in Poem LXVIII, which ends (note the capitals):

—Who wields a poem huger than the grave?
from only Whom shall time no refuge keep
though all the weird worlds must be opened?
)Love

One last event of 1931 important to Cummings' career was the first one-
man exhibition of his painting and drawing, held at the Painters and
Sculptors Gallery in December. He was beyond mingling with the herd
at the Independent Artists shows now. For this exhibition he used the
same pattern of assembly that he had followed in his book of reproduc-
tions, and chose work in charcoal, ink, oil, pencil, and watercolor. Al-
though his new direction in representational painting dominated the
show, the work still had a distinct "modern" appearance. The reviewer
for the *New York Times* looked favorably upon the whole presentation,
aware that Cummings was an experimental poet and tried to relate the
painting and the poetry: "Failing a ready-made device—such as the sub-
stitution of lower-case for the traditional capitals—with which to flabber-
gast the Rotarians, Cummings imparts an outré air to his drawings by
startling eliminations and equally startling emphases. In the A-B-C-D
landscape series he lets himself go in a synchromatic orgy; in the portrait
group—"eyes" "face" "hair"—he tries an interesting psychological trick.
Here after all is the keynote of the show. Cummings the painter, like
Cummings the poet, is first of all an intelligent experimenter." For Cum-
mings the high point of the review was the remark that his New Hamp-
shire landscape entitled "day" "recalls Cézanne both in technique and
composition."[8]

II

When Anne left Joy Farm in the fall of 1931 to take Diana down to school,
she sent back a mixed collection of reports. The studio at Patchin Place
was in good shape. The repainting of the apartment at 55 Charles Street
was not completed yet. Slater Brown had quarreled with his wife; Anne
took him in one night and let him sleep on the couch. Other news
reflected the worsening effects of the depression. The Provincetown
Playhouse had closed two years ago and Jimmie and Patti Light were
temporarily down and out. "Everyone terribly depressed and depressing.
Jimmie Light sleeps on a Dr.'s operating table—Patty somewhere else
since they are broke and homeless—Bunny [Edmund Wilson] came to see
me—he has a furnished room on 7th Avenue. Broke but cheerful—ex-
pects a revolution."[9] Business was so bad that the next year even Douglas,

*Anne Barton, pencil drawing
by E. E. Cummings.*

Anne's "merchant prince", lost the executive position he had with a cosmetic company.

Cummings had spent so little time in New York since the 1929 crash that he was not very conscious of the widespread unemployment and general economic distress that afflicted the nation. It is true that his books did not sell very well, but then he never had expected commercial success. The one exception was the English edition of *The Enormous Room*, which had been reprinted twice since it was issued in 1928—English readers took an avid interest in war memoirs. But Cummings was aware that his sources of income were drying up. He had now reached the point where without protest he accepted an "allowance" of $100 a month from his mother (her own income from the estate was $250 per month).[10] She also paid the taxes and insurance on Joy Farm and sent generous checks for his birthday and other occasions. When he paid $325 for the electric generator for the Farm in 1931, she sent a check for $325 for his birthday in October.

Money troubles very likely lay behind some of Anne's dissatisfactions with the marriage during this time. But her sexual restlessness continued to be a source of trouble too. Werner said that during this time he had to comfort Cummings often. "Once when they were still together but she had taken up with another man and was humiliating him, I urged him to throw her out. He said feebly, 'But she has the keys'."[11] Werner calmly advised him to have the lock changed. But Cummings would never do such a thing. He could not bear to part from her.

Anne had a cruel tongue when her vicious moods descended upon her. She accused him of New England snobbery; she made fun of the Boston manner of his mother and most particularly of his sister. She called Cummings names—a fairy, a cocksucker. She goaded him for his slight physique, "my puny husband." She publicly humiliated him before his friends, and "frequently made jokes," Brown reports, "about what she considered the inadequate proportions of his virile development."[12] Malcolm Cowley gives a depressing picture of their marriage at the time it was breaking up in 1932: "She was at that time very entertaining, beautiful, a heavy drinker, and a perfect bitch. There was a party at our place in Chelsea during which she embarrassed Estlin in such a painful way that I didn't feel comfortable with him afterwards and I saw him only a dozen times in his later years."[13]

But no matter what Anne did, Cummings was forbearing; he could not stand the pain of losing another wife. Anne stuck to Cummings for perhaps other reasons, as one of Werner's anecdotes reveals: "Just the three of us were at dinner in Marte's and she kept picking on him and I said to her bluntly, 'If you feel that way why don't you get out?' 'I want that property,' she said brutally. I told her she was a bitch, and she seemed to enjoy the role."[14]

The strained marriage finally came apart sometime in 1932 when Anne became attracted to a New York surgeon, Dr. Joseph Girdansky— the attractions were not only the wealth and position he could offer but also his big muscular body and masculine assertiveness. Presumably Anne's father complex was at work. Indeed, reports indicate that the doctor was also sadistically inclined and perhaps Anne was even fatally attracted to his bruising manner.[15] At any rate, the first evidence of his presence in Cummings' life is a doctor's bill, February 4, 1932 for a nighttime house call to treat Mrs. E. E. Cummings. His fee was "one picture by E. E. Cummings or autographed copy of his next book."

Anne and Girdansky finally traveled to Mexico sometime in mid-1932, where she obtained a divorce. But she then returned to claim Joy Farm since she was one of its owners. Cummings was so demoralized by the break-up of his marriage and so weak in dealing with someone as aggressive as Anne that he would have let her take over the farm if Werner had not dug up a lawyer to help him.

Anne's situation was complicated by the fact that she was pregnant by now. She wanted to marry Girdansky soon so that the child would be legitimately their own. Cummings' lawyer, however, intervened. He filed a claim for Cummings, holding that the Mexican decree was not valid, and this held up Anne's marriage. Anne then sought compromise. In mid-August she came to Cummings and said that if he wanted an American divorce he could have it in exchange for everything she had put into the farm in the way of furnishings plus $3500. Diana needed an education, she declared, (and probably also pointed out that the child's inheritance from Barton was only $2500). Cummings' lawyer advised him to wait, he reported to his mother: "the dope . . . for everybody is to lie low, *put nothing in writing where Anne is concerned,* and let her eventually come to me asking for a divorce on my own terms, namely: Yes, she can have whatever furniture she put into the farm; No, she can't have 1 (one) cent, let alone any dollars; And, willynilly, she must deed her half of the farm back to you (whereupon I do the same)."[16]

No doubt, something of this sort eventually took place, for Anne married Dr. Girdansky October 31, 1932, and the following March, after Cummings' threat of legal action to declare the marriage void, Anne signed over her half of the farm to Rebecca Cummings. Estlin was now completely free of the dazzling, vivacious wife who had turned into a harpy.

XXI

The Unworld Visited

How cold I grew, how faint with fearfulness,
Ask me not, Reader; I shall not waste breath
Telling what words are powerless to express;
This was not life, and yet it was not death. . . .
                                        DANTE, *Inferno*

During the painful period of severance from Anne, Cummings was composing his most important prose work, *Eimi*, a development and expansion, about ten times the length, of the travel diary he kept during the trip to Russia. The title, which means "I am" in Greek, is his personal banner, the assertion of the individual against the forces of collectivism.

The book was well in progress by the early part of 1932, for Cummings wrote to Watson that he was trying to raise some money by finding a publisher for a new book and he feared that it would please even fewer people than *ViVa*, which had not sold well at all.[1] But one day Paschal Covici of Covici-Friede asked Cummings to lunch and halfway through the meal said he wanted a book from Cummings:

> "What sort of a book?" Cummings asked.
> "Any sort."
> "I have a Russian diary."
> "Great. I know that everybody in the U.S. has been sold lock, stock, & barrel on Karl Marx's Paradise."
> "But this book is against Russia. I spent [five weeks] there and I loathed it."

"So what. Did you write this book?"
"I sure did."
"Then I want it."[2]

Work continued and a final draft was being typed by a young friend and neighbor, Shelly Hamilton, in September. Lincoln Kirstein, the editor of *Hound and Horn,* a really prestigious little magazine which had published some of Cummings' poems the previous year, was persuaded to accept two excerpts, the opening section—up through the first day in Moscow—and the episode of the visit to Lenin's tomb. They appeared in two installments, in April and October, 1932.

At about the same time, Cummings was having trouble with the linotype operators who were setting the book for Covici-Friede. When the machine kept breaking down, Cummings suspected that the union printers did not approve of the anti-Communist slant of the book and were sabotaging its publication. He felt his suspicions confirmed when it was reported that one typesetter objected to a particular passage in the book. He persuaded Covici to turn the rest of the job over to Jacobs, who then set the remainder of the book by hand, in time to meet the publication schedule. *Eimi* came off the press on March 28, 1933, in an edition of only 1381 copies, which was the number of prepublication orders that Covici-Friede had received for the book. Each copy was signed by Cummings, a task he did not relish. "I expect to write my name 13 hundred times in a day or so," he wrote to his mother. "I hope someone's there to blot!"[3] A second printing, unsigned, followed later in the year.

Very few people have read *Eimi,* for it is much too long, and it is written in a highly idiosyncratic style that demands a patient, linguistically supple reader. For a later edition in 1958, Cummings added a brief explanatory preface, giving the itinerary he followed, describing some of the characters he encountered, and offering a brief outline of the day-to-day experiences he was recording. To this he appended a glossary of the Russian words which he used in the book. As a result, *Eimi* is a little easier to read now. But a few more details about its composition may be helpful.

Once again, Cummings chose to place his narrative within a mythic framework—this time choosing the Journey to the Underworld (or the Unworld as he referred to Soviet Russia). He began to organize his sequence on the basis of the six Sundays he spent in travel, in order to develop the motif of "Sunday, the day I was born," the day which did not exist in the new Russian week. Thus in the conclusion, his return to France on the final Sunday could represent a birth back into the real world. Soon, he added the pattern of a journey through another underworld, Dante's allegory in the *Inferno*. At the beginning of the *Inferno*, the character Dante, "in the middle of the journey of life," has become lost for he has strayed from the true path. His beloved Beatrice, who represents Grace, sends Virgil to guide the wandering man down through the nine circles of Hell to its depth, where he perceives Satan himself, the very essence of Evil. As *La Divina Commedia* continues, Dante passes through Purgatory and eventually reaches Paradise and a mystical vision of God.

Although Cummings does not strive to duplicate the complexity of allegorical points in Dante's poem, he picks up correspondences wherever he can in order to give a shape and extra dimension to his book. Cummings himself was in the middle of his life, thirty-six years old, and wandering in search of some answers about life and society. Dana, his first guide in Moscow, is called Virgil throughout most of the book (although sometimes he is called Sibyl in reference to Aeneas's guide in the descent to Avernus). The gracious Joan Malamuth is Beatrice. The visit to Lenin's Tomb becomes the view of Satan. The time spent in Turkey is in Purgatory. Paris is Paradise and the book ends with Cummings' mystical identification with the forces of creativity.

For the central figure of this narrative, Cummings has created a character named Comrade Kem-min-kz, the Russian pronunciation of his name, usually referred to as Comrade K. He is a bumbling, bewildered character, much in need of aid in order to cope, much put-upon because he cannot understand the language and customs. This "heroless hero" struggles persistently to carry out his simple intentions, which are to eat, sleep, and collect his mail, to see a few common sights, to present a few letters of introduction, to deliver a few gifts, and to satisfy his curiosity or follow whims of the moment. The inner self of Comrade K is called I or me, a person who joins Comrade K in all his activities and sometimes asserts to himself his views about life or existence in opposition to all the negation he sees around him. Once in a while, he is Cummings the American, a foreigner in Russia. Occasionally he is Peesahtel and Hoodozhnik (Writer and Painter) meeting artists and intellectuals. From time to time, all five selves come together into a wholeness—for example, when he is sharing the third-class compartment with the Russian workers:

> everybody's eating now;as for comrades Kem-min-kz and Cummings, together with comrades peesahtel and hoodozhnik and also comrade me-myself,that oaf,why we're all 5 aplunging and awhirling into our ambrosia like nothing even a Russian ever saw and ever heard.[4]

Cummings conveys the essential qualities of the Unworld that Comrade K travels through by means of linguistic negatives. As a visitor to

the "cityless city," he changes his money at the "bankless bank." At
dinner he inspects something on his plate which is "nonmeat." The
Russian women are so lacking in femininity that they can only be called
"nonmales." Further, in describing what he sees, Cummings employs
words that build up an accumulative impression of a place in which
things are either repellent or worn out. Adjectives like shoddy, rickety,
mouldy, mildewed are frequent, along with nouns like dirt, filth, run-
downness, outatheelness, neglectedness, and so on. Sometimes an item is
referred to only by some negative condition: thus windows are always
shut and eventually each one he encounters is called a shutness.

But Cummings is not always depressing in his linguistic play. He
twists a great many allusions or ordinary sayings into forms which have
some Russian or Marxist reference and many of them are quite amusing:
"Marx helps those who help themselves," "argue until the comrade cows
come home," "this earthly paradise enow," "comrade weather permit-
ting," "where in capitalism did the comrade get that idea?" "looking as
if he had been hit by a batch of 5 year plans and several collective farms
to boot." Some of the word play is just Cummingsesque fun without too
much satirical reference to the socialist state: eyes which "Red Riding
Hoodishly survey grandma," difficulties which "spoil the best laid mice,"
and arguments that the new economics "makes sun while the hay shines,
opens the key of life with the lock of science, juggles (without dropping)
the unworld the unflesh and the undevil, and justifies from soup to nuts
the ways of Marx to man."

But to describe certain features in this way does not really indicate
anything about the stylistic richness of the book or the difficulties which
that stylistic richness presents to the common reader. Some readers have
found a superficial resemblance to Joyce's *Finnegans Wake.* But if that is
so, the likeness is in spirit, not in manner. The style is a unique Cum-
mings creation, one he had been developing for some time in letters to
literary intimates, and it bears more likeness to his own experimental
verse than to Joyce's final opus. One might try to generalize about the
stylistic practice by saying that Cummings liked to play with language
in a great many ways: 1) by distorting popular sayings and well known
quotations, as described above, 2) by using puns, spoonerisms, portman-
teau words, and witty combinations of any sort, 3) by violating common
grammatical usage (e.g. adjectives and adverbs used as nouns; nouns used
as verbs, etc.), 4) by jumbling the accepted syntactical order within sent-
ences, 5) by substituting an allusive reference for a direct reference
(barbed wire is "worldwarwire") 6) by devising his own private epithets
for people and things (a "semimiddleaged demifairy" is soon called
"semidemi"; a "glad-to-see-you-ish" consul is soon known as "gtsy,") 7)

by using common words and phrases of foreign languages—in this book, Russian is added to French, German, and Italian—as well as phonetically rendered dialects of English, 8) by mixing slang or colloquial phrasing with learned or archaic terms, 9) by juggling punctuation marks and capital letters for special effects, 10) by using any and all the devices of verse: rhyme, alliteration, spacing, metaphor, etc. The intermingling of all these ways of manipulating words produces a kind of linguistic vaudeville act that is Cummings' very own. And we do not do wrong to call it poetry.

This stylistic display is additionally complicated by Cummings' abrupt jumps into new events with no explanation of what is taking place, although most of the time a patient reading is rewarded by understanding. But patience and persistence are really needed before a reader becomes accustomed to Cummings' idiom. The author helps out by restraining himself at the beginning, but he becomes quite prodigal as his narrative goes on. Sometimes he employs a simple stream-of-consciousness style for presenting first impressions of a scene, for instance, an early look at Moscow streets, in company with Dana:

> Fresh Air,burgeoning with amorphous beings:sunlight,tucked with swarming closeups of oldfashioned streetcars("don't they remind you of Harvard Square" the Sibyl mused,whimsically). "I was just thinking how somehow Athens-of-America everything seems" agreed(dimly)Aeneas;who never(no, not even in Bosting)beheld so frank a flaunting of optical atrocities. Eheu fugaces . . . posthumously the mostly becapped men wear anything;the nonmen(especially those who are of maternal construction)show an indubitable preference for kiddiefrocks(reaching less than 1/2way to the knee)and socklets;as a result,only comrade God can make a tree—but even comrade Kem-min-kz knows that the sum total would be not quite 1/2 worse if women were present.[5]

At the beginning of the book, the passages are easy to follow. Here, an entry on the second day gives us Cummings on the train seeking breakfast and at first going in the wrong direction:

> seek the diner,semiexpecting(thanks to my American procommunists-living-in-Paris—The Horrors of Capitalist Poland)to be brutally cheated;if not softly knocked down and simply robbed. Frank E. Campbell turns me round with a word of his own,supposed to be a "wagon restaurant":march tipsily back through train,past living corpses hit with Fresh Air and luxuriously outstretched on authentic wood. Promptly and courteously I'm supplied with excellent coffee butter bread and cheese:at nearby table,a plutocrat,insisting that the only waiter(who's obviously Robinson Crusoe)accept

one entire American dollar;R.C. obliges with footprint-in-the-sand reflex—
my own(less immodest)generosity provokes the more hysterical thanks of 5
languages.[6]

Later Cummings makes full use of his complex style, especially when he
wishes to express action or suggest confusion. Here, for example, is the
experience of Comrade K trying to board a train in Kiev. He is aided by
"weazel," an Intourist flunkey, and by "bum," a porter:

> "SCHNELL!" weazel twitters exultant tumbling over a toandfro rocking
> moaning beshawled mountain of maternalish miseryful makes for restaur-
> perhapsant(behind him I,fully I recovered,I completely restored,boosting
> him by the scruff of his weazelneck over lesser objects smaller unthings)fran-
> tic wavings the bum sees us & now (fallreeling)gallops with my baggage—
> "beelyet?" [ticket]—"da" I cry,squeezing into his handclawfin all my
> change sicklemyhammers my all contentedly—"au revoir,monsieur" salu-
> tes(beaming)almost (tearful)"bon voyage!"(I seize valise,weazel knapsack)
> rush at into through against &
> "—nyet!" a guard snarls;blocking the gate to the trains—& and immedi-
> ately weazel chatters and the & expostulates denies yes affirms no the argues
> "NYET!!"[7]

Cummings has created an experience for the reader—one which
approximates his five kaleidoscopic weeks in Russia. But as the whole
structure has implied and as the stylistic emphasis on negation has ham-
mered home, the book has its thesis, which is stated in a variety of ways:
the regimented life of the Communist state crushes the individual and
thus life. "A Russian's soul belongs to the state," a minor official had
bluntly put it. To make clear his opposition, Cummings has included in
the book a number of meditations on his special terms of value: celebra-
tions of "Is," declarations of "I am," and assertions of being "alive."

This basic view of life pushed Cummings toward sympathy with
something that Russia had rejected—religion, which he associated with
that whole side of human life which he revered—feeling, spirit, inner-
ness, and all qualities which cannot be measured. In the narrative this
partisanship emerges in the repeated contrasts between the baroque glo-
ries of St. Basil's, the church he refers to as "Arabian Nights" or "Some-
thing Fabulous," and the bleak structure of Lenin's Mausoleum. The visit
to Lenin's tomb has its countervisit to St. Basil's, where Cummings sees
what he calls the Madonna of the String. He describes entering a sanctu-
ary where he finds "on this crude easel, a cruder image—a woman with
a big baby in her wide hands." Underneath the picture is a notice in
Russian, No Admittance. He moves toward the picture:

halts.   —Goosefleshed from head to toe
:touched
yes!because(but more lightly than by a whisper;more
fatally than by a sword)touched
   . . .quivering,scared;I:look—down. ı hair of string,so
thin as to be almost invisible,warned,whispered to,me
(touched). . . .

The word "touched" communicates to us that he has been moved in his
inner being. But the word is literal too. The string is stretched across the
entrance to keep people out, but it is placed just at knee level, a circum-
stance which Cummings immediately perceives to have meaning: "speak-
ing very strangely to knees which must no longer kneel."

The motif of religious opposition to the Soviet regime is picked up
again vigorously at the end of the book. The first instance is the prayer
inspired by the vastness of St. Sophia, where Cummings senses some-
thing within himself, a "dark poet; blindman," "darkly communing with
impossible light." The language in this passage is full of paradoxes but
it helps to explain the conclusion of the book. Cummings appears to be
addressing the power of creativity within himself:

>   . . . his
> voice is made of silence and when his voice pauses the
> silence is made of voice.
>   (Silently
>   as now to
>   whom my,pray-
>   ing my
> self;bows)

The second instance of religiously tinged definace is an address to the
locomotive of the the Orient Express, a "metal steed," an "unspontaneous
sterility," a false "wheelgod," a mere "go-toy." In this pronouncement,
Cummings speaks as Poietes, "a totally adventuring Is," who is the em-
bodiment of "a moving within feelfully Himself Artist, Whose will is to
dream, only Whose language is silence."[10] The words, like those in St.
Sophia, take on a religious tone the effect of which is to personify the
concept of unconscious life within all human beings, the concept which
is also the power behind creativity.

These preliminary events, the prayer in St. Sophia and the address
to the locomotive, prepare the reader for the concluding passage of the
book, which by itself is very puzzling, almost incoherent. Cummings is

attempting to present an Emersonian transcendental experience, a mystical union of the speaker with the creative force. In the final passage the speaker identifies himself, first, with the advance of the seasons toward winter and snow (star-rise and moonrise are also taking place) and, then, with the "Voice of silence" itself:

> leaning I am this hurling inexhaustibly from june huge rushing
> upon august until whirlingly with
> harvest huger happens bloodily prodigious october
> . . . .
> finally
> (and what
> stars)descendingly assuming
> only shutting gradually this
> perfection(and I am)becoming
>
> silently
>   made
>   of
>   silent.
>   &
>
> silence is made of
> (behind perfectly or
> final rising
> humbly
> more dark
> most luminous proudly
> whereless fragrant whenlessly erect
> a sudden the!entirely blossoming)
>
> Voice
>   (Who:
>   Loves;
>   Creates,
>   Imagines)
>   OPENS[11]

It seems that it took a trip to Russia to make a full-fledged New England Transcendentalist out of Cummings.

In Cummings' career, *Eimi* represents more than its existence as a complex and powerful literary work. It stands as a turning point in his life. He grew more deeply committed to his philosophy of life when he saw how it could be threatened by a governmental system. The energy that he devoted to expressing his values in *Eimi* strengthened him in his defense of individualism so that he became much more confident and assertive about his views—in time, even dogmatic. He became at the same time less tolerant of differing opinions. At length, he grew so obsessed by his anti-Soviet position that he came to despise not only Communists but even liberals. As the United States passed into the liberal dominance of the Roosevelt-Truman era, he gradually turned even more hostile toward American culture than he had been in the 1920's. In the end, his conservatism changed to reactionary bitterness, and old friends who were moderate liberals found they could not even discuss social or political issues in his presence. There were of course many other contributing causes for the change in Cummings' personality, but the creation of this admirable literary work which bore upon important social and political matters of the decade seems to have marked the scarcely perceptible beginning of a new and, at times, less attractive Estlin Cummings.

XXII

Marion

Lady! in beauty and in favour rare,
Of favour, not of due, I favour crave.
Nature to thee beauty and favour gave;
Fair then thou art, and favour thou may'st spare!

HENRY CONSTABLE

One time in his later years when Cummings was musing on his psychic ups and downs, he recorded some observations which reflect on his emotional state during the period after the break with Anne:

> If I am losing, become separated from, some deep spiritual influence—represented perhaps by a parent or relative, perhaps by a girl with whom I've been (& cannot even suspect that I am not still) entirely in love—I suffer torments: the loss, the separation, is intolerable: every moment of my experience is a new & differing agony to me, & the sum of these agonies equals the mystery of being born. But sooner or later, if I live and do not die, it suddenly occurs to me that this very experience was the most fortunate of my life: then (& only then) does the curse wonderfully become a blessing, the disappearance an emergence, the agonizing departure an ecstatic arrival. . . .

This resilience was a feature of his own psychic make-up, to be sure, but in 1932, while the divorce with Anne was being negotiated, his recovery was greatly helped when a new and more generous-natured woman floated into his life.

Marion Morehouse was a Midwesterner, twelve years younger than Cummings. She was born March 9, 1906 in South Bend, Indiana. After her parents, who were Roman Catholics, moved east to Hartford, Connecticut, she was sent, it is reported, to a Roman Catholic school in that city for her education.[1] Her early background is sketchy. One friend remembers that her parents were circus people and that she cherished a desire to be a female clown; another that Marion told her she had run away to join the circus when she was a teenager. In any case, it is evident that she left home without finishing high school to live by her beauty and her wits in New York. By the mid-1920's she was trying for a stage career. Since she was much taller than the usual New York actress, she had a hard time finding roles, but she was able to get jobs as a showgirl in one or another of the musical revues such as the Ziegfeld Follies or to find bit parts here and there in plays (for example, she played the "First Corinthian Woman" in Gilbert Seldes' adaptation of *Lysistrata* in 1930). She was very serious about her acting, and one summer she had even studied at Richard Boleslavsky's school at Pleasantville, New York. But she was not sufficiently talented for a future in the theater and she turned to fashion modeling, a career in which she had great success.[2]

She was one of the great beauties of her time, with a long slim body, ideal for modeling clothes. Indeed, a number of her features merged to suggest an over-all willowy slimness. She had a long elliptical face with high cheekbones (she had some remote Choctaw Indian ancestry), a swan-like neck that rivaled Queen Nefertiti's, delicately curved breasts, a short waist, narrow hips (ideal for wearing slacks, a fashion which she helped to promote), and long shapely legs. Her training in the theater helped her to become a renowned fashion model, for she had the knack of adapting herself to the character of the clothes that were chosen for her. "When she put on the clothes that were to be photographed," said Edward Steichen, "she transformed herself into a woman who really would wear that gown or that riding habit or whatever the outfit." She was, he declared, "the greatest fashion model I ever shot."[3] Although she was very young and her background was limited, she adopted a regal manner, which was greatly aided by her height and her large boldly frank eyes. "The aim of models at this time was to be grand ladies," said Cecil Beaton, "and Marion Morehouse, with her particularly personal ways of twisting her neck, her fingers and feet, was at home in the grandest circumstances."[4]

Cummings met Marion through Patti and Jimmy Light, to whom he had turned for confidences and support during the troubles with

Anne. On June 23, 1932, the three stopped backstage, after the perform-
ance of a play in which Marion had a small part, to take her to dinner.[5]
As they walked along the street together toward Felix's, one of Cum-
mings' favorite restaurants, his first impression was "This girl's too tall
for me." But her lustrous expressive eyes and her friendly openness
soon banished any negative qualms and within a short time they were
seeing each other regularly. The first time she came to Patchin Place to
stay with him he could not believe his good fortune: he sent her a great
bouquet of flowers the next day to mark the occasion. She later told him
that she had not been sure he really loved her until the flowers came
and then she knew.

That summer Marion was living over on Long Island with Dudley
and Mae Clements, a theatrical couple; and since Cummings did not
have a telephone, the notes and telegrams they sent to each other allow
a few glimpses into their early months together. Cummings' first letter
records his readiness to take her into his own poetic realm: "let us move
our minds out of smallness, out of ideas, out of cities; let us pack all our
minds carefully (without breaking anything) and carry them carefully
away and unfold them very carefully among hills and rivers: come with
me among mountains and oceans, let's change our minds, let's go away
from not and from must and from if carefully into growing and into
being and into loving."[6] He was apparently inviting her to a weekend
in the country.

This kind of talk was welcome but not when he became too compli-
cated. One night when they were "drinking red ink" out of teacups "in
a prohibition woprestaurant," he launched into a lyrical, allusive paean
of his love for her, but it became clear that his poetic flight had left her
on the ground. His momentary thought was "she's not my equal (can't
follow me) mentally" but her eyes looked imploringly across at him and
he stopped. Brought down to earth, he knew that henceforth he would
have to adopt a different idiolect for her. With Marion he would live in
a simpler kind of world.

But there was plenty for them to enjoy together and Cummings
began to return to the less sophisticated life he had followed in his youth
before he met Anne Barton—walking about the Village, calling on his
mother or sister, visiting the aquarium, watching the tugboats, having tea
with friends, working diligently in his studio—and sending his girl
friend notes and cartoons composed by the *petit garçon*. His notes were
usually signed with a drawing of a scurrying elephant carrying a banner
in his trunk announcing "LOVE." One early phonetic picture-message
reads "I'm tremendously glad of you."[7]

glad of you!

Another invites her to Khoury's:

or why   or

don't   if you

you come to   'd like some

see   stuffed squash with vine

me   leaves crushed eggplant

at   with sesame

about six o'clock   oil and laban and

                    watermelon and

             ahhwhich[?] come at one

                  o'clock and

             we'll go down to the Syrian

                  restaurant[8]

Another is a complete "elephant-picture" letter, formed by the words "I'm feeling much better thank you it's now about a quarter of two and I've worked hard tonight so am about to retire this elephant takes my good night to Miss Morehouse down down with Teny's son up with life liberty and the pursuit of happ[eye]-ness." "how are you" forms an elephant ear, and "love" forms a little elephant penis.[9]

She was charmed by this unique new man; she had never known anyone remotely like him. One of her early letters thanks him for his drawings and then declares: "You're such a wonderfully marvelous Comrade, Kem-minkz, and I'm so much in love with you I don't know what to do. I might fly the Atlantic up & down—everybody goes across—and in great white words of smoke in the sky tell everyone how I feel."[10]

Cummings seems not to have gone to New Hampshire in the summer of 1932 but stayed around town to be with Marion. He had found the woman he wanted to spend his life with. Often in his meditative scribblings of later years he made comparisons among the three women he married and the resulting judgments were always similar: with Elaine he had an idealized relationship, with Anne he had sexual fulfillment, but with Marion he combined both and found real love for the first time. As time went on, she became the person who filled his every need. She played the role of mistress, mother, housekeeper, nurse, hostess, cook, accountant, model, courier, secretary, muse, and a great many other parts in a lifelong companionship.

During the late summer Marion moved in from Long Island to a small walk-up apartment at 43 West 8th Street. She took on a variety of modeling assignments over the next few months. In the fall she was working at Steichen's studio and during the winter she worked for the designer Francis Clyne. She was at the height of her loveliness. Estlin wrote proudly to his mother in the spring of 1933, "Marion's been working ('modelling' clothes uptown) since last Monday . . . and her boss (a couturière of note)—NOTE THE feminine gender—likes her greatly and tells her several times a day that she's the most beautiful girl in N.Y."[11] Kind, warm Rebecca Cummings, greatly relieved to see Estlin happy once again, opened her heart to Marion, as she had to Elaine and Anne. But Marion, unlike the other two, developed a deep affection for Mrs. Cummings in return, combined with a respect that never wavered into the jealousy that gnawed at Anne. Mrs. Cummings was in her seventies now, but she wanted to make herself useful to her fellow beings, so she became a volunteer worker at the Traveler's Aid center in Grand Central Station.

Cummings was having money troubles during 1932, and possibly another reason that he had not gone to New Hampshire in the summer was the fact that he owed over $300 to the various helpers and handymen of Silver Lake. These financial worries were banished, however, when in the spring of 1933 he was awarded a Guggenheim Fellowship. It paid only $1500, one-half of what the annual stipend had been before the depression set in, and it carried a further stipulation that the recipient had to spend the year "abroad." Marion, who had never been to Europe, had often yearned for travel when she went down to the piers to see her friends off on the big Atlantic liners. Now she was ecstatic when Cummings asked her to go with him to France for the year, even though it would mean a financial squeeze for the two of them to live on the fellowship money.

II

Cummings had applied to the Guggenheim Foundation at the suggestion of Henry Allen Moe, executive secretary of the Foundation, who was an admirer of his work. His application contained what must be the briefest description of a proposed project in the history of the Foundation: "a book of poems." When he received the good news, he elected to take the award as soon as possible. As a consequence, his fellowship year was set to begin April 15, 1933, and he and Marion sailed for France the last week of April. On board the ship was a troupe of black entertainers who were billed for a Parisian Music Hall, "Les Ambassadorz." Marion knew one of the performers and thus their voyage in the second-class area turned out to be a gay week-long party.

When they arrived in Paris, Walter Lowenfels, a poet whom Cummings had known in New York,[12] was vacating his apartment at 10 rue du Douanier, near the Porte D'Orleans, and let them sublet at $225 for the quarter. It had a big studio with an eighteen-foot ceiling, two bedrooms, a kitchenette, their own bathroom and toilet, and a roof garden over the studio which allowed a splendid view of Paris at sunset. It was their first home together and Marion was soon turning out delicious French meals. Estlin did the shopping and selected wine and cognac. Marion paid a call at the headquarters of *Paris Vogue* for modeling work and, not surprisingly, made an impact upon the editors there who, in Estlin's words, were very shortly "doting on her slightest whim, creeping about the boulevards on hands and knees to buy her orange juice."[13] In time she became the favorite of Baron George Hoyingen-Huene, the international fashion photographer, and he used her for some of his best work. The Baron later invited Estlin and Marion to visit his villa in Tunisia.

Cummings took great pleasure in introducing Marion to the nooks and crannies of his favorite city. His sketchbook for the summer shows the familiar Paris scenes, fishermen along the Seine, the gardens of the Tuileries, a fireworks display, children in Luxembourg Gardens, and reveals that he took her to the Opéra, to the Folies-Bergère, to the Gingerbread Fair, to the prize fight, and to the Cirque. They enjoyed the Paris galleries, especially a large Renoir exhibition, including "a huge canvas of R's late years worth 50 1/2 times all the world's so-called 'gold'."[14] His painting took on new vigor and Marion occasionally had time to model for him.

Many friends were in Paris that summer. They spent evenings with Pound and his wife, Margaret and John Peale Bishop, George Malkine, the Surrealist painter, and his wife. Cummings describes dinner with Dudley and Mae Clements in an outdoor restaurant at one of his old haunts, the place du Tertre on Montmartre: "we all dined out in the twilight the acrobat stood on his head on a caraffe, a walking race ('le foo-teeng') happened across the street, our hosts drank in accordion music and starlight."[15] There were more indecorous gambols too. One night, which included Cummings dancing on top of a friend's sedan, ended up with his having lost both his passport and the signature card for his letter of credit. Before the whole matter was straightened out, Cummings had some distressing moments and eventually he was obliged to borrow money from Lincoln Kirstein, who happened also to be in Paris.

Lincoln Kirstein, a poet and one of the founding editors of the *Hound and Horn* at Harvard, was a Greenwich Village neighbor of Cummings. Although he was more than a dozen years younger than Cummings, they

Marion, pencil sketch by E. E. Cummings. HOUGHTON LIBRARY

had met through Cummings' classmate, the poet John Brooks Wheel-wright. Kirstein had moved the *Hound and Horn* to New York in 1930, and soon after, Cummings became a contributor. Kirstein had developed a great admiration for Cummings, even going so far as keeping notes on Cummings' conversation in his diary.

In his devotion to art, Kirstein was in many ways like a young Scofield Thayer. He was very wealthy (the son of one of the owners of Filene's department store in Boston) and wanted to use his money to promote the arts in every way. Under his control, and with the guidance of the two regional editors he chose, Allen Tate and Yvor Winters, the *Hound and Horn* became very much like a continuation of the *Dial.* Just now, his new interest was the ballet ("Leaping Link," Cummings called him) and he was attempting to form an American ballet company. Since he considered it important for all the arts to intermingle, he approached Cummings as a poet to compose a ballet scenario. Estlin, attracted by the idea, talked it over with Marion, who suggested an adaptation of *Uncle Tom's Cabin,* perhaps because she knew that a dramatic version of the book had proved to be one of the most popular presentations of the nineteenth-century American theater. When Cummings proposed it to Kirstein, he agreed, and on July 10 he made a first payment to bind the verbal contract.

Another episode of the summer was Cummings' renewed contact with Elaine, who came forth with a strange request. Two years before, in 1931, Elaine had been compelled to struggle with a scheme to have her marriages to both Thayer and Cummings annulled by the Catholic Church so that she and Frank MacDermot could be married in a Roman Catholic ceremony. MacDermot's political ambitions in Ireland to try for a seat in the Irish Dáil as representative for Roscommon, made it neces-sary for him to have been married in the Church. Stewart Mitchell had already agreed to testify about Thayer's mental breakdown so that Elaine's first marriage could be annulled. But the grounds upon which they hoped to annul her second marriage were more tenuous—as Mac-Dermot later explained them in a letter to Cummings: "Your marriage to her, though valid legally, was not valid canonically from a Roman Catholic point of view, because of the agreement between you before-hand that it could be terminated at the desire of either party."[16] But Cummings was so disgusted at the treachery of the MacDermots in cut-ting him off from Nancy that he ignored their petition to him in 1931.*

---

*My mother had a pathological dislike of religious matters (something to do with the holiday schoolmistresses perhaps.) When I once accompanied her to a Roman Catholic church in London in about 1929, because she was crying I had to know why; she replied she had to take religious instruction from a priest, but I was to tell NO ONE; I was left

Early in 1933, they had tried to use Stewart Mitchell to persuade him to cooperate with them. Cummings' reply to Mitchell exists only in a draft of a telegram (or perhaps notes for a letter) which he jotted on the back of Mitchell's letter dated February 18, 1933:

have seen Elaine once that's enough she would tell me nothing definite about Nancy she didn't mention evidence or legal procedure so please write me exactly and completely she asked me for clerical annulment I said I would consult lawyers shall refuse all favors until she changes her attitude appreciate tremendously your friendship[17]

As soon as he arrived in Paris, Cummings was approached once again. Elaine, who had his address from John Peale Bishop, wrote him a note in which she was very specific about procedure: "All I want is that you should agree to make a statement in writing to my local parish priest here confirming the fact that when you & I married it was on the understanding we would each agree to divorce if the other wanted."[18] But she said not a word about Nancy, who was now thirteen. Cummings, it seems, did not reply.

Later he was coming out of the bank one day when, as he wrote in a manner of high burlesque to his mother: "a cry pursued him, a cry followed by an apparition: there was Mrs. Frank MacDermot, alias Mrs. me, alias Mrs. Thayer, alias Helen of Troy New York. And she begged me for a rendez-vous, of course. . . . 'Sure,' I agreed unperturbedly."[19]

The proposed meeting afforded an opportunity to achieve a mild triumph. Cummings decided to bring Marion along. He no doubt wanted Elaine to see that she had been replaced by a young woman whom Baron Huene called "the most beautiful woman and the most poised in Paris."[20] Thus it came about that Marion first met

the redoubtable queen of "Old Erin." . . . both of us lunched Elaine at an ancient haunt on la rue de l'Echelle where the management honorably warns you of at least 1000 hors d'oeuvres. Well—of course—Madame wanted me to see a "bright-eyed priest" who was also "little" and "awfully nice". . . . With this testimony of mine Elaine would be able to marry her Frank

in the church to wait. Shortly afterwards I went to see her in a nursing home at Penshurst where she had a nervous collapse for a few weeks.

When I told my father later about this, he seemed unaware how much she had suffered, and added then he was glad he had "given her what she wanted. It happened like this," he went on: "suddenly, without any warning, a priest arrived at my front door and asked me to sign a declaration that my marriage to Elaine had not been consummated. You can imagine my feelings." [The joke is I imagined them wrong.] "Eventually I agreed; what difference could it make to the truth?"—N T A in the Catholic Church. Without this testimony, her Frank's numerous enemies (political, especially) would undoubtedly dig up a wicked past.—So far, as per usual: but now (to my amazement) comes the question, what do you want in exchange for this favor to me?

Taken by surprise, Cummings began to ask questions about Nancy and heard the first detailed news in seven years. She was presently attending a school at Bexhill in England:

I was told that Nancy was not big, but was very intelligent and athletic and etc. I then asked Elaine to write me a letter saying that, if at anytime I (or my "fiancée") were in the Frank vicinity, the Franks would be glad to see us. She balked. . . . She dissolved into tears. . . . Finally I regretted I could

Marion Morehouse. GEORGE HOYINGEN-HUENE, CONDÉ NAST PUBLICATIONS

not see her bright-eyed priest unless the above-mentioned invitations were forthcoming. She said, then, that we'd both be welcome as far as she went but "Frank" didn't like me too much. I then agreed to immediately write him, asking for his okay.[21]

Cummings wrote. MacDermot's reply was redolent of benevolence and cunning: "both my fiancée and I would be welcome as soon as the McD church marriage went through; he himself felt flattered by 'my offer of friendship,' etc. etc. etc."[22] Nevertheless, Cummings finally consented. His account of his going to see the priest is treated with even more levity in a letter to Werner:

> I rise at dawn, take a taxi to a Catholic Refectory or Archbishopric rather or Archiveque (whatever that means) wait 20 minutes then talk 105 to a pugnacious prelate while a gentle little p scrivens busily and meantime—I said mean—am alternately misunderstanding what am not supposed to say and standing up and swearing that all these lies (circa 1,000,000,000,000 per cu in) are the god's truth and still pond no moving (all in French, my favorite tongue) also turn the other cheek frequently. . . . I then give a gore soon oon frawng to 'phone for me and I then take a taxi, myself, not g-s, to a hot jumbled implausible dump called Beri on the elysian fields and there I patiently peevoh [drink beer] until wife number 1 appears, as per appointment plus the usual lateness, when I explain that the interview with the pope's retainers for the purpose of annuling my marriage to hoo-eyef noombear hoo-wone (referred to by the scrivening p as "Ellen Whore") hereinafter to be called the putty of the zTH part has to all intents succeeded; whereupon she says well and she never regretted anything and someday maybe she won't have to bother me like this. . . . Wish you . . . could have seen Marion & i dining with Mister MacDermot of high yaller Erin and the charming Mrs, dining in quotes, it was very hot, it was soe sheeque u no, eye doan. They (Marion and la MacD) got onn likee l piece knittingcircle; that is they so utterly and incomparably despised each other's out-&inwards that everything was nice—pronounce "niece"—and polite.[23]

When he would ever be able to see Nancy, who never seemed to be on the scene, was still a question.

Rebecca Cummings replied to Estlin's news that she was "delighted the affair with Elaine is settled,"[24] and she wrote later to Marion, expressing her gratitude to her for making her son happy and adding, "I'm thankful the Elaine episode is over. I only wish I might have a photograph of Nancy & know whether she has ever received my birthday gifts."[25] Part of her wish was granted in September when Elaine sent some snapshots of herself and Nancy at the beach. Something further happened when Nancy began writing thank-you letters after receiving her 1934 birthday-Christmas gift.[26] But Nancy still did not know why this nice Mrs. Cummings sent her these books year after year from America.

The opportunity for the vacation trip to Tunisia was fascinating to Cummings and Marion, and the prospect of rent-free quarters was most welcome. The Baron Huene's villa at Hammamet, "The City of Doves," was, they found, a palace built around a court. In the town nearby, Cummings reported, there "patter donkeys and lurch camels (the worst put together of all creatures) and howls a trumpeting phonograph and loll ay-rabz galore."[27] Behind them was a mountain range, before them the warm, blue Mediterranean. Estlin did a great many sketches and water-colors. They swam every day in the nude and they began to turn a deep tan all over. They took a siesta during the heavy mid-day heat, swam again, had a drink at five, and dined at eight (such delicacies as "partridges with wine sauce.") These were the details he sent his mother. Letters to others add his amazement at the open homosexuality of the Tunisian men ("hear wee have faggots aliarse fayreez, hoo spen thair taim encluering arrabbz. Eye amb sory tew sa. Enculer is a frensche verbe. Wee keepe awa from tham eye meen thee quearz as mutsh az pozbul.")[28] During the fall, Cummings composed a great many poems and worked in a desultory way on his ballet scenario.

On the way back from Tunisia, Marion had her first chance to see Italy. Estlin especially wanted her to see the Sistine Chapel in Rome, for a view of Michaelangelo's frescos. A slow train back to France got them to Paris at the end of November. As soon as the quarterly money was available from the Guggenheim Foundation, they sailed on the *Bremen* for home in mid-December.

Cummings had been hoping that his Guggenheim Fellowship could be renewed for one more year, so he reapplied in January 1934, and submitted his "book of poems" as a sample of his accomplishment during the previous nine months. The request was denied.

It had been hard for him to stretch the money in Europe but his mother's "allowances" and a check from Sibley Watson had helped. Now, the problem continued. Liveright did not want to publish the new vol-ume of poems: *Is 5* and *Viva* were not selling and Horace Liveright was no longer in control of the firm. Nor was Covici-Friede interested: in the first half of 1934, [*No Title*] had no sale; *Eimi* had no sale (6 returns had only made the unearned balance a little heavier). Cummings turned to mild, modest Lincoln Kirstein with a rather blunt request for money: "am now ready to work on TOM; shall need $100 a week for 5 weeks; if you want me to do the ballet, please enclose one century by what some-body loosely called return mail."[29] Kirstein was even more generous: he also took some poems for the *Hound and Horn*.

Cummings wanted Marion to be with him at Joy Farm for the summer, and he countered his mother's worries about propriety by asserting that she would go as his common-law wife: "the idea that the natives of Madison would high hat Marion is just a trifle idiotic. She will be my wife, introduced thus by me—as she has been in New York, Paris, Philadelphia, Tunis and many other parts of the world. 'Honi soit' might apply to Cambridge, Mass, but the Wards and the Gilmans—believe me —will never give a thought to such matters. They're better than that and they have something else to keep their so-called minds busy."[30] He could report in mid-July, "All the natives seem to be crazy over my wife and she's obviously feeling slicker'n a weazel—how be you?"[31]

But he did take steps to make marriage possible. The Mexican divorce that Anne had secured without his knowledge two years before did not seem to him valid. So in May he had sued Anne for an American divorce charging adultery: The divorce was granted by the Nassau County Supreme Court on August 31, 1934. It is uncertain whether he and Marion ever did go through a marriage ceremony. But from this time forward, Marion held the position of wife. She was introduced as his wife, she was (some years later) registered at a hospital as Mrs. E. E. Cummings, their stationery sometimes carried the imprint Mr. and Mrs. E. E. Cummings, and in Cummings' first will, written in his own hand, he left all his property to "my wife Marion (Morehouse) Cummings."[32]

XXIII

Gratitude to
Almost No One

The birthday of Christianity meant the birthday of a new epoch in human history, just because the guiding star of love has never ceased to shine above the cradle of the humblest child, from that first Christmas day till now. It still stands above the humblest tenements of this great city and of every city.

EDWARD CUMMINGS, Christmas Sermon, 1905

Lincoln Kirstein had mentioned a production of the ballet *Tom* for fall 1934. But there were problems about the music. Although he had chosen Roger Sessions to compose a musical score, Sessions kept postponing the job. Cummings then hoped he could get Louis Siegel, who had done the music for Sibley Watson's experimental film, *Lot in Sodom,* but Kirstein decided to wait for Sessions.

Meanwhile, Cummings was having no luck placing his new book of poems with a publisher. His own efforts, those of his agent, Bernice Baumgarten of Brandt and Brandt, and those of Jacobs, who was ready to print the book, all came to nothing. This situation makes abundantly clear the struggle that Cummings had in achieving recognition as an important American writer. In the previous dozen years, he had published five volumes of poetry, a play, a collection of his art work, and two remarkable prose narratives, but now fourteen publishers had refused to undertake the publication of one of his most important collections of poems. Certainly the depression had a good deal to do with it. In the last half of 1934, Covici-Friede had sold exactly one copy of *Eimi.* In the first six months of 1935, Boni and Liveright had sold only thirteen copies of

Is 5 and two copies of *ViVa*. Cummings was only able to get his book in print when his mother offered to put up a three-hundred-dollar subsidy for the printing bill, and the book was published under Jacobs' imprint, The Golden Eagle Press. Cummings entitled his book *No Thanks* and dedicated it to the publishers who had turned him down, their names carefully listed to form the shape of a funeral urn. The book came out finally in the spring of 1935, bound in a unique way. The pages were gathered at the top rather than at the left side: a two-page poem could then be read continuously rather than breaking for a page.

No Thanks contained more linguistic experiments and more obscurities than any volume Cummings ever produced. He was always uncritical about his published work and ready to include jokes, ephemeral epigrams, and private poems along with memorable lyrics and technically brilliant linguistic constructions. Since in this collection the doubtful items were found in the first half of the book, this placement in itself must have helped to discourage publishers. Thus we can be grateful that the book got into print at all, so that we can now stand back from the work to see it as a whole, before we look more closely at some of the individual poems.

When we do, we can become aware of two distinct aspects of *No Thanks:* the pattern in which the poems are arranged and the highly individual view of life that the totality of the work reveals. Here, as in his other books, Cummings consciously strove to put his materials in a carefully planned order. When he first assembled his poems for publication, he arranged them in a "schema" (he learned the term in his Dante course at Harvard) which he thought of in the shape of a caret. Starting with a piece about "snow," he set up a pattern of three poems followed by a sonnet, then three more poems and another sonnet, and so on up to "poem 35," again a "snow" poem; then a peak of three sonnets; then descending on the other side he began with "poem 39," which had "star" as its subject, and again the pattern of three poems followed each time by a sonnet, until the end, "Sonnet XIX," another "star" poem.[1]

Revision and reworking brought about the final schema which governs the book. Cummings visualized it in the shape of a V: the movement from two "moon" poems, descending to "earth" poems at the center of the book, and then rising to two "star" poems at the conclusion.[2]

The other distinctive feature of the book is the fully developed presentation of Cummings' view of life, which is here revealed even more clearly than in *The Enourmous Room* and *Eimi*. Cummings held that the essential self of any human being was an instinctive complex of conciousness which responded harmoniously to the world by "feeling"; hence, he regarded mind and its analytical powers as only a suppressant, and he

FIRST SCHEMA   "sonnet entitled" etc
                                         SONNET X
                            SONNET IX   SONNET XI

                            . . . .
                          SNOW 3 poems   3 poems   star (poem 39)
                      (poem 35) SONNET VIII   SONNET XII
                              3 poems   3 poems
                            Sonnet VII   SONNET XIII
                              3 poems   3 poems
                             SONNET VI   SONNET XIV
                              3 poems   3 poems
                             SONNET V   SONNET XV
                              3 poems   3 poems
                             SONNET IV   SONNET XVI
                              3 poems   3 poems
                            SONNET III   schema   SONNET XVII
                              3 poems   3 poems
                             SONNET II   SONNET XVIII
                              3 poems   3 poems
                             SONNET I   SONNET XIX   star
                              3 poems   . . . (SONNET XIX)
                          snow . . .
                          (poem 1)

FINAL SCHEMA
                    °2 moons   *2 stars
                ('mOOn Over tOwns mOOn')   ('brIght')
                ('moon over gai')   ('morsel miraculous and
                                                    meaningless')

                        NO THANKS:schema of construction
                    °2 poems   2 poems*
                    sonnet I   sonnet XVIII
                    3 poems   3 poems
                    sonnet II   sonnet XVII
                    3 poems   3 poems
                    sonnet III   sonnet XVI
                    3 poems   3 poems
                    sonnet IV   sonnet XV
                    3 poems   3 poems
                    sonnet V   sonnet XIV
                    3 poems   3 poems
                    sonnet VI   sonnet XIII
                    3 poems   3 poems
                    sonnet VII   sonnet XII
                    3 poems   3 poems
                    sonnet VIII   sonnet XI
                    3 poems   3 poems
    ('how dark and single,where—sonnet IX sonnet X—('conceive a man,should he
            he ends,the earth')   I poem   have anything')
                        ('into a truly')

considered intellectual systems (usually referred to as "science") to be
the enemy of happiness for the instinctive self. Whatever the instinc-
tive self desires to express is good: one should follow impulse; one
should thrust aside caution or restraint. He saw the population of the
world as a multifarious mixture of unique selves, each of whom can
achieve the good life if he freely acts out his uniqueness and avoids
the pressures imposed by society to behave otherwise. This is an opti-
mistic view, too, because Cummings considered that the essential self
is in its tendencies good and loving and that it would only become
twisted into evil by outside forces. Socially and politically this is an
anarchistic view because Cummings had come to feel that society in
general and government in particular are always attempting to curb
the activities of the individual.

Early in *No Thanks* these views are exhibited negatively. "sonnet
entitled how to run the world" gives a succinct answer, "don't." (Note
that in the first schema, Cummings had placed this poem at the apex of
his caret.) Poem 23 invites us to observe a man who "does not have to feel
because he thinks," and if that is not bad enough for him, the thoughts
are supplied by other people. Certainty is even worse: "he does not have
to think because he knows." Thus Life (reverently capitalized) looks
down upon one whose natural emotional existence is crushed, making
him one of the living dead. American life, it is implied, is especially
repressive because of its demands for conformity. Again and again in
other poems, Cummings hoots at pretentions to "progress" which over-
value technological achievement and at advertising ballyhoo which pro-
motes the commercialization of modern culture. These are forces which
encourage the standardization of human life. But he reserves his greatest
scorn for the totalitarian state which makes complete and willing slaves
out of its "kumrads."

More positively, the poems celebrate an openly felt response to the
beauties of the natural world—stars, snow, birds, flowers, and even such
minor miracles as grasshoppers or mice. The poems optimistically ex-
press joy in the time of beginnings, spring, and they give first place to
love among all the feelings—love in all of its manifestations, especially
in fully shared sexual intercourse.

These attitudes give rise to a special evaluative vocabulary, to which
Cummings sometimes gives additional emphasis when he alters normal
grammatical usages. Of course, since "Alive" is one of the chief value
terms and the verb "is" the essence of being alive, these terms will be
isolated for special veneration, for example, the "isful" star in the last line
of the book, or the affirmative declaration in Poem 67 that "Is will still
occur" in spite of the threats of "knowings" and their "credos." "Guess"

is one of the good words, along with "dare," "open," "dream," and "yes." "Reason" is a bad one, as well as "same," "shut," "numb," and "most (people" or "most)people." When Cummings is speaking of people, the good relative pronoun is "who" because it refers to human beings; the bad one is "which" because it refers to things.

When we see that the poems in a cumulative way express a totality of outlook, we are then less inclined to regret Cummings' lack of taste when he includes something on the level of a college humor magazine like "may i feel said he," or his self-indulgence when he includes a private poem like Poem 27, a hexameter sonnet in praise of Joe Gould, the ultimate urban romantic:

> little joe gould has lost his teeth and doesn't know where
> to find them(and found a secondhand set which click)little
> gould used to amputate his appetite with bad brittle
> candy but just(nude eel)now little joe lives on air
>
> Harvard Brevis Est for Handkerchief read Papernapkin no laundry
> bills likes People preferring Negroes Indians Youse
> n.b. ye twang of little joe(yankee)gould irketh sundry
> who are trying to find their minds(but never had any to lose)
>
> and a myth is as good as a smile but little joe gould's quote oral
> history unquote might(publishers note)be entitled a wraith's
> progress or mainly awash while chiefly submerged or an amoral
> morality sort-of-aliveing by innumerable kind-of-deaths
>
> (Amérique Je T'Aime and it may be fun to be fooled
> but it's more fun to be more to be fun to be little joe gould)

Cumming's manipulation of language may provide aesthetic pleasure no matter what kind of material he is treating. With him, nothing can be considered "not a proper subject for poetry." A case in point is Poem 9, which satirizes the custom that the president of the United States will throw out the first baseball of the season. Cummings' ingenious spatial handling brings aesthetic life to this unpromising subject. Cummings pitches an initial "o" past a whole team of eleven lines, before we realize that it has the roundness of a baseball. It is then picked up, after we have forgotten it, to be used again for "supposedly" and "throwing":

o pr
    gress verily thou art m
    mentous superc
    lossal hyperpr
    digious etc i kn
    w & if you d

    n't why g
     to yonder s
    called newsreel s
    called theatre & with your
    wn eyes beh

ld The
            (The president The
            president of The president
            of the The)president of

            the(united The president of the
            united states The president of the united
            states of The President Of The)United States

            Of America unde negant redire quemquam supp
sedly thr
w
    i

        n

            g

                a

                    b

                    aseball

The spacing both horizontal and vertical toward the end of the poem is appropriately representative of the throwing down of the ball, and the letters that Cummings has isolated to show its fall can be seen, after a moment's look, to divide into "win" and "gab," two words which are part of the season's activity. The accumulative repetition of words, "The/ (The president The/president of The president/of the . . ." and so on, mounts like fanfare preceding the president's act, and the Latin words which Cummings then supplies "unde negant redire quemquam" (hence denying anyone to say again) adds to the factitious pomp.

If we remember that years earlier Cummings had thought of doing away with the word "poem" and substituting the word *"fait,"* we may think how wonderfully suitable that term is to describe some of the work we find in *No Thanks*. The grasshopper poem is a brilliant instance. In this linguistic construct everything depends upon devices that are in no way associated with traditional poetry:

                                        r-p-o-p-h-e-s-s-a-g-r
                            who
            a)s w(e loo)k
            upnowgath
                        PPEGORHRASS
                                        eringint(o-
            aThe):l
                    eA
                        !p:
        S   a
                        (r
            rIvInG   gRrEaPsPhOs)
                                                to
            rea(be)rran(com)gi(e)ngly
            ,grasshopper;

The two "star" poems which conclude *No Thanks* represent something new in Cummings' poetry—a religious tone—a further development of the tendency revealed at the end of *Eimi*. Earlier in *No Thanks*, his ballade, Poem 54, had begun its envoi with the lines "King Christ, this world is all aleak;/and lifepreservers there are none," but the Christ reference here, I think, is only an echo of the François Villon tradition, for that medieval maker of ballades also called upon "Prince Christ" in his envois. Cummings was not a Christian; he had been brought up in that halfway station, the Unitarian Church, which regards Christ not as God but as a holy man who brought a special message about worshipping God and living the moral life. Yet for twenty years now, Estlin had professed none of the beliefs of his father's Unitarianism. By 1935, however, he had been through a lot of anguish and the heartbreak of two divorces. Married now to a woman who was brought up a Roman Catholic, he was open to the religious views which she had learned from the nuns at school, although she herself was not active in her religion. Furthermore, almost ten years had past since Edward Cummings' death, and

Estlin had been moving gradually toward a reconciliation with what he had rejected.

But whatever the reasons—the influence of Marion, a gesture toward the memory of his father, or an extension of his own sense of cosmic order—these star poems introduce a new note into Cummings' book of poems. They suggest Edward Cummings' "religion of the star," as he called it. Edward Cummings disliked the Christian emphasis on the crucifixion as the central event in the Christian theology, because of the stress on sin and suffering. He preferred a religion of joy and brotherly love, and he selected the star of Bethlehem rather than the cross as his principal religious symbol. To him it signified not only a joyful sense of newness in a rebirth of the world but also the light that shone down on all humankind, rich and poor, in all the nations of the earth. The angels' song of "peace and good will to men" was for him the message of "the religion of the star."[3]

A few words and phrases, like "holy," "miraculous," "lifting hopes and hands," and an attitude of wonder and humility before some higher otherness add the religious coloration to the star poems. The final one is a syntactical scramble, too complex for explication here.[4] But the penultimate poem is one of Cummings' most pleasingly patterned linguistic experiments. As Robert McIlvaine has pointed out, there are only eleven discrete words used in the fifteen-line poem but they are deployed in such a way that they make up a total of forty-four words: the three-letter words "big," "yes," and "who" are used three times; the four-letter words "soft," near," "calm," "holy," "deep," and "star," four times; the five-letter word "alone," five times; the six-letter word "bright," six times.[5] There is no English sentence at all—only a construct of words. But a statement emerges by means of patterns:

brIght

bRight s??? big
(soft)

soft near calm
(Bright)
calm st?? holy

(soft briGht deep)
yeS near sta? calm star big yEs
alone
(wHo

> Yes
> near deep whO big alone soft near
> deep calm deep
> ????Ht ?????T)
> Who(holy alone)holy(alone holy)alone

The lines are arranged in a numerical progression from the first line standing alone to a five-line final group. Another progression moves from "s???" to the full spelling of star," as if star gradually comes into being. "Bright" orthographically disappears into "?????T," as if dawn comes isolating the morning star and then causes it to fade. Suggestion builds into meaning that this is a poem about the star of Bethlehem, a meaning greatly aided by the conjunction of words like "bright," "holy," and "calm" in their allusion to the Christmas hymn "Silent night, holy night./ All is calm, all is bright." The pattern of capital letters at length spells out BRIGHT, YES, and WHO and is completed with the last line when the capital "Who" remains "(holy alone) holy(alone holy)alone." Edward Cummings would have been gratified.

Cummings placed his dedication to his mother, "AND THANKS TO R.H.C." at the end of the book. It is appropriate in its place next to the star poems, memorials of her husband's religious symbols. Her money was well spent.

XXIV

A Stranger in the
Supercolossal West, 1935

I believe I could do it if it were in my nature to aim at this sort of
excellence, or to be enamoured of the fame and immediate influence
which would be its consequence and reward. But it is not in my
nature.

COLERIDGE, on Junius

Cummings was used to mixed reviews of his books but he was not pre-
pared for the negative responses to his work in the early 1930s. *Eimi*,
which was reviewed in over sixty newspapers and magazines when it
came out in spring 1933 had caused a widespread outcry over its stylistic
acrobatics. A few headlines and titles give an idea of the general recep-
tion. "New Type of Novel Baffles with an Odd Style," "A Super Atrocity
in the Much Abused Name of the Novel," "Eimi Worser than Quite
Necessary," "Eimi—Irregular as a Greek Verb."[1] The *Boston Transcript*,
always learned in its references, pronounced it more obscure than
Browning's *Sordello*.[2] One reviewer admitted he did not finish the book;
others declared it impossible to read. Even those who admired the stance
of individualism or welcomed his report on the Russian scene warned
readers about the style in such phrasings as "if you have the courage to
wade through the typography," "almost as Greek as its title, in spots,"
or "the reader's powers of instantaneous response become exhausted
before he gets through many of the 432 pages."[3]

The trouble began when the *American Spectator*, edited by George
Jean Nathan, who had hated Cummings' *Him*, named *Eimi* "The Worst
Book of the Month" in the April issue. Since the book had still not been

delivered from the printer, Pat Covici offered to donate $100 to charity if anyone on the staff of the *American Spectator* could prove he had read the book. The challenge was not taken up, but a great many critics mentioned the *American Spectator*'s judgment in their reviews.

A few of Cummings' friends were on hand, however, to give a sympathetic and intelligent assessment: Foster Damon in the *Providence Journal,* Gilbert Seldes in the *New York Journal,* and Marianne Moore in the August issue of *Poetry* magazine, who called the entire book a poem.[4] But only one reviewer revealed any understanding of the full meaning of *Eimi* —"Saintly Paul," the rotund, walrus-moustached Paul Rosenfeld, whom Cummings had known well as the music critic for the *Dial.* Rosenfeld declared the book "a comic masterpiece" and then went on to say in what special respect it was comic: "The book indeed is purely aristophanic[,] communicating an idea of God through a literary expression of the exuberant, leaping, dancing, shouting dionysiac energy of which He is the inexhaustible spring: the energy which rises spontaneously from the unfathomable quick of nature independently of external excitement . . . and takes form in the gambols of animals, the activity of children, the riot and frolic of men; in caricature, in farce, and finally in humane comedy." At length he offered a sound reading of the mystical recognition of this force which Cummings had expressed in the conclusion of *Eimi.*[5]

In spite of the leftward shift that had taken place in the literary circles of the United States, there was no heavy political attack on the book. Only Nathan Asch's dismissal of it in the *New Republic* was politically motivated.[6] The *New Masses* ignored the book. But Cummings did sense the personal disapproval of many of his acquaintances. Before the publication of *Eimi,* he himself had generally been regarded as a voice in the radical camp, not only because of his hard-hitting antimilitary poems but also because one passage in *The Enormous Room* had been interpreted as threatening the revolt of the masses (the passage in which, referring to the little Machine Fixer, Cummings apostrophized, "O *gouvernement français,* I think it was not very clever of you to put this terrible doll in La Ferté; I should have left him in Belgium with his little doll-wife if I had been You; for when Governments are found dead there is always a little doll on top of them, pulling and tweaking with his little hands to get back the microscopic knife which sticks firmly in the quiet meat of their hearts.")[7] No doubt some people had felt the betrayal of a position that they thought Cummings had shared with them. Certainly Muriel Draper, Cummings' friend and former lover, felt this way when she broke with him at this time. Edmund Wilson and Malcolm Cowley did not seem to be as friendly with him as formerly. Two other friends crossed the street to the other side one day rather than meet him.[8] In speaking of this period in later years, Cummings possibly exaggerated the rejection he experienced, but one way or another, there was a definite change in a good many of his relationships with people who believed in the new political solutions to the problems and ills of the world. In the 1920's he had enjoyed being a part of a literary movement which opposed the tastes of the general public. In the 1930's he found himself isolated, still not accepted by the general reader but now separated also from the literary world, which had become largely sympathetic to Russia, to Communism, and to literary expression which supported social action.

As for *No Thanks*, it got very few notices when it appeared in 1935. Since it was not in the hands of a major publisher, it got no advertising, and outside New York it received little attention. There were, of course, many friendly words for the book, but there was also a tone of "we have heard this before' and an air of impatience with "the naughty boy of modern American poetry."[9] (Cummings was now in his forties.) *No Thanks* was frequently reviewed along with *Poems* by Kenneth Fearing, whose satirical work was more in tune with the sober concerns of the time. A good example of the mid-1930's attitude toward Cummings as being somewhat too frivolous is the comment by Kenneth Burke, a former friend from the *Dial* period whose Marxist seriousness now caused him to feel irritated with Cummings: "As we read 'No Thanks' carefully, the following picture emerges: For delights, there is sexual dalliance, into which the poet sometimes reads cosmic implications (though a communicative emphasis is lacking). For politics, an abrupt willingness to let the whole thing go smash. For character building, the rigors of the proud and lonely, eventually crystallizing in rapt adulation of the single star, which is big, bright, deep, near, soft, calm, alone, and holy. . . ."[10]

Joe Gould, needless to say, was mightily pleased at his place of honor in the book. On the strength of his notoriety, he tried, with Cummings' help, to get a piece of his Oral History published in *Esquire* magazine, but the editor was not persuaded.

One event of the spring was a harbinger of things to come, although Cummings had no notion of it. He was invited to Bennington College, the new, educationally avant-garde college for women in Vermont, to give a reading of his poems. Helen Stewart, a member of the junior class with literary leanings, had become acquainted with his verse and had happened to meet him at a cocktail party in November 1934. At the party, Cummings was very natural, very open, sat on the floor chatting playfully, and Helen was enchanted. During that winter she and her fellow-student, Dorothy Case, decided to promote a Cummings visit to the campus, and as a result of their efforts the administration authorized her

Joe Gould, pencil drawing by E. E. Cummings.

to send him an invitation to come in April to read for a fee of twenty-five dollars plus travel expenses. She also arranged for her father, who was on the board of trustees, to accompany him up on the train and to see that he was properly accommodated at the Bennington Inn.[11]

Cummings agreed to come because he thought she showed very good judgment in the poems she suggested for the reading. Helen and Dorothy felt triumphant in securing him, and they began to prepare for his visit by acquainting their classmates with Cummings' poems. Soon the Bennington girls were striding down the corridor or into the shower, declaiming to each other that "the Cambridge ladies live in furnished souls" or "Buffalo Bill's defunct." When the day arrived for the performance, Helen was supposed to introduce him but she became too filled with stage fright when the girls in the auditorium began to recite in unison the Buffalo Bill poem. Cummings finally stepped out on the stage alone as the audience was chanting the poem for the third time. He was so overcome by the whole display that he did not know what to say. Flustered, he took the handkerchief from his breast pocket and waved it at them.

Money was scarce this spring of 1935, so even $25.00 helped. The promised production of the ballet had still not come off, nor were any of his publications bringing in money. Cummings began to look in a new direction for income. In the summer of 1934, a recent friend, the lawyer Maurice Speiser, who was a tireless promoter of literature and the arts, had arranged an offer for Cummings to work as a script writer at Paramount Studios in Hollywood, at a salary of $100 a week for several weeks.[12] Immersed in his ballet scenario, Cummings had turned it down, saying he was not interested in writing "movie junk." But another finger also beckoned from California. During the lean winter of 1934–35, Cummings received several letters from his friend, Eric Knight, who was working for Fox Studios at "a princely salary" and who urged him to come to the West Coast.

Eric Knight, who is best known to American readers for his stories in *The Flying Yorkshireman* and his novel, *Lassie Come-Home,* had come to the United States when he was thirteen years old. He had attended the Cambridge Latin School a few years later than Cummings, thus the two found much in common when "Moe" Speiser introduced them in the early 1930's. Knight was an extraordinarily lively man, full of verbal effervescence, who had abandoned an interest in art to become a newspaper writer and eventually a film critic for the *Philadelphia Evening Ledger.* He and his wife Jere, a sprightly dark-haired Philadelphian, enjoyed Cummings and Marion thoroughly and invited them to visit their farm, Pentacres, in Valley Forge, Pennsylvania, in the summer of 1934. Since Knight had a serious interest in film, he accepted a contract as a script writer when Fox Studios offered it in the fall of 1934. Although he went to Hollywood with great expectations, he soon came to feel that fools and ignoramuses were running the studios. His letters to Cummings are hilarious excoriations of Hollywood, though he did concede "I'm making a silly amount of money." In spite of his misgivings, he suggested that Cummings should give Hollywood a try—to some extent for personal reasons ("You would be life to us out here")—and he assured him, "if you dare this specialist's shack of celluloid excreta, if you do, here are the Knights waiting with White Rock. . . ."[13] Cummings still did not consider the suggestion seriously: "Quand a Hollywood cinq mille dollars par semaine pendant un (1) mois (and no effing options) me tempterait peut-etre. Mais je crois que les movies, étant sur leur last legs, sont probablement trop far gone pour inviter un specialiste authentique et expensive comme moi. Tant pis!"[14]

But Knight's urgings and the sore need of money made their impact. Early in 1935, Estlin and Marion decided to go to California. As he later explained in a letter to his Aunt Jane, "I'd had my hardest (to date) year in New York . . . and our only chance of $ seemed to be Hollywood, where 2 of Marion's old friends were highlights in the socalled motionpictureindustry (one a director, one an actress)."[15] The director may have

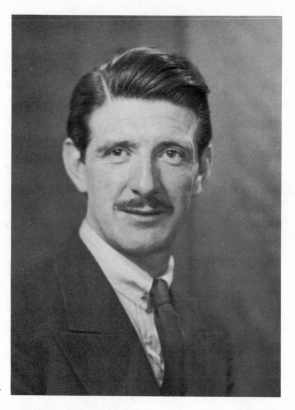

Eric Knight.
COURTESY JERE KNIGHT

been Joseph von Sternberg, for his name crops up a few times in Cummings letters during this 1935 period. The actress was Aline MacMahon with whom Marion had maintained a warm friendship ever since they met at Boleslavsky's acting school. In the mid-1920's Aline had shared her apartment at 796 Sixth Avenue in New York with Marion, until she finally had to tell Marion to move out: none of her boy friends, she said, would look at her when Marion was around.

An opportunity for the Cummingses to begin their Hollywood venture arose when the son of Edward Titus, their Paris friend, appeared on the scene. He had been recently married and he and his bride now planned a trip to California with a stop-over in Mexico. He invited Estlin and Marion to go along as his guests.

The party set out in late May, traveling, Cummings pointedly commented, in an eight-cylinder Packard ("never did like Cadillacs.") They stopped in Washington, affording the Cummingses their first look at the national capitol, and then went down through the South to New Orleans, where John Peale Bishop, who was visiting there, showed them around the French Quarter. After they crossed the Mexican border a series of troubles occurred: a landslide blocked the road to Mexico City, the car had to be abandoned for the train, and the difficulties of travel had begun to strain the relations between the couples, especially between Marion and Mrs. Titus, who "turned out to be a complete moron of the omnivorously show-off type."[16] By the time they reached Mexico City, the Cummingses had decided to break off from the Tituses. But now they were no longer guests and their small supply of money had evaporated during the journey south. Nevertheless, they took a room in a pension and decided to "trust to Luck," which meant wiring Rebecca Cummings for help.

Mrs. Cummings, who was now seventy-seven years old, had been packed off to live with Aunt Jane at 104 Irving Street in Cambridge, for Estlin did not know when he would return. There was no one to look after her in New York now, for Elizabeth had married Carlton Qualey, a young history scholar who had the promise of a job at Bard College in Annandale-on-Hudson, and they were soon to move out of the city. Cummings discovered that not only was his mother ready with some helpful cash but also Aunt Jane had five hundred dollars waiting for him that she had been planning to send later in the year. This windfall made possible a real Mexican holiday, during which they roamed all over the city, viewed the murals of the modern Mexican painters, took Marion to her first bullfight (Estlin with flying fingers filled sheets with sketches of picadors, horses, bulls, toreadors)[17], and made side trips to the pre-Columbian cities of Tlaxco, Xochimilco with its floating gardens, Cuernavaca, and Teotihuacan with its giant pyramid of the sun.[18] Because of a recent civil insurgence, Mexico City was a turmoil of uniforms. This coupled with the fact that the communized municipal services were not functioning well gave Cummings a poor opinion of the Mexicans, but characteristically, he found the Indians "superb." "Seeing them you see beyond Orozco—and clear through 'Dago' Rivera."[19]

After two weeks, they splurged $220 for airplane tickets to Los Angeles. During the flight, the copilot showed them through the control cabin. When Cummings saw the instrument panel he thought it "looked so like NY-by-night that I might have wept."[20] In Los Angeles they were met by the Knights, who soon had them bedded down in their snug Santa Monica house at 303 9th Street, where they found a cheery flower garden and orange trees in bloom. Other friends were soon offering a welcome. In the Los Angeles area, where it is impossible to get around except by automobile, the Cummingses were driven about by the Knights or by David Hertz, a friend of Marion's and a writer at Metro-Goldwyn-Mayer. Aline MacMahon, who was very busy at the studio, put at their disposal a limosine driven by a female chauffeur.

A week later they rented a small furnished apartment with a bed that folded into the wall, at 849 11th Street in Santa Monica. When Marion was apologizing to Aline about its inadequacies, Cummings allowed that there was nothing to complain about: it had a view of the Santa Monica mountains and it was only eleven blocks from the ocean. "You see what a nice man he is," Marion beamed. Cummings was amazed and delighted at the physical beauty of Southern California—its profusion of flowers (many of which he had never seen), its serene skies and balmy Mediterranean weather, and its lengths of sparkling beach backed by imposing mountains. He began painting right away. They swam as often as possible; "God bless the Pacific" was his cry. But he described the people as "chiefly Iowa farmers of unmitigated docility" and he thought of them as "sterile".[21]

His friends tried to help him find work in the motion picture studios. Aline introduced him to Irving Thalberg, the production chief at MGM, and David Hertz tried to interest Joseph von Sternberg in Cummings as a script writer. Cummings also talked with Kenneth MacGowan, formerly of the Provincetown Playhouse, who was temporarily with one of the studios, and Samuel Hoffenstein, who confessed he was prostituting his talents at another. Nothing seems to have come of all this. Although Cummings spoke of trying to sell a scenario to MGM, there is no record of what it may have been. His lack of success is not surprising. He had no promise as a screen writer: all his narrative publication had come from personal experience, his play was too avant-garde in its dialogue, and generally speaking, there was no place for a lyric poet in Hollywood, let alone a satirical one. There was, however, one center of a newly developing cinematic form that could have used his talents: Eric Knight took him to Walt Disney studios. Knight was an enthusiastic admirer of animated cartoons and recognized too that Cummings' imaginative playfulness in company with his skills in line drawing would have been useful to Disney. But nothing came of this attempt either and there are no details about it in his letters or notes.

Marion was applying for modeling jobs and had a whole series of photographs made for a dossier. Estlin thought that her beauty should have overwhelmed the film directors and producers: "I personally don't see why Blue Angel Joe (von S) shouldn't spend the rest of his career photographing her."[22] Although a screen test was scheduled for Marion, it somehow did not come off. Once again perhaps, she was thought to be too tall.

The Cummingses spent two months in California, much of the time at the beach or in lively talk with the Knights. By this time, Eric had been fired from Fox Studios, whose executives did not care for his frank opinions about their products. He and David Hertz were able to supply Estlin with all of the Hollywood gossip and the general lore of the studios, including many of the oft-told sayings of Samuel Goldwyn ("Who is this Dickens? Maybe he'll sue us.") Another subject for endless talk between Eric and Estlin was the loss of their children. Eric had been previously married and his former wife, like Elaine, had thrown obstacles between him and his daughters. When deep in drink, he and Estlin would exchange accounts of their deprivations and reopen old wounds for each other's inspection.

During this time, Estlin and Marion had a glimpse of the Hollywood social and cultural life but did not care for it. Southern California had a thin culture, dominated by the film industry and its commercialization. Certainly this was enough for Cummings' scorn, but he developed a snobbery that seemed independently gratuitous. Noguchi, the sculptor, took the Cummingses and Aline to a concert at the Hollywood Bowl, which Cummings described as "an open air auditorium seating 30,000 morons."[23] Aline invited them to a party at the Trocadero with, Cummings wrote, "a group of distinguished numbskulls."[24] Since Aline went to some trouble to arrange social invitations for them, she was annoyed when the naïveté of the Hollywood parties became the target of Cummings' ridicule. The film folk, she explained in later years, were still at the stage where "they enjoyed party games like post office."[25] Cummings describes one of these evenings in a letter to Jacobs:

Speaking of which, ecco a sample: the only in any way spirited "executive" have as yet encountered gives a birthday party for his wife. Guests arrive at 6, continue until 9. No symptom of either host or -ess. Meanwhile old fashioneds & martinis & empty stomachs & hysteria & continual puttingsout of all lights and everybodygettingunderfurniture so as sort of kind of to surprise them when they do. They do. Guests detonate from beneath tables chairs etc arisingly chant "hap pee Burr thd a y, 2 yoU"—lights go up: dinner for 16 with magnolia flowers at every plate, hostess & host very appreciative & fairly soused, Sherry wine (NOT champagne) throughout meal, toasts by totterers etc., everybody adjourns to parlour, host immediately insists everybody play the following game: a piece of toilet paper is brought in, about 6 inches long & 2 broad; host hangs it on his upper lip, holding it by suction of indrawing breath via nostrils[;] he rubs noses with lady adjoining who thereupon indraws via nostrils breath whereat host ceases inspirating thereby both of them succeed in transferring the toiletpaper from him to her & so on. I was especially honoured: Mr. Lazarus (the host) Laughed & (in person, not a picture) rubbed noses with mere me & then blew, causing toiletpaper to descend & other merrymakers to suppose I had failed & a gwate diwector to cry out "thazza guywe gutta washow tfo rheezuh fay rea"—all of which surprized me no end comma as I was not a lady nor adjoining either; but as it were singled out for this by no means negligible shall we say attention¿ however, have recovered (I trust) and beg to remain yours for *l'esprit!*[26]

Although some of these attitudes reflect a familiar East Coast response to any place west of the Appalachians, Cummings' ill-tempered comments were also revealing a resentment over the fact that the film studios had not found him worth hiring. As the summer wore on, his injured ego began to find a refuge in offensive remarks about Jews. His letters become sprinkled with references to the "cinema-factory" people as "kikes." Samuel "Goldfish" and his studio run by "a kike named Irving Thalberg"[27] come in for special attention, and he quotes with evident agreement a quip by one of his friends that Hollywood was "the Christian wailing wall."[28]

By late August, Cummings was ready to head for home but he had absolutely no money. He wrote to Jacobs "asking the Golden Eagle for a few feathers," but *No Thanks* had no earnings to send. The problem was partly solved by Isama Noguchi, the charming, beautifully mannered Eurasian sculptor, a friend of Marion's with whom Cummings had developed a good rapport. Noguchi had lost his driver's license for speeding and he needed someone to drive him in his touring car to the Texas-Mexican border. Cummings and Marion set off with him in his heavily loaded car for the journey over mountains and through desert. Cummings' sketchbook is filled with his drawings of the Grand Canyon and desert scenery—cacti, buttes, mesas.[29] From Texas he wired 104 Irving Street to get money for the train journey to New York. By late September, they were at Joy Farm, which Cummings appreciated more deeply than ever before.

The anti-Semitic upsurge in Cummings while he was in Hollywood came to a strange conclusion. On September 24, 1935, Joe Louis, the promising young Negro boxer, knocked out Max Baer, the former heavyweight champion, who was a Jew. Cummings interpreted this as personally symbolic: "Something whispers to yours truly that the Big Year for the Kikes is o'er."[30] He saw in the event the exorcism of forces that had frustrated him in Hollywood. "This suggested," he jotted in a sketchbook, "à propos of, & inspired directly by, Thomas Mann's 'Joseph & His Brethren'—that now my destiny is coalescing w. a universal one: ⌐ ⌐ which, more & more, I impress myself & it expresses itself through me?"[31] This is a powerful illustration of how the poetic mind can take something as irrational as a religio-ethnic dislike and shape it into a myth. It also illustrates the potential dangers of romanticism: if feeling ("Something whispers to me") rather than reason is allowed to dominate, then some strongly felt prejudice can be used to justify action. More than this,

Cummings had developed a tendency to see any event in the world as emblematic of himself and his problems. Only a few days later he went to see John Ford's great film about the Irish rebellion, "The Informer," and afterwards he wrote in his notebook, "situation (Ireland, her grouped individuals vs black and tans) ∽ myself vs 'mechanism'."[32]

His bruised ego needed Joy Farm, and he gave himself fully to the familiar setting and its natural phenomena for healing. During the next month, his sketchbook became filled with notes on his observations of the night sky: the northern lights, a "little starkite rising," the "plunging" of a "youngish silver moon," "the handle of the Big Dipper sticking out of the roof of the barn." He quotes from Mann's *Joseph and His Brothers* about spheres and their mystery, then on another page draws sketches of a moon coming into its fullness. He notes, "O the mystery of that round-ness! Here she was, all lopsided, only two days ago, & badly warped even yesterday—yet tonight I cannot find a stopping place in all of her edge; everywhere it begins and nowhere." There are notes and sketches of sunsets, birds of all varieties, bees, a snake, seedlings sprouting in the meadow, a mouse "that decided to leave its body in a pail of water" (sketch: "extraordinary beautiful ear.") Observations of this sort often begin a diarylike entry: "Thursday/ a grasshopper leaped into my coffee —kicked! wasn't."[33] As the years go on now, Joy Farm comes to mean more and more. There are only two times in the future when even part of a summer is spent in travel.

extraordinary beautiful ear

Patchin Place, Cummings' home in New York from 1924 to 1962. MARION MOREHOUSE, COURTESY JERE KNIGHT

XXV

The Undanced *Tom*

"So you're the little woman who made the book that made this great war."

ABRAHAM LINCOLN to Harriet Beecher Stowe

The return to Patchin Place in the fall of 1935 was attended by a piece of luck in finding an apartment for Marion at number 8. All these years since 1924, Cummings had continued to rent the studio, a room fourteen by twenty on the third floor at the rear of number 4, most of the time living there as well as using it for his painting and writing. From now on, Marion would also have an apartment in Patchin Place. First it was number 8; soon it would be the ground floor of number 4: a narrow sitting room with a table which could be opened for dining, a tiny kitchen, a small bedroom, and a bathroom. But it would always be her apartment, even though they furnished and decorated it together, took their meals there together, and used the small sitting space as their common room. Estlin spent the days and most of the evenings upstairs in the studio and he slept there as well.

The activities of the next year were not fruitful. Estlin struggled once more with his undeveloped play but without success. Bad news had come about the ballet scenario. Balanchine, who was Kirstein's choreographer did not like it. He was baffled by its verbal emphasis. Kirstein commented, years later, that the scenario "was not about dancing." It might have worked as a film but it was "unsuitable for production as a ballet."[1] Cummings had already made arrangements to have it published.

Bernice Baumgarten had placed it with Arrow Editions, a small press
owned by an old acquaintance from the Cambridge Latin School, Walter
Charak. The small book, *Tom*, with a frontispiece by Ben Shahn, a strik-
ingly apt picture of the all-enduring Tom, was issued on October 1, 1935,
dedicated to Marion.

During the fall, reports in the newspapers announced that Kir-
stein's American Ballet Company was going to present a ballet based
on *Uncle Tom's Cabin* in the next season. Cummings thought that suc-
cess had come at last and a composer was at work on the music, but
when his publisher telephoned to find out the details, Kirstein told
him that it was not Cummings' *Tom* but another version "apparently
by Kirstein, with music by [Nicholas] Nabokoff."[2] Rumors had it that
Muriel Draper was involved in the production too, and Cummings let
his imagination roam about the result: "Kumrads Kirstein and Dra-
per, Inc." would end their ballet with "a white and black chorus de-
claiming 'Workers of the World Unite'."[3] He was bitterly angry with
Kirstein, and though the supposedly rival ballet never came into
being, their friendship cooled to nonexistence. But a new friend soon
replaced him. In January 1936, Cummings received a letter from a
composer, not yet twenty-one years old, named David Diamond, ask-
ing permission to create a musical score for *Tom*. Since Cummings
felt freed from any obligation to Kirstein about the ballet, he sent the
scenario to this young stranger. It led to a friendship that lasted for
the rest of his life.

David Diamond was another Rochesterian, a musical one this time,
who had trained early at the Eastman School and then gone on to the
Dalcroze Institute in New York, where he worked under Roger Sessions
and Aaron Copland. He came from a poor family, and the depression
years made his life even harder; nevertheless, he lived from hand to
mouth in New York City devoting all his time to musical composition.
Since he had long revered Cummings' works, he was amazed when he
heard, through Copland, that no composer had been found to write the
music for *Tom*, and at the urging of Hildegarde Watson, who had been
an early patroness, he wrote directly to Cummings, volunteering for the
task. His response to the scenario was the first encouraging judgment that
Cummings had heard: "This is a real ballet script you have given me,"
and later, "The ballet is perfectly proportioned in good theatrical varia-
tions," and still later, when Diamond was finishing the musical draft of
the final episode, "You should have subtitled *Tom* 'a spectacle to be
danced, sung and mimed'."[4] Cummings had added at Diamond's request
a short original spiritual to be sung by the chorus of slaves for the dance
of Religious Ecstasy:

Lawd
    My
        Hope

(my-saviour
my-saviour)

Lawd
    My
        Life

(pre-serveme
pre-serveme)

may-de-light-of-yo-face-shine-up On Me
and give me
        Peace
and give me
        Joy

(O
Lawd
). my-Lawd[5]

Diamond's opinions were sound. *Tom* is a skillfully arranged series of scenes which capture the essence of Harriet Beecher Stowe's novel. In fact, it seems heavily dependent, in its scenic division, on the published text of George Aiken's stage version of *Uncle Tom's Cabin,* which had recently been revived by Otis Skinner.[6] Despite some Cummingesque peculiarities of language (which no doubt mystified Balanchine), it is a genuine modern ballet in two important respects. First of all, the principal actions, relationships, attitudes, and ideas are expressed by means of dance. Eliza dances the Crossing of the Icechoked River among spots of shifting brightness on the stage; The Shelbys dance the Benevolent Master and Mistress through stiffly executed platitudes of classical ballet; Tom's love of the Bible is rendered in the dance of the Book; the slave auction is conceived as the dance of the Rival Bidders, who make their bids by climbing one, two, three on up to seven stairs toward the top of the auction block.

But more than this, Cummings perceived in Stowe's story the elements of Christian epic that have given her work its continued interest over the decades. As a consequence, his treatment of the characters invests them with that mythic quality which is essential to good ballet stories: Legree is made truly Satanic, Tom is a Christ figure, Eva is angelic, Topsy is "Instinct Unsubdued." In this vein, *Tom* reaches its climax, as the final scene is presented in images of the Anglo-American Evangelical tradition: "outward goldenly slowly the huge doors open— revealing an immeasurable radiance and which, prodigiously forthpouring upon a stage drowned in glory, becomes angels in white robes with harps of gold and crowns."[7] (Dante's vision of the multifoliate rose at the end of *La Divina Commedia* may have influenced this final scene.)

The music was finished by the end of 1936 and Cummings continued his quest for a producer because of his love for the ballet as an art and his wish to contribute creatively to it. Ever since his youthful raptures at seeing Pavlova and Nijinsky in Boston and *Petrouchka* and *Parade* in Paris, he had been a genuine balletomane. Diamond approached Massine; others sought producers in both London and Paris. Kirstein even had the whole of the scenario translated into Russian for Stravinsky to read. But to this day the work has never been performed. Diamond went on, over the years, to set various Cummings poems to music and even composed a musical rendering of the snowfall passage in *The Enormous Room*. Cummings continued to value Diamond's work but especially what he had created for *Tom*. His opinion, including a summary of some of the refusals, is given in a letter of recommendation that he wrote when Diamond applied for a Guggenheim Fellowship:

> I had scarcely heard of him when he came to me and asked for a job which American composers famous infamous and neither hadn't cared or dared to tackle. . . . Roger Sessions had said he would need a year. Virgil Thomson sidestepped gracefully. Aaron Copeland [*sic*] never peeped. Lehman Engel regretted. Paul Boles [*sic*] wouldn't touch it with a television ray. Even George Gershwin later died. David Diamond not only did the job, but created—strictly on his own initiative—a musical original which is also a musical equivalent. If you don't consider that an achievement beyond any mere "abilities," read "Tom"; then get Diamond to play you a pianoversion of "Tom," stand at the piano, and follow my script which he has copied over his score.[8]

In the spring of 1936 Helen Stewart and Dorothy Case took an apartment in Greenwich Village not far from Patchin Place. About this time, Helen's father commissioned a portrait of his daughter, thus she came to the studio for a series of sittings and occasionally stayed on for tea with Marion. These visits laid the foundation for a solid friendship and she became almost a daughter to the Cummingses. For a time, she saw them

E. E. Cummings at Patchin Place,
1938. DAVID DUNHAM, COURTESY
HOUGHTON LIBRARY

almost every day. She took them to dinner once in a while at Charles, a restaurant of rather old-fashioned elegance on Sixth Avenue, which Estlin and Marion could never afford. She invited them down to Gladstone, New Jersey, where her father had built a fine country place and where a Sunday champagne breakfast was frequently served. Her roommate, "Casey," became a frequent caller and firm friend too. Later she would make a habit of driving the Cummingses up to Joy Farm in the spring and staying over for a day or two. Later, in 1939, Helen and Casey provided money, through their fathers, for David Diamond (at Cummings' suggestion) at a time when he was in desperate financial need.

In their friendship, Helen Stewart, Dorothy Case, and David Diamond (and even earlier Lincoln Kirstein) were the first of a series of young people who attached themselves to Cummings and came to love Marion. As the years went by, he increasingly enjoyed the discipleship of young friends. He had his devotion to art and his gospel of individualism to preach, and they enjoyed absorbing it. Their response to Cummings was partly personal—the young women (and sometimes the men) fell in love with him—but he also represented for them the glamor of the 1920's, which in these grim depression years began to appear golden.

These young people filled another need. Very gradually Cummings had been losing the intimate friends of his youth. Lachaise died of leuke-mia in 1935. Nagel had a mental breakdown. Thayer was, of course, still under private care. Mitchell took a Ph.D. degree (horror to think!) and later became the director of the Massachusetts Historical Society in Boston. Brown had wandered out of Cummings' life during a divorce and remarriage. Crane had committed suicide in 1932. Malcolm Cowley and Edmund Wilson, though never really close to Cummings, were some-what estranged from him because of wide political differences. Werner was in Washington ("Tugwell Junction"). Dos Passos was off in other parts of the country, or the world. Only the Watsons would continue to be in frequent contact, although they lived in Rochester and came down only occasionally to New York City. There was scarcely a remnant of Cummings' 1920's world left.

The presidential election of 1936 made him feel even more out of touch with his time. His opinions about domestic politics had always been improvisational, and he often did not even vote. But generally he sided with the Republican party because this political leaning had been traditional in the Cummings family: his father had fought against the Democratic organization in Boston which was controlled by John Fitz-gerald ("Honey Fitz"), the grandfather of the later president, John Kennedy. But he told Morrie Werner that he supported the Republicans because he preferred elephants to jackasses. When Roosevelt was elected president in 1932, Cummings was at first pleased by the return of 3.2 beer and the prospect of repeal of the Prohibition amendment, but Roosevelt's program of social action soon turned him away, for he thought he saw signposts on the road to Moscow. From mid-1933 on, he made continual fun of the New Deal ("nude eel") and "Noodle" Roosevelt (or "rusey felt"), and he drew a cartoon of the NRA blue eagle as a crow, with the slogan "Of Caws" under it. As Roosevelt's legislative program continued to be enacted he would offer such remarks as, "You'd never guess that karl marx's Whiskers were on the point of taking over uncle sam's chin Would you now."[9] But after the United States recognized Soviet Russia and the two nations exchanged diplomatic representatives, he became convinced that Roosevelt was a Communist sympathizer and he always had his ear open for confirmation of the opinion—as in 1935 when he said he heard that Stalin had broadcast an appeal to all good Communists "to cooperate with the New Deal and Noodle Roosy."[10] When eighty percent of the United States press was anti-Roosevelt during the 1936 election campaign and thus created the impression that the public was going to end his stay in office, Cummings felt some support for his opinions, but when Roosevelt won in a landslide and carried all the states except Maine and Vermont, he thought that Communism was right around the corner.

Yet his reaction on election night had the familiar doubleness: dislike for the behavior of the group but interest in the unique situation of an individual, even the President. "I was depressed by the fishhorn blowers & torn newspaper hustlers at times square = the mob. I was renewed, transformed by 1 little guy selling extras at 14th—where I got off to avoid Hunter[11] & gal; & there was this Shakespearian comic—this clown bursting with Joy—& he just said 'Roosevelt ran away with it this time' but in him was All; through him whatever is Eternal Laughed. 'Yes' I said, smiling—though wryly. And (because I felt him all good & gay, all gladly triumphant—nothing small or mean, nothing great; but simply & gladly Everything) I added quite without conscious wishing "up at Times Square they flashed that he was elected—already." The little Man, Mr. Everywhere, beamed. . . . Whitman's ("the divine average") Force [.] Nothing succeeds like success[.] Roosevelt, the crippled, the partial man (deformed) becomes—<u>with the vote of All</u>—transfigured: the triumph over even paralysis, the man whose spirit conquered disease of body, the Superman . . . the essential meaning of the election: All is only what matters & All arrives always through *change*. "The Verb," on earth = to move. Noone can live spiritually who allows himself to become rigid, noone can die spiritually who keeps himself atune to Nature—I touch the tree."[12]

The bitterness of the previous year had certainly waned for a time if he could engage in this benign mythmaking about the political leader who he feared would become a despot.

XXVI

The War Years

Last night went to the pub to listen to the 9 o'clock news, and arriving there a few minutes late, asked the landlady what the news had been. "Oh, we never turn it on. Nobody listens to it, you see. And they've got the piano playing in the other bar, and they won't turn it off just for the news." This is at a moment when there is a most deadly threat to the Suez Canal. Cf. during the worst moment of the Dunkirk campaign, when the barmaid would not have turned on the news unless I had asked her.

GEORGE ORWELL, *War-Time Diary*

The recognition that had been long withheld from Cummings by the literary world was finally granted in 1938 with the publication of *Collected Poems.* The event came about through the perceptiveness of a brilliant editor at Harcourt Brace, Charles A. Pearce, known to his friends as "Cap." Over the years he had become a Cummings admirer and realizing with the publication of *No Thanks* that Cummings' poems lay scattered in books which were difficult to procure, issued by a series of different publishers, he approached his superiors and got "reluctant approval" to gather a collection of his poems.[1] Cummings bought up the copyrights for *Tulips and Chimneys* from Thomas Seltzer and for *XLI Poems* from the Dial Press. After he made additional arrangements with Liveright, the way was clear for a book that would show Cummings' development over the years from the Harvard poems up to the present. Pearce and Cummings wrote back and forth deciding which poems would be included. Cummings first submitted a list of his choices, saying, "the enclosed list represents what I like, irrespective of whether it's obscene or unsetup-able."[2] Since he had got around the obscenity problem with the poems in *&* by using the method of a "privately printed" volume, there were some questions about such poems as "i like my body when it is with your" and "my girl's tall with hard long eyes," but the Harcourt lawyers finally gave their opinion that none of the poems were going to invite prosecution.

With a royalty advance of $400 from Harcourt Brace, another advance from a British publisher for a twenty-poem book of selections entitled *1/20*, and $300 from Jacobs that had accrued from reprint fees from anthologists, Cummings had enough money to repay his mother the $300 she had put up for *No Thanks* and to take Marion to Europe again. An invitation to visit Oxford had come from the British zoologist, Solly Zuckerman, whom he had met recently in New York. Marion would be able to see London for the first time, perhaps also do some more modeling for Baron Huene in Paris, and, if the money held out, get to see Florence and Venice. They sailed in June 1937 and remained abroad for two months.

In London, they looked up the MacDermots, hoping for some time with Nancy. They knew from Rebecca Cummings that Nancy had been spending the year in Austria, for she had received a letter at Christmas time in which Nancy, who had just turned seventeen, reported her plans in a charming and surprisingly mature manner: "In a few weeks, I am going off to stay for a few months with a family in Vienna, to learn German, and to go on with music which interests me very much. I have learnt the piano ever since I was six or so, but I would really like to take up some string instrument as well. Next winter I may either go to a domestic school over here, or spend a few months in Italy as I have started Italian and like it very much. Anyway, I have finished with school and am now starting with the 'finishing'—an arduous business."[3] The Mac-Dermots were living in England now, since Frank had given up politics for a time, and they obligingly asked Estlin and Marion to tea at the Carlton Hotel. They told them that Nancy was still in Vienna and gave them a scattering of news about her, including plans for her to be "brought out" next year and to be presented at court.

Everyone in England and France was jittery about the threat of war breaking out. The Spanish Civil War, with all its horrors, had been raging for almost a year, and Hitler and Mussolini had sent arms, planes, and troops to help the insurgents. "Herr Franco," as Cummings called him, had just captured Bilbao and was crushing the Basque resistance in Northern Spain. In Paris on Bastille Day, Cummings saw the city teeming with "garde mobile, tanks and zouaves" because the government

feared a Communist demonstration. But only a few Communists in
trucks appeared waving red flags and shaking clenched fists. The Euro-
pean political turmoil this summer provoked Cummings' grim nursery
rhyme:

> red-rag and pink-flag
> blackshirt and brown
> strut-mince and stink-brag
> have all come to town
>
> some like it shot
> some like it hung
> and some like it in the twot
> nine months young

Since money ran short, the plans for Florence and Venice had to be
abandoned. They returned home in August to Joy Farm.

There had been some give and take between Cummings and Pearce
about the choice of poems for the new volume, but they had become two
warm and accommodating friends by this time. Pearce was reassuring
about the pagination of the book so that the appearance of any "picture
poems" would be preserved; and Cummings, who had demanded the
reinstatement of fourteen poems which Pearce had cut, was ready to
compromise by suggesting others that could be dropped to make room
for his favorites.[4] There is no particular pattern of likeness which lies
behind the fourteen poems he was willing to fight for, but it is notable
that "brIght" and his anti-Communist lampoon, "kumrads die because
they're told," are among them. The volume was to have the freshness of
twenty-two "New Poems," which had appeared in periodicals since *No
Thanks.* The two most worthy of comment are a tribute to the comedian,
Jimmy Savo, "so little he is"—one more appreciation of a Chaplinesque,
Petrouchka-like, comic-pathetic underling—and "(of Ever-Ever Land i
speak/ sweet morons gather roun,'" a broadside against standardization
and conformity in life.

Most important was the preface that Cummings wrote by request for
Collected Poems. It contains a special quality of address that many people
have described as a feature of Cummings' personality, namely, his mak-
ing a person feel that he was speaking to him alone and that there was
no one else in the world but the two of them. The preface sets forth, as
we might expect, Cummings' views about the value of being "alive":
"The poems to come are for you and for me and are not for mostpeople
—it's no use trying to pretend that mostpeople and ourselves are alike.

*Rebecca Cummings pencil drawing
by E. E. Cummings.*
HOUGHTON LIBRARY

Mostpeople have less in common with ourselves than the squarerootof-minusone. You and I are human beings;mostpeople are snobs. Take the matter of being born. What does being born mean to mostpeople? Catastrophe unmitigated. . . . you and I are not snobs. We can never be born enough. We are human beings;for whom birth is a supremely welcome mystery,the mystery of growing:the mystery which happens only and whenever we are faithful to ourselves. You and I wear the dangerous looseness of doom and find it becoming. Life,for eternal us,is now. . . ."

Pearce conceived of a unique device to promote the book. He arranged for Cummings to make a phonograph recording of several poems, including "Buffalo Bill's," "since feeling is first," and "somewhere i have never travelled,gladly beyond." His scheme was to have the Harcourt Brace salesmen distribute it as they took orders for the book from bookstore managers.

When *Collected Poems* was published in February 1938, it was more widely reviewed and more charitably received than any book Cummings had ever put before the public. Aside from the scornful dismissal by the *Daily Worker,* only two reviews did not give the book a good reception: the grave voice of Yvor Winters pronounced it "infantile exhibitionism" and the eye of Horace Gregory sought and did not find a demonstration that Cummings had developed over the years.[5] More representative of American literary opinion was Dudley Fitts in the *Saturday Review of Literature*, who began by saying, "It was time for this book," and ended by praising the poet himself. "With all its failures and beauties, its clashing styles, its brainsmashing complexities and moving simplicities, this is the poetry of a man of complete artistic integrity."[6] This was the book, then, that was soon to be found in public libraries all over the country. This was the book from which anthologists were to choose selections which made Cummings' name familiar to the reader of poetry and to the college student.

Rebecca Cummings was pleased, as always, and she happily pasted the reviews into "the doomsday book," the scrapbook of clippings she had been keeping since 1922. She was almost eighty now and "cheerful as a chipmunk." In his notes Cummings gives a very loving picture of her in her old age:

> being unique, she had her own way of welcoming you at a distance: suddenly the stocky body's right arm would fly up like a glad flag and its hand begin vividly sailing and slowly leaping to and fro, while over herself tumbled and rushed and lived a brook a river a fiery ocean of recognition; until every radiant aspect and each glowing atom of her flesh and her spirit expressed joy alone and nothing but joy, joy . . . as if, when the man who is her son takes her in his arms, she can feel his unborn wish kicking at her heart.

But the book sold very slowly. Even though it was priced at only $3.00, it was, after all, a volume of poetry, and besides that, the economic depression lay hard upon the book trade. The Cummingses began to feel the economic pinch once more. Marion was doing some modeling again, the Watsons occasionally helped out by buying a painting, anthologists paid for reprint rights once in a while, but Cummings fell so far in debt in 1939 that he had to turn to Watson and ask directly for a loan, confessing he had absolutely no security to put up against it, for his mother was still the owner of Joy Farm. Watson sent $300 by return mail, and Cummings, thanking him, conceded, "am literally American enough to hope I'll be able to 'make my own way' 'some day' 'soon'."[7] His mother was providing a check for the monthly rent of the studio and the apartment (which in a few years rose to $70.00 per month) and giving him an additional check for $75.00.

The Knights returned East during this time and bought another farm about thirty miles up the Hudson from New York City. When the Cummingses visited them, they were able to renew acquaintance with neighbors of the Knights, Max Eastman and his wife, Eliena Krylenko,

E. E. Cummings, Max Eastman, Marion Morehouse, Eliena Krylenko at Martha's Vineyard. COURTESY JERE KNIGHT

who had painted a splendid portrait of Cummings in 1933. Max was a literary critic, author of *The Enjoyment of Poetry*, a book which Cummings knew well. He also had a strong interest in social issues and had been one of the editors of the *Liberator* when Cummings was a contributor in the 1920's. In politics, he was a Trotskyist and had just published a translation of Trotsky's *History of the Russian Revolution*. Although he was an anti-Stalinist, one would anticipate a clash with Cummings, who these days was outspoken against socialism in any form. But Eastman was a hearty man, full of good humor, and deeply committed to the value of art, and he and Cummings became good friends. In addition to their farm, the Eastmans had a summer place on Martha's Vineyard that had a private beach which allowed for nude bathing. When the Cummingses came down for weekends, Marion especially enjoyed it, for, proud of the beauty of her body, she liked to share it with intimate friends.

Some new acquaintances of these years were Paul Nordoff, a composer and music teacher, and his wife Sabrina, a dancer. Nordoff later set some of Cummings' poems to music, the best settings that Cummings had ever heard—"luminous," he called them. On one occasion, Nordoff invited the Cummingses to hear him play and sing "if there are any heavens," "little tree," and several other compositions. He was a first-rate performer and hearing the poems brought to life musically, Cummings "turned red with surprise and pleasure."[8] Cummings wrote to thank him, calling the music "beyond praise (sorry, therefore, I tried to praise—& how clumsily!)"[9]

A new and very close friendship that began around this time was that with Lloyd Frankenberg and his wife, Loren MacIver, who lived nearby the Cummingses at 61 Perry Street in the Village. Lloyd, a handsome six-foot-two poet, had just published his first book, *The Red Kite*. He had long admired Cummings' work, and the culmination of his regard was an article he wrote for the *Harvard Wake*, "Cummings Times One," which showed, Cummings thought, the best understanding of his work that had yet been printed. When anyone asked Cummings questions about his poetry, he would say, "Ask the maestro," Frankenberg. Loren, quiet, gentle, and loving, was a painter who shared Cummings' romantic view of life and his dislike of machines and appliances. She painted a picture for Cummings that gave him more pleasure than anything since the sculptured head by Lachaise. It was a spring scene, complete with balloonman and organ grinder, called "Lilac Time." Cummings hung it over the mantelpiece of the apartment at Patchin Place.[10]

A most important new figure in Cummings' life was the poet, Theodore Spencer, who was an assistant professor of English at Harvard. Cummings met him in spring 1939 when he was invited to give a poetry reading at Harvard—again $25.00 plus travel money. Spencer, tall and blond, had the magnetism and good looks of a matinee idol and whenever he taught in the Extension Division in the evening, he fluttered the hearts of the Boston ladies. Striding across the Harvard yard, wearing his trench coat over his shoulders like a cape, he seemed almost theatrically professorial. In the lecture hall, he leaned over the lectern toward his audience of Harvard men, stirring them into an enthusiasm for Shakespeare or Donne. When Cummings came for the poetry reading, he provided a sharp contrast. He played the role of Bohemian poet, and, what is more, he was in an anti-Cambridge mood. A short note among his papers records his experience on that occasion: "Some years ago I returned to Cambridge (& Harvard) to read poems for Ted S.   Felt wretched before, & nervous during, the ordeal. Was bombarded by my own words bouncing back at me from hardrubber audience—1 Chinaman excepted." Helen Schevill, who was in the audience, remembers details which illuminate this note. The reading took place in the rather battered lecture auditorium, Room 11 of Sever Hall. Cummings, looking very youthful, appeared in a white turtleneck sweater wearing dirty sneakers, one of which was untied. A rather small audience, including several old ladies (Aunt Jane and some neighbors?), sparsely filled the room. When in the course of the reading he came to "the Cambridge ladies live in furnished souls," the old ladies stiffened and became obviously restless for the remainder of the hour.[11]

Nevertheless, the occasion was a valuable one for Cummings because he was able to spend a good deal of time with Spencer and "his goddess-tall girl friend," and he found an important new force in his life. Spencer was in the midst of work on his book, *Shakespeare and the Nature of Man,* an admirable study, which placed Shakespeare in the intellectual milieu of his time and examined the moral issues which his major plays confronted. He and Cummings discussed some of his ideas: "Ted had a great influence on me at the time. Mighty concerned with 'the problem of evil,' he wanted me to write about simple things; & I resented this: 'The problem,' I maintained, doesn't exist. But am pretty sure it was after meeting him that I finished a poem to my father: a poem of which one line . . . doomed me to a moral life—the line being 'No liar looked him in the head' . . . but this feeling of doom was vastly more than counterbalanced by a sense of freedom & exileration—a feeling that I was developing a newer deeper dimension."

The writing of this poem represents a real psychological breakthrough for Cummings. The preparation apparently began with some plunges into memory and some meditation about his father, followed by some jotting down of notes. Some were simple statements like "My father was the handsomest man I ever saw." Other notes were poetic, nostalgic reminiscences or impressions such as "Big was my father and strong with lightblue skies for eyes. Everywhere he went, people looked up at him wonderingly, and (recognizing something more than human in the truth of his height—feeling that out of him came generosities like mountains and a forgiveness like morning) everyone smiled and my (moving like a god) father smiled at everyone as gently as tomorrow, being afraid of nothing and noone."[12] Yet, when he came to write the poem, what took shape was a piece that employed his own characteristic manipulation of language:

> my father moved through dooms of love
> through sames of am through haves of give
> singing each morning out of each night
> my father moved through depths of height

He seems to have removed some restriction from his deepest self, a release which then allowed him to identify himself with his father, for he even transfers to duty-filled Edward Cummings his own self-directed philosophy of life:

Scorning the pomp of must and shall
my father moved through dooms of feel

The poem builds toward a climax in which the spirit of Edward Cummings becomes an optimistic force which can overcome all evil:

i say though hate were why men breathe—
because my father lived his soul
love is the whole and more than all

Looking back many years after this poem "wrote itself," Cummings felt that it was the beginning of a new poetic period for him, one in which he spoke with a more responsible, more morally concerned voice. "I'd long ago written a poem to my mother—'if there are any heavens,' & in life, had (after revolting against) become friends with my father. . . . I'd won my freedom, & he (being *great of soul*) had congratulated me! . . . but in my art I'd never celebrated this [reconciliation]. Now I felt that I'd done so; & in so doing had shown the world how to move, what direction to take[.] Did this culminating stage of "religion" threaten to prove severe and spartan (if not meagre and moral)? if so I remembered Montaigne's assertion that 'la bonté' has 'luxe' of its own. Or I reflected that every titan of art—a Michelangelo, a Shakespeare—has been conscious of moral values—moral myths I almost wrote!" Cummings in his reminiscence is a little premature, this development did not take place as early as 1939. But it is worth noting that he saw the origin of it in this creative act of reconciliation with his father. It was, without question, a crucial episode in his life.

Not only were there new friends, but old friends had their brief return. Dos Passos brushed through town now and then. In September 1937, he had come from adventurous months in Spain trying to make a film about the Spanish war with Hemingway and MacLeish. He was fed up with Stalin and the Communists now because the Communists, after gaining supremacy in the Spanish government, had summarily executed his friend, José Robles, who had long been a Loyalist fighter. In his writings at this time, Dos Passos, the man who had been the brightest star in the literary galaxy of the left, was admitting that the methods of dictatorship made the aims of Communism impossible of achievement.

Dos heard the phonograph record that Harcourt Brace had distributed and was delighted with the mellifluous voice of "Franklin D. Cummings." When he wrote Cummings about it, he mentioned that Mike Gold in the *New Masses* had accused him of backsliding into immaturity.[13] Cummings reply was his usual breezy dismissal: "Thee can tell All That Glitters from mee that if twenty pianomovers with forty hands carried worldrevolution all yee way up yee Empire State and dropped it into yee East River, yee splash wouldn't fill a pissant's vagina."[14]

Another long-absent friend visited the United States in spring 1939, but, alas, seemed to be mentally wobbling. Ezra Pound was very much changed and more concerned with his peculiar monetary theories than with poetry. Cummings wrote Watson about it, for Pound was about to receive an honorary degree from Hamilton College in Clinton, New York, and Cummings thought Watson might travel over from Rochester to see Pound: "You may be surprised to learn that the recently endowed . . . Patchin Institute has been studying an Ezra. We don't know if he's a spy or merely schizo, but we do feel he's incredibly lonesome. Gargling anti-semitism from morning till morning doesn't (apparently) help a human throat to sing. He continually tackles dummies, while uttering ferocious poopyawps & screechburps, as though he suspected somevast-invisible footballgameaudience were surrounding bad-guy Titan-him. Etc if you don't know money you don't know nothing. . . . He's very fond of me incidentally."[15] After a few days, he and Marion "literally fled" to New Hampshire. But he was fond of Ezra too. As Cummings later remarked, he wore his clothes and his friends forever; when they needed repair they were not thrown away; he patched or mended them in whatever way he could. After Pound returned to Italy, they continued their decade-old correspondence, full of linguistic jabberwocky.

II

When the European war that seemed inevitable broke out in September 1939, Cummings hoped fervently that the United States would stay out this time. He looked with a suspicious eye at war news from the Allied governments thinking it doctored to lure the United States into participation. Right from the start, he had no faith in Roosevelt's isolationist pronouncements. He referred to him as "Woodrow Wilson." At the same time, he assured his mother: "Something tells me that this time the propaganda department will have to hand out something hotter than the Lusitania—or else Uncle Sam (nay Ward) will keep right on minding his small ize."[16] His grief the next year over the fall of France was shared by all his friends to whom Paris had been paradise. Yet he was so obsessive in his desire for a hands-off policy that he actually became anti-British in 1940, fearful that U.S. aid to Britain in various forms would draw the country in as a belligerent.

But never consistent or logical in any views on foreign affairs, he
seemed to want some kind of protective action on the part of the United
States when Russia attacked Finland. Or so his little epigram implied:

o to be in finland
now that russia's here)

swing low
sweet ca

rr
y on

(pass the freedoms pappy or
uncle shylock not interested[17]

It was the fate of the small weak country that always moved him ("I've
a leftward green truly American fondness for underdogs")[18] and he
cheered louder for the Greeks when they came under German attack than
he did for the English who withstood the months of aerial bombardment
by the Luftwaffe.

One of the reasons for his superficial knowledge of world happen-
ings was the fact that, even though he seldom read newspapers, he would
not allow a radio in the house. His violent dislike of the radio had a
mixture of sources. His prejudice against "mechanism" and "science"
was part of it. The irritation that extraneous noise caused him con-
tributed too. But what really made him hate radio "like piesun" was his
perception that the radio networks could be used for political and social
persuasion. His resentment of Roosevelt's ability to use his radio ad-
dresses to maintain the confidence of the public was only matched by his
antipathy toward Churchill ("his jakes") and the rhetorical skill with
which he moved American hearers to support the English cause.

When he heard that "Herr Roosevelt" was going to run for a third
term, he thought it a dictatorial tactic, and he became an ardent supporter
of Wendell Willkie, although he had his doubts about Willkie, who
seemed to him suspiciously liberal. After Roosevelt's third election vic-
tory, he saw with dismay the movement toward involvement in the
European war, with the passage of the Lend-Lease Bill, the Roosevelt-
Churchill signing of the Atlantic Charter, the arming of merchant ships,
and other acts of aid to Britain or hostility toward the Axis powers. He
did not know what to think of the German invasion of Russia, and
reluctant to cheer for the Soviets, he juggled his mixed feelings. From Joy

Farm he wrote to Eric Knight that "crapsheets down the valley (thank God our hill has no radio) claim that the world isn't big enough yet; so Adolph Hoi and Joseph Polloi are sensibly butchering each other by the billions. Perhaps."[19] Like thousands of other Americans, he began reading Tolstoy's *War and Peace* as the war on the Russian front ground on.

But now he heard a clamor from another direction, this time for aid to Russia, that he feared might pull the country into the conflict. He wrote to Pound in answer to his "latest queeries" that Max Eastman "has gone off in a c-nd-m in a pamphlet arguing everybody should support Russia for the nonce" and he showed his resentment too at the pro-Allied efforts by "macarchibald maclapdog macleash," who as Librarian of Congress was helping Roosevelt with his speeches. He ended his letter giving his views of Roosevelt as a dictator and offering a nonsense limerick about the push toward entering the war:

> "make haste" spake the Lord Of New Dealings
> "neutrality's hard on my feelings"
> —they returned from the bank
> with the furter in frank:
> & the walls;& the floors,& the ceilings[20]

As the fervor in the nation developed in 1941, he took an interest in the America First party that had become the strongest voice for the antiwar position. He even went so far as to visit a neighbor to hear a radio speech by Charles Lindbergh in favor of continued isolationism.

Almost lost sight of during the war years was his new book, *50 Poems*, published by Cap Pearce under the imprint of his own publishing firm, Duell, Sloane, and Pearce. The collection shows some movement in expression toward compactness and an increase in philosophizing about mankind, but this development is scarcely noticeable among the satirical epigrams, love poems, and syntactical anagrams that resemble the work he had published before. The book contained some outstanding pieces which are frequently anthologized: among them are the wistful myth about his secret self, "anyone lived in a pretty how town;" the poem in memory of his father (which would have been more effective if it had been shorter); and a poem remarkably expressive of the staunchness of a serene individual, which begins:

> wherelings whenlings
> (daughters of ifbut offspring of hopefear
> sons of unless and children of almost)
> never shall guess the dimension of

him whose
each
foot likes the
here of this earth

whose both
eyes
love
this now of the sky

Critics were not all kind to the book. Nor did it do well in the market-place. Once the royalty advance had been earned, Cummings received royalty checks for the six-month periods that amounted to $14.94, $6.00, $.75, $9.75, and so on. But it did have a constant sale over the next twenty years as Cummings' reputation rose. By the 1960's it was bringing in about $400 a year.

III

In 1941 Cummings began to have health problems. He had recurrent pains in his left leg and increasingly severe backaches. By the end of the year, he was in misery. Diathermy treatments did no good and os-teopathic sessions gave only temporary relief. Fed up with both his New York physician and the osteopath that Hildegarde Watson had recommended, he finally went to Dr. Frank Ober, an orthopedic spe-cialist in Boston, in January 1942. Dr. Ober X-rayed his back and legs. He gave him a lift to wear in his left shoe and advised him on a new pattern of living which Cummings described in a letter to his mother, "I . . . am told to 'baby' myself, to keep as comfortable as possible— preferably on a bed—&, as I gather, to cheer up. . . . what I need is a hot water bag on my hip, & aspirin or empirin when I can't sleep—I don't need heat-machines or osteopathy or (apparently) anything but beaucoup de patience."

When Dr. Ober studied the X-ray plates, he found the presence of osteoarthritis in the spine. Cummings was soon wearing a specially de-signed corset. "It resembles armour; but I feel like somebody living in a drain-pipe (with his legs and arms & head sticking out) rather than like any ancient Roman, though stoicism comes in mighty handy these days! The corset has so many straps I've got to learn trigonometry. You should see Marion ensconsing me!"[21]

Although he hated his confinement in "The Iron Maiden," his life became more liveable under Dr. Ober's treatment. But Cummings was never without physical limitation or pain for the rest of his life. As a result, the irritability which he had been displaying in recent years became more frequent and his growlings about social issues, domestic politics, or the course of the war grew proportionately ill-tempered. When the war finally came to the United States on December 7, 1941, Cummings seemed at first to blame Roosevelt for his international policies rather than Japan for its attack (or Germany or Italy for their declarations of war on the United States), and he continued in this frame of mind even as the Japanese conquests spread over the South Pacific. When he was visiting in Boston and Mitchell told him that "he took to his bed for 12 hours after Singapore's collapse," Cummings was not in sympathy—"Manifest Destiny will have its; etc. etc."[22] The hatred that began to be engendered against the Japanese troubled him, and he was inspired to write a skillfully patterned satire about the inarticulate sputterings of that racially tinged rage:

ygUDuh

     ydoan
     yunnuhstan

     ydoan o
     yunnuhstan dem
     yguduh ged

     yunnuhstan dem doidee
     yguduh ged riduh
     ydoan o nudn
LISN bud LISN

       dem
       gud
       am

       lidl yelluh bas
       tuds weer goin

   duhSIVILEYEzum

Eric Knight, who felt loyalties to both of his countries, went to England in 1941 to help out, but when the United States was forced into the war, he volunteered for duty in the American army and was commissioned a major in the Special Services Corps. He and Cummings had words over the decision: Cummings told him he was a damned fool for getting himself involved; but Knight felt, "This war is too big to make any one man or his life of the slightest importance."[23] That summer when the Selective Service threatened to take single men of Cummings' age, he roared out his protest, and, stamping about with his game leg, declared (as if he really believed he might be drafted) that they "couldn't make me fight Germans twice."[24] These were bad years for Cummings. His letters fumed about the United States as the "home of the slave" and charged hypocrisy whenever an expression of idealism came from the president or any other national leader.

He did not follow the war news. Information came to him only in scattered ways ("occasionally glimpse a newspaper headline and sometimes talk with militarized friends").[25] His general position seemed to be totally against the war and anyone involved in it. He did not like to have people in uniform visit his house, and the friend whom he respected most for his response to the war was Lloyd Frankenberg, who was serving as a conscientious objector in a hospital in Washington, D.C. His feelings were so bitter that the word pacifist does not seem quite suitable. A poem that expresses his complex attitude most accurately appeared in 1944. It was his own way of saying. "War is hell" and at the same time blaming the United States for selling material for military build-up to other nations:

plato told

him:he couldn't
believe it(jesus

told him;he
wouldn't believe
it)lao

tsze
certainly told
him,and general
(yes

mam)
sherman;
and even

                    (believe it
                    or

                    not)you
                    told him:i told
                    him;we told him
                    (he didn't believe it,no

                    sir)it took
                    a nipponized bit of
                    the old sixth

                    avenue
                    el;in the top of his head:to tell

                    him

But one can overstress his querulousness. He had his changes of mood and periods of good will toward everyone, especially when he was at Joy Farm. And individual soldiers found him warm and generous. He maintained a long correspondence with a young Marine named Howard Nelson, a total stranger who wrote to him from the Pacific, and he sent young John Cheever, whom he had met through Morrie Werner, a letter containing a ten-dollar bill, an autumn leaf, and sympathetic words, "I too have slept with someone else's boot in the corner of my smile."[26]

As might be expected, he did not grieve at the death of President Roosevelt. Nor yet did he feel cheered about Truman as president. Altogether, his comments to his mother about the change in the White House make him sound more like a Wall Street banker than a poet: "Not being a monarchist, I felt vastly relieved when Mr. R. disappeared. As for his successor, as somebody remarked, 'Now we won't have to hear about The Common Man anymore because he's right where he belongs: in the White House."[27]

The sense of alienation that reverberates from Cummings' words during the war years had other sources besides the state of the world and his own bodily aches. A staggering blow had fallen upon the inhabitants of 4 Patchin Place. Marion became seriously ill with arthritis: she was so severely stricken that for a time it seemed she would never walk again. In recent years, she had occasionally experienced pains in her joints. As early as age thirty-two, she had some trouble with the sacrum; then three years later she was hospitalized with an attack of bursitis in her shoulder. Now in February 1944, just at a time when Cummings was preparing a painting exhibit at the American-British Art Gallery, his first in a dozen years, Marion was again hospitalized—this time for pains in her legs, back, and arms. The diagnosis by her physician, Dr. Frank Peters, was rheumatoid arthritis.

At first, Cummings expected her to be home in a few days, but at the time of her birthday, March 9, when Estlin brought her a cake, Dr. Peters said it would be two or three weeks more. None of the treatments seemed to help her. Specialists were consulted, new medications were prescribed, her tonsils were removed, special diets were tried. Any relief was only temporary. After three months of daily pain and of growing weakness because of her confinement in bed, her doctor began to give her gold injections, and very gradually her condition began to improve. During this time, Estlin suffered the greatest anguish of his life, though his friends thought him very stoical. Friends and relatives rallied around. Aunt Jane volunteered to pay all the hospital bills, the Watsons were ready to pay doctors' bills. A stream of visitors called upon her. Room 1206 of the New York Hospital was an indoor garden of flowers from Estlin and other well-wishers. Aline MacMahon thought a beautiful woman needed some jewelry to make her feel less like a patient, so she sent her the gold earrings she had bought from Alexander Calder, a pair of tiny mobiles.

Cummings visited almost every day, frequently going up in a taxi with Loren MacIver and having tea or dinner with her afterward. It was a lonely time, the first separation from Marion in twelve years. Besides sending flowers, he wrote letters to her, typed out poems from anthologies, drew cartoons to cheer her, told her how empty the apartment was without her, how he missed La Cuisine Morehouse. His letters are signed by the banner-bearing elephant or by Pengy, a penguin drawing. We are familiar with the elephant symbol but the penguin was a new one. Cummings knew that the penguin, a comical, clumsy creature on land, is a graceful swimmer capable of terrific speed in the water. He thought of himself as having a "penguin soul," by which he seemed to mean that, although he was comical and awkward in his outward manner, he had an inner self, an unconscious being, of beauty and power. In his tenderness of expression in his letters, he is once more the *petit garçon:* he types a letter beginning, "Mlle. Corona asked to be allowed to write you"; he speaks of himself as "little worthless" or "petit sans valeur." Under the stress of his sorrow for her afflictions, his religious feeling burgeoned. Commenting on Santayana's remarks in *The Sense of Beauty* that it was regrettable that Protestant iconoclasm deprived men of the contemplation of the Virgin Mary as an ideal, he wrote to Marion: "imagine being the sort of person to whom such miracles don't mean anything whatever!

We must deal very simply and kindly with those people: they're not merely 'deaf' and 'dumb' and 'blind,' they're so infinitely sick that any 'sickness' we suffer is riproaringlyhealthy by comparison—to put it mildly."[28]

Occasional passages in the letters show his feeling of isolation from his fellow citizens and even a little self-pity because Marion was not on hand to take care of his needs: "You, looking and being (in spite of all your troubles) so beautiful and so gay, made myself completely forget there was any such thing as a "war," all filled with lies and curses; or a "city," crammed with hurting selfish hysterical people: or even any such fearsome concoction as 'black bean soup' (which, by the way, looked tan & tasted worse) à la me."[29] Sometimes a concerned friend sent a cleaning woman around to Patchin Place to wash the stacks of dishes Estlin let pile up or to chase the roaches that were appearing.

By June, Marion was able to be helped into a warm pool to get her limbs moving again and she was taken to the gymnasium to use some arm-exercising devices. They had hoped she might be able to go up to Joy Farm late in the summer but she was not strong enough. In August Estlin went to the farm by himself for three weeks and visited his sister and mother at Abenaki. But the farm was not the same without Marion: "I realize, being up here alone, how a pagan must have felt after christianity had marched noisily into his favorite grove and blessed away the protecting spirit whom he silently worshipped there. You are the Tutelary Genius of Joy Farm; you are its Guardian Angel. Without you, this hilltop and all its inhabitants—its birds and crickets and butterflies and flowers—are lonely. They all want you and miss you; because you are theirs, and they love you dearly."[30] As usual a stay at Joy Farm softened his mood: "God is certainly and marvellously kind! Last night there wasn't a star & everything prophecied rain. today is heavenly—brilliant hot sun; birds singing (I heard a finch) everywhere."[31] By the time he returned to New York and had heard of her many visitors, their flowers and gifts, he was ready to concede that "Maybe America isn't such a bad place . . . and Van 'wick' Brooks was totally correct in murmuring chez PR [Paul Rosenfeld?] 'but it'll come out right in the end.' "[32]

By December Marion was able to get out of bed and go about on crutches, but it was the end of January before she could leave the hospital. At first, they went to the Hotel Earle in New Jersey so that Marion could be waited upon ("little helpless" was not much good at that sort of thing), but Marion was unhappy in the hotel atmosphere and wanted to be at home in her apartment. After the return to Patchin Place, friends helped out, especially Hazel Werner, Morrie's wife, and Miriam Patchen, wife of the poet, Kenneth Patchen. Marion's treatments were continued and she was able to travel to Joy Farm by June 1945. Cummings was back into his routine of writing and painting, although he frequently had to rest his back. He spent a good part of the summer writing and rewriting an introduction to a collection of George Herriman's Krazy Kat comic strips. When the war with Japan came to an end in August, he allowed less credit to Truman for his leadership in bringing it about than he gave blame to Roosevelt for its beginning. He could never forgive Truman for ordering the atomic bombing of Hiroshima and Nagasaki.

IV

Cummings occasionally published poems in magazines that did not pay. Sometimes he was returning a favor that the editor had done him, as when he contributed to Edward Titus's *This Quarter,* but at other times, he was just helping a little magazine to get started, as when he contributed to *Furioso,* a Yale publication begun by two undergraduates, Reed Whittemore, a young poet, and James Angleton, a literary entrepreneur who was an admirer of Pound. For their first issue in 1939, Cummings had sent them a rhymed squib that seemed to be directed at Auden and Spender, "flotsam and jetsam/ are gentlemen poeds," and he continued to contribute up to 1943. James Angleton, having called at Patchin Place, gradually came to know Cummings, and on one visit he brought his fiancée, Cecily d'Autremont, who was a junior at Vassar. Cecily was really thrilled by Cummings, who represented to her the essence of the "lost generation"—World War I, postwar Paris, and the literary florescence of the 1920's. After the couple married and they came to know about Marion's illness, Cecily arranged for the Cummingses to spend the winter in Arizona, where her parents had a family compound, "Brule Wisconci," near Tucson, an establishment large enough so that the Cummingses could have a private cottage of their own.

Estlin and Marion arrived in Tucson in December 1945, shortly before Christmas, to find a gracious welcome and a snug house within a walled courtyard alongside the main household and facing a large swimming pool. Their host, Mr. Hubert d'Autremont, was a bronzed, good-humored, open-hearted Westerner, president of the Southern Arizona Bank and president of the Arizona State Senate. Cummings took to him right away; he was very much surprised, for he never thought he would like a banker.[33] Mrs. Helen d'Autremont was very beautiful: "This lady looks like Renoir's Madame Charpentier," he wrote Watson. "She and her husband love each other. Together they're a bulwark against those sub-human vulgarities which = democracy. Separately, he's a lively limited authentic man & she's a shy incredibly generous perfectly sincere doer-of-good. Neither of them have any pretentions or pomposities; both are merely dimly aware that the arts exist. Let me add that Marion & I truly like them both & each: & I think they each & both like us truly— anyhow they could not be more morethan-kind."[34] Cecily was on hand, too, to be additionally hospitable; James Angleton, who was now a captain in the O.S.S., was still in Italy. (In later years he was to become head of the CIA's Counterintelligence Division.)

Estlin and Marion soon came to know the relatives and friends, especially as the weather was warm enough for swimming and the d'Autremonts were very generous about use of their pool. Cummings took special interest in Juan Xavier, an Arizona Indian, whose wife, Gwenyth Harrington, an anthropologist, was from Cambridge, Massachusetts. Juan was a dark, silent, self-possessed man with a magnificent physique, a real D. H. Lawrence primitive, who filled every requirement as the genuine human being, uncorrupted by civilization, that Cummings admired. He and his wife lived in a tent on the d'Autremont land. Gwenyth had been all over Europe and the Balkans with her researches and Cummings was fascinated by her stories of her adventurous life.

The Cummings celebrated Christmas at the d'Autremonts with a most unusual collection of guests: "On Christmas Eve I sat opposite a Papago Indian (married to a New England archeoethnologist; both, let me reassure you tres sympathique) simultaneously discussing the fall of Catholicism with a kind & impoverished granddaughter of Majeska & the rise of aesthetics with Waldo-Pierce-the-painter's lively and enormous sister."[35] Juan sang a Christmas song he had learned in the mission school, a long but familiar-sounding chant that ended suddenly with its only intelligible words, "glory to the new-born king." When they began to play charades, Estlin retreated to the cottage, but Marion stayed and displayed her very considerable talents.

The weather did not stay pleasant and Cummings complained that the Tucson Chamber of Commerce "grossly exaggerated the benefits of an Arizona winter."[36] He soon began to be bored, ("liveliness, nil. Culture, none.") and he did not appreciate the Arizona landscape that he was painting, the desert, the cactus, the clear bright blue skies. He especially disliked the aridity, the sparseness of plant life. "This is the country of death," he pronounced. Marion liked it, however, and they both benefited from the mildness of the climate, until one night when the temperature dropped below freezing and the pipes froze. Cummings' letters began to reflect his restlessness: bewilderment because of the contrast with the New York City ethos, "almost nobody seems quite real" and "almost everybody appears bent on gooddoing";[37] and impatience because of the lack of variety, "Marion and I are temporary denizens of a freakish part of the cosmos. . . . Occasionally some subinfantile pillarofpresociety will get drunk & (suddenly taking up l'homme blanc's burden) accidentally shoots a Mexican; generally, however, Tucson's higlif [*sic*] oscillates between merely chronic alcoholism & an irremediable infatuation with the american indian. Yet my lady and I are guests of a nonalcoholic host & hostess. And the Cambridge lass (our excellent friend) whose husband is a Papago brave (our excellent friend) loves him truly."[38] Even the Papago brave turned out to be an alcoholic who would disappear for days at a time before being hauled home from a town bar.

In mid-February, New York had a great snowstorm that shut down the whole city. But "opening or shutting, N.Y. will be a change," Cummings wrote, "& many things (my unreason tells me) are worse than a change."[39] They entrained from Arizona March 1, 1946, and after two months of spring in New York, they were at Joy Farm once more. "I wouldn't give an inch of New Hampshire for all the rest of New England,"[40] Estlin had once written his mother. He wouldn't have given an inch of New England for all the Rocky Mountain states either. Joy Farm was becoming his real home and its rock-strewn, mountain-rimmed austerity seemed to offer a womblike security.

XXVII

Oneness and
Santa Claus

Thus may we gather honey from the weed
SHAKESPEARE, *Henry V*

In 1942, Helen Stewart had taken a job in the publishing world at Henry Holt and Company, where William Sloane was manager of the trade book department. Since word was out that Duell, Sloane and Pearce was disappointed with the sale of *50 Poems*, both Miss Stewart and Mr. Sloane had hopes they might secure Cummings' next book of poems.[1] As a result of their combined efforts, Holt became Cummings' publisher for the next few years while he was at the peak of his career. In 1944, Holt issued *One Times One*, his most important volume of poems, and in 1946 *Santa Claus*, a short play which has become a Christmas perennial. It is curious that creative products of this quality emerged during a time when he was fulminating about the general state of the world and suffering physically himself and mentally in sympathy with the woman he loved.

Some years later, reflecting on the changes that took place in his career he set down some notes of self examination. In the earliest period when he was a youngster, he said, he tried to write poetry that would "help people." Of the second period, which began at Harvard, he observed that " 'the community' sinks into limbo: it's *I* who count. I am (or shall be) an artist, & an artist is responsible only to himself. He has no goal other than to enjoy life & thereby to create it. In so far as the world helps him, the world is good; but when it tries to crush him, to overcome

his individuality—through a war, a social program—down & to hell with
it!"

The third period "begins with 'my father moved through dooms of
love' & is continuing as I write these words (February 14, '48)." Cum-
mings saw this third period as moving back toward greater concern for
other human beings: ". . . the 2nd 'world war' finds me trying to cheer
up my native land; I feel responsible to certain anonymous-or-otherwise
admirers."

The statement is surprising in two respects. First, it is hard to see
the change going back as far as 1939, and second, it is hard to understand
the phrase, "trying to cheer up my native land," unless we discount
heavily the censorious remarks that Cummings was constantly making in
his letters. However that may be, something did happen as a result of the
broader national recognition that came to him. By 1943, the year he
brought *One Times One* into being, Cummings was producing a great
many poems that reflected universal concerns, and he was expressing a
greater joy in life through poems about love and natural phenomena. He
was also finding less need to write satirical poems and most of the ones
he did write have the sobriety of a Juvenal rather than the sardonic bite
of a Martial.

One Times One has a three-part structure which follows the same
progression from darkness to light that some of Cummings' volumes had
done before, but the tones are more pronounced. Section one ("1") begins
with a scrambled imagistic piece about a bleak day in November, when
the sky shows only a "nonsun blob." It moves on shortly to a modern
rendering of the fall of man—a little apple-stealing:

> then over our thief goes
> (you go and i)
> has pulled(for he's we)
> such fruit from what bough
> that someone called they
> made him pay with his now.

Early on, we also find a poem analyzing the behavior of the mob, "this
collective pseudobeast," the animal without a heart. Along with these
dark musings are clustered all the satires in the book, rather few this time.
Besides the antiwar poems we have already noted, those against salesmen
and politicians (is there any difference? Cummings would ask) are the
sharpest. The culmination is a very savage sonnet, "Pity this monster

manunkind/not," in which the speaker suggests that the only remedy for
human evil may be to start over again:

> We doctors know
>
> a hopeless case if—listen:there's a hell
> of a good universe next door;let's go

It is not until the end of section one that Cummings strikes his main
theme for the first time. This book is about oneness and the means (one
times one) whereby that oneness is achieved—love. Variations on that
theme are played throughout the book and Poem XVI offers the first:
"one's not half two. It's two are halves of one."

In section two ("X") we have a mixture of materials. Cummings
seems to have placed here a good many of his most linguistically com-
pact and sometimes obscure poems. Some of the poems in *One Times
One* are written in a more elliptical style than we have found before.
To give an example and one which also offers Cummings' explanation
of his many and varying selves as a poet, Poem XXII could be set up
in this way:

[He is]	no man,if men are gods;but if gods must
	be men,the sometimes only man is this [one.]
	([This is] most common,for each anguish is his grief;
	and,for his joy is more than joy,[this is] most rare)
[He is]	a fiend,if fiends speak truth;if angels burn
	by their own generous completely light,
[he is]	an angel;or(as various worlds he'll spurn
	rather than fail immeasurable fate)
[he is a]	coward,clown,traitor,idiot,dreamer,beast—
	such was a poet and shall be and is. . . .

Other poems use anagrammatical syntax or fragmented words,
such as this cheery portrait of one of the New Hampshire natives, old
Mr. Lyman, who has just come from a funeral. These are the opening
stanzas:

old mr ly
fresh from a fu
ruddy as a sun
with blue true two

man
neral
rise
eyes

Besides Mr. Lyman, the book contains poems about a number of the
ordinary folk in New Hampshire or Greenwich Village whom Cum-
mings knew and loved. The most memorable is an elegy for Sam
Ward, the handyman at Silver Lake, who had died in 1942. Cummings
thought a lot about Sam and tried to bring him into his writing when
he could. One time when he was drafting an essay which had to do
with some Renoir paintings at the Metropolitan Museum of Art,
some of his notes, very much scratched over, are about Sam. "Rugged
as a bar and stout as a bridge, Sam Ward of Silver Lake used to [be]
able to tell you pretty nigh always what the weather would do. Now
he don't know. The weather come out of a black box on the mant-
lepiece clear from Portland and wife she kinda like to hear the young
fellow talk and leastways you don't have to worrow none cause he is
wrong. So Sam don't know no more but at 78 he can still [spout star-
lore?], for her not me, & if you ask him the state of his health you'll
see him smile & hear him say Slickern a weazel, howbe you?"[2] With
notes like this, or more likely, with some of Sam's phrases revolving
in his memory, Cummings created a unique modern elegy, making
use of a very Unitarian concept of the afterlife, calling it "what":

rain or hail
sam done
the best he kin
till they digged his hole

:sam was a man

stout as a bridge
rugged as a bear
slickern a weazel
how be you

(sun or snow)

gone into what
like all them kings
you read about
and on him sings

a whippoorwill;

heart was big
as the world aint square
with room for the devil
and his angels too

yes,sir

what may be better
or what may be worse
and what may be clover
clover clover

(nobody'll know)

sam was a man
grinned his grin
done his chores
laid him down.

Sleep well

The theme of "one times one" is variously expressed in section two, mostly in love poems which are grouped toward the end.

In section three ("1"), Cummings is completely lyric in manner and optimistic in outlook. He moves from oneness in the natural world to oneness in human life, with poems about the developmental process in a flower, about the coming of dawn, about the miracle of spring, about Mr. Gorgas on the corner with his flower cart and on to a series of love poems, a couple of which are even shamelessly sentimental. He concludes the book with two poems that not only play upon the theme of one times one but also reach back into the innocent atmosphere of childhood. In the first one, a wish which has to do with the oneness of "you-i" is treated in terms of a kite:

> with a swoop and a dart
> out flew his wish
> it dived like a fish
> but it climbed like a dream

The final poem in the book uses the lilt of a nursery rhyme for its stanzas, which express the joy of life, love, and oneness and which set up a contrast to those symbols of intellectual life, books:

> if everything happens that can't be done
> (and anything's righter
> than books
> could plan)
> the stupidest teacher will almost guess
> (with a run
> skip
> around we go yes)
> there's nothing as something as one

Cummings placed the dedication "marion's book" at the end because as the book progresses it grows in love and joy. Its final lines seem to lead to the dedication:

> now i love you and you love me
> (and books are shuter
> than books
> can be)
> and deep in the high that does nothing but fall
> (with a shout
> each
> around we go all)
> there's somebody calling who's we
>
> we're anything brighter than even the sun
> (we're everything greater
> than books
> might mean)
> we're everyanything more than believe
> (with a spin
> leap
> alive we're alive)
> we're wonderful one times one

One Times One got a good reception from reviewers. Glancing through the reviews, one can see what gave Cummings the notion that he had cheered up his native land, for critics in a war-weary nation were obviously refreshed by the exultation that rises from the pages of Cummings' book. Theodore Spencer called it "a poetry of joy, that seeks for joy and, perhaps at the cost of wearing blinkers, finds and succeeds, to our great delight, in expressing it."[3] Marianne Moore took a similar view, "this writing is an apex of positiveness and of indivisible, undismemberable joy."[4] Cummings' broadening of concern and his readiness to write about mankind rather than self was recognized too, even in the hinterlands. William Reisen in the *Cincinnati Enquirer* commented on the change in this way, "Cummings, whose lower case poems were once regarded as the 'dernier cri' in modernism, has developed beyond mere sensationalism into a sincere and responsible artist although he still clings to his forms."[5]

The book sold well at first and eventually went into second and third printings. It even helped to boost the sale of *50 Poems* and *Collected Poems* for a time. But by 1947 sales dwindled and it was allowed to go out of print in 1950. One happy result of the success of *One Times One* was Cummings' receipt of the Shelley Memorial Award for 1944 from the Poetry Society of America, a money prize of $670. The judges were David Daiches, Josephine Miles, and Jean Starr Untermeyer. Mrs. Untermeyer was more amused than offended by Cummings' little rhyme about her husband in the book:

> mr u will not be missed
> who as an anthologist
> sold the many on the few
> not excluding mr u

The chief irony of the event, however, was the fact that the award was announced by the president of the Society, Harold Vinal, whom Cummings had ridiculed so mercilessly in "POEM, OR BEAUTY HURTS MR. VINAL" back in the 1920's.

If the response to *One Times One* brightened the war years for Cummings, there were certainly other events that brought sorrow or distress. One was the death of Eric Knight, who was killed in a plane crash on the way to North Africa in January 1943. Another was the arrest of Ezra Pound in 1945, who was charged with treason because of his short-wave radio broadcasts from Rome during 1942 and 1943. As transcripts from the broadcasts show, they were addled, rambling diatribes against "Roosevelt and his Jews" and "the hyper-kikes on the London gold exchange firms"[6]

or discourses about his peculiar monetary theories, and it would be diffi-
cult to prove that they gave aid to the enemy, let alone interested any
American soldiers. Nevertheless, he was brought before a federal court,
even though a number of literary figures published statements urging his
release. As it turned out, his already-distorted mental state had become
worse during the period of his imprisonment, especially because he had
been kept in a cage in the Italian sun for a week by the U.S. Army, and
he was judged mentally unfit to stand trial.

Cummings, always intensely loyal to friends, wanted to help in
whatever way he could. Generally, he felt that a true artist could do no
wrong, but in particular, he regarded Pound as America's greatest poet
and therefore entitled to a privileged position. For the first time in his
life he joined hands with others in a "cause." Along with William Carlos
Williams, Karl Shapiro, Conrad Aiken and others, he published a state-
ment in defense of Pound in the newspaper *PM,* November 26, 1945. His
statement was weakened by his use of his own special terminology but
the point that he tried to argue is best summed up in one of his sentences,
"Every artist's strictly illimitable country is himself."

When Pound's lawyer, Julien Cornell, paid a call at Patchin Place in
November 1945, he told Cummings about Pound's need for medical treat-
ment and explained that all of Pound's money was tied up by the Alien
Property Act and that Mrs. Pound's money in England was blocked
because of wartime restriction on transfers of funds. Cummings had just
received a check for $1000 from the Rochester Memorial Art gallery for
a painting of Mount Chocorua, a purchase-gift arranged by the Watsons.
Without hesitation he turned the check over to Cornell to help with
Pound's medical and hospital bills, saying he did not need the money.
Cornell was "moved by this spontaneous generosity."[7] Even so, he knew
nothing of the recent avalanche of bills for Marion's illness nor of the fact
that Cummings was able to sell paintings only when friends were trying
to help him out. Later when Mrs. Pound's funds were released, she
insisted on paying him back, but at the time, Cummings intended it as
a freely offered contribution.

Not all the news about those dear to him was bad. He heard from
Elaine that Nancy was married on December 23, 1943, to Willard Roose-
velt, the grandson of Theodore Roosevelt. Willard was a composer who
had volunteered for the Navy and, after obtaining a commission as
Lieutenant, served first as executive officer of a destroyer in the Atlan-
tic and later commanded his own ship in the Pacific. Nancy had been
living in the United States since 1940, but much as the thought of her
haunted him, Cummings had grave doubts about the wisdom of seeing
her now.

II

Cummings' next publication was even more unusual than *Tom*. It was a cross between a medieval "morality play," as he called it, and a children's Christmas pantomime. Its true genre is the puppet play, for its archetypal characters and its basic action with sudden reversals are straight from the tradition of the Guignol performances in the Champs Elysées, the Toon puppets in Brussels, or the marionette theater of Remo Bufano in Greenwich Village.[8] It emerged sometime in 1945, perhaps in the fall when Cummings was at work once more trying to write a play. His intermittent efforts since 1928 had never produced more than ideas, schematic patterns, outlines, and fragments. But now an offshoot from one of those dramatic schemes grew into the short play, *Santa Claus*, which was published by Holt in book form just before Christmas in 1946.

Santa Claus is really two plays entwined together, one using the plot line of the Faust story, the other the story of lost loved ones reunited. In the first part of the play, Death, strolling across the stage (the same street-wise tempter who had spoken in 1916 in "Death and the Young Girl"), encounters a mournful Santa Claus, who is troubled because "he has so much to give and no one will take." Death offers his advice, for in Faust stories the Mephistophelian character usually has a perceptiveness about the ways of the world. He tells Santa Claus that this is an age of salesmanship and convinces him that "knowledge without understanding" is the easiest thing in the world to sell, and what is more, if the salesman is a scientist, the job is even easier. They exchange masks so that Santa Claus can appear with a death mask as "Science." (A grim reminder, by the way, of Cummings' reflections on the development of the atomic bomb.) Death recommends that Santa Claus try to sell stock in a wheelmine because not only does a wheelmine sound "scientific" but it does not even exist—and people find things that do not exist even more desirable than things that do.

In this way, Santa Claus is lured into devilish work, but since this is an American version of a Faust story he has to display his fallen condition in an American way. In the next scene we find him acting the part of a fast-talking confidence man as he sells shares in the wheelmine to the gullible Mob. His success is soon his undoing, however, for in the following scene he enters pursued by the Mob who wish to lynch Science because of the rumor that an accident has taken place in the wheelmine injuring the wheelminers. Death warns Santa Claus that the only means of escape is to prove that he does not exist. When the Mob catches him, Santa Claus denies he is Science and risks his fate on the testimony of a little girl in the crowd. When he says to her, "Who am I?" and she replies,

"You are Santa Claus," he escapes the wrath of the Mob because, as they freely acknowledge, "There ain't no Santa Claus." Faust has been saved by the intercession of an innocent little girl.

In this Faust story, the female savior is divided into two characters, the "Child" in the first part of the play and the "Woman" in the second part, which now develops the story of the reunion of lost loved ones. Santa Claus, grateful to Death for suggesting the ruse of nonexistence that saved him from the Mob, agrees to change clothes with him, for Death has need for a plump body in order to impress "a swell jane up the street." Thus when Santa Claus, dressed in his skeleton costume, meets the Woman, she thinks he is Death. She greets him with resignation, for she has lost her love and has also lost her joy that was born from love. When Santa Claus agrees to take her "now and forever," she regains hope in life because she has heard a voice reminiscent of her lost beloved. She now recoils from the figure she assumes to be Death and refuses his invitation. As if she has passed a test by conquering despair, her decision seems to trigger the next action. The Child enters dancing and rushes into her arms. The Woman greets the Child as her lost "Joy." Santa Claus removes his death mask, revealing the face of a young man, whereupon the Woman, "kneeling to Santa Claus" and holding the Child, declaims the single word, "Ours."

With this abrupt denouement, the little Christmas play is over and all the members of the audience who believe in love and Santa Claus can go away feeling joyous that the family is secure. One can readily see that the play has some of the same appeals as other dramatic favorites of the Christmas season. It has, for example, the fantasy found in *Peter Pan* and the logical treatment of absurdities found in *Alice in Wonderland.* But there are some darker undercurrents in the play that are also characteristic of nursery stories or children's plays. *Hansel and Gretel,* for instance, played every Christmas season by the Metropolitan Opera Company, has its threats of cannibalism and parental abandonment. In *Santa Claus,* the activities of the Mob constitute a more negative dramatic force than Death himself. They are shown to be greedy and easily duped because they live in a world:

> so blurred
> that its inhabitants are one another
> —an idiotic monster of negation:
> so timid it would rather starve itself
> eternally than run the risk of choking;
> so greedy,nothing satisfies its hunger
> but always huger quantities of nothing—
> a world so lazy that it cannot dream . . .

They are also capable of violence. Toward the end of the play, they enter carrying the lynched, dangling body of Death dressed in the costume of Santa Claus, for the Child has told them he was an imposter.

Negative dramatic action of this kind can invigorate a play if it is handled appropriately, but it can trouble a comic work if the moral tensions it produces are unrelieved. The mob behavior in *Santa Claus* needs some kind of comic resolution. They are not trolls or goblins, nor are they an abstraction like Death. They are people, and their unreproved violence constitutes an incongruous element in a romantic fantasy of the sort Cummings has created. In a Christmas play, no vigilantes, however American in tradition, should have their way. Their presence in the play is evidence that Cummings' basic feelings about the American populace had really not mellowed, despite his concessions on occasion that "maybe America isn't such a bad place."

Since Cummings dedicated his play to Dr. Fritz Wittels, it is worth a moment's speculation to wonder why. We do not know the details of his psychoanalytic sessions with Wittels back in 1929. Although he continued to consult Wittels for advice from time to time, even calling him on the telephone when a stressful situation or a nagging worry arose, again there is not much evidence available about the problems he discussed. But he did at some time talk with Wittels about his nonrelationship with Nancy. The dedication of *Santa Claus* may now indicate that there is some connection between the play and Cummings' psychic needs. The first point to consider is the fact that Cummings has the little girl in the play telling Santa Claus that she is looking for "somebody very beautiful" and that they both have lost "somebody else." She then exits: "dances away." At her reappearance in the conclusion, the stage direction reads, "Enter dancing Child." The only reason for her to be described this way lies completely outside the play. Cummings' memory of Nancy as a child, he later wrote in a letter he never sent to her, was "the you who danced up&down with joy all over your bed every evening before saying goodnight."[9]

The second point to consider is that the conclusion of the play seems not necessarily to have arisen out of the previous action. Since this is so, we might venture a guess that a play about a young man's reunion with a kneeling woman and a dancing child seems to be like a wishful dream, Cummings' attempt to create a reality out of an imagined situation, a triumphant reunion that never took place.

XXVIII

Reunion and Revelation

She was quite sure that she heard the words. They came plainly to her ears, leaving on her brain their proper sense, but yet she could not move or make any sign that she had understood them.

TROLLOPE, *Framley Parsonage*

Cummings was fifty-two years old now and was beginning to lose his hair. Yet aside from a slight wrinkling around the mouth when he talked and laughed, he was still very youthful in appearance. But he did not feel that way. Five years in the Iron Maiden was not a cheering experience and frequent stiffness in his legs or a pain in his arm reminded him that his condition would worsen rather than get better. Although he bore his bodily ills as best he could, friends noticed his growing cantankerousness, especially in his objections to noise. He would not allow a vacuum cleaner in the house, not just because it was a "mechanism" but because its sound harrowed his nerves. His usual welcome to pleasant spring weather was now somewhat spoiled because radios blared the popular tunes of the day from the open windows of neighbors. He had begun to withdraw more from contact with others, and one of the ironies of his slowly spreading fame is that more people now sought him out, invited him to participate in literary gatherings, asked him to speak, to give poetry readings. Students from New York University or Columbia knocked on the door at Patchin Place to question him about his poems. Retreating, he let Marion take care of these problems and intrusions. He was fond of quoting Cézanne, "Je suis faible dans la vie."

As time went on, Marion became increasingly protective. She handled the telephone (they had one since 1937), answered the door while he shrank out of sight, kept people away from him when he was in his studio. One afternoon when Cecily Angleton had joined them for tea, a knock came at the door. Estlin flew to flatten himself against the wall out of view. It was a young girl asking for Mr. Cummings; she wanted to get some information about a poem. "Mr. Cummings is not here," Marion said forbiddingly. After the caller had gone, Marion was remorseful: "She really looked so disappointed. I think maybe you should go after her." "How can I?" said Cummings, "I am not here."[1]

Marion was more sociable and gregarious than he. Nothing pleased her more than to exercise her imperious manner at tea or a small dinner party or, in a restaurant, at an after-theater supper. She had a fashion model's appreciation for fine clothes and wore them with innate chic, but lack of money forced her to be very careful. It helped that she was allowed to keep some of the clothes she modeled. She had one or two evening dresses in which she looked elegant, but she had to be seen in them time after time. She loved to go to plays, gallery openings, concerts, movies. She often went without Estlin, who hated crowds and was very fussy about the plays he saw, usually wanting to leave after the first act. He loathed the movies and made great fun of his young friends' enthusiasm for them, but Marion would frequently go out to see a film in the afternoon while he was at work upstairs. She found it very pleasant when friends or literary associates would invite them to dinner—it lightened her chores and it introduced some social gaiety. She would sweep in grandeur over to Charles' with an editor, Cummings trailing along in the role of little Estlin saying, "All I really need is a gnarled crust." Since they seldom could reciprocate, she was uneasily conscious of their state of poetic poverty, but she carried off her part with great style. Friends reported that, like a queen, she could always make them feel that she was doing them a great favor in allowing them to offer entertainment.

Estlin and Marion had become a more devoted couple than before Marion's illness. If he once had a roving eye, it fastened now only on her. If she had once tended to respond to the attentions that men showered upon her, she did so no more. They leaned together, and although they still presented a fine appearance, they were a trifle creaky and needed each other's support. For all Cummings' abhorence of leading the bourgeois life, they were settling into their own middle-life routines.

Marion's role as protector and caretaker seemed to enlarge as Rebecca Cummings had less involvement in her son's life. Mrs. Cummings was in her late eighties now. During the war she had lived with Aunt Jane in Cambridge, in somewhat contentious fashion, or with Eliza-

beth in Annandale-on-Hudson and later in Swarthmore, Pennsylvania,
in a very happy situation. She was still very heavy, and very jolly despite
a series of mild strokes which had caused falls and broken bones. She now
walked with a noticeable limp. Although she was getting quite deaf, she
delighted in Elizabeth's two children, John and Mary, and they in turn
responded with open-hearted love for their grandmother. Estlin saw her
chiefly during the summer when Elizabeth and Carlton brought her up
to Abenaki. In 1946 he and Marion went over for a visit one afternoon
and found her "at once flaccid & edged, bulgy and angular; & how old!"
Later back at Joy Farm, when he and Marion were looking at the full
moon, he associated it with his mother as she had looked when Charles
Hopkinson painted her portrait in the 1890's:

> How beautiful she is! My remembering eye. Young strong, aglow with
> confidence, & supremely childlike; yet heroic: a naive fortitude, essentially
> Christian & fundamentally (as she would say) "of the earth earthy." A
> woman!
>
> The recognition of this symbol stirs within me all sorts of queries &
> wonderings; & my subliminal tentacles are reaching for life's Mystery.
> Who is the old mask which kissed me twice today? Not (most certainly!)
> *my mother*—as she probably knows: indeed, during our time together she
> touched (with a tragic lightness) quite frankly on her death, "Of course I
> may go anytime, or I may live to be a hundred!" (I've had, I think, five?
> of those . . shocks—& didn't know it!) as if to prove she *was* mine and
> *was* mother. . . .
>
> Meanwhile she has always been the purposeful mom, who (also) changes
> —growing and ungrowing, becoming & aging—& la lune (by whom my
> father sent me his love when I was in a French concentration camp!) always
> has been my mother. Such is not merely "a fact"; such is the Truth only.
> Should RHC die, she would no more cease than the moon ceases—this
> Truth, too, she knows; for Mae Ward told me that "your mother" (like Mae)
> told her, long ago, that she—the woman who bore me—was willing to rejoin
> my father: patiently (I felt) & cheerfully waiting; but with a deep eagerness
> [in getting?] thru this half. . . .
>
> Alas, mother dear! I love you truly—but *you*, You; YOU[2]

When Carlton Qualey took a teaching position at Carleton College
in Northfield, Minnesota, in September 1946, Mrs. Cummings moved
there with the Qualey family. Estlin was reassuring about the change,
pointing out that "our brief experience in Tucson would lead us to
believe that the further West you go the gladder folks are to see you."[3]
Although she was stone deaf and could not move around too easily, she
could still read to the children and she enjoyed doing the household

mending. In January 1947, however, she had a severe stroke, which left her helpless. After a week in a nursing home she went into a coma; she died without regaining consciousness in the middle of the month. Estlin had been expecting her death. He had said his good-bye in the summer, to her and to the July full moon. He was "deeply touched" when he learned that two of his poems (one was "if there are any heavens") were included in the funeral service.[4]

II

Nancy Thayer was now Nancy Roosevelt. In her twenty-six years, she had led a strange life. She certainly did not have a normal childhood. Elaine had taken her back and forth across the Atlantic and up and down the European continent, with a succession of trained nurses to look after her. Elaine had thought herself too young to be a matron and seemed to behave as if the reality of the child's presence could be pushed aside, nineteenth-century fashion, because there was enough money to arrange it. Nancy was early treated as a doll, something to dress up and to show off to guests. Later, she was shuttled between the nursery and grownup behaviour at table and found herself expected to discuss world events with MacDermot, who humorously insisted, "Always ask yourself: is this worth saying? *before* you speak!"[5]

Elaine's marriage to MacDermot took her in a new direction. She had been neglected by two previous husbands, and her needs, developed out of her orphaned childhood, were for protection. Yet when she did find a dominant husband, he was perhaps too overbearing; still she made the best of it and tried to ease Nancy's adjustment to the new master of the household too. MacDermot was responsible for securing Nancy's first governess, Mademoiselle Chevassus, originally from the Jura, who had lived with a noble family in Russia before reaching America. She began teaching Nancy, age five, to read and write in both French and English. Mademoiselle made costumes for Nancy to wear in short musical sketches at Christmas. Cummings was present for one of these, (probably in New York in 1925) in the dark at the back of the room.

But Nancy was troubled by the new marriage, not only because Frank MacDermot was a martinet but also because her mother did not have as much time for her now:

—she took her punishment
as will all children, in the backward silence of the disguised
        unlovable . . .

So begins a poem she wrote in later years, remembering her difficulties.[6] Her worried little self, confused by an exposure to conflicting cultures, displayed the anxieties in various ways—nightmares, tantrums, sullen spells. As a bright child, she found school both oppressive and stimulating, but felt almost as unhappy at home; then a sense of further neglect entered when Elaine brought a little brother into her world when Nancy was eleven. He was the new center of attention—more so because he was Frank's child and because he was a boy.

Nancy retained her original name, Thayer, and refused to change it to MacDermot. She was enrolled in a series of boarding schools in France and England; in the fifth grade she discovered oil painting and Impressionism but was forbidden to continue "because it was messy." Meanwhile, the MacDermot household moved about, from Ireland, to France, to England. It seemed to Nancy that she was always at school in a different country from the family and traveling long and lonely journeys home for Christmas or for summer vacation. Very early she displayed the same verbal facility and literary inclinations that Estlin had shown as a child. She read very widely and she had an extensive personal library by the time she was fifteen. She spoke and read French and for a time even partially forgot English; she began Italian but chose to go to Vienna, after completing school, for musical studies. There she lived with a family and learned German. Because of her language skills, MacDermot wanted to take her with him to Czechoslovakia during the Sudeten crisis, but Elaine would not allow it.

As Estlin and Marion had been told in advance, Nancy was compelled to be "brought out" in 1938, but she refused to be presented at court (Elaine and Frank were presented, instead: Elaine with all her annulments no longer had the taint of divorce upon her). For Nancy, the winter of 1938–39 was a series of debutante parties, which at eighteen she proclaimed, in one of her earliest poems, to be "contemptuous cacophony."[7]

As she remembered it, Nancy first came to know the poems of E. E. Cummings in Vienna when a friend with an interest in modern poetry had asked her—have you read Eliot? have you read Cummings? She had read *The Enormous Room* earlier but the poetry was new: she felt that the love poems were a revelation in modern language. She was further attracted because she was beginning to write poetry herself now. She had no notion of her mother's early literary associations—Elaine's secrecy about the past had kept hidden even the fact that she had been married to Cummings, although she occasionally referred to Dos Passos, and other members of the *Dial* group. Nancy felt that something had been left out, and MacDermot clearly discouraged references to the fun of her mother's youth. But Nancy's resentment at feeling left in the dark rose to shock and anger, when one day, very casually while they rose in a hotel elevator, Elaine let drop the phrase, "when I was married to Cummings." Nancy's insistent questions about this revelation were brushed aside: it had been for such a short time and it was so long ago.

Elaine had early told Nancy that her "father," Scofield Thayer, was dead, and since the girl had lost contact with the American part of her life, the subterfuge was easy. Later the story was changed. He was alive but divorced, therefore it was impossible to communicate with him. Elaine gave her a small snapshot of him for school, where "everyone else had a father." The first time Nancy was able to visualize her mother in the old days came in 1938 when Arthur McComb, a Harvard friend of Cummings and Dos Passos, visited Elaine in London: he talked and laughed with her about Harvard and the war, Paris and New York in the early twenties.

When the MacDermots moved to Dublin after war was declared in 1939, Nancy remained behind in England and studied to pass the Oxford entrance examinations. Since the bombing did not start, as feared, Nancy arranged for a room at Oxford, planning to begin study there as a "Home Student" in September 1940. After Germany began the air attacks on England, Frank MacDermot sent Nancy a plane ticket to Dublin and demanded that she return to the family home in June 1940. Although she was still determined to attend Oxford in September, she discovered only after her arrival in Dublin that the Irish border was now closed and she was unable to return to England. She was furious at not having been consulted but now MacDermot did give her a choice: she had twenty-four hours to decide whether to remain with them in Dublin or travel to the United States to stay with her Aunt Alexis till the war was over. Although she did not want to go to the United States, it represented the unknown and thus seemed the more attractive course. In mid-June, she sailed from Galway on the S. S. *United States* with a shipload of European refugees. It was the last American passenger ship to leave the British Isles during the war.

Fearing Nancy's determined curiosity about her background, Elaine chose to warn her, the night before leaving, not to look up Scofield Thayer and revealed that he had suffered a mental breakdown and was under private care. "But you needn't worry," she reassured her. "It is not hereditary. I have looked into it." Shocked at this disclosure, Nancy was distraught at what seemed to her to be inhuman callousness toward her "father." When Nancy reached the United States, she did contact the attorney who handled Thayer's affairs but he refused to let her see him, "because you are said to resemble your mother."

Nancy spent the war years in New York and Washington, D.C. She trained as a Morse code operator at RCA and earned a telegrapher's license and a radio-telephone operator's license. But she took her first job as a typist in Mrs. Kermit Roosevelt's agency, Your Secretary Incorporated, in New York City. Mrs. Roosevelt, who was very actively pro-British, felt sympathetic toward the young uprooted British-American girl. It was at Mrs. Roosevelt's house that Nancy met Willard, her second son, who used to come there and play the piano in the evenings during the period he was in Naval training. After Willard was sent on Atlantic duty, Nancy took a job in Washington D.C., using her linguistic skills for the Foreign Broadcast Intelligence Service. In 1943, when Willard had a leave, they were married in New York, and Nancy quit her job to become a mobile Navy wife, often living near the U.S. Naval Base in Norfolk, Virginia. By this time, the MacDermots had come to New York, where Frank was a correspondent for the *Sunday Times* (London).

Fate has its curious windings and among them was a path that led Nancy Roosevelt to New Hampshire in the summer of 1945. Mrs. Kermit Roosevelt had rented a summer place near Chocorua, and Nancy, now pregnant, her husband back on duty in the Pacific, was spending the summer there with her in-laws. Near neighbors were the William Jameses—the Billy James who was Estlin's friend and former neighbor in Cambridge days.

When Cummings had first heard of Nancy's presence in the United States at the time of her marriage, uncertain feelings stirred within him about whether or not to seek her out. But Marion, for whatever reasons, urged him not to reveal himself to her or to have any contact with her because she said it would upset him and "interfere with his work." Cummings, readier than ever to avoid a stressful situation, was persuaded. Sometime in the early 1940's Dos Passos had met Nancy in New York and, no doubt, brought a report to Cummings. In 1941 Dorothy Case offered to invite Nancy for lunch and to bring Cummings up to date on what she was like,[8] but Cummings apparently dissuaded her. Thus for five years, Cummings' knowledge of his daughter and her activities was sparse and secondhand. Worried about a sudden confrontation, he talked the matter over with Dr. Wittels, who told him not to be concerned, that the truth would come out eventually and his perplexity would be resolved in some perfectly natural way.

In the summer of 1945, a near-miss took place. Cummings wrote to Hildegarde Watson on August 9 that he and Marion had bumped into "spry old Mrs. Willard" at the James's and "discovered that madame's grandson = Nancy's husband. Apparently Nancy had just left Chocorua for New York to have a baby." When Simon Roosevelt was born on

September 6, William James, who knew about Nancy's parentage, brought the news to Cummings that he was a grandfather. Far from interfering with his work, the new awareness of Nancy and her ongoing life seems to have stimulated Cummings into literary activity. In writing *Santa Claus* with its sublimated wish for a negation of the 1924 divorce, he had his first success at completing a play since 1928, and when the play first appeared in the special Cummings number of the *Harvard Wake*, it was also accompanied by his fairy tale, "The Old Man who said 'Why,' " a story that he used to tell Nancy back in the early 1920's. Once Cummings realized that contact with Nancy would not be upsetting for his work, he seems to have changed his mind about keeping away from her. The following autumn, he asked William James to bring Nancy and her husband to tea at Joy Farm.

Nancy later remembered the events of the day in vivid detail. When she received the invitation, she was very excited: she was about to meet the famous poet who had once been married to her mother. William and Alice James with Willard and Nancy in tow appeared at the farm on the appointed afternoon. When they first entered the house, Marion kept the others outside, leaving Estlin and Nancy alone to enter together a somewhat darkened downstairs room. At the first sound of his voice talking of perfectly ordinary matters, Nancy felt eerie. She took a cigarette, her hand shook, she could not smoke, she felt unable to control her movements. As she later recalled, "His voice seemed extraordinary, like a bell, like something come from afar, almost echoing." Finally the others came in and the spell was broken. They all had tea. Every time Cummings spoke, it had a compelling effect on Nancy, but she "had no place to put this feeling."[9]

By the following year, she was pregnant once more and on August 30, 1947, she gave birth to her daughter Elizabeth. By now she felt she had a friendly acquaintance with Cummings, so she wrote to him in October telling him about the new baby and about the family move into a new apartment complex at 5901 39th Street in Long Island City. During the winter in early 1948, she called at Patchin Place, and Cummings asked if she would sit for a portrait.

By May 1, 1948, he had painted a small portrait—of the head only, a semiprofile, a rather meditative pose which showed none of the dancing sparkle of her blue eyes.[10] He went on to do a larger canvas of a seated figure. It is even possible that this second portrait was not begun until the late fall, for Cummings spent the usual June-to-October months at Joy Farm. In any case, the picture was not finished for a long time. Since it was difficult for Nancy to arrange for a babysitter and to travel from Long Island City to Greenwich Village, the sittings were few and far

Nancy, May 1 1948, oil sketch by E. E. Cummings. RICHARD S. KENNEDY
COLLECTION

between. Nevertheless, she always enjoyed them, and these meetings
lingered long and clearly in her memory. It was the first time she was
alone with him since the initial meeting in the darkened room. As he
painted, he did not say much, he would drop into some aimless talk—
about himself, about tangential matters. She tried on these occasions to
draw him out with questions about the old days and delighted to hear that
low musical voice rolling out wittily phrased reminiscences. She also felt
an odd sensation at times that she knew what he was going to say before
he said it.

She would stay for tea but since Marion was always there, she
could not ask him about the days when he was married to her mother.[11]
She hoped he might talk about his writing, for she was interested in his
ideas and longed to know something of the way he created his poems.
But he never discussed his work with anyone—and Marion's presence

even discouraged general literary conversation. Nancy's sessions with Cummings, whether sitting to be painted or at tea, were pleasant escapes from her domestic duties, for her life at home was filled with diaper-changing and child-feeding and beset by difficulties with troublesome neighbors.

As the months wore on, these visits became oases of pleasure and relaxation for her. She found herself more and more fascinated by Cummings, wondering how on earth her mother could have broken off from such an attractive man. Moreover, her own marriage was not going well during this time. Willard was absorbed in his music and in his difficulties in finding employment as a musician; she felt isolated with the children and at her wits' end with loneliness. As she sat for Cummings, she began to feel, "I am falling in love with this man." This new development was perplexing for her and invited a complex of problems. Marion was very much present. Nancy had two babies she was responsible for. Willard seemed to sense something of the situation. But she could not help responding to Cummings as she did, and she knew she would have to take some action. In this odd predicament, she decided finally to try to save her marriage. She resolved to stop seeing him. The painting was finished now, a rather dark portrait and one that made her look as if she were wearing a fur collar:[12] there was no more need for sittings. She went once more to Patchin Place for tea, uncertain what she was going to say, but she had decided it would be the last time.

As Nancy remembered the occasion, Marion was on hand as usual and Cummings' talk ran in and around trivial subjects, until a knock came on the door and Marion had to go out. Since they were alone now for the first time out of the studio, Nancy could continue her probings about the early days at 3 Washington Square. In answer to questions, Cummings talked about her Aunt Alexis, who he had once thought was in love with him, and about her Aunt Constance, whom he regarded as the finest of the three sisters, and went on to talk about Scofield. Since Nancy had never known Thayer as a father, it was an effort for her to use the word as she then asked Cummings a question about "my father." There was a distinct halt in the conversation. Finally he said, "Did anyone ever tell you I was your father?"

There was a long pause, for she did not fully understand. "You cannot mean it," she said, feeling this was of the order of fairy tales. Perhaps fearful of being rejected, Cummings was not sure what the long pause meant: "You don't have to choose between us," he added. The situation had finally been confronted, but just then Marion returned. As she came in and saw them together, looking as if some special exchange had taken place, she made some inquiring remark. Cum-

Cummings with his painting of Mount Chocorua, Rochester, 1950.

mings turned to her and said solemnly, "We know who we are."[13]

Nancy had never doubted that Thayer was her father, even though she had been told bewildering things—that he was dead, that he was alive, that he was under private care. Her name had been her own special identification. Now stunned by this sudden explosion of truth, it took her several days to absorb her new feelings. Cummings had made an engagement with her to return, for on that crucial day she had been forced to rush home to relieve the babysitter. "You can ask me anything you like," he said. And, on subsequent visits, she did: "How can you be sure? How do you know Mamma did not trick you?" But she was soon convinced that he was certain. He even offered to take a blood test, as if that would be final proof for her. What Nancy had never realized was that she so resembled Cummings in appearance that Cummings' close friends had always known she was his child. Even when Nancy was a baby, Elizabeth

Cummings did not want her friend Peggy Gay (then on a trip to New York) to see her for fear she would note the resemblance and be scandalized.[14] As time went on, Nancy discovered in talking with William James, with Loren MacIver, with her mother's friends, that everyone knew she was Cummings' daughter except herself. It made her feel the center of a vast conspiracy.

But her relationship with Marion was now going to be a problem, for Marion over the years had grown possessively jealous about Estlin. Marion herself had wanted to have a child, but Cummings would not let her. Now here came Nancy and the grandchildren intruding their emotions and family demands upon Estlin. Nancy sensed the difficulty and, as she later reported, tried to handle her new relationship with delicacy. She was immensely happy to have found a father at last and she did not want anything to happen to spoil it or, in some way, make it all untrue after all.

Well might she worry. Cummings had so sealed himself off from any emotional outlet toward Nancy after the heart blows he had been dealt in 1925 that it was very difficult for him to allow himself any new flow of feeling toward her again. He had told Nancy that she could ask him anything she wanted, but when the occasion came he was more elusive than she expected him to be. When she tried to call him "father," he drew back: "My name is Estlin." A greater difficulty was Marion's dominance of the household at Patchin Place. Nancy wanted to spend time with her father, to come to know him intimately. For her, he was a magnet for a new set of emotions for which she had never had an outlet. But she found she could not drop in to see him. She had to make appointments. She could not speak to him by telephone: Marion always answered and Estlin was not to be disturbed at his work. When she did get to see him, she felt somehow that she was being permitted to be there; she was not treated like a member of the family but rather like an inquiring student from NYU.

She was not easily daunted, however; she was determined to be more a part of his life: she felt it was her right. She went to an exhibition of his pictures. She went to the YMHA to hear his poetry reading and sat with him on the platform. She wrote him letters, personal communications about herself and her life. She invited Cummings and Marion to visit the summer place in New Boston, Massachusetts, which she and Willard owned. She asked if she and Willard could come to Joy Farm. Estlin was very cordial "of course you and Willard can 'spend a night or two'; why not 3?"[15] Finally at his request and with great trepidation, she sent him some of her poems to read. Among them was a recent composition:

To Estlin

May I pay my debt with spring
stifle you with green and gold,
all I have of everything
I will give to you to hold—
gave me yours instead too soon!
I'm ashamed and very sad;
in my hands your gold and green
seem so much more than I had

January 1950 (Groundhog)[16]

She later suppressed this early trial at expressing her new emotions and
wrote a sonnet taut with controlled feelings:

dedication

perhaps it's natural that I seem to see
chiefly within your spring how glorious
the sky you breathe, the sun you warm; to say
your shadow sings is but the more, alas,
being the less able to be you;
and yet of all the love I never lived
you've proved most given, holding to the true
the only words that know you always moved
in beauty; if you ever wonder why
I try to find your shadow where it sings
what you have chosen as a simple yes
to worlds that grow and gather gentleness
of flowers just to give away in spring—
Life chose the sun and circumscribed the sky[17]

In the batch of material that January, Estlin liked best the poem ad-
dressed to him but offered no criticism. As he told her, it was against his
personal policy to comment on anyone's work.

In spite of Marion's efforts to keep her at a safe distance, Nancy did
come to know her father better and Marion gradually adjusted herself to
a new presence in their life. Nancy felt that she came to have a special
rapport with him in one respect, a shared wit and humor that went
beyond Marion's matter-of-factness. She loved his mimicry—she had
once had a talent for it herself, which was firmly repressed as unsuitable
for "young ladies." They could talk about literature, but she discovered
that his viewpoint was not as international as her own and many of his

Marion Morehouse in the 1950's.
COURTESY JERE KNIGHT

opinions about contemporary writers were scornful. His politics did not seem to her consistent with his ethics but she was careful to leave that alone. His opinions often seemed to her irrational, yet occasionally showed an intuitive insight that cut through his own prejudices.

Indeed, she came to see a good many of his limitations, that he was quite tyrannical about certain aspects of domestic life: he would not allow Marion to learn to drive a car, he would not allow her to have a radio, he would not allow the smell of clorox in the house. She saw too that from Marion's readiness to let him have his way there were two results: first, she got him into the habit of expecting reverence from everyone for his opinions and attitudes (indeed, she promoted it among their acquaintances); second, she so shielded him from whatever irritated him that she really dominated his life, while he slipped acquiescently into the role of "poor little Estlin who couldn't do anything practical." Indeed, beyond her managing the practicalities of their household, she seemed at times to protect him from life itself, so that he became less able to bear the stresses of the outside world.

As for Estlin's response to Nancy, it was very mixed, largely because he feared to plunge himself into a new emotional relationship, much as he really loved this fresh vision of youth who had come into his life. Some of this complexity of feeling crops up in a notation he made about her, probably in the spring of 1950:

> Nancy was never more darling than this evening, when she & Willard dined chez nous; nor could anyone have been lovelier, as—with his guiding silence next herself—she slowly disappeared; holding only four flowers (narcissus, yellow tulip, daffodil, iris) & gaily to me with her eyes smiling from the darkness of the car.
>
> Yet . . . am aware that my child's loveliness is like a summer, a season or surface; that while a part of me forever is her tragic & immediate father, wholly I (shall be &) am (& have been always) somebody else whose fate is never of this world . . . so that while part of me is her tragic & immediate father, I am wholly & permanently someone else. . . .[18]

In July 1950, Nancy visited Joy Farm without Willard for a weekend. She arrived on the train on Friday and they had a very lively evening— in fact, Cummings had to take a Nembutal tablet that night in order to quiet himself down for sleep. On Saturday, he "felt the presence of a strain (nothing hostile, something which made me uneasy, though). Drove her to the village—she in a blouse-&-little-else, showing lovely legs almost to the hip ("Aunt Alexis gave me that")—& then around Chocorua. finally it broke." It seems that Nancy was bursting to tell him of a decision she had made. She had decided to write her mother and tell her that she now knew who her true father was, and she had been worrying about Elaine's response. She had not told the Roosevelts about her new parent either and that too was part of her worry. She had made up her mind to unveil her mother's deceptions completely and to make her new self known to the world—partly for the sake of her children, she told him. Later that afternoon, William James came to tea. With a touch of envy, Estlin saw him "put his arms gently around her smallness; with real fatherhood."

That night they dined with friends and Nancy was rather quiet, "semiretiring (psychologically) from the party; though now & then making a good point (to my delight!)." Later as they chatted on the porch in the dark, Estlin had a moment of remorse about his past lack of assertiveness in claiming her, "plead guilty to being a failure, at taking responsibility." Nancy was comforting, saying that she knew he was a responsible person.

The next day, a chance happening gave Nancy a jarring glimpse into the past. Cummings was going through an old Harvard footlocker, digging out letters from Mitchell, Watson, and Thayer in order to satisfy Nancy's curiosity about the days surrounding her early life. Cummings began reading Thayer's letters aloud, including one thanking him for the "Epithalamion." "N's eager to see the letters, & I give her the whole group, explaining that I don't know what's in it. Later she confronts me with a card, from ST, reading: 'For value received.' I suggest it's something he wrote when crazy. 'But it isn't' N. states almost vehemently '—look at the date!' I look, sans enlightenment. 'Do you know when that was?' she asks intensely. 'No,' 'The day after I was born.' Well (I tell her) I still don't understand the message: unless 'it's a grim attempt at humor.' Half contemptuously, wholly disgusted, she gives me back the letters, saying something like 'well I don't want it!' (with a laugh of horror) & I feel how distinctly her opinion of ST has fallen. did I do right or wrong?" He did not perceive that, in her eyes, he too had fallen.

Although this mishap dashed their spirits, the remainder of the visit was apparently pleasant, and on Monday afternoon, Nancy departed on the train, with little Estlin trying to help her with her luggage and demonstrating that he had not improved much in this line of activity since the wedding journey with Elaine. He brought her bag onto the train but was confused by the conductor's remark that the train was about to move and he dumped the bag on the first seat and hurried to get off. He "turned to glimpse a gentle pitying look on my child's face; her indulgent but a little sad smile as she picked the big thing up to move it elsewhere. My failure (at the climactic moment) upset me so fearfully that I almost didn't stand & wait for her car to pass—almost but not quite. . . . As she passed, I (scarcely knowing what I did) kissed my hand to this forgiving vision: & beautifully smiling, who kissed her slender hand to me."

The emotional stimulus of her visit sent him into a severe depression the next day and a fit of self-scrutiny: "it seems to me that she is real, & my life here (with M) isn't. What are all my salutings of [Mount] Chocorua [at sunset] & worshipings of birds & smellings of flowers & fillings of humming bird cups, etc. They're sorry substitutes for human intercourse generally & particularly[,] for spiritual give-&-take with a child or a child-woman whom I adore—someone vital & young—& gay! . . . M can't have a child now, or if she can, we've neither of us money to support ourselves, let alone a child. And if I think of having a child by someone else (who?) my heart smites me for faithful M.—Sunt lacrimae." He then went up on the roof and lay in the sun and recited the Lord's Prayer for relief from his inner distresses.

When Nancy wrote to thank them for the hospitality, she reported that she had acted upon her decision to announce her identity to the world, but what is really remarkable in the letter is her tone of overflowing love for Estlin:

My dearest Father
This is all I can call you I find. To be alive is very wonderful when at

last one is, and I thank you for a most substantial part of it (after all so, from the very beginning!) Willard's mother reacted in a—probably characteristic —way surprising to me & she insisted that all along *had* I been Scofield's daughter, I would have worried about my eventual sanity always. . . .

Never mind it's done. And I have just achieved the letter to Mama (hence the airmail paper to you. For I dare not come out of hiding while the children & all responsibilities lurk everywhere) a copy of pertinent matter [and] which I send you for your files ho ho.

I hope you will accept how glad I am to be me and loving you. . . .[19]

Cummings' response to this daughterly affection shows how really distorted his personality had become by this time of life. "Tuesday July 18 receive a wonderful letter from N beginning "My dearest Father"— & am almost prostrated. The very thing which I'd have given my heart for 25 years ago, today knocks me down. my terror now isn't, je crois, that of old age (being 'a grandfather'). It's le grappin dessus [the dominating grip] (in a social sense: terror of being made into a bon bourgeois; fear of the 'respectable' collectivity, of the makers of categories & pigeon-holes[)]." Part of his emotional confusion arose, perhaps, from a question Nancy asked him in the letter, wondering what her children should call him. He did not want to be a family man.

The whole effect of the weekend with Nancy was reaching into some deep recesses of his memory. He asked himself over and over, "why did the first words of Nancy's letter so strangle my heart in guilt-fear?" He finally accounted for it when a memory floated forth of his father's warning him, when they had their one and only sex talk, that he must control his sexual drives until marriage, for if by chance he made some girl pregnant, it could ruin his whole life. The ethic of 104 Irving Street was making him pay its price years afterward.

He sat down to reply to Nancy's letter and to make it plain that he was not going to accept the role of grandpa. Marion read it and judged it "pretty stiff"; so Estlin composed a second, more open-hearted version. The next day he felt tense and upset and was so disagreeable that Marion said "All right then send the 1st letter." Cummings exploded, raising the question of Nancy's inheritance from Thayer, "If I were Thayer's lawyer, & knew his 'daughter' was declaring she wasn't his, I'd cut off her allowance" (for he erroneously believed she had income from Thayer). He decided finally to write a third letter. "The 2nd had entirely repressed my resentment at N's pigeonholing of myself. And that (I believe) is what is wrong with me now—so I'll tell the truth to N: gently, to be sure, but I'll tell it."[20]

When he had finished, it was not a forbidding document, but it did convey that sense of constraint which his feelings of guilt-fear imposed:

> darling Nancy—
> thank you for a loving and wonderful letter
> it makes me happy & very miserable: very happy, that you can love me so richly; very miserable, that I must love you so poorly in return. For (as I've already tried to tell you) I'm a wholly selfish individual, whose work—or play—is his life
> but one thing in your letter makes me entirely glad, perfectly & without sorrow joyful: the expression of your love for Marion.[21] O Nancy, this is very sweet. What a galant [*sic*] & candid human being you are!
> am naturally delighted to enclose the two fairy tales which you so kindly copied; because I wrote them (with a couple of others) long ago for you.
>
> —X
E
>
> "E.E." is all right, but isn't "Estlin" an even better pet name?[22]

Nancy accepted it all in good fashion, even offering some cheery encouragement: "Thank you for your letter it is very nice to have. Don't be sad though, Willard is the same way & we're all three porcupines really—even to leaving the odd quills lying around for unwary visitors." The children were delighted with the stories and requested illustrations. As for the name they were to call him, "they are both enchanted with the name Estlin only Elizabeth likes Hestlin better. They want to know when you are coming to sleep here—stay for supper?"[23]

It took a long time for Elaine to reply about Nancy's decision, and when she did, she handled it with her characteristic brushing away of reality. All she said about Nancy's announcement was "Yes, I did receive your last two letters" and then went on to other matters, "but in a noticeably rigid and formal style."[24] She told Nancy later, "Your children will blame you for what you have done." On the only occasion Nancy had eventually succeeded in confronting her mother directly with the demand, "I want, just once, to hear *you* say who my father was," she received the implacable answer, "It was *my* life, and has nothing whatever to do with you!" Estlin had said of Elaine that "she lived with stage furniture; though make-believe, it hurt when you bumped into it." But the only play in which Nancy, their child, had a part, began with each parent walking off the stage that was her life. "Who then had written the play they would not perform," she asked herself, "and whose part have I been given instead?"[25]

One more revelation of Cummings' inner turmoil at this time comes

in a few reflections that he set down several days after Nancy's stay at
Joy Farm. They show a current worry that his creativity was drying up.
Indeed, self-flagellation leads him to downgrade all his achievement since
1925. But above all, these reflections tell us how his withdrawal from the
world had produced a loneliness that apparently even Marion could not
dispel. His statements are those of a very pathetic human being, made so
partly by what the world had done to him and partly by what he himself
had done to bring about the world's reaction:

> since Nancy's latest visit, am feeling: O, for such a love! The lack of it
> is what makes me write merely short poems: keeps me from achieving great
> works: when the EO-N thread broke, I broke too. Since then, have been lost
> in a fragmentary world (my "unworld"!) of abstraction & generalities, of
> hatreds & scorns & satires, of la vie politique et pratique et toujour banale.
>
> All this has been anaesthetic—a way of *not* suffering, of avoiding pain
> —i.e., Life.
>
> yes to Live is to Suffer; (ergo) & to Enjoy.
>
> if I had a N[ancy], Nature would drop into the background (where she
> belongs): it's my loneliness (& nothing else) has heaved her into the fore-
> ground."

The next day things were no better: "waking, run into a wicked depres-
sion, re N. Pray. Finally write imaginary letter to Wittels—& feel better."
In the imaginary letter, he summarized Nancy's visit and then went on
to say, "I feel that the child N is trying to get in—that I have closed myself
(the wound has healed) but she must enter me and be warm. . . . Perhaps
the trouble is, not that I don't love my child (for I do, according to my
power) but that she suggests Elaine (her mother) so strongly—& being
young & lively & attractive, not to mention (if I dare say it!) like me, so
flatteringly—that the old scar becomes a new wound." To her, however,
he gave no hint of being troubled by anything between them; he seemed
so impassively self-contained, she later wrote, that she often "felt her own
repressed emotional turmoil to be in bad taste."[26]

Later in the summer, Nancy and Willard visited Joy Farm briefly,
but she did not see much of Estlin during the year. One letter written
in the fall of 1950 refers perhaps to some problem about her freedom to
drop in to see him at Patchin Place. In it, her plea to be treated like a
member of the family is touching, and her loving words suggest that
perhaps she could have, over time, helped to repair Cummings' vulnera-
bility—if Marion had allowed it:

> After today something changed. I shall have you always with thirty extra
> years crowding in to fit smoothly, & they can't. And that is my grief, since

it must be uncomfortable for *you*. . . . I want to be allowed the most rare of all: to be taken sometimes for granted—or for usual.[27]

In August of 1951, Nancy came alone to Joy Farm to spend a week. This time Estlin and Marion were both more tense about her presence. Cummings retreated to the security of his studio each morning and left the two women to occupy themselves as they pleased. But he drove Marion and Nancy about on errands, and when Marion introduced her to the local New Hampshire folk as Estlin's daughter, one old man, perhaps Mr. Lyman, was taken aback: "I didn't know you were married!" he said, looking puzzled, then joined in the general laughter. Marion taught Nancy to bake bread (Dr. Ober had recommended against commercial bread for Estlin). Marion had begun to take up photography, having learned its techniques from one of the great masters, Edward Steichen. On this visit she took some effective photographs of Nancy and one of her and Estlin together, Nancy standing proudly but shyly at his side, Estlin grinning amiably, wearing one of his well-dented old hats. About five o'clock every day, Estlin came down for tea and afterward there was the twilight ritual of watching the sun set behind Mount Chocorua. As she remembered these afternoons, Nancy really wanted to talk about literature with Cummings, but he only wanted to talk about humming birds or the latest sayings of Mae Ward or Jesse Shackford.

It happened, however, that Nancy slept at night in the studio, and although Cummings' writings were usually put away every evening, one day Nancy came upon about twenty-five versions of a poem lying on the desk. She examined them with interest and that evening asked Cummings about his methods of composition, for she too revised in the same way, by writing a poem over and over. An awkward silence fell. Cummings looked at Marion and remarked that perhaps he would have to take more care in tidying up his desk. Nancy had violated one of his rules of privacy, looking at an unfinished poem. No one had ever seen his work in manuscript or his revisions on typescript while he was composing—not even a roommate like Brown. This occurrence seemed to give Marion a reason for pushing Nancy further back from their lives. The next day Marion told her she had been at the farm long enough and it would be better if she went home. "You know how hard it is for your father to have anyone around when he is trying to work. You have been here since Monday. It is time to go." Marion had never been rude to her before, but there was no mistaking her manner now. Nancy felt, as she later recalled, "booted out."[28] Whether Estlin knew or not how abruptly Marion had issued her orders is uncertain. In any case, Nancy's "bread and butter letter" made no mention of it.[29]

Nancy at Joy Farm, summer 1950.

As time went on, Nancy continued to be warm and courteous in her relations with Estlin. She had opened her heart to him and he filled a psychic need that had been long in want. But their relationship had undergone a distinct change, and she no longer sought him out as she had done before. After three years, the door that she thought had opened was now seen to be only slightly ajar. Nancy had feared that this might happen, for in her life there had been a series of losses and deprivations. Even when Cummings had said those fateful words to her at Patchin Place, she could not, as she said, quite believe in "this parcel from heaven—because I was afraid it would be whisked away."[30] But it was not a parcel from heaven: it turned out to be only a battered, very much earth-traveled package that had sat in the lost-and-found for thirty years, and its contents, though still inside, were too broken to be of much use to her.

XXIX

The Nonprofessor at Harvard

... yet I sometimes saw in him a man whom I had not seen before, and I did not know whether he was as wise as Shakespeare or as simply ignorant as a child, whether to suspect him of a fine poetic consciousness or of stupidity.

THOREAU

The principal literary event of Cummings' career during this time of reunion with Nancy was the publication of *Xaipe* by the Oxford University Press on March 30, 1950. Apparently Holt had now joined the list of publishers who could not stand further losses in publishing Cummings' work. The Krazy Kat collection had been a flop and *Santa Claus* had not done well since the first Christmas. The new book was entitled *Xaipe*, pronounced Kyereh ("almost rhymes with 'fiery' "), the Greek imperative, "Rejoice." It was a collection of seventy-one poems, beginning with a sunset and ending with a new moon, "luminous tendril of celestial wish." It contained an elegy for Cummings' dear friend, Paul Rosenfeld, and another for Peter Munro Jack, the literary critic, in addition to poems about other friends and local personalities. It had more satires than his previous book, including one horrific sonnet about the atom bomb: "whose are these (wraith clinging with a wraith)/ ghosts drowning in surpreme thunder? ours." But this book and the award given to Cummings some months after its publication by the Academy of American Poets were the center of the most unpleasant controversy Cummings ever provoked. At issue was a slant-rhymed epigram that brought accusations of anti-Semitism:

> a kike is the most dangerous
> machine as yet invented
> by even yankee ingenu
> ity(out of a jew a few
> dead dollars and some twisted laws)
> it comes both prigged and canted

The reaction would have been even more angry if the last line had been printed as Cummings originally wrote it, "it comes both pricked and cunted," but he changed the wording when publication problems arose as early as 1945, the year he sent it to the *Quarterly Review of Literature.*

On that occasion he explained to Allen Tate that he had intended no insult to Jews, "quite incidentally: anyone who resents [poem] 3 on the unground that it's 'antiJewish' must either be méchant or eed-yoh— since my Good American point = that the kike isn't (hélas) a Jew—so heraus mit said objector."[1] But the objections did come, from friends and enemies alike, and the question of Cummings' anti-Semitism was the subject of a symposium in the *Congress Weekly,* in which Cummings was both attacked and defended by a number of Jewish critics. Stanton Coblenz, an old foe of Cummings as head of the "League for Sanity in Poetry," was the principal attacker and William Carlos Williams, the chief defender.

The hostility distressed Cummings greatly, and professing surprise and bewilderment, he went running to discuss the situation with Dr. Wittels, who, no doubt, applied verbal balm. But Cummings certainly could not deny that he had been given plenty of warning. When he sent the manuscript of *Xaipe* to Lloyd Frankenberg to look over before publication, he received a letter from Lloyd which hinted (Cummings' friends knew how touchy he was about freedom to say what he pleased) that Cummings should drop two of the poems. One was a poorly developed myth about a Negro who caught hold of a star ("one day, a nigger"), an inoffensive piece, on the whole, but Frankenberg thought the word, nigger, was objectionable and tried to point out why. He was more forthright in his comment about the second poem:

> Two misgivings: in poem 24 and 46 the words nigger and kike. The first is used affectionately; the second, if I read it right refers to an abstraction. But I have fears that both will be mistaken for unkindness. By a black magic they seem to hold within them all the accumulated hatred with which they have ever been used. . . .
>
> The word kike I grew up with. I can hardly remember my Christian family getting together but what "the kikes" were discussed, as if we were

speculating about a leper colony. It was a truly contagious word, and came to convey, for me, nothing but a group attitude: a group of gentiles hating Jews. . . .[2]

Cummings replied blithely, as if somehow the Boston Watch and Ward Society were trying to suppress his usage of four-letter words in print:

> . . . it is more than most kind of thee, monsieur, to warn me of le public's reaction to 2 Wild Words (see how they run). And yet the (however painful) fact that America is not a free country doesn't, I feel, justify anyone's behaving like a slave or three or (in the lines of the Bad Bald Poet) steady
> there once was a cuntry of owe
> such lofty ideals that know
> man ever could mension
> (imagine the tention)
> what might have offended jane dough
> selah[3]

Nor was Frankenberg's the only cautioning voice. Early in December 1949 Evelyn Buff Segal, a young artist from Rochester whom Cummings had met through Sibley Watson, came by Patchin Place bringing with her the photographer, Nancy Newhall, to chat with Marion about her new photographic interests. Cummings' words best tell the story in a letter to Hildegarde Watson:

> wishing to entertain E (& also, no doubt, hoping for a patontheback from someone I like) I offered to show her the galley-proofs of my new book. E seemed all eagerness as I produced a set. She exclaimed over the fact that the book was dedicated to you; then uncannily Et Comment—she lifted out of all my 71 poems the one and only poem in any way related to her race, & immediately objected to it; began telling me what I should & shouldn't Write, etc. Oddly enough, the little poem states (in effect) that a "kike" is what becomes of a jew—not every jew & not any—thanks to the machine-world of corrupted American materialism: i.e. that America (which turns Hungarian into "hunky" & Irishman into "mick" & Norwegian into "squarehead") is to blame for the "kike." That's the point—but I couldn't make E see it; & even Paul Rosenfeld misunderstood this poem until I explained its "meaning" (as people say) to him, personally & patiently: & then we were friends again[4]

As Evelyn Segal remembers the occasion, she told him, "A lot of Americans are not going to like this," an admonition which he greeted with glee. Just another chance *pour épater le bourgeois*. After they left, Nancy Newhall was downright angry and resolved to call Oxford University Press to remonstrate. She urged Evelyn to see Cummings' editor and try to dissuade him from publishing the poem. Evelyn had lunch at the Warwick with Mr. Philip Vaudrin of the Press, who explained that he was helpless to do anything. He had pleaded with Cummings to drop the "kike" poem, but with no success. With understated apprehension, he concluded, "This is most unfortunate."[5]

Cummings, the foe of tyranny and the defender of the underling, does not fit the definition of an anti-Semite, even though he was not above pinning a pejorative ethnic or racial tag on someone he did not like and claiming his inalienable right to do so. But in the matter of this objectionable epigram, he showed puzzling insensitivity. In the first place, he seemed unaware that the word "kike" has a resonance (to use Leslie Fiedler's word) which echoes down centuries of Jewish persecution. But in the second place, coming as it did, just a short time after the full horrors of Hitler's death camps in Eastern Europe had become known, Cummings' contribution to anti-Jewish literature is unforgivable. People who love literature, however, have forgiven him, including Jewish friends and critics who accept his protestations of innocence and prefer to remember the quality of his work in general and his fearless opposition to overweening authority in particular. Speaking for these readers, Leslie Fiedler has presented a sensible,—or perhaps rather generous—judgment of the case:

> In short, Cummings is like everyone else (somewhat) evil, and like few others, a remarkable artist. There is scarcely any work of art that is not somewhere marred by the spite, violence, self-pity, wrong-headedness, smugness, false humility or abject terror of its maker. When the human weaknesses of a writer find formal expression in anti-Semitism (rather than anti-feminism, sentimentality about sex, a lust for death, etc.) it is especially difficult for me as a Jew to get past the evil to the beauty—past the partial response to the whole one that a work of art deserves. But after all, what is extraordinary is not that Cummings may be an anti-Semite (this he shares with innumerable jerks) but that he is able to make orderly and beautiful things out of his chaotic and imperfect heart—and for this he is to be honored.
>
> Certainly, when the attackers of Cummings (or Eliot or Ezra Pound or Celine) are revealed as men motivated not so much by a love for Jews as by a hatred for art, I know where to take my stand.[6]

Cummings never removed this item from his collected works. It was his way ever to let his past record stand: he never revised, never "improved" an early poem published in one of his books. But he never included this epigram in any of his poetry readings either.

II

After the death of his mother in 1947, Cummings had received an inheri-
tance of almost $7300 from her estate. But postwar living expenses, medi-
cal bills, and the real estate taxes on Joy Farm soon swallowed that up.
Moreover, he no longer had the $150 a month "allowance" that she used
to provide. He turned for help to those he knew most intimately. Early
in 1949, Stewart Mitchell came through with a gift of $1000. In August
of that year, Elizabeth and Carlton offered to buy Joy Farm and give him
life tenure on it, thereby providing him with a monthly income for
twenty years and relief from paying the real estate taxes.[7] He did not
accept the offer, perhaps because he expected Marion to outlive him by
many years and wanted her to have the farm. By January 1950, he was in
severe financial straits, and he turned, as was his wont, to Sibley Watson
and laid matters before him:

> perhaps you can help me. I cannot see how to go on unless am sure of 5000$
> a year. While my mother lived I had a very small but regular income; & after
> she died, my father's sister used to give me as much as 2 or 3 hundred$ from
> time to time—but the aunt's money is now tied up. I "earn" anyhow 1000$
> a year in "royalties" & "permissions"—that I can depend upon; with a dollar
> worth 30 cents. Marion's photographing helps out, & sometimes we sell a
> watercolour, rarely an oil. With herself cooking-in, our bills here (including
> 125$ for rent, all our food, laundry, occasionally even a cleaning-woman,
> electricity & telephone, & about 50$ for medicines: but not including the
> doctor or the dentist) come to 350$ a month. The taxes on Joy Farm were
> 306$ last year; & the upkeep of the place is something, though very little. I
> owe only 800$, somebody owes me 75$, & have 30$ on hand. Recently the
> socalled Bollingen Foundation seemed eager to produce a "grant," but that
> fell through. Shall try Guggenheim people again, but they (after awarding
> me a scholarship, years ago) refused a "renewal." I can't (& should never
> pretend to) teach; but can, & do, "read": always "clearing expenses" &
> generally "making" a few $
>
> —vive la vie!
>
> The only thing I have of any value is the farm; which I'd be glad to offer
> as security (if that's the proper word)[8]

What Watson's laconic reply may have been is unknown, but it appears
that Hildegarde bestirred herself to arrange for a poetry reading at the
University of Rochester in the spring, together with an exhibition of his
paintings at the Rochester Memorial Art Gallery. The Guggenheim
Foundation, however, turned down his application for a renewal of the
fellowship.

Cummings now approached Aunt Jane for some kind of help. Jane Cummings at age 97 was quite wealthy, for she not only was the last surviving member of the older generation of Cummingses and holder of whatever wealth the family had possessed but she had also inherited $50,000 from Mr. Philip Davis, a Cambridge neighbor who, after his house burned down in 1918, had lived in the third-floor studio at 104 Irving Street. Cummings knew that a $15,000 bequest to him was an item in Aunt Jane's will and he tried in his present need for some arrangement whereby he could draw some of that money out of her estate. But Aunt Jane in her old age was convinced that everyone was after her money and she refused to cooperate.

Other happy windfalls dropped instead. In June 1950, Cummings was awarded the Harriet Monroe Prize of $500 by *Poetry* magazine. About this time, Nancy bought a self-portrait for $300, as a friendly gesture. Then at the end of the year, he received the most distinguished literary award given in the United States, the $5000 Fellowhip of the Academy of American Poets. In 1951 two other events coincided which solved Cummings' financial problems for years to come. In February, Aunt Jane died and his legacy plus interest and some additional residue came to $17,423.64. At about the same time, Cummings received news that Henry Allen Moe had resubmitted the 1950 application to the Guggenheim Foundation without his knowledge and that he had been granted a fellowship for 1951. Moe's letter announcing the fellowship was so generous in its praise and encouragement that Cummings replied, "If I had to choose between your letter and the award, I'd take your letter."[9] Cummings immediately planned a European trip.

He and Marion had not traveled abroad for thirteen years. Although Cummings had some misgivings about travel because of his back miseries, he was fully aware that Marion had long deserved a vacation trip and besides she still had not seen Venice and Florence. Their tour was to begin in Italy, then to go on to Athens and the Greek Isles, and finally to end with two months in Paris. They sailed early in May.

Cummings was overjoyed to see that the European cities had made such a quick recovery and that American visitors were receiving a genuine welcome everywhere, even in Italy. Athens was something of a disappointment, except for the climate "& the miraculous MAIDEN & one view of a skyhigh monkery."[10] He and Marion both fell ill while in Athens and were further troubled by the fact that Cummings could not handle modern Greek: for the first time in his life he found himself in a country where he did not have some rudimentary command of the language. After feeling almost bored with Athens, Cummings felt some trepidation about returning to paradisical Paris, "I wonder if I'd be too old for so young a mistress."[11] He had some apprehension too about the activities of the Communist party, for France had the largest membership of any of the European democracies. Once there, however, his worries lifted and he was soon revisiting the favorite sites: his sketchbook shows the familiar street scenes, the old French faces, and the ever-fascinating rooftops. No war damage was perceptible and Cummings was thankful that nothing seemed "socialized, communized, or otherwised." Shortly, however, he began to yearn for Joy Farm, the first time he had ever been homesick in Paris. Although Marion was reluctant to leave, he changed the date for sailing home from August 2 to July 12. "I can't wait to arrive," he wrote to Paul Nordoff.[12]

When Cummings had applied for a Guggenheim Fellowship in 1943, he had been lightheartedly frivolous in his first inquiry:

> somewhat (but hope not too)
> tardily am writing to ask
> a renewal of my fellowship
>
> on what grounds? No grounds,
> my dear sir
>
> skies[13]

But upon being asked for specific details about plans for work, he replied: "hope one day to finish my second play . . . ; to achieve a small collection of (original) fairytales for children, and to write as many poems as possible."[14] When he applied in 1950, he stated, "as for my project: I'd like to write a prose account of myself (which would probably be called 'a novel') as unlike Eimi as it is unlike The Enormous Room."[15] Now in 1951 when he settled down at Joy Farm, he seems to have worked on the play from time to time and to have spent a great deal of time typewriting a copy of his multivolumed diary and compiling reminiscences of his childhood and youth as if in preparation for another autobiographical narrative. Even so, no finished or even partially finished work of these sorts emerged at the end of the Guggenheim year, only short poems, some of which were published in a scattering of little magazines over the months.

Cummings must have carried out a good deal of desultory reading, however, for his time was his own: he was not having to travel about giving poetry readings at colleges and universities. The previous year, he had remarked in a letter to the poet, Eve Triem, that he did not read books any more, that after Harvard "my books disappeared; almost." Since he worried about this, he talked it over one time with Dr. Wittels, who provided, then, a "soothing dictum": "you don't need to read. You write."[16]

But for a person who claimed not to read much, he seems to have ranged over quite a varied body of reading, for he accumulated stacks of notes on books and articles that he read. It appears that whenever he was reading anything, he would take notes and copy out passages that interested him. Thumbing through the pages of notes that are among his papers in the Harvard Library, one can produce any number of sample lists of the books he was reading and they would all show the heterogeneity of his taste.

Here, for instance, are some titles: Shelley's *Prometheus Unbound,* Rumer Godden's *Black Narcissus, The Letters of D. H. Lawrence, Hedda Gabler, The House of Seven Gables,* Graham Greene's *British Dramatists,* Rilke's *Letters to a Young Poet* (he admired this greatly and gave copies as gifts to young people), a biography of Gertrude Stein by Donald Southerland, *Anna Karenina,* Lincoln's letters, Camus' *Le Mythe de Sisyphe,* Foster Damon's critical study of Blake, M. D. Landon's *Anna and the King of Siam,* Isak Dinesen's *Out of Africa* and *Seven Gothic Tales* (he loved her unusual handling of the English language), several books by Jung, Georg Groddeck's *The Unknown Self,* Joyce's letters, Santayana's *Persons and Places* and *Realms of Being,* a book on the Haiku by R. H. Blythe (lent by John Cage), a book on the *Nibelungenlied,* Malraux's *The Psychology of Art,* the essays of Ananda Coomaraswamy, Keyserling's *Travel Diary of a Philosopher* (this was a favorite), Byron's letters.[17]

There are notes from a jumble of periodicals too, mostly popular magazines: they range from *Harper's* and *Scientific American* down to *Esquire* and *Paris Match.* The kinds of notes he took are illuminating, for out of this flotsam arose some of his poems. There are notes on advertisements, scientific discoveries, politics and current affairs, speeches and sayings by both prominent figures and ordinary people, cartoon captions, the literary scene, the theater, sex, anthropology, animal life, art, psychology, mythology, and theology.[18] It appears then, that Cummings did a great deal more reading than he himself was aware of, and from the quantity of notes that he took, it seems that he was busy writing even when he was reading.

III

In February 1952, Cummings had reason to meditate on his dislike of Boston and Cambridge and his aversion to Harvard as a wellspring of intellectualism, for he received a letter inviting him to fill the Charles

Eliot Norton Professorship at Harvard for the year 1952–53. Archibald MacLeish, who was now Boyleston Professor of Oratory and Rhetoric in the Harvard English Department had suggested his name. The Norton Professorship was Harvard's most distinguished chair for visiting scholars in the area of the Humanities, and as the letter from Professor John Finley had pointed out, some of the recent holders of the professorship had been Gilbert Murray, T. S. Eliot, C. M. Bowra, and Thornton Wilder.[19] It carried a salary of $15,000 and required only a minimum of six lectures and the option of their publication by the Harvard University Press. All of this was staggering enough for one who had been a baiter of intellectuals all his adult life, but there was one further stipulation: residence in Cambridge from October 1 to Christmas and February 1 to May 1. The prospect was very tempting—if only he could perform six times, employing his own special linguistic utterance, and then skip town after each appearance. When he met Slater Brown in the Village one day, he groaned over his decision, for he wanted to accept the honor that had been so graciously tendered to him, but he dreaded a year of "unmitigated boredom" in Cambridge. He was also apprehensive about just what he would have to do to fulfill his lecture obligation. A further inquiry brought a concession that he would not have to appear until October 15 and an explanation that he would not have any teaching duties outside the six lectures, which would be open to the whole university community, and that the lectures could be on any topic he chose and could include the reading of poems. In the course of answering the questions, Professor Finley actually suggested the form which Cummings later adopted (and he could not have chosen more persuasive phrases to attract Cummings interest and consent):

> There seems to me here much scope for freshness and individuality. Mr. Copland has hit upon the novel scheme this year of talking himself rather generally about certain specific musical aims or problems and then at the conclusion of his lecture having a small concert, sometimes with a singer or two, occasionally with three or four instruments. These concerts, as I understand them, do not specifically illustrate points made by him but have only a general relationship to his earlier argument. My reason for bringing up Mr. Copland's practice is simply to make clear that interesting departures from the conventional procedure of lectures are more than welcome. What such a departure might be in your case I of course do not know. I can imagine a far more analytical and detailed treatment of certain poems, your own or those of others, than has been common hitherto. Conversely a more philosophic and speculative attack on the nature of poetry would seem more than possible. Special understanding might be evoked and communicated by reading poetry, with appropriate comment. One could conceive a scheme

like Mr. Copland's, by which certain general points were made first and these then followed simply by reading. . . .[20]

With great trepidation Cummings finally accepted the appointment and began casting about for advice on what might make suitable lecture topics for the series.

He was at this time in correspondence with a Harvard graduate student named Norman Friedman, who had written his honors thesis on Cummings' poetry in 1947. When Cummings asked him what the Harvard students would be interested in hearing from him, Friedman suggested that Cummings talk about his own life and "the things you and people you knew were talking about and doing after World War I. This could be assisted by readings from your (and their work)."[21] This suggestion fitted admirably with what Cummings had been trying to do earlier with some narrative account of his own life. Thus during the spring and summer of 1952, he worked at writing what became the "nonlectures" that he delivered during the college year. By September he had only finished three of them. Nonlecture 1 comprised character sketches of his mother and father, nonlecture 2 an account of his Cambridge childhood, and nonlecture 3 some reminiscences of his Harvard days, ending with remarks that New York and Paris had also provided an atmosphere for learning about life and art. By October 1, Marion reported that Cummings had never worked harder in his life than he did during the summer and that he threatened several times to resign the professorship.[22]

In order to make his task easier he had decided to lecture for only the first forty-five minutes and to spend the last fifteen minutes reading aloud poems, by various poets, that would be appropriate to each topic. For the end of nonlecture 1, he chose to read Wordsworth's "Ode. Intimations of Immortality from Recollections of Early Childhood"; after nonlecture 2, five poems about spring, by Nashe, Chaucer, Swinburne, Charles d'Orleans (in French), and Shakespeare; after nonlecture 3, five poems about love, by Dante (in Italian), Shakespeare, Burns, Donne, and Walter von der Vogelweide (in German).

That Cummings could have had such terrible difficulty putting together these brief autobiographical vignettes and would have awakened in the morning, "writing and rewriting letters of resignation," seems to suggest that age was creeping up on him, especially when it appears that he had been unable to produce anything more than a few short lyrics and linguistic constructs during the whole of his Guggenheim Fellowship the previous year. What he had bemoaned about loss of creative power when he was meditating on his relationship with Nancy in 1950 was perhaps an indication of something even more serious: that only with great effort was it possible for him to write even simple narrative composition that required little or no imaginative power.

Just before going to Cambridge, Cummings and Marion planned to return to New York to bid bon voyage to Nancy who was going to Austria for the winter with her children. Estlin had seen Nancy infrequently during this period. Marion had once said to her that it was a good thing she was married and busy with her family, for Estlin would not have had much time to spare from his work to see her. Only once had Nancy managed to arrange to have dinner with him alone, when they spent a noncommunicative hour together in a Chinese restaurant. Estlin was so disappointingly withdrawn that Nancy resolved never to try that again. Nor was she able to develop his interest very steadily in his grandchildren, although he did appreciate each as a person: Simon, who had just turned seven years old, and Elizabeth five. He chose Christmas gifts for them and in his letters to Nancy enclosed his own special drawings for them. They delighted in these and responded with their own drawings of family members and elephants. But he seemed to her more like a relative who lived across the country rather than one who lived a few miles from their apartment in Long Island City or later at 1239 Madison Avenue in New York.

But it was Nancy's own relationship with him that counted most to her and she offered her love freely whenever an opportunity opened. Very seldom did she allow herself to call his constrained behavior into question, as she did, for instance, in a letter she sent him just before her departure for Europe: "This feeling comes over me—what are you doing at the other end of fathership? And how in my naked presumption did I manage *my* end? I hope never to forget the force of rejection, (at the moment of discovery) of what was too much dreamed about to be real— so that the force was the measure of the dream. You are so damned real yourself, though. . . ."[23] Now, with Nancy and her family in Europe during the coming year, it would really be easier for him to carry on their father-daughter relationship without strain. The mails allow reflection before saying anything; letters create less stress for the writer than personal presence.

On October 15, Cummings and Marion moved into a house at 6 Wyman Road in Cambridge, a little cul-de-sac far enough away from Harvard Yard to allow Cummings to feel secure from too much intrusion and far enough from Harvard Square to make Marion feel housebound. His strains began to ease when the lectures began, for they proved to be a great popular success. The first night, October 25, Sanders Theater in Memorial Hall, the scene of Estlin's commencement triumph in 1915, was packed, and students who were turned away at the door climbed fire escapes and tapped on the windows with coins, asking to be allowed to slip in and sit in the aisles. Professor Finley provided a suitably literary and personal atmosphere when he introduced Cummings "in the guise of Odysseus returning to Ithaca."[24] Cummings strolled on stage with an "erect carriage," much assisted by Dr. Ober's corset, displaying "an elegance of manner" and "supreme indifference" as he took his seat behind the reading desk.[25] But when he began to speak, he achieved instant communication. He spoke slowly and quietly to a hushed hall, where despite the help of a public address system some had to strain to hear because of the bad acoustics. He wove a spell that still captures, for the nonlectures were recorded, and now, listening to the Caedmon records, we can hear that resonant voice and perceive the rapport he established with the assembled group of students, faculty, and local visitors.

After the first lecture William and Alice James had a little social gathering at which everyone was cheerily congratulatory. Marion, however, was annoyed because Alice James forgot to introduce her to the other guests. As the months went by, Cummings managed to dodge "social phenomena" as much as he could. The one person who could have made Cambridge pleasanter for him, Theodore Spencer, was no longer there. He had died of a heart attack in 1949. Others, however, offered hospitality to the Norton Professor. Archibald MacLeish, generous-hearted as ever; shy, witty Douglas Bush, the great Renaissance scholar; Perry Miller, the gruff, hard-drinking authority on Puritanism—all entertained him. At Professor Miller's, Cummings met with glad surprise Werner Jaeger, the author of *Paideia, The Ideals of Greek Culture,* one of his favorite books of all time,[26] and he was impressed by the diffident courtesy of the old man, who helped him off with his coat. He made two very good friends during the year. One was cheery Jack Sweeney, the librarian of the Lamont Poetry Room (for which Cummings made phonograph recordings of poems by Edward Lear and Lewis Carroll). On later trips to Boston, especially after the death of Stewart Mitchell in 1958, Cummings would often stop over with Jack and his wife Máire. The other was genial, courteous John Finley, the professor of Greek literature who became his "guardian angel" during the year and helped him to fend off social invitations. On the whole, everyone was as cordial and welcoming as Cummings allowed them to be. Harvard was distinctly not Marion's milieu, however, and as Cummings wrote to Nancy, Cambridge life was "perhaps harder on Marion than even on myself."[27]

One source of tension was politics. In the fall of 1952, the Eisenhower and Stevenson presidential campaigns were at the peak of their intensity, and the Republicans were pressing hard on all the charges made by Senator Joseph McCarthy that the Democrats had allowed Communists to infiltrate the government. Cummings was a passionate supporter of McCarthy and felt, as he told his sister, that McCarthy's strident voice "came as a direct result of exactly what it decries: namely, procommunist-&-how activities throughout the USA, sponsored by Mrs. FD Roosevelt & her messianicallyminded partner plus a conglomeration of worthy pals."[28] Harvard University had stood up against McCarthy when his anti-Communist investigations came to Cambridge, and the officials refused to discharge any faculty member for any political affiliations past or present. In Cummings' view, then, the local political scene had the wrong coloring. "Have yet to encounter anybody in any manner connected with Harvard who isn't primevally pink."[29] He kept his opinions to himself, however, and no one recalls that Cummings revealed in any way his support for McCarthy and the Eisenhower-Nixon Republican effort. He only smiled quietly to himself at Stevenson's defeat in November and wrote to his sister, "What will happen to intellectual (pink) Cambridge when it awakes from its election trance, non so."[30]

The nonlectures continued to be an immense popular success among the undergraduates and the visitors. Professor Frederick Packard's class in "Oral Interpretation" regarded them as model presentations. "The audience couldn't be more appreciative,"[31] Cummings reported to Elizabeth after he had gone back to New York for Christmas. The graduate students and faculty, however, were disappointed with them. "I thought them elegantly phrased and delivered but empty of content. This was the general response of students and faculty,"[32] reported David Perkins, one of the few graduate students whom Cummings came to know during the year.

Cummings began work on the last three lectures right after Christmas. These would not even be autobiographical reminiscences. They would be made up of snippets from his miscellaneous writings strung together with very little comment. He was worried about the success of this method, for he did not want to let his generous audience down "theatrically." He had somewhere acquired the notion that part of his function was to entertain.[33] In the spring, however, the audience continued to be faithful in attendance and enthusiastic in response. Some of his friends traveled a good distance to attend the nonlectures. Hildegarde Watson came all the way from Rochester. His old roommate, Arthur Wilson, now a landscape painter calling himself Winslow Wilson, came in from Rockport, Massachusetts, to join Hildegarde. Lloyd and Loren traveled up from New York; although too late and locked out of the first one, they managed to hear the rest. Cummings' former playmate, Betty Thaxter, still lived in Cambridge and walked over to attend after she heard that her name had been mentioned in nonlecture two. She even called one afternoon at 6 Wyman Road to renew old acquaintance. She felt aware of her age when Marion answered the door, barefooted, her hair in braids, looking like a schoolgirl.[34] Another Irving Street neighbor, Esther Lanman organized a cocktail party for Cummings with as many of the old Cambridge crowd as she could locate. Amy Gozzaldi was there, her jet-black hair now grey. She and Estlin looked at each other and grinned self-consciously, feeling what the years had done to them. He raised his hand to his bald head.[35]

He was still slaving over the last lectures during the spring, tirelessly revising and polishing their phrasing. One of the reasons his delivery was so masterful was his conscientious rehearsal and his preparation of the text with every pause and emphasis carefully marked. However below expectations these last three nonlectures may have been to the more discerning hearers, he was doing the best job that he knew how and the strain told upon him. He was taking Nembutal every night in order to sleep but still waking after about five hours, bothered by a barking dog or a honking automobile. Thus the return to Patchin Place May 1 was a great relief in many ways. He was soon "making a rapid recovery from ektdemocratic Cantabridgian semiexistence."[36] He had been unwilling and actually unable to fit in at Harvard, despite the graciousness extended from all sides and his outward courtesy in responding to it. The discomfort this caused him found expression in disparaging statements about the whole experience after he had departed the Cambridge scene. He was more at ease now in Greenwich Village, seeing literary friends or dealing with the local service people, Mr. and Mrs. Psomas at the florist shop, I. Schwartz the stationery man, or Dominico de Paulo, the ice man with the truck named Zoom Doom. He could hardly wait to get to New Hampshire.

XXX

Verbal Vibrations:
A New Career

His delivery was good, his voice admirable, and his power over his audience was evident. He was probably an orator by right of inheritance, though he had never cared to assert the claim, perferring to rest his distinction on his poetry.

HENRY ADAMS, *The Life of George Cabot Lodge*

Cummings had long known he could not live by verse alone, but by the 1950's he began to draw a helpful income through his poetry readings. With practice, he had grown beyond the uncertain presentations of the 1930's to become, during the last dozen years of his life, a superb reader of his own work, both poetry and prose. With the exception of Dylan Thomas, he was the best reader of his time. Through these performances, he became possibly the best-known poet in the country to a whole generation of students at colleges and universities on the East Coast and in the Great Lakes area. He also helped bring a love of poetry to the ordinary follower of the arts through his readings in such public forums as the YM-YWHA Poetry Center in New York, the Museum of Modern Art, the Institute for Contemporary Art in Washington D. C., and the Great Northern Theater in Chicago.

Unlike other poets, who read standing behind a lectern, Cummings always sat in a straight-backed chair behind a table equipped with a gooseneck lamp and a microphone. He read slowly and precisely, offering every nuance that the typographical arrangements of his poems held. His New England accent conveyed a tone of high culture, which seemed more pronounced alongside his brilliant mimicry of the harsh edges of a New York City dialect or the high whine of a caricatured female. What many hearers remember most vividly was the singing intonation he used for his simplest lyrics. A typical program lasting about an hour would consist, usually, of a half hour of narrative or dramatic selections, from *Eimi, Him, The Enormous Room,* or *Santa Claus,* followed by a ten-minute intermission, after which would come a dozen or more selections from his poems. He would often add one more poem after the applause, as an "encore." A sample program is one he gave at the Museum of Modern Art, March 14, 1950. He began by reading three scenes from *Santa Claus.* Then after a ten-minute break, he read a sequence of poems that ran from satire to springtime and love time, as these notations have preserved the occasion:

> Now I should like to try to read you a few poems. And we may as well begin with a portrait—a portrait of 100 & some million super-sub-morons—a portrait which might be entitled "this is a free country, because compulsory education"
>   "of all the blessings [which to man]"
> Next we have two candid close-ups
>   "a salesman [is an it that stinks Excuse/me]"
>   "a politician [is an arse upon]"
> & here comes—a dirge
>   "plato told"
> Now having paid tribute to socalled reality, we are free to enter Life
>   "anyone [lived in a pretty how town]"
>   "my father [moved through dooms of love]"
> & so, from life we move (very naturally) into More-than-life
>   "nothing false and possible is love"
>   "except in your [honour,/my loveliest]"
>   "all ignorance toboggans into know"
>   "sweet spring is your [/time]"[1]

His "best by much" audience was at the YM-YWHA Poetry Center, which, because of its well-planned subscription series every season, became known as the "Carnegie Hall" of poetry readings. The readings were held in the evening from 8:40 to 10:15, the theater and concert hour. John Malcolm Brinnin, the witty and learned director of the Center, introduced the poet, who was advised to begin with short poems at first, for ushers were instructed not to seat late-comers during the reading of a poem, only between poems. The whole procedure and atmosphere in the large auditorium seating about a thousand people helped to formalize and dignify this newly established genre of the performing arts. By reading at the YM-YWHA, Cummings probably learned how to stage his performances elsewhere. "He was an enormously effective and careful reader," Brinnin recalls, "slightly 'stagey' and perhaps slightly narcissistic. . . . He drew large audiences and . . . the core of these were young people who brought with them the air and enthusiasms of a cult."[2]

He learned how he could earn more money too. It was at the Poetry Center that he met Betty Kray, the assistant director, a vivacious blonde recently graduated from the University of Washington who soon became a perceptive admirer and a friend who dropped in for tea every Friday afternoon at Patchin Place. She later formed Craymore Associates and became Cummings' agent for his readings. She organized a reading schedule for him each fall and spring at colleges and other educational institutions such as museums and art centers. She formalized in advance all of Cummings' stipulations about the physical arrangement of the reading, plus other details such as "There will be no provision for autographing books, attending dinners, receptions, and other social functions as part of the total reading engagement," and "there will be no commentary with the reading."[3] She also undertook all the arrangements for travel by train and airplane. But the most important outcome of their association was the establishment of a standard fee schedule that made Cummings' travels worthwhile. After the war when he was making his own arrangements he had been getting paid about $100 plus travel expenses. But in 1955, Betty Kray set a $400 flat fee (he paid his own plane fare) and organized tours to certain areas of the country where he would have three or four engagements. As years went by, this fee rose to $600 and $700, depending on geographical location. At first, he was willing to accept lower fees but she argued him out of that backsliding. She contended that a poet should be treated like a musician. Should Menuhin or Horowitz take less money just because Michigan State University had a tight budget?

Because the conditions he imposed were exacting, the college officials expected a cantankerous man. But, as Betty Kray recalls, "they were amazed to find Cummings, unlike his rules, charming, soft-spoken and thoughtful." Although he refused any press, radio, or television interviews, he would allow students to ask him questions for their college newspapers. "They sent him garbled versions of his quite clear statements, which he took great pains to read to me," Miss Kray remembers; "nevertheless, I suspect that he liked the attention."[4]

In the fall season of her management in 1955, Cummings read during October at Northwestern, the University of Chicago, and the Chicago Art Center (here the former Mrs. Adlai Stevenson—it was O. K., she was a Republican—also arranged an exhibition of his paintings and drawings); during November at Harvard, Dartmouth, the Metropolitan Museum, Queens College in North Carolina, Duke, and the Institute for Contemporary Art in Washington, D. C.; and during December at the YM-YWHA and Barnard College.

In this way, Cummings began, really, a new career. He reached a much wider audience than he ever dreamed possible for his poetry, a fact which began to show up in sales figures of his books, especially *Collected Poems*. He also accepted engagements for lectures, something he had never been willing or able to do before. He would warn ahead of time that it would be a "nonlecture," and then read nonlecture 4, devoting the last fifteen minutes to reading a group of his own poems rather than using the selections from Child's *Ballads* that appear in the published version. · His fame as a poetry reader spread rapidly so that now his coming to a college campus was regarded as a major cultural event. At the University of Michigan in May 1957, two thousand students and faculty jammed Rackham Auditorium, while a thousand more clamored outside for admission. He appeared on stage, "a casually dressed elderly man" walking "stiff-legged, with one shoulder raised as though bearing a chip of contention."[5] He read nonlecture 4 and then several poems to this huge, keenly responsive audience.

Since Cummings was over sixty now, these tours were physically hard on him. At this time of his life, he could not stand or even sit for extended periods of time: he had to spend part of each day lying down to ease his back. Long plane rides were especially torturesome. He had to turn down a $1000 offer from the University of Texas because of the four-and-a-half-hour plane flight. Getting to out-of-the-way places was particularly burdensome. In early May 1957, he endured "a fantastically murderous reading in the State of William Penn," when he visited Pennsylvania State University and Millersville State College, both buried in the middle of the Appalachian range. He did not get any enjoyment out of the travel itself. He had long ago lost any interest in visiting cities of the United States and now expressed such views as, "To me Hell holds few horrors worse than spending so much as a weekend in such a desolatingly mediocre hole as Indianapolis."[6] The nervous tension of a performance did not lessen much over the years. "What I generally experience before a reading," he told Elizabeth in 1954, "is a conglomeration of anxieties involving bellyache, hearttrouble, arthritis, diarrhoea, & (temporary) blindness. But feel I'm somehow gradually evolving; despite selfpity narcissism an inferiority complex & possibly several other psychic ailments. . . ."[7]

But he continued to do it—and not just for the money. He enjoyed performing, for he knew he did it to perfection, and he loved the applause and adulation of the student audiences. He treasured certain tidbits of praise that came his way and reported them unabashedly to Marion and others. On one occasion, a student told him that his English professor described him as a man who "has the guts to say what he thinks and the ability to say it in poetry."[8] These were rewards that had long been denied him.

II

Even life at home can have its miseries for a man who is ailing. In the winter at Patchin Place, he got no heat in the studio after 10 P.M. "and rarely enough in the day." He was still abnormally sensitive to noise. When the tenant in the third-floor-front of 4 Patchin Place moved out, Hildegarde Watson rented the room from the landlord, Mr. Keenan, so that Estlin could have the peace and quiet of an empty apartment next to him. His previous neighbor had been too "radioactive." But even this was no help when wreckers destroyed a building nearby, only to be followed by a construction gang who, with pounding and riveting, went to work on a new structure.

Why not leave New York and all its assaults upon the nerves and the senses? Marion had work with her photography now that kept them in New York. She had a photography studio both for sittings and for dark-room development on the second floor at Patchin. That was the excuse. But Marion could never have left New York permanently, to become just an old man's nurse as she had seemed to be in Cambridge. And Estlin himself was too set in his cycle of winter life in the city and summers on the farm to change his habits. He escaped from noise when necessary by sleeping in a room nearby which was lent him by Elliot Coleman, a professor at Johns Hopkins University in Baltimore. It was so small "that only half of me can turn around at a time," but was "celestially quiet."[9]

Other ailments afflicted him. His hands broke out into "little drooling (weeping) sore spots."[10] He tried salves, X-ray treatments, wearing gloves while painting in case of allergy from the paints—all to no avail. As Dr. Peters said, "nobody knows" what was wrong. In addition, Cummings continued to slide into depressions of the sort he had suffered when Nancy's reentry into his life upset him. When these melancholy fits would befall him he felt cowardly, guilty, feeble, good-for-nothing, and old. Sometimes he had peculiar emotional responses that can best be described as paranoid. Even in the midst of a reading performance with an enthusiastic audience, he would warn himself: don't forget, they applaud you on Monday but they would hang you on Friday.[11] One woman friend whose husband was a psychiatrist, speculated about a psychologi-

cal basis for Cummings' illnesses as early as 1949. In a letter to Evelyn
Segal, she mentioned talking to Cummings about the problem of her
young son's asking so many questions about death and religion:

> Cummings took me seriously, and gave the most wonderful answers—noth-
> ing canned, but something truly imaginative and releasing. . . . He has a
> marvellous quality as a teacher and he has affected us a great deal. The sad
> thing is, he is really sick (psychosomatically, with emphasis on the psyche,
> I guess), and quite a bit crazy and I hope he won't become moreso. . . .[12]

Her pronouncement is hasty and exaggerated, but it illustrates the way
in which some of Cummings' friends worried about him. The healthiest
thing for Cummings to do was to turn to his work, especially if he could
create something out of his miseries, whether physical or psychological.
One splendid example of what could be done and one which had obvious
therapeutic uplift is the following poem, written in the mid-1950's, which
draws upon the darker aspects of self-recognition:

> a total stranger one black day
> knocked living the hell out of me—
>
> who found forgiveness hard because
> my(as it happened)self he was
>
> —but now that fiend and i are such
> immortal friends the other's each

Cummings no longer had Dr. Fritz Wittels to turn to in times of
stress. He had died in the fall of 1950. The absence of Wittels may be one
of the reasons why Cummings, now more religiously inclined, turned
toward Jung and somewhat away from Freud in his late years, for he
thought Freud's pessimistic discourse on religion, *The Future of an Illusion*,
was "Freud's gaffe." Cummings was obviously attracted by Jung's mar-
riage of psychoanalysis and religion, and one of Jung's statements fitted
nicely with Cummings' views about twentieth-century followership in
politics. In writing to Elizabeth in 1954, he affirmed the validity of "Jung's
classic pronunciamento: that, to worship being as human as human can
be, if you take Someone Worth Worshipping (alias "God") away from
human beings, they'll (without realizing what they're doing) worship
someone-unworthy-of-worship); e.g., a Roosevelt or Stalin or Hitler—
alias themselves."[13]

A belief in God was most important for Cummings these days.

Prayer helped him out of his depressions and seemed also to ease his pains. The God he prayed to was the classic God of New England Unitarianism, the idea of a comprehensive Oneness, together with a sense of the presence of this Oneness in Nature. When he expressed his belief in a poem most clearly, he combined both the form of prayer and the idea of the presence of God in Nature:

> i thank You God for most this amazing
> day:for the leaping greenly spirits of trees
> and a blue true dream of sky;and for everything
> which is natural which is infinite which is yes
>
> (i who have died am alive again today,
> and this is the sun's birthday;this is the birth
> day of life and of love and wings;and of the gay
> great happening illimitably earth)
>
> how should tasting touching hearing seeing
> breathing any—lifted from the no
> of all nothing—human merely being
> doubt unimaginable You?
>
> (now the ears of my ears awake and
> now the eyes of my eyes are opened)

If creation of individual poems was therapeutic, so was the publication of whole volumes. *i: six nonlectures* was published by the Harvard University Press in 1953 and was sympathetically treated by reviewers. Much more important was the garnering of all his published poems into one volume, an undertaking carried out by Harcourt Brace under the title, *Poems 1923–1954*. Since the book opened with "Epithalamion," the first poem of *Tulips and Chimneys,* and ended with that "luminous tendril" of a new moon sonnet at the end of *Xaipe,* it gave testimony to the course of Cummings' development and stood as the record of years of achievement. The collection was extensively reviewed and highly praised, and even though the praise was frequently tempered by strictures on one aspect or another of his work, there was a genuine acknowledgment that Cummings must be counted among the foremost poets of the country. Also because of the continuing freshness of his outlook, there was surprise in realizing that Cummings was a sixty-year-old poet ("a SEXagenarian" is the way he would have preferred to bill himself).[14]

But even so, the witholding of unqualified praise annoyed Cummings. Randall Jarrell made Cummings as angry as "a whitearsed hornet" when, on the front page of the *New York Times Book Review,* he boggled at the phrase "great poet," which the publishers had used on the book jacket and became very condescending about Cummings' place in the literary scene.[15] At first, Cummings declared that the " 'intellectual' gangsters" were out to get him, but his sense of humor soon returned to calm him down.[16]

When the National Book Award Committee[17] met in 1955 to consider the merits of the books of poetry published during the previous year, they had a delicate decision to make because two leading poets had brought out their collected poems in 1954. Wallace Stevens's cold, cerebral, precise, and philosophical verse had to be weighed against the joyous, vital, careless experimentalism of Cummings. A compromise was reached. The award was given to Stevens, who was now seventy-five years old (he was to die within the year), and a Special Citation was declared for Cummings. Not everyone was happy about the outcome, including Cummings, because Stevens had been given the award in 1951. (Besides, Cummings despised Stevens as "a business man": how could he be an artist?) Nevertheless, it was greater honorary recognition than any publication of Cummings had ever received, and there were further reverberations. Trumpeting the citation, Harcourt Brace mounted a new advertising campaign to sell the book. *Poems 1923–1954* was also selected by a book club, *The Reader's Subscription,* for distribution to its members, who constituted an extensive but discriminating readership.[18]

III

People at Harvard who knew Cummings and who had no idea how he felt about Boston were continuing to do him favors that had the effect of getting him to return. Early in 1957, he received a letter inviting him to be the Festival Poet at the Boston Arts Festival in June. The Poetry Committee which had chosen him was made up of Archibald MacLeish, Paul Brooks, and David McCord, the unofficial poet laureate of Harvard, famous for his witty epigrams.[19] The Boston Arts Festival was a pleasant civic affair held outdoors every summer in the Public Garden with no admission charge for most of its events. For a period of three or four weeks, it featured concerts, choral singing groups, musical comedies (such as a Gilbert and Sullivan operetta), plays (light summer fare such as O'Neill's *Ah Wilderness!*), an exhibition of paintings hung in a tent-gallery, and one evening devoted to a poetry reading by the Festival

Poet.[20] Everything was in the good old-fashioned Boston spirit of pop concerts and lemonade. The three previous Festival Poets had been Robert Frost, Carl Sandburg, and MacLeish himself. For the occasion, Cummings would be paid $500 plus expenses and have the honor of being listened to by an audience of several thousand people under the summer stars. The only requirement was that the poet write a poem for the festival.

After some correspondence with McCord, who was the chairman of the Poetry Committee, Cummings perceived the nature of the occasion as a kind of civic jolly-up, and he told McCord that, "I realize what a 'festival poem' should be; something quite foreign to my own feeling." He declined the honor.[21]

But McCord returned to persuade a change of mind, indicating that the festival poem could be on any subject whatever, be of any length, and need not be written especially for the occasion—any new poem would do. He badly wanted Cummings, whose reputation as a performer was very high in the Boston area. Cumming was persuaded, and as if to challenge all he had been told, he sent McCord "THANKSGIVING (1956)," a savage release of his deepest feelings about the Hungarian Revolution. The poem was distinctly not in the pop-concert vein.

"THANKSGIVING (1956)" is one of Cummings' most impressive later satires. The reader who lived through that period will remember that in the autumn of 1956 when unrest shook the Eastern European nations under Soviet domination, Hungary was the scene of a full-scale anti-Communist uprising which expelled the resident Russian troops from its territory. As a result, a government coalition under Imre Nagy withdrew Hungary from the Warsaw pact and took steps to establish an independent socialist state free of Soviet power. On November 1, Russian Premier Nikita Khrushchev recognized a puppet government in Hungary and sent a heavy reinforcement of Soviet troops and tanks to suppress the rebellious forces. The Hungarians were brutally crushed in a few days of fighting, during which Radio Free Europe continued its encouraging broadcasts to the Hungarians from the United States. At the same time the debate in the United Nations Assembly over the Russian invasion was simply a futile verbal exercise.

In the United States, feelings raged helplessly during these calamitous days, but no one was racked more painfully than Cummings. In a letter written on Thanksgiving Day to Elizabeth Kaiser-Braem, his German translator, he said:

> . . . [I] doubt if any European can conceive the reaction of an American *born & bred*. Picture "God's country" (alias earth's richest nation)—the sworn

enemy of brute force, the foremost friend of democratic freedom, perpetu-
ally dedicated to an unconditional defense of all oppressed peoples & (with
this sacred mission in view) armed to the hyperangelic teeth with every not
imaginable implement of supersatanic destruction—urging (via night&day
broadcasts) the socalled satellite nations to revolt from colossal Russia; &,
when diminutive Hungary miraculously did so, lauding Hungarian heroism
to the skies & offering the gallant Hungarian people millions of dollars &
promising the immediate dispatch of all kinds of desperately needed materi-
als . . . until Moscow, enraged hurled her whole hugeness ABSOLUTELY
UNOPPOSED against that handful of patriots; & began blowing their cities
& their women & their hopes & their children to hell . . . whereupon the
never defeated United States Of America shrugged her peaceloving shoul-
ders & murmured "too bad"[22]

He had been, he told Nancy in an earlier letter, in a "shaggyblack chasm
of shame & anger created by UNamerica's absolute d'abord encourage-
ment & utter ensuite abandonment of that handful of humanbeings who
did the bravest thing since Finland."[23]

The only way he could do anything to vent his anger at the Eisen-
hower-Dulles response to the Hungarian crisis and to try to express to
the world his admiration for the courage of the Hungarians was to turn
his feelings into verse. He began tapping out Satyric doggerel on his
Corona:

> a monstering horror swallows
> the living spirit of man
> while all america wallows
> in dollars up to her chin
> (if anything goes ~~really~~ wrong
> please notify the un)
>
> fresh marvels
> the wonders of democracy
> are broadcast night & day
> you're told to overthrow tyranny
> who's a golem with feet of clay
> "just make like us" the lowdown is
> "and all your earthly woes will cease

As he went on to describe the Hungarian uprising in his Hudibrastic
stanzas, he turned his attack toward Eisenhower for the very opposite
reasons that he used to berate Roosevelt:

so ~~she just~~ america shrugs her pretty
shoulders as smooth as snow
& murmurs "it's a pity
but i'm awfully busy right now
reelecting general icinghoar
because he'll keep us out of woar."[24]

As he revised and rephrased his lurching lines, a Satyric poem emerged that came down very hard on the United States, the United Nations, and Radio Free Europe and seemed to imply that the United States should have intervened on the side of Hungary and hurled the Russian troops and tanks beyond the Hungarian borders (a curious reversal for the antimilitaristic nonhero). His ironical title "THANKSGIVING (1956)" reflects the widespread grief for the fate of Hungary which was felt by the Americans during their celebration of the national holiday that year.

Problems arose when the Boston Arts Festival chairman received the festival poem. It was so contrary to the spirit of the Festival that the business manager, Peter Temple, felt he could not submit that poem to the Boston papers to print on the day of the reading and tried to persuade Cummings to give them something else. Cummings' ever-ready stubbornness rose, as if someone were imposing the censor's clamp upon him. Fortunately, however, he had learned something during the fracas over the "kike" epigram, namely that a lack of concern for others' feelings would ultimately bounce back upon himself and that his own nerves would undergo exacerbation in the end. His change of mind is recorded in a letter to his sister, as he described "the climax of this war with the Boston Arts Festival bize":

during an interview with this gang's least objectionable member (its businessmanager) I discovered that, while nobody would dare refuse to accept Thanksgiving (1956) as "the festival poem," neither would anybody dare to give it the slightest publicity as such. Presently came a feeling that if I insisted on reading Thanksgiving as the festival poem, the BAF mike might just accidentally go dead on me—& a realization that I was deep in the muck with a bunch which would stop at literally nothing to protect its sacred honour[.] well aware that another 24 hours of said muck could more than than easily spoil my holy summer, I stopped fighting at once; wrote the enclosed letter: & with it enclosed the enclosed (in case you haven't seen Encounter magazine lately) festival poem. The bm's telephonic response was truly touching.[25]

What he had done was to substitute the following as the festival poem:

> i am a little church(no great cathedral)
> far from the splendor and squalor of hurrying cities
> —i do not worry if briefer days grow briefest,
> i am not sorry when sun and rain make april
>
> my life is the life of the reaper and the sower;
> my prayers are prayers of earth's own clumsily striving
> (finding and losing and laughing and crying)children
> whose any sadness or joy is my grief or my gladness
>
> around me surges a miracle of unceasing
> birth and glory and death and resurrection:
> over my sleeping self float flaming symbols
> of hope,and i wake to a perfect patience of mountains
>
> i am a little church(far from the frantic
> world with its rapture and anguish)at peace with nature
> —i do not worry if longer nights grow longest;
> i am not sorry when silence becomes singing
>
> winter by spring,i lift my diminutive spire to
> merciful Him Whose only now is forever:
> standing erect in the deathless truth of His presence
> (welcoming humbly His light and proudly His darkness)

Having thus humbled himself, both in the poem and in the gesture he made toward the Festival Committee, he insisted, nevertheless, that he would also read "THANKSGIVING (1956)" as part of the program.

On the oppressively hot evening of June 23, 1957, Cummings sat before the largest audience he had ever drawn, about seven thousand people, some sprawled on the grass, some a little less comfortable, seated on hard folding chairs. Archibald MacLeish introduced him, presented him with the festival medal, and went out of his way to call Cummings "the original anti-Communist" and to express the hope that he would read the poem he had written about the Hungarian crisis. Cummings was in top form, as reported by "Mr. Harper" [Russell Lynes?] in *Harper's* magazine:

> Perhaps this is one of the last romantic individuals to spring from the
> Concord-and-vicinity breed; a plain, outspoken personality; cantankerous,

unorthodox, patriotic in the old set-my-country-right-when-wrong sense of the word. But the big crowd loved him. He read slowly, meaningfully, lovingly—lingering on each syllable without losing for an instant the drive and surge of his poems. With something of the ancient magic that puts the "right" spell in the right place, he took ordinary sounds and made them sing. And his slow, clear gift of full value to every word unfolded to the ear the rhyme and rhythm that his verses may not convey to the eye. Though it is banal to say over and over that poetry is something to be *heard*, one must say it—and say it again—to describe Cummings' impact on his listeners.

They clapped each poem, and they would not let him go without an encore. Even the tough items—like "Thanksgiving, 1956" apropos of Hungary and what MacLeish called our "unState Department"—they took in stride.[26]

A reviewer for the *Boston Herald* commented: "With unalloyed disdain he read a poem (called "thanksgiving") denouncing official apathy during the Hungarian revolt. Expressing a strong point of view with Swiftian savagery, it caused gasps among the audience, but was warmly received."[27]

The poem that made them first gasp and then applaud was this:

THANKSGIVING (1956)

a monstering horror swallows
this unworld me by you
as the god of our fathers' fathers bows
to a which that walks like a who

but the voice-with-a-smile of democracy
announces night & day
"all poor little peoples that want to be free
just trust in the u s a"

suddenly uprose hungary
and she gave a terrible cry
"no slave's unlife shall murder me
for i will freely die"

she cried so high thermopylae
heard her and marathon
and all prehuman history
and finally The UN

"be quiet little hungary
and do as you are bid
a good kind bear is angary
we fear for the quo pro quid"

uncle sam shrugs his pretty
pink shoulders you know how
and he twitches a liberal titty
and lisps "i'm busy right now"

so rah-rah-rah democracy
let's all be as thankful as hell
and bury the statue of liberty
(because it begins to smell)

Cummings told Elizabeth, "I never had a better microphone. Nor did I ever receive such applause as followed my brief salutation to the statue of liberty."[28]

He drew that heavy applause because he had touched something deep in their feelings that needed expression. Over the next few years, whenever Cummings read "THANKSGIVING (1956)" during his performances at colleges and universities, it was always met with a spontaneous burst of applause, the only poem in a program that the audience would single out for this treatment. The response was partly to the intensity of feeling that Cummings conveyed when he read it, but it was partly something else. He was reawakening that sense of helplessness and frustration that had descended upon the American public in November 1956. However, quixotic the political implications of the poem, Cummings had spoken for all those who felt, "Why can't somebody do something?" as the Russian tanks swept their fire across Budapest and rounded up rebels for execution or prison camp. It is a poem that will take its place in the literature of American social protest, along with the poems of Whittier and Lowell in the antislavery cause and the literary outcries of Dos Passos and Millay after the execution of Sacco and Vanzetti. Cummings was part of a Boston tradition whether he wanted to be or not.

XXXI

Oneliness: Loneliness

When, when, Peace, will you, Peace? I'll not play hypocrite
To my own heart: I yield you do come sometimes; but
That piecemeal peace is poor peace.

G. M. HOPKINS

Health problems were his curse. In recent years, he had done what he could to take care of himself. His diet was moderate; his waist slim. He did no excessive drinking any more: he had long ago gone on what he called "the three-drink wagon" and he seldom took more than one. He stopped smoking a number of times, and once went without a cigarette for eighteen months in 1955–56, but he slipped back under the stress of the poetry readings. In addition to his arthritis and the skin eruptions on his hands, he had new health concerns. He was beset by occasional fibrillation of the heart ("paroxysmal cardiac arhythmia"), which always scared him, although Dr. Ober's prescription of Quinidine stopped it. Further, his poetry reading tours caused increasing intestinal or digestive upset.

At length, while visiting the Watsons in Rochester in May 1955, he entered the outpatient clinic at Strong Memorial Hospital for a full physical examination, including a barium enema examination and a full set of gastrointestinal tests. His physician was tall, lean Dr. Harry Segal, a medical colleague of Watson's[1] and the husband of Evelyn Segal. Cummings had known both Evelyn and Harry, the "dear seagulls," for years, and he and Harry enjoyed a warm relationship. Harry was a quick-witted man with a ready joke and a burbling laugh, whose geniality and kindness were widely acknowledged. Cummings had utter confidence in his professional judgment and from this time on, began to turn to him like a medical Fritz Wittels whenever a disturbing problem arose, telephoning him from New York or New Hampshire if necessary.

The clinical report from the hospital described Cummings as a "thin, high-strung, middle-aged man who does not appear to be ill," although he had "symptoms of bloating, lower abdominal discomfort, diarrhea, all since lectures at Harvard and re-inforced by anti-cancer propaganda." Dr. Segal soothed his worries, for he found no real medical problem. The record reads "nervous colon about which the patient is not overly concerned" and "anxiety state seems to be the cause of the present GI symptoms."[2] This was in the spring of 1955.

Cummings' schedule of readings the next two years was heavier than he had undertaken before, and the stresses of the Boston Arts Festival created further tension. At the same time, Dr. Ober had observed that he was taking as much as three grains of Nembutal each night in order to sleep and prescribed a tranquilizer instead: three tablets per day of Equanil. This calmed Cummings' nerves so that now he was able to sleep with a mere half-grain dose of Nembutal.[3]

But the tranquilizers were insufficient to steady him down for sustained literary work. In the spring of 1957, Cummings received a most cordial invitation from Professor James Phillips of the UCLA English Department to give the Ewing Lectures that year on November 18 and 20. Marianne Moore had been the 1956 lecturer, and after she assured Cummings that the arrangements and the hospitable treatment would be much to his satisfaction, he accepted. He was to be paid $2500 for two "nonlectures" on any aspect of English or American literature that he chose.[4] He decided to call them "an appendix to *i; six nonlectures,*" thinking perhaps that an expanded edition of the Harvard Press book might push it to a second edition.

He worked all summer trying to prepare two more sets of autobiographical reminiscences. The notes and fragments indicate that he considered talking about such experiences as his tour of duty with the Norton-Harjes Ambulance Corps and how *The Enormous Room* came to be written; his service in the U.S. Army and how he met "Olaf"; his associations with Thayer, Watson, Lachaise and the *Dial;* and about his friendship with Ezra Pound. These were glances back to the "pre-fall world" of his youth: "America (in those far-off days) symbolized a veritable Promised Land, Christian and Protestant, where anyone was free to work out his or her particular destiny—not an atheistic Eldorado, where nobody could help becoming not merely just as good as, but a little bit better than a hundred million other people, [—] & an American could be defined as a human being who stood up straight & looked his or her God in the eye and was only afraid of being false to himself or herself."[5]

But on September 22, he wrote to Elizabeth that the California non-lectures "so far have declined to write themselves." Betty Kray had prepared an elaborate reading schedule centering on the UCLA lecture date. During November, Cummings was to read at Oberlin, University of Tulsa, University of Colorado, University of Oregon, University of Washington, University of California at Berkeley, and then on the way home from Los Angeles, to stop for a reading at the University of Texas. Marion planned to go along.

But Cummings broke down under these impending demands. He was stricken with intermittent diarrhea and abdominal pains, "left-handed appendicitis," he called it. Under the stress of trying to put together the UCLA lectures, he had begun to have these attacks at Joy Farm, where he had hitherto always found relief from the nervous indigestion he suffered during winter and spring. He cancelled the entire schedule of engagements and the lectures were never written.

The sequence of events seems to be that, about October 1, Hildegarde Watson appeared in New Hampshire and seeing his distressed situation took him back to Strong Memorial Hospital for a further checkup.[6] Cummings arrived just at the time Dr. Segal himself was about to undergo surgery, but, still in charge, Harry talked cheerily to Cummings by phone from his hospital bed and assigned him to his colleague Dr. Robert Burton. Dr. Burton sought the source of Cummings' intestinal troubles[7] and in the course of his investigation found a large polyp in the lower colon which bled readily. After they agreed that an operation for removal should take place, the surgery was carried out through the abdomen by Dr. W. J. Merle Scott on October 10, 1957. During the operation everything else seemed normal but Dr. Scott removed the appendix before sewing up the surgical incision. The polyp proved to be benign. Cummings spent his sixty-third birthday in a hospital bed.

Eight days after the operation, Cummings was discharged to the Watson home, "that blessedly quiet house," to convalesce, and Marion returned to New York. He was still in great pain but would take no medication from Watson. He wanted, he said, everything from life including the pain.[8] He was deluged with letters from friends and received many floral encouragements, including a dozen roses from the poet, Theodore Roethke. After ten days of hovering care from Hildegarde and her servants, he could walk to the end of the block and back. It would take six months before the soreness completely disappeared, but he felt better and more relaxed already, if only from the enforced reprieve from the composition of the Ewing lectures. "Medically, it seems, am a case of 'anxiety hysteria' i.e., I worry and therefore produce 'symptoms' (like the indigestion which was bothering me when H[ildegarde] appeared."[9] There would be no more public performances for several months. That fact alone must have contributed to his recovery, which was really quite speedy for a man of his age.

II

1958 was a big year for Cummings. At the outset he was awarded the prestigious Bollingen Prize of $1000 from Yale University. He published a collection of his fugitive prose pieces and a new volume of poems. A new issue of *Eimi* was launched by the Grove Press in both cloth and paperback editions. A biography of his life appeared. Further, his work was the focus of a full-length critical study and a complete bibliography, both of which were not published, however, until 1960.

The story behind the appearance of *A Miscellany*, a heterogeneous collection of short prose items, begins with S. A. Jacobs, the printer, whose "enthusiasm for my work," Cummings wrote, "extended even to essays published in *Vanity Fair;* he urged me to make a book of them & insisted on presenting me with a collection torn from issues of Mr. Crowninshield's lively periodical: whereat I thanked him and did nothing." Sometime in 1957, a new figure appeared at Patchin Place, "bearing gifts of jams and jellies, & expressing great enthusiasm re his 'unhero' (alias me)."[10] This was George Firmage, an NYU graduate who had continued his literary interests even though he was working in a bank. He was the author of a bibliography of the writings of Gertrude Stein and now wished to develop a similar descriptive listing of Cummings' publications. In the course of searching out all his published work, Firmage saw the possibilities for a side project, a volume of all of Cummings' uncollected prose, to be published under the title *Et Cetera,* the first book issuing from Deborah Benson's Argophile Press. Soon both Marion and Cummings were working to collect material (Cummings insisted on changing the title to *A Miscellany*), and Firmage dug through the Condé Nast files to find the cancelled checks which identified all of Cummings' *Vanity Fair* items.[11] The book was, in the end, a valuable effort, but particularly because it included Cummings' commencement speech, "The New Art," and his essays written for the *Dial.* In 1965, Firmage revised and expanded it to include additional items, among them a complete illustrated version of [*No Title*].

95 Poems, the last book of new poems published in Cummings' lifetime, appeared October 8, 1958. This book, coming from a sixty-four year old poet, is remarkable for its vigor and freshness, for its lively interest in certain ordinary individuals—like Dominic, the ice man, or the Greenwich Village organ grinder who carried a cockatoo—, and for its perceptive focus on certain ordinary entities of the natural world, a cheery whippoorwill, sentinel robins, "twofroing" hummingbirds, a bee in a rosebush, thrushes, a "raucous rogue" of a bluejay, white roses from "my mother's greatgrandmother's rosebush," a forest pool, and "the good rain farmers pray for." Somewhere deep within the cluster of bodily aches named E. E. Cummings, at the still center of a roil of anger and hostility, was a sweet wellspring of creativity that released occasional trickles of pure Hippocrene. The first poem in the book is the most delicately beautiful literary construct that Cummings ever created. It consists of the phrase "a leaf falls" and the word "loneliness": that is all, although the two are intertwined. After the first line, "l(a," the rest of the letters of the parenthetical intrusion, "a leaf falls)," are scattered down the page, five more lines in a pattern of alternating consonants and vowels, as if to demonstrate how the leaf drifts to and fro in falling. Then comes the word "one," which continues the spelling of "loneliness." Then an "l" by itself, reminding us that an "l" and a numeral one are the same key on a typewriter. Then the rest of the word "loneliness" (which also contains "oneliness") is completed:

> l(a
>
> le
> af
> fa
>
> ll
>
> s)
> one
> l
>
> iness

Mitchell Morse has called it, "in spirit a perfect haiku."[12]

In the middle of the book is a sonnet about the birth of a baby, probably inspired by some meditations on the meaning of new life after Nancy gave birth to Ioanna, the first grandchild to come along since the reunion of father and daughter:

from spiralling ecstatically this

proud nowhere of earth's most prodigious night
blossoms a newborn babe:around him,eyes
—gifted with every keener appetite
than mere unmiracle can quite appease—
humbly in their imagined bodies kneel
(over time space doom dream while floats the whole

perhapsless mystery of paradise)

mind without soul may blast some universe
to might have been,and stop ten thousand stars
but not one heartbeat of this child;nor shall
even prevail a million questionings
against the silence of his mother's smile

—whose only secret all creation sings

For the first time too, real children, not abstractions, make their entry into Cummings' poetry. Poem 67, "this little huge/ -eyed per-/son," (a copy of which he sent to Nancy for Ioanna) and poem 68, "the (oo) is/ look," are observations of expressively inarticulate children.

Another poem, which had already become a favorite with student audiences, deals with the conflicts between youth and age:

old age sticks
up Keep
Off
signs)&

youth yanks them
down(old
age
cries No

Tres)&(pas)
youth laughs
(sing
old age

scolds Forbid

        den Stop
        Must
        n't Don't

        &)youth goes
        right on
        gr
        owing old

Looking at items of this sort, we may note that in *95 Poems* Cummings
displays a greater awareness of the cycle of human life than in any of his
previous volumes. It comes as a surprise to think that, in this respect, he
had produced a book of poems with a "mature" outlook, although it still
reflected his youthful gratitude for whatever life offers: looking back
from sixty-four years, he did not hesitate to assert, "Time's a strange
fellow: more he gives than takes."

The new edition of *Eimi* by Grove Press contained Cummings'
"Sketch for a Preface to the Fourth Edition of Eimi," the helpful com-
mentary on the method and the characters of the book and an outline-
summary, day by day, of its contents. It was Cummings' first paperback,
a format which became common for his reprinted books during the two
succeeding decades.

In the fall appeared *The Magic Maker* by Charles Norman, the first
biography of Cummings, a book about which he had ambivalent feelings.
Charles Norman was a newspaperman whom Cummings had met in the
1930's and who later arranged some publicity interviews with him. Out
of his interviews, Norman had created two very good puffs for Cum-
mings and his work, which were carried by the Associated Press Feature
Service and thus made available to newspapers all over the country. But
Norman was also a poet and a biographer, having published popular
treatments of the lives of Shakespeare, Marlowe, and Johnson. One day
he came to Patchin Place with horrifying news: he wanted to do a biog-
raphy of Cummings. Estlin's first reaction was a scuttling retreat and
Marion was ready for a formidable refusal, but when Norman announced
that he had already signed a contract with Macmillan, Cummings gave
in, on condition that he should read through and approve the manuscript
before publication.[13] Although he was very leary of what he considered
an invasion of his privacy, he cooperated by answering questions and by
supplying him with the correspondence about La Ferté-Macé that Ed-
ward Cummings had so carefully organized. Marion turned over the
scrapbooks of clippings that Rebecca Cummings had filled in and that she
herself had continued to keep up to date after Mrs. Cummings' death.

Elizabeth gave information about ancestry and childhood days. Slater Brown, Morrie Werner and other Greenwich Village friends gave aid, and gradually a full narrative came into being.

But Estlin and Marion began to interfere with Norman's book as soon as they received the manuscript, and only after Cummings' own cutting and rewriting of sections was poor Norman free to publish.[14] The resulting biography was the only kind of work that could have passed muster with Cummings. It was grossly flattering, yet it was sufficiently superficial that he could look down on it as "mere journalism."[15] He also had protected himself from real scrutiny: although the publisher claimed that Norman had access to family papers, Cummings boasted to Nancy that "the access was negligible (indeed microscopic)." But the sincerity of Norman's efforts to please him eventually made its impact. Cummings finally conceded, "I can't help liking it, as a whole, because he writes with genuine affection."[16]

A far more important publication with Cummings at the center was Norman Friedman's book, *E. E. Cummings: The Art of His Poetry* published by the Johns Hopkins University Press in 1960. Friedman had sent Cummings his first critical essay on the poetry in 1954, and Cummings received it with evident curiosity and cheerful foreboding: "Although slightly terrified of your scholarship, am daring your opus by degrees; & flatter myself I may possibly become a wiser ignoramus in consequence."[17] Evidently impressed by the young man's work, Cummings was cooperative when Friedman undertook a book-length study of his poetry and even lent him a stack of 175 work sheets that he had used for the poem, "rosetree, rosetree," as a sample of his working methods, a highly unusual gesture. Thus Friedman was able to add a chapter on the creative process that Cummings carried out in writing a poem. His critical study still stands as the best treatment of Cummings' poetry that has ever been done. An equally definitive publication, George Firmage's *E. E. Cummings: A Bibliography*, appeared the same year and immediately became a standard reference work on Cummings.

III

Cummings was able to return to the reading circuit as early as the spring of 1958. Some of the excitement he once felt in performing for the huge audiences of vibrant young people had begun to wear off. He had begun to change his tastes in audiences too. The era of the beatnik had altered the appearance and manners of the student groups in New York and some of the other urban universities, and Cummings did not much care for the unshaven faces and matted hair, the ragged clothes, and the generational protest of marijuana smoking. " 'An asbestos curtain,' I heard myself observe not long ago, 'came down between my era and the present nonepoch'."[18] As a consequence, he now found himself newly attracted to certain special groups.

He had at first been wary of an excursion into the South. But now he loved the courtesy and order that he found at southern colleges. He returned from readings in North Carolina in May 1958 saying, "What a surprise—to enter a peacefully homogeneous community where money is never mentioned, where no racial tension exists either on or under any surface; & where instead of colliding with indoctrinated automata, one meets courteous individuals! For the first time I realize what 'America' might have been. It may have taken a century hereabouts to prove that whoever wins a war loses it; but if somebody doubts that the soidisant North is now defeated, let him or her wander Greenwich Village on a Friday or Saturday (or even Sunday) night; experiencing the total triumph of murderous muckerdom & 'liberal' fanaticism (inc.)."[19]

He also found Roman Catholic institutions to his liking. This was in part because of their political and social conservatism. Of a trip to Notre Dame in 1957 he had speculated, "Maybe—who knows—a dash of honest-toGod RC fanaticism may prove agreeable after the sickening pinkery of NYC's hypocritical 'liberals'."[20] But the students themselves appealed to him because they seemed better mannered and more unsophisticated than the students at other institutions. "I recently read at Boston College, on behalf of a Catholic group composed chiefly of young people ("teenagers"). And you cannot begin to imagine how entirely refreshing they were—cheerful, open & honest, very lively, extraordinarily well mannered, & extremely attractive. That single contact taught me something much deeper than any amount of il-'liberal' propaganda will ever erase."[21] He chose his material carefully for these readings, omitting anything likely to shock because of its sexual reference and including material religious in theme and often forthrightly anti-Communist.[22] He had begun to note "that the only 'religious group' which seems to honestly detest a Soviet Pigman yclept 'Mr.' (sic)K is the RCChurch, believe it or dis-"[23]

Women's colleges had never lost their appeal. The young women had always been openly and intensely responsive to his performances. A reading at Bryn Mawr, April 20, 1959, was one of his most enjoyable experiences. He felt "from the moment my infinitely kind mentor (Miss Mary [Katherine] Woodworth) materialized at Philadelphia's 30th Street station till we said goodbye . . . I was always among—previously unimagined!—fearlessly enthusiastic *friends*."[24] Since at women's colleges he generally read more love poems than he did at other institutions, this time he began with "it is so long since my heart has been with yours" and went on to live up to his reputation (so the student newspaper reporter thought) as "the finest lyric voice of any contemporary poet."[25] Later the audience interrupted with spontaneous applause after "THANKSGIVING (1956)." Miss Woodworth's letter to Cummings a few days later conveyed to him the success of his appearance. She wished he were present on campus to "hear some of the expressions of pleasure with which people rush up to say how carried away they were by Monday night's reading. The students are truly in an exalted mood. I've never known anything like it. You heard the applause and you saw the hall, its walls were draped with undergraduates and heaven knows who else. No commencement looks like that I assure you. I'm told the students started to pack the hall by six thirty, two hours ahead of time."[26]

IV

The schedule of readings did not leave much time for creating new work. Only the summers on the farm seemed to allow for the uninterrupted daily concentration that was necessary before anything could come forth. But even those periods found creativity clogged for longer efforts. A friend who was a composer (Paul Nordoff?) had for some years urged him to collaborate on an opera, yet after Cummings developed a number of scenes for an opera based on the life of Pushkin and his relations with the Tsar Peter, the friend was not interested in the results.[27] As Cummings mentioned to Henry Allen Moe some years earlier, he wanted to complete a book of fairy stories for children. He had written three as early as the 1920's when Nancy was a little girl. He finished a fourth one in 1950, during the summer that Nancy visited Joy Farm. He wanted a book of seven stories; "yet can't seem to write another 3," he confessed to Elizabeth in 1957.[28]

But the real bugaboo was the play. Summer after summer he had spent time on it. Ideas multiplied, schemes were considered, scenes begun, but except for the offshoot that blossomed into *Santa Claus*, nothing ever developed. Since Cummings tried so hard and so continuously to shape another play and since he wasted so much creative energy on the project, it will be worthwhile to look briefly at some of the different schemes that he tried to work with, for this is evidence of the fertility of his imagination, yet at the same time of his ineffectualness in building large structural wholes.

When one examines the notes and fragments, it is possible, because of a few dates and references, to see what Cummings had in mind at different stages of his efforts from 1928 to 1958. In its earliest form, the play appears to have centered on a character named Seul, who was an artist. The "Speech (from a forthcoming play)" published in 1936 comes from this period: the speaker admonishes his hearers to stop thinking and return to instinctual responses and he urges civilization to "pull in your eyes and kiss all your beautiful machines good night."[29] In the 1930's, after Cummings met Marion, Seul has become, additionally, a new archetype, "the ever-alive human type:/ vagabond: Seul, Alone, (Quo Vadis, The Wandering Jew) ♂ —SPERM/ Chaplin . . . A Nous La Liberté/ Whitman 'the open road'."[30] The principal action involves Seul's love for the Ragged Girl, who is his female counterpart. The action of the play would bring them together, achieving a oneness of soul (as some notes indicate) or bringing to birth a new world (as other notes suggest). A good many characters that he considered for the play are attached to one or another pattern of ideas that he toyed with. For instance, when he attempted to erect a symbolic Freudian scheme, Uncle Tom was to represent the unconscious, Uncle Sam the conscious, and Seul the "superconscious."

Sometime later he worked with an epic American scheme about "the birth of a nation," which was to feature Lincoln and his cabinet and the Mayflower Pilgrims. This dramatic idea was not to be merely historical, for the variety of characterizations indicates an expressionistic extravaganza, far more complex than *Him*, in which Seul, Lincoln, Uncle Tom and others would be involved with Joan of Arc, De Lawd and Gabriel, Jesus Christ and Ghost (the Spirit of Science), Mary Magdalene, Miss Youessay, Columbia (a golddigger), The White Rock Girl and the Drowned Man, and others. Every folder of notes shows additional complexities and variations in patterns as trivial as boy-meets-girl and as vast as the fall and redemption of humankind.

Sometime later, perhaps in the early 1950's when Cummings saw the musical comedy, *The King and I*, which included a Siamese dance-play based on *Uncle Tom's Cabin*, he considered developing a musical-comedy version of his material. Certain songs are listed, either by title or by a few lines, such as, "my girl's the sweetest thing in shoes," "the devil crep' in eden wood," "funny money blooz" (about the dollar that is worth only thirty cents), "but if it's Miami, try Annie" (a bawdy song beginning, "There's a girl in our town named Mamie"), "orchids don't grow in ostrich eggs," "I want-to-be-all over-you-like Heaven/ with a kick like Judgement Day." Also to be featured was a chorus of vagabonds and nudes going through a number called "gimme gin and bitters/ to open my eyes."[31]

However bewildering or grotesque Cummings' plethora of ideas seems, they are full of vigor and surprise, and no matter how mundane or silly, the images and plot outlines always had symbolic or allegorical intention behind them. "if I could find a myth (old story),"[32] he jotted at one point. He wanted something that would give his play structure and dimension, the way *Pilgrim's Progress* and Dante's *Inferno* had done with his prose narratives. For he aspired high: "my gift is (I pray) to create a form as greatly deep as tragic drama—as Sophocles' Oedipus or Shakespeare's Antony and Cleopatra; & in no wise imitative of them! Wholly new!"[33]

The aspiration was not always that high, and sensibly so: *Santa Claus* had proved that the puppet play or the children's play was a good medium for his talent. In the late 1950's he was following this vein once more, and this direction for his play was taken at the same time he was attempting to write more fairy tales for children. Some notes show that he tried out two autobiographical characters, i and mySelf, and sometimes Little Estlin and Pengy. At this stage of work, characters had their real-life counterparts in order to give his ideas solidity. For example, for dual aspects of Pengy, the penguin, he thought of his friends. Pengy on land was Loren MacIver, "Xian (Doestoyevsky)—GOODNESS—*life*/ S[ibley] W[atson] no distinctions, love-for-all/ clumsy (homely)—but sweet of nature generous of heart." Pengy in the water was Scofield Thayer "all style, form, technique, skill—BEAUTY—*art*/ a Dingansich/ taking her prey perfectly."[34] On another page, a cast of characters is listed as follows:

1 Pengy
2 Blessed One
3 Everybody (a mouse)————Nagle?
4 Hurrah (a flea)—European
5 Whose (a mind always wandering)
[6] Noone (a cat) whom Everybody fears
[7] Somebody (a dog)————Brown?[35]

These later stages of work on a play or plays almost always involve dualisms of one sort of another, usually the mixture of good and evil. Here Cummings was reflecting the thoroughness with which he had absorbed Dr. Fritz Wittels' idea of moral doubleness, or as he put it in his Viennese accent, "Everysing iss two." Cummings was even able to apply it to the Hungarian revolution: "USA nothelping Hungary ag R —EVIL but: the whole Western world is so shocked thereby that R, through her very unhinderedness, loses more prestige than she could have lost in any other way (if we'd stopped her, a lot of people would have always believed in communism, who now are horrified at it)."[36]

However mechanical this ethical formula may seem, it did invite an effective approach to symbolic drama for Cummings because he wished to present opposites in conflict and then provide a resolution between them. Seul was alone because he was selfish, "can't even love his own child,"[37] but would, as an artist, discover he was an unselfish person. Marion at one point represents the merging of the extremes of Elaine and Anne, at another point, the Virgin Mary and Marilyn Monroe. In the dramatic schemes, eros and agape were always to reach some golden mean. Paradoxes both personal and religious crowd Cummings' pages; a force of love was generally planned as the agent which would resolve the paradoxes and bring about a denouement in the dramatic action. But no matter how profound or intriguing these ideas and schemes may seem, Cummings was unable to give them literary life in a finished play.

Does all of this tell us anything about Cummings' imaginative strengths and weaknesses? Or about his creative genius and what it was able to bring forth? Perhaps. Throughout his career, Cummings would spend his time sitting at the typewriter or with pencil in hand, setting down images, sayings, fleeting concepts, reminiscences, observations about his friends, thoughts from books he had read, slogans, parodies, streams of association, patterns of correspondences, typographical manipulations, and at some point a creative spark would catalyze some of this linguistic doodling and a form would emerge: a poem would "write itself." It could be rewritten, revised, or polished, perhaps a great many times, but that original burst of creative coalescence was the essential act. Although this process worked for short poems, it was much more difficult to keep in operation for larger narrative or dramatic structure. This was why autobiography played such a large part in his longer works: a time sequence offered structure. But even with autobiography to depend on, those works tended to be made up of short units just strung together, sometimes even insecurely. The bulk of *The Enormous Room* was comprised of character sketches and anecdotes; *Him* was chiefly a vaudeville revue; *Eimi* was a daily diary of entries governed by the chance of life. In this perspective, the little morality play, *Santa Claus,* appears to be the most fully sustained imaginative effort that Cummings ever produced. But with the play about Seul, the creative spark that was needed to pull a chaos of material together never flashed. To our regret, the play occupies a place in that limbo where are found unwritten epics, undeveloped tragedies, and novels with only a title page and a dedication—that limbo out of which major writers as well as aspiring nonentities have been unable to coax an elusive idea into literary existence.

V

European travel still had its attractions for Estlin and Marion in the later 1950's, but the state of their health, especially Estlin's made their leaving home rather precarious. They went by ship (Marion did not like to fly) and they arranged for comfortable hotel accommodations, Estlin taking the harder of the two beds and sometimes having to order a bed board. In 1956 they planned a twelve-week tour. They sailed March 17 and Estlin was able to show Marion southern Spain for three weeks, but they returned home two weeks later. "Spain was icy." Italy was "cold, cold, cold." In Venice they encountered motorboats and television, in Florence roaring motorcycles, and in Rome even at their favorite spot, the Piazza Navona, a variety of buzzing motor bicycles. On the return trip, Marion slipped on the deck and injured her knees. She arrived home in a wheel-chair.[38] Estlin decided against further peregrinations.

But in 1959 when a representative of the Ford Foundation visited Patchin Place and, out of the blue, offered Cummings a two-year grant of $15,000, he thought they might try a carefully planned trip once more. (Cummings maintained that the grant was awarded to him because he still drove a 1929 Ford up at Joy Farm.) Jack and Máire Sweeney had invited them to visit them on their farm in Corofin, County Clare, Ireland. They sailed on the *Queen Mary* in mid-May to Southampton, and after a brief stay in London, flew over to Dublin. Cummings liked the old-fashioned atmosphere of Dublin, reminiscent of the European cities he knew during his youth. Their hotel, the Sheffield, struck him as "the disguising of a past culture skilfully blended w. modern tendencies & the effect is perfect harmony."[39]

When they arrived in County Clare on May 28, Marion was suffering from a bad cold and was confined to bed all during the visit to the Sweeneys. But Jack drove Estlin around the county and over into Galway. Sweeney recalled "that Cummings was pleased by the dry stone walls and the limestone terrain and also the mushroom soup which was served at a Galway restaurant called 'The Twelve Pins.' He was also interested in what he called 'the vocality of the locality.' He liked the turns of phrase he heard and gleefully reported them to us."[40] On June 4, Sweeney motored them from Corofin to Dublin, and after an overnight rest, the Cummingses went on to Paris for a stop-over before their return to the United States in mid-June. Respitory troubles ruined most of the holiday for Marion, and Estlin had his usual daily pain, which was aggravated whenever they shifted to a new city. He was no longer keen to travel.

In the summer of 1960, Nancy bore her fourth child, Alexis, in

Athens, where she was now living. Shortly afterward, she became very
ill and "almost perished, of Greek doctors,"[41] but she flew to London,
where she received proper medical attention and surgery. Estlin was
deeply concerned, and coping as best he could to make a transatlantic
telephone call, finally reached her in her hospital bed where she, sur-
prised and weak, had difficulty in talking to him. Although earlier that
year, he had written to Elizabeth that "my most recent glimpse of What-
wasonceEurope taught me . . . not to travel,"[42] he and Marion now
planned a trip to the Mediterranean area, their principal object to see
Nancy when she returned to Greece.

Nancy's marriage to Willard Roosevelt had ended in divorce, and in
1954 she married Kevin Andrews, "a wild man"—that is to say, he was
a primitivist, just the sort of man Cummings admired. Born in Peking,
the stepson of Roy Chapman Andrews the explorer, he was partly
brought up in England. After enduring the Italian campaign as a G.I.,
he was graduated *summa cum laude* from Harvard, where, as a prize
student of Professor John Finley in Greek literature, he won a postgradu-
ate grant to the American School of Classical Studies in Athens. Very
soon finding archaeology too academic, he got himself a permit to travel
about the country to study medieval fortresses, casually moving between
the rival Greek groups in a civil war. The results of his field research were
published as *Castles of the Morea*, 1953;[43] but an account of his travels, a
more interesting book drawing freely upon his association with shep-
herds, fishermen, and guerilla fighters called *The Flight of Ikaros*, was
published by Houghton Mifflin in 1959.

Cummings had become acquainted with Kevin as early as 1953, and
Kevin and Nancy had visited Joy Farm briefly that summer. But in 1955,
Nancy, Kevin, and Nancy's children all went to Europe to live, going
first to the Swiss mountains and later to the Greek islands, where the
"simple life" proved too complicated, and then to Athens, where they
acquired a house halfway up Mount Lycabettos with a direct view of the
Acropolis out of their living room window.

On September 30, 1960, Estlin and Marion sailed on the *Vulcania*,
first-class this time, for a first stop in Sicily. After a week in Palermo and
a tour of the principal sights of the island, they crossed to southern Italy.
Naples, Sorrento, and Rome depressed them, for there were so many
tourists they felt crowded everywhere they went. Since Estlin's back was
troubling him, he almost decided to turn back, but he was determined to
see Nancy. About November 1, they went on to Athens, where they put
up at the newly renovated Hotel Grande Bretagne, whose rooms had
been turned into little boxes and whose uncarpeted corridors echoed like
an empty hospital. Everything began badly. Cummings winced at the

hotel noise, his back was giving him twinges of pain, and his heating pad would not plug into the Greek electrical outlet. When Marion tried to reach Nancy, she discovered that the Andrews had no telephone. Very cross about the difficulties of communication, she sent a note to Nancy asking her to call at the hotel. When Nancy finally got the message and telephoned from downstairs, Marion did not seem in the least interested in seeing them. She was only full of complaint about everything, especially the Greek electrical plug. Kevin hastened to the rescue, having with great difficulty procured a suitable heating pad, but at the hotel room Marion took it from him and shut the door without even letting him greet them properly. Not having waited to hear Kevin's instructions about the heating pad, she was further upset when it sputtered and blew the fuse. Eventually the heating pad was made to work.

On November 3, Nancy with some trepidation sent a note to her father: "We are as Kevin tried to say, at your disposal at all times but, not wishing to intrude & being perhaps rather too much aware of this possibility it seems best to leave the modus up to you—even at the risk of seeming, Estlin, less loving toward yourself than I feel; this has always seemed the lesser/ or better/ risk & very possibly I have always been wrong; I have very little to go on."[44]

Estlin replied that they would like to see them the next day, and at length, the Cummingses were invited to lunch, Kevin by now having got over his annoyance at Marion's rudeness. But Marion was next, as Nancy recalls, behaving in a hoity-toity fashion about being invited to a mere family lunch with grandchildren present, implying that Cummings was too important a man to be asked to join the children at the family table. One happy development, however, was an excursion Kevin, Estlin, Marion, and five-year old Ioanna made to a beautiful Byzantine monastery halfway up Hymettos.

It had been years since Nancy and Estlin had seen each other; yet in the few days the Cummingses spent in Athens, they were alone only once. They took a short walk down the street, Cummings very restrained as usual. "You love your children very much," he said, as if with some surprise. He smiled and smiled, Nancy remembers, walking erect with his head thrown back, but what he had to say seemed far off, as if the conversation were taking place with someone else.[45] She learned for the first time that afternoon that he had come all that way just to see her.[46] When he and Marion were leaving, there was a momentary relaxation of constraint: he waved good-bye to them all at the window and then came back to say with delight that the baby, Alexis, "was the spitting image of my Uncle George."

For Nancy, the visit to Athens was saddening. Estlin, wrapped in

*E. E. Cummings, Paris, early
1920s.*
COURTESY NANCY T. ANDREWS

his problems and his pains, was never aware what a disappointment it had all been for her. He and Marion made a quick trip home. After a flight to Rome, they went on to Paris, where the strains of travel were eased in the Hotel Continental overlooking the Tuileries: the Ford Foundation money made it possible for them to stay at the hotel where Thayer used to stop. They flew home in eight hours by superjet. It was easier for him to communicate with Nancy by letter. He told her how much he had enjoyed the Greek visit and described the speedy flight home. He was then able to express his genuine concern for her well-being and for her recovery from the surgery: "if I'm worried about you, it's partly because you obviously need rest&relaxation & don't seem to be getting it, but chiefly because am by no means sure you'll have the uncommonsense to LEAVE Greece every 6 months for a 'checkup' via some A 1 (e.g. English) doctor." He also dropped a detail or two about another health problem of his own: ". . . have you, as I every so often have had, a 'fibrillating' heart, which (apropos of nothing discoverable) suddenly goes on a frightening spree & hammers Fast&Loud? If so you're lucky; because this nuisance is not 'organic' & can be controlled by *quinidine* ("kwin-id-een"). And don't lose any time getting a cardiogram from that A 1 doctor. . . ."[47] In a later letter he enclosed a small photograph, as she requested, which showed him as he looked in the last days at 3 Washington Square. It was a picture of Cummings, about age twenty-eight, in a sheepskin coat, in profile, with a little moustache.

When Nancy received it, she felt vibrations from a long-ago self: "Do you know at all, I wonder," she wrote him, "what you sent me? perhaps. Anyway I do; & like that first, or last, visit with the James', being-recognized-&-recognizing in dimness, . . . although this is a piece of paper that doesn't vanish or doesn't change, curiously isn't reallythere, it did produce an initial shock just as truthful as onceuponatime. So you were you, after all, and I was with you. Strange that I should be able to forget so long."[48] There was, then, real communication between father and daughter, but it took an exquisitely responsive sensor like Nancy to make it possible.

XXXII

Now I Lay Me Down
to Dream

Old age is respectable so long as it asserts itself, maintains its rights, is subservient to no one, and retains its sway to the last breath. I like a young man who has a touch of the old, and I like an old man who has a touch of the young.

CICERO

Cummings' last years in Patchin Place were little different from those a decade earlier. He rose about eleven A.M. and came down to a good breakfast—no orange juice because of his tender intestinal tract—and took a Donnatal tablet to ease digestion. For his morning walk he went over to Washington Square to note what "urbs" allowed Nature to display there; even rain did not deter him: he took an umbrella. He still appeared as he had described himself a few years earlier, with exaggerated deprecation, "a little old lopsided New Englander; self-consciously hiding his baldness under a decayed Stetson."[1] Upon return, he disappeared upstairs for his daily stint in the studio. He was writing captions now for a book of Marion's photographs ("they're superb!") to be published by Harcourt Brace in 1962.

Marion was allowed to have a radio now. She would only turn it on after he had gone upstairs. If a visitor called, Marion would go out in the hall and clang the Indian "elephant bell" as a signal for him to come down. If it were late in the day, a cup of lapsong suchong, perhaps laced with rum, would provide festivity. If the visitor, sitting on the sagging couch or the frayed Eastlake chair, looked around, he would see books stacked all about, a line of elephant figurines marching across the mantelpiece, a little mouse made by Marion perched beside them, a French carriage clock dangling on the wall telling the time, Estlin's paintings hung around in all the available wall spaces, a self-portrait in a red pom-pommed beret placed by the door, and Loren's "Lilac Time" given the place of honor over the fireplace. The Lachaise head of Cummings would be seen standing with a grandeur of its own on a side table.

Marion would be in and out from the tiny curtained-off kitchen with the tea things. Estlin would perhaps be eating a pear in the French manner—with a fork piercing its top as he sliced chunks off of its side. Or he might be tilting back and forth on his straight-backed rush-bottomed chair, offering his latest complaint about a decision of the Supreme Court[2] or describing his latest put-down of an authority figure. When President Kennedy in a display of support for the arts invited a crowd of distinguished writers and artists to dine at the White House in the spring of 1962, Cummings was on the guest list. But in his peevish way, he would have none of it. To him, "the Kennedy-Kulcher (Mick-kike) tie-up" was "an Abie's Irish Rosary."[3] He turned down the invitation.

If the weather were pleasant, there might be an evening stroll. Betty Kray remembers, "For a while I was living near Patchin Place in the Village and every night around ten o'clock he would come by, tap on my window, and I would then go with him on a long prowl through the Village streets. We walked and I listened and he talked about himself, about the world, about the things he loved. I disagreed with much of his political belief but held my tongue; he was quite vulnerable during this period. . . . . He would disprove over and over again the critics' charge that neither his poems nor his paintings showed 'development'; this was the most intolerable of all the criticism. What I liked best was to have him reminisce about his early years in New York, and he told some fine stories. I checked one once with Slater Brown, who appreciated the drama of the story but doubted that he, at least, had participated in it. Cummings had the two of them commandeering and driving like Roman charioteers a garbage wagon with two large white horses; I can visualize yet Cummings whipping them onward like Ben Hur."[4]

If it were Christmas-time at Patchin Place, Estlin made much of the rituals. The sitting room was gaily decorated with a tree as large as the room would permit. The big wooden elephant by the fireplace was all shined up and had a big red bow tied around his neck. Each visitor dropping in for a drink would bring an ornament for the tree. Dominic the ice man, also stopping by for a drink, would bring a huge ice cake and place it in the bathtub as a spare. One Christmas he returned several times, until he had so much to drink that the bathtub was full of ice blocks. "Nothing's too good for Mr. Cummings" was the cheery departing cry.[5]

Although Cummings felt that New York grew "noisily slummier every minute" and was now "the world's filthiest bigspot,"[6] he and Marion actually had to struggle to stay in Patchin Place. First, Commissioner Robert Moses had marked it, as well as the nearby Jefferson Market Tower, for demolition in the urban renewal program. But, as Estlin wrote Elizabeth, "a lively & indignant Jewish advertisingwriter & Marion leaped into action: a committeefordefense (inspired by a fighting female radioscenarist & a hardworking also female, authentic Southern aristocrat) was formed."[7] Urban renewal was fended off. But in 1961, Mr. Hugh Keenan, tired of his small rental income held down by rent control, decided to do a complete renovation of 4 Patchin Place in order to create five new studio apartments, and gave notice to Estlin and Marion to vacate. Marion fought this order through three court hearings. At length, someone apprised Mayor Robert Wagner that a venerable elderly poet was being harassed into moving by his landlord, and City Hall denied Keenan a building permit. Patchin Place was no *Better Homes and Gardens* beauty spot, but it was a New York home for Estlin and Marion and as quiet a cul-de-sac as one could find in the city, with its ailanthus trees, "trees of heaven," providing an unusual bit of greenery in the midst of all the Greenwich Village concrete. Or it was quiet until construction began on a fourteen-story apartment house (which Marion referred to as the "hatchery") next to Estlin's studio window.

Nights were quiet now, though, for the Cummingses controlled all the units at 4 Patchin Place except the second floor front, and Estlin could still work after dinner until quite late. One chance set of notes among his papers gives us a glimpse of him late at night and at the same time shows us how clearly he could still recapture his childhood:

Saying goodnight to my trees of heaven, i hear—at the edge of an imagined horizon Westward—the (through the raindarkness floating) chuh-chuh-chuh-chuh which means an engine, the locomotive of a train
I stand (in the light of my room, listening; hearing) myself—now & here
    then I shut both lights off; & stand in my room's darkness; becoming (as I listen & hear) the I of long ago & of elsewhere—a child in his mother's bedroom at Cambridge, listening & hearing; a very little boy whose mind

goes up & over & down a hill (into Somerville) while his (lying in a toobig
bed of dreadful uninhabited emptiness) body's self feels the invisibility of
engines moving on his flesh, almost over whom pouring are continually
distant trains."[8]

It was at moments like this that he could project himself, at age sixty-
seven, into a poem recreating an earlier self:

> who are you,little i
>
> (five or six years old)
> peering from some high
>
> window;at the gold
>
> of november sunset
>
> (and feeling:that if day
> has to become night
>
> this is a beautiful way)

The many selves were still here in 1962, the last year of his life. The
petit garçon was still very active. He went to the circus on Saturday, May
5, and drew elephants, trapeze artists, tightrope walkers.[9] The sexually
alert youth was still writing erotic poems:[10]

> N W
> o
> H
> s
> lOw
> h
> G
> My oD

The vociferous angry man was there too. One afternoon in May he
argued so hotly with Dorothy Case about Freud that he bit a piece out
of his tongue.[11] The sensitive artist was still chastising himself:

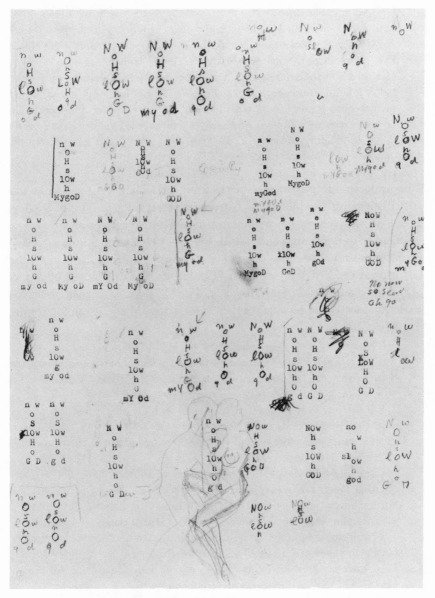

Working drafts of "n w." HOUGHTON LIBRARY

I never knew anyone as shy as me—today (cold March wind; sun in-&-outing) as I stood outside the wildanimalbars of WSq's NE playpen, sketching kids inside, became aware that the only sympathetique-looking Negro I've seen since UNamerica's hideous egalitarianism began (a vaguely glimpsed human darkness with sensitive eyes, sitting merely & to my right; sad & lonesome) was eagerly watching me. Instantly I stop—slamshutting my notebook & hurry away what I *wanted to do* was express my appreciation of his (obviously quite genuine) interest, by saying, "They're cute, aren't they" & nodding toward the children—but what I did was exactly the opposite & now, how I hate myself![12]

The understanding man who patronized individual young people was still dispensing kindness. He befriended and defended John Qualey, Elizabeth's mixed-up son who had dropped out of college and was now engaged in generational battle with his parents. The mellifluous-voiced reader of poetry was still occasionally in action. In March, he read for the last time at the YM-YWHA Poetry Center; he was introduced by a poet of the new generation, James Dickey. The old man concerned about his health and lessening powers was very much present and given to groping introspection:

wake, morning of 24th Jan., downstairs (it's 22 degrees outside) with the thought that my "impotence" was caused by The World ("popularity")—false values getting in between M & me.

—that my only salvation is to abandon wholly all previous schemes & systems (Groddeck, Jung, les Symbolistes, etc) & watch out for the dear, distinct uniqueness (the turn of the Spring worm in the earth) who's DIFFERENT: individual, here&now

spiritual—Marion, vs the Bitch Goddess of Success (R[agged] G[irl], etc) that I *must* take *wholly* seriously, as a symbol of My LIVING Self, the "little church (no great cathedral)" with her

standing erect in the deathless truth of His presence

(welcoming humbly His light and proudly His darkness) as against any Goethean superman figure of a stuffedshirt colossus

—that my *only social* thesis must = each individual being for him-or herself ALONE: a Whole—vs *all* (conforming)[13]

II

Joy Farm in these last years had been his Elysian Fields. His personality always underwent a softening after he arrived. He once wrote

Loren MacIver after a return to the farm: ". . . that Bad Kem-min-kz is Over the Hill; & a sweet-natured fellow (with chipmunk tendencies) has taken his place—for how long, personne ne sait."[14] He had less complaint now about "mechanism." He had electric wiring installed at the farm so that Marion could print photographs in the summer. This also meant she could have a refrigerator. The electric lights would be useful too in the future, especially since Mina Curtiss, Lincoln Kirstein's sister and a very old friend, arranged in 1962 to have a heating system installed at the farm so that they could stay on as late as December if they wished.

Elizabeth and Carlton came back every summer, so there was a Cummings family presence there at Silver Lake, as well as the old familiar places of Estlin's childhood. Elizabeth had been writing down the reminiscences of her own childhood and compiled them into a book, "When I Was a Little Girl." Estlin delighted in reading it and tried placing it with New York publishers where he had friends, but editors did not think its interest would extend to the general public. Elizabeth hoped, however, that her stories would inspire Estlin to write about the Joy Farm days himself.

Although the older generation of New Hampshire natives was dying off, their sons and daughters were becoming part of Cummings' summer life. Cliff Ward, Sam's boy, and young Roland Lyman, Bud Shackford, and others were repairing fireplaces, cutting wood, fixing roofs, and performing various services—and reminding Cummings of the ongoing replacement of human beings.

But the features of nonhuman nature interested him more. His letters from the summer are crammed with news about raccoons, deer, a red fox who chased crickets, a grey fox, a porcupine who taught her young one to eat apples, woodchucks, chipmunks who were threatened by a marauding cat (Estlin still had the Remington 38 that Watson had procured for him to arm himself against MacDermot and he was determined to use it to protect the chipmunks.) Birds became an important part of his summer life. He pored over Pearson's *Birds of America,* Mathews' *Fieldbook of Wild Birds* and Reed's *Bird Guide.* One Christmas Elizabeth sent him a phonograph recording of bird songs to help him identify their notes. Hummingbirds were Estlin's special bird pets. He would not allow himself to eat breakfast until he had filled their cups with sugar water. Gentleman Buzz and his lady then filled the air with grateful sound. The flowers in their succession were a shared joy for both Marion and himself; Marion was the chief flower gardener. But the old perennials and wild flowers were the principal pleasure-givers.

All of the natural phenomena swirled into one great symphony of sight and sound for him as soon as he arrived each May or June. A letter to Hildegarde describes one of these first-responses: "Humming-birds, a robin, phoebes, an indigo bunting, thrushes, a purple finch, swallows—buttercup, vetch, iris, sweet rocket & wild roses—backed by our seven mountains—what more could any human creature ask?"[15]

What indeed? The last entry Cummings made in any notebook, on September 2, 1962, was about flowers: "M's new delphiniums (which I preserved, with a wire cage, from woodchucks & alas! chipmunks) have long since lost their blue-glorious blossoms & gone to seed. But yester-day I noticed a lovely light-blue (& far smaller) blossomer who'd come to her beauty all alone!"[16] On that hot September afternoon, Cummings was out by the barn splitting wood. After he finished, he turned the grindstone and sharpened the axe, leaving it all ready for the next time, just as his father had taught him. He went inside and walked upstairs. Marion heard a fall and rushing up found him lying in the hall uncon-scious.[17] An ambulance took him to the hospital in North Conway. It was a brain hemorrhage. He died the following morning, September 3, at 1:15 A.M. All day the flags flew at half-staff in the town center at Madi-son.[18]

Marion was stunned with grief. Helpless to cope with funeral ar-rangements, she planned a private service in Boston. Mina Curtiss came in from the country and took care of her at the Copley-Plaza the day of the funeral. Only three or four people were present. Est-lin's grandchildren, Simon and Elizabeth Roosevelt, were the only rel-atives able to attend.[19] He was buried in Forest Hills Cemetery near his father and mother. He could no longer object to a return to Boston.

During the summer, Cummings had been gathering a group of poems for another book. Working through the sheaf of material and searching through periodicals for his published but uncollected poems, George Firmage helped Marion assemble an orderly volume, which be-came *73 Poems,* published by Harcourt Brace in 1963. The collection was made up of the usual mixture, with a heavier emphasis on poems dealing with the natural world, from the "rawrOO" of the morning cock to a "drea(chipmunk)ming." It is, on the whole, a peaceful book about birds and flowers, stars and moon, springtime and church bells, and it contains the last poem Cummings ever published in his lifetime,[20] one that could well serve as his epitaph:

                          one

                          t
                          hi
                          s

                          snowflake

                          (a
                            li
                              ght
                                  in
                          g)

                          is upon a gra

                          v
                          es
                          t

                          one

So passed from the joys and pains of his life one of America's unfor-
gettable poets. It is hard to imagine the development of poetry in mid-
twentieth century without him, although when truly original break-
throughs are achieved in any field of art or knowledge they seem not only
to come as a surprise but also to carry with them a sense of inevitability.
After Cummings burst upon the literary scene with his unique visual and
linguistic presentations in 1920, however, none of his imitators achieved
what he could do at his best when juggling a few words and their con-
stituent possibilities. The anthologies of American poetry will always
include him, whether the taste of the editor run to satire, singable lyric,
or linguistic play.

What has become gradually more clear as the years pass by is that,
although Cummings did not change his basic poetic styles during his
career, he mingled them and perfected them. Even though he was uncriti-
cal enough to publish some of his inferior efforts and to give more promi-
nence to his bagatelles than they deserved, he continued to create memo-
rable poems into his late sixties, long after the age at which many poets
lose their creative spark or become numb with the burdens and afflictions
of later life. However out of tune with his time he may have been in his

later years, he did not alter his principles of individualism or his habits of work. He managed to stay at his artistic task day after day, keeping his creative powers supple by persistent, though tiring, exercise, and he used whatever strategies of role-playing he felt necessary in order to keep himself productive—*petit garçon,* idealizing lover, scourge of conformity, worshipper of nature, judicious elder, or irascible old crank. What he produced will long amuse, titillate, thrill, provoke, or enthrall his readers, and the best of his work will continue to create that serenity which is the peculiar feature of aesthetic experience.

Chronological List of
E. E. Cummings' Works

Bibliographical Essay

George J. Firmage, *E. E. Cummings: A Bibliography* (Middletown, Conn.: Wesleyan University Press, 1960) is the authoritative bibliographical study. It contains a full descriptive bibliography of Cummings' writings and lists contributions to periodicals, translations of his writings, musical settings of poems, and recorded readings. Guy L. Rotella, *E. E. Cummings, A Reference Guide* (Boston: G. K. Hall, 1979) is the fullest and most accurate of the lists of criticism, and it gives a clear, concise summary of every important item.

The Cummings Collection at the Houghton Library, Harvard University, contains almost all of Cummings' papers that were in the author's possession at the time of his death, including his letters to his mother and father, carbon copies of most of the letters from the later years of his career, manuscripts, working drafts, notes, diaries, sketchbooks, travel notebooks, drawings, photographs, correspondence received, and the miscellaneous associational items of a lifetime. The books in Cummings' personal library that have his annotations are part of the collection. At Marion Morehouse's request, the diaries are sealed until 1991. A few similar batches of personal notes, such as records of his dreams while he was in psychoanalytic consultation with Dr. Fritz Wittels, fall under the same restriction.

The Humanities Research Center, University of Texas, has the next largest Cummings collection, chiefly manuscripts, notes, and academic materials associated with Cummings' childhood or his years at Cambridge Latin School and Harvard. The remainder of Cummings' personal library, including some books with marks and annotations, are also here. The Clifton Waller Barrett Library at the University of Virginia has manuscripts and drafts for several of Cummings' books, including *The Enormous Room, Eimi, Is 5,* and *No Thanks,* as well as his letters to S. A. Jacobs. His letters to John Dos Passos are in the Alderman Library, University of Virginia. The Princeton University Library holds Cummings' letters to Allen Tate and John Peale Bishop. The Yale University Library has a large body of important material in the *Dial* Collection, as well as Cummings' letters to Marianne Moore and Lincoln Kirstein. The Massachusetts Historical Society has Cummings' letters to Stewart Mitchell, as well as a sizable collection of papers and diaries of the Cummings family. Cummings' letters to Theodore Spencer are in the Harvard Archives, Harvard College Library.

The National Archives has three files that contain the complete documentation about Cummings' and Brown's imprisonment at La Ferté-Macé. Since they are difficult to locate I will give the specific references: 1) RG59, General Records of the Department of State, 1910–1929, Decimal File, 351.112B81; 2) RG84, Records of Foreign Service Posts of the United States, Correspondence, American Embassy Paris, 1917, Volume 28, "Cummings"; and 3) the same, 1918, Volume 53, "Cummings."

Although Cummings was a prolific letter writer and one who had a fascinating epistolary style, there has been only one published volume, rather limited in scope: *Selected Letters of E. E. Cummings,* F. W. Dupee and George Stade, eds. (New York: Harcourt Brace Jovanovich, 1969). An edition of Cummings' letters to his parents would illuminate in rich detail his early career. His letters to his sister and to his friends Sibley and Hildegarde Watson would do the same for his later years.

There is very little biographical publication on Cummings. Charles Norman, *E. E. Cummings: The Magic Maker* in all three of its editions (Macmillan, 1958; Duell, Sloane and Pearce, 1964; and Bobbs-Merrill, 1972), carries authority in its facts because Cummings himself read and corrected the manuscript of the earliest version. Cummings' *i: six nonlectures* (Cambridge: Harvard University Press, 1953) provides reminiscences of his early life. Nicholas Joost's books, *Scofield Thayer and The Dial* (Carbondale: Southern Illinois University Press, 1964) and *Years of Transition, The Dial 1912–1920* (Barre, Mass.: Barre Publishers, 1967) give good background for Cummings in the 1920s, as also does William Wasserstrom, *The Years of The Dial* (Syracuse: Syracuse University Press, 1963). J.P. Hallais' unpublished master's thesis "Facts and Fancies in *The Enormous Room,*" University of Rouen, contains valuable research on Cummings' imprisonment. George Wickes' *Americans in Paris 1903–1939* (New York: Doubleday, 1969) treats *The Enormous Room* as well as giving the best background on Cummings in France.

The only critical books on Cummings that are worthwhile are both by Norman Friedman, *E.E.Cummings: The Art of His Poetry* (Baltimore: Johns Hopkins Press, 1960) and *E. E. Cummings: The Growth of a Writer* (Carbondale: Southern Illinois University Press, 1964). The other book-length critical studies are either introductory or contain critical commentary that any educated reader could make. More valuable are the collections of critical essays. The Cummings issue of *Wake* (Spring 1976) contains memoirs and appreciations as well as Theodore Spencer's critical assessment of Cummings as a poet. S. V. Baum has collected a high-quality group of essays by various hands in *EΣTI:eec: E. E. Cummings and the Critics* (East Lansing: Michigan State University, 1962) and has prefaced the whole with his own perceptive study of Cummings' poetic techniques. Norman Friedman in *E. E. Cummings: A Collection of Critical Essays* (Englewood Cliffs, New Jersey: Prentice-Hall, 1972) has drawn together the best of the more recent critical studies, including Robert E. Maurer's outstanding discussion of Cummings' development as a poet, "Latter-Day Notes on E. E. Cummings' Language." The Cummings number of *The Journal of Modern Literature* (April 1979) reflects the latest trends in Cummings criticism: research on Cummings' early manuscripts in the Cummings Collection at the Houghton Library and study of Cummings' language habits by linguisticians.

This brings us to one book-length study that stands by itself, Irene Fairley, *E. E. Cummings & Ungrammar; a Study of Syntactic Deviance in His Poems* (Stamford, Conn.: Windmill Press, 1975). Fairley's linguistic analysis of Cummings' games with language takes an entirely new approach to the poems and demonstrates the extraordinary complexity of the statements they make.

In recent years, Rushworth Kidder has published several articles on the relationship between Cummings' painting and his poetry, the most important of which is "E. E. Cummings, Painter," *Harvard Library Bulletin* (April 1975). His book, *E. E. Cummings and Modern Art*, with a generous selection of illustrations in color, will, when it is published, allow readers a fuller knowledge of an area of Cummings' career that has been difficult to understand because his work has been little seen and never adequately reproduced.

Notes

The following abbreviations are used in the notes:

CP   *Complete Poems 1923–1962* (New York: Harcourt Brace Jovanovich, 1972).
EC   Edward Cummings, E. E. Cummings' father.
EEC   Edward Estlin Cummings.
EFC   Elizabeth Frances Cummings, E. E. Cummings' sister.
RHC   Rebecca Haswell Cummings, E. E. Cummings' mother.
HL   Houghton Library, Harvard University. (Call numbers are given for items in the Cummings' manuscript collection, e.g., bMS Am 1892.10.)
HRC,UT   Humanities Research Center, University of Texas.
NTA   Nancy T. Andrews, E. E. Cummings' daughter. Her poetry is published under the pen name, Nancy Cummings de Forêt.
RSK   Richard S. Kennedy.
SL   *Selected Letters of E. E. Cummings,* F. W. Dupee and George Stade, eds. (New York: Harcourt Brace Jovanovich, 1969).
T&C   *Tulips and Chimneys.*

I

An Introduction to Someone and anyone

1. Interview with RSK, September 1971.
2. *A Second Flowering,* (New York: Viking Press, 1973), p. 97.
3. Archibald MacLeish, quoted in Charles Norman, *E. E. Cummings: The Magic Maker* (New York: Bobbs-Merrill, 1972), p. 192; Cecily Angleton, interview with RSK, March 1978; Lincoln Kirstein, interview with RSK, March 1978; John Dos Passos, *The Best Times* (New York: New American Library, 1966), p. 84.
4. Letter to RSK, April 4, 1978.
5. *We Were Interrupted* (New York: Doubleday, 1947), pp. 188–89.

6. bMS Am 1823.1 (156), EEC to RHC, January 10, 1922.

7. bMS Am 1892.7 (149).

8. Dos Passos, *The Best Times,* p. 85.

9. "anyone lived in a pretty how town," *50 Poems,* 1940.

10. bMS Am 1823.1 (510), EEC to EFC, undated letter, number 67.

11. SL, p. 275.

II
Origins

1. bMS Am 1892.10.

2. E. E. Cummings *i: six nonlectures* (Cambridge, Mass.: Harvard University Press, 1953), p. 23.

3. Material on Cambridge in this chapter is based upon Arthur Gilman, ed., *The Cambridge of Eighteen and Ninety Six,* (Cambridge, Mass. 1896); Estelle M. H. Merrill, ed., *Cambridge Sketches by Cambridge Authors,* (Cambridge, Mass. 1896); "Reminiscences of Cambridge Days" by Mrs. Eliot Hubbard, Jr., and Mrs. Robert Cushman (unpublished manuscript); "Where the Old Professors Lived" by Mrs. Robert Cushman (unpublished manuscript); volumes of the *Proceedings of the Cambridge Historical Society;* and scattered references in the Cummings papers.

4. *And Gladly Teach* (Boston: Houghton Mifflin, 1935), p. 227.

5. Sherburn R. Merrill was the oldest son of Samuel and Fanny Bancroft Merrill (who was a native Scot and a relative of George Bancroft). He was born in Newbury, New Hampshire, January 2, 1810, and struggled manfully from the age of sixteen, at which time his father died, in farming, hauling, trading, shipping, and milling, until he reached a position of wealth and power in Coos County. His story, told in *The History of Coos County,* ed. Georgia Merrill, 1888, reads like the summary of a historical novel distributed by the Literary Guild.

6. EEC himself refers to this family tradition in *The Enormous Room* (1922; rpt. New York: Liveright, 1978), p. 11.

7. "Isaac Cummings of Topsfield, Mass., and Some of His Descendants," *The His-*

torical *Collections of The Topsfield Historical Society,* (Topsfield, 1899), 5: pp. 1–39.

8. Henry Ames Blood, *History of Temple, New Hampshire* (Boston: Rand and Avery, 1860), p. 117.

9. Information about Archelaus Cummings III is drawn from William H. Gifford, *Colebrook: A Place up back of New Hampshire* (Colebrook News and Sentinel, 1970) and from Merrill, *The History of Coos County.*

10. bMS Am 1892.10 (19).

11. Information about Edward Norris Cummings, including details about his uneventful service as a Quartermaster in the Union army, is based upon Gifford *Colebrook;* Merrill, *The History of Coos County;* Military Service Records (NNCC), National Archives, Washington, D.C.; *Soldiers and Sailors of New Hampshire in the War of the Rebellion,* 1861–1865 (Concord: Ira C. Evans, 1895); details from EFC; and from EEC's notes in Houghton Library.

12. bMS Am 1892.10 (19). Actually, the phrase, in Aunt Jane's family register, is "over the Cutler store." Edward Norris's first partner was Henry Cutler.

13. Information about Edward Cummings's early career is drawn from a press release by the South Congregational Church published in the *Boston Transcript* and the *Boston Herald,* August 21, 1900; newspaper accounts in the *Woburn News,* August 21, 1900, *Boston Advertiser* October 8, 1900, and *Boston Herald,* November 21, 1913; a newspaper interview by Edith Talbot, July 8, 1916, and other newspaper clippings in the Harvard University Archives; the Unitarian Yearbook, 1927–28; interviews with EFC and others who knew him; and various materials in the Cummings papers.

14. Edward Cummings *The Layman's Answer,* chosen by the Unitarian Layman's League as one of the three best sermons preached June 1919, on the general subject "Unitarianism, What It Means and What It Can Do under Existing Conditions for the Help of Mankind." Published in pamphlet form, Boston, 1920. A copy is in the Andover-Harvard Divinity School Library.

15. I have skipped over many details here. He spent a term in the Harvard Law

School in 1883 before entering Divinity School. He was a graduate assistant in Elocution at Harvard during his two years in Divinity School. He received an A.M. degree in 1885 and became a graduate assistant in the English department teaching composition and forensics, but studied social science on the side. He held an appointment as instructor in English for one year, 1887–1888, and continued his sociological studies until he was awarded the Robert Treat Paine Traveling Fellowship. Upon his return from his European investigations of cooperatives, labor organizations, and charitable institutions in 1891 he was appointed an instructor in Political Economy (for Harvard had no faculty titles in Sociology) and he taught the first course in The Principles of Sociology ever offered at Harvard. The following year when the Department of Political Economy changed its name to the Department of Economics, his own faculty title was changed to instructor in Sociology, although he remained in the Department of Economics.

16. Information on Edward Cummings' sermons and other writings is drawn from manuscript materials which I examined when they were in the possession of Marion Morehouse.

17. *i: six nonlectures*, p. 9.

18. Philip Smith, interview with RSK, October 1978.

19. bMS Am 1823.9 (68), EFC, "When I Was a Little Girl," an unpublished memoir of her childhood years.

20. Information about RHC's ancestors is drawn from Louise Diman, *Leaves from a Family Tree* (Providence: Roger Williams Press, 1941); John Sparago, *Anthony Haswell, Printer-Patriot Balladeer* (Rutland, Vermont: Tuttle Co., 1925); and F. W. Horway, "A Short Account of Robert Haswell," *Washington Historical Quarterly*, 24 (1933): 83–90.

21. Diman, *Leaves*, p. 83.

22. Diman, *Leaves*, p. 114.

23. The little that is known about the Hanson side of the family emerged after Rebecca's death, when Elizabeth found some letters and pictures locked in the false top of Rebecca's jewel case. It appears that John Hanson, son of Tobias

Hanson, a tailor, was born in Salem, Massachusetts, September 25, 1810. He married Mary L. Clarke, his second wife, September 28, 1858. Details are in bMS Am 1892 (707), EFC to EEC, September 3 and 14, 1948, along with an enclosed letter from Anna Bumstead to RHC, January 28, 1903; and in bMS Am 1892.13 (321), EEC to EFC, September 7, 1948. Mary Clarke Hanson's diary, 1864–1871, is in the Massachusetts Historical Society, but in her entires she seems very loving toward her husband, "Mr. Hanson."

24. EFC, "When I Was a Little Girl."

III

The Realm of the Goat-footed Balloonman

1. bMS Am 1892.10 (21).

2. The name actually has Unitarian connections going back to the Rev. John Prior Estlin, a Unitarian leader in Bristol who was Coleridge's friend and religious advisor, bMS Am 1892.4, Marie Estlin Helms to RHC, September 21, 1936.

3. bMS Am 1892.10 (21) and Am 1823.9 (60).

4. Antoinette F. Downing, Elisabeth MacDougall, and Eleanor Pearson, *Survey of Architectural History in Cambridge, Report Two: Mid Cambridge* (Cambridge Historical Commission, 1967).

5. CP, p. 352.

6. Details of the house are based on EEC's annotated floor plan and his notes bMS Am 1892.7, Cambridge, and on my own visit to the house through the courtesy of Dr. Eleanor Wagner.

7. Information about the neighborhood activities comes from bMS Am 1892.7, Cambridge; from EFC, "When I Was a Little Girl"; and from interviews with Robert Cushman, Esther Lanman Cushman, Elizabeth Thaxter Hubbard, and Franklin Hammond. I am especially grateful to Mrs. Cushman for allowing me to read her childhood diary.

8. bMS Am 1892.7 and 1892.8.

9. Charles F. Whiting, "Francis Avenue and the Norton Estate: The Development of a Community," *Cambridge His-*

torical Society: Proceedings for the Years 1967–69, 41: 16–39.

10. Information about Joy Farm is drawn from bMS Am 1923.9 (16), Joy Farm Log, 6 volumes; bMS Am 1892.7 (89), New Hampshire; EFC, "When I Was a Little Girl"; and my visit to the farm in 1964 through the courtesy of Marion Morehouse.

11. bMS Am 1892.7 (89), New Hampshire.

12. bMS Am 1823.9 (16), Joy Farm Log, Volume II. Educators were cookies.

13. All the following quotations are from bMS Am 1823.7 (2a), Journal for 1900–01–02.

14. Information about the Cambridge Schools and their requirements is based on the Annual Reports of the School Committee and Superintendent of Schools, 1900–1911.

15. EFC makes this statement in "When I Was a Little Girl." On the other hand, her mother's datebook, bMS Am 1892.10 (25), records for October 3, "Elizabeth Frances went to school for 1st time in her life 1910 (Buckingham School)." She was nine years old at that time.

16. The earliest surviving report cards for 1902–03 and 1903–04 are in HRC, UT.

17. bMS Am 1892.10 (11).

18. bMS Am 1892.7 (177).

19. Ibid.

20. See, for example, "come, gaze with me," CP, p. 273; "Poem, or Beauty Hurts Mr. Vinal," CP, p. 230; and "next to of course god america i/love you," CP, p. 268.

21. A pleasant reminiscence of the Peabody School may be found in Richard C. Evarts, "The Class of 1903," *Cambridge Historical Society: Proceedings for the Years 1967–69*, 41:132–140.

22. bMS Am 1892.7, Academic Notes, and HRC, UT, School Essays.

23. bMS Am 1892.7, Academic Notes.

24. SL, p. 95.

25. HRC, UT, Graduation Program, Peabody School.

26. The information about EEC's early reading has been drawn from the Joy Farm Log; bMS Am 1892.7, Cambridge; bMS Am 1823.4 (103 and 104), Notes for nonlectures; and elsewhere in the Cummings papers. Some of the actual volumes he read have been preserved. See, for example, Houghton Library

69C-135, 236, and 294. Others are in HRC, UT.

27. bMS Am 1823.6 (27).

28. bMS Am 1892.7, Cambridge.

29. bMS Am 1823.7 (5) and 1892.8 (1).

30. bMS Am 1823.7 (1) and 1892.8 (1).

31. bMS Am 1823.7 (1).

32. All these stories and pictures, and those which follow, are found in bMS Am 1892.6, 1892.7, and 1892.8. A typescript of the story of Sir Gareth is in HRC, UT.

IV
Longfellow's Latest Disciple

1. bMS Am 1892.10 (13).

2. bMS Am 1892.10 (24).

3. bMS Am 1892.10 (21).

4. bMS Am 1823.7 (2a).

5. bMS Am 1892.

6. bMS Am 1892.10 (21).

7. bMS Am 1892.

8. bMS Am 1892.10 (21).

9. English High provided programs for girls in the commercial course, the normal (preparing for teacher training) course, and the domestic science course. Nearby Rindge Manual Training School provided the vocational programs for boys.

10. bMS Am 1892.7, Cambridge.

11. The account of Cummings' studies is based upon bMS Am 1823.8 (33), his application for admission to Harvard; the Annual Report of the School Committee and Superintendent of Schools, Cambridge, for 1902 which describes the Latin School program in detail; his official record at the School; interviews with Cecil T. Derry and Robert Cawley; and information scattered among the Cummings papers.

12. The School Committee report prescribes a course in History of England, but Cummings' application indicates that he used George Willis Botsford, *Ancient History* in his first-year study of history.

13. If he had followed the five-year program, he would have taken physics or chemistry.

14. His well-worn copy is in the Harvard Collection, 69C-56.

15. John Williams White, *The First Greek Book* (Boston: Ginn and Co., 1896).
16. Interviews with Cecil T. Derry and Joseph MacCarthy; *Cambridge Chronicle,* July 30, 1970.
17. Copies of the *Cambridge Review* containing all of Cummings' publications (and some with his annotations) are in HRC, UT. The issue for January 1910, containing "The Little Quarter," is also in bMS Am 1892.11, F.
18. bMS Am 1892.7, Cambridge.
19. Ibid.
20. bMS Am 1823.7 (5a)
21. Ibid.
22. bMS Am 1892.
23. bMS Am 1892.
24. It is clear that Cummings had a copy of the American edition, edited with three additional chapters on the sonnet and on the French forms by Arthur Penn (New York: D. Appleton, 1882).
25. bMS Am 1892.5 (632).
26. bMS Am 1892.5 (200).
27. bMS Am 1892.
28. bMS Am 1892.5 (172).
29. HRC, UT, dated July 20; bMS Am 1892.5 (174), no date but on Joy Farm stationery. The last summer the Cummings family spent at Joy Farm was 1910.
30. bMS Am 1892.6 (20).
31. All poems are in bMS Am 1892.5.
32. HRC, UT, Poems and Stray Thoughts.
33. bMS Am 1892.5 (178).
34. bMS Am 1892.5 (31) and (378).
35. bMS Am 1823.9 (16).
36. HRC, UT, Poems, Works.
37. bMS Am 1823.9 (68).
38. HRC, UT, Rex.
39. bMS Am 1823.9 (16), Vol. VI.
40. A copy of the program is in HRC, UT.
41. HRC, UT, Poems, Works.

V
The Harvard Experience: Studies

1. Samuel Eliot Morison, ed., *The Development of Harvard University 1869–1929* (Cambridge: Harvard University Press, 1930), pp. xxiii–i.
2. bMS Am 1892 (598), Theodore A. Miller to EEC, October 11, 1914.
3. For a more extended study of Cummings' college education, see my article, "E. E. Cummings at Harvard: Studies," *Harvard Library Bulletin,* 24 (July 1976): 267–297.
4. bMS Am 1892.5 (742).
5. Keats to Benjamin Bailey, November 22, 1817.
6. bMS Am 1892 (598), August 14, 1912.
7. HL 69c-257, 7, and 7a.
8. For example in *The Greek Anthology:* "But if the while I think on thee, dear friend,/All losses are restored and sorrows end./To my dear friend Estlin Cummings on his 19th birthday October 14, 1913."
9. *i: six nonlectures* (Cambridge: Harvard University Press, 1953), p. 25.
10. bMS Am 1892 (598), Letters, Theodore A. Miller to EEC; 1892.4 (104), (106), Notes for nonlectures; 1892.7 (4), Sketchbook. Although Miller was always inviting EEC to visit him in Rochester or in Princeton, EEC never accepted these invitations. The friendship waned. Miller died early—June 30, 1929 in Paris.
11. bMS Am 1892.7, Class Notes; and HRC, UT, Cummings, Misc., Harvard Course Notes.
12. His professor was perhaps Clifford H. Moore, the editor of his textbook, *Horace The Odes, Epodes, and Carmen Seculare* (New York: American Book, 1902). EEC's copy is HL 69c-163.
13. bMS Am 1892.5 (742). The typescript has the error "leas."
14. Ibid.
15. Ibid.
16. Boston: Heath, 1913. EEC's copy is HL 69c-143.
17. New York: Duffield and Co., 1916.
18. Constant Southworth to RSK, September 8, 1970. Southworth was not one of the sleepers.
19. bMS Am 1823.7 (23).
20. He mentions having read "Chrétien de Troyes, Marie de France, and Tristan & Iseult," bMS Am 1892.7.
21. A rather solemn biography of this fascinating man is C. K. Hyder, *George Lyman Kittredge* (Lawrence: University of Kansas Press, 1962).
22. bMS Am 1823.4 (104).
23. UT, HRC, Cummings, Misc., Harvard Course Notes.

24. Paul Brooks and T. Gordon Upton (Cambridge: Harvard Lampoon, 1931).

25. Letter to RSK, August 30, 1970.

26. bMS Am 1823.7 (23), p. 136.

27. Boston: Houghton Mifflin, 1902. EEC's copy is HL 69c-228.

28. Harvard Archives, HUC 8913.315.12, G. H. Shaw's notes for Comparative Literature 12, 1913–14.

29. bMS Am 1892.6.

30. HRC, UT. Cummings, Works.

31. Morison, *Development of Harvard*, p. 76.

32. It is with a nostalgic flourish that I include Knibbs, the author of one of my favorite books from grammar school days, *The Riding Kid from Powder River.*

33. HRC, UT, Cummings, Misc., English Notebook. In EEC's handwriting, the man's name is indecipherable—something like Hinchman.

34. *i: six nonlectures*, pp. 29–30.

35. Published in *Harvard Monthly*, 55 (February 1913): 170.

36. Published in *Harvard Monthly*, 60 (April 1915): 37.

37. bMS Am 1892, August 5, 1913.

38. Rollo Walter Brown, *Dean Briggs* (New York: Harper, 1926), p. 57. Brown gives a fully detailed account of his career and of the students' love and admiration for him.

39. "P. S. to Dean Briggs" in Brooks Atkinson, ed., *College in a Yard* (Cambridge: Harvard University Press, 1957).

40. bMS Am 1892.6 (114).

41. bMS Am 1892.6 (124).

42. bMS Am 1892.6, "The Young Man," an allegory in a Greek setting, about Death visiting a tyrant, written March 1, 1915.

43. bMS Am 1892.6 (94).

44. Published in *Harvard Monthly*, 60 (July 1915): 132–136.

45. bMS Am 1892.6 (84).

VI

The Harvard Experience:
Verse, Friends, Rebellion

1. HRC, UT, Cummings, Workbook, dated February 1, 1912. For a more detailed treatment of Cummings' development during these years, see my article, "E. E. Cummings at Harvard: Verse, Friends, Rebellion," *Harvard Library Bulletin* 25 (July 1977): 253–291.

2. HRC, UT, Cummings, Works, "A World of Men and Women."

3. HRC, UT, Cummings, Workbook.

4. bMS Am 1892.5 (3).

5. bMS Am 1892.5 (505), dated August 1912. Miller's letter, bMS Am 1892 (598), August 27 [1912].

6. Published in *Harvard Advocate* 95 (March 21, 1913): 25–56. Cummings made a few changes in phrasing, such as "drowsy-fair" for "milky-fair" when he included it in *T & C.*

7. bMS Am 1892, May 16, 1913.

8. In his term paper for Fine Arts 9b "The Significance of El Greco," Cummings elaborated on the "modernism."

9. bMS Am 1892.5 (71).

10. See Dos Passos' "Camera Eye (25)" in *The 42nd Parallel,* (New York: Harper's, 1930) in which he offers a sardonic summary of his studies at Harvard. The best picture of young Dos Passos is found in Townsend Ludington, ed., *The Fourteenth Chronicle, Letters and Diaries of John Dos Passos* (Boston: Gambit Inc., 1973).

11. bMS Am 1892.7 (90), Notes for nonlectures.

12. New York: John Lane, 1915, Houghton Library, 69c-312.

13. *Harvard Monthly*, 62 (June 1916): 123. The best account of Thayer is Nicholas Joost, *Scofield Thayer and the Dial* (Carbondale: Southern Illinois University Press, 1964).

14. bMS Am 1892.5 (495).

15. bMS Am 1892, April 2, 1913.

16. Published in *Harvard Monthly*, 59 (December 1914): 86–99. It is likely that they objected to the fact that the Radcliffe girl in the story was the mistress of a middle-aged man and also that she took off her dress, a theatrical costume, while she talked to the young Harvard student.

17. I perhaps should add another item of information that has literary significance. He was the central figure in a tragic accident that formed the basis for "The Camera Eye (20)" in Dos Passos' *The 42nd Parallel.* He and his classmate, Merle Britten, became strike-breaking

motormen during a street car strike in Boston. On July 4, 1912, while Wilson was moving his car in the City Point carbarn, he accidently killed Britten, whose head was crushed between two cars. (*Boston Daily Globe*, July 5, 1912.) I am indebted to Ruth Marshall of the Boston Public Library for help in gathering the details of this terrible story.

In later years Wilson became a painter in Rockport, Massachusetts, and changed his name to A. Winslow Wilson.

18. HRC, UT, Cummings, Workbook.

19. *Harvard Monthly*, 62 (March 1916): 8–9. Later published in *T & C*.

20. bMS 1892.6.

21. The essay reflects not only his reading of Wright's *Modern Art* but also Arthur Jerome Eddy's *Cubism and Post-Impressionism* (Chicago: McClurg, 1914), from which he took profuse notes.

22. The text of the commencement part is published in George Firmage, ed., *A Miscellany Revised* (New York: October House, 1965), pp. 5–11.

23. bMS Am 1892.7 (90).

24. bMS Am 1892.7, Note to an unidentified correspondent, probably Dean Briggs.

25. bMS Am 1892.7 (90).

26. An informal history is given in Richard W. Hall, "Recollections of the Cambridge Social Dramatic Club," *Proceedings of the Cambridge Historical Society* 38 (1961): 51–67. Miss de Gozzaldi is now Mrs. Richard Hall. I am grateful to her for her reminiscences of Cummings.

27. *Harvard Monthly*, 54 (June 1913):128.

28. bMS Am 1892, May 10, 1915.

29. bMS Am 1823.7 (23), 199–200; AMS version entitled "Doris," 102.

30. Ibid., 101.

31. bMS Am 1892, September 15 [1915].

32. bMS Am 1892.7, Cambridge.

33. bMS Am 1892.7, Notes dated "December 21."

34. bMS Am 1892.7, Cambridge.

35. bMS Am 1892.5 (601).

36. bMS Am 1892.7, Miscellaneous Notes.

37. I am grateful to Miss Mary Meehan of the Harvard University Archives for digging out Brigg's class list.

38. Dudley Poore to RSK, August 10, 1975.

39. bMS Am 1892.5 (750), Poems written for classes; and HRC, UT, Cummings, Poems for College Composition Class.

40. bMS Am 1823.7 (23) 104; HRC, UT, Cummings, Poems for College Composition Classes; and bMS Am 1892.5 (237).

41. bMS Am 1892.5 (730). Cummings worked this over in several versions before publishing it in *T & C*. For a full discussion of them, see Irene Fairley, "Syntactic Deviation and Cohesion," *Language and Style* 6 (1973): 216–229.

42. bMS Am 1823.7 (21), 184. Healy's Palace was at 642 Washington Street.

43. HRC, UT, Cummings, Miscellaneous.

44. bMS Am 1892.5 (476).

45. HRC, UT, Cummings, Miscellaneous.

46. bMS Am 1823.5 (165).

47. bMS Am 1823.5 (358). For the final version, see CP, p. 51.

48. bMS Am 1823.7 (21), 7. An earlier version somewhat longer and rougher is bMS Am 1823.7 (25), 203. For the final version, see CP, p. 61.

49. Cummings turned this reversal around again when the poem was published in the *Dial*, 67 (May 1920): 582, much to the distress of Edward Cummings, who wrote to him objecting to the word "slobber."

50. bMS Am 1823.5 (354).

51. bMS Am 1892.7, Cambridge.

52. *i: six nonlectures*, pp. 8–9.

53. bMS Am 1892.7, Cambridge.

54. bMS Am 1892.7, Notes beginning "By the family."

55. bMS Am 1892.7, Cambridge.

56. bMS Am 1892.5 (375).

57. bMS Am 1892.7, Cambridge.

58. Ibid.

59. bMS Am 1823.4 (104), Notes for nonlectures.

VII

The Poet Finds
a Patron

1. A good account of the whole transaction is found in Charles Norman, *E. E. Cummings The Magic Maker* (New York: Bobbs-Merrill, 1972), pp. 50–64.

2. bMS Am 1892.7 (90), Notes for nonlectures.

3. *Des Imagistes* (New York: Albert and Charles Boni, 1914).
4. bMS Am 1823.4 (104), Notes for nonlectures.
5. *Paradise Lost*, IX, pp. 427–433. Norman, p. 39, confirms my sense of association with Milton.
6. bMS Am 1823.5 (146).
7. In the various early typescripts of these poems, "Crepuscule" is the only one which uses the "i." It appears in the third and tenth lines.
8. bMS Am 1892.4 (121)., November 29, 1929. Cummings revealed the source of the small "i" in an interview with Harvey Breit, "Talk with E. E. Cummings," *New York Times*, December 31, 1950, p. 10.
9. CP, p. 568.
10. bMS Am 1892.7, (23).
11. SL, p. 13.
12. Letter to RSK, October 27, 1978.
13. bMS Am 1823.5 (760).

VIII

The Emergent Styles

1. bMS Am 1892.7, Miscellaneous Notes [for a poetic theory, p. 4].
2. bMS Am 1823.7 (23), p. 208.
3. bMS Am 1823.7 (21), p. 8.
4. bMS Am 1823.7 (21), p. 1.
5. bMS Am 1823.7 (23), p. 44 Verso.
6. bMS Am 1823.7 (23), p. 44.
7. bMS Am 1823.7 (23), p. 150.
8. bMS Am 1823.7 (23), p. 142.
9. bMS Am 1823.7 (23), p. 201.
10. bMS Am 1823.5 (359).
11. bMS Am 1892.5 (760).
12. bMS Am 1823.7 (22), p. 73. For a more extended discussion of EEC's experiments, see my article, "E. E. Cummings: The Emergent Styles, 1916," *Journal of Modern Literature*, 7 (April 1979).
13. bMS Am 1823.7 (22), p. 95.
14. bMS Am 1823.7 (18).
15. E. E. Cummings, "Three Poems in the Modernist Manner," *Vanity Fair*, 21 (December 1923):160.
16. bMS Am 1823.7 (23), p. 139.
17. bMS Am 1892.7, Miscellaneous notes.
18. Ibid. [for a poetic theory, p. 4a].
19. bMS Am 1823.1 (156), January 2, 1917.
20. bMS Am 1823.7 (21), 120. Rushworth Kidder, in a brilliant article, "Buffalo Bill's —an Early Cummings Manuscript," *Harvard Library Bulletin*, 4 (October 1976), 373–380, has identified the newspaper and reproduced the two work sheets.
21. bMS Am 1823.7 (21), 80.
22. bMS Am 1823.1 (156), January 2, 1917.
23. bMS Am 1892, Dillwyn Parrish to EEC [undated, mid-1917].
24. bMS Am 1823.1 (156), March 18, 1917.
25. bMS Am 1892.1, EEC to F. J. Reynolds.
26. bMS Am 1823.1 (156), March 13, 1917.
27. bMS Am 1892, Dillwyn Parrish to EEC [undated, mid-1917].
28. bMS Am 1823.1 (156), April 2, 1917.

IX

The Pacifist Warrior, 1917

1. For a full discussion of his theology, see my article, "Edward Cummings, The Father of the Poet," *Bulletin of the New York Public Library*, 70 (1966): 437–449.
2. Published in *Poems 1905–1962*, (London: Marchim Press, 1973) p. 616.
3. bMS Am 1892.5 (729).
4. Sheets and working notes for a five-stanza poem are in bMS Am 1892.5 (729). The five-stanza version that he wrote for Briggs is in HRC, UT: Cummings, Works, Poems for College Composition Classes.
5. bMS Am 1892.5 (760).
6. Samuel Eliot Morison, *Three Centuries of Harvard 1636–1936* (Cambridge: Harvard University Press, 1946), pp. 450–457.
7. The articles ran from October 1914 to April 1915. When the United States declared war on Germany, the editorial board was split between patriots and pacifists. As a result, the magazine ceased publication.
8. HRC, UT, Cummings, Works, Poems for College Composition Classes.
9. Ibid.
10. bMS Am 1892, February 6, 1917.
11. bMS Am 1823.10 (12), Edward Cummings to EEC, May 25, 1917.
12. bMS Am 1823.1 (152), [April 18, 1917]. EEC's letter to Eliot Norton volunteering for Norton-Harjes is dated April 7, 1917, Houghton Library, H 795. 148.25 F, Bx 18 (370), Richard Norton papers.

13. bMS Am 1823 (296), [April 28, 1917].

14. bMS Am 1823.7 (18), p. 6.

15. Ibid., p. 4.

16. The details of the account of Cummings and Brown in Paris are drawn from bMS Am 1823.7 (7) to (20), Sketchbooks, and 1892.7 (122) to (147), Notebooks; from letters to his parents; and from an interview with William Slater Brown, September 3, 1971. The detail about seeing Satie's ballet is from George Wickes's wonderful book, *Americans in Paris* (New York: Doubleday, 1969), p. 70.

17. SL, p. 25.

18. HRC, UT, EEC to Dillwyn Parrish, May 12, 1917.

19. Ibid.

20. SL, p. 27.

21. bMS Am 1892.7, Cambridge.

22. bMS Am 1892.7 (181) to (185).

23. bMS Am 1892.7 (137). See also (81).

24. Ibid.

25. Ibid. See also bMS Am 1823.7 (17). Later published as one of the "Sonnets-Realities" in *T&C*.

26. From a draft of the letter in his sketchbook, bMS Am 1823.7 (19).

27. bMS Am 1823.1 (156), [July 18, 1917].

28. Letter to RSK, November 28, 1978.

29. Georgia Slater Bartlett to RHC, September 16, 1917, in which she quotes from Brown's letter of August 19, 1917. Massachusetts Historical Society Manuscripts, "Cummings." The French inscription reads, "Respect the mutilated Virgin because she cannot defend herself."

30. SL, p. 36. "The present head of the section, formerly sub-head, is a rather stupid man without education." [About Richard Norton]: "A skinny man, rather lofty, who talks without moving his mouth, has one eye blocked by a monocle; in a word, a pleasant ass and without reason for existence . . . shit for him."

31. There is uncertainty about exactly what the letter said. Richard Norton's summary of the letter, published in the Norton Critical Edition of *The Enormous Room*, contradicts what Cummings says in ER, p. 18.

32. Houghton Library, H 795.148.25 F, Bx 18 (370), Richard Norton Papers.

33. National Archives, RG84, American Embassy, Paris, Vol. 28. Norman prints in full the three censored letters that Brown wrote, *E. E. Cummings*, pp. 83–88.

34. Houghton Library, H 795.148.25 F, Bx 18 (378). "Notes on Mr. Anderson's verbal report to Mr. Norton," Richard Norton Papers.

35. ER, p. 14.

36. The details of the account of Cummings and Brown at La Ferté-Macé are drawn from J. P. Hallais, "Facts and Fancy in the Enormous Room," (Master's thesis, University of Rouen 1970); interview, William Slater Brown with RSK, September 3, 1971, plus Brown's letters and his annotation of the Hallais thesis; my visits to La Ferté-Macé; and, of course, Cummings own account in ER.

37. SL, p. 38.

38. ER, p. 128.

39. bMS Am 1892, November 29, 1917.

40. bMS Am 1823.7 (19).

41. bMS Am 1823.7 (17).

42. bMS Am 1892, Brentano's Bookstore to EEC, December 6, 1917. The books are now in HRC, UT.

43. bMS Am 1892, September 28, 1917.

44. It is uncertain just when during late 1917 the book appeared. Although Gomme says in August (Norman, *E. E. Cummings*, p. 64), RHC in a letter, December 7, 1917, reported that the family had just received their first copies of the book from Gomme.

45. bMS Am 1823.10 (38).

46. bMS Am 1823.10 (12), October 18, 1917.

47. bMS Am 1823.10 (9), October 17, 1917. A very full account of Edward Cummings' correspondence with Paris and Washington will be found in the Norton Critical Edition of *The Enormous Room*.

48. bMS Am 1823.10 (28), a pencil draft, later misdated October 18 in another hand.

49. SL, pp. 39–40.

50. bMS Am 1823.10 (38).

51. bMS Am 1892 (196), November 23, 1917.

52. bMS Am 1892 (193), November 29, 1917.

53. SL, p. 40.

54. Hallais, p. 11.

55. December 10, 1917. This letter was discovered by Professor J. P. Vernier of the University of Rouen. He has published it in the *Journal of Modern Literature*, April 1979.

56. Hallais, p. 43. These are Hallais' words as he summarized the official's report.
57. Hallais, p. 13.
58. bMS Am 1892.7 (124), Paris notebook, Bloc-memo. A draft of the letter to Marie Louise in pencil is so faint and illegible that not all of its sentences are readable.
59. bMS Am 1892.7 (5), 18. The early draft is bMS Am 1892.7 (127), Paris notebook, Bloc-memo.
60. bMS Am 1892.7 (124), Paris notebook, Bloc-memo. "If you think that I have forgotten the days and nights that we spent together, you are mistaken, Marie Louise.... Until my return, accept these kisses."
61. CP, p. 120.

X

A Wartime Interlude

1. bMS Am 1823.10 (14), February 20, 1918.
2. bMS Am 1823 (296), EC to EEC, March 19, 1918, and November 28, 1919.
3. bMS Am 1823.7 (23), 149. "And everyone will always be dancing, singing, and getting drunk on the most costly nectar, to the sound of golden harps of my very own orchestra which plays in the heavenly cafe all night long, including Sundays."
4. bMS Am 1823.7 (23), 83.
5. bMS Am 1823.7 (17), 40.
6. "You aren't Mad, Am I," George J. Firmage, ed., *A Miscellany Revised*, (New York: October House, 1965), p. 128.
7. HRC, UT, February 17, 1934. It was probably Brown, not Dos Passos who accompanied him.
8. bMS Am 1823.1 (156), June 14, 1918.
9. bMS Am 1823.1 (152), June 26, 1918.
10. SL, p. 49.
11. bMS Am 1823.7 (21), 134.
12. Later published in *&*, 1925.
13. Later published in *XLI Poems*, 1925.
14. bMS Am 1823.7 (23), 162.
15. Both published in *&*, 1925.
16. bMS Am 1823.7 (21).116.
17. bMS Am 1823.7 (21), 223.
18. bMS Am 1892, May 31, 1918.
19. SL, pp. 47–48.

20. bMS Am 1823 (296).
21. Quoted in John B. McMaster, *The United States in the World War, 1918–1920* (New York: Appleton, 1920) p. 35.
22. bMS Am 1823.1 (152), May 24, 1918.
23. bMS Am 1823.1 (156), April 15, 1918.
24. SL, p. 47.
25. bMS Am 1823.7 (23), 151.

XI

Private Cummings, 1918

1. BMS Am 1823.4 (104), Notes for nonlectures.
2. bMS Am 1823.1 (156), July 29, 1918.
3. bMS Am 1823.1 (156), August 31, 1918.
4. bMS Am 1823.1 (156), July 29, 1918.
5. bMS Am 1823.4 (104), Notes for nonlectures. EEC exaggerated about Perry. A letter from Perry to EEC is still extant in the Harvard Library.
6. SL, p. 49.
7. SL, p. 53.
8. SL, p. 51.
9. bMS Am 1823.1 (156) EEC to Charles Anderson, December 31, 1918.
10. SL, p. 52. I have translated the second sentence from French into English.
11. EEC's footnote, "Grk: $\pi o \iota \eta \tau o \varsigma$" poetry.
12. bMS Am 1892.7 (69), draft of letter to unknown correspondent, fall 1918.
13. bMS Am 1892.7 (70). In later years, Cummings forgot the admiration he had once had for Nijinsky. He remarked once to his daughter that "Nijinsky was a zero."
14. bMS Am 1892.7 (122).
15. bMS Am 1892.7 (70).
16. Ibid.
17. Ibid.
18. Ibid.
19. Later published in *XLI Poems*, 1925.
20. Ibid.
21. bMS Am 1892, November 1, 1918.
22. Later published in *&*, 1925.
23. Several pages of his La Ferté-Macé notebook have lists of this sort, bMS Am 1823.7 (17).
24. bMS Am 1892.7 (69).
25. Later published in *&*, 1925.
26. bMS Am 1892.7 (69), draft, fall 1918.
27. All published later in *&*, 1925.
28. bMS Am 1892.7 (69).

29. Phrases from sonnets published in *&*, 1925.
30. bMS Am 1892.7 (69).
31. Poems published later in *&* and *XLI Poems*, 1925.
32. bMS Am 1823.1 (56), ECC to Charles Anderson, December 31, 1918.
33. bMS Am 1892, October 5, 1918.
34. bMS Am 1892, November 8, 1918.
35. Later published in *XLI Poems*, 1925.
36. EEC to EC, January 13, 1919, SL, p. 55.

XII
Elaine

1. bMS Am 1823.1 (156), EEC to RHC, March 15, 1924.
2. Details of the story of Cummings and his first wife are drawn from interviews with Elaine Orr MacDermot, Sibley Watson, Slater Brown, and Nancy Thayer Andrews and from letters and notes among the Cummings papers.
3. I am grateful to J. W. Nystrom, President of Bennett College, for information about Elaine Orr at Miss Bennett's school.
4. bMS Am 1892.5 (405).
5. bMS Am 1892 (861), Scofield Thayer to EEC, September 13, 1916.
6. Caroline F. Ware, *Greenwich Village, 1920–1930*, (New York: Harper, 1935), pp. 235–263.
7. John Dos Passos, *The Best Times* (New York: New American Library, 1966), p. 82.
8. bMS Am 1892 (545), Elaine to EEC, November 9, 1924.
9. Ibid. (861), Scofield Thayer to EEC, May 21, 1918.
10. These and other poems were found in EEC's Camp Devens notebook, bMS Am 1892.7 (122) or were among a group of thirty-four poems found in Elaine MacDermot's papers after her death.
11. bMS Am 1892.7 (69).
12. bMS Am 1892 (861), Scofield Thayer to EEC, September 11, 1918. The rendezvous took place in Boston at the Hotel Touraine.
13. Found among Elaine MacDermot's papers.

14. Thayer and his friends disliked Roosevelt because he so actively espoused the entry of the United States into the European war.
15. The Y.M.C.A. stationery at Camp Devens had a motto printed at the top "With the Colors." EEC apparently wrote "premeditated?" after it as a joke at his own expense (since he was trapped by his own volunteering for the 12th Infantry Division).
16. bMS Am 1892, Slater Brown to EEC, undated, ca. January 6, 1919. Lucretius's poem *De Rerum Natura* presents his theory of the atomic make-up of matter.
17. bMS Am 1892.7 (69). The Watsons now lived near Elaine at 6 Washington Square.
18. bMS Am 1892 (545), Elaine to EEC, undated letter, fall 1918.
19. Cummings later apparently forgot about this. Nancy states "he told me about that early time as if he had not known she *contemplated* abortion," NTA to RSK, December 2, 1978.
20. bMS Am 1823.1 (152), EEC to EC, January 5, 1921.
21. bMS Am 1892 (861).
22. Slater Brown to RSK, January 24, 1979.
23. bMS Am 1823.1 (510).
24. SL, p. 73.
25. Slater Brown to RSK, January 24, 1979.

XIII
Some Firsts

1. bMS Am 1892, Scofield Thayer to EEC, April 1, 1919.
2. bMS Am 1892.7, Miscellaneous Notes.
3. bMS Am 1823.1 (156), EC to RHC, April 7 and March 2, 1919.
4. Catalogue of the First Annual Exhibition of the Society of Independent Artists, 1917.
5. bMS Am 1823.1 (156), EEC to RHC, March 18, 1919.
6. Ibid., April 24, and May 6, 1919.
7. Ibid., April 7, 1919.
8. bMS Am 1823 (296), EC to EEC, April 26, 1919.
9. bMS Am 1823.1 (152), EEC to EC, August 19, 1918.

10. bMS Am 1823 (296), EC to EEC, August 30, 1918.
11. bMS Am 1823.1 (152), EEC to EC, August 19, 1918.
12. Ibid., June 22, 1920.
13. Ibid., May 6, 1919.
14. Ibid., November 3, 1919.
15. bMS Am 1823.7 (27), 20.
16. For the full details of the change in ownership, see Nicholas Joost, *Years of Transition, The Dial, 1912–1920* (Barre, Mass.: Barre Publishers, 1967).
17. The essay is reprinted in George J. Firmage, ed., *A Miscellany Revised,* (New York: October House, 1965), pp. 12–24.
18. bMS Am 1823.1 (156), EEC to RHC, January 9, 1920.
19. Interview with M. R. Werner, August 1976.
20. *Dial* Collection, Yale University Library. Cummings' notes to the essay indicate that an editor had objected to the obscurity of some of his references. See also SL, p. 69.
21. The essay is reprinted in George J. Firmage, ed., *A Miscellany Revised,* (New York: October House, 1965), pp. 25–29.
22. bMS Am 1892, Scofield Thayer to EEC, September 24, 1920.
23. bMS Am 1823 (296), EC to EEC, May 7, 1920.
24. bMS Am 1823.1 (152), EEC to EC, May 22, 1920.
25. bMS Am 1823.1 (156), EEC to RHC, May 9, 1920.
26. bMS Am 1823.1 (152), EEC to EC, November 3, 1919.
27. bMS Am 1823.1 (156), EEC to RHC, November 25, 1919.
28. Ibid., June 2, 1920. Some additional letters about the plans to "follow the sea" are in the Massachusetts Historical Society, July 8, 13, and 17, 1920.
29. Ibid., November 25, 1919.
30. bMS Am 1823.1 (152), EEC to EC, June 17, 1920.
31. bMS Am 1823.7 (10) and (12).
32. bMS Am 1823.7 (17).
33. bMS Am 1892 (193), EC to EEC, October 2, 1920.
34. bMS Am 1892.7, Miscellaneous Notes, "Myself a Chromatic Individual."
35. SL, p. 74.
36. Clipping from a New York newspaper in the Catalogue of the Society of Independent Artists, Fifth Annual Exhibition, 1921, in the New York Public Library.
37. bMS Am 1823.10 (5), Slater Brown to EC, June 12, 1921.
38. bMS Am 1892 (861), Scofield Thayer to EEC, September 27 and November 1, 1918.
39. bMS Am 1823.1 (152), EEC to EC, November 23, 1921.

XIV

The Great War

1. bMS Am 1823.7 (23), 107.
2. All quotations from *The Enormous Room* follow the text of the Typescript edition, edited by George J. Firmage, (New York: Liveright, 1978).

XV

Europe 1921–1924

1. John Dos Passos, *The Best Times* (New York: New American Library, 1966), pp. 86–87.
2. bMS Am 1892.8 (12).
3. SL, p. 76.
4. bMS Am 1892.8 (31) and Firmage, *A Miscellany Revised,* p. 167.
5. bMS Am 1892.8 (44) and Edmund Wilson, *The Twenties,* ed. Leon Edel (New York: Farrar, Strauss, 1975), p. 207.
6. SL, p. 96.
7. bMS Am 1823.1 (156), EEC to RHC, May 17, 1921.
8. bMS Am 1892.7, Miscellaneous Notes.
9. bMS Am 1892.7 (77).
10. bMS Am 1892.7 (90).
11. bMS Am 1823.1 (156), EEC to RHC, July 6, 1921.
12. bMS Am 1892.7 (126).
13. bMS Am 1823.1 (156) EEC to RHC, undated, folder 49.
14. Ibid.
15. bMS Am 1892.7 (90).
16. bMS Am 1823.1 (152) EEC to RHC, December 23, 1921.

17. Dos Passos, *The Best Times*, p. 83.
18. SL, pp. 82–83.
19. August 10, 1922, quoted in Norman Friedman, *E. E. Cummings The Growth of a Writer* (Carbondale: Southern Illinois Univ. Press, 1964), p. 37.
20. bMS Am 1823.1 (156) EEC to RHC, January 13, 1922.
21. bMS Am 1892.5 (39).
22. Published in *Is 5*, 1926.
23. Dos Passos, *The Best Times*, p. 89.
24. May 14, 1922, Section IV, p. 7.
25. John Peale Bishop, "Incorrect English," *Vanity Fair*, 18 (July 1922): 20.
26. John F. Carter, Jr., *The Literary Review*, 20 (May 1922).
27. Gorham B. Munson, "Syrinx," *Secession*, 5 (July 1923): 9–10.
28. John Dos Passos, "Off The Shoals," *Dial*, 73, (July 1922): 99.
29. bMS Am 1823.1 (152), EEC to EC, April 2, 1922.
30. Ibid., June 19, 1922.
31. SL, pp. 84–86.
32. bMS Am 1892 (707), EFC to EEC, December 29, 1960.
33. *Dial* Collection, Yale University, Scofield Thayer to Sibley Watson, March 23 and 31, 1923.
34. Interview, Elaine MacDermot with RSK, July 1973.
35. bMS Am 1823.1 (152), EEC to EC, July 26, 1923.
36. Ibid., EEC to RHC (with letter to Father), April 11, 1923.
37. bMS Am 1823.1 (156), EEC to RHC, May 17, 1923.
38. bMS Am 1823.1 (152) EEC to EC, December 5, 1923.
39. bMS Am 1823.1 (156).

XVI
Disaster

1. This piece was published after Cummings' death as one of his collection, "Fairy Tales."
2. Dos Passos, *The Best Times*, pp. 83–84.
3. bMS Am 1823.1 (156), EEC to RHC, April 4, 1924.
4. Ibid., May 26, 1924.
5. *Broom*, 6 (January 1924): 26–28.
6. *Dial* 76 (January 1924): 49–52.

7. November 8, 1923, p. 9.
8. bMS Am 1823.10 (24), EEC to EC and RHC, July 9, 1924.
9. bMS Am 1892 (545), Elaine to EEC, November 9, 1924.
10. bMS Am 1892.7, Miscellaneous notes.
11. SL, p. 185.
12. bMS Am 1823.1 (152), EEC to EC, July 26, 1926.
13. bMS Am 1892 (545), Elaine to EEC, August 6, 1924.
14. Ibid., July 18, 1924.
15. bMS Am 1823.1 (156), August 12, 1924.
16. bMS Am 1892 (545).
17. bMS Am 1892.7, Miscellaneous notes.
18. bMS Am 1892.7 (90), Notes for additional nonlectures. The person was probably Winifred, Nancy's English nurse, who would have had an accent like MacDermot. In his version of the story to Nancy the shot he almost fired might have killed her, not the maid, Eva Prior.
19. Divorce decree of the 3rd court of the Civil Tribunal, December 4, 1924, translated by Jean Lenoir.
20. bMS Am 1892 (545), Elaine to EEC, November 29, 1924.

XVII
The Struggle for Nancy

1. One of the difficulties, as he later explained to Nancy, was that according to French law you cannot adopt your own child. Thus by adopting Nancy he would have, in the eyes of the French courts, given up any legal pretension to being her father.
2. bMS Am 1892 (545).
3. bMS Am 1823.10 (41), January 28, 1925.
4. bMS Am 1892 (193) January 30, 1925.
5. bMS Am 18992.5 (159).
6. bMS Am 1892.4 (104).
7. Joe Gould died in 1957 after having been confined to Pilgrim State (Mental) Hospital since 1952. In a moving and sympathetic book, *Joe Gould's Secret* (New York: Viking Press, 1965), Joseph Mitchell has given an anecdotal biography of Gould and also revealed that the "Oral History of Our Time" did not exist. For thirty years, Gould had

written and rewritten four or five di-
gressive essays on such topics as the
death of his father or the dangers of
eating tomatoes and had given himself
dignity among the Village literati by
being the author of a great unfinished
work.

8. bMS Am 1823 (156), EC to RHC, March
   20, 1925.
9. bMS Am 1823, September 25, 1924.
10. HRC, UT, November 27, 1925.
11. bMS Am 1892 (546), May 4, 1925.
12. bMS Am 1892.7, Miscellaneous notes.
13. bMS Am 1892 (193), July 19, 1925.
14. bMS Am 1823.10 (24), August 22, 1925.
15. Ibid.
16. bMS Am 1823.10 (25), EEC to RHC Au-
    gust 22 and August 30, 1925.
17. Ibid., September 3, 1925.
18. On July 24, Cummings had dinner with
    Scofield Thayer, who reported about
    Elaine's paralyses. Thayer theorized
    that she seemed to be adopting her sister
    Constance's lameness. Constance had
    been lamed in childhood by a crochet
    hook and walked with a cane.
19. bMS Am 1892.1 (156) EEC to RHC, Octo-
    ber 22, 1926.
20. bMS Am 1892.4 (46). A copy of the letter
    survives because Estlin wrote it out to
    show to his sister before he mailed the
    original back to Cambridge.
21. When the invitation was offered, the
    MacDermots had perhaps not yet re-
    ceived Rebecca's letter, for MacDer-
    mot called Cummings later and told
    him everyone had been exposed to
    mumps and perhaps he would not
    wish to come.
22. bMS Am 1892.1 (156), EEC to RHC,
    March 4, 1927.
23. SL, p. 269.

XVIII

Anne and *Him*

1. bMS Am 1823.1 (196), February 4, 1926.
2. Ibid., September 13, 1926.
3. bMS Am 1892.7.
4. Information about Anne Barton is
   drawn from her letters to Cummings in

the Houghton Library and his scattered
notes and letters and from my inter-
views with M. R. Werner and Slater
Brown.

5. In September 1926, he told his mother
   that he was "painting in a new direc-
   tion" and in January 1927 he described
   the two small paintings he was sending
   as 1) flowers and part of a chair-back,
   done on cardboard with a palette knife
   and 2) a portrait of "Corway [?]."
6. bMS Am 1892.7 (121), p. 116.
7. bMS Am 1892 (331).
8. Brom Weber, ed., *The Letters of Hart
   Crane*, (Berkeley: University of Califor-
   nia Press, 1952), pp. 310–11. Letter to an
   unnamed correspondent, November 16,
   1927.
9. bMS Am 1823.4 (15), Notes for *Him*.
10. In his notes and schematae for the play,
    Cummings sets down the "sexual as-
    pect" of each of the scenes in Act II such
    as "unconscious," "sterile" "conven-
    tional sex" "female invert," etc. bMS
    Am 1823.4 (15), p. 305.
11. bMS Am 1823.4 (15), a description of "The
    Structure of the Play" states, "The chief
    motif of the play is pregnancy."
12. In a number of the early plans for the
    play the Doctor is referred to as the
    Abortionist. Cummings seems to have
    changed his mind about this, but the
    outcome of the hospital action is left am-
    biguous.
13. In one earlier version, Him cries out
    "Mother!" at this point.
14. *i: six nonlectures*, p. 12.
15. *Dial Papers*, Yale University, November
    12, 1926.
16. Ibid., March 2, 1927.
17. Helen Deutsch and Stella Hanau, *The
    Provincetown; A Story of the Theatre* (New
    York: Russell and Russell, 1959), p. 170.
18. bMS Am 1892. (291), M. R. Werner to
    EEC, June 11 [1936?].
19. bMS Am 1823.8 (39).
20. Ibid. Clippings in the scrapbook kept by
    Rebecca Cummings.
21. Ibid.
22. Quoted in Deutsch and Hanau, *The
    Provincetown*, pp. 176–77.
23. bMS Am 1823.1 (156), September 17, 1927.
24. bMS Am 1892.1 (156), October 22, 1927.

25. bMS Am 1892.1 (156), November 8, 1927.
26. Ibid., December 30, 1927. Rody is Monroe Hall, Cummings' friend who worked for the State Department. Mary, later his wife, was the sister-in-law of Gilbert Seldes.
27. bMS Am 1892.1 (35), January or February 1928. The letter is undated and unfinished.
28. bMS Am 1892.1 (35).
29. bMS Am 1823 (1418) and 1892.7 (58), p. 45.
30. bMS Am 1892.7.
31. bMS Am 1823.1 (156), March 26, 1929.
32. bMS Am 1823.8 (40).
33. Leon Edel, ed., *The Twenties* (New York: Farrar, Straus, 1975), p. 429.

XIX

Anne and Russia

1. She was an avant-garde composer, one of the group known as Les Six.
2. bMS Am 1892.8 (46).
3. The torn pieces are in the Houghton Library.
4. bMS Am 1892.8 (46).
5. bMS Am 1823.1 (156), September 29, 1930.
6. bMS Am 1823.7.
7. bMS Am 1892.4 (63), Anne Barton to RHC, July 21, 1930.
8. bMS Am 1823.1 (156), EEC to RHC, January 7, 1931.
9. Ibid., April 9, 1931.
10. bMS Am 1892 (331).
11. *Eimi*, (1933, rpt. New York: Grove Press, 1958), p. 312. There is no mention of this in his diary.
12. bMS Am 1892.7 (90).
13. David Sinclair remembers Dana as "quite a character. He reminded me of Jack Benny in his comical moments. He even carried a violin in a case." Interview with RSK, June 24, 1978.
14. bMS Am 1823.4 (100), May 14.
15. Meyerhold's talents led, unfortunately, to his downfall; he was later arrested and charged with bourgeois attitudes alien to Soviet art. He died in prison in 1940.
16. bMS Am 1823.4 (100), May 15, 1931?
17. David Sinclair felt that Cummings was overapprehensive. He said that he was aware of the GPU presence but that he himself felt safe, unless he were to do something like try to buy rubles in the black market. Interview with RSK, June 24, 1978.
18. bMS Am 1823.4 (100), May 19, 1931.
19. Ibid. The diary actually reads " 'K' (as she asks me to call her.)" But after that she is always referred to as "J" (in quotation marks) in the diary.
20. Ibid., May 22. The best and most detailed picture of Moscow in 1931 and the operations of the Soviet system at the time of Cummings' visit is the book by Eugene Lyons, United press correspondent in Moscow 1927–1933, entitled *Assignment in Utopia* (New York: Harcourt Brace, 1937). Although he was vacationing in America at the time of Cummings' stay in 1931, his apartment in Moscow was the one the Malamuths were occupying when they took Cummings in. Lyons' comment on Cummings' account of the Russian trip testifies to its accuracy: " … what I understood of that book, *Eimi*, was so good, so penetrating, that I still wish he had not written it in puzzlewords" (p. 418).
21. bMS Am 1892 (331), May 31, 1931. Details about Barton are taken from the *New York Times*, May 21 and 24, 1931.
22. bMS Am 1823.4 (100), June 1.
23. *Eimi*, pp. 261–62.
24. bMS Am 1823.4 (100), June 2.
25. *Eimi*, pp. 284–85.
26. bMS Am 1823.4 (100), June 2.
27. Ibid., June 6.
28. Ibid., June 9.

XX

The Ordeals of Olaf and Estlin

1. A limited edition of 491 copies, each signed by the author.
2. [*No Title*], 1930; rptd., George J. Firmage, ed., *A Miscellany Revised* (New York: October House, 1965), p. 230.
3. May 1927. Reprinted in Firmage, *A Miscellany Revised*, pp. 195–96.

4. bMS Am 1892.8 (41).
5. *SL*, p. 261.
6. bMS Am 1892.7 (90).
7. *SL*, pp. 54–55.
8. "An Experimentalist's Exhibition," signed K. G. S., *New York Times*, December 6, 1931, II, 8.
9. bMS Am 1892 (295), October 27, 1931.
10. bMS Am 1892 (196), July 7, 1936. It appears that the $100 to Estlin was in addition to the $250 she drew from the estate. Even so, her "money man," Duncan Spencer, handled her affairs so well that between 1932 and 1936 her account grew from $30,000 to $44,612.
11. Werner to RSK, August 18, 1976.
12. Brown to RSK, July 31, 1977.
13. Cowley to RSK, November 15, 1977.
14. Werner to RSK, August 8, 1976.
15. Werner reports that she later turned up at social gatherings, wearing dark glasses to cover black eyes. Another story has its origin with her sister. It seems that Anne, off one night with Girdansky while she was still married to Cummings, asked him what he would do if she treated him in that fashion. "I'd wait till I got you on the operating table," was the reply. Brown to RSK, July 31, 1977.
16. bMS Am 1823.1 (156), August 24, 1932. It may be that the legal action was taken after, rather than before, this reported meeting.

XXI

The Unworld Visited

1. EEC to J. Sibley Watson, March 28, 1932.
2. bMS Am 1892.7 (90).
3. bMS Am 1823.1 (156), March 4, 1933.
4. *Eimi* (1933; rpt. New York: Grove Press, 1958), p. 282.
5. *Eimi*, p. 21. "Eheu fugaces" is an allusion to Horace's Ode XIV, Book II, "Alas, my Postumus, our years slip silently away. . . ."
6. *Eimi*, p. 6.
7. *Eimi*, p. 278.
8. *Eimi*, p. 90.
9. *Eimi*, p. 406.
10. *Eimi*, p. 418.
11. *Eimi*, pp. 431–32.

XXII

Marion

1. The New York Times obituary of Marion Morehouse, May 19, 1969, reports that she was "educated at St. Anne's Academy in Hartford," but there is no record of her ever having been enrolled at St. Anne's School (for French-speaking girls) or St. Joseph's Academy in Hartford. Her sister has failed to reply to any of my inquiries about Marion.
2. I am grateful to Aline MacMahon Stein for information about Marion's life in New York.
3. Edward Steichen, *A Life in Photography* (New York: Doubleday, 1968).
4. Quoted in the *New York Times*, May 19, 1969.
5. Marion Morehouse, interview with RSK, August 1964.
6. bMS Am 1892.1 (99).
7. bMS Am 1892.1 (99).
8. Ibid.
9. Ibid.
10. bMS Am 1892.3 (11), July 31, 1932.
11. bMS Am 1823.1 (156), March 4, 1933.
12. In 1932 Cummings and Lowenfels had divided the $500 Richard Aldington Prize for the best poetry appearing in *This Quarter*. The editor had chosen Cummings, but the donor had objected, wishing Lowenfels to receive the prize. The difference of opinion was compromised.
13. bMS Am 1823.1 (156), May 26, 1933.
14. Ibid., July 11, 1933.
15. Ibid.
16. bMS Am 1892, May 30, 1933.
17. bMS Am 1892, on Mitchell's letter dated February 18, 1933.
18. bMS Am 1892, May 12, [1933].
19. bMS Am 1823.1 (156), July 2, 1933.
20. Ibid., May 26, 1933.
21. Ibid., July 2, 1933.
22. Ibid.
23. EEC to Werner, July 20, 1933.
24. HRC, UT, July 22, 1933
25. bMS Am 1892.4, August 4, 1933.
26. bMS Am 1892.4 (6), January 15, 1935.
27. bMS Am 1823.1 (156), September 13, 1935.
28. EEC to S. A. Jacobs, Undated 1933, Alderman Library, University of Virginia.

29. EEC to Kerstein, Undated, Yale University Library. Used by permission.
30. bMS Am 1823.1 (156), July 8, 1934.
31. Ibid., July 17, 1934.
32. bMS Am 1892.11 (88), October 25, 1948.

XXIII

Gratitude to
Almost No One

1. bMS Am 1823.7 (22).
2. George Firmage discovered this manuscript in the Clifton Waller Barrett Library, University of Virginia, Deposit 6246-a.
3. For a full discussion of Edward Cummings' theology, see my article, "Edward Cummings, the Father of the Poet," *Bulletin of the New York Public Library*, 70 (September 1966): 437–449.
4. For a full explication, see Valarie Arms, "A Catholic Reading of Cummings' 'morsel miraculous and meaningless,'" *Journal of Modern Literature*, 7 (April 1979).
5. Robert McIlvaine, "Cummings' BrIght,'" *Explicator*, 30 (September 1971): 6.

XXIV

A Stranger in the
Supercolossal West, 1935

1. *New York Daily News*, April 9, 1933; *Boston Herald*, April 3, 1933; *Rocky Mountain News*, April 2, 1933; and *Philadelphia Public Ledger*, April 1, 1933.
2. April 1. 1933.
3. Lewis Gannett, *New York Herald-Tribune*, April 4, 1933; Frances Dawson, *St. Louis Globe-Democrat*, April 29, 1933; and William Troy in *The Nation*, April 12, 1933.
4. April 23, 1933; April 1, 1933; and August, 1933.
5. Rosenfeld, *Contempo*, 3 (July 25, 1933): 1–3.
6. "Descent into Russia," April 26, 1933.
7. New York: Liveright, 1978, p. 117. He had also recently translated Louis Aragon's *The Red Front*, which appeared in *Literature of the World Revolution*, August 1931. The translation had been done as a gesture of thanks to Aragon, who had written a letter of introduction for him to his sister-in-law in Moscow in 1931.
8. Not only does Cummings refer to this incident in his notes, bMS Am 1892.7 (90), but Marion reported it in an interview with RSK in August 1964. The friends were not identified.
9. W.T.S. in the *Providence Journal*, May 5, 1935.
10. Kenneth Burke "Two Kinds of Against," *The New Republic*, June 26, 1935.
11. Helen Stewart, interview with RSK, November 29, 1977.
12. In one letter, Cummings says three weeks, in another ten weeks.
13. bMS Am 1892 (469), October 13, 1934.
14. Undated letter, 1934. I am grateful to Jere Knight for information about Eric Knight and for allowing me to see Cummings' letters to him.
15. SL, p. 143.
16. Ibid.
17. bMS Am 1823.7 (44).
18. Details of the trip come from a letter, EEC to M. R. Werner, June 16, 1935, and from bMS Am 1823.1 (156), EEC to RHC, July 10, 1935.
19. bMS Am 1892.13 (95), EEC to RHC, undated, June 1935.
20. SL, p. 113.
21. bMS Am 1823.1 (156), EEC to RHC, July 9, 1935 and bMS Am 1892.13 (95), EEC to RHC, July 2, 1935.
22. bMS Am 1825.1, EEC to RHC, July 10, 1935.
23. Ibid., July 19, 1935.
24. Ibid., July 25, 1935.
25. Interview with RSK, March 20, 1978. I am deeply grateful to Miss MacMahon for information about Marion's early career and for details about Cummings in California.
26. EEC to S. A. Jacobs, undated, Alderman Library, University of Virginia.
27. bMS Am 1823.1, July 15, 1935.
28. EEC to Hildegarde Watson, September 30, 1935.
29. bMS Am 1892.8 (22). Cummings usually referred to Samuel Goldwyn by his earlier name, Samuel Goldfish.

30. bMS Am 1823.1 (156), EEC to RHC, September 26, 1935.
31. bMS Am 1823.7 (45).
32. Ibid.
33. Ibid.

XXV

The Undanced *Tom*

1. Interview with RSK, April 3, 1978.
2. bMS Am 1892.1 (41), EEC to David Diamond, January 1936.
3. EEC to Hildegarde Watson, December 24, 1935. Lincoln Kirstein denied that another ballet based on *Uncle Tom's Cabin* was ever presented. (Interview with RSK, April 3, 1978).
4. bMS Am 1892 (227), January 30, 1936; July 24, 1936; and August 7, 1936.
5. I am grateful to David Diamond for allowing me to reproduce this song, the manuscript for which is in his possession.
6. This text of 1852, used loosely by the many traveling "Tom shows" of the nineteenth century, was easily available in the public library.
7. *Tom*, 1935. Reprinted in *Three Plays and A Ballet*, ed. George J. Firmage (New York: October House, 1967), p. 170.
8. EEC to Henry Allen Moe, October 25, 1937. I am grateful to the John Simon Guggenheim Foundation for access to this letter in their files.
9. bMS Am 1823.1 (156), EEC to RHC, October 28, 1933.
10. Ibid., August 20, 1935.
11. Reginald ("Rex") Hunter, a New Zealander who occupied the third floor front at 4 Patchin Place.
12. bMS Am 1892.7 (121), p. 107.

XXVI

The War Years

1. Norman, *E. E. Cummings*, p. 287. Norman quotes Pearce's letters to him, giving full details of the development of this book.
2. Ibid.
3. bMS Am 1892.4 (6), December 26, 1936.
4. bMS Am 1823.1, July 25, 1944.
5. *American Literature*, January 1939, and *The New Republic*, April 27, 1938.
6. March 19, 1938.
7. SL, p. 148.
8. Paul Nordoff, interview with RSK, April 1964.
9. bMS Am 1892.13 (284), undated letter, [1948?].
10. Loren MacIver, interview with RSK, September 1977. Frankenberg's essay was later reprinted in his book, *Pleasure Dome* (New York: Houghton Mifflin, 1949).
11. Helen Schevill, interview with RSK, March 4, 1978.
12. bMS Am 1892.7.
13. Dos Passos, *The Fourteenth Chronicle*, p. 508.
14. EEC to Dos Passos, September 13, 1937, University of Virginia Library.
15. EEC to Watson May 30, 1939.
16. bMS Am 1823.1 (156), EEC to RHC, September 9, 1939.
17. The date of this poem is uncertain. On January 19, 1940, he placed a "Viva Finland" at the end of a letter to his mother. I assume the poem was written shortly afterward when the Russians took over Finland, although it was not published until Summer 1944 in the *Maryland Quarterly*.
18. bMS Am 1892.1 (142), EEC to Allen Tate, June 18, 1946.
19. EEC to Eric Knight, July 12, 1940.
20. SL, pp. 161–62.
21. bMS Am 1823.1 (156), January 9 and February 22, 1942.
22. Ibid., February 22, 1942.
23. Quoted in the *New York Times*, January 22, 1943. These words are taken from his last letter to his publisher.
24. EEC to Hildegarde Watson, *ca.* January 1950.
25. EEC to Howard Nelson, September 1, 1944.
26. Quoted in the *New York Times*, March 26, 1978.
27. bMS Am 1823.1 (156), May 15, 1945.
28. bMS Am 1892.1 (99), April 23, 1944, and March 23, 1944.

29. Ibid., March or April, 1944.
30. Ibid., August 17, 1944.
31. Ibid., August 12, 1944.
32. Ibid., August 25, 1944.
33. I am grateful to Mrs. Cecily Angleton for many of the details about Cummings in Arizona.
34. EEC to Watson January 23, 1946.
35. SL, pp. 170–71.
36. bMS Am 1823.1 (156), EEC to RHC, December 26, 1945.
37. SL, p. 170.
38. Harvard University Archives, EEC to Theodore Spencer, February 6, 1946.
39. EEC to Paul Nordoff, February 17, 1946, courtesy of F.W. Duppee.
40. bMS Am 1823.1 (156), May 8, 1938.

XXVII

Oneness and *Santa Claus*

1. It appears that Duell, Sloan and Pearce rejected Cummings' book, for a letter from Pearce, November 5, 1943, indicates that he was considering it for publication at that time, bMS 1892, (166).
2. bMS Am 1892.7 (121). Cummings may have been trying to work out his introduction to *Collected Poems*, which in its published version ends with a description of Renoir painting with his arthritic hands in his old age.
3. *New Republic*, April 3, 1944.
4. *The Nation*, April 1, 1944.
5. March 18, 1944.
6. Quoted from the two transcripts in Julien Cornell, *The Trial of Ezra Pound*, (New York: John Day, 1966) appendix. Five other transcripts appear in Olga Rudge, *If This Be Treason*, privately printed 1948. Excerpts from the broadcasts may be found in a number of studies of Pound's career. Complete transcripts are available in the Library of Congress.
7. Cornell, *The Trial of Ezra Pound*, p. 39.
8. Cummings invited Bufano to dine at Patchin Place in April 1941, but it is uncertain how well he knew him. bMS Am 1823.1 (156), EEC to RHC, April 17, 1941.

9. bMS Am 1892.13 (15), draft of a letter, EEC to NTA, March 5, 1957.

XXVIII

Reunion and Revelation

1. Cecily Angleton, Interview with RSK, April 1978.
2. bMS Am 1823.7 (46).
3. bMS Am 1823.13 (95), EEC to RHC, October 2, 1946.
4. bMS Am 1823.1 (510) EEC to EFC, undated, early 1947. The other poem was "life is more true than reason will deceive."
5. Information about Nancy's life is drawn from a series of interviews with her beginning in July 1972.
6. Nancy Cummings de Forêt, *Charon's Daughter, A Passion of Identity* (New York: Liveright, 1977) p. 41. NTA asked me to explain that she was "echoing her mother" here, "suggesting a repetition of my mother's original behavior in Quai Bourbon." "All of Charon's Daughter is echoes," she added, "and this one is central to the Cummings-Orr situation."
7. Ibid., p. 7.
8. bMS Am 1892 (646), May 8, 1941.
9. Nancy T. Andrews, Interview with RSK, July 1972.
10. This portrait is owned by RSK.
11. Marion one day gave Nancy a photograph of Estlin as a golden-curled child in a sailor suit, saying, "Here is a picture of your father." Nancy was very embarrassed at what she took to be Marion's error and was careful to make no comment.
12. This portrait has disappeared.
13. Nancy T. Andrews, Interview with RSK, July 1972.
14. bMS Am 1823 (157), EFC to RHC, April 20, 1921.
15. bMS Am 1892.13 (15), EEC to Nancy Roosevelt, September 1, 1949.
16. bMS Am 1892 (28), Nancy Roosevelt to EEC, January 9, 1950.
17. Nancy Cummings de Forêt, *Charon's Daughter*, p. 38.

18. bMS Am 1892.7.

19. bMS Am 1892 (28), Nancy Roosevelt to EEC, July 22, 1950.

20. Nancy never understood from Cummings that he had legally adopted her. On one occasion, he had perhaps given some indication when he suggested that she could change her name to Cummings if she wished. She replied that, since she was married now, it would seem to be too late to make any difference. It was not until 1973 that she first had knowledge from Thayer's lawyers of the adoption papers.

21. Years later, Nancy commented on this reference to her expression of love for Marion, which was nowhere in the letter: "I distinctly remember I was rather mystified by this—uncomfortable—it seemed out of place (as well as untrue, and I couldn't very well say so!)" NTA to RSK, December 13, 1978.

22. bMS Am 1892.1 (4), July 28, 1950.

23. bMS Am 1892 (28), Nancy Roosevelt to EEC, August 10, 1950.

24. Ibid., September 10, 1950.

25. NTA to RSK, December 13, 1978.

26. Ibid.

27 bMS Am 1892 (28), Nancy Roosevelt to EEC, November 1, 1950.

28 Nancy T. Andrews, interview with RSK, May 1978.

29 bMS Am 1892 (28), August 1951.

30 Nancy T. Andrews, interview with RSK, May 1978.

XXIX

The Nonprofessor at Harvard

1. bMS Am 1892.1 (142), EEC to Allen Tate, July 20, 1945.

2. bMS Am 1892 (308), August 6, 1949.

3. SL, p. 184.

4. December 20, 1949.

5. Evelyn Segal, interview with RSK, November 1977.

6. *Congress Weekly*, August 20, 1951.

7. bMS Am 1823 (1074), EFC to EEC, August 8, 1949. The letter of thanks to Mitchell is bMS Am 1892.13 (266), February 14, 1949.

8. SL, p. 202.

9. EEC to Henry Allen Moe, April 1, 1950, John Simon Guggenheim Foundation.

10. bMS Am 1892.13 (15), EEC to NTA, November 8, 1956.

11. bMS Am 1823.7 (47).

12. bMS Am 1823.1 (443), undated letter, [1951].

13. EEC to Henry Allen Moe, December 5, 1943.

14. Ibid., December 8, 1943.

15. Ibid., February 20, 1950.

16. SL, pp. 207–8.

17. bMS Am 1823.7 (64) and scattered throughout the Cummings papers.

18. Ibid.

19. See Norman, *E.E. Cummings*, pp. 340–44 for a fairly full representation of Cummings' correspondence with Harvard.

20. bMS Am 1892 (289), John Finley to EEC, February 26, 1952.

21. bMS Am 1823 (448), Norman Friedman to EEC, April 18, 1952.

22. Letter, a friend to Evelyn Segal, October 1, 1952.

23. bMS Am 1892 (28), Nancy Roosevelt to EEC, September 19, 1952.

24. bMS Am 1892.13 (15), EEC to Nancy Roosevelt, October 29, 1952.

25. bMS Am 1892.10, Hildegarde Watson's memoir of Cummings, August 30, 1967.

26. Cummings' copies of both volumes of *Paideia*, gifts from Marion, Volume I in 1934 and Volume II in 1943, are Houghton Library 69c–169.

27. bMS Am 1892.13 (15), EEC to Nancy Roosevelt, October 29, 1952.

28. SL, p. 223.

29. EEC to Hildegarde Watson, November 9, 1952.

30. bMS Am 1892.1 (510), EEC to EFC November 13, 1952.

31. bMS Am 1892.13 (321), EEC to EFC January 19, 1973.

32. David Perkins to RSK, April 11, 1977.

33. EEC to Hildegarde Watson, December 27, 1952.

34. Mrs. Eliot Hubbard (Betty Thaxter) interview with RSK, June 1970.

35. Mrs. Richard Hall (Amy Gozzaldi), interview with RSK, March 1973.

36. bMS Am 1892.13 (321), EEC to EFC, May 5, 1953.

XXX
Verbal Vibrations:
A New Career

1. EEC to Sibley Watson, March 14, 1950.
2. John Malcolm Brinnin to RSK, September 7, 1978.
3. bMS Am 1823 (707), April 11, 1955.
4. Betty Kray to RSK, March 19, 1979.
5. John Nist, "E. E. Cummings Speaks to the Academic World," *Artesian*, May—June 1957.
6. bMS Am 1823 (510), EEC to EFC, May 3, 1959.
7. SL, p. 238.
8. EEC to Hildegarde Watson, May 7, 1957.
9. bMS Am 1823 (510), EEC to EFC, undated letter, 1948–1950.
10. Ibid., December 1, 1951.
11. bMS Am 1892.7 (56), p. 127, and bMS Am 1823.1 (443), EEC to Howard Nelson, July 18, 1960. Twice this is associated with the audience at the nonlectures.
12. Letter, a friend to Evelyn Segal, January 24, 1949.
13. bMS Am 1892.13 (321), EEC to EFC May 16, 1954.
14. bMS Am 1823.1 (443), EEC to Howard Nelson, June 14, 1958.
15. October 31, 1954.
16. bMS Am 1892.13 (321), EEC to EFC, November 23, 1954.
17. Oscar Cargill, Richard Eberhart, Dudley Fitts, Randell Jarrell, and Christopher Lafarge.
18. The old established book clubs never chose poetry, except an occasional anthology. The Reader's Subscription, founded in 1951, aimed at a more discriminating taste. The editors had recently chosen volumes of collected poems by Yeats, Eliot, Lawrence, and Thomas and had also offered the phonograph album, "Caedmon Treasury of Modern Poets," which included Cummings.
19. bMS Am 1892 (542), David McCord to EEC, February 5, 1957. For a fairly full representation of the correspondence, see Norman, *E.E. Cummings*, pp. 328–35. Although McCord's letter stated that Jack Sweeney was a member of the committee, this is in error. Sweeney had

chaired the committee in 1956.
20. The hippie movement and the Vietnam War demonstrations combined to bring an end to the Festivals in the mid-1960's.
21. bMS Am 1823.1 (87), EEC to David McCord, February 19, 1957.
22. SL, p. 235.
23. bMS Am 1892.13 (15), EEC to NTA, November 8, 1956.
24. bMS Am 1823.5.
25. bMS Am 1823.1 (510), EEC to EFC July 9, 1957. Cummings had consulted with Jack Sweeney, who had then suggested the compromise. Cummings reported back to him, "following your suggestion (made to Marion by telephone) our un-hero sent the enclosed letter and poem to T[emple]; who 'phoned that he considered my (id est your) gesture 'magnificent' & felt 'stunned.'" bMS Am 1823.1 (597), undated letter [May 1957]. Cummings also asked Sweeney's advice on what other poems to read for the Festival audience.
26. "Bard in Boston," *Harper's*, September 1957, pp. 86–87.
27. June 24, 1957, signed RST. Norman identifies the writer as Robert Taylor.
28. bMS Am 1823.1 (510), ECC to EFC, July 9, 1957.

XXXI
Oneliness: Loneliness

1. It seems appropriate at this point to explain a few details about the later career of Cummings' best friend, Dr. James Sibley Watson. After taking his medical degree, Watson did not go into practice, but spent his time, first, working in a department of physiology in a Chicago hospital, then returning to Rochester to work for Eastman Kodak, while at the same time making the avant-garde motion pictures, *Lot in Sodom* and *The Fall of the House of Usher*. In the later 1930's, Watson began to combine his knowledge of medicine and photography. He envisioned making a camera that would take pictures inside the human stomach and came to consult Dr. Harry Segal about it. After

extensive work and with the help of a watchmaker, Watson and Segal finally succeeded in making a tiny camera that took the first internal photograph in the history of medicine. This association reawakened Watson's interest in medicine, and with Segal's encouragement, he enrolled for some refresher courses and then in the 1940's took a residency at Strong Memorial Hospital in radiology. Afterward he became one of Harry Segal's medical partners, and the two went on to make the University of Rochester Medical School the most famous in the country in the field of cinefluorography.

2. Strong Memorial Hospital record on Edward Cummings, Unit 39–65–51, Number 262 396 551. Report dated 5/10/55.

3. EEC to Hildegarde Watson, undated, [August 1957].

4. bMS Am 1823 (177), James Phillips to EEC, April 23, 1957.

5. bMS Am 1892.7 (90).

6. The exact details are uncertain. EEC may have written a letter describing his situation and then been invited to Rochester by Hildegarde. See, however, the letter to Marion Morehouse cited in footnote 10.

7. Dr. Burton's report on Cummings' recent intestinal troubles reads as follows: "For 4 or 5 years, the patient noted increased gas after meals, particularly exacerbated by fatty and fried foods, with pain in the lower abdomen, improved by decreasing fatty meals. No medication except recent use of Donnatal which relieved his discomfort. During past summer, he had an episode of severe bloating pains which kept him awake all night, subsiding spontaneously the next day. About two weeks ago, he was awakened by left lower quadrant discomfort which subsided spontaneously." Strong Memorial Hospital Record. Report dated 10/3/57.

8. J. Sibley Watson, interview with RSK, November 1977.

9. bMS Am 1892.1 (99), EEC to Marion Morehouse, October 26, 1957.

10. EEC to Hildegarde Watson, June 25, 1958.

11. George J. Firmage, interview with RSK, December 13, 1978.

12. Morse to RSK, July 21, 1978.

13. Marion Morehouse, Interview with RSK, January 28, 1964. I am giving Marion's version of how the biographical project began, although it differs from that described on page 235 of Charles Norman, *E. E. Cummings: The Magic Maker* (New York: Duell, Sloan, and Pearce, 1964), a revised and expanded edition. Both versions are, I am sure, true. Cummings was a courteous man and probably did not let Norman know his real feelings. There is ample evidence in Cummings' letters, however, that he insisted on seeing the manuscript and that he wielded a blue pencil over it.

14. EEC to Hildegarde Watson, undated, [1958].

15. bMS Am 1823.1 (510), EEC to EFC, November 17, 1958. Norman's third revised and expanded edition (New York: Bobbs-Merrill, 1972) is a much more satisfactory book because he did not have Estlin and Marion looking over his shoulder while he was preparing it. He did, however, remove the final chapter of the second edition, to which Marion had objected. The chapter had contained a remark by Cummings in May 1961, "All I ask is one more year," and an account of his death.

16. bMS Am 1892.13 (15), EEC to NTA December 1, 1958, and 1892.1 (4), EEC to NTA, April 13, 1959.

17. bMS Am 1892.13 (141), EEC to Norman Friedman, February 28, 1954.

18. bMS Am 1892.13 (321), EEC to EFC, October 30, 1954.

19. Ibid., May 3, 1958.

20. Ibid., January 5, 1957.

21. bMS Am 1823.1 (510), EEC to EFC, November 21, 1959.

22. bMS Am 1823.1 (597), EEC to Jack Sweeney, November 16, 1959. Cummings enclosed a list of the selections he planned to read at Boston College and asked Sweeney to see if there was anything that the Catholic audience would find objectionable. It included four passages from *Eimi* and nineteen poems. Betty Kray had received a telephone call

from Father Sweeney (no relative of Jack) of Boston College who expressed a hope that Cummings would not include anything that his audience would find objectionable.

23. bMS Am 1823.1 (443), EEC to Howard Nelson, December 21, 1959.

24. EEC to Hildegarde Watson, April 21, 1959.

25. Deborah Ham, "E. E. Cummings Lectures, Attracts Capacity Crowds," *The College News*, April 22, 1959. She was quoting Archibald MacLeish's opinion, which he had pronounced at the Boston Arts Festival.

26. bMS Am 1823 (153), Mary K. Woodworth to EEC April 22, 1959.

27. bMS Am 1892.7 (92) contains the notes and scenes. There is only one date indicating the period of this work, September 1958.

28. bMS Am 1892.13 (321), EEC to EFC, January 5, 1957.

29. *The New American Caravan*, 1936, pp. 476–77; reprinted as "Speech from an Unfinished Play: I" in Firmage, *A Miscellany Revised*, p. 296–97.

30. bMS Am 1823.7 (55), p. 13.

31. bMS Am 1823.7 (61).

32. bMS Am 1823.7 (56), p. 80.

33. Ibid., p. 167.

34. bMS Am 1823.7 (69a), p. 1.

35. Ibid., p. 13.

36. bMS Am 1823.7 (56), p. 125.

37. Ibid., p. 51.

38. bMS Am 1892.13 (293), EEC to Kenneth Patchen, May 15, 1956, and (266), EEC to Paul Roche, undated.

39. bMS Am 1892.7 (121), p. 161.

40. Jack Sweeney to RSK, August 9, 1978.

41. bMS Am 1892.13 (321), EEC to EFC, September 24, 1960.

42. Ibid., April 15, 1960.

43. Gennadeion Monographs, 4 "American School of Classical Studies at Athens," (Princeton University Press, 1953).

44. bMS Am 1892 (28), NTA to EEC, November 3, 1960.

45. Nancy T. Andrews, interview with RSK, May 1978.

46. bMS Am 1892 (28), NTA to EEC, December 7, 1960.

47. bMS Am 1892.1 (4), EEC to NTA, November 19, 1960.

48. bMS Am 1892 (28), NTA to EEC, December 30, 1960.

XXXII
Now I Lay Me Down to Dream

1. bMS Am 1892.13 (430), EEC to Scott Verner, October 14, 1954.

2. bMS Am 1823.1 (510), EEC to EFC, July 22, 1957: "Maybe things would be better if the 'Supreme'! 'Court' in full conclave, were accidentally blown into the stratosphere a few times."

3. bMS Am 1892.7 (131). See further details about the Kennedy invitation, SL, p. 275.

4. Betty Kray to RSK, March 19, 1979.

5. Loren MacIver, interview with RSK, August 1977.

6. bMS Am 1823.1 (510), EEC to EFC, November 21, 1959.

7. Ibid., undated letter, number 88, [November 1953].

8. bMS Am 1892.7, Miscellaneous notes.

9. bMS Am 1892.7 (131).

10. bMS Am 1892.5 (371), dated February 16, 1962. It is clear that Cummings intended to introduce ambiguity by means of religious suggestion.

11. bMS Am 1892.7 (129).

12. bMS Am 1892.7 (133).

13. bMS Am 1823.7 (54), p. 3. Although it cannot be dated 1962 for certain, it is, without doubt, near to the end of Cummings' life.

14. bMS Am 1892.1 (90), EEC to Loren MacIver, October 6, 1949.

15. EEC to Hildegarde Watson, June 9, 1555.

16. bMS Am 1892.7 (132).

17. Marion Morehouse, interview with RSK, August 1964.

18. Mary Meier, "e. e. cummings Gave Madison a Big 'M,'" *Boston Globe*, September 4, 1962.

19. Mina Curtiss, interview with RSK, September 1977.

20. *The Wormwood Review*, 1 (Winter 1960): 1.

Index